WELCOME TO YOUR AFRICAN SAFARI

African safaris produce unforgettable moments, whether a lion's powerful roar shakes your core, a hyena's maniacal laugh tingles your spine, or a mountain gorilla's piercing gaze freezes you in your tracks. These singular events hold you in thrall and profoundly connect you to your environment. And what environments they are: the golden plains of the Serengeti, the pristine waterways of the Okavango Delta, the star-shaped sand dunes of the Namibian desert. Africa's varied landscapes stage nature's most spectacular wonders, and a safari is your front-row seat.

TOP REASONS TO GO

★ **Accommodations:** Supremely comfortable lodges and camps surrounded by wilderness.

★ **Parks and Reserves:** Africa's protected areas are home to the most animals on earth.

★ **Village Visits:** Fascinating tours of Himba, Maasai, Zulu, and other local communities.

★ **Beaches:** Coastal towns such as Zanzibar and Mombasa have beautiful shores.

★ **Epic Landscapes:** Mt. Kilimanjaro, Victoria Falls, the Bwindi rainforest, and more.

★ **Adventure:** Walking safaris, balloon flights, and camel treks are thrilling journeys.

Fodor's THE COMPLETE GUIDE TO AFRICAN SAFARIS

Editorial: Douglas Stallings, *Editorial Director*; Margaret Kelly, Jacinta O'Halloran, *Senior Editors*; Kayla Becker, Alexis Kelly, Amanda Sadlowski, *Editors*; Teddy Minford, *Content Editor*; Rachael Roth, *Content Manager*

Design: Tina Malaney, *Design and Production Director*; Jessica Gonzalez, *Production Designer*

Photography: Jennifer Arnow, *Senior Photo Editor*

Maps: Rebecca Baer, *Senior Map Editor*; David Lindroth, Mark Stroud (Moon Street Cartography), *Cartographers*

Production: Jennifer DePrima, *Editorial Production Manager*; Carrie Parker, *Senior Production Editor*; Elyse Rozelle, *Production Editor*

Business & Operations: Chuck Hoover, *Chief Marketing Officer*; Joy Lai, *Vice President and General Manager*; Stephen Horowitz, *Director of Business Development and Revenue Operations*; Tara McCrillis, *Director of Publishing Operations*; Eliza D. Aceves, *Content Operations Manager and Strategist*

Public Relations and Marketing: Joe Ewaskiw, *Manager*; Esther Su, *Marketing Manager*

Writers: Claire Baranowski, Charlotte Beauvoisin, Colleen Blaine, Christopher Clark, Leah Feiger, James Gifford, Mary Holland, Barbara Noe Kennedy, Linda Markovina, Lee Middleton, Lizzie Williams

Editor: Alexis Kelly

Production Editor: Elyse Rozelle

5th Edition

ISBN 978-1-64097-028-1

ISSN 1941-0336

All details in this book are based on information supplied to us at press time. Always confirm information when it matters, especially if you're making a detour to visit a specific place. Fodor's expressly disclaims any liability, loss, or risk, personal or otherwise, that is incurred as a consequence of the use of any of the contents of this book.

SPECIAL SALES

This book is available at special discounts for bulk purchases for sales promotions or premiums. For more information, e-mail SpecialMarkets@fodors.com.

PRINTED IN THE UNITED STATES OF AMERICA

10 9 8 7 6 5 4 3 2 1

CONTENTS

CONTENTS

MAPS

ABOUT
THIS GUIDE

Fodor's Recommendations

Everything in this guide is worth doing—we don't cover what isn't—but exceptional sights, hotels, and restaurants are recognized with additional accolades. **Fodor's Choice** ★ indicates our top recommendations; and **Best Bets** call attention to notable hotels and restaurants in various categories. Care to nominate a new place? Visit Fodors.com/contact-us.

Trip Costs

We list prices wherever possible to help you budget well. Hotel and restaurant price categories from **$** to **$$$$** are noted alongside each recommendation. For hotels, we include the lowest cost of a standard double room in high season. For restaurants, we cite the average price of a main course at dinner or, if dinner isn't served, at lunch. For attractions, we always list adult admission fees; discounts are usually available for children, students, and senior citizens.

Hotels

Our local writers vet every hotel to recommend the best overnights in each price category, from budget to expensive. Unless otherwise specified, you can expect private bath, phone, and TV in your room. For expanded hotel reviews, facilities, and deals visit Fodors.com.

Top Picks	Hotels &
★ **Fodor's**Choice	**Restaurants**
	🏨 Hotel
Listings	🛏 Number of
✉ Address	rooms
✉ Branch address	⍢ Meal plans
☎ Telephone	✕ Restaurant
📠 Fax	⍧ Reservations
⊕ Website	👗 Dress code
✉ E-mail	▭ No credit cards
🎫 Admission fee	$ Price
⊙ Open/closed	
times	**Other**
Ⓜ Subway	⇨ See also
⊹ Directions or	☞ Take note
Map coordinates	🏌 Golf facilities

Restaurants

Unless we state otherwise, restaurants are open for lunch and dinner daily. We mention dress code only when there's a specific requirement and reservations only when they're essential or not accepted. To make restaurant reservations, visit Fodors.com.

Credit Cards

The hotels and restaurants in this guide typically accept credit cards. If not, we'll say so.

EUGENE FODOR

Hungarian-born Eugene Fodor (1905–91) began his travel career as an interpreter on a French cruise ship. The experience inspired him to write *On the Continent* (1936), the first guidebook to receive annual updates and discuss a country's way of life as well as its sights. Fodor later joined the U.S. Army and worked for the OSS in World War II. After the war, he kept up his intelligence work while expanding his guidebook series. During the Cold War, many guides were written by fellow agents who understood the value of insider information. Today's guides continue Fodor's legacy by providing travelers with timely coverage, insider tips, and cultural context.

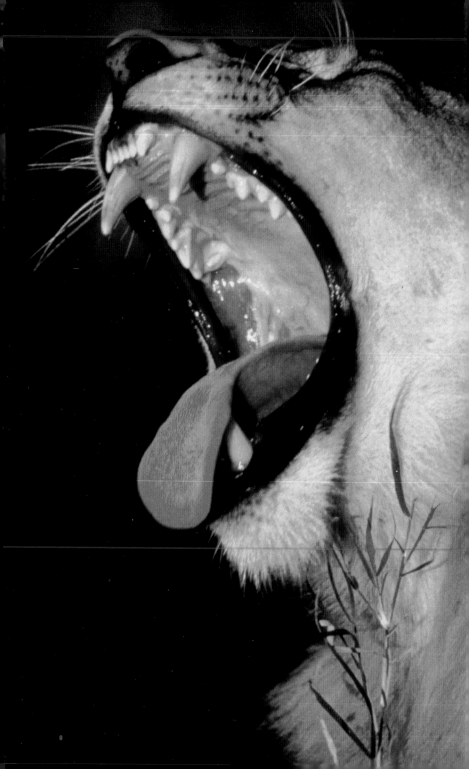

EXPERIENCE AN AFRICAN SAFARI

WHAT'S WHERE

The following numbers refer to chapters.

4 Kenya. Expect golden lions, red-robed warriors, snowcapped mountains, pristine white beaches, orange sunsets, and coral-pink dawns. You'll also experience some of the world's most famous safari destinations—Masai Mara, the Rift Valley—and world-class beach destinations like Diani Beach and the tiny town of Lamu.

5 Tanzania. Also part of East Africa, Tanzania attracts far fewer tourists than Kenya and South Africa, even though it boasts some of Africa's greatest tourist attractions—the Serengeti, the Great Migration, Olduvai Gorge, Ngorongoro Crater, Selous Game Reserve, and Lake Victoria.

6 South Africa. Africa's most developed country, at the very tip of the continent, is many worlds in one: modern bustling cities, ancient rock art, gorgeous beaches, fabulous game lodges, well-run national parks, mountain ranges, desert, and wine lands. It's home to Kruger National Park and the KwaZulu-Natal Parks.

7 Rwanda and Uganda. Trekking mountain gorillas in these countries of undulating hills, terraced farmlands, volcanic mountain chains, and dense rain forests is an experience unlike any other.

8 Botswana. The country itself is a natural wonder with terrain that varies from vast salt pans to the pristine waterways of the Okavango Delta. Expect lots of game, few tourists, and stars brighter than you'll ever see—the Kalahari Bushmen say that you can hear them sing.

9 Namibia. From the Namib Desert—the earth's oldest—to the fog-enshrouded Skeleton Coast. The great game park of Etosha, Damaraland's stark beauty, desert elephants, small cities with a fascinating mix of colonial and modern: you've never been anywhere like Namibia.

10 Victoria Falls. Shared by Zambia and Zimbabwe, Vic Falls is one of the greatest natural wonders of the world. It's the adventure center of Africa where adventurers can try everything from bungee jumping and white-water rafting to canoeing, rappelling, and Jet Skiing.

Etosha Pan

SKELETON COAST

NAMIB DESERT

DAMARALAND

Swakopmund
Walvis Bay

Luдеritz

IF YOU LIKE

The Out of Africa Experience

Turn back the clock to the great, glorious days of the early safaris, when Ernest Hemingway and Teddy Roosevelt stalked the golden grass of the plains with the Big Five in their rifle sights. Forget the rifles, but shoot as much as you like—with cameras. We have the perfect spots.

Cottars 1920s Safari Camp, Kenya. For an original safari replay it doesn't get much better than this—claw-foot tubs, antique rugs, wrought-iron candlesticks, old gramophones, polished butlers' trays—all under white safari tents.

Finch Hattons, Kenya. Live your every African dream at this classy camp where you'll dine at a table sparkling with silver and crystal as strains of Mozart softly fill the African night.

Il Moran, Kenya. Situated where Kenya's first colonial governors used to twirl their handlebar moustaches and sip their G&Ts while on safari, you'll enjoy the exclusive location, teeming game, and bygone elegance.

King's Pool, Botswana. From the ancient tree dominating the main deck to the lush accommodations, everything is on a regal scale—a tribute to the European royalty who used to hunt in this area.

Sabi Sabi Selati Camp, South Africa. Formerly a private hunting lodge, the early-1900s ambience stems from genuine train memorabilia. Old leather suitcases, antique wooden chairs, and signals recall the days of an 1870s train line.

To See the Great Migration

No matter where you stay during the Great Migration, you'll be assured of unforgettable sights. But we've highlighted a few camps where sightings may be even more spectacular. Remember that world weather cycles are changing—there's no guarantee that at that particular place and time your game-viewing will live up to the National Geographic TV Channel.

Grumeti River Camp, Tanzania. Watch out for galloping wildebeest at this exclusive camp on the banks of the famed Grumeti River, where you'll be perfectly positioned to witness one of the greatest shows on earth.

Little Governors' Camp, Kenya. A ferry ride across the Mara River and a short walk escorted by armed guides takes you to this lovely camp sited directly in the path of the wildebeest migration.

Mara Serena Safari Lodge, Kenya. If you get tired of looking at the endless grasslands where the migration takes place in front of your eyes, then spot game at the lodge's own busy waterhole.

Naibor Camp, Kenya. Situated in a particularly game-rich area 20 minutes away from one of the legendary migration river crossings, this is the perfect base for watching the migration.

Sayari Camp, Tanzania. This camp is perfectly poised for watching the Mara River crossing, when hundreds of thousands of wildebeest plunge into the crocodile-infested water on their journey north.

Serengeti Under Canvas, Tanzania. This luxury mobile camp follows the migration, staying put for a couple of months and then moving north with the herds. Not cheap but worth every penny.

Drop-Dead Luxury

So you want the whole game experience but don't want to rough it? No problem. Our favorites will tempt you to defect from the real world and live like kings and queens.

Great Fish River Lodge, Kwandwe, South Africa. Colonial luxury with genuine antiques combine with stunning river views in this malaria-free Big Five reserve.

MalaMala Game Reserve, Mpumalanga, South Africa. One of the oldest and most distinguished of all Southern African bush lodges, this is the haunt of royalty, celebs, and the jet set.

Mombo Camp, Botswana. The spacious, graciously decorated en suite rooms of this legendary camp may have a tented feel, but they're ultraluxurious with great game-viewing.

Ngorongoro Crater Lodge, Tanzania. The theme here is Great Zimbabwe ruins meets SS *Titanic* baroque, and your abode will be palatial and the game-viewing equally fabulous.

Singita Sabi Sand, Kruger, South Africa. Hide yourself away at these multi-award-winning bush getaways, with superb game and service to match.

Thanda Main Lodge, KwaZulu-Natal, South Africa. This exquisite lodge has beehive-shape dwellings that blend elements of royal Zulu with an eclectic pan-African feel. Shaka never had it this good.

Vlei Lodge, Phinda, South Africa Six sumptuous secluded suites with private plunge pools look out over an open wetland stretching to the horizon. Expect game galore, magnificent wildlife, and superb service.

Animal Encounters

David Sheldrick Orphanage for Rhinos and Elephants, Kenya. Orphaned elephants are hand-raised here until they are old enough to be reintroduced into the wild. Watch the youngsters playing as they are washed and fed by their handlers.

Clouds Mountain Gorilla Lodge, Uganda. Profits from this luxury lodge fund local community conservation projects, helping support the future of this critically endangered ape.

Desert Rhino Camp, Namibia. If it's rhinos you're after, especially the rare black rhino, then this remote tented camp in the heart of the private Palmwag Reserve is a must.

Greystoke Mahale, Tanzania. About 60 of the area's 1,000 or so wild chimpanzees live in the forest near this gorgeous lodge on a deserted beach, so you have an excellent chance of spotting them.

Londolozi, South Africa. This is the place to see leopards. The most beautiful and successful of all feline predators, watching a leopard move through the bush is a truly awesome sight.

Ol Kanjau Camp, Kenya. The focus is on elephants, which have been studied here for nearly 40 years. You'll never forget the thrill of your nose-to-trunk introduction to one of the 52 great matriarchal herds.

To Get Away from the Crowds

If you choose any of the following camps and lodges you'll be assured privacy and exclusivity.

Duba Plains, Botswana. Deep in the Okavango Delta, this tiny camp on an isolated island has superb game-viewing. Only two 4x4 open game vehicles operate in the whole reserve.

Jack's Camp, Botswana. If you're bold-spirited, reasonably fit, and enjoy a rugged pioneer experience, then Jack's is for you. Try quad-biking, horseback safaris, or walking with the bushmen.

Mnemba Island Lodge, Tanzania. For the ultimate beach escape where time stands still and where sand, sea, and horizon melt into each other, this exclusive lodge with only 20 guests is hard to beat.

Tswalu Kalahari, South Africa. South Africa's largest private game reserve is also malaria-free, and only 30 guests at a time can stay at the two properties, The Motse and Tarkuni. Explore the vast wilderness by 4x4, on foot, or on a horse.

Ruzizi Tented Lodge, Rwanda. Far from the gorilla-trek hordes, the grunt of baboons and the splash of bathing elephants are all you'll hear at this secluded eco-lodge in Akagera National Park.

Sand Rivers Selous, Tanzania. Above a wide bend of the Rufiji River—hundreds of miles away from touristy Africa—this lodge is just about as isolated and exclusive as you can get.

Sarara Tented Camp, Kenya. At this small remote tented camp below the Mathews Mountains in the 75,000-acre Namunyuk Wildlife Conservation Trust, the only strangers in the night you'll see are the wildlife residents.

!Xaus Lodge, South Africa. In one of South Africa's most remote parks, !Xaus (pronounced "Kaus") provides great hospitality, game drives, desert walks, and introductions to local bushmen.

To Interact with the Locals

Many of the cultural and village visits aren't entirely authentic given the need for tourist dollars, but we've identified a few genuine experiences.

Deception Valley Lodge, Botswana. At this lodge in the Central Kalahari Game Reserve you'll meet the desert-dwelling Naru people, who built it entirely by hand. Expect pure magic during a three-hour walk with the bushmen themselves.

Forest Lodge, Phinda, South Africa. Learn about the fascinating customs, traditions, and beliefs of the legendary Zulu nation on a village tour. The local *sangoma* (traditional healer) will even foretell your future.

Il'Ngwesi Lodge, Kenya. Learn about hunting, gathering honey, animal trapping with indigenous poisons, and fashioning beadwork at the nearby Maasai village.

Lake Manyara Serena Lodge, Tanzania. Take a guided walk to Mto wa Mbu, a small town that's home to more than 100 different tribes. Here you'll visit homes, a school, a church, the market, and a banana-leaf bar.

Ol Seki Hemingway's Mara, Kenya. At this eco-friendly camp you'll visit authentic, nontouristy Maasai villages, where you might be lucky enough to witness a genuine betrothal or post-initiation ceremony.

Serra Cafema, Namibia. Only the nomadic Himba people share this awesome remote area, and a visit to a local village will be a life-changing experience.

To Go to the Beach

Going on safari is also about where you're going to go before or after your game-viewing, and there are plenty of beach resort options to choose from.

The Majlis, Kenya. Set on the beach on Manda Island, close to Lamu, The Majlis combines Swahili, Arabic, and Indian influences to make a seriously stylish retreat furnished with African antiques and world-class artworks.

Mnemba Lodge Tanzania. For the ultimate beach escape head to this tiny island off the tip of Zanzibar. You can dive and snorkel off a pristine coral reef, and you might just rub elbows with the rich and famous.

Oyster Box, South Africa. A South African icon for more than half a century, this gorgeous hotel, which seamlessly blends old colonial decor with contemporary African art, sits on a golden beach guarded by a lighthouse.

Zawadi Hotel, Tanzania. Nine spacious villas are on a clifftop setting that overlooks the Indian Ocean's turquoise waters on the southeast coast of Zanzibar. Ideal for a romantic break, the amenities here include a small spa and an infinity pool, as well as gourmet dining.

Rocktail Beach Camp South Africa. If you're in the mood for pristine beaches, surf fishing, amazing scuba diving, and snorkeling, then coming to this lodge nestled in the Maputaland Coastal Reserve will be the perfect beach getaway after your safari.

Natural Wonders

Sub-Saharan Africa is home to some awe-inspiring natural wonders.

Explosion Crater Drive. This stunning three-hour drive traverses the Katwe crater field in Uganda. It's littered with steep-sided volcanic craters, each containing its own microhabitat from ancient rain forest to a sulfurous lake.

The Great Migration. This annual journey of more than 2 million animals through Kenya and Tanzania is a safari seeker's Holy Grail; some consider it to be one of the world's greatest natural wonders.

Mt. Kilimanjaro. Kili, as it's fondly called, is the continent's highest peak and the tallest freestanding mountain in the world. It's one of the easier mountains to climb; about 25,000 people each year set out for the summit.

The Namibia Dunes. In Namib Naukluft Park, the largest game park in Africa, lie the mythical Namibia sand dunes. Said to be the highest dunes in the world, this is an adventure seeker's dream.

The Ngorongoro Crater. Nearly 3 million years old, this UNESCO World Heritage Site in northern Tanzania is a haven for wild game. Though it does get busy during high season, your experiences far outweigh the annoyances.

Okavango Delta. At its peak, the world's largest inland delta covers some 16,000 square km (6,177 square miles) of northwest Botswana.

Victoria Falls. More than 91 meters (300 feet) high and visible from 50 km (31 miles) away, the Falls are one of the world's seven natural wonders.

FINDING THE BIG 5

The fauna that can be found on an African safari is as varied and vast as the continent's landscape. Africa has more large animals than anywhere else in the world and is the only place on earth where vast herds still roam the plains.

		African Buffalo	Elephant	Leopard	Lion	Rhino
BOTSWANA	The Okavango Delta	●	●	●	●	●
	Moremi Wildlife Reserve	●	●	●	●	●
	Chobe Nat'l Park	●	●	●	●	●
	Kwando Game Reserve	●	●	●	●	○
KENYA	Masai Mara	●	●	●	●	●
	Amboseli Nat'l Park	●	●	●	●	●
	Tsavo Nat'l Park	●	●	●	●	●
	Laikipia Plateau	●	●	●	●	●
NAMIBIA	Namib Naukluft Park*	○	○	◑	◑	○
	Damaraland	○	●	○	○	●
	Etosha Nat'l Park	●	●	●	●	●
SOUTH AFRICA	Kruger Nat'l Park	●	●	●	●	●
	Sabi Sands Game Reserve	●	●	●	●	●
	KwaZulu-Natal Parks	●	●	●	●	●
	Kgalagadi Transfrontier Park	○	○	●	●	○
TANZANIA	Serengeti Nat'l Park	●	●	●	●	●
	Ngorongoro Crater	●	●	●	●	●
	Lake Manyara Nat'l Park	●	●	●	●	○
	Selous Game Reserve	●	●	●	●	●
	Gombe Stream and Mahale Mountains Nat'l Parks**	○	○	○	○	○

*This park is noted for its stunning scenic beauty - not game
**These parks are primarily for primate viewing - chimpanzees and monkeys
KEY: ● = yes ◑ = Rarely ○ = No

THE BIG 5

There's nothing quite like the feeling of first setting eyes on one of the Big Five—buffalo, elephant, leopard, lion, and rhino—in the African bush. Being just a few feet from these majestic creatures is both terrifying and exhilarating, even for the most seasoned safari-goer.

The Big Five was originally a hunting term referring to those animals that posed the greatest risk to hunters on foot—buffalo, elephant, leopard, lion, and rhino. Today it has become one of the most important criteria used in evaluating a lodge or reserve, though it should never be your only criterion.

THE AFRICAN BUFFALO

Often referred to as the Cape buffalo, this is considered by many to be the most dangerous of the Big Five because of its unpredictability and speed. Do not confuse it with the docile Asian water buffalo as the Cape buffalo is a more powerful and untameable beast with a massive build and short strong legs. They have few predators other than human hunters and lions. It generally takes an entire lion pride to bring down an adult buffalo, although calves or weak and sick adults can be taken by wild dog and spotted hyena. Lions risk being mobbed by the herd when they do attack, and are sometimes trampled and gored.

Cape buffalo can reach up to 1,900 pounds and in the wild can live up to 15 or so years, much longer if they are in captivity. Never found very far from water, they are grazers and widespread throughout sub-Saharan Africa, especially in Kenya, Tanzania, Botswana, Zambia, Zimbabwe, and South Africa. Large, mixed herds can number up to a few hundred, and in the Serengeti, during the rains, in their thousands. You shouldn't fear a herd, but beware lone old males, which have mostly been thrown out of the herd and are now bad-tempered and volatile. Known as "Dagha Boys"—dagha is the clay mixture used for building traditional huts—they spend much of their days in mud wallows and are usually thickly coated in the stuff. While seemingly lethargic these old boys can turn on a dime and charge like lightning. If you are charged, run for cover or climb the nearest tree.

THE ELEPHANT

The largest of the land animals, it once roamed the continent by the millions. Today, according to the World Wildlife Fund (WWF), the population, mainly about 415,000, with a quarter to a third of the population being forest elephants.

African elephants are divided into two species. Savannah elephants are the largest, at 13 feet and 7 tons, and can be found by lakes, marshes, or grasslands. Forest elephants have an average height of 10 feet and weight of 10,000 pounds. They're usually found in central and West African rainforests.

An elephant's gestation period is 22 months—the longest of any land animal. The average calf is 265 pounds. When calves are born, they are raised and protected by the entire herd—a group of about 10 females led by the oldest and largest. Males leave the herd after 15 years, often living with other males or alone.

When an elephant trumpets in a showy manner, head up and ears spread, it's a mock charge—frightening but not physically dangerous. If an elephant stomps the ground, holds its ears back and head forward, and issues a loud, high-pitched screech, this means real trouble. A charging elephant is extremely fast and surprisingly agile. If you're on foot make for the nearest big tree or embankment; elephants seldom negotiate these obstacles. If you're in a vehicle, hit the gas.

THE RHINO

There are two species of these massive primeval-looking animals in Africa: the black, or hook-lipped rhino, and the white, or square-lipped rhino. Both species have poor eyesight but excellent hearing, and because of their erratic tempers, they may sometimes charge without apparent reason. These animals are surprisingly agile for their size. The white rhino is slighter taller (up to 60 inches at the shoulder) and heavier at over two tons, the black rhino is shorter and stockier by a few inches and can weigh up to one and a half tons. Although they share habitats, the white rhino is a grazer eating only grasses, the black, a browser, eating leaves and shrubs. The black rhino which is more aggressive than the white, prefers thick thornveld and dense vegetation, while the white sticks more to open grassland and the plains. Both love to wallow in mud. They mark their territory by means of defecating in individual middens, or dung heaps, which they make along rhino paths and territorial boundaries, regularly patrolling these 'signposts' on the look out for intruders.

The black rhino tends to be more solitary unless it is a very small mother/father/calf group; the white rhino stays together in small groups called crashes. Calves of both species stay with their mothers until they are four or five, when they leave to find a new territory.

Sadly, the survival of this incredible mammal is under serious threat from poaching; according to Save the Rhino, poaching increased 9,000% from 2007 to 2014. Today, many are protected in sanctuaries or reserves, but poaching continues–in South Africa's Kruger National Park, 1,054 rhinos were killed in 2016. These are traded on the black market as aphrodisiacs (an empty claim) and as potential dagger handles in the Middle East to symbolize wealth and power. While major efforts by conservationists are in hand to try to stem the problem, poaching is moving into Kenya, Zimbabwe, and Namibia.

THE LION

Known as the king of beasts—the Swahili word for lion, "simba," also means "king," "strong," and "aggressive"—this proud animal was once found throughout the world. Today, the majority of the estimated 20,000 lions are found in sub-Saharan Africa—a small population is also found in India—in grasslands, savannah, and dense bush.

Watching a lion stalk its prey can be one of the most exciting safari encounters. Females do most of the hunting, typically setting up a plan of attack, which is then carried out by the pride. Lionesses take turns hunting and this collective labor allows them to conserve their energy and survive longer in the bush. They are most active from dusk to dawn. A pride consists of between four and six adults but occasionally may go up to 20 or even 30. Botswana's Savute region is known for its large prides. The males, identified by their gorgeous golden-red or black manes, are often brothers who behave territorially; their main task is to protect the females and the cubs. Typically, the females in the pride will give birth at approximately the same time, and the cubs will be raised together. Litters usually consist of two to three cubs that weigh about three pounds each. Sometimes, males that take over a pride will kill existing cubs so that they can sire their own with the lioness.

Lions can sleep for up to 18 hours a day. Lounging about in the grass, lions will often lick each other, rub heads, and play. But don't be fooled by their charms. When a lion moves, it can do so with awesome speed and power—a charging lion can cover 330 feet in four seconds. If you come face to face with a lion, never, ever turn your back and try to run—that is your death warrant. Your best bet is to stand as still as possible and try to outface the lion.

THE LEOPARD

Secretive, stealthy and shrewd, the leopard is the most successful predator of all Africa's big cats. They are often difficult to spot on safari, primarily because they are nocturnal, but if you go on a night game drive your chances will increase tremendously.

Leopard can vary in appearance, their coat ranging from a light tawny hue in dry areas to darker shades in the forest. Their spots, called rosettes, are round in East Africa, but square in Southern Africa. Leopard can also be found in India, China, Siberia, and Korea. The female leopard, whose litter usually ranges from about one to three cubs, will keep her young hidden for about two months after birth, then feed and nurse them for an additional three months or so until her cubs are strong enough to roam with her. What about dad? Male leopards play no part in rearing the cubs. In fact, the male is usually long gone by the time the female gives birth. He leaves her after they mate, although he has been known to return to kill the cubs, hence the reasoning behind keeping them hidden for the first few months of their lives.

Leopard use a combination of teeth and razor-sharp claws to kill their prey; it's not uncommon for a leopard's lunch to be taken away by lion or hyena. In order to avoid this, the leopard will often drag their larger kills up a tree where they can dine amongst the leaves in relative peace and quiet.

THE LITTLE 5

We've all heard of the Big Five, but keep a look out for the Little Five, a term given to the animals with names that include the Big Five: antlion, buffalo weaver, elephant shrew, leopard tortoise, and rhinoceros beetle.

RHINOCEROS BEETLE

The rhinoceros beetle grows up to two inches long. It has large spikes—similar in appearance to a rhino's horns—which are used in battle with other rhino beetles, or for digging, climbing, and mating.

LEOPARD TORTOISE

The largest tortoise in sub-Saharan Africa, the leopard tortoise can grow up to two feet long and weigh up to 100 pounds. It lives in the grasslands of East and Southern Africa and doesn't mate until it's at least 10 years old. Its name stems from its black and yellow-spotted shell, which resembles a leopard's coat.

ELEPHANT SHREW

These ground-dwelling mammals range in size from that of a mouse to a large rabbit. They live in lowland forests, woodlands, rocky outcrops, and deserts and eat small fruits and plants. They get their name from their long nose, which resembles a miniature elephant's trunk.

ANTLION

Also known as a "doodlebug" because of the winding patterns it leaves in the sand when building traps, the antlion makes its home on dry, sandy slopes sheltered from the wind. Essentially larva, it eventually grows into an insect akin to a dragonfly.

RED-BILLED BUFFALO WEAVERS

These black birds with red bills and legs make big sturdy communal nests out of sticks which are defended by the dominant male and nearly always face westward. Inside, the nests are separate chambers with individual tunnels leading to the outside. Their mating is unique amongst birds as it lasts up to two minutes instead of seconds as in most birds.

FAUNA

OTHER ANIMALS

You'll be amazed by how many visitors ignore a gorgeous animal that doesn't "rank" in the Big Five or lose interest in a species once they've checked it off their list. After you've spent a few days in the bush, you'll hopefully understand the idiocy of racing about in search of five animals when there are 150 equally fascinating species all around you. Here are a few to look out for.

Baboons

(A) These are the most adaptable of the ground-dwelling primates and can live in all manner of habitats as long as they have water and a safe place to sleep. Baboons travel in groups of up to 40, sleeping, eating, and socializing together. Although they're hugely entertaining to watch, always keep your vehicle windows rolled up. Like other animals, they can be vicious when they feel threatened, and they have huge canine teeth. They eat mainly plants, but will also consume small quantities of meat.

Cheetah

(B) Reaching speeds of 70 mph, cheetahs are the world's fastest land animals—they have slender, muscular legs and special pads on their feet for traction. With its characteristic dark spots, the cheetah also has a distinctive black "tear" line running from the inside corner of its eye to the mouth. A solitary, timid creature, cheetahs are found mainly in open savanna. Males and females can sometimes be seen together after mating, but usually one or two males—often brothers—are alone and females are with the cubs. Cheetahs generally prey on gazelles and impalas. Sadly, this stunning cat is one of the most endangered animals, due to shrinking habitat, loss of prey, and disease.

Giraffe

(C) The biggest ruminant and tallest living animal, giraffes are social creatures that live in loose herds that can spread out over half a mile. Although there are no leaders, the males fight over females using a "necking" technique, winding their necks around each other, pushing and shoving. Giraffes either walk or gallop and are ubiquitous in most national parks. It's easy to tell the difference between males and females. The tops of the male's horns are bare and shiny from fighting; the females have bushy tips like paintbrushes.

Hippo

(D) Though they may be comical looking, these are actually one of Africa's most dangerous animals. The most common threat display is the yawn, which is telling you to back off. Most guides will give them a wide berth. Never get between a hippo and its water, as this will appear to them that you're trying to corner them and may result in an attack. The comical nighttime sounds of hippos snorting and chortling will be one of your safari's most memorable experiences.

Impala

(E) One of the most populous animals in the African bush, impalas can be found in grasslands and wooded areas, usually near water. Similar in appearance to a deer, these one-of-a-kind antelopes are reddish-brown with white and black markings. A typical herd has one dominant male ruling over his harem, although bachelor herds are usually in the vicinity, with hopeful individuals awaiting their turn to oust the ruling male. It's a hugely successful animal, because it's both a grazer and a browser.

FAUNA

African Wild Dogs
(F) Also called the "painted dog" or "painted wolf" because of each uniquely spotted coat, the wild dog is headed toward extinction with numbers of approximately 6,600 and shrinking. This highly social animal lives in small packs of about 15; only the alpha male and female are allowed to breed. Intelligent and quick, wild dogs hunt as a coordinated pack running down their prey, which varies from antelopes to zebras, until exhausted. They have an amazingly successful catch rate of 85%.

Bush Baby
(G) These small nocturnal primates, which make cries similar to that of a human baby, range in size from 2 ounces to 3 pounds. During the day, they stay in tree hollows and nests, but at night you'll see them leaping and bouncing from tree to tree in pursuit of night-flying insects.

Their main predators are some of the larger carnivores, genets, and snakes.

Hyena
(H) Hyenas live in groups called clans and make their homes in dens. They mark their territory with gland secretions or droppings. Cubs are nursed for about 18 months, at which point they head out on hunting and scavenging sprees with their mothers. Both strategic hunters and opportunists, hyenas will feed on their own kill as well as that of others. Aggressive and dangerous, African folklore links the hyena with witchcraft and legends.

Nile Crocodile
(I) Averaging about 16 feet and 700 pounds, this croc can be found in sub-Saharan Africa, the Nile River, and Madagascar. They eat mainly fish but will eat almost anything, including a baby hippo or a human. Although fearsome looking and lightning quick in their attack, they're unusually sensitive with their young,

carefully guarding their nests until their babies hatch. Their numbers have been slashed by poachers, who seek their skins for shoemakers.

Springbok

(J)This cinnamon-color antelope has a dark brown stripe on its flanks, a white underside, and short, slender horns. It often engages in a mysterious activity known as "pronking," a seemingly sudden spurt of high jumps into the air with its back bowed. Breeding takes place twice a year, and the young will stay with their mothers for about four months. These herbivores travel in herds that usually include a few territorial males.

Wildebeest

(K)This ubiquitous herbivore is an odd-looking creature: large head and front end, curved horns, and slender body and rear. Often called "the clowns of the veld" they toss their heads as they run and kick up their back legs. Mothers give birth to their young in the middle of the herd, and calves can stand and run within three minutes and keep up with the herd after two days.

Zebra

(L)Africa has three species: the Burchell's (or common) zebra, East Africa's Grevy's zebra (named after former French president Jules Grevy), and the mountain zebra of southern and southwestern Africa. All have striped coats and strong teeth for chewing grass and often travel in large herds. A mother keeps its foal close for the first few hours after birth so it can remember her stripes and not get lost. Bold and courageous, a male zebra can break an attacking lion's jaw with one powerful kick.

FAUNA

BIRDS

Many people come to Africa solely for the birds. There are thousands of winged beauties to "ooh" and "aah" over; we mention a few to look out for.

Bateleur Eagle
(A) This spectacular bird, which looks as if it's "balancing" in the air, is found throughout sub-Saharan Africa and is probably one of the best known birds in Africa. Mainly black with a red back, legs, and beak and white underneath its wings, the Bateleur eagle can fly up to 322 km (200 miles) at a time in search of prey, which includes antelope, mice, other birds, snakes, and carrion. They mate for life, often using the same nest for several years.

Lappet-Faced Vulture
(B) The largest and most dominant of the vultures, this scavenger feeds mainly on carrion and carcasses that have been killed by other animals. The most aggressive of the African vultures, it will also, on occasion, kill other weaker birds or attack the nests of young birds as prey. The Lappet-faced vulture has a bald head and is pink in color with a wingspan of up to 8½ feet.

Lilacbreasted Roller
(C) This stunning-looking bird with a blue-and-lilac-color breast is found in the open woodland and savanna throughout sub-Saharan Africa. It's usually solo or in pairs sitting in bushes or trees. Both parents nurture the nest and are extremely territorial and aggressive when it comes to defending it. During mating, the male flies up high and then rolls over and over as it descends, making screeching cries.

Kori Bustard

(D) One of the world's heaviest flying birds is found all over southern and East Africa. Reaching almost 30 pounds and about 3½ feet in length, the male is much larger than the female but both are gray in color, have crests, and gray-and-white necks. Although it does fly, the majority of its time is spent on land where it can find insects, lizards, snakes, and seeds. One male mates with several females, which then raise the young on their own.

Pel's Fishing Owl

(E) A large, monogamous, ginger-brown owl with no ears, bare legs, and dark eyes, it lives along the banks of rivers in Kruger Park, South Africa's Kwa-Zulu Natal province, Botswana's Okavango Delta, and Zimbabwe. One of only three fishing owls in the world, it hunts at night with its sharp talons and dozes in tall trees during the day. The owls communicate with each other through synchronized hooting at night as they guard their stretch of riverbank.

Wattled Crane

(F) The rarest African crane is found in Ethiopia, Zambia, Botswana, Mozambique, and South Africa. A gray-and-white bird, it can reach up to 5 feet tall and, while mating, will nest in pairs along the shallow wetlands of large rivers. They're omnivorous and sometimes wander onto farmlands where they're vulnerable to poisoning by farmers. They occur in pairs or sometimes in large flocks, especially in the Okavango Delta.

FLORA

Although the mammals and birds of Africa are spectacular, we'd be remiss if we didn't mention the amazing plant life of this varied landscape. The floral wealth of the African continent is astounding, with unique, endemic species growing in all parts—the South African Cape has one of the richest of the world's six floral kingdoms. There are also several species of non-native plants and trees in Africa that have become the subject of lively environmental debates due to their effect on the environment.

TREES

African Mahogany

(A)Originally from West Africa, you'll find this majestic tree in warm humid climates like riverine forests; you'll also find them in the Florida everglades. A member of the Khaya genus, the mahogany requires significant rainfall in order to thrive and can reach up to 140 feet with a 6-foot trunk diameter. Its much-prized, strong, richly colored wood is sought after for furniture making and boat building.

Baobab

(B)A huge, quirky-looking deciduous tree that grows throughout mainland Africa, the baobab has a round, hollow trunk with spiny-looking branches growing out at the top in all directions—it almost looks like it's upside down with the roots sprouting out at the top. Known for storing water in its trunk, the baobab is found in dry regions and can live up to 400 years; some have lived for more than 1,000 years. The hollow trunks have been home to a prison and a post office.

Fever

(C)The fabled fever tree, which thrives in damp, swampy habitats throughout sub-Saharan Africa, has a luminous, yellow-green bark that's smooth and flaky, and its branches have white thorns and clusters of yellow flowers. It's so named because

before mosquitoes were known to carry malaria, travelers often contracted the disease where fever trees grew and thus they were wrongly thought to transmit malaria. Bees are attracted by the sweet smell of the flowers, and birds often nest in its branches as the thorns offer extra protection against predators.

Fig

(D)There are as many as 50 species of fig trees in southern and East Africa, where they may reach almost gigantic proportions, growing wherever water is nearby. Although figs provide nourishment for a variety of birds, bats, and other animals, they're most noted for their symbiotic relationship with wasps, which pollinate the fig flowers while reproducing. The fig seed is dispersed throughout the bush in the droppings of animals who feed on the rich, juicy fruit.

Jackalberry

(E)The large, graceful jackalberry, also known as the African ebony, is a riverine tree found all over sub-Saharan Africa. It can grow up to 80 feet tall and 16 feet wide. It bears fragrant white flowers and a fleshy yellow fruit that jackals, monkeys, baboons, and fruit-eating birds love. Its bark and leaves are used in traditional medicine with proven pharmacological benefits.

Sausage

(F)This unique tree, found in southern Africa, bears sausagelike fruit that hangs from ropelike stalks. The tree grows to be about 40 feet with fragrant red flowers that bloom at night and are pollinated by bats, insects, and the occasional bird. The fresh fruit, which can grow up to 2 feet long and weigh as much as 15 pounds, is poisonous but can be made into various medicines and an alcohol similar to beer.

FLORA

PLANTS

Magic Guarri

This round shrub grows along floodplains and rivers. It has dark green leaves and white or cream-color flowers, and its fruit is fleshy and purple with a seed in its center. The fruit can be fermented to produce an alcoholic beverage, and the bark is used as a dye in basket making. The twigs have been used as toothbrushes, while the root can be used as mouthwash. The wood, sometimes used to make furniture, is said to have magical or supernatural powers and is never burned as firewood.

Strelitzia Flower

(G)Also known as Bird of Paradise or the crane flower, the strelitzia is indigenous to South Africa. It grows up to 6½ feet tall with a beautiful fan-shape crown with bright orange and bluish-purple petals that grow perpendicular to the stem, giving it the appearance of a graceful bird.

Welwitschia mirabilis

(H)With its long, wide leathery leaves creeping over the ground, this somewhat surreal-looking plant is also one of the world's oldest plants; it's estimated that welwitschia live to about 1,500 years, though botanists believe some can live to be 2,000 years old. It's found in the Namib Desert and consists solely of two leaves, a stem base, and roots. The plant's two permanent leaves lie on the ground getting tattered and torn, but grow longer and longer each summer.

Wild Thyme

(I)Also called creeping thyme, wild thyme grows mainly in rocky soil and outcrops. Its fragrant flowers are purple or white, and its leaves are used to make herbal tea. Honeybees use the plant as an important source of nectar. There's also a species of butterfly whose diet consists solely of wild thyme.

Cape Fynbos

(J)There are six plant kingdoms—an area with a relatively uniform plant population—in the world. The smallest, known as the Cape Floral Kingdom or Capensis, is found in South Africa's southwestern and southern Cape; it's roughly the size of Portugal or Indiana and is made up of eight different protected areas. In 2004 it became the sixth South African site to be added to the UNESCO World Heritage list.

Fynbos, a term given to the collection of plants found in the Cape, accounts for four-fifths of the Cape Floral Kingdom; the term has been around since the Dutch first settled here in the 1600s. It includes no less than 8,600 plant species including shrubs, proteas, bulbous plants like gladiolus and lachenalia (in the hydrangea family), aloe, and grass-like flowering plants. Table Mountain alone hosts approximately 1,500 species of plants and 69 protea species—there are 112 protea species worldwide.

From a distance, fynbos may just look like random clusters of sharp growth that cover the mountainous regions of the Cape, but up close you'll see the beauty and diversity of this colorful growth. Many of the bright blooms in gardens in the United States and Europe, such as daisies, gladioli, lilies, and irises, come from indigenous Cape plants.

PLANNING A SAFARI

2

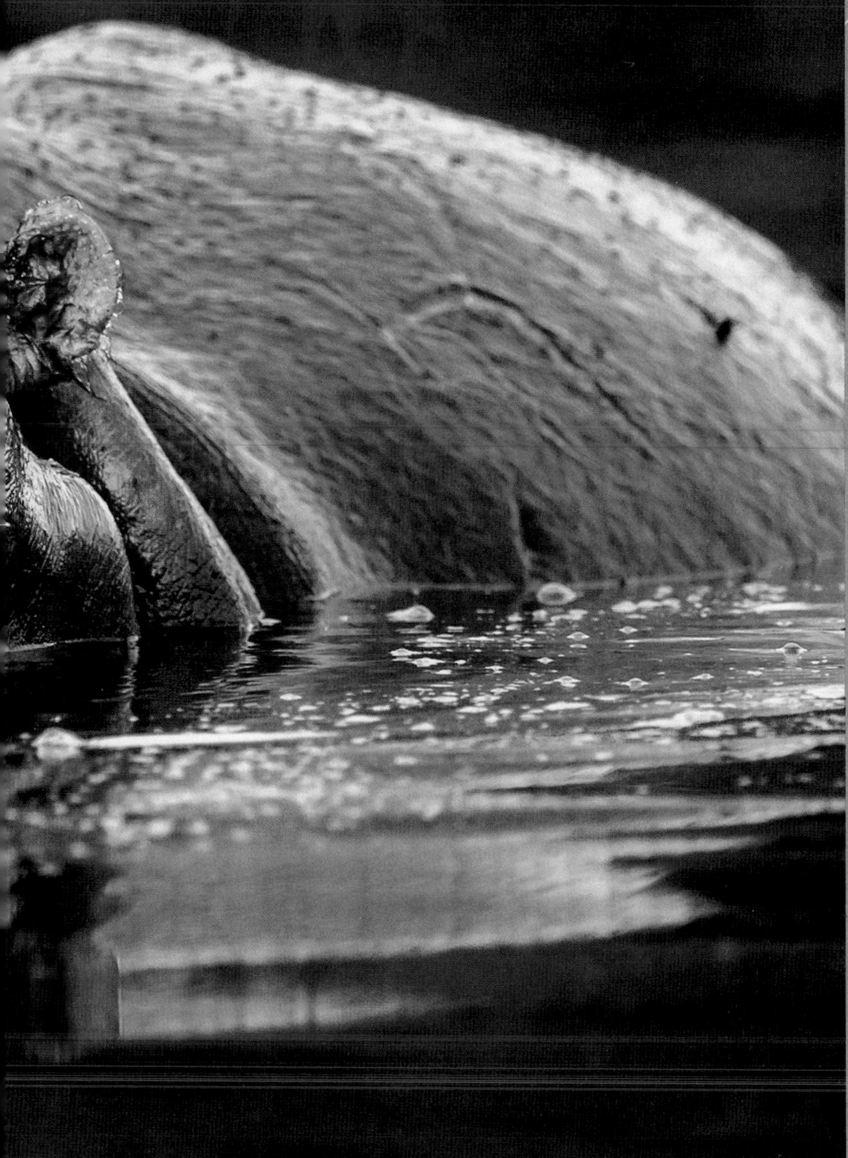

Updated
by Claire
Baranowski

A safari is one of the biggest travel adventures you can have. Planning well is crucial to ensure you get the most out of it. Even a basic question like "What should I wear?" is extremely important. In this safari section, we'll cover all the special considerations and lingo you'll need, with plenty of insider tips along the way.

Most people start planning a safari six to nine months in advance, but it's never too soon to start planning your trip. In fact, planning your trip 12 months in advance isn't unreasonable, especially if you want to travel during peak season—November through February in South Africa, July through October elsewhere—and have your heart set on a particular lodge.

If you're keen to see big game, particularly the Big Five *(see feature in Chapter 1)*, then your best bets for success will be in East Africa and South Africa. The Serengeti National Park *(Chapter 5)* in Tanzania is known for its plentiful game and is the stomping ground for approximately 2 million wildebeest, 250,000 zebra, and 500,000 antelope that race more than 1,931 km (1,200 miles) every July to find enough water and grass to survive during the Great Migration. The Masai Mara National Reserve *(Chapter 4)* in neighboring Kenya is probably best known for its large population of big cats, as well as hippos and the rare black rhino and spotted hyena. In South Africa, Kruger National Park and the private Sabi Sand game reserve just outside of Kruger *(Chapter 6)* are ideal places to observe the Big Five as well as leopards and hundreds of other species. In Kruger alone, there are an estimated 1,200 species of flora and fauna, as well as endangered African wild dogs. You'll see the African elephant everywhere in the park, with lions more abundant in the central and eastern regions; rhinos and buffalo make their home in the woods of southwest Kruger.

Deciding where you want to go and choosing the right safari operator *(Chapter 3)* are the most important things you need to do. Start planning for your safari the way you would any trip. Read travel books about the areas that most interest you. Talk to people who have been on a similar trip; word-of-mouth advice can be invaluable. Surf the 'net. Get inspired. Line up your priorities. And find someone you trust to help plan your trip.

GETTING STARTED

AIR TRAVEL

Traveling by plane is the best and most viable means of transportation to most safari destinations. If you're visiting a game lodge deep in the bush, you'll be arriving by light plane—and you really will be restricted in what you can bring. Excess luggage can usually be stored with the operator until your return. Don't just gloss over this: charter operators take weight very seriously, and some will charge you for an extra ticket if you insist on bringing excess baggage. *For airline contact information and specific information for each country, see Air Travel, in the Getting Here and Around section of each chapter.*

AIR PASS

If you're planning to fly between a few of the countries mentioned in this book, consider the Star Alliance African Airpass, which can be purchased only by international passengers arriving in Africa on a Star Alliance carrier (Lufthansa, United, US Airways, Air Canada, South African Airways, etc.); it's good for 3 to 10 flights on Ethiopian Airways, South African Airways, Brussels Airlines, and EgyptAir. The flights are sold in segments, priced by the distance between cities. These are a bargain for the longer routes, such as from Nairobi to Johannesburg. If your itinerary includes more than 2 of the 23 cities served in Africa, this may be a good choice.

If you're flying on British Airways or its affiliate Comair, another option is the Visit Africa Pass by Oneworld Alliance (there are 14 airlines in the alliance), which uses a zone system between cities in South Africa, Namibia, Zambia, and Zimbabwe. The minimum purchase is two segments. It's a great value when compared to regular fares.

Air Pass Information Oneworld Alliance. ⊕ *www.oneworld.com.* **Star Alliance.** ⊕ *www.staralliance.com.*

CHARTER FLIGHTS

Charter flights are a common mode of transportation when getting to safari lodges and remote destinations throughout Southern and East Africa. These aircraft are well maintained and are almost always booked by your lodge or travel agent.

On-demand flights, those made at times other than those scheduled, are very expensive for independent travelers, as they require minimum passenger loads. If it's just two passengers, you'll be charged for the vacant seats. Keep in mind that you probably won't get to choose the charter company you fly with. The aircraft you get depends on the number of passengers flying and can vary from very small (you'll sit in the co-pilot's seat) to a much more comfortable commuter plane. Those with a severe fear of small planes might consider road travel instead.

Luggage limits: Due to the limited space and size of the aircraft, charter carriers observe strict luggage regulations: luggage must be soft sided, preferably with no wheels, and usually must weigh no more than 15 kg (33 lbs); weight allowances may vary by company, so be sure to ask what the limits are before packing.

For information regarding charter companies in each country, see the Air Travel section in each country chapter.

CUSTOMS AND DUTIES

Visitors traveling to South Africa or other Southern Africa Customs Union (SACU) countries (Botswana, Lesotho, Namibia, and Swaziland) may bring in new or used gifts and souvenirs up to a total value of R5,000 (in South African rand, US$377 at this writing; *See individual chapters for currency values*) duty-free. For additional goods (new or used) up to a value of R20,000, a fee of 20% is levied. In addition, each person may bring up to 200 cigarettes, 20 cigars, 250 grams of tobacco, 2 liters of wine, 1 liter of spirits, 50 ml of perfume, and 250 ml of eau de toilette. The tobacco and alcohol allowance applies only to people 18 and over. If you enter a SACU country from or through another in the union, you aren't liable for any duties. You will, however, need to complete a form listing items imported.

The United States is a signatory to CITES, a wildlife protection treaty, and therefore doesn't allow the importation of living or dead endangered animals, or their body parts, such as rhino horns or ivory. If you purchase an antique that's made partly or wholly of ivory, you must obtain a CITES preconvention certificate that clearly states the item is at least 100 years old. The import of zebra skin or other tourist products also requires a CITES permit.

U.S. Information U.S. Customs and Border Protection. ⊕ *www.cbp.gov.* **U.S. Fish and Wildlife Service.** ⊕ *www.fws.gov.*

INTERNATIONAL DRIVER'S LICENSE

If you're taking a self-driving safari or renting a car in countries other than South Africa and Namibia, you'll need an international driver's license. These licenses are valid for one year and are issued at any American Automobile Association (AAA) office in the United States; you must have a current U.S. driver's license. You need to bring two passport-type photographs with you for the license. A valid U.S. driver's license is acceptable in South Africa and Namibia.

MONEY MATTERS

Most safaris are paid in advance, so you need money only to cover personal purchases and gratuities. (The cash you take should include small denominations, like US$1, US$5, and US$10, for tips.) If you're self-driving, note that many places prefer to be paid in the local currency, so make sure you change money where you can. Local currency information is discussed in individual chapters. MasterCard and Visa are accepted almost everywhere; American Express is not accepted in Botswana. Neither Diners Club nor Discover is recognized in most African countries. ■TIP→ **It's a good idea to notify your credit-card**

You never know who or what will stop traffic when you're on safari. This elephant in South Africa's Kruger National Park was just passing through and caused a slight traffic jam.

company that you'll be traveling to Africa so that unusual-looking transactions aren't denied.

Reporting Lost Cards American Express. ☎ *800/992–3404 in U.S., 336/393–1111 outside U.S.* ⊕ *www.americanexpress.com.* **MasterCard.** ☎ *800/627–8372 in U.S., 636/722–7111 collect from outside U.S.* ⊕ *www. mastercard.com.* **Visa.** ☎ *800/847–2911 in U.S., 303/967–1096 collect from outside U.S.* ⊕ *www.visa.com.*

FIGURING YOUR BUDGET

Consider three things: your flight, the actual safari costs, and extras. You can have a low-budget self-catering trip in a national park or spend a great deal for a small, exclusive camp. Almost every market has high-priced options as well as some economical ones.

Besides airfare and safari costs, make sure you budget for visas, tips, medications, and other sundries such as souvenirs. You'll likely stay at a hotel in your arrival/departure city on your first and last nights in Africa. Rates range from US$75 for basic accommodations to US$750 a night in the most luxurious hotels. If you do splurge on your safari, but want to keep costs down elsewhere, look for special offers—sometimes South African lodges will throw in a free night's accommodation in Cape Town, for example.

Plan to spend US$15–US$25 a day per traveler on gratuities *(see Tipping below)*. In South Africa tips are on the higher end of this range and usually are paid in rand; you may also use U.S. dollars for tips, however. Elsewhere in Southern Africa, local currency is preferred except in Kenya, Tanzania, and Zimbabwe where U.S. dollars are preferred.

LUXURY
SAFARIS

The most popular option is to book with a tour operator and stay in private lodges, which are owned and run by an individual or company rather than a country's government *(See Chapter 3, Choosing an Outfitter)*. Prices at these lodges include all meals and, in some cases, alcoholic beverages, as well as two three- to five-hour-long game-viewing expeditions a day. Occasionally high-end lodges offer extra services such as spa treatments, boat trips, or special-occasion meals served alfresco in the bush. Prices range approximately from US$300 to US$2,000 per person per night sharing a double room. If you travel alone, expect to pay a single supplement because all safari-lodge rooms are doubles; exceptions may be made depending on the property, the size of your group, and/or the season.

SAFARIS ON A
SHOESTRING
BUDGET

Don't let a tight budget deter you. There are many opportunities for great big-game experiences without going over the top. And, you won't have to completely abandon the idea of comfort and style either. Here are some money-saving tips that every budget can appreciate.

Drive yourself and/or self-cater. The least expensive option is to choose a public game park—Kruger National Park in South Africa, for example—where you drive yourself and self-cater (shop for and prepare all meals yourself). Most South Africans travel this way, but we only recommend this for extremely seasoned safari travelers. Driving yourself can be enjoyable, but keep in mind that you'll have to identify (and watch out for) all the animals yourself, and you can't go off-road.

Stay in accommodations outside the park or in a nearby town. This cuts down on the "mark-ups" that you may experience for the convenience of staying inside a park, and you can come into the park on day trips, so you won't miss anything.

Stick to one park or visit a lesser-known one, and keep your trip short. The high-end safari-goer may visit up to four different parks in different terrains and areas of the country, but the budget traveler would do well to stick to just one. Lesser-known parks can be just as good as famous ones, and sometimes being far from the madding crowds is a luxury in itself. Many travelers tack a two- or three-day safari onto the end of a beach holiday; this is enough time to see the Big Five and get a good understanding of the animals you'll encounter.

Consider mobile-camping safaris. Travel is by 4x4 (often something that looks like a bus), and you sleep in tents at public or private campsites. There are different levels of comfort and service, and the price varies accordingly: at the lower end, you'll pitch your own tent and help with cooking; but with a full-service mobile-camping safari, your driver/guide and a cook will do all the setup. The cost will also vary according to the number of people on the tour. You'll really feel at one with nature and the wildlife if you take this option, but you'll need to be able to put up with a certain level of roughing it. A full-service safari costs in the region of US$200–US$500 a day, depending on the comfort level.

2

Book a private lodge in the off-season. Many lodges—South Africa's Sabi Sands area, for example—cost on average about US$700–$1,200 per person, per night during the high season but can drop to about US$350 a night in the very low season; on average savings can be 30%–40%. In the rainy season, however, roads may be impassable in some areas and the wildlife hard to spot, so do your research beforehand. Sometimes the high season merely correlates with the European long vacation. In South Africa, the low season is from May to September, mostly because Cape Town is cold and wet during this time. Regions north of the country, such as Kruger, are excellent for game-viewing during this time, as the winter is the dry season and grasses are short. Early morning and nighttime can get cold, but the daytime is usually dry and sunny. You'll also have the benefit of fewer crowds, although if you're very social, you may find the off-season too quiet. If you're a honeymooner, it's perfect.

Cheap flights are out there, but you'll have to work for them. Aggregators such as Skyscanner.net and ebookers.com can help you search for the best fares that meet your requirements. American travelers can sometimes save money by flying through Europe. Book a flight to a regional hub like Nairobi or Johannesburg, and then catch a connecting flight to your destination. Many of Kenya's budget airlines fly from Nairobi to destinations in Tanzania, and South Africa's budget airline Kulula Airlines (⊕ *www.kulula.com*) flies from South Africa to Kenya, Namibia, Zambia, and Zimbabwe. For flights to South Africa, look into flying via Dubai or Doha. You'll add extra time to your flight, but you could save big. Always book at least two months in advance, especially during the high season.

Budget for all aspects of your trip and watch out for hidden extras. Most safaris are all-inclusive, so you don't think about the cost of your sundowner drink, snacks on your game drive, or cocktails at mealtime. However, some lodges charge extra for drinks and excursions (e.g., a visit to a Maasai village in Kenya). You can keep your costs down by going to a place where things are à la carte and pay only for the things you deem important. ■TIP➡ **Local beer is usually cheap, but wines are often imported (outside of South Africa) and are quite expensive.**

When you book your trip, be clear as to whether extras such as airport transfers, use of equipment (including sleeping bags on some mobile-camping safaris), and entry fees are included in the price.

Book your trip locally, or at the last minute. Last-minute deals can offer massive discounts, as long as you're prepared to be flexible about everything to do with your trip. Alternatively, book a trip locally once you're at your destination. This is popular in Kenya and Tanzania. You can also gather a group of people at your lodging and do a group booking. This way you'll have the benefit of a guide, too, with the cost shared among a number of people. You can also save money by booking with a tour operator that is based in the country you are visiting, as you will be cutting out the commission charged by an American agent. Make sure that you thoroughly research your prospective tour operator first, however, to ensure they have a consistently good reputation.

TIPPING

Ranger/Guide: About US$10 per person, per day.

General staff: Per day/per couple: roughly $10 a day into the general tip box and $5 to your tracker; $5 per trip for a vehicle transfer (i.e. from the airport/airstrip to your hotel/lodge). ■TIP➔ Note that some safari operators, such as Micato, include tips in their price, so you don't have to worry about carrying around the correct denominations.

The amount you tip depends on your budget and what you're comfortable with, but when in doubt, it's always better to tip too much than too little; it's not unusual for a member of staff to be supporting an entire extended family on one salary and they are grateful for any help. Never tip children as it could discourage them from attending school if tourists are seen as a lucrative form of income. Hand your tip (preferably in a sealed envelope; many lodges provide them) directly to a member of staff or hand to management to distribute. Some lodges have collection tins for general staff tips. It's a nice gesture to bring small gifts—pens, T-shirts, soccer balls with pumps, etc.—to give to the staff.

ONLINE TRAVEL TOOLS *All Africa* culls English-language news articles from regional papers.

All About Africa Africa Adventure. ⊕ *www.africa-adventure.org.*

Media All Africa. ⊕ *www.allafrica.com.* **Getaway.** ⊕ *www.getawayafrica.com.* **Independent Newspapers.** ⊕ *www.iol.co.za.*

PASSPORTS AND VISAS

A valid passport is a must for travel to any African country. ■TIP➔ Certain countries, such as South Africa, won't let you enter with a soon-to-expire passport; also, you need two blank pages in your passport to enter South Africa. If you don't have a passport, apply immediately, because the process takes approximately five to six weeks. For a greatly increased fee, the application process can be shortened to as little as one week, but leaving this detail to the last minute can be stressful. If you have a passport, check the expiration date. If it's due to expire within six months of your return date, you need to renew it at once.

■TIP➔ If you're planning a honeymoon safari, make sure the bride's airline ticket, passport, and visas all use the same last name. Any discrepancies, especially between a passport and an airline ticket, will result in your trip being grounded before you even take off. Brides may want to consider waiting to change their last name until after the honeymoon. Do be sure to let the lodge know in advance that you're on your honeymoon. You'll get lots of special goodies and extra-special pampering thrown in. *For country-specific information regarding passports and visas, see the Passports and Visas section, under Planning, in each country chapter.*

U.S. Passport Information U.S. Department of State. ☎ *877/487–2778* ⊕ *www.travel.state.gov.*

U.S. Passport and Visa Expediters A. Briggs Passport & Visa Expediters. ☎ *800/806–0581* ⊕ *www.abriggs.com.* **American Passport Express.** ☎ *800/455–5166* ⊕ *www.americanpassport.com.* **Passport Express.**

DOCUMENT CHECKLIST

- Passport
- Visas, if necessary
- Airline tickets
- Proof of yellow-fever inoculation, if necessary
- Accommodation and transfer vouchers
- Car-rental reservation forms
- International driver's license (if needed)
- Copy of information page of your passport

- Copy of airline tickets
- Copy of medical prescriptions
- List of credit-card numbers and international contact information for each card issuer
- Copy of travel insurance and medical-emergency evacuation policies
- Travel agent's contact numbers
- Notarized letter of consent from one parent if the other parent is traveling alone with their children (if needed)

☎ 877/387–7277 ⊕ *www.uspassportexpressinc.com.* **Travel Document Systems.** ☎ 800/874–5100 ⊕ *www.traveldocs.com.* **Travel the World Visas.** ☎ 202/223–8822 ⊕ *www.world-visa.com.*

SAFETY AND PRECAUTIONS

Although most countries in Southern and East Africa are stable and safe, it's a good idea to do your homework and be fully aware of the areas you'll be traveling to before planning that once-in-a-lifetime trip.

The CIA's online World Factbook has maps and facts on the people, government, economy, and more for countries from Afghanistan to Zimbabwe. It's the fastest way to get a snapshot of a nation. It's also updated regularly and, obviously, well researched.

There's nothing like the local paper for putting your finger on the pulse. World-Newspapers.com has links to English-language newspapers, magazines, and websites in countries the world over.

The U.S. State Department's advice on the safety of a given country is probably the most conservative you'll encounter. That said, the information is updated regularly, and nearly every nation is covered. Just try to parse the language carefully. For example, a warning to "avoid all travel" carries more weight than "avoid nonessential travel," and both are much stronger than a plea to "exercise caution." A travel warning is more permanent (though not necessarily more serious) than a so-called public announcement, which carries an expiration date.

Travel Warnings Central Intelligence Agency (*CIA*). ⊕ *www.cia.gov.* **U.S. State Department.** ⊕ *www.travel.state.gov.* **World-Newspapers.com.** ⊕ *www. world-newspapers.com.*

TRAVEL INSURANCE

You may want to consider a comprehensive travel-insurance policy in addition to any primary insurance you already have. Travel insurance incorporates trip cancellation; trip interruption or travel delay; loss or theft of, or

SAFARI PLANNING TIMELINE

SIX MONTHS AHEAD
■ Research destinations and options and make a list of sights you want to see.

■ Start a safari file to keep track of information.

■ Set a budget.

■ Search the Internet. Post questions on bulletin boards and narrow your choices. Watch out for fake trip reviews posted by unscrupulous travel agents.

■ Choose your destination and make your reservations.

■ Apply for a passport, or renew yours if it's due to expire within six months of travel time. Many countries now require at least two empty pages in your passport.

■ Buy travel insurance.

THREE TO SIX MONTHS AHEAD
■ Find out which travel documents you need.

■ Confirm whether your destination requires visas and certified health documents.

■ Arrange vaccinations or medical clearances.

■ Research malaria precautions.

■ Book excursions, tours, and side trips.

ONE TO THREE MONTHS AHEAD
■ Create a packing checklist. *See Packing.*

■ Fill prescriptions for antimalarial and regular medications. Buy mosquito repellent.

■ Shop for safari clothing and equipment.

■ Arrange for a house and pet sitter.

ONE MONTH AHEAD
■ Get copies of any prescriptions and make sure you have enough of any needed medicine to last you a few days longer than your trip.

■ Confirm international flights, transfers, and lodging reservations directly with your travel agent.

■ Using your packing list, start buying articles you don't have. Update the list as you go.

ONE WEEK AHEAD
■ Suspend newspaper and mail delivery.

■ Collect small denominations of U.S. currency ($1 and $5) for tips (note that this is only the case in Kenya, Tanzania, and Zimbabwe).

■ Check antimalarial prescriptions to see whether you need to start taking medication now.

■ Arrange transportation to the airport.

■ Make two copies of your passport's data page. Leave one copy, and a copy of your itinerary, with someone at home; pack the other separately from your passport. Make a PDF of these pages and email them to yourself for access.

damage to, baggage; baggage delay; medical expenses; emergency medical transportation; and collision damage waiver if renting a car. These policies are offered by most travel-insurance companies in one comprehensive policy and vary in price based on both your total trip cost and your age.

It's important to note that travel insurance doesn't always include coverage for threats of a terrorist incident or for any war-related activity. It's important that you speak with your operator before you book to find out how they would handle such occurrences. For example, would you be fully refunded if your trip was canceled because of war or a threat of a terrorist incident? Would your trip be postponed at no additional cost to you?

■ TIP→ **Purchase travel insurance within seven days of paying your initial trip deposit. For most policies this will not only ensure your trip deposit, but also cover you for any preexisting medical conditions.**

Many travel agents and tour operators stipulate that travel insurance offering coverage for medical emergencies and medical evacuations due to injury or illness is mandatory, as this often involves the use of jet aircraft with hospital equipment and doctors on board and can amount to many thousands of dollars.

Consider signing up with a medical-evacuation assistance company. A membership in one of these companies gets you doctor referrals, emergency evacuation or repatriation, 24-hour hotlines for medical consultation, and other assistance. International SOS and AirMed International provide evacuation services and medical referrals. MedjetAssist offers medical evacuation.

Insurance Allianz Travel Insurance. ⊕ *www.allianztravelinsurance.com.* **HTH Worldwide.** ⊕ *www.hthworldwide.com.* **International Medical Group.** ⊕ *www. imglobal.com.* **Travel Guard.** ⊕ *www.travelguard.com.* **Wallach & Company.** ⊕ *www.wallach.com.*

Medical-Assistance Companies Air Med. ⊕ *www.airmed.com.* **International SOS.** ⊕ *www.internationalsos.com.* **MedJet Assistance.** ⊕ *www.medjetassist. com.*

VACCINATIONS

Traveling overseas is daunting enough without having to worry about all the scary illnesses you could contract. But if you do your research and plan accordingly, there will be no reason to worry.

The Centers for Disease Control, or CDC, has an extremely helpful and informative website where you can find out country by country what you'll need. Remember that the CDC is going to be extremely conservative, so it's a good idea to meet with a trusted health-care professional to decide what you'll really need, which will be determined by your itinerary. We've also included the basic information on the countries we cover in the preceding chart.

Keep in mind that there's a time frame for vaccines. You should see your health provider four to six weeks before you leave for your trip. Also keep in mind that vaccines and prescriptions could run you from $1,000 upwards. It's important to factor this into your budget when planning, especially if your plans include a large group.

	Yellow Fever	Malaria	Hepatitis A	Hepatitis B	Typhoid	Rabies	Polio	Other
Kenya	●	●	●	●	●	●	●	Meningitis
Tanzania	●	●	●	●	●	●	●	
South Africa	◐	●	●	●	●	●	●	
Botswana	◐	●	●	●	●	●	●	
Namibia	◐	●	●	●	●	●	●	
Zambia	◐	●	●	●	●	●	●	
Zimbabwe	◐	●	●	●	●	●	●	

KEY: ● = Necessary
     ● = Recommended
     ◐ = The government requires travelers arriving from countries where yellow fever
         is present to have proof that they got the vaccination

You must be up-to-date with all of your routine shots such as the measles/mumps/rubella (MMR) vaccine, and diphtheria/pertussis/tetanus (DPT) vaccine. If you're not up-to-date, usually a simple booster shot will bring you up to par. If you're traveling to northern Kenya December through June, don't be surprised if your doctor advises you to get inoculated against meningitis, as this part of the continent tends to see an outbreak during this time.

We can't stress enough the importance of taking malaria prophylactics. But be warned that all malaria medications aren't equal. Chloroquine is *not* an effective antimalarial drug in sub-Saharan Africa, as the mosquitoes have developed resistance. And halofantrine (marketed as Halfan), which is widely used overseas to treat malaria, has serious heart-related side effects, including death. The CDC recommend that you do *not* use halofantrine. Their website has a comprehensive list of the different malaria medications available, and which are recommended for each country. *For more information on malaria, or other health issues while on safari, see Health below.*

Health Warnings Centers for Disease Control (*CDC*). ☎ 800/232–4636 international travelers' health line ⊕ wwwnc.cdc.gov/travel.

HEPATITIS A AND B AND OTHER BOOSTERS
Hepatitis A can be transmitted via contaminated seafood, water, or fruits and vegetables. According to the CDC, hepatitis A is the most common vaccine-preventable disease in travelers. Immunization consists of a series of two shots received six months apart. You only need

to have received the first one before you travel. This should be given at least four weeks before your trip.

The CDC recommends vaccination for hepatitis B only if you might be exposed to blood (if you're a health-care worker, for example), have sexual contact with the local population, stay longer than six months, or risk exposure during medical treatment. As needed, you should receive booster shots for tetanus-diphtheria (every 10 years), measles (you're usually immunized as a child), and polio (you're usually immunized as a child).

YELLOW FEVER

Yellow fever isn't inherent in any of the countries discussed in this book. Some countries, however, such as Kenya, will require you to present a valid yellow-fever inoculation certificate if prior to arrival you traveled to a region infected with yellow fever.

ZIKA VIRUS

Zika virus is a risk in Kenya and Tanzania. Zika infection can cause serious birth defects, so pregnant women should not travel to these destinations at the time of writing. All travelers should protect themselves against mosquito bites and exposure through sexual contact during their trip.

PACKING

You'll be allowed one duffel-type bag, approximately 36 inches by 18 inches and a maximum of 26 kilos (57 pounds)—less on some airlines, so it's essential you check ahead—so that it can be easily packed into the baggage pods of a small plane. A personal-effects bag can go on your lap. Keep all your documents and money in this personal bag.

■TIP➔ At O.R. Tambo International Airport in Johannesburg and Cape Town International Airport you can store your bags at Ateck (011/390–2318 in Johannesburg and 72/384–2954 in Cape Town). The cost is approximately US$8 per bag per day, and the facility is open 24 hours a day, 7 days a week. Many travelers also pay to have their luggage wrapped in shrinkwrap, but locking your suitcase should be sufficient.

BINOCULARS

Binoculars are essential and come in many types and sizes. You get what you pay for, so avoid buying a cheap pair—the optics will be poor and the lenses usually don't stay aligned for long, especially if they get bumped, which they will on safari. Whatever strength you choose, pick the most lightweight pair, otherwise you'll be in for neck and shoulder strain. Take them with you on a night drive; you'll get great visuals of nocturnal animals and birds by the light of the tracker's spotlight. Many people find that when they start using binoculars and stop documenting each trip detail on film, they have a much better safari experience. ■TIP➔ Many high-end camps provide binoculars, so ask before purchasing and packing them.

PACKING CHECKLIST

Light, khaki, or neutral-color clothes are universally worn on safari and were first used in Africa as camouflage by the South African Boers, and then by the British Army that fought them during the South African War. Light colors also help to deflect the harsh sun and are less likely than dark colors to attract mosquitoes. Don't wear camouflage gear. Do wear layers of clothing that you can strip off as the sun gets hotter and put back on as the sun goes down.

■ Smartphone or tablet to check emails, send texts, and store photos (also handy as an alarm clock), plus an adapter. If electricity will be limited, you may wish to bring a portable charger.

■ Three cotton T-shirts

■ Two long-sleeve cotton shirts

■ Two pairs shorts or two skirts in summer

■ Two pairs long pants (three pairs in winter) in light earth colors

■ Optional: sweatshirt and sweatpants, which can double as sleepwear

■ One smart-casual dinner outfit

■ Underwear and socks

■ Walking shoes or sneakers

■ Sandals/flip-flops

■ Bathing suit and sarong to use as a cover-up

■ Warm thigh-length padded jacket and sweater in winter

■ Windbreaker or rain poncho

■ Camera equipment, extra batteries or charger, and memory cards; a photographer's vest and cargo pants are great for storage

■ Contact lenses, including extras

■ Eyeglasses

■ Binoculars

■ Small flashlight

■ Personal toiletries

■ Malaria tablets

■ Sunscreen and lip balm with SPF 30 or higher, moisturizer, and hair conditioner

■ Antihistamine cream

■ Insect repellent that is at least 20% DEET and is sweat-resistant

■ Tissues and/or premoistened wipes

■ Warm hat, scarf, and gloves in winter

■ Sun hat and sunglasses (Polaroid and UV-protected ones)

■ Documents and money (cash, credit cards, etc.).

■ A notebook and pens

■ Travel and field guide books

■ A couple of large white plastic garbage bags

■ Ziplock bags to keep documents dry and protect electronics from dust

■ U.S. dollars in small denominations ($1, $5, $10) for tipping

CLOTHING

You should need only three changes of clothing for an entire trip; almost all safaris include laundry as part of the package. If you're self-driving you can carry more, but washing is still easy, especially if you use drip-dry fabrics that need no ironing. On mobile safaris you can wear tops and bottoms more than once, and either bring enough underwear to last a week between lodges, or wash as you go in the bathroom sink. Unless there's continual rain (unlikely), clothes dry overnight in the hot, dry African air.

■TIP→ In certain countries—Botswana and Tanzania, for example—the staff won't wash undergarments because it's against cultural custom.

For game walks, pack sturdy but light walking shoes or boots—in most cases durable sneakers suffice for this option. For a walking-based safari, you need sturdy, lightweight boots. Buy them well in advance of your trip so you can break them in. If possible, isolate the clothes used on your walk from the remainder of the clean garments in your bag. Bring a couple of large white plastic garbage bags for dirty laundry.

ELECTRICITY

Most of Southern Africa is on 220/240-volt alternating current (AC). The plug points are round. However, there are both large 15-amp three-prong sockets (with a ground connection) and smaller 5-amp two-prong sockets. Most lodges have adapter plugs, especially for recharging camera batteries; check before you go, or purchase a universal plug adapter before you leave home.

Safari hotels in the Serengeti, the private reserve areas outside Kruger National Park, and the less rustic private lodges in South Africa are likely to provide you with plug points and plugs, and some offer hair dryers and electric-razor sockets as well (check this before you go). Lodges on limited generator and solar power are usually able to charge cameras, as long as you have the right plug.

TOILETRIES AND SUNDRIES

Most hotels and game lodges provide toiletries such as soap, shampoo, and insect repellent, so you don't need to overpack these items. In the larger lodges in South Africa's national parks and private game reserves, stores and gift shops are fairly well stocked with clothing and guidebooks; in self-drive and self-catering areas, shops also carry food and drink. Many lodges have small shops with a selection of books, clothing, and curios.

■TIP→ The African sun is harsh, and if you're even remotely susceptible to burning, especially coming from a northern winter, don't skimp on sunscreens and moisturizers.

ON SAFARI

Your safari will be one of the most memorable trips you'll ever take, and it's essential that your African experience matches the one you've always imagined. Nothing should be left to chance, and that includes where you'll stay and how you'll get around.

Safari Photo Tips

All the safaris included in this book are photographic (game-viewing) safaris. That said, if you spend your entire safari with one eye closed and the other peering through a camera lens, you may miss all the other sensual elements that contribute to the great show that is the African bush. And more than likely, your pictures won't look like the photos you see in books about African safaris. A professional photographer can spend a full year in the field to produce a book, so your time might be better spent taking snaps of your trip and buying a book to take home.

■ TIP→ No matter what kind of camera you bring, be sure to keep it tightly sealed in plastic bags while you're traveling to protect it from dust. (Dust is especially troublesome in Namibia.) Tuck your equipment away when the wind kicks up. You should have one or more cloth covers while you're working, and clean your equipment every day if you can.

Learning some basics about the wildlife that you expect to see on your safari will help you capture some terrific shots of the animals. If you know something about their behavior patterns ahead of time, you'll be primed to capture action, like when the hippos start to roar. Learning from your guide and carefully observing the wildlife once you're there will also help you gauge just when to click your shutter.

The trick to taking great pictures has three components: first is always good light. An hour after sunrise and before sunset are the magical times, because the light is softer and textures pop.

For the few hours of harsh light each side of midday, you might as well put your camera away. The second component is framing. Framing a scene so that the composition is simple gives an image potency; with close-ups, fill the frame for maximum impact. Using objects of known size in the foreground or middle ground will help establish scale. The third component is capturing sharp images: use a tripod or a beanbag to rest the camera on while in a vehicle. When using a long lens (upward of 200mm), you can't hand-hold a steady shot; you must have some support if you want your photos to be clear.

DIGITAL CAMERAS AND SMART-PHONES

Cameras with eight megapixels of resolution can print high-quality, smooth A4 or letter-size prints; images with five-megapixel resolution are fine as well. Recent-generation smart-phones (e.g., iPhone, Samsung Galaxy, Motorola Droid) work pretty well, too. You might consider investing in a telephoto lens to shoot wildlife, as you are often too far away from the animals to capture details with the zoom lenses generally built into most smartphones and point-and-shoot cameras. This may mean upgrading to a more robust camera. A tripod or beanbag is also helpful; it'll stabilize your camera, especially when a zoom lens is extended.

Buy or borrow as many memory cards as you can—you'll use them. You may want to use multiple smaller memory cards to minimize the risk of losing an entire card's worth of images. And, as always, remember to bring extra batteries or your battery charger.

2

The whos, whats, and hows still need to come into focus. If you have questions like, "Where's the best place to sit in a game-drive vehicle? Can you get near a honey badger? Where do you go to the bathroom in the bush?," then read on.

By the way, "bush" is a term used to describe the natural setting of your safari—be it in forests, plains, or on riverbanks. The expression "going to the bush" means going away from urban areas and into the wilderness.

ACCOMMODATIONS

The days are long gone when legendary 19th-century explorer Dr. David Livingstone pitched his travel-stained tent under a tree and ate his sparse rations. But whether you go simple in a basic safari tent with an adjacent bucket shower and long-drop toilet, choose ultracomfort in a megatent or canvas-and-thatch chalet, or go totally over the top in a glass-walled aerie-cum-penthouse with a state-of-the-art designer interior, you'll still feel very much part of the bush.

LUXURY LODGES

Some would say that using the word "luxury" with "safari lodge" is redundant, as all such lodges fall into this category. But there's luxurious, and then there's *luxurious*. Options in the latter category range from *Out of Africa*–type accommodations with antique furniture, crystal, and wrought-iron chandeliers to thatch-roofed stone chalets, Tuscan villas, and suites that wouldn't seem out of place in midtown Manhattan. In nearly all, you can expect to find air-conditioning; in many there will be a small library, a spa, a gift shop, and Internet service—often in a "business center" (a computer in the main lodge) or Wi-Fi. You may even have your own plunge pool.

PERMANENT TENTED CAMPS

Think luxurious, oh-so-comfortable, and spacious…in a tent. This is no ordinary tent, though. Each has its own bathroom, usually with an outdoor shower; a wooden deck with table and chairs that overlooks the bush; carpet or wooden floors; big "windows"; and an inviting four-poster (usually) bed with puffy pillows and fluffy blankets (for those cold winter months). The public space will comprise a bar, a lounge, dining areas, viewing decks, usually a pool, and a curio shop. Some will have Wi-Fi, air-conditioning, and private plunge pools.

MOBILE TENTED CAMPS

This option varies enormously. You could have the original, roomy walk-in dome tent (complete with canvas bedrolls, crisp cotton bedding on G.I. stretchers, open-air flush toilets, and bucket showers) that's ready and waiting for you at day's end. Or you could have luxury tents (with crystal chandeliers, antique rugs, and shining silver) that stay in one place for a few months during peak seasons. They're all fully serviced (the staff travels with the tents), and you'll dine under the stars or sip coffee as the sun rises.

NATIONAL PARK ACCOMMODATIONS

What you'll get in this category depends on which park you're in and what type of lodgings you're looking for. Accommodations can vary from campsites to simple one-room rondavels, or round huts, with en suite bathrooms; safari tents to two- to four-bed cottages; or possibly a top-of-the-range guesthouse that sleeps eight people. With the exception of some camping sites, and some places in South Africa, all national-park accommodations are fully serviced with staff to look after you.

CHILDREN ON SAFARI

Most safari operators and private game reserves don't accept children under a certain age, usually under eight, but sometimes the age limit is as high as 12. This age limit is largely for safety reasons. Animals often respond, not in a positive manner, to something that is younger, slower, or smaller than they are. And even though you might think your six- or seven-year-old adores all sorts of animals and bugs, you'd be surprised how overwhelmed kids can become, out of the comfort of their home and backyard, by the size and multitude of African insects and wildlife.

Take into account, also, that when you're following a strange schedule (with jet lag) and getting in and out of small planes, safari vehicles, boats, and the like with other people whom you probably won't know, there often is no time to deal with recalcitrant children—and fussing will, you can be guaranteed, annoy the other people in your plane or lodge, who have spent a great deal of money for what may be a once-in-a-lifetime safari trip.

One option, if you can afford it, is to book a private safari where no other people are involved and you dictate the schedule. Many private lodges will rent you the entire property for the length of your stay; this is often the only way these camps allow children under age eight on safari. At the very least, a camp will require that you pay for a private safari vehicle and guide if you have children under 12. Be advised that, even if you're renting the whole camp, babies and toddlers still aren't allowed out on game-viewing trips.

Another great family option is to stay with &Beyond, a safari operator with children's programs at several of its upscale camps throughout Southern and East Africa. While you follow your own program, your kids pursue their own wilderness activities, and you all meet up later for meals and other activities.

It's best not to visit malarial areas with children under age 10. Young kidneys are especially vulnerable to both the effects of malaria and the side effects of malaria prophylactics. You might opt to practice stringent nonchemical preventive measures, but know the risks: malaria's effects on young children are much worse than they are on older people.

Babies aren't allowed in safari vehicles. Some lodges, such as those at MalaMala, provide babysitting services for infants. The sound of an infant crying puts most predators on alert—dangerous to other passengers as well as the child. Keep in mind also that the bush is often a hot and dusty place with little in the way of baby-friendly amenities. You'd have to bring all your own supplies, and if something were to go wrong there would be no way to get immediate help until a flight could be arranged.

CONSIDERATIONS FOR CHILDREN

Consider the following if you're thinking about bringing children to a private safari lodge:

■ **Are they afraid of the dark?** A safari camp that runs on generator-powered batteries will have minimal lights at night.

■ **Are they startled easily?** Large animals may come quite close to rooms or tents or near safari vehicles.

■ **Are they comfortable with strangers?** Most meals at safari lodges are at communal tables, and shared six-seat planes are the basic form of transportation between remote safari camps.

■ **Are they troubled by bugs?** The African bush can be filled with moths as big as small birds as well as a host of other flying and crawling insects.

■ **Are they picky eaters?** Meals are usually buffet-style and food for camps is often ordered at least a month in advance, so your child's favorite food may not be available.

COMMUNICATIONS

It's estimated that about half the population of Africa has a cell phone, and areas with 3G reception are widespread and can include remote areas (4G is reception is available in South Africa, too). Don't count on it, though. This is Africa, and networks can be down. If you urgently need to get in touch with home, all camps have a radio or satellite phone. ■TIP➡ Leave your contact details with folks back home so they can call you if there's an emergency.

INTERNET

Most lodges have Wi-Fi, although the service can be erratic and slow. Availability and speed varies widely by location and camp; South African lodges have pretty good capability but elsewhere it can be poor, especially in remote areas of Zambia, Botswana, and Namibia.

PHONES

If you really want to save on international phone calls, the best advice is to provide a detailed itinerary back home and agree on a schedule for calls. Internet calling like Skype may work well from the United States, but it's not always functional in Africa, unless you're on a reliable high-speed Wi-Fi, or a 3G or 4G connection. However, if you have a South African "free" cell phone (meaning you can receive calls for free; all phones using a South Africa SIM card do this), someone in the United States can call you from their Skype account, for reasonable per-minute charges, and you won't be charged. You can also buy a cheap local SIM card, but remember that any phone that you take abroad must be unlocked by your company in order for it to accept a different SIM card.

Cell phones can be rented by the day, week, or longer from the airport on your arrival, but this is an expensive option. The least complicated (but potentially expensive) way to make and receive phone calls is to obtain international roaming service for your mobile phone before you leave home—make sure it's activated before you leave. Turn off your phone's roaming capabilities to avoid incurring steep charges and draining the battery. If you don't text message at home, you'll learn to in Africa, where a simple text message costs a fraction of the cost of making an actual call. This is a handy option for meeting up with friends or keeping in touch with home, but for making hotel reservations, it's best to make the call. You can use Skype to make calls to local landlines or mobile numbers, if there is a decent 3G connection—it's cheaper than a straight call and reception is often better. ■TIP→ **Make sure you bring an universal adaptor so you can charge your phone.**

Most people use the time on safari to "switch off" from modern life. Conducting business or making phone calls in the lodge's public areas is generally frowned upon, as is using your phone on a game drive. If you think you'll be too tempted to fiddle with your phone, leave it back at camp.

For country-specific information on phones, see the Communication section, under Planning, in each country chapter.

TELEPHONE COUNTRY CODES
■ United States: 1
■ Botswana: 267
■ Kenya: 254
■ Namibia: 264
■ South Africa: 27
■ Tanzania: 255
■ Zambia: 260
■ Zimbabwe: 263
Note: When dialing from abroad, drop the initial 0 from local area codes.

GAME DRIVES

In most regions the best time to find game is in the early morning and early evening, when the animals are most active, although old Africa hands will tell you that you can come across good game at any time of day. Stick to the philosophy "you never know what's around the next corner," and keep your eyes and ears wide open all the time. If your rest camp offers guided night drives on open vehicles with spotlights—go for it. You'll rarely be disappointed, seeing not only big game but also a lot of fascinating little critters that surface only at night. Book your night drive in advance or as soon as you get to camp.

Arm yourself with specialized books on mammals and birds rather than a more general one that tries to cover too much. Airports, lodges, and camp shops stock a good range, but try to bring one with you and do a bit of boning up in advance. Any bird guide by Ken Newman (Struik Publishers) and the *Sasol Guide to Birds* are recommended.

Many national parks have reception areas with charts that show the most recent sightings of wildlife in the area. To be sure you see everything you want to, stop at the nearest reception and ask about a spotting chart, or just chat with the other drivers, rangers, and tourists you may encounter there, who can tell you what they've seen and where.

BATHROOM BREAKS

On your game drive you'll very likely be pointed to a nearby bush (which the ranger checks out before you use it). Tissues and toilet paper are usually available in the vehicle (but you may want to make sure).

Making friends with giraffes in South Africa.

Sometimes there might be a toilet—well, actually, it'll very likely be a hole in the ground below a toilet seat—called drop toilets. Either way, bring the paper back with you—don't bury it. If you have an emergency, ask your ranger to stop the vehicle and he or she will scout a suitable spot.

GAME RANGERS AND TRACKERS

Game rangers (sometimes referred to as guides) have vast experience with and knowledge of the bush and the animals that inhabit it. Rangers often work in conjunction with trackers, who spot animals, and advise the rangers where to go. Often a tracker will be busy searching out animal tracks, spoor, and other clues to nearby wildlife while the ranger drives and discusses the animals and their environment. Rangers often communicate with each other via radio when there's been a good sighting.

The quality of your bush experience depends heavily on your guide or game ranger and tracker. A ranger wears many hats while on safari: he's there to entertain you, protect you, and put you as close to the wilderness as possible while serving as bush mechanic, first-aid specialist, and host. He'll often eat meals with you, will explain animal habits and behavior while out in the bush, and, if you're on foot, will keep you alive in the presence of an excitable elephant, buffalo, hippo, or lion. This is no small feat, and each ranger has his particular strengths. Because of the intensity of the safari experience, with its exposure to potentially dangerous animals and tricky situations, your relationship with your guide or ranger is one of trust, friendliness, and respect.

Acknowledge that your guide is a professional and an expert in the field, and defer to his knowledge. Instead of trying to show how much you know, follow the example of the hunter, which is to walk quietly and take notice of all the little signs around you. Save social chatter with the guide for when you're back at camp, not out on a game drive. Rangers appreciate questions, which give them an idea of your range of knowledge and of how much detail to include in their animal descriptions. However, if you like to ask a lot of questions, save some for later, especially as several other people are likely to be in the safari vehicle with you. Carry a pocket notebook on game drives and jot down questions as they occur; you can then bring them up at dinner or around the campfire, when your ranger has more time to talk and everyone can participate in the discussion.

Don't let your ranger "guide by the numbers"—providing only a list of an animal's attributes. Politely ask questions and show you'd like to know more. Even the best guides may experience "bush burnout" by the end of a busy safari season with demanding clients, but any guide worthy of the title always goes out of his way to give you the best possible experience. If you suspect yours has a case of burnout, or just laziness, you have a right to ask for certain things. There's never any harm in asking, and you can't expect your guide to read your mind about what you like. If, for example, you have a preference for birds, insects, or whatever, ask your guide to spend time on these subjects. You may be surprised by how happy he is to oblige.

BUSH WALKS Guided bush walks vary, but usually a maximum of eight guests walk in single file with the armed ranger up front and the tracker at the back. A bush walk is a more intimate experience than a drive. You're up close with the bush and with your fellow walkers and guides. Your guide will brief you thoroughly about where and how to walk, emergency procedures, and the like. If you're in a national park, you'll most likely have to pay an additional fee to have an armed park ranger escort you on your walk.

VEHICLES ON GAME DRIVES
Your safari transportation is determined by your destination and could range from custom-made game-viewing vehicles (full-service safari) to a combi or minivan (basic safari or self-drive). There shouldn't be more than six people per vehicle. To make sure you experience every view, suggest to your ranger that visitors rotate seats for each drive.

In closed vehicles, which are used by private touring companies operating in Kruger National Park, sit as close to the driver-guide as possible so you can get in and out of the vehicle more easily and get the best views.

OPEN-SIDED
LAND ROVERS This is the most common game-viewing vehicle, especially in **South Africa, Tanzania,** and **Botswana,** and is usually a Land Rover or a Land Cruiser. Each vehicle seats six to eight people. Vehicles that have raised, stepped seating—meaning the seats in back are higher than the ones in front—are used for game drives. There are usually three rows of seats after the driver's row; the norm at a luxury lodge is to have two people per row. The more expensive the camp, the fewer people in the vehicle.

Sit beside the ranger/driver if you're a bit unsteady, because you won't have to climb up into the rear. In the front row you'll have the clearest conversations with the ranger, but farther back you'll have a clearer, elevated view over the front of the car. The back seats tend to be bumpy, but you get great views.

POP TOPS   Used mainly in **Kenya,** because of dirt, dust, and rain (and cheetahs, who like to jump on the roof or hood of the vehicle!), these hard-topped minivans pop up so you can stand up, get a better view, and take photos in every direction. If you're claustrophobic or very tall, this might not be the vehicle for you, but there are outfitters that have larger vehicles that can "stretch." If it gets really hot outside, you'll be happy to close up and turn on the air-conditioning. Make sure water and sodas are available.

MINIVANS   It's unlikely that you'll use one of these unless you're on a very cheap safari or a self-drive—they are, however, perfect for the **Namibia Desert.** The advantage is that they sit high off the ground and provide much better views; some outfitters offer vehicles that can expand. If you're self-driving, make sure you get a van with air-conditioning and power steering. The farther north you go, check out your prospective vehicle's year and make sure it's as recent as possible.

SMALL PLANES   As many camps and lodges are inaccessible by land, or are in very remote places, you'll often fly in a 6- to 10-seat plane. Always take a bottle of water with you (small planes can get very hot), and make sure you have medication ready if you're prone to motion sickness. Keep in mind the strictly enforced luggage restriction: usually 12 kg (26 lbs) of luggage in a soft bag that can squeeze into the plane's small hold, but check in advance. Flights can be bumpy, and landing strips are often just baked earth. Also keep in mind there are no bathrooms on these planes, which, if you're practicing good hydration, can be problematic for flights that are more than an hour!

WATERCRAFT   If your lodge is on or near a river, expect to go out in a boat. Options range from the big sunset safari boats with bars and bathrooms on the **Zambezi** and **Chobe rivers** to a six- or eight-seater along the **Okavango** and smaller rivers, where your amenities include a cool box of drinks and snacks but no toilet. One of the highlights of your stay in the Okavango Delta will be gliding in a *mokoro* (a canoe) poled by an expert local waterman through papyrus-fringed channels where hippos and crocs lurk.

HEALTH

Of all the horror stories and fantastic nightmares about meeting your end in the bush, the problem you're most likely to encounter will be of your own doing: dehydration. Also be wary of malaria, motion sickness, and intestinal problems. By taking commonsense precautions, your safari will be uneventful from a health perspective but memorable in every other way.

The Center for Disease Control (CDC) has information on health risks associated with almost every country on the planet, as well as what precautions to take. The World Health Organization (WHO) is the health arm of the United Nations and has information by topic and by country.

The International Travel and Health section of the WHO's website covers everything you need to know about staying healthy abroad.

Health Warnings Centers for Disease Control (*CDC*). ☎ 800/232–4636 *international travelers' health line* ⊕ *wwwnc.cdc.gov/travel.* **Travel Health Online.** ⊕ *www.tripprep.com.* **World Health Organization** (*WHO*). ⊕ *www.who.int.*

DEHYDRATION AND OVERHEATING

The African sun is hot and the air is dry, and sweat evaporates quickly in these conditions. You might not realize how much bodily fluid you're losing as a result. Wear a hat, lightweight clothing, and sunscreen—all of which will help your body cope with high temperatures. If you're prone to low blood sugar or have a sensitive stomach, consider bringing along rehydration salts, available at camping stores, to balance your body's fluids and keep you going when you feel listless.

Drink at least two to three quarts of water a day, and in extreme heat conditions as much as three to four quarts of water or juice. Drink more if you're exerting yourself physically. Alcohol is dehydrating, so try to limit consumption on hot or long travel days. If you do overdo it at dinner with wine or spirits, or even caffeine, you need to drink even more water to recover the fluid lost as your body processes the alcohol. Antimalarial medications are also very dehydrating, so it's important to drink water while you're taking this medicine.

Don't rely on thirst to tell you when to drink; people often don't feel thirsty until they're a little dehydrated. At the first sign of dry mouth, exhaustion, or headache, drink water, because dehydration is the likely culprit. ■TIP➜ **To test for dehydration, pinch the skin on the back of your hand and see if it stays in a peak; if it does, you're dehydrated.** Drink a solution of ½ teaspoon salt and 4 tablespoons sugar dissolved in a quart of water to replace electrolytes.

Heat cramps stem from a low salt level due to excessive sweating. These muscle pains usually occur in the abdomen, arms, or legs. When cramps occur, stop all activity and sit quietly in a cool spot and drink water. Don't do anything strenuous for a few hours after the cramps subside. If heat cramps persist for more than an hour, seek medical assistance.

INSECTS

In summer ticks may be a problem, even in open areas close to cities. If you intend to walk or hike anywhere, use a suitable insect repellent. After your walk, examine your body and clothes for ticks, looking carefully for pepper ticks, which are tiny but may cause tick-bite fever. If you're bitten, keep an eye on the bite. Most people suffer no more than an itchy bump, so don't panic. If the tick is infected, however, the bite will swell, itch, and develop a black necrotic center. This is a sure sign that you'll develop tick-bite fever, which usually hits after about eight to 12 days. Symptoms may be mild or severe, depending on the patient. This disease isn't usually life-threatening in healthy adults, but it's horribly unpleasant. ■TIP➜ **Check your boots for spiders and other crawlies and shake your clothes out before getting dressed.**

Always keep a lookout for mosquitoes. Even in nonmalarial areas they're extremely irritating. When walking anywhere in the bush, watch

If you're traveling with kids, consdier a stay with &Beyond, which offers children's programs at several of its upscale camps throughout Southern and East Africa.

out for snakes. If you see one, give it a wide berth and you should be fine. Snakes really bite only when they're taken by surprise, so you don't want to step on a napping mamba.

INTESTINAL UPSET

Micro-fauna and -flora differ in every region of Africa, so if you drink unfiltered water, add ice to your soda, or eat fruit from a roadside stand, you might get traveler's diarrhea. All reputable hotels and lodges have filtered, clean tap water or provide sterilized drinking water, and nearly all camps and lodges have supplies of bottled water. If you're traveling outside organized safari camps in rural Africa or are unsure of local water, carry plenty of bottled water and follow the CDC's advice for fruits and vegetables: boil it, cook it, peel it, or forget it. If you're going on a mobile safari, ask about drinking water.

MALARIA

The most serious health problem facing travelers is malaria. The risk is medium at the height of the summer and very low in winter. All travelers heading into malaria-endemic regions should consult a health-care professional at least one month before departure for advice. Unfortunately, the malarial agent *Plasmodium* seems to be able to develop a hardy resistance to new prophylactic drugs quickly, so the best prevention is to avoid being bitten by mosquitoes in the first place.

After sunset, wear light-color (mosquitoes and tsetse flies are attracted to dark surfaces), loose, long-sleeve shirts, long pants, and shoes and socks, and apply mosquito repellent (containing DEET) generously. Always sleep in a mosquito-proof room or tent, and if possible, keep a fan going in your room. If you're pregnant or trying to conceive, some malaria medicines are safe to use but in general it's best to avoid malaria areas entirely.

Generally speaking, the risk is much lower in the dry season (May–October) and peaks immediately after the first rains, which should be in November, but El Niño has made that a lot less predictable.

If you've been bitten by an infected mosquito, you can expect to feel the effects anywhere from seven to 90 days afterward. Typically you'll feel like you have the flu, with worsening high fever, chills and sweats, headache, and muscle aches. In some cases this is accompanied by abdominal pain, diarrhea, and a cough. If it's not treated you could die. It's possible to treat malaria after you've contracted it, but this shouldn't be your long-term strategy for dealing with the disease. ■ TIP→ **If you feel ill even several months after you return home, tell your doctor that you've been in a malaria-infected area.**

MEDICAL CARE AND MEDICINE
As a foreigner, you'll be expected to pay in full for any medical services, so check your existing health plan to see whether you're covered while abroad, and supplement it if necessary. South African doctors are generally excellent. The equipment and training in private clinics rival the best in the world, but public hospitals tend to suffer from overcrowding and underfunding and are best avoided.

OVER-THE-COUNTER REMEDIES
You can buy over-the-counter medication in pharmacies and supermarkets. For expediency, however, you should bring your own supply for your trip and rely on pharmacies just for emergency medication.

MOTION SICKNESS
If you're prone to motion sickness, be sure to examine your safari itinerary closely. Though most landing strips for chartered planes aren't paved but rather grass, earth, or gravel, landings are smooth most of the time. If you're going on safari to northern Botswana (the Okavango Delta, specifically), know that small planes and unpaved airstrips are the main means of transportation between camps; these trips can be very bumpy, hot, and a little dizzying even if you're not prone to motion sickness. If you're not sure how you'll react, take motion-sickness pills just in case. Most of the air transfers take an average of only 30 minutes and the rewards will be infinitely greater than the pains.

■ TIP→ When you fly in small planes, take a sun hat and a pair of sunglasses. If you sit in the front seat next to the pilot, or on the side of the sun, you'll experience harsh glare that could give you a severe headache and exacerbate motion sickness.

SWIMMING
■ TIP→ **Don't swim in lakes or streams.** Many lakes and streams, particularly east of the watershed divide (i.e., in rivers flowing toward the Indian Ocean), are infected with *bilharzia* (schistosomiasis), a parasite carried by a small freshwater snail. The microscopic fluke enters through the skin of swimmers or waders, attaches itself to the intestines or bladder, and lays eggs. Avoid wading in still waters or in areas close to reeds. If you've been wading or swimming in dubious water, dry yourself off vigorously with a towel immediately upon exiting the water,

as this may help to dislodge any flukes before they can burrow into your skin. Fast-moving water is considered safe. If you've been exposed, pop into a pharmacy and purchase a course of treatment and take it to be safe. If your trip is ending shortly after your exposure, take the medicine home and have a check-up once you get home. Bilharzia is easily diagnosed, and it's also easily treated in the early stages.

PEOPLE WITH DISABILITIES

Having a disability doesn't mean you can't go on safari. It's important, however, to plan carefully to ensure that your needs can be adequately met. South African lodges, especially the high-end private ones, are the easiest to navigate and have the fewest steps. Keep in mind that all-terrain 4x4 vehicles don't have seat belts, so you need enough muscle control to keep yourself upright while the vehicle bumps along the unpaved roads. Getting in and out of these elevated vehicles can also be challenging. MalaMala Game Reserve in South Africa is completely accessible and even has specially equipped four-wheel-drive safari vehicles with harness seat belts. Many of Kruger's camps have special accommodations. There are a number of tour operators offering wheelchair-accessible safaris, such as Endeavour Safaris (⊕ *www. endeavour-safaris.com*).

SEASONS

The seasons in sub-Saharan Africa are opposite of those in North America. Summer is December through March, autumn is April and May, winter is June through September, and spring is October and November.

HIGH SEASON/DRY SEASON

High season, also called dry season, refers to the winter months in Southern and East Africa when there's little to no rain at all. Days are sunny and bright, but the nights are cool. In the desert, temperatures can plummet to below freezing, but you'll be snug and warm in your tent wherever you stay. The landscape will be barren and dry (read: not very attractive), but vegetation is low and surface water is scarce, making it easier to spot game. This is the busiest tourist time.

The exception is South Africa, where high season is linked with the summer vacation schedules of South Africans (December–mid-January), and both the European summer vacations (July and August) and Christmas holidays (December and January) in the Seychelles.

LOW SEASON/RAINY SEASON

When we say "low season," we're saying that this is the rainy season. Although the rains are intermittent—often occurring in late afternoon—the bush and vegetation are high and it's more difficult to spot game. It can also get very hot and humid during this time. However, the upside is that there are far fewer tourists, lodge rates are much cheaper (often half price), and the bush is beautifully lush and green. Plus there are lots of baby animals, and if you're a birder all the migrant species are back from their winter habitats.

SHOULDER SEASON

The shoulder season occurs between summer and winter; it's fall in the United States. The rains are just beginning, tourist numbers are decreasing, and the vegetation is starting to die off. Lodges will offer cheaper rates.

TYPES OF SAFARIS

FLY-IN SAFARIS

The mode of transportation for fly-in safaris is as central to the experience as the accommodations. In places such as northern Botswana, where few roads are paved, or northern Namibia, where distances make road transfers impractical, small bush planes take you from lodge to lodge. These planes are usually six-seat Cessna 206 craft flown by bush pilots. The planes have no air-conditioning and in summer can be very hot, especially in the afternoon. Bring a bottle of water with you. And go to the bathroom before flying; there are no restrooms on these planes. Most flights are short—approximately 30 minutes or so—but some can be up to an hour.

Flying from destination to destination is a special experience. The planes stay at low altitudes, allowing you to spot game along the way: you might see elephant and buffalo herds lined up drinking along the edges of remote water holes, or large numbers of zebras walking across the plains. Fly-in safaris also allow you to cover more territory than other types of safaris. In Botswana, for example, the trip between the diverse game destinations of the Moremi Wildlife Reserve in the Okavango Delta and northern Chobe National Park is 40 minutes by plane; it would take six hours by vehicle, if a road between these locations existed.

Hopping from place to place by plane is so easy and fast that many travelers make the mistake of cramming their itineraries with too many lodges. Plan your trip this way and you'll spend more time at airstrips, in planes, and shuttling to and from the airfields than tracking animals or enjoying the bush. You'll glimpse animals as you travel back and forth—sometimes you'll even see them on the airstrips—but you won't have time to stop and really take in the sights. Try to spend at least two nights at any one lodge; three nights is better.

The best way to set up a fly-in safari is to book an all-inclusive package that includes airfare. (It's impractical to try to do it yourself.) A tour operator makes all the arrangements, and many offer standard trips that visit several lodges.

■ TIP→ If your bag is over the weight limit, or if you weigh more than 220 pounds, you'll be required to purchase an additional plane seat (usually about US$100).

LUXURY LODGE–BASED SAFARIS

The majority of safari-goers base their trips at luxury lodges, which pack the double punch of outstanding game-viewing and stylish, atmospheric accommodations. A lodge may be made up of stone chalets, thatch-roof huts, rondavels, or large suitelike tents. Mosquito nets, leather furnishings, and mounted trophies add to the ambience. Dinners are served inside or in an open-air boma. All have hot-and-cold

		Summer				Fall		Winter				Spring	
		Dec	Jan	Feb	Mar	Apr	May	Jun	Jul	Aug	Sep	Oct	Nov
BOTSWANA	The Okavango Delta	●	●	●	●	●	●	●	●	●	●	●	●
	Moremi Wildlife Reserve	●	●	●	●	●	●	●	●	●	●	●	●
	Chobe Nat'l Park	●	●	●	●	●	●	●	●	●	●	●	●
	Kwando Game Reserve	●	●	●	●	●	●	●	●	●	●	●	●
KENYA	Masai Mara	●	●	●	●	●	●	●	●	●	●	●	●
	Amboseli Nat'l Park	●	●	●	●	●	●	●	●	●	●	●	●
	Tsavo Nat'l Park	●	●	●	●	●	●	●	●	●	●	●	●
	Laikipia Plateau	●	●	●	●	●	●	●	●	●	●	●	●
NAMIBIA	Namib Naukluft Park	●	●	●	●	●	●	●	●	●	●	●	●
	Damaraland	●	●	●	●	●	●	●	●	●	●	●	●
	Etosha Nat'l Park	●	●	●	●	●	●	●	●	●	●	●	●
SOUTH AFRICA	Kruger Nat'l Park	●	●	●	●	●	●	●	●	●	●	●	●
	Sabi Sands Game Reserve	●	●	●	●	●	●	●	●	●	●	●	●
	KwaZulu-Natal Parks	●	●	●	●	●	●	●	●	●	●	●	●
	Kgalagadi Transfrontier Park	●	●	●	●	●	●	●	●	●	●	●	●
TANZANIA	Serengeti Nat'l Park	●	●	●	●	●	●	●	●	●	●	●	●
	Ngorongoro Conservation Area	●	●	●	●	●	●	●	●	●	●	●	●
	Lake Manyara Nat'l Park	●	●	●	●	●	●	●	●	●	●	●	●
	Selous Game Reserve	●	●	●	○	○	○	●	●	●	●	●	●
	Gombe Stream and Mahale Mountains Nat'l Parks	●	●	●	●	●	●	●	●	●	●	●	●

KEY: ● = Low Season, Park Open   ● = Shoulder Season Park Open   ● = High Season Park Open
○ = Low Season, Park Closed   ○ = Shoulder Season Park Closed   ○ = High Season Park Closed

Watercraft safaris such as those offered in Chobe National Park, Botswana, provide special wildlife encounters.

running water, flush toilets, toiletries, laundry service, electricity, and, in most cases, swimming pools. Some lodges also have air-conditioning, telephones, hair dryers, and minibars. The most lavish places also have private plunge pools.

Make no mistake: you pay for all this pampering. Expect to spend anywhere from US$500 to US$1,800 per person per night, depending on the season. All meals, beverages, house wines, game drives, and walks are included. A three-night stay is ideal, but two nights are usually sufficient to see the big game.

The time you spend at a private lodge is tightly structured. With some exceptions, the lodges offer almost identical programs of events. There are usually two three- to four-hour game drives a day, one in the early morning and another in the evening. You spend a lot of time sitting and eating, and in the afternoon you can nap and relax. However, you can always opt for an after-breakfast bush walk, and many lodges now have spas and gyms. If you're tired after your night drive, ask for something to be sent to your room, but don't miss the bush *braai* (barbecue) and at least one night in the boma (if your lodge offers it).

On game drives at bigger camps, rangers stay in contact with one another via radio. If one finds a rhino, for example, he relays its location to the others so they can bring their guests. The more vehicles you have in the field, the more wildlife everyone is likely to see. But don't worry, most lodges are well disciplined with their vehicles, and there are rarely more than three or four at a sighting. As your vehicle arrives, one already there will drive away. In choosing a game lodge, remember to check how much land a lodge can traverse and how many vehicles it uses.

Try to go on a bush walk with an armed ranger—an unforgettable experience, as the ranger can point out fascinating details along the way.

All lodges arrange transfers from nearby airports, train stations, or drop-off points. In more remote areas most have their own private airstrips carved out of the bush and fly guests in on chartered aircraft at extra cost. If you're driving yourself, the lodge will send you detailed instructions because many of the roads don't appear on maps and lack names.

A VOYAGE OF DISCOVERY

As you embark on your safari, consider how lucky you are to be witnessing these rare species in their natural habitat. To this day, researchers in Africa continue to unearth new species. In the summer of 2007, for example, a group of scientists in the Democratic Republic of the Congo discovered six new species (a bat, a rodent, two shrews, and two frogs) in a remote forest, and in 2013 an international team of scientists discovered five new species of bat in West Africa. A study in 2016 found that there are actually four species of giraffe in Africa, with nine subspecies, not one, as previously thought. One can't help but wonder what else is out there or who will find it and when.

MOBILE AND OVERLAND SAFARIS

Most mobile-safari operations are expertly run but are aimed at budget-conscious travelers. They're mostly self-sufficient camping affairs with overnights at either public or private campgrounds, depending on the safari's itinerary and price. Sometimes you stay at basic lodges along the way. Travel is often by something that looks like a 4x4 bus.

For young, hardy people, or the young at heart, mobile safaris are a great way to see the land from ground level. You taste the dust, smell the bacon cooking, stop where and when you want (within reason), and get to see some of the best places in the region. Trips usually run 14 to 21 days, although you can find shorter ones that cover fewer destinations. Prices start at US$750 and climb to US$2,500 for all-inclusive trips. Not sure whether all-inclusive is right for you? Consider combining a mobile safari with a lodge-based one, which gives you the best of both worlds. A minimum of 10 nights is recommended for such an itinerary.

WALKING SAFARIS

Many lodges offer walks as an optional way to view game. On a walking safari, however, you spend most, if not all, of your time in the bush on foot, accompanied by an armed guide. Because you're trekking through big-game country, there's an element of danger. But it's the proximity to wilderness that makes this type of trip so enchanting—and exciting. Of course, you can't stop every step of the way or you'd never get very far, but you'll stop frequently to be shown something—from a native flower to spoor to animals—or to discuss some aspect of animal behavior or of tracking.

Walking treks take place on what are known as wilderness trails, which are natural tracks made by animals and are traversed only on foot, never

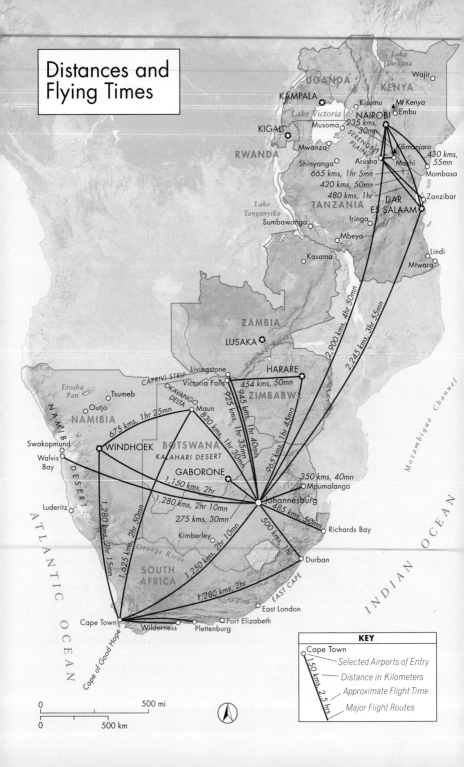

Distances and Flying Times

KAMPALA
UGANDA
Lake Turkana
Wajir
Lake Victoria
Kisumu
NAIROBI
235 kms, 30mn
KIGALI
Mt Kenya
Embu
Musoma
RWANDA
Mwanza
Shinyanga
SERENGETI PLAIN
Arusha
Moshi
Kilimanjaro
430 kms, 55mn
Mombasa
665 kms, 1hr 5mn
420 kms, 50mn
480 kms, 1hr
TANZANIA
DAR ES SALAAM
Zanzibar
Lake Tanganyika
Iringa
Sumbawanga
Mbeya
Lindi
Kasama
Mtwara
ZAMBIA
Mozambique Channel
LUSAKA
2,900 kms, 4hr 50mn
2,245 kms, 3hr 55mn
Livingstone
HARARE
Victoria Falls
454 kms, 50mn
CAPRIVI STRIP
ZIMBABWE
Etosha Pan
Tsumeb
925 kms, 1hr 35mn
945 kms, 1hr 40mn
965 kms, 1hr 45mn
KAVANGO DELTA
Outjo
Maun
830 kms, 1hr 30mn
675 kms, 1hr 25mn
NAMIBIA
Swakopmund
WINDHOEK
BOTSWANA
KALAHARI DESERT
Walvis Bay
GABORONE
1,150 kms, 2hr
350 kms, 40mn
Mpumalanga
1,280 kms, 2hr 10mn
Johannesburg
485 kms, 50mn
Luderitz
275 kms, 30mn
500 kms, 1hr
Richards Bay
1,280 kms, 2hr 15mn
1,625 kms, 2hr 50mn
Kimberley
2hr 10mn
Orange River
1,250 kms, 2hr 10mn
Durban
SOUTH AFRICA
EAST CAPE
1,280 kms, 2hr
ATLANTIC OCEAN
East London
Port Elizabeth
INDIAN OCEAN
Cape Town
Wilderness
Plettenburg
Cape of Good Hope

KEY
Cape Town
Selected Airports of Entry
Distance in Kilometers
1,150 kms, 2.5 hrs
Approximate Flight Time
Major Flight Routes

0   500 mi
0   500 km

CLOSE UP

Safari Do's and Don'ts

Do observe animals silently. Talking loudly frightens animals and disturbs their activities.

Don't attempt to attract an animal's attention. Don't imitate sounds, clap hands, pound the vehicle, or throw objects.

Do respect your driver and guide's judgment. They have more knowledge and experience than you. If they say no, there's a good reason.

Don't leave your vehicle. On self-drives, drive slowly, and keep ample distance between you and the wildlife.

Do dress in neutral tones. If everyone is wearing earth tones, the animal sees one large vegetation-color mass.

Don't litter. Any tossed item can choke or poison animals.

Don't attempt to feed or approach animals. This is especially important at lodges and campgrounds where animals are accustomed to humans.

Don't smoke. The bush ignites easily.

by vehicle, to maintain their pristine condition. These trails usually lead into remote areas that you would never see on a typical safari. In some cases porters carry the supplies and bags. Accommodations are usually in remote camps or occasionally in tents.

■TIP➔ **Consider your physical condition for walking safaris.** You should be in good health and be able to walk between 6.4 and 16 km (4 and 10 miles) a day, depending on the scope of the trip. Some trips don't allow hikers under age 12 or over age 60 (but Kruger Park makes exceptions for those over 60 if you produce a doctor's certificate). Also, you shouldn't scare easily. No guide has time for people who freeze up at the sight of a beetle, spider, or something more menacing; guides need to keep their attention on the wilds around them and on the group as a whole. Guides are armed, and they take great caution to keep you away from trouble. To stay safe, always listen to your guide and follow instructions.

WILDLIFE SAFETY AND RESPECT

Nature is neither kind nor sentimental. Don't be tempted to interfere with natural processes. The animals are going about the business of survival in a harsh environment, and you can unwittingly make this business more difficult. Don't get too close to the animals and don't try to help them cross some perceived obstacle; you have no idea what it's really trying to do or where it wants to go. If you're intrusive, you could drive animals away from feeding and, even worse, from drinking at water holes, where they're very skittish and vulnerable to predators. That time at the water hole may be their only opportunity to drink that day.

Never feed any wild creature. Not a cute monkey, not an inquisitive baboon, not a baby tree squirrel, or a young bird out of its nest. In some camps and lodges, however, animals have gotten used to being fed or steal food. The most common animals in this category are baboons and monkeys; in some places they sneak into huts, tents, and even occupied vehicles to snatch food. If you see primates around, keep all food out of sight, and keep your windows rolled up. (If a baboon manages to get into your vehicle, he will trash the interior as he searches for food and use the vehicle as a toilet.)

> **STARSTRUCK**
>
> You'll be awed by the brilliance of the night skies on safari, especially if you live in a city. To add romance and interest to your stargazing, study up on the southern skies and bring a star guide. Also, most guides are knowledgeable about the stars, so ask questions.

Never try to get an animal to pose with you. This is probably the biggest cause of death and injury on safaris, when visitors don't listen to or believe the warnings from their rangers or posted notices in public parks. Regardless of how cute or harmless they may look, these animals aren't tame. An herbivore hippo, giraffe, or ostrich can kill you just as easily as a lion, elephant, or buffalo can.

Immersion in the African safari lands is a privilege. In order to preserve this privilege for later generations, it's important that you view wildlife with minimal disturbance and avoid upsetting the delicate balance of nature at all costs. You're the visitor, so act like you would in someone else's home: respect their space. Caution is your most trusted safety measure. Keep your distance, keep quiet, and keep your hands to yourself, and you should be fine.

VOCABULARY

Mastering the basics of just two foreign languages, Zulu and Swahili, should make you well equipped for travel through much of the region. Zulu is the most common of the Southern African Nguni family of languages (Zulu, Shangaan, Ndebele, Swazi, Xhosa) and is understood in South Africa and Zimbabwe. Swahili is a mixture of Arabic and Bantu and is used across East Africa. In Namibia, Botswana, and Zambia your best bet initially is to stick with English.

SAFARI SPEAK

Ablution blocks: public bathrooms

Banda: bungalow or hut

Big Five: buffalo, elephants, leopards, lions, and rhinoceroses, collectively

Boma: a fenced-in, open-air eating area, usually circular

Braai: barbecue

Bushveld: general safari area in South Africa, usually with scattered shrubs and trees and lots of game; also referred to as the bush or the veld

Camp: used interchangeably with lodge

Campground: a place used for camping that encompasses several campsites and often includes some shared facilities

Campsite: may or may not be part of a campground

Concession: game-area lease that's granted to a safari company and gives it exclusive access to the land

Game guide: used interchangeably with ranger; usually a man

Hides: small, partially camouflaged shelters from which to view game and birds; blinds

Kopje/Koppies: hills or rocky outcrops

Kraal: traditional rural settlement of huts and houses

Lodge: accommodation in rustic yet stylish tents, rondavels, or lavish suites; prices at lodges usually include all meals and game-viewing

Marula: tree from which *amarula* (the liquor) gets its name

Mobile or overland safari: usually a self-sufficient camping affair set up at a different location (public or private campgrounds) each night

Mokoro: dugout canoe; plural *mekoro*

Ranger: safari guide with vast experience with and knowledge of the bush and the animals that inhabit it; used interchangeably with *game guide*

Rest camp: camp in a national park

Rondavel/rondawel: a traditional round dwelling with a conical roof

Sala: outdoor covered deck

Self-catering: with some kind of kitchen facilities, so you can store food and prepare meals yourself

Self-drive safari: budget safari option in which you drive, and guide, yourself in a rented vehicle

Sundowner: cocktails at sunset

Tracker: works in conjunction with a ranger, spotting animals from a special seat on the front of the 4x4 game-viewing vehicle

Veld: a grassland; see *bushveld*

Vlei: wetland or marsh

SOUTH AFRICAN WORDS AND PHRASES
BASICS

Abseil: rappel

Bakkie: pickup truck (pronounced "bucky")

Berg: mountain

Boot: trunk (of a car)

Bottle store: liquor store

Bra/bru/my bra: brother (term of affection or familiarity)

Buck: antelope

Chommie: mate, chum

Dagga: marijuana, sometimes called *zol*

Djembes: drums

Dorp: village

Fanagalo: a mix of Zulu, English, Afrikaans, Sotho, and Xhosa

Highveld: the country's high interior plateau, including Johannesburg

Howzit?: literally, "How are you?" but used as a general greeting

Indaba: literally, a meeting, but also a problem, as in "That's your indaba."

Ja: yes

Jol: a party or night on the town

Kloof: river gorge

Kokerbooms: quiver trees

Lekker: nice

Lowveld: land at lower elevation, including Kruger National Park

Mopane: nutrient-poor land

More-ish: so good you'll want more, mouthwatering

Muthi: traditional (non-Western) medicine (pronounced "mooti")

Petrol: gasoline

Plaas: farm

Robot: traffic light

Sangoma: traditional healer or mystic

Shebeen: a place to drink, often used for taverns in townships

Sis: gross, disgusting

Sisi or usisi: sister (term of affection or respect)

Spar: name of grocery market chain in Africa

Spaza shop: an informal shop, usually from a truck or container

Stoep: veranda

Takkie: sneaker (pronounced "tacky")

FOOD AND DRINK

Biltong: spiced air-dried (not smoked) meat, made of everything from beef to kudu

Bobotie: spiced, minced beef or lamb topped with savory custard; a Cape Malay dish

Boerewors: Afrikaner term for a spicy farmer's sausage, often used for a braai (pronounced "boo- *rah-vorse*")

Bredie: a casserole or stew, usually lamb with tomatoes

Bunny chow: not a fancy name for salad—it's a half loaf of bread hollowed out and filled with meat or vegetable curry

Chakalaka: a spicy relish

Gatsby: a loaf of bread cut lengthwise and filled with fish or meat, salad, and fries

Kabeljou: one of the varieties of line fish

Kingklip: a native fish

Koeksister: a deep-fried, braided, sugared dough

Malva: sponge cake dessert, usually including apricot jam and served with custard or ice-cream

Melktert: a sweet custard tart

Mogodu: beef or ox tripe

Moroho: mopane worms

Pap: also called *mielie pap,* a maize-based porridge

Peppadew: a patented vegetable, so you may see it under different names, usually with the word *dew* in them; it's a sort of a cross between a sweet pepper and a chili and is usually pickled.

Peri-peri: a spicy chili marinade, Portuguese in origin, based on the searing hot *piri-piri* chili; some recipes are tomato-based, others use garlic, olive oil, and brandy

Potjie: pronounced "poy- *key*" and also called *potjiekos,* a traditional stew cooked in a three-legged pot

Rocket: arugula

Rooibos: an indigenous, earthy-tasting red-leaf tea

Samp: corn porridge

Snoek: a barracudalike fish, often smoked, sometimes *smoorsnoek* (braised)

Sosaties: local version of a kebab, with spiced, grilled chunks of meat

Waterblommetjie: water lilies, sometimes used in stews

Witblitz: moonshine

SWAHILI ESSENTIALS
ANIMALS

Buffalo: nyati

Cheetah: duma

Crocodile: mamba

Elephant: tembo

Giraffe: twiga

Hippo: kiboko

Impala: swala

Leopard: chui

Lion: simba

Rhino: kifalu

BASICS

Yes: ndio

No: hapana

Please: tafadhali

Excuse me: samahani

Thank you (very much): asante (sana)

Welcome: karibu

Hello: jambo

Beautiful: nzuri

Good-bye: kwaheri

Cheers: kwahafya njema

FOOD AND DRINK

Food: chakula

Water: maji

Bread: mkate

Fruit(s): (ma)tunda

Vegetable: mboga

Salt: chumvi

Sugar: sukari

Coffee: kahawa

Tea: chai

Beer: pombe

USEFUL PHRASES

What's your name?: Jina lako nani?

My name is … : Jina langu ni…

How are you?: Habari?

Where are you from?: Unatoka wapi?

I come from … : Mimi ninatoka…

Do you speak English?: Una sema Kiingereza?

I don't speak Swahili.: Sisemi Kiswahili.

I don't understand.: Sifahamu.

How do you say this in Swahili?: Unasemaje kwa Kiswahili?

How much is it?: Ngapi shillings?

May I take your picture?: Mikupige picha?

Where is the bathroom?: Choo kiko wapi?

I need … : Mimi natafuta…

I want to buy … : Mimi nataka kununua…

No problem.: Hakuna matata.

ZULU ESSENTIALS

BASICS

Yes: yebo

No: cha

Please/Excuse me: uxolo

Thank you: ngiyabonga

You're welcome: nami ngiyabonga

Good morning/hello: sawubona

Good-bye: sala kahle

FOOD AND DRINK

Food: ukudla

Water: amanzi

Bread: isinkwa

2

Fruit: isthelo
Vegetable: uhlaza
Salt: usawoti
Sugar: ushekela
Coffee: ikhofi
Tea: itiye
Beer: utshwala

USEFUL PHRASES
What's your name?: Ubani igama lakho?
My name is … : Igama lami ngingu…
Do you speak English?: Uya khuluma isingisi?
I don't understand.: Angizwa ukuthi uthini.
How much is it?: Kuyimalini lokhu?
May I take your picture?: Mikupige picha?
Where is the bathroom?: Likuphi itholethe?
I would like … : Ngidinga…
I want to buy … : Ngicela…

CHOOSING AN OUTFITTER

3

WHY GO WITH AN OPERATOR?

Booking a vacation yourself online is now very much the norm, and there's a widespread perception that you'll get a more authentic and reasonably priced experience if you do it all yourself.

This approach often works for American or European city visits, but not as frequently for a safari in Africa. You may save money, but you could end up with hassles that outweigh the savings.

An exception is an overland safari, or a self-drive safari in South Africa *(See Planning Your Safari for more about the various types of safaris)*. One of the main reasons to book yourself is to choose what you want to do and when, but all of the outfitters we feature offer customized trips.

THINGS TO CONSIDER

Do you have only 12 days or less? Africa is huge and infrastructure isn't well developed outside South Africa. Flights from the United States and Europe are long and seldom direct, and if one leg is delayed you can miss your connection and derail your whole itinerary. Just getting to a lodge from an airstrip can be a time-consuming journey, too. A tour operator will know the ins and outs of local travel so you're aware of traveling times in advance, and they'll sort things out if they don't go as planned. They also know the best ways to contact lodges and airlines, which can be challenging due to time differences between countries on the continent and the United States, as well as unreliable phone and Internet.

Safety and surprises. Although the countries you're likely to visit are largely stable and safe, first-time travelers in particular can be anxious about their virgin journey into unknown terrain. Political climates can change quickly, and news can be slow to filter out through traditional news channels. Your operator has contacts on the ground who keep them up-to-date with relevant information. Natural disasters, or even heavier-than-expected rainfall, can make roads dangerous or impassable, and a tour operator can adjust your itinerary accordingly. And they will be accountable if anything goes wrong or if you don't receive the service you paid for.

Specific requests or interests. When you plan a safari, you're presented with multiple countries and infinite options, depending on your budget, the time of year, whether you want to see animals and landscape in a vehicle, on foot, on horseback, or on a boat, and whether you want to stay in a canvas tent or a hotel. You may have dietary or health issues, or want an eco-holiday rather than a butler and private plunge pool. You might want to see three countries in 10 days or just one in a week. A good tour operator will discuss your preferences and tailor an experience that delivers exactly what you want and how you want it, saving you weeks of research. Tour operators also have the kind of overview of an area and its various options that you can't pick up from reading individual reviews of places online.

Details, big and small. Weight allowance on planes, yellow-fever certificates, visas, tipping—these are just some of the easily overlooked details that a good outfitter will tend to. You'll also receive valuable information about local culture and customs.

Choices and prices. Hotels and lodges have two sets of prices—rack rates, which are what the public pays, and a cheaper rate for tour operators. The operator will add their own markup, but you often still pay less, and you'll be aware of all the costs involved up-front, which allows you to budget better. Tour operators will also buffer you against currency fluctuations—the price you'll pay months in advance of a trip will be guaranteed. Also, many lodges don't take bookings directly from the public because they also prefer their clients to go through an operator, so you'll automatically lose out on a lot of good choices.

TYPES OF SAFARI OPERATORS

African tour operator. Usually based in the United States, this type of company specializes in tours and safaris to Africa and works with a safari operator that provides support on the ground. Start dates and itineraries are set for some trips, but customized vacations can almost always be arranged. Travelers can find out the details of these trips through retail travel agents but can also deal directly with the company, usually by talking with them about their preferences on the phone and then receiving a personalized itinerary and quote via email.

African safari operator/ground operator. This type of outfitter is a company in Africa that provides logistical support to a U.S.-based tour operator by seeing to the details of your safari. An operator might charter flights, pick you up at the airport, and take you on game-viewing trips. Some operators own or manage safari lodges. In addition, a safari operator communicates changing trends and developments in the region to tour operators and serves as your on-site contact in cases of illness, injury, or other unexpected situations. For example, &Beyond is an African tour operator that uses a ground operator to handle logistics and accommodations. Micato and Wilderness Safaris on the other hand, handle every stage of your trip themselves.

Retail travel agent. In general, a travel agent sells trip packages directly to consumers. In most cases an agent doesn't have a geographical specialty. When called on to arrange a trip to Africa, the travel agent turns to an African tour operator for details.

Before you entrust your trip to tour operators or travel agents, do your best to determine the extent of their knowledge as well as the level of enthusiasm they have for the destination. There are as many travel companies claiming to specialize in Africa as there are hippos in the Zambezi, so it's especially important to determine which operators and agents are up to the challenge. *We've featured some of the best further on in this chapter.*

After choosing a tour operator or travel agent, it's a good idea to discuss with him or her the logistics and details of the itinerary so you know what to expect each day. Ask questions about lodging, even if you're traveling on a group tour. A lodge that's completely open to the elements may be a highlight for some travelers and terrifying for others, particularly at night when a lion roars nearby. Also ask about the amount of time you'll spend with other travelers. If you're planning a safari honeymoon, find out if you can dine alone when you want to, and ask about honeymoon packages.

QUESTIONS TO ASK A SAFARI SPECIALIST

We recommend you withhold your deposit until you've considered your operator's answers to most of the following questions. Once you pay the deposit, you're liable for a penalty if you decide to cancel the arrangements for any reason.

■ How many years have you been selling tours in Africa?

■ How many people does your company take on safari every year?

■ Where do you have offices—do you have any in the destination itself?

■ Can you provide past traveler references?

■ To which professional organizations do you belong? For example, the American Society of Travel Agents (ASTA) or the United States Tour Operators Association (USTOA)? International Airlines Travel Agent Network (IATAN) members must have annual sales exceeding US$250,000 and carry a US$1 million liability insurance policy, which eliminates fly-by-night operators.

■ Do you have bonding insurance? (This protects you if the company goes under and your agent defaults before your trip.)

■ What is your security policy? How do you mitigate risks and stay informed of potential threats?

■ What are your cancellation policies in the event of a U.S. State Department or World Health Organization travel warning, or a natural disaster?

■ What are the payment terms? Do you offer optional trip cancellation insurance in case I need to cancel?

■ Can you handle arrangements from start to finish, including flights? Is there a 24-hour support line if needed?

■ Who will lead my trip, and what are their qualifications? Will they be with me the whole time, or will I be with different local guides at each place?

■ Do you have your own guides and vehicles? What certification and/or training is required for your guides?

■ What kind of vehicles do you use for game drives, and can a window seat be guaranteed?

■ Do you charge a fee? (Agents and operators usually make their money through commissions.)

■ What's included in the cost? For instance, are all tips, permits, departure taxes, and game park fees included? What about meals and drinks?

■ What is the maximum and minimum size of a group? And, is the trip guaranteed to operate regardless of the number of travelers?

■ What level of fitness is required for this trip?

■ Do you operate any social and environmental responsibility programs, or support any NGOs? Can I get involved with your philanthropic efforts or learn about volunteering efforts?

■ Do you have any affiliation to a particular lodge chain, or will you refer me to lodges or camps you own yourself only? (An operator can keep costs down by doing this, but you'll benefit the most from impartial advice.)

■ Has your company won any industry or magazine awards?

■ Will you be able to arrange any add-on experiences, such as a beach break or a city stay afterwards?

■ Do you accept bookings from single travelers? If so, will I have to pay a single supplement, or, are there ways around the fee, i.e. traveling at a different time of year?

■ TIP→ Consider how responsive the agent is to your queries. If they take a long time to get back to you, aren't easy to get hold of on the phone, don't read your emails properly, or make mistakes with details in the beginning stages, it's not a good sign. The level of service you receive when gathering information and booking the trip is a strong indicator of the company's professionalism.

GOING GREEN

How do you ensure that your operator is committed to sustainability, works with the local community, and leaves as light an impact on the landscape as possible? It can be tricky because many companies "green-wash"—they apply an eco tag to their trips or services without any real follow-through. Until an official ratings system is in place, you'll have to do the research yourself—though Kenya has a reliable website with ratings *(See box in Chapter 4)*. Helpful watchdog agencies include: Tourism Concern (⊕ *www.tourismconcern.org.uk*) and Green Globe (⊕ *www.greenglobe.com*). Conservation organizations such as World Wildlife Fund (⊕ *www.worldwildlife.org*) or the African Wildlife Foundation (⊕ *www.awf.org*) also promote green tourism standards. Another excellent resource is Africa's Finest (⊕ *africasfinest.co.za*), a website started by the renowned conservationist Colin Bell and travel journalist and environmental scientist David Bristow. Bell, Bristow, and their team spent two years independently assessing hundreds of lodges in order to pinpoint those with truly eco credentials; although the list on their website is not exhaustive, it's a very useful resource. There's also a list of NGOS they consider worthy of support.

Private conservancies are usually able to offer a more environmentally sustainable model than national parks. Conservancies are created out of tracts of land, usually adjacent to a national park, that have been leased from the local community for the purpose of wildlife conservation. They have strict usage conditions—meaning no overcrowding—and experiences that national parks can't offer, such as night drives and walking safaris. Although lodges on conservancies can be expensive to stay in, the fees go directly towards supporting conservation and local communities.

Ask your operator the following questions to find out where they stand on the 4 C's: Commerce, Conservation, Community, and Culture.

■ Are the lodges on the itineraries solar-powered? Solar energy is inexpensive and reliable and can now be used for heating water, lighting, and cooking, so there's really no excuse.

■ What are the recycling, water conservation, and waste management practices? Are environmentally friendly cleaning products used, and does the lodge purify its own water rather than bringing in hundreds of plastic water bottles?

■ Does the lodge's dining menu use local ingredients? Or, even better, are ingredients sourced on-site from local communities? Is leftover food composted?

■ Do the safari guides, rangers, and trackers belong to tribes from the region in which you're traveling?

■ Do the chefs and porters hail from the surrounding area?

■ Does the company, or the lodges it uses, provide educational and economic opportunities for local communities?

■ Does the company have any philanthropic or "voluntourism" projects such as building and maintaining a school or a health clinic?

■ Does the lodge offer low-impact activities such as walking, horseback riding, cycling, or canoe excursions? The experience should be about more than just ticking off the Big Five.

■ Does the lodge support academic and scientific research, or is it involved in any programs to support or reintroduce endangered species?

Many reputable outfitters have established foundations that make donations to local peoples or wildlife, and some will arrange trips to nearby schools, orphanages, or neighborhoods. *We've highlighted the philanthropic endeavors of a number of top operators in our Tour Operators list below.*

TOUR OPERATORS

Our list of tour operators hardly exhausts the number of reputable companies, but the following operators, sorted alphabetically, are well-established firms that offer a good selection of itineraries ranging from overland safaris to walking and fly-in safaris, under-canvas safaris, and safari lodges. They all offer fully customizable trips, too. *(See Planning Your Safari for more about the various types of safaris.)*

If you want to experience original safari ambience like Ernest Hemingway enjoyed, Cottars 1920s Safari Camp in Kenya's Masai Mara National Reseve is the place to do it.

TOP 10 OUTFITTERS

Abercrombie & Kent. In business since 1962, this company is considered one of the best in the business and is consistently given high marks by former clients. From your first decision to go on safari to its successful conclusion, A&K offers seamless service. Their tailor-made safaris hearken back to days past when intrepid adventurers such as Teddy Roosevelt and Ernest Hemingway relied on private guides to create a safari program and escort them through the bush from start to finish. The company has a professional network of local A&K offices in all its destination countries, staffed by full-time A&K experts, and maintains its own fleet of four-wheel-drive safari vehicles and trains its own drivers. The head office in the U.S. is in Illinois. **Destinations:** Botswana, Kenya, Namibia, South Africa, Tanzania, Uganda, Zambia, Zimbabwe. **Popular packages:** Kenya & Tanzania, 12 days, from $7,995. **Philanthropy:** Extensive projects benefit ecosystems and wildlife, communities and cultures, and health and education. Guests can meet local people making a difference in their communities. Many guests build their safari around several of these projects. **What they do best:** Destination knowledge—they have some of the most experienced guides on the continent. ✉ *1411 Opus Pl., Downers Grove* ☎ *888/611–4711* ⊕ *www.abercrombiekent.com.*

Access2Tanzania. After living in Tanzania for two years as a Peace Corps volunteer, owner Brian Singer set up Access2Tanzania in 2004 with his wife Karen and Tanzanian partner Michael Musa. Brian and Karen handle all pre-safari planning, and Michael takes care of ground logistics. They are one of few companies in Tanzania that do

Outfitter	Location	Tel. no.	Website	Countries Covered
&Beyond	South Africa	27/11809-4300 888/882-3742	www.andbeyond.com	All
Abercrombie & Kent	USA	888/611–4711	www.abercrombiekent.com	All
Access2Tanzania	USA	718/715-1353	www.access2tanzania.com	Rwanda, Tanzania
Africa Adventure Company	USA	800/882–9453	www.africa-adventure.com	All
Africa Serendipity	USA	212/288-1714	www.africanserendipity.com	Kenya, Tanzania
African Portfolio	USA	800/700-3677	www.onsafari.com	All
Black Tomato	USA	646/558-3644	www.blacktomato.com	All
Cheli & Peacock	Kenya	254/20/60–4053	www.chelipeacock.com	Kenya
Deeper Africa	USA	888/658-7102	www.deeperafrica.com	Kenya, Tanzania
Doug Macdonald Safaris	Zimbabwe	263/778-219208	www.dougmacsafaris.com	All
Earthlife Expeditions	Tanzania	255/753-891310	www.earthlifeexpeditions.com	All
Eyes on Africa	USA	888/450-9247	www.eyesonafrica.net	All
Extraordinary Journeys	USA	212/226-7331	www.extraordinaryjourneys.com	All
Gamewatchers Safaris	Kenya	877/710-3014	www.porini.com	Kenya, Tanzania, South Africa, Botswana, Zambia
Ker & Downey	USA	800/423–4236	www.kerdowneysafaris.com	All
Micato Safaris	USA	212/545-7111	www.micatosafaris.com	All
Natural Habitat Adventures	USA	800/543-8917	www.nathab.com	All
Nomad Tanzania	Tanzania	255/784-734490	www.nomad-tanzania.com	Tanzania
Premier Tours	USA	800/545–1910	www.premiertours.com	All
ROAR Africa	USA	855/666-7627	www.roarafrica.com	All
Roy Safaris	Tanzania	255/272-502115	www.roysafaris.com	Kenya, Tanzania
Safari Infinity	Tanzania	255/688-285354	www.safari-infinity.com	Tanzania
Wilderness Safaris	South Africa	27-11/807–1800	www.wilderness-safaris.com	South Africa, Botswana, Namibia, Zambia, Zimbabwe
Travel Beyond	USA	800/ 876-3131	www.travelbeyond.com	All
The Wild Source	USA	720/497-1250	www.thewildsource.com	Tanzania, Botswana

not subcontract their guides; each one is a full-time employee and they all consistently receive rave reviews. They own and maintain their own air-conditioned vehicles, which have unlimited mileage and pop-up roofs to allow 360-degree views. A new operation in Rwanda run by the company under the same principles is called Treks2Rwanda. **Destinations:** Rwanda, Tanzania. **Popular packages:** Adventures through Northern Tanzania, 7 nights, from $3,165; Rwanda Gorilla Trekking, 3 nights, from $2,515. **Philanthropy:** The owners run a nonprofit, Project Zawadi, which supports the educational needs of orphans and other vulnerable Tanzanian children. Hundreds of children are put through school each year, and it has also built several classrooms, teacher's accommodations, and a vocational training center. **What they do best:** Itineraries are custom-made and private only; the team works hard to ensure that the individual needs of each client are met. They have offices in both Tanzania and the United States, meaning service is superb before, during, and after the safari. ⊠ *253 Duke St., St. Paul* ☏ *718/715–1353* ⊕ *www.access2tanzania.com.*

African Portfolio. African Portfolio's team members visit each in-country operator annually and are on a first-name basis with the managers of the properties they use. They pride themselves on discovering the best places, whether they're hidden gems, up-and-coming properties, or well-established classics. With each client, they're committed to providing a safari reminiscent of what captivates them about Africa. Their mission is to provide unique and memorable experiences through nature-based travel that educate, entertain, inspire, and provide participants with opportunities to directly contribute to conservation. **Destinations:** Botswana, Kenya, Malawi, Mauritius, Mozambique, Namibia, Rwanda, Seychelles, South Africa, Tanzania, Uganda, Zambia, Zimbabwe. **Popular packages:** Chobe, Victoria Falls and Hwange, 9 days, from $5,500; Great Rift Valley Safari, Tanzania, 12 days, from $9,000. **Philanthropy:** African Portfolio was started in Zimbabwe and their philanthropic efforts are directed there; this includes support for education, orphanages, and a wildlife sanctuary. **What they do best:** Creating tailor-made safaris incorporating unique, genuine, and "off the beaten path" experiences. ⊠ *146 Sound Beach Ave., Greenwich* ☏ *800/700–3677* ⊕ *www.onsafari.com.*

Deeper Africa. This small, hands-on company, based in Colorado, has built its reputation on three things: excellent service, quality guides, and amazing wildlife viewing. Owners Wil Smith and Karen Zulauf have spent nearly two decades developing unique contacts that enable privileged access for their guests. Their knowledge of wildlife migration and movement patterns means that Deeper Africa travelers are in the right places, at the right time. They highly recommend having one of their guides join guests for their entire safari, allowing for discovery of the people, culture, and politics of Africa beyond wildlife basics. **Destinations:** Botswana, the Congo, Kenya, Rwanda, Namibia, Tanzania, Uganda, Zimbabwe. **Popular packages:** Kenya and Tanzania: Safaris in Style, 13 days, from $11,749. **Philanthropy:** Deeper Africa supports conservation and community programs and creates opportunities for travelers to do the same both personally and monetarily. **What**

they do best: Great wildlife viewing delivered by expert guides and authentic cultural experiences that give unique insights into African culture. ✉ *5353 Manhattan Circle, Suite 202, Boulder* ☎ *303/415–2574* ⊕ *www.deeperafrica.com.*

Gamewatchers Safaris. This Nairobi-based company specializes in delivering luxury tailor-made safaris to small camps and lodges in the top game-viewing areas of East Africa. Every traveler is guaranteed a personal, authentic safari and the opportunity to experience the magic of the African bush while helping protect Africa's wildlife, ecosystems, and cultures. Gamewatchers run their own ground operations, ensuring guests are well looked after from the start of their trip to the finish. Guests often add beach trips to the end of their safaris. **Destinations:** Botswana, Kenya, Mauritius, Rwanda, Seychelles, South Africa, Tanzania, Uganda, Zambia. **Popular packages:** African Splendours Safari, 12 nights, from $5,755; Gamewatchers Adventure Camping Safari, 6 nights, from $1,995. **Philanthropy:** Pioneers of the conservancy concept, here habitat is conserved in cooperation with local communities. They also support a school in Kibera, Nairobi, and more than 1,000 Maasai families are direct beneficiaries of their conservancies. They have also set up outreach programs to assist with water provision, education, and predator protection. **What they do best:** A personal, authentic experience, as far from mass-market tourism as it's possible to get. ☎ *877/710–3014* ⊕ *www.porini.com.*

Micato Safaris. Family-owned and -operated, this New York–based operator offers ultraluxurious trips driven by a sustainable ethos. Safari lodges enchant with such unadulterated luxuries as private plunge pools and personal butlers. Cultured safari guides educate, instruct, and amuse, while itineraries offer an irresistible array of experiences from the sophisticated pleasures of Cape Town to the celebrated savannas of the Serengeti and the near-spiritual beauty of the Kalahari. Micato has been long praised for its ability to deliver seamless personalized "un-group-like" service and over-the-top luxury without sacrificing true immersion in the "real Africa." Stand-out inclusions on Micato programs include time-saving bush flights between lodges and an "all included" policy that covers all gratuities, meals, alcoholic beverages, laundry, and just about anything else one could think of. **Destinations:** Botswana, Kenya, Mozambique, Namibia, Rwanda, South Africa, Tanzania, Uganda, Zambia, Zimbabwe. **Popular packages:** The Hemingway Wing Safari, Kenya, 14 days, from $14,650 per person. **Philanthropy:** Their charitable endeavours are impressive, with visits to the Micato-AmericaShare Harambee Community Center, a highlight for many clients. In addition, every safari sold puts one Kenyan child in school through Micato-AmericaShare's One for One program. **What they do best:** Impeccable service from start to finish alongside excellent community projects. ✉ *15 W. 26th St., New York* ☎ *212/545–7111* ⊕ *www.micatosafaris.com.*

Natural Habitat Adventures. Nicknamed "The Nature People," this operator is known for its focus on wildlife and conservation. Nat Hab's headquarters are in Colorado, and although they organize trips to destinations around the world they have a good reputation for arranging incredible safari itineraries. They always choose the best destinations for viewing wildlife in its natural habitat and focus on small groups and intimate lodges in secluded, off-the-beaten-track settings. Their online safari-building tool, iSafari.com, is a useful starting point for getting an idea of what's possible before speaking to one of the experts in their team. They can also arrange photo expeditions and family safaris. **Destinations:** Botswana, Ethiopia, Kenya, Madagascar, Namibia, Rwanda, South Africa, Tanzania, Zambia, Zimbabwe, Uganda. **Popular packages:** Secluded Botswana (includes Victoria Falls on the Zambia side), 10 or 13 days, from $11,195. **Philanthropy:** NHA has been the official conservation partner of the World Wildlife Fund (WWF) since 2003. This unique alliance allows NHA and its guests to play a role in the WWF's mission to conserve nature and reduce threats. This is accomplished through economic support for communities visited, educational outreach, and direct financial support to the WWF. **What they do best:** Sustainable ecotourism for small groups with a focus on wildlife and conservation. ✉ *833 W. South Boulder Rd., Boulder* ☎ *800/543–8917* ⊕ *www.nathab.com.*

Roy Safaris. Based in Arusha in Tanzania, and going strong for 28 years, Roy Safaris maintains a mid-size operation with a clear focus on adding value at every stage of your trip. They are dependable and responsive, offering both tailor-made and small group tours, and more than 70% of their business comes from repeat customers or referrals. They can also arrange photographic safaris with specially customized vehicles. The company owns two hotels, the African Tulip in Arusha, and The Retreat at Ngorongoro Lodge, although they do not influence clients to stay at their properties. **Destinations:** Kenya and Tanzania. **Popular packages:** Majestic Tanzania, 11 days, from $4,900; Tanzania Migration Safari, 12 days, from $5,500. **Philanthropy:** Their Sasha Foundation has an annual budget of about $40,000 and picks one project to see through per year. This includes education grants, building classrooms, and clean water development. Unused marketing funds from both the company and hotel are allocated to the foundation, as well as parts of the proceeds of safari and room sales. **What they do best:** Excellent, personalized service, and good value. ✉ *2 Serengeti Rd., Arusha* ☎ *255/272–502–115* ⊕ *www.roysafaris.com.*

The Wild Source. Bill Given, a wildlife biologist and African big cat researcher, started taking small groups of people on private safaris in 2004 and essentially became a one-man safari operator. As his clients increased due to word of mouth, he formed the Wild Source, and the operation evolved to partnering directly with exceptional local guides to create ownership opportunities in ground operations and safari camps. Their Tanzanian guide team in particular receives rave reviews for providing "hard core" game viewing, with all-day game drives and no mileage limits. The Wild Source has assisted in developing the Okavango Delta's only majority Bushman–owned camp, Bushman Plains Camp, which utilizes ancient tracking skills to find predators. **Destinations:** Botswana, Kenya, Mozambique, Namibia, Rwanda, South Africa, Tanzania, Uganda, Zambia, Zimbabwe. **Popular packages:** Big Cats and the Migration, Tanzania, 11 days, from $6,950. **Philanthropy:** The Wild

Source has a wide range of programs that focus on enriching the lives of local people and conserving wildlife, including the hiring and training of local wildlife biologists, sponsoring students, and improving health clinics—they are the first safari operator to employ Tanzanian wildlife biologists to conduct big cat research. **What they do best**: Wild Source's belief that the direct economic empowerment of African guides through ownership is critical to establishing lasting conservation sets the company apart. ✉ *Golden* ☎ *720/497–1250* ⊕ *www.thewildsource.com.*

Wilderness Safaris. Wilderness Safaris specializes in creating memorable journeys in some of Africa's most remote and pristine areas, while also helping to ensure the future of the continent's spectacular wildlife. The company operates a wide array of safari camps and lodges, from "seven star" premier accommodation to mobile safaris known as Explorations, to tailor-made itineraries and honeymoon packages. Wilderness has more than 50 lodges and camps, all with different styles, so there is something for everyone. They have a regional office in each country in which they operate, as well as a head office in Gaborone, Botswana, ensuring that their ground operations run very smoothly. **Destinations**: Botswana, Kenya, Namibia, Rwanda, Seychelles, South Africa, Zambia, Zimbabwe. **Popular packages:** The Great Wilderness Journey, Botswana, 11 days, from $10,403; Desert Dune Safari, 10 days, from $5,300. **Philanthropy:** In addition to a 4C's sustainability program (Conservation, Community, Culture, and Commerce), Wilderness has also created two nonprofit programs to further its aims of helping children in Africa: Children in the Wilderness and the Wilderness Wildlife Trust. **What they do best:** Incredible destinations, authentic experiences, and seamless service from start to finish. ✉ *373 Rivonia Blvd., Rivonia* ☎ *11/257–5000* ⊕ *www.wilderness-safaris.com.*

HIGHLY RECOMMENDED OUTFITTERS

Africa Adventure Company. Based in Florida, Africa Adventure Company is renowned for arranging personalized travel with a strong focus on sustainable tourism and eco-conservation. Their experienced staff listen closely to what kind of experience their clients are after and match it with a suitable itinerary according to their budget, from affordable to high-end. Owner Mark Nolting has spent more than 30 years exploring and researching Africa and has written several guidebooks. His partner Alison managed safari camps for many years and now works on developing new safari programs for both repeat and new clients as well organizing community and volunteer programs. They promote camps that are symbiotic with nature and the community, and offer exquisite game viewing with top-notch guides. They also offer add-on tours, such as beach escapes and honeymoon packages. ✉ *2601 E. Oakland Blvd., Suite 600, Fort Lauderdale* ☎ *800/882–9453* ⊕ *www. africanadventure.com.*

Africa Serendipity. This New York–based company has excellent Africa-based operators and specializes in Kenya and Tanzania exclusively. Although they offer suggested itineraries, the trip is ultimately custom-designed for the client based on what they want to see and do, their budget, and the time of the year. Clients often combine Kenya and

Tanzania into one trip, often tacking on a beach escape at the end. ⊠ *New York* ☎ *212/288–1714* ⊕ *www.africaserendipity.com.*

&Beyond. One of the world's leading luxury experiential travel companies, &Beyond designs personalized high-end tours in 15 countries in Africa as well as Asia and South America. They offer some of the best accommodations in Africa—and manage 29 of their own highly regarded properties—from the Okovango Delta to remote Indian Ocean islands. The company's commitment to responsible travel, conservation, and community empowerment is combined with warm local hospitality and highly skilled guides and rangers. ⊠ *Pinmill Farm, 164 Katherine St., Sandton* ☎ *11/809–4300 in South Africa, 888/882–3742 in U.S.* ⊕ *www.andbeyond.com.*

Black Tomato. A luxury travel company based in London and New York City, Black Tomato specializes in tailor-made experiential travel to destinations around the world. When planning trips for their clients, the destination is taken into consideration, as are the clients' needs, passions, and interests so each trip is unique. African itineraries include Namibia's Skeleton Coast, gorilla trekking in Rwanda, and romantic safari and beach trips. ⊠ *119 W. 24th St., New York* ☎ *646/558–3644* ⊕ *www.blacktomato.com.*

Cheli & Peacock. Born out of a passion to conserve Kenya's wildlife and wilderness areas, this upmarket company specializes in tailor-made safaris and has offices in Nairobi, Kenya and Arusha, Tanzania. It has developed over the years to become one of East Africa's leading destination-management companies and inbound tour operators. The variety of locations covers a broad selection of ecosystems, game, and conservation, and features small luxury camps and lodges in top national parks and reserves. Their trips are very creative—for example, helicopter rides across the Great Rift Valley, or walking with camels across the Laikipia plateau. They manage all ground arrangements themselves. Beach escapes can be added to safari trips. ⊠ *Lengai House, Wilson Airport, Nairobi* ☎ *730/721–000* ⊕ *www.chelipeacock.com.*

Doug Macdonald Safaris. Founded by professional Zimbabwean walking guide Doug Macdonald, this small, hands-on company has a diverse range of clients—over 90% come from referrals—all of whom have one thing in common: a deep desire to connect with Africa in a way that resonates with them. With 23 years of experience working in the bush, Macdonald has endless enthusiasm for Africa and is constantly looking for new and different places to introduce to his guests. This passion carries over to his team, all specialists in their own right, who pay attention to every detail of a trip and offer around-the-clock support should it be needed. ⊠ *Macorrs Bldg., Suite 3* ☎ *778/219–208* ⊕ *www.dougmacsafaris.com.*

Earthlife Expeditions. Based in Tanzania and locally-owned, this small company has earned rave reviews for their knowledgeable guides and trips in Tanzania, Kenya, Uganda, and Rwanda. With a focus on value for money, along with highly personalized service, Earthlife's consultants work closely with guests to arrange the perfect once-in-a-lifetime trip. A percentage of the company's revenue goes to local community projects, such as school libraries and hospitals, which guests are encouraged to visit as part of their trip. ✉ *PO Box 16353, Kimandolo Area, Arusha* ☎ *753/891–310* ⊕ *www.earthlifeexpeditions.com.*

Extraordinary Journeys. Founded and operated by a mother-daughter team who have over half a century of combined safari knowledge, Extraordinary Journeys specializes in creating unique, custom safari experiences to Southern and East Africa. Itineraries mix and match safari camps, lodges, and private villas to create a true sense of being on an exotic adventure, with travel by private plane, 4x4, hot air balloon, horse, and/or camel. The Extraordinary Journeys team has planned well over 4,000 unique safaris, but all bear the hallmarks of first-hand knowledge, personalized service, and social responsibility. ✉ *345 W. 58th St., New York* ☎ *212/226–7331* ⊕ *www.extraordinaryjourneys.com.*

Eyes on Africa. Whether you're a honeymooner, wildlife enthusiast, or photographer, Chicago-based Eyes on Africa will find a trip to match your budget. A wide range of interests and preferences can be catered to, and they have a long list of budget options, too. Along with safaris, they also cover mountainous destinations and beaches. They are becoming well-known for their occasional group photography trips, and have expanded to South America, India, and Sri Lanka in order to service requests from their existing customer base. ✉ *1743 W. Fletcher St., Chicago* ☎ *800/457–9575* ⊕ *www.eyesonafrica.net.*

Ker & Downey. With more than 50 years of experience in the travel industry, Ker & Downey is one of the oldest and most respected safari companies in Africa; they also have an office in Texas. The company utilizes its exclusive camps to provide luxury safari experiences and offers in-house expertise for all destinations as well as excellent on-the-ground service. They work hard to get to know their clients so they can best customize each itinerary. ✉ *6703 Highway Blvd., Katy* ☎ *800/423–4236* ⊕ *www.kerdowney.com.*

Nomad Tanzania. Nomad Tanzania owns and operates a collection of unique camps and privately guided safaris across Tanzania. They also offer an efficient ground-handling (airport pickup and drop-off, on-the-ground support, etc.) and safari-planning service throughout Tanzania and Zanzibar. They have excellent guides on staff and pride themselves on "going the extra mile for their guests." While each trip is fully customized, the website has sample itineraries for inspiration. ☎ *787/595–908* ⊕ *www.nomad-tanzania.com.*

Premier Tours. Although it's based in Philadelphia, Premier Tours is owned and managed by people born and raised in Africa who have organized all kinds of safaris, from basic camping trips to celebrity vacations. CEO Julian Harrison specializes in the development of ecotourism on the continent and is the founding member (and first USA tour operator) of The UN's Environment Program's Initiative on Sustainable Tourism Development. Other team members lead tour groups as naturalist guides, and participate in research projects in various African countries. Beach escapes can be added to safaris. ✉ *1120 South St., Philadelphia* ☎ *800/545–1910* ⊕ *www.premiertours.com.*

ROAR AFRICA. ROAR AFRICA offers a one-of-a-kind travel service for personalized, curated tours. The founder's family dates back to 1688, ensuring a wealth of information and well-established network that can only come from years of actually living in Africa. Clients have had memorable and life-changing adventures, such as meeting with artists and tribesmen, sleeping under the stars in the Kalahari, dinner with a CEO from their industry, participation in rhino conservation efforts, the opportunity to meet wildlife documentary producers Dereck and Beverly Joubert, VIP wine tours by helicopter, and visiting township schools. ROAR is headquartered in New York but also has offices in South Africa. They run their own ground operation, which enables concierge-level service and support during both the planning phase and travel. They also meet clients at the door of the airplane upon arrival, whisk them through customs, and can offer their own plane for private flights. ✉ *110 E. 25th St., New York* ☎ *855/666–7627* ⊕ *www. roarafrica.com.*

Safari Infinity. You can be sure of high-quality guides and excellent customer service with a personal touch from this luxury boutique tour operator based in Tanzania. All of their safari, mountain, and Zanzibar packages are completely customizable. From the moment you send your first inquiry to the end of your journey, staff are attentive and professional, ensuring a well-planned trip that is exactly how you imagined. ✉ *Box 14345, Arusha* ☎ *688/285–354* ⊕ *www.safari-infinity.com.*

Travel Beyond. Founded in 1975, Travel Beyond was the first US-based safari agency and tour operator to plan luxury photographic (i.e. non-hunting) safaris to Africa. Their safari consultants have lived and worked in Africa and eagerly share their firsthand knowledge of a combined 150 years of travel planning expertise. The company does not own any properties in Africa, ensuring their recommendations are only from personal experience. All trips are custom-designed for each client and can include primate treks and beach extensions along with traditional wildlife safaris. ✉ *106 Broadway Ave. S, Wayzata* ☎ *800/876–3131* ⊕ *www.travelbeyond.com.*

KENYA

WELCOME TO KENYA

TOP REASONS TO GO

★ **The Great Migration:** Millions of plains game move in an endless cycle of birth and death from Tanzania's Serengeti to Kenya's Masai Mara.

★ **Eyeball Big Game:** Visiting Kenya's legendary national parks and game reserves almost guarantees that you'll see the Big Five as well as huge herds of plains animals and hundreds of colorful birds.

★ **Africa's Fabled Tribe:** The tall and dignified red-robed Maasai have held explorers, adventurers, and writers in thrall for centuries.

★ **Beach Escapes:** Miles of white sandy beaches lined by an azure ocean and water sports galore. From diving and snorkeling to windsurfing, there's something for everyone.

★ **Turn Back the Clock:** Check out ancient history along the coast where Arab traders and Vasco da Gama once sailed. In the tiny UNESCO World Heritage town of Lamu you'll find an Arabic way of life unchanged for centuries.

Kenya lies on Africa's east coast. It's bordered by Uganda to the west, Tanzania to the south, South Sudan and Ethiopia to the north, Somalia to the northeast, and the Indian Ocean to the southeast. It's a land of amazing diversity with extraordinary tourist attractions: great game reserves like the Masai Mara and Amboseli; the Great Rift Valley dotted with a string of lakes including Nakuru and Naivasha; fertile highlands with towering peaks such as Mt. Kenya; and a coastline and islands with long pristine sandy beaches and marine parks full of coral reefs and colorful fish. Its two major cities couldn't be more different. Nairobi, the capital, is a bustling city where colonial buildings rub shoulders with modern skyscrapers, while steamy, coastal Mombasa retains its strong Arabic influence and history as it continues to be Kenya's largest and busiest port.

1 Masai Mara. Located in Southern Kenya's Great Rift Valley, the Mara is considered to be one of the world's greatest game parks.

After the Great Migration reaches here, you can see hundreds of thousands of wildebeest, zebra, and gazelle, followed by dozens of predators.

2 Amboseli National Park. Kilimanjaro's snowcapped peak, huge herds of elephants, and quintessential Kenyan landscape (open plains, acacia woodland, grasslands, bush, and marshland) greet you along the Tanzanian border.

3 Tsavo West and East National Parks. Tsavo West and Tsavo East are home to peaceful lion prides and loads of other game. Split by the Mombasa Highway, their proximity to the coast makes them a great choice for those who want to combine beach and beasts.

4 Laikipia Plateau. This region has become one of Kenya's hottest game destinations with some of its classiest camps and lodges. The nearby Samburu National Reserve boasts unusual dry-country species of animals and birds.

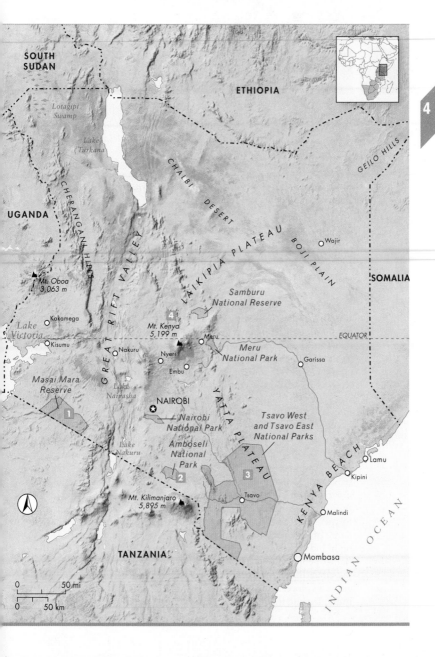

4

SOUTH
SUDAN

ETHIOPIA

*Lotagipi
Swamp*

*Lake
Turkana*

CHALBI DESERT

UGANDA

C H E R A N G A N I   H I L L S

▲ Mt. Oboa
3,063 m

L A I K I P I A   P L A T E A U

B O J I   P L A I N

○ Wajir

SOMALIA

Kakamega ○

*Lake
Victoria*

Kisumu ○

G R E A T   R I F T   V A L L E Y

4

Mt. Kenya
5,199 m ▲

Samburu
National Reserve

Nakuru ○

Nyeri ○

Meru ○

EQUATOR

Meru
National Park

Garissa ○

Embu ○

*Lake
Naivasha*

Masai Mara
Reserve

1

*Lake
Nakuru*

★
NAIROBI

Nairobi
National Park

Y A T T A   P L A T E A U

Tsavo West
and Tsavo East
National Parks

Amboseli
National
Park

2

3

K E N Y A   B E A C H

Lamu ○

Kipini ○

Tsavo ○

▲ Mt. Kilimanjaro
5,895 m

Malindi ○

I N D I A N   O C E A N

TANZANIA

Mombasa ○

0 ────── 50 mi

0 ────── 50 km

Updated by
Lizzie Williams

Kenya is where "going on safari" started. A hundred years or so ago, visitors from all over the world, including Teddy Roosevelt, started traveling to Africa, lured by stories of multitudes of wild animals; there were more than 3 million large mammals roving East Africa's plains at the time. Today visitors continue to flock to this East African nation each year. Although humans have made their mark, Kenya still holds onto its pristine wilderness.

But Kenya's tourism industry, the main source of foreign revenue, is very susceptible to perceptions of tourist safety. Tourism declined following the 1998 terrorist bombing of the U.S. Embassies in Nairobi and Dar es Salaam in Tanzania, but visitor numbers were on the rise again before the crisis in 2007–08. Widely televised at the time, the ethnic violence that arose after disputed election results still tarnishes Kenya's reputation, even though no tourists were in danger. The crisis was, however, a large contributing factor to a new constitution signed into law in 2010, which is aimed at limiting presidential powers and keeping corruption in check. It'll take years to implement, but there's a new optimism among Kenyans and little reason to consider Kenya unsafe as a tourist destination.

Kenya's human history dates back at least 6 million years; the controversial Millennium Man was discovered near Lake Baringo in the northwest in 2001. Today, Kenya hase more than 70 ethnic groups that range from the Maasai, Samburu, Kikuyu, and Turkana tribes to the Arabs and Indians that settled on the coast and the descendants of the first white settlers in and around Nairobi and the Kenya highlands. In Nairobi, about 40% of the population is Kikuyu—a Bantu people numbering more than 6 million. Islam arrived along the coast in the 8th century, followed in the 15th century by Portuguese explorers and sailors who came looking for the sea route to India. During the rule of Seyyid Said of Oman in the 1830s, German,

British, and American merchants established themselves on the coast, and the notorious slave routes were created.

The British created what was then known as British East Africa in the late 1800s. After a much publicized and often sensationalized struggle by native Kenyans against British rule in the 1950s, known as the Mau Mau era, Kenya finally won independence in 1963.

The perennial African life-and-death drama plays out among vast populations of prey and predators in what's widely called one of the world's greatest wildlife destinations. But, Kenya isn't just about big game. It has a gorgeous tropical coastline with white sandy beaches, coral gardens, superb fishing, and snorkeling, diving, and vibey beach resorts. Traditional triangular-sailed *dhows* still ply their trade providing unforgettable seafood to the surrounding restaurants. You'll discover unique islands with ancient stone Arab buildings, where a donkey is the main means of transport, and where time really does seem to stand still.

PLANNING

WHEN TO GO

Generally speaking, Kenya has one of the best climates in the world with long, sunny, dry days. The country's equator-straddling position means the length of a day hardly changes and sunrise is always 7 am–8 am and sunset 6 pm–7pm, with daytime temperatures average between 20°C (68°F) and 25°C (77°F). The coast can get hot and humid, though sea breezes cool things down, and the mountainous regions can get very cold—remember there's snow all year round on the highest peaks. Try to avoid the long rains of March and April or the short rains of October, November, and December because park roads can become impassable and mosquitoes are at their most prolific. Game-viewing is at its best during the driest seasons (May–September, January, and February) because the lack of surface water forces game to congregate at waterholes. Safari high season runs July through November when the annual wildebeest migration is in full swing, but it's much cheaper to go in the low season (April and May) when rates drop dramatically. High season at the coast is September through January (the hottest time is December and January), but avoid Christmas and New Year periods as holiday resorts are packed. If you're a birder, aim to visit between October and April when the migrant species have arrived.

GETTING HERE AND AROUND

AIR TRAVEL

Most flight options from the United States to Kenya involve a change of planes or airlines in Europe, the Middle East, or elsewhere in Africa. Nairobi is not only the principal arrival city for Kenya, but is a hub for East Africa and has good air connections to neighboring countries such as Tanzania, Uganda, and Rwanda.

In Kenya, there are a number of domestic and regional airlines that fly from both Jomo Kenyatta International Airport and Wilson Airport in Nairobi, as well as from Moi International Airport in Mombasa. Several major towns have airports, and Kenya also has a wide network of well-maintained airstrips at the safari destinations. One airstrip will service an entire park or reserve, or in some parks like the popular Masai Mara, there are several airstrips that each serve a group of safari lodges and camps. In most cases, transfers are provided from the airstrip to your accommodations. Schedules for the safari airlines often work in circuits and drop off and pick up at a number of destinations and may often return on the same route.

Airports Jomo Kenyatta International Airport (JKIA) (NBO). ✉ Mombasa Rd. (A104), Nairobi ✈ 16 km (10 miles) southeast of CBD ☎ 020/682-2111 ⊕ www. kaa.go.ke. **Moi International Airport** (MBA). ✉ Airport Rd., Mombasa ✈ 11 km (6.6 miles) northwest of city center ☎ 020/357-7508, ⊕ www.kaa.go.ke. **Wilson Airport** (WIL). ✉ Langata Rd., Nairobi ✈ 5.5 km (3.4 miles) southwest of CBD ☎ 072/425-6837, 425-5343 ⊕ www.kaa.go.ke.

Air Travel Resources in Kenya Kenya Airports Authority. ☎ 020/682-2111 ⊕ www.kaa.go.ke.

INTERNA-
TIONAL
FLIGHTS

Most major international airlines fly into Jomo Kenyatta International Airport (JKIA), Kenya's largest airport and the major airline hub for East Africa. At the time of writing, there are no direct flights from the United States to Kenya, however, Kenya Airways is expected to begin direct flights between Nairobi and JFK–New York in May 2018. There are also a number of indirect flights; British Airways via London, Ethiopian Airlines via Addis Ababa, Emirates via Dubai, KLM via Amsterdam, Lufthansa via Frankfurt, Turkish Airlines via Istanbul, and Qatar Airways via Doha. Another option is to go to Europe and continue with the national carrier Kenya Airways, which flies from London, Paris, Amsterdam, and Rome to Nairobi. Moi International Airport in Mombasa is mostly used for regional flights and seasonal air charter flights from European cities, often for package holidays that are inclusive of accommodations. Only Ethiopian Airlines and Turkish Airlines make scheduled stops in Mombasa as part of their Nairobi or Kilimanjaro routes. The usual connections between Nairobi and Mombasa are with Airkenya, Jambojet, Kenya Airways, or Fly540.

International Airlines British Airways. ☎ 0844/493-0787 in U.K. ⊕ www. britishairways.com. **Emirates.** ☎ 0344/800-2777 in U.K., 0800/777-3999 in U.S. ⊕ www.emirates.com. **Ethiopian Airlines.** ☎ 0800/016-3449 in U.K., 0800/445-2733 in U.S. ⊕ www.ethiopianairlines.com. **Kenya Airways.** ☎ 020/327-4747 in Kenya, 866/536-9224 in U.S. ⊕ www.kenya-airways.com. **KLM.** ☎ 207/660-0293 in U.K., 866/434-0320 in U.S. ⊕ www.klm.com. **Lufthansa.** ☎ 371/945-9747 in U.K., 800/645-3880 in U.S. ⊕ www.lufthansa.com. **Qatar Airways.** ☎ 330/024-0125 in U.K., 877/777-2827 in U.S. ⊕ www.qatarairways.com. **Turkish Airlines.** ☎ 844/375-4254 in U.K., 800/874-8875 in U.S. ⊕ www.turkishairlines.com.

DOMESTIC
FLIGHTS

There are plenty of efficient domestic airlines offering daily flights. Kenya Airways flies between Nairobi JKIA and Eldoret, Kisumu, Malindi and Mombasa and several regional destinations including Entebbe in Uganda, Kigali in Rwanda, and Kilimanjaro, Dar es Salaam, and Zanzibar in Tanzania. Kenya Airway's no-frills airline, Jambojet, flies between Nairobi JKIA and Diani Beach (Ukunda), Eldoret, Kisumu, Lamu, Malindi, and Mombasa. Fly540 flies from Nairobi JKIA to Eldoret, Kisumu, Lamu, Lodwar, Malindi, and Mombasa, and Kilimanjaro and Zanzibar in Tanzania. From Nairobi's Wilson Airport, Airkenya flies to Amboseli, Diani Beach (Ukunda), Lamu, Lewa Downs, Loisaba, Malindi, the Masai Mara, Meru, Nanyuki, and Samburu, and Kilimanjaro in Tanzania. Also from Wilson Airport, Safarilink flies to Amboseli, Diani Beach (Ukunda), Lamu, Lewa Downs, Lodwar, Loisaba, the Masai Mara, Naivasha, Nanyuki, Tsavo West, Samburu, and Kilimanjaro, and from the Masai Mara to Migori, which links travelers from the Mara to the Serengeti National Park in Tanzania. Mombasa Air Safari has its hub at Moi International Airport and flies in circuits from Mombasa, Diani Beach (Ukunda), and Malindi on the coast to Amboseli, the Masai Mara, and Tsavo West.

If you want to arrange your own timetable to the safari destinations or coast, there are several air charter companies based at Nairobi's Wilson Airport such as East African Air Charters and Reliance Air Charters. Small planes like Cessnas are utilized which can seat 5–13 passengers. Although more expensive than scheduled flights, charters are convenient and are an option for families and groups.

All domestic, regional and charter flights can be booked directly with the airlines, or alternatively ask your travel agent, or local accommodation or a Kenyan tour operator, to book as part of your package. Airport departure tax is included in all scheduled flight tickets but may be additional on charter flights. Be aware that on the small planes to the airstrips in the parks, the baggage allowance is usually 15 kg (33 pounds) per person, including hand luggage and camera equipment, and bags should be soft-sided. In the event you are carrying more than this, most hotels in Nairobi will store extra luggage or ask your airline if they have facilities.

Domestic Airlines Airkenya. ☎ *020/391–6000* ⊕ *www.airkenya.com.* **East African Air Charters.** ☎ *0735/880–011* ⊕ *eaaircharters.co.ke.* **Fly540.** ☎ *0740/540–540* ⊕ *www.fly540.com.* **Jambojet.** ☎ *020/327–4545* ⊕ *www.jambojet.com.* **Mombasa Air Safari.** ☎ *0734/500–500* ⊕ *www.mombasaair-safari.com.* **Reliance Air Charters.** ☎ *020/600–7778* ⊕ *www.relianceair.co.ke.* **Safarilink.** ☎ *020/669–0000* ⊕ *www.flysafarilink.com.*

CAR TRAVEL

Self-drive safaris are an option, however, poor road conditions in many places means there's often a big difference between distance on a map and driving time (for example, it takes about five hours to drive from Nairobi to the Masai Mara, a 150-mile/240-km journey). There are a number of car rental companies that specialize in 4x4s, and most will also offer the services of a driver. Expect to pay from $110 a day to hire a 4x4 and $20 a day for a driver.

Self-drive Safari Companies Central Rent-a-Car. ✉ *Downtown Nairobi* ☎ *020/222–2888* ⊕ *www.carhirekenya.com.* **Concorde Car Hire & Safaris.** ✉ *Westlands, Nairobi* ☎ *020/444–8953* ⊕ *www.concorde.co.ke.*

ESSENTIALS
COMMUNICATIONS

PHONES Local landline and mobile calls are quite cheap, but hotels add hefty surcharges to phone calls. The need for public telephones in Kenya has fallen away given that the majority of people carry a mobile phone, so most have been decommissioned or removed. If you don't want to use your own mobile phone because of expensive international roaming fees, buy a Kenyan pay-as-you-go SIM card (from one of the service-provider stores or street vendors—there's no shortage of them) and add airtime as you need it. The local providers are Airtel, Safaricom, and Telkom. Coverage is good throughout most of the country, but can be patchy in remote places—don't expect to get a signal at an out-of-the-way safari lodge or camp.

Calling Within Kenya: City codes are (020) for Nairobi, (041) for Mombasa, (040) for Diani Beach, and (012) for Lamu; include the first 0 when you dial within the country. When making a phone call in Kenya, always use the full 10-digit number, including the area code, even if you're in the same area.

Calling Outside Kenya: When dialing out from Kenya, dial 000 before the international code. So, for example, you would dial 000 (0001) for the United States. Other country codes are 00044 for the U.K and 00027 for South Africa.

Internet: Internet is widely available in Kenya. Free Wi-Fi is available in many public places in Nairobi and Mombasa such as restaurants and coffee shops and at almost all hotels—although again, in remote places you won't be able to connect. You can top up your own phone with data on a Kenyan pay-as-you-go SIM card.

Mobile Phones Airtel. 🕾 100 from an Airtel number, 0733/100–100 from another number ⊕ www.africa.airtel.com/kenya. **Telkom.** 🕾 100 from a Telkom number, 020/222–1000 from another number ⊕ www.telkom.co.ke. **Safaricom.** 🕾 100 from Safaricom number, 0722/002–100 from another number ⊕ www. safaricom.co.ke.

CUSTOMS AND DUTIES

Each person may bring 200 cigarettes (or 50 cigars or 250 grams of tobacco), 1 liter of spirits or 2 liters of wine, and up to 568 ml of perfume. The tobacco and alcohol allowance applies only to people 18 and over.

Contact Kenya Revenue Authority. 🕾 020/499–9999 ⊕ www.kra.go.ke.

HEALTH AND SAFETY

Kenya is a relatively safe country, but occasional incidents of crime are a reality for residents and tourists alike; follow these basic precautions for a safe trip.

Mugging, purse snatching, and pickpocketing can occur in big towns. Leave good jewelry and watches at home, and unless you're on safari, keep cameras, camcorders, and binoculars out of sight. Always lock valuables in the hotel or lodge safe. If you must carry valuables, use a money belt under your clothes; keep some cash handy so you don't reveal your money belt in public. Don't leave belongings out on balconies or terraces or on show in a vehicle. If you're unfortunate to be a victim of a robbery, you will need a police report to make an insurance claim. Bring copies of all your important documents and stash them away from the originals. Carry extra passport photos in case you need new documents fast.

Always take a taxi after dark, and never take food or drinks from strangers—it could be drugged. Be on the lookout for street scams like hard-luck stories or appeals to finance a scholarship. If you're driving, be polite but firm if you're stopped by police officers charging you with an "instant fine" for a minor infraction. If you ask to go to the police station, the charges are often dismissed.

A yellow fever vaccination card is *not* needed for entry to Kenya, unless you're traveling from a country with risk of yellow fever; this does not include the United States or neighboring Tanzania, but does include Uganda and some other African countries. Always use sunscreen and bug repellent with DEET. The HIV infection rate is high so exercise caution. Malaria is an issue in certain areas (not in Nairobi but definitely on the coast and low-lying game reserves). Consult your health-provider well in advance about the best malaria prophylactics to take as most medication needs to start prior to arrival in Kenya.

You'll need full medical travel insurance that includes repatriation in the event of a medical emergency. If you're planning to dive, trek, or climb, make sure your insurance covers active pursuits. Medical bills are often paid upfront in Kenya, so keep all paperwork to make an insurance claim. The AMREF Flying Doctors service provides air evacuation and transportation between health-care facilities for medical emergencies in Kenya, Tanzania, and Uganda, or anywhere within a 1,000 km (621 miles) radius of Nairobi. The planes fly out of Nairobi's Wilson Airport 24 hours a day, 365 days a year.

Embassies U.S. Embassy. ✉ *Gigiri, Nairobi, United Nations Ave., Gigiri* ☎ *020/363–6000* ⊕ *ke.usembassy.gov.*

Emergencies Kenya Police. ☎ *999* ⊕ *www.kenyapolice.go.ke.*

Medical-Assistance Companies AMREF Flying Doctors. ☎ *020/699–2299 emergencies, 020/334–4170 customer service* ⊕ *www.flydoc.org.*

MONEY MATTERS

The official currency is the Kenya shilling (KSh). Available notes are 50, 100, 200, 500, and 1,000 shillings. Available coins are 1, 5, 10, and 20 shillings. At this writing, the shilling exchange is about KSh103 to US$1.

Most things are priced and paid for in KSh. However many businesses in the tourist industry like hotels, safari companies, and airlines may quote in U.S. dollars as well as shillings. If you pay with dollars, check that you're getting a fair exchange rate. Credit cards are widely accepted, but for small amounts like restaurants, shopping, taxi fares, fuel and tips, it's easiest to withdraw shillings from an ATM once you're in the country. Most ATMs dispense large denomination notes; try and break these when you can as taxi drivers and souvenir vendors often don't have change for large bills.

If you are exchanging U.S. dollars at a bank or bureau de change, bring new notes; any old, worn, or damaged bills will not be accepted.

ATMS AND BANKS Banks open at 8:30 on weekdays and close at 4; on Saturday they open at 9 and close at noon. Banks are closed on Sundays and public holidays. Most ATMs are open 24 hours. Many banks can perform foreign-exchange services or international electronic transfers. Try to avoid banks at their busiest times—at 9 and from noon to 2 on Friday, and at month's end—unless you're willing to arrive early and line up with the locals. Major banks are Kenya Commercial Bank (KCB), which has the largest branch network in the country, and Barclays, National Bank of Kenya, and Standard Chartered.

Major credit cards such as Visa and MasterCard are accepted at Kenyan banks and by ATMs. Most ATMs accept Cirrus, Plus, Maestro, Visa Electron, and Visa and MasterCard; the best place to withdraw cash is at an indoor ATM, preferably one at the airport, in a shopping mall, or guarded by a security officer.

Contacts Kenya Commercial Bank (KCB). ☎ *020/228–7000 customer care* ⊕ *ke.kcbbankgroup.com.*

TIPPING Tipping isn't mandatory, but porters do expect something, and 10% is customary in restaurants. Some hotels and most safari lodges and tented camps have a gratuity box for you to put a tip for all of the staff at the end of your stay. Tip your safari driver and guide approximately US$10–US$15 per person, per day. It's not necessary to tip taxi drivers as the fare is determined before you set off.

PASSPORTS AND VISAS
Your passport must have at least two blank pages and be valid for a minimum of six months after your date of entry into Kenya. Most nationalities require a visa, including citizens of the United States. Single-entry visas (US$50) are valid for three months and allow reentry to Kenya after going to Tanzania and Uganda. Children under 16 years accompanying their parent(s) *do not* require visas. Prior to travel eVisas can be obtained online, or visas are also available in cash only (US$, euros, or UK pounds) at Nairobi's Jomo Kenyatta International Airport, Mombasa's Moi International Airport, and all land borders. To avoid queues, it's easier to get them online beforehand.

Contacts eVisa Kenya. ⊕ *www.evisa.go.ke.* **Kenya Embassy.** ☎ *202/387–6101 Embassy, Washington D.C., 212/421–4741 Consulate, NYC* ⊕ *www.kenyaembassy.com.*

TAXES
In Kenya the value-added tax (V.A.T.) of 16% is included in the price of most goods and services, including accommodations and food. To get a V.A.T. refund on items taken out of the country such as souvenirs, foreign visitors must present receipts at the V.A.T. refund desk in the departures halls of the international airports (Nairobi and Mombasa) or at land borders. Refunds are paid by check, which can be cashed immediately at an airport bank or refunded to your credit card with a small transaction fee.

Contacts Kenya Revenue Authority. ☎ *020/499–9999* ⊕ *www.kra.go.ke.*

ABOUT THE RESTAURANTS

Kenya prides itself on game meat and seafood, organically grown vegetables, and tropical fruits (such as passion fruit, papaya, and mangoes) are excellent. Sample traditional Indian and Arabic food when you're near the coast, and look for Kenyan-grown tea and coffee and Tusker beer, a local brew. "Swahili tea" is very similar to chai in India. You'll find most cuisines, from Chinese to French to Ethiopian, in restaurants in Nairobi.

For information on what you can expect at the restaurants and hotels on the Kenyan coast, see the Beach Escapes section below. Restaurant reviews have been shortened. For full information, visit Fodors.com.

KEEPING IT GREEN

Ecotourism Kenya (⊕ *www. ecotourismkenya.org*) is an organization that promotes responsible practices in the Kenyan tourism industry. They provide guidelines for attaining sustainable solutions for the conservation of the environment and improving the well-being of local people, and each year they present awards to hotels, lodges, camps, and tour operators for their efforts in keeping it green.

ABOUT THE HOTELS AND LODGES

Kenya has a broad choice of accommodations ranging from intimate tented camps and luxurious boutique hotels to mid-range safari lodges and beach resorts as well as local lodgings and campsites. Hotel rates in Nairobi and other towns tend to stay the same throughout the year (although there could be midweek specials), but all room prices in the wildlife and coastal areas are seasonal. It's essential to book in advance in high season and look out for specials during the low season, while during rainy months some establishments close altogether.

There's a bewildering choice of safari lodges and tented camps in the national parks, game reserves, and wildlife conservancies. Lodges tend to be large solid structures with hotel-like rooms and restaurants. Most are family-friendly, and many have extra facilities like a swimming pool. Smaller tented camps have spacious and often luxuriously appointed walk-in tents with bathrooms, meals are taken communally in a dining tent or outside, and most are unfenced allowing for greater connection with the wildlife (as such, children aren't always permitted). Prices at lodges are almost always all-inclusive, which includes accommodations, meals, and activities such as game drives and walks; find out in advance if park fees (US$40 to US$100 per day) are included. Campsites in the wildlife areas have few or no facilities and aren't really an option for a visitor with time restrictions or for first-timers, but there is the option of going on a camping safari with a tour operator.

Nairobi has hundreds of hotels and many of the international chains are represented, but there are also charming independent hotels and some older establishments with colonial ambience. Standard prices usually include a full English breakfast and other meals are available in the hotel's restaurant. All kinds of accommodations can be found on the coast, from luxurious honeymoon-hideaways to all-inclusive family beach resorts, and on Lamu, some beautifully restored historic Arabic houses have opened as hotels. *Hotel reviews have been shortened. For full information, visit Fodors.com.*

WHAT IT COSTS IN U.S. DOLLARS				
	$	**$$**	**$$$**	**$$$$**
Restaurants	under $12	$12–$20	$21–$30	over $30
Hotels	under $250	$250–$450	$451–$600	over $600

Restaurant prices are the average cost of a main course at dinner or, if dinner is not served, at lunch. Hotel prices are the lowest cost of a standard double room in high season.

ABOUT THE PARKS

Unfortunately, you probably won't be able to see all of Kenya in one trip. So our listings are broken down into **Must-See Parks** (Masai Mara National Reserve, Amboseli National Park, Tsavo West and East National Parks, and the Laikipia Plateau) and **If You Have Time Parks** (Nairobi National Park, Meru National Park, Samburu National Reserve, and Lakes Nakuru and Naivasha) to help you better organize your time. It's suggested, though, that you research *all* of them before you make your decision.

VISITOR INFORMATION

There's no official tourist office in Nairobi and the one in Mombasa is not official or much good. Your best option is to consult the Kenya Tourist Board website before you leave home. The website for the Kenya Wildlife Service is a good source if you're going to the national parks and reserves.

Visitor Information Kenya Tourism Board. ☎ *020/271–1262* ⊕ *www. magicalkenya.com.* **Kenya Tourism Federation.** ☎ *020/600–4767 tourist helpline* ⊕ *www.ktf.co.ke.* **Kenya Wildlife Service (KWS).** ☎ *0800/597–000* ⊕ *www.kws.go.ke.*

MASAI MARA NATIONAL RESERVE

4

Game
★★★★★
Park Accessibility
★★★★★
Getting Around
★★★★★
Accommodations
★★★★★
Scenic Beauty
★★★★

The legendary Masai Mara National Reserve ranks right up there with Tanzania's Serengeti National Park and South Africa's Kruger National Park in terms of the world's finest wildlife sanctuaries.

Established in 1961, some 275 km (171 miles) southwest of Nairobi, the Mara covers an area of 1,800 square km (702 square miles) and includes part of the Serengeti ecosystem that extends from northern Tanzania into southern Kenya. This ecosystem of well-watered plains supports one of the largest populations of numerous animal groups on earth. There are more than 1 million wildebeests; 250,000 Thomson's gazelles; 250,000 zebras; 70,000 impalas; 30,000 Grant's gazelles; and a huge number of predators including lions, leopards, cheetahs, jackals, and hyenas. There are also more than 470 species of bird, including 57 species of raptor. Every January the wildebeest start to move in a time-honored clockwise movement around the Serengeti toward the new, fresh grazing in the Masai Mara. It's an unforgettable experience.

Local communities, not the Kenya Wildlife Service, manage this reserve giving the Maasai, who are pastoralists, the rights to graze their stock on the perimeters of the reserve. Although stock is lost to wild animals, the Maasai manage to coexist peacefully with the game, and rely only on their own cattle for subsistence; in Maasai communities wealth is measured by the number of cattle owned. You'll see the Maasai's *man-yattas*—beehive huts made of mud and cow dung—at the entrances to the reserve. The striking appearance of the Maasai, with their red robes and ochre-dyed and braided hair, is one of the abiding images of Kenya. Many lodges offer visits to traditional Maasai villages and homes, and although inevitably these visits have become touristy, they're still well worth doing. Witnessing the dramatic *ipid,* a dance in which the *moran* (warriors) take turns leaping high into the air, will keep your camera clicking nonstop. The Maasai people named the reserve *mara*, which means "spotted," but whether mara applies to the landscape, which is

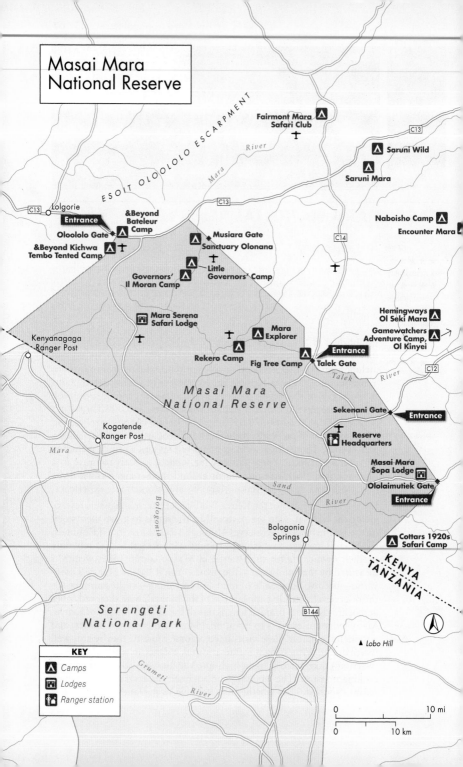

Masai Mara National Reserve

Fairmont Mara Safari Club

Saruni Wild

Saruni Mara

Naboisho Camp

Encounter Mara

Lolgorie

Entrance

&Beyond Bateleur Camp

Oloololo Gate

&Beyond Kichwa Tembo Tented Camp

Musiara Gate

Sanctuary Olonana

Little Governors' Camp

Governors' Il Moran Camp

Mara Serena Safari Lodge

Hemingways Ol Seki Mara

Gamewatchers Adventure Camp, Ol Kinyei

Kenyanagaga Ranger Post

Mara Explorer

Rekero Camp

Entrance

Fig Tree Camp

Talek Gate

Masai Mara National Reserve

Kogatende Ranger Post

Sekenani Gate

Entrance

Reserve Headquarters

Mara

Masai Mara Sopa Lodge

Ololaimutiek Gate

Entrance

Bologonia Springs

Cottars 1920s Safari Camp

KENYA

TANZANIA

Serengeti National Park

Lobo Hill

KEY

- **Camps**
- **Lodges**
- **Ranger station**

0   10 mi

0   10 km

ESOIT OLOOLOLO ESCARPMENT

Mara River

Talek River

Sand River

Bologonia River

Grumeti River

C13

C13

C14

C12

B144

spotted with vegetation, or the hundreds of thousands of wildebeest and other game that spot the landscape, is anybody's guess.

WHEN TO GO

There's no real best time to visit the Mara, but most people come in the July–October dry season, when the Great Migration is taking place and there are plenty of wildebeest and zebras for the lions, leopards, and cheetahs to prey on. There's no guarantee of seeing any epic river crossings, however. The rainy season is April and May and November, and many roads become difficult or even inaccessible.

GETTING HERE AND AROUND

Most people fly to the Mara from Nairobi's Wilson Airport, and scheduled daily air services (about 45 minutes) land at eight airstrips in the area. The cost is approximately $185 each way (some lodges include this flight and transfer in their rates). If you're a nervous flyer, note that you'll usually travel in small turboprop aircraft and there could be a couple of touchdowns at other airstrips, too, as the flights operate in circuits. However, tour operators can offer a driving option; the Mara is 270 km (168 miles) from Nairobi and takes approximately six hours by road. Once in the park, there are few signposts, so make sure you know exactly where you're going before you depart. The park fee is $80 per person per 24 hours, which is often included in package tours.

WHERE TO STAY

$$$$ RESORT 🏨 **&Beyond Bateleur Camp.** If you're among the many who saw *Out of Africa* and began fantasizing about your own African experience, then you'll be happy to know that this totally private and very romantic world-class camp is just below the famous hill from the unforgettable final scene. **Pros:** the service is excellent; there are unexpected surprise touches along the way; good-sized swimming pool. **Cons:** intermittent mobile phone and Wi-Fi reception; no bath (showers only); electric generator is generally switched off overnight. [$] *Rooms from: $2470* ✉ *Masai Mara National Reserve* ☎ *27/11–809–4300 reservations, South Africa* 🌐 *www.andbeyond.com* 🕓 *Closed Jan.–Mar.* 🛏 *18 tents* 🍴 *All-inclusive.*

$$$$ RESORT FAMILY 🏨 **&Beyond Kichwa Tembo Tented Camp.** Kichwa Tembo, which means head of the elephant in Kiswahili, is one of Kenya's most sought-after camps. **Pros:** there's an excellent curio shop; day and night game drives and bush walks along the Mara River; infinity swimming pool. **Cons:** no baths (showers only); hair dryers in luxury tents only; a large camp, it may not be intimate enough for some. [$] *Rooms from: $900* ✉ *Masai Mara National Reserve* ☎ *27/11–809–4300* 🌐 *www.andbeyond.com* 🛏 *40 tents* 🍴 *All-inclusive.*

$$$$ RESORT FAMILY Fodor's Choice ★ 🏨 **Cottars 1920s Safari Camp.** If you want to turn back the clock and immerse yourself in the kind of original safari ambience that Ernest Hemingway enjoyed, this is the place to do it. **Pros:** complimentary massages; you will seldom see another game vehicle; highly trained guides. **Cons:** hair dryers can be used only in the office; minimum two nights booking; conservancy fees $116 extra. [$] *Rooms from: $2072*

✉ *Olderkesi Conservancy* ☎ *0733/773–377 reservations* 🌐 *www.cottars.com* 🛏 *10 tents* 🍴 *All-inclusive.*

$$$$ RESORT FAMILY 🏨 **Encounter Mara.** Tucked within a shady acacia forest on the exclusive Mara Naboisho Conservancy, the luxury tents at this comfortable and contemporary-styled camp have great views across the plains. **Pros:** a game-viewing hide experience in camp; exclusive game drives in the Mara Naboisho Conservancy; excellent Maasai guides. **Cons:** the camp is fenced but bushy so parents need to supervise young children; a full day is required for a game drive into the Mara; a 45-minute drive from the airstrip. [$] *Rooms from: $1250* ✉ *Mara Naboisho Conservancy, Masai Mara National Reserve* ☎ *020/232–4904 reservations* 🌐 *www.asiliaafrica.com* 🕓 *Closed May* 🛏 *10 tents* 🍴 *All meals.*

$$$ RESORT FAMILY 🏨 **Fairmont Mara Safari Club.** Although the Fairmont's camp area has manicured lawns and flowers, it is surrounded on three sides by the croc- and hippo-filled Mara River, so you are always close to the wildlife. **Pros:** rooms have hair dryers; the views of the Mara River from the tents are excellent; good-sized pool with sun-beds and bar. **Cons:** some distance to the reserve itself or near any migration routes; game drives and bush walks cost extra; a large camp so can feel a little impersonal. [$] *Rooms from: $498* ✉ *Ol-Choro Oiroua Conservation Area, Masai Mara National Reserve* ☎ *020/226–5000 reservations* 🌐 *www.fairmont.com/masai-mara-safari* 🛏 *51 tents* 🍴 *All meals.*

$$$ RESORT FAMILY 🏨 **Fig Tree Camp.** This budget option on the banks of the Talek River overlooks the plains and its location on the northeastern boundary of the reserve gives it easy access to all the game areas. **Pros:** there is a lovely pool area; there's evening entertainment with Maasai dancers or music; 24-hour complimentary hot drinks in the lobby. **Cons:** no fans or air-conditioning; tents are located close to each other so can be noisy; electricity only from 5 to 9 am, noon to 3 pm, and 6 pm to midnight. [$] *Rooms from: $580* ✉ *Masai Mara National Reserve* ☎ *0722/202–564 reservations* 🌐 *www.madahotels.com* 🛏 *80 rooms* 🍴 *All meals.*

$$$$ RESORT 🏨 **Gamewatchers Adventure Camp, Ol Kinyei.** Gamewatchers Adventure Camp offers the same exclusivity as luxurious camps, but with more basic accommodation in large Coleman camping tents. **Pros:** the conservancy is very exclusive; the guides are fantastic; picnic lunches are included on game drives. **Cons:** the fence surrounding the tents entirely blocks the view; walks are often undertaken without the security of an armed ranger; you must bring your own sleeping bag or rent one. [$] *Rooms from: $1385* ✉ *Ol Kinyei Conservancy, Masai Mara National Reserve* ☎ *0774/136–523* 🌐 *www.porini.com* 💳 *No credit cards* 🕓 *Closed Apr.–June, Nov., and Dec.* 🛏 *9 rooms* 🍴 *All meals.*

$$$$ RESORT 🏨 **Governors' IL Moran Camp.** One of the famous Governors' Camps, Il Moran is where Kenya's first colonial governors used to twirl their handlebar moustaches and sip their gin and tonics while on safari—as you can imagine, it boasts an exclusive location that's teeming with game. **Pros:** the beds are very comfortable; there's a maximum of four guests per game vehicle; the tents are well-spaced along the banks of the Mara River. **Cons:** unfenced so no children under eight; electricity only from 5 to 11 am and 3:30 to 11 pm; paths run in front of the tents' verandas making them not very private. [$] *Rooms from: $1376*

Lion cubs out for an early morning prowl in the Masai Mara National Reserve.

✉ *Masai Mara National Reserve* ☎ *020/273–4000 reservations* ⊕ *www.governorscamp.com* ✈ *10 tents* ⦿ *All meals.*

$$$$
RESORT
FAMILY
🏕 **Hemingways Ol Seki Mara.** This eco-friendly camp in the middle of the exclusive Mara Naboisho Conservancy is named after the *olseki* or sandpaper tree, which is a Maasai symbol of peace, harmony, and wealth. **Pros:** positioned on an elevated ridge with great views across the plains; afternoon tea is delivered to your tent; exclusive game-driving area where you won't encounter many other vehicles. **Cons:** you'll need to enter the Mara proper to see the best migration river spots; the bathrooms are small, although the showers are reasonably spacious; the steep wooden walkways around camp would be a problem for very young children. ⓢ *Rooms from: $1360* ✉ *Mara Naboisho Conservancy, Masai Mara National Reserve* ☎ *020/229–5011 reservations* ⊕ *www.hemingways-collection.com/mara* ✈ *10 tents* ⦿ *All meals.*

$$$$
RESORT
FAMILY
🏕 **Little Governors' Camp.** Getting to this camp is a mini adventure in itself. **Pros:** the camp sits directly in the path of the wildebeest migration; the tents are situated around a busy waterhole; 15-minute from the Musiara Airstrip and transfers are included. **Cons:** the tents are close together, and there is not much privacy on the verandas; there are steep flights of steps on both sides of the river crossing; furnishings are adequate but a little plain. ⓢ *Rooms from: $1176* ✉ *Masai Mara National Reserve* ☎ *020/273–4000 reservations* ⊕ *www.governorscamp.com* ✈ *17 tents* ⦿ *All meals.*

$$$$
RESORT
🏕 **Mara Explorer.** At this intimate little camp tucked in a riverine forest on a bend on the Talek River, you'll be able to watch elephants wading, hippos snorting, and all other sorts of game from your outdoor clawfoot bathtub that overlooks the river. **Pros:** the camp is a short drive

Ol Seki

Mara Explorer

Bateleur

from the Mara River, where thousands of wildebeest make their perilous crossing every year between July and September; all tents overlook the Talek River; a three-minute drive from the nearest airstrip. **Cons:** hot water is available only at fixed times; Wi-Fi only in the public areas; hippos can be loud at night. [$] *Rooms from: $684* ✉ *Masai Mara National Reserve* ☎ *020/444–6651 reservations* 🌐 *www.heritage-eastafrica.com* 🛏 *10 tents* 🍴 *All meals.*

$$$$ RESORT FAMILY 🏨 **Mara Serena Safari Lodge.** Perched high on a hill deep inside the Mara Triangle part of the reserve, attractive domed huts echo the style and shape of the traditional Maasai *manyattas*. **Pros:** amazing views from the bedrooms; the breakfasts at the hippo pool; has its own airstrip. **Cons:** the decor is a bit dated; rooms lack tea- and coffee-making facilities; some rooms are far away and downhill from the public areas. [$] *Rooms from: $638* ✉ *Masai Mara National Reserve* ☎ *0732/123–333 reservations* 🌐 *www.serenahotels.com* 🛏 *74 rooms* 🍴 *All meals.*

$$ RESORT FAMILY 🏨 **Masai Mara Sopa Lodge.** On a hillside near the Ololaimutiek Gate, this well-priced family-style lodge (*sopa* means welcome in the Maasai language) is one of the most popular in the reserve. **Pros:** it's very close to the eastern entrance to the Mara; there's a bushbaby feeding table; the great pool is ideal to cool off in after a game drive. **Cons:** hot water is available only at limited times; rondavels are located close to each other; because you're more than 6,000 feet above sea level, you'll need some warm clothes. [$] *Rooms from: $347* ✉ *Masai Mara National Reserve* ☎ *020/375–0235 reservations,* 🌐 *www.sopalodges.com* 🛏 *50 rondavels* 🍴 *All meals.*

$$$$ RESORT FAMILY Fodor's Choice ★ 🏨 **Naboisho Camp.** Quite possibly the best camp in all of the Mara area, Naboisho Camp is in the 210-sq-km (82-sq-mile) Mara Naboisho Conservancy, which has exclusive use for only those guests staying at the handful of lodges there—there are no hordes of safari vehicles here. **Pros:** the guides at this camp are excellent; the conservancy is very exclusive, allowing for uninterrupted game drives; high level of personalized service. **Cons:** Wi-Fi but mobile phone reception is poor; need to allow for a full day to do a game drive into the Mara proper; the camp is unfenced, so kids' supervision is essential at all times. [$] *Rooms from: $1790* ✉ *Mara Naboisho Conservancy, Masai Mara National Reserve* ☎ *020/232–4904 reservations* 🌐 *www.asiliaafrica.com* ⊗ *Closed April* 🛏 *9 tents* 🍴 *All-inclusive.*

$$$$ RESORT Fodor's Choice ★ 🏨 **Rekero Camp.** Rekero is beautifully situated deep within the Masai Mara National Reserve and is tucked away in a grove of trees on a river bank near the confluence of the Talek and Mara rivers. **Pros:** each tent is tucked into the bush along the river and offers absolute privacy; excellent location next to a migration river crossing point; first-class guiding. **Cons:** the access road is particularly rough; the area can be busy with game-viewing vehicles from other camps; children over five are welcome, but must be carefully supervised. [$] *Rooms from: $1740* ✉ *Masai Mara National Reserve* ☎ *020/232–4904 reservations* 🌐 *www.asiliaafrica.com* ⊗ *Closed Apr. and May* 🛏 *9 tents* 🍴 *All-inclusive.*

$$$$ RESORT FAMILY 🏨 **Sanctuary Olonana.** Named after an honored Maasai chief, this attractive eco-friendly camp in game-rich country rests just outside the northwestern border of the reserve, overlooking the Mara River and the Ooloololo Escarpment. **Pros:** the honeymoon tents are beautiful and

The circle of life: a cheetah chases his prey.

have outdoor showers; you can watch hippos in the Mara River from your tent; relaxing spa with a riverside deck. **Cons:** rates exclude park fees; peak season rates are high, but drop by about half in low season; the farthest tents are quite a long walk from the main facilities. $ *Rooms from: $1750* ✉ *Masai Mara National Reserve* ☎ *1242 /546–609 reservations, U.K.* ⊕ *www.sanctuaryretreats.com* ⌨ *14 tents* ⏣ *All-inclusive.*

$$$$
RESORT
FAMILY
⌂ **Saruni Mara.** This exclusive eco-friendly lodge lies just outside the Masai Mara National Reserve, inside the Mara North Conservancy in a remote valley of olive and cedar trees. **Pros:** specialized guiding, such as bird-watching, is available; night drives are permitted on Mara North Conservancy; excellent Italian food. **Cons:** the camp is at least a 40-minute drive to the Masai Mara National Reserve; can be a little cool at night because of the altitude; a small lodge, reservations are required well in advance. $ *Rooms from: $1560* ✉ *Masai Mara National Reserve* ☎ *020/218–0497 reservations,* ⊕ *www.sarunimara. com* ⌨ *6 cottages* ⏣ *All meals.*

$$$$
RESORT
FAMILY
⌂ **Saruni Wild.** You certainly won't come across another vehicle at this exclusively sited camp in the northern section of the Masai Mara ecosystem on the border between the Lemek Conservancy and the Mara North Conservancy. **Pros:** because the camp is in a conservancy, you'll hardly see another vehicle; there's a high chance of seeing rare nocturnal species; very small with an exclusive and intimate feel. **Cons:** it's far from the prime viewing spots during migration time; won't appeal to those wanting more facilities like a pool; the conservancy fee of $116 per person per night is not included in rates. $ *Rooms from: $1560* ✉ *Lemek Conservancy, Masai Mara National Reserve* ☎ *020/218–0497 reservations,* ⊕ *www.saruniwild.com* ⌨ *3 tents* ⏣ *All-inclusive.*

AMBOSELI NATIONAL PARK

Game	★★★★★
Park Accessibility	★★★★
Getting Around	★★★★
Accommodations	★★★★
Scenic Beauty	★★★★★
	★★★★★

Amboseli National Park, immediately northwest of Mt. Kilimanjaro and 220 km (140 miles) southeast of Nairobi on the Tanzanian border, is certainly one of the most picturesque places in the whole of Africa to watch game. Where else could you watch a great herd of elephants on a wide empty plain dominated by Africa's highest mountain, Kilimanjaro?

At dawn, as the cloud cover breaks and the first rays of sun illuminate the snowcapped 5,895-meter (19,340-foot) peak, the sky, colored by rosy pinks and soft reds, provides the perfect backdrop for the plains below. It gets even better at dusk, when the mountain stands out in stark relief against the fiery sun.

Amboseli has a checkered history. First established as a natural reserve in 1948, it was returned to Maasai ownership and management in 1961 but soon became environmentally degraded with too many cattle and too many tourists. Some 10 years later, 392 square km (151 square miles) were designated a national park, and cattle-grazing was forbidden. This angered the pastoral Maasai, who took their revenge by killing a majority of the rhino population. Eventually peace was restored with some expedient land swapping, and today there's a responsible environmental program that controls the well-being of the game, puts limits on tourist numbers, and enforces a strict policy on off-road driving.

There are five different habitats in Amboseli: open plains, acacia woodland, thornscrub, swamps, and marshlands. To the west is the Ol Donyo Orok massif and Lake Amboseli, which is usually dry. But when the heavy rains return, the surrounding area becomes green and lush again and migratory birds flock to the park. Expect some impassable roads at these times, as well as when the lake is completely dry because the fine alkaline dust that blows up from the lake bed is hell for tires—the name "Amboseli" comes from a Maasai term that means "salty dust."

Amboseli is filled with great game: zebra, warthog, giraffe, buffalo, hippo, impala, wildebeest, unusual antelopes like the fringe-eared oryx and long-necked mini giraffe-like gerenuk, and baboons galore. The park, however, is not home to rhino and your chances of seeing predators are not quite as good as in the Masai Mara. Maasai hunters once almost killed off Amboseli's lions because they preyed on their herds of cattle, but after many years of tolerance from the local communities, populations have increased steadily and lucky visitors may spot not only lion, but hyena, jackal, and cheetah, too. If it's elephants you're after, then Amboseli is the place to come. Perhaps the oldest and most studied elephant population in sub-Saharan Africa lives here. There are more than 1,200 of these great pachyderms today, and because they're accustomed to visitors and vehicles you'll experience eyeball-to-knee-high close encounters.

Birdlife is also prolific, with more than 420 recorded species. There are dozens of birds of prey including more than 10 different kinds of eagles. In the swamp areas, which are fed by the melting snow of Kilimanjaro, seasonal flamingo, pelican, and more than 12 species of heron are among the profusion of water birds.

Game-viewing is best around Enkongo Narok, which means "black and benevolent." This belt of swamps in the middle of the park is home to hippos, numerous birds, beds of papyrus and waterlilies, herbivores coming to drink, and elephants taking baths. At Observation Hill, the Amboseli landmark just to the west of Lake Kioko, you are permitted to park and walk to the top for a surefire opportunity to spot game as you gaze out over the plains.

WHEN TO GO

January and February, and June through September are the best times to come here. During the rainy season (April and May), roads might become rough but it's a favorite time for photographers and birders to be here, when everything is green. There might also be rain in November and December.

GETTING HERE AND AROUND

Amboseli is 220 km (140 miles) from Nairobi. The best approach by road is to the gates on the southeastern side of the park via the fairly new tarred road from Emali on the Mombasa road (A109)—do not take the old route from Nairobi via the Namanga road (A104) as this is now rarely used and in poor shape. There's no public transportation within the park and the roads are gravel; a 4x4 is a good idea and essential if it's wet. Amboseli's airstrip is served by scheduled flights from Nairobi's Wilson Airport as well as from Mombasa's Moi International Airport; some of which go via the Ukunda airstrip at Diani Beach.

Contacts Kenya Wildlife Service. ✉ *Amboseli National Park* ☎ *0716/493–335* ⊕ *www.kws.go.ke.*

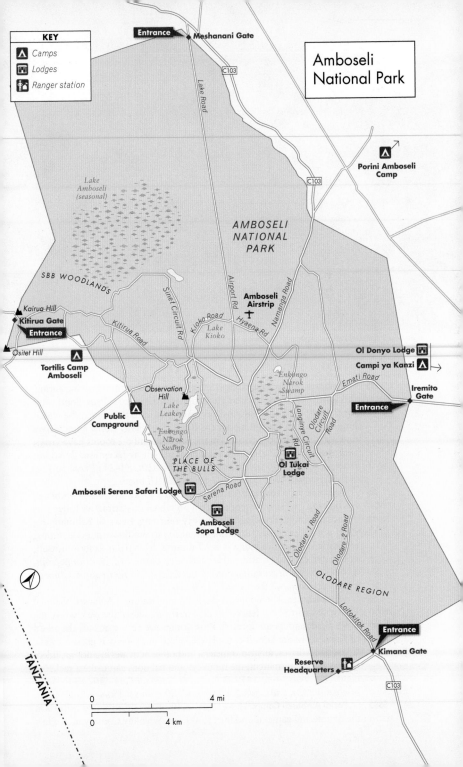

KEY

- ⛺ *Camps*
- 🏠 *Lodges*
- 👫 *Ranger station*

Amboseli National Park

Entrance ◆ Meshanani Gate

C103

C103

Lake Road

Lake Amboseli (seasonal)

AMBOSELI NATIONAL PARK

⛺→ Porini Amboseli Camp

S B B   W O O D L A N D S

Simet Circuit Rd

Airport Rd

Kioko Road

Lake Kioko

Hyaena Rd

Namanga Road

✈ **Amboseli Airstrip**

Kairua Hill
◆ **Kitirua Gate**
Entrance

Kitirua Road

◆ *Ositet Hill*

⛺ **Tortilis Camp Amboseli**

Observation Hill
Lake Leakey

Enkongo Narok Swamp

Ol Donyo Lodge 🏠
Campi ya Kanzi ⛺ →

Emati Road

Iremito Gate

Entrance ←

⛺ **Public Campground**

Enkongo Narok Swamp

P L A C E   O F   T H E   B U L L S

Longinye Rd

Olodare Circuit Road

🏠 **Ol Tukai Lodge**

Amboseli Serena Safari Lodge 🏠

Serena Road

🏠 **Amboseli Sopa Lodge**

Olodare-1 Road

Olodare-2 Road

O L O D A R E   R E G I O N

Loitokitok Road

Entrance
◆ **Kimana Gate**

Reserve Headquarters 👫

C103

T A N Z A N I A

0 _____ 4 mi

0 _____ 4 km

In Amboseli National Park, cheetah and wildebeest keep a watchful eye on each other.

WHERE TO STAY

$$ RESORT FAMILY **Amboseli Serena Safari Lodge.** Situated beside a natural flowing spring, this lodge enjoys spectacular views of Mt. Kilimanjaro. **Pros:** good value for money; the lodge balcony has views out onto the plains; the waterhole in front of the dining area is floodlit at night. **Cons:** game drives and activities are not included in the price; not all the rooms have views; rooms don't have safes and valuables are left at reception. [$] *Rooms from: $392* ✉ *Amboseli National Park* ☎ *020/284–2333 reservations* 🌐 *www.serenahotels.com* 🛏 *92 rooms* 🍴 *All meals.*

$$ RESORT FAMILY **Amboseli Sopa Lodge.** When Ernest Hemingway wrote *The Snows of Kilimanjaro,* he stayed near the area on which this attractive lodge was eventually built. **Pros:** excellent early-morning views of Kilimanjaro; great pool with comfy sun loungers; plenty of wildlife around including elephants. **Cons:** the lodge is a 20-minute drive from Amboseli itself; hot water can be erratic; safari activities cost extra. [$] *Rooms from: $314* ✉ *Amboseli National Park* ☎ *020/375–0235 reservations* 🌐 *www.sopalodges.com* 🛏 *83 rooms* 🍴 *All meals.*

$$ RESORT FAMILY **Ol Tukai Lodge.** This popular lodge is a central feature of Amboseli National Park as it's part of the fenced-off area in the middle of the park where the KWS headquarters are located. **Pros:** rooms are very spacious; the views of Kilimanjaro are fantastic; the large, fenced-in property is great for kids. **Cons:** game drives, airstrip transfers, and other activities are not included; Wi-Fi can be intermittent; the monkeys and baboons can make a racket at night. [$] *Rooms from: $450* ✉ *Amboseli National Park* ☎ *020/444–5514 reservations* 🌐 *www.oltukailodge.com* 🛏 *80 rooms* 🍴 *Some meals.*

$$$$ RESORT **Porini Amboseli Camp.** This exclusive, back-to-nature tented camp is in the remote and game-abundant 15,000-acre Selenkay Conservancy, a few

miles north of Amboseli National Park. **Pros:** the camp benefits the local community and is eco-friendly; there are few visitors but lots of game; the gift shop is superb—do all your curio shopping here. **Cons:** as with most camps, you'll struggle to get a phone signal; children under eight are not permitted; no laundry facilities. $ *Rooms from: $3020* ☒ *Selenkay Conservancy, Amboseli National Park* ☎ *0774/136–523 reservations* ⊕ *www.porini.com* ☽ *Closed mid-Apr.–May* ↗ *10 tents* ⦿| *All-inclusive.*

$$$$
RESORT
FAMILY

🏕 **Tortilis Camp Amboseli.** This rustic bush camp is named after the flat-topped *Acacia tortilis* trees that surround the main thatch-roof open bar, lounge, and dining room, which also overlooks a waterhole and have superb views of Mt. Kilimanjaro and Mt. Meru in neighboring Tanzania. **Pros:** stunning views of Mt. Kilimanjaro; excellent library; lots of elephants and great birdlife. **Cons:** the tents are accessed by steep steps; it's about a 45-minute drive to Amboseli's central swampy regions; accommodations are nice but lighting is insufficient. $ *Rooms from: $1210* ☒ *Amboseli National Park* ☎ *0730/127–000 reservations* ⊕ *www.elewanacollection.com* ↗ *17 tents, 1 private house* ⦿| *All-inclusive.*

NEAR AMBOSELI AND TSAVO WEST

The Chyulu Hills are a deeply green volcanic ridge of low hills between Amboseli and Tsavo West National Parks. It's a beautiful rugged wilderness and habitats include riverine bush and high mountain forests, although there are few roads and this region is fairly impenetrable unless you fly there. The altitude (up to 2160 meters/7087 feet above sea level) does not attract huge numbers of game, but elephant and buffalo are common and you'll find numerous antelope and more than 400 species of birds. The hills give a tremendous outlook across the broad African plains that spread out from their base and there's always a staggering view of Mount Kilimanjaro to the west. It's a good destination for hiking, bird-watching, horse-riding, or simply relaxing at the Chyulu's luxury lodges.

$$$$
RESORT
FAMILY
Fodor'sChoice
★

🏕 **Campi ya Kanzi.** One of the most environmentally friendly camps in Kenya, this lovely camp—in the Kuku Group Ranch, the natural corridor between Amboseli and Tsavo West National Parks—is owned by an Italian couple who are deeply committed to the environment and the local Maasai community. **Pros:** the tented cottages are very private; staff are from the local Maasai community; owners Luca and Antonella are superb hosts. **Cons:** animals are around but not in big quantities; not an overnight stop and 3–4 nights are needed to enjoy it; no Wi-Fi and intermittent mobile phone reception. $ *Rooms from: $1500* ☒ *Chyulu Hills* ☎ *0720/461–300* ⊕ *www.maasai.com* ↗ *8 tents, 1 villa* ⦿| *All-inclusive.*

$$$$
RESORT
FAMILY
Fodor'sChoice
★

🏕 **Ol Donyo Lodge.** Located on the Maasai-owned Mbirikani Group Ranch on the southwestern flank of the volcanic Chyulu Hills, this stylishly romantic and superluxurious lodge is considered one of the best in southern Kenya. **Pros:** the horizon pool has stunning views of Mt. Kilimanjaro; suites have indoor and outdoor showers as well as bathtubs; the "star beds" are an indescribable experience. **Cons:** there's less concentrated game than in Amboseli, but no other people; the access road is long and rough; it's better to fly to the private airstrip; the US$120 conservancy fee is extra. $ *Rooms from: $2310* ☒ *Chyulu Hills, Mbirikani Group Ranch* ☎ *87/354–6591 reservations, South Africa* ⊕ *www.greatplainsconservation.com* ☽ *Closed Apr.* ↗ *10 suites, 1 house* ⦿| *All-inclusive.*

Ambroseli Serena Safari Lodge Bedroom interior

Camp ya Kanzi

Ol Donyo

4

TSAVO WEST AND EAST NATIONAL PARKS

Game
★★★
Park Accessibility
★★★★
Getting Around
★★★★
Accommodations
★★★★
Scenic Beauty
★★★★

Covering almost 21,000 square km (8,108 square miles), the combined Tsavo West and Tsavo East National Parks is Kenya's largest protected game area. They are two distinct parks with different ecosystems: Tsavo West features wooded and hilly volcanic landscapes, while Tsavo East is much flatter with scattered bush on more open plains. They are administered separately, have separate entry fees and are split geographically by the Mombasa Highway—the main A109 road between Nairobi and Mombasa—as well as the railway that runs more or less alongside. Both stretch for about 130 km (80 miles) along the highway where a number of park gates provide access to the west and east. It's amazing that just a few miles away from the constant thunder of motor traffic on Kenya's busiest road is some of Kenya's best wildlife viewing.

TSAVO WEST

Tsavo West covers 7,065 square km (2,728 square miles), which is a little less than a third of the total area comprising all of Kenya's national parks. With its diverse habitats of riverine forest, palm thickets, rocky outcrops and ridges, mountains and plains, it's more attractive and certainly more accessible than Tsavo East. In the north, magnificent landscapes of heavily wooded hills dominate and this is where most of the lodges and game-viewing tracks are concentrated; it's generally known as the "Developed

Area." The south of Tsavo West is flatter with more open plains, but access is tricky as parts of the park are disjointed and crossed by another highway between Voi and Taveta. There's evidence of volcanic activity everywhere in the park, especially where ancient lava flows absorb the rainfall. In one spectacular spot, this rainfall, having traveled underground for 40 km (25 miles) or so, gushes up in a pair of pools at Mzima Springs, in the north of the park. There's a submerged hippo blind here, but the hippos have gotten wise to tourists and often move to the far side of the pools. Because of the fertile volcanic soil and abundance of water, the park is brimming with animal, bird, and plant life. There are large numbers of elephant and you may see lion and cheetah—especially in the dry season when the grass is low—plus spotted hyena, buffalo, the beautiful Masai giraffe, and all kinds of antelope, including Thomson's and Grant's gazelle—the prettiest of the antelope. The birdlife in the park is outstanding, with more than 400 species including eight types of hornbills.

WHEN TO GO

You'll have a good experience whenever you go, but bear in mind that the long rains are from March to May, and the short rains are October to December—vegetation is dense in these wet months, making it more difficult to see animals.

GETTING HERE AND AROUND

It's 240 km (150 miles) from Nairobi to Tsavo West's Mtito Andei Gate, which takes around five hours to drive. The park's Tsavo Gate in the southeast is approximately 200 km (125 miles) north of Mombasa and takes about four hours. There's no public transport to or in the park, and if you drive yourself, keep an eye on the park signage (cairns at numbered junctions) or use a GPS. There are three airstrips in the park and you can fly from Nairobi's Wilson Airport, Mombasa's Moi International, and the Ukunda airstrip at Diani Beach.

Contacts **Kenya Wildlife Service.** ✉ *Tsavo West National Park* ☎ *0720/968–527* 🌐 *www.kws.go.ke.*

WHERE TO STAY

$$$$ RESORT Fodor's Choice ★ 🏨 **Finch Hattons.** If you saw the movie *Out of Africa,* then you'll have some idea, even if it's rather over-romanticized, of who Denys Finch Hatton was. **Pros:** you'll see an extraordinary array of wildlife right in the camp; food and service are outstanding; game drives, airstrip transfers, and sundowners are included. **Cons:** park fees of $60 per night are extra; the generator is switched off at 11:30 pm; no children under six years. [$] *Rooms from: $1960* ✉ *Tsavo West* ☎ *020/357–7500 reservations* 🌐 *www.finchhattons.com* 🛏 *17 tents* 🍴 *All-inclusive.*

$$ RESORT FAMILY 🏨 **Kilaguni Serena Safari Lodge.** This lovely old lodge was Kenya's first lodge to open in a national park (1962). **Pros:** the waterhole is floodlit at night; the airstrip is less than 1 km away; family-friendly with babysitting and kids' dining. **Cons:** not all rooms have great views; room decor is a bit dated; can be full with large tour groups. [$] *Rooms from: $332* ✉ *Tsavo West* ☎ *020/284–2333 reservations* 🌐 *www.serenahotels.com* 🛏 *56 rooms* 🍴 *All meals.*

$ RESORT 🏨 **Sarova Salt Lick Game Lodge.** This truly uniquely designed lodge is set in the Taita Hills Wildlife Sanctuary just outside Tsavo West and

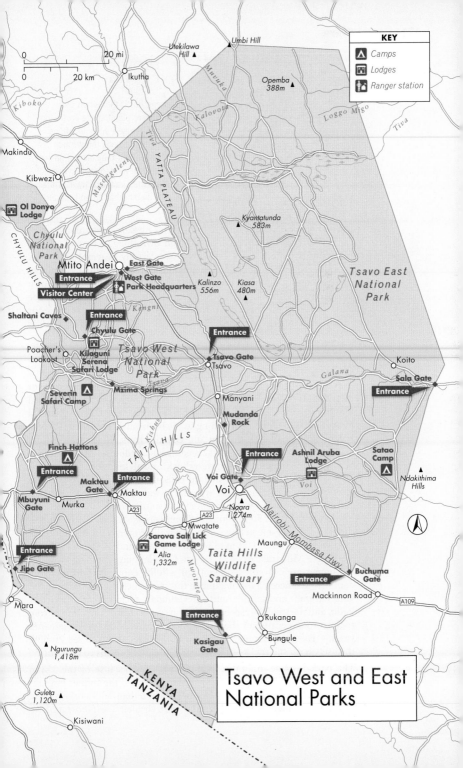

off the main Voi-Taveta road (A23). **Pros:** the underground viewing room; watching animals from your bed; fantastic architecture. **Cons:** no pool; the half-moon shaped rooms are small; stairs and bridges make it not suitable for small kids. $ *Rooms from: $193* ✉ *Taita Hills Wildlife Sanctuary, Tsavo West* ✚ *40 km (25 miles) east of Voi* ☎ *0728/608–765 reservations* ⊕ *www.sarovahotels.com* ➥ *96 rooms* ◯ *Some meals.*

$$
RESORT 🏕 **Severin Safari Camp.** With 27 rooms this upscale, meticulously kept camp is large enough for you to do your own thing, yet small enough to retain its tented camp feel with a wonderfully peaceful ambience. **Pros:** lovely, relaxing pool area, with a little spa and gym; a 10-minute drive from the Mzima Springs; good views of Mt. Kilimanjaro. **Cons:** most activities, including game drives, cost extra; water pressure can be a little low at times in the bathrooms; it's unfenced so not suitable for small children. $ *Rooms from: $397* ✉ *Tsavo West* ☎ *041/211–1000 reservations* ⊕ *www.severinsafaricamp.com* ➥ *27 tents* ◯ *All meals.*

TSAVO EAST

Tsavo East—11,747 square km (4,535 square miles)—is the larger of the two Tsavos and has a fairly harsh landscape of scrubland dotted with huge baobab trees; photographers will revel in the great natural light and the vast plains stretching to the horizon. There's lots of greenery along the banks of the Voi and Galana rivers, and the big Aruba Dam, built across the Voi, attracts game and birdlife galore. You'll see herds of elephant and buffalo, waterbuck, and all kinds of animals coming to drink at the dam. The Lugard Falls, on the Galana River, is more a series of rapids than actual waterfalls; walk along the riverbank to catch a glimpse of the water-sculpted rocks. Another fascinating feature in the park is the 290-km-long (180-mile-long) Yatta Plateau, one of the world's longest lava flows. It runs parallel to the Nairobi-Mombasa Highway and is 5 to 10 km (3 to 6 miles) wide and 305 meters (1,000 feet) high. Mudanda Rock, a 1.5-km (2-mile) outcropping, is a water catchment area. You'll see plenty of wildlife coming to drink at the dam below. There's a lot of game in this park, including zebra, impala, lion, cheetah, and giraffe, and rarer animals such as the oryx, lesser kudu, and the small klipspringer antelope, which can jump nimbly from rock to rock because of the sticky suction pads under their feet. And yes, it's true: those fat and hairy marmotlike creatures you see sunning themselves on the rocks—the hyraxes—are first cousins to elephants.

The park became infamous in the late 1890s because of the "Man Eaters of Tsavo," a pride of lions that preyed on the Indian migrant laborers who were building the railway. More than 130 workers were killed; the incident was retold in the 1996 thriller, *The Ghost and the*

Darkness, starring Val Kilmer. In the 1970s and '80s Tsavo became notorious once again for the widespread poaching that decimated the elephant population and nearly wiped out rhinos altogether. Today, thanks to responsible management, enlightened environmental vision, and proper funding, both elephant and rhino populations are on the rise and are carefully monitored.

WHEN TO GO

Tsavo East is accessible year-round, so the peak season is actually based on demand months such as migration time in Kenya (July–October) and also vacationers getting away during the winter months—especially Europeans. That being said, March through May is the rainy season, and there are short rains in October and December. Humidity is high from December to April.

GETTING HERE AND AROUND

There are several gates to Tsavo East and Mtito Andei Gate is 233 km (148 miles) southeast of Nairobi. Voi Gate, 157 km (98 miles) north-west of Mombasa, and Buchuma Gate, 100 km (62 miles) northwest of Mombasa, are the routes often used on organized safaris from the coast. There are nine airstrips but no scheduled flights; most visitors drive up from Mombasa or charter flights are an option. There's no public transport within the park.

Contacts Kenya Wildlife Service. ⊠ *Tsavo Rast National Park* ⊕ *www.kws.go.ke.*

WHERE TO STAY

$$ 🏨 **Ashnil Aruba Lodge.** This large mid-range safari lodge may not have **RESORT** the intimacy of a small tented camp, but its location is superb as it **FAMILY** overlooks the Aruba Dam—one of the best places to see wildlife in the whole of Tsavo East. **Pros:** elephants can be seen from the swimming pool; hospitable and well-organized staff; easy access from Voi Gate. **Cons:** it has a large resort feel but will suit those who like hotel rooms; park fees and activities cost extra; Wi-Fi only in the lounge. $ *Rooms from: $270* ⊠ *Tsavo East* ☎ *020/356–6970 reservations* ⊕ *www.ashnilhotels.com* 🛏 *40 rooms* ⦿ *Some meals.*

$$ 🏨 **Satao Camp.** This small and friendly camp lies on a traditional migra-**RESORT** tion route, so it's not short of game. **Pros:** excellent views of the water-**FAMILY** hole; it's fully equipped for people with disabilities; up to 50% discounts for children under 12. **Cons:** parts of the camp look onto unsightly power lines; rates do not include park fees or game drives; hot water for showers only in the evening. $ *Rooms from: $436* ⊠ *Tsavo National Park East* ☎ *020/243–4610 reservations* ⊕ *www.sataocamp.com* 🛏 *20 tents* ⦿ *All meals.*

LAIKIPIA PLATEAU

Game
★★★★
Park Accessibility
★★★
Getting Around
★★★
Accommodations
★★★★
Scenic Beauty
★★★★

Stretching northwest of Mt. Kenya, the Laikipia Plateau isn't in itself a national park or reserve, but it's a broadly defined region of community group ranches and private conservancies. It has become one of Kenya's most successful conservation successes, with many landowners turning cattle ranches into wildlife sanctuaries, too, and it is where traditional ways of pastoral life continue side by side with an abundance of free-roaming game.

This huge region covers around 9,500 square km (3,668 square miles), and the conservancies are crisscrossed by dirt roads. The Ol Pejeta Conservancy, famous for its black rhino and chimpanzee sanctuary, is open to day visitors and it's the easiest to get to from Nairobi. The Lewa Wildlife Conservancy, which was founded in the 1970s, has become a globally recognized black and white rhino conservation; it can also be reached by road from Nairobi. Some other conservancies on the fringe of Kenya's northern territory are accessible by those who stay in one of their exclusive lodges and who usually arrive by plane. This is high country, with altitudes from 1,700 meters (5,577 feet) to 2,600 meters (8,530 feet), so bring those sweaters and jackets.

Laikipia's habitats range from arid semidesert, scrubland, and sprawling open plains in the north and south, to the thick forests of cedar and olive trees in the east. The area has one of the biggest and most diverse mammal populations in Kenya—only the Masai Mara can boast more game. The Big Five are all present, and it's the only area in Kenya to have a burgeoning population of wild dogs. Many northern Kenyan animals can be spotted such as the gerenuk, Grevy's zebra, Jackson's hartebeest, and reticulated giraffe.

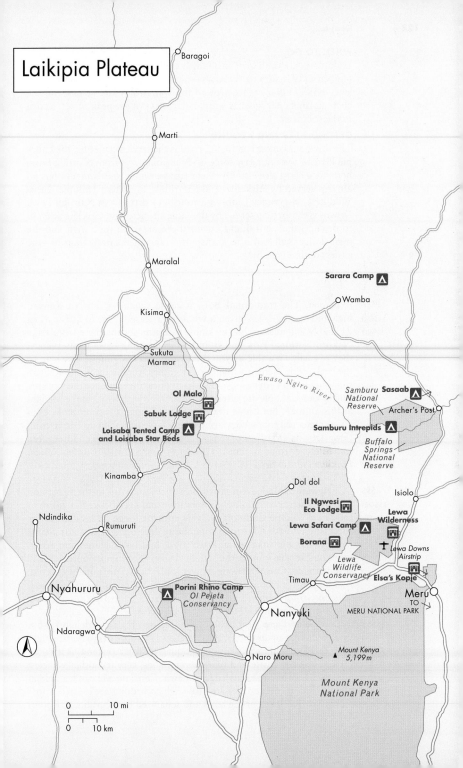

WHEN TO GO

Laikipia is good all year around, but the dry seasons—May to September and January to February—tend to offer the best game viewing since wildlife congregate around the waterholes and creeks and the clear air offers particularly spectacular views of the peak of Mt. Kenya in the southeast.

GETTING HERE AND AROUND

The town of Nanyuki on the A2 road is the service center for the Laikipia Plateau and is an easy three- to four-hour drive from Nairobi. From here it's a short drive to Ol Pejeta Conservancy, and Nanyuki has an airstrip served by Airkenya and Safarilink. In eastern Laikipia, Lewa Wildlife Conservancy is about a four-hour drive from Nairobi; Lewa Downs is the airstrip served by the same airlines. Few travelers attempt to drive to the central and far northern areas on their own and the many lodges will look after transport arrangements from Nairobi—the easiest option is to fly.

WHERE TO STAY

$$$$
RESORT
FAMILY
Fodor's Choice
★

Borana. The traditional Borana cattle ranch—a part of Kenyan highland history—was given a whole new lease on life in 2013, when 21 highly endangered black rhinos were translocated here from Lake Nakuru National Park and from the neighboring Lewa Conservancy; they're easily viewable as you drive around. **Pros:** unique views up to the peak of Mt. Kenya; a chance to meet the Dyer family, one of Kenya's founding farming dynasties; lots of activities to experience the working ranch. **Cons:** people are often surprised at how chilly it can be at night at this altitude, but hot-water bottles and romantic open fireplaces in all cottages add to the cozy atmosphere; at least one hour's drive from Lewa Downs airstrip; not fenced and steep in places so children need to be supervised at all times. $ *Rooms from: $1280* ⊠ *Borana Ranch, Laikipia Plateau* ☎ *020/211–5453* ⊕ *www.borana.co.ke* ⊘ *Closed Nov.* ⟋ *8 cottages* ⦿❘*All-inclusive.*

$$$
RESORT
FAMILY

Il Ngwesi Eco Lodge. Situated on a rocky outcrop in the Il Ngwesi Group Ranch, a community conservation and livestock region north of the Lewa Wildlife Conservancy, this intimate lodge prides itself on its successful efforts to integrate community development and sustainable environmental management. **Pros:** good children's facilities and activities; you can sleep under the stars; excellent community outreach and sustainability. **Cons:** open-air showers only; drinks are not always cold; two-hour drive from Lewa Downs airstrip. $ *Rooms from: $600* ⊠ *Il Ngwesi Group Ranch, Laikipia Plateau* ☎ *020/203–3122 reservations* ⊕ *www.ilngwesi.com* ⟋ *6 rooms* ⦿❘*All-inclusive.*

$$$$
RESORT
FAMILY

Lewa Safari Camp. If it's rhinos you're after, then this delightful but small tented camp in the 65,000-acre Lewa Wildlife Conservancy, right where the old Rhino Sanctuary headquarters used to stand, is for you. **Pros:** tents are private and two sleep families; very few other vehicles; guides have intimate knowledge of Lewa. **Cons:** no a/c; can get cold at night, but hot water bottles are provided; bathrooms are located a little close to the bed area of the tents and separated by a curtain. $ *Rooms*

Finding a leopard in the wild is very rare. This leopard was spotted in Samburu on a twilight game drive.

Sabuk

Sabuk

Il'Ngwesi Lodge

from: $1228 ⊠ *Lewa Wildlife Conservancy* ☎ *0730/127–700 reservations* ⊕ *www.elewanacollection.com* ⇥ *13 tents* ⦿ *All-inclusive.*

$$$$
RESORT
FAMILY
Fodor's Choice
★

📷 **Lewa Wilderness.** Lewa Downs is another one of Laikipia's conservation successes. **Pros:** it's ideal for families; there's a huge range of activities available; all drinks are included from the self-service bar. **Cons:** very popular and with many repeat guests, you need to book well in advance; it can get a little chilly in the evening; at least three nights are needed here to enjoy the experience. $ *Rooms from: $1590* ⊠ *Lewa Wildlife Conservancy, Laikipia Plateau* ☎ *0796/035–177 reservations,* ⊕ *www.lewawilderness.com* ⇥ *10 rooms* ⦿ *All-inclusive.*

$$$$
RESORT
FAMILY

📷 **Loisaba Tented Camp and Loisaba Star Beds.** The Loisaba Tented Camp sits plumb in the middle of the game-rich Loisaba Conservancy in the northern reaches of Laikipia and is part of the Ewaso Nyiro River ecosystem. **Pros:** small, intimate and peaceful with excellent service; good interaction with Laikipia's local people; both the tents and star beds have family options. **Cons:** no a/c, although the elevation means it's hardly needed; Wi-Fi can be erratic; not ideal if it's windy or wet. $ *Rooms from: $1100* ⊠ *Loisaba Conservancy, Laikipia Plateau* ☎ *0730/127–000 reservations* ⊕ *www.elewanacollection.com* ⇥ *6 tents, 4 star beds* ⦿ *All meals.*

$$$$
RESORT
FAMILY

📷 **Ol Malo.** Perched on an escarpment with views towards Mt. Kenya in the south, this lovely lodge is on a privately owned family ranch in the wild northern Laikipia Plateau. **Pros:** it's very child-friendly; the afternoon tea is excellent; rates include conservancy fees and activities. **Cons:** no a/c in rooms, but open walls make it airy; transfers from Loisaba airstrip cost extra; Wi-Fi has spasmodic reception. $ *Rooms from: $1800* ⊠ *Laikipia Plateau* ☎ *020/600–0457 reservations* ⊕ *www.olmalo.com* ☉ *Closed Apr., May, and Nov.* ⇥ *4 cottages, 1 house* ⦿ *All-inclusive.*

$$$$
RESORT

📷 **Porini Rhino Camp.** This delightful eco-friendly tented camp is nestled among Kenya's ubiquitous *Acacia tortilis* trees in a secluded valley in the Ol Pejeta Conservancy. **Pros:** the camp benefits the local community and is eco-friendly; the waterhole in front of the camp attracts a lot of wildlife; the price includes conservancy fees and a visit to the chimpanzee sanctuary. **Cons:** it can be cooler than reserves south of the country; no Wi-Fi and limited phone reception; not recommended for children under eight. $ *Rooms from: $2810* ⊠ *Ol Pejeta Conservancy, Laikipia Plateau* ☎ *0774/136–523,* ⊕ *www.porini.com* ☉ *Closed mid-Apr.–May* ⇥ *7 tents* ⦿ *All-inclusive.*

$$$$
RESORT
FAMILY

📷 **Sabuk Lodge.** This lodge organically created out of local thatch, stone, and wood clings to a hillside on the conservancy of the same name in the northwest of the Laikipia Plateau. **Pros:** excellent Laikipia Maasai guides; the camel safaris are highly recommended; families can opt for Eagle Cottage with two bedrooms and a plunge pool. **Cons:** rooms are fairly rustic, but do have charm; no phone reception or Wi-Fi; at least a four-hour drive north of Nanyuki so it's best to fly. $ *Rooms from: $1460* ⊠ *Sabuk Conservancy, Laikipia Plateau* ☎ *020/266–3397 reservations,* ⊕ *www.sabuklodge.com* ⇥ *8 cottages* ⦿ *All-inclusive.*

IF YOU HAVE TIME

Although the reviews go into great detail about the must-see parks in Kenya, there are many others to explore if you have time. Here, a few good ones are mentioned.

NAIROBI NATIONAL PARK

The most striking thing about Nairobi National Park, Kenya's oldest national park (established in 1946), is the very fact that it exists at all. This sliver of unspoiled Africa survives on the edge of a city of more than 3.5 million people. Where else can you get a photo of animals in their natural habitat with skyscrapers in the background?

The park is tiny compared with Kenya's other game parks and reserves; it covers only 117 square km (44 square miles). It's characterized by open plains that slope gently from west to east and rocky ridges that are covered with rich vegetation. Seasonal streams run southeast into the Mbagathi River, which is lined with yellow-color fever and acacia trees.

Despite the urban pressures, the park contains a good variety of wildlife, even during the dry season, as there's always a source of permanent water. It's home to four of the Big Five; elephant are absent as the area isn't big enough to support them. ■TIP→ If you want to see baby elephants, visit the orphanage at the David Sheldrick Wildlife Trust close to the main entrance of the park. Zebra, impala, Grant's and Thomson's gazelles, warthog, and ostrich are common on the open plains. Good populations of lion and cheetah can be seen on the grasslands, Masai giraffes browse in the woodlands, black rhinos are sometimes found around the forest area, and more than 400 species of permanent and migratory birds have been recorded in the park.

Nairobi National Park has very pleasant picnic sites, a boardwalk to see a hippo pool, and a monument to Kenya's famous ivory-burning site. Both the Kenya Wildlife Service's Nairobi Safari Walk and the Animal Orphanage are near the KWS headquarters at the main gate of the park. Each has a separate entry fee and offers the opportunity to walk around for an hour or so and get close to many of Kenya's animals that you might see on safari, all of which are kept at these facilities in spacious natural enclosures.

GETTING HERE AND AROUND

A 20-minute drive from downtown Nairobi (7 km/4 miles), the park's network of paved and all-weather dirt roads can be negotiated by regular cars; junctions are signposted and clearly marked on the official park map, which you can pick up at the gate. Most safari operators will arrange a half-day trip; otherwise hire a taxi for a few hours. Rangers keep a careful note of the movements of the larger animals, so it's worth asking at the gate where to look for lion or rhino.

Contact **Kenya Wildlife Service.** ✉ *Langata Rd.* ☎ *0800/597–000 KWS headquarters, 020/242–3423 Nairobi National Park* ⊕ *www.kws.go.ke.*

Continued on page 138

Blue wildebeest in Tanzania's Serengeti National Park

THE GREAT MIGRATION

Nothing will prepare you for the spectacle that is the Great Migration. This annual journey of more than 2 million animals is a safari-seeker's Holy Grail, the ultimate in wildlife experiences. Some say it's one of the world's greatest natural wonders.

The greater Serengeti ecosystem, which includes Kenya's Masai Mara (north) and Tanzania's Serengeti (south), is the main arena for this awesome sight. At the end of each year during the short rains—November to early December—the herds disperse into the southeast plains of Tanzania's Seronera. After calving early in the new year (wildebeests drop up to 8,000 babies a day), huge numbers of animals start the 800-km (497-mile) trek from these now bare southeast plains to lush northern pastures. On the way they will face terrible, unavoidable danger. In June and July braying columns—40 km (25 miles) long—have to cross the crocodile-infested Grumeti River. Half of the great herds which successfully survive the crossing will stay in northern Tanzania, the other half will cross over into Kenya's Masai Mara. In early October the animals begin their return journey back to Seronera and come full circle, only to begin their relentless trek once again early the following year.

WHO'S MIGRATING

What will you see during the migration?

More than **2 million** wildebeest
250,000 Thompson's gazelle
200,000 zebra
70,000 impala
30,000 Grant's gazelle

In addition, huge numbers of predators follow the herds. You're likely to see lion, leopard, cheetah, jackal, hyena, and numerous smaller predators.

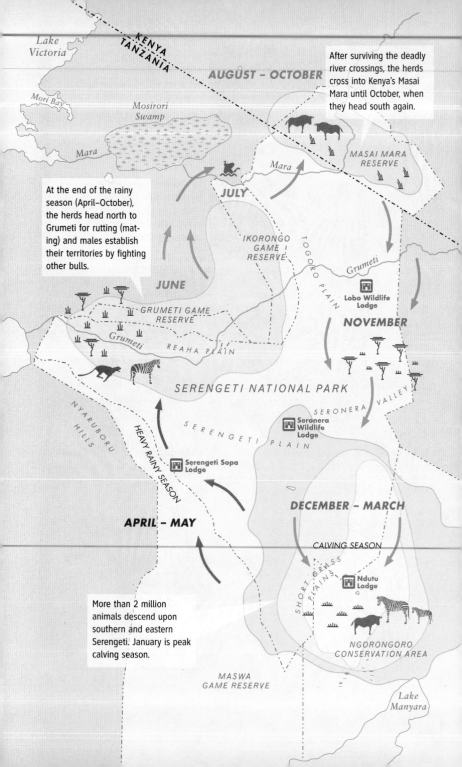

KENYA
TANZANIA

Lake Victoria

Mori Bay

Mara

Mosirori Swamp

AUGUST – OCTOBER

After surviving the deadly river crossings, the herds cross into Kenya's Masai Mara until October, when they head south again.

Mara

JULY

MASAI MARA RESERVE

At the end of the rainy season (April–October), the herds head north to Grumeti for rutting (mating) and males establish their territories by fighting other bulls.

IKORONGO GAME RESERVE

TOGORO PLAIN

Grumeti

JUNE

Lobo Wildlife Lodge

GRUMETI GAME RESERVE

NOVEMBER

Grumeti

REAHA PLAIN

SERENGETI NATIONAL PARK

SERONERA VALLEY

NYARUBORU HILLS

SERONERA PLAIN

Seronera Wildlife Lodge

HEAVY RAINY SEASON

Serengeti Sopa Lodge

DECEMBER – MARCH

CALVING SEASON

APRIL – MAY

SHORT GRASS PLAINS

Ndutu Lodge

More than 2 million animals descend upon southern and eastern Serengeti. January is peak calving season.

NGORONGORO CONSERVATION AREA

MASWA GAME RESERVE

Lake Manyara

DRIVEN BY DINNER

WHERE THE MAGIC HAPPENS

The Serengeti more then lives up to its awesome reputation as an amazing spot to see wildlife and it's here that the Great Migration begins and ends. The park's ecosystem supports some of the most abundant mammal populations left anywhere on earth and it covers almost 15,000 square km (9,320 square miles) of seemingly endless plains, riverine bush, forest and scrubland roughly the size of Northern Ireland or Connecticut. It stretches between the Ngorongoro highlands, Lake Victoria, and Tanzania's northern border with Kenya. It was named a UNESCO World Heritage Site in 1978 and an International Biosphere Reserve (a UNESCO international conservation area) in 1981.

WHEN TO GO

Because rainfall patterns are unpredictable, it's difficult to anticipate timings for the migration. But usually, by the beginning of each year, the grazing on the southeast plains of Serengeti's Seronera is exhausted and the herds start to move northwest into Tanzania's Western Corridor. The actual crossing of the Grumeti River, usually between June and July, when an unrivalled bloody spectacle of terrified frantic wildebeest and huge lashing crocodiles unfolds, is a gruesome, unforgettable spectacle. You'll see hundreds of thousands of animals between March and November, including predators. Seronera in March, April, and May is an ideal time for a safari because there are huge concentrations of predators preying on all the baby animals. Safaris are much cheaper between April and June, and although you may not witness the actual river crossings, you'll still be privy to prime game-viewing experiences. Plus there will be far fewer vehicles.

STAGGERING NUMBERS

The Great Migration, as we know it, is a fairly young phenomenon, having only started in the 1960s when wildebeest numbers exploded. However, an estimated 250,000 wildebeests don't survive the annual migration.

4

IN FOCUS THE GREAT MIGRATION

WHERE TO STAY

Nairobi National Park is easy enough to visit on a day trip from accommodations in Nairobi. However, the one lodge and a tented camp in the park are a good way to kick-start your safari. Stay here and you could be viewing lion and rhino within an hour of stepping off your plane.

$$$$ RESORT FAMILY 🏨 **The Emakoko.** A 45-minute drive from Nairobi's Jomo Kenyatta International Airport is a luxurious paradise bush lodge in a seemingly remote and hidden valley. **Pros:** close to both of Nairobi's airports, but in a remote area; dinner by the pool is a starlit experience; log fires in the rooms turn cooler nights into sheer romance. **Cons:** windows and doors might have to be closed because of monkeys; the upper-level rooms are reached by steps; the access road is steep and tricky for drivers. [$] *Rooms from: $940* ✉ *Nairobi National Park, Nairobi* ☎ *0724/156–044* 🌐 *www.emakoko.com* 🛏 *10 rooms* 🍴 *All-inclusive.*

$$ RESORT 🏨 **Nairobi Tented Camp.** Insulated by a hidden glade—home to leopard, lion, and hyena—Nairobi Tented Camp is in a secluded part of Nairobi National Park, providing an authentic bush experience within a few miles of the city center. **Pros:** short transfers from JKIA and Wilson airports; if your plane lands after dark you'll be treated to a night drive en route to the camp; hammocks are strung in the trees for afternoon siestas. **Cons:** Nairobi National Park entrance and camping fees are extra; the access road is bumpy with the last 200 meters being on foot; the tents are quite close together. [$] *Rooms from: $260* ✉ *Nairobi National Park, Nairobi* ☎ *0774/136–524* 🌐 *www.nairobitentedcamp.com* 🛏 *9 tents* 🍴 *Breakfast.*

MERU NATIONAL PARK

Situated 348 km (216 miles) northeast of Nairobi and west of Mt. Kenya, this little-visited park (1,810 square km/699 square miles) offers some of Kenya's wildest country, but was taken off the mainstream safari circuit because of the lawless poachers who wiped out a considerable amount of wildlife in the 1980s. But starting in 2000, the Kenya Wildlife Service embarked on a restoration mission and restocked the park with many large mammals—including elephant and black and white rhino—which have since thrived, and today the park is home to all of the Big Five. It's yet to attract large numbers of safari-goers, but Meru is a safe and fulfilling destination again—after all, this is the place where wildlife champions Joy and George Adamson hand-reared Elsa the lioness made famous by the 1966 film *Born Free.*

Game here includes buffalo, lion, leopard, cheetah, hippo, lesser kudu, hartebeest, Grevy's and Burchell's zebra, the gerenuk, the reticulated or Somali giraffe, waterbuck, oryx, and Grant's gazelle. The park is part of an ecosystem that includes Kora National Park and Mwingi, Rahole, and Bisanadi reserves. It straddles the equator and is home to a great variety of habitats, including scrubland dotted with baobab trees, lush green grasslands, and riverine forests. Tana, Kenya's longest river, is fed by 13 rivers that create a superb habitat for birdlife, including the Somali ostrich and raptors such as the red-necked falcon and the palm-nut vulture. You may also see that megascore on a serious birder's "life list," the Pel's fishing owl, which hides in the huge ancient trees along the rivers.

GETTING HERE AND AROUND

There's a daily flight between Nairobi's Wilson Airport and Meru National Park with Airkenya, which takes one hour. You can drive from Nairobi; the road isn't particularly bad but it takes five to six hours. If you're already at a property in the area, say at Laikipia or Samburu, it can make sense to drive, but a 4x4 vehicle is required for driving within the park.

Contact Kenya Wildlife Service. ⊠ *Meru National Park* ☎ *0786/348–875* ⊕ *www.kws.go.ke.*

WHERE TO STAY

$$$$
RESORT
FAMILY
Fodor'sChoice
★

Elsa's Kopje. The best place to stay in Meru, this stylish and romantic lodge is set above George Adamson's original campsite, where he and his wife, author Joy Adamson, released their lioness Elsa (after which the lodge is named) back into the wild. **Pros:** high standard of food with homegrown vegetables; free laundry service; spectacular views across Meru. **Cons:** not all rooms have tubs; room lighting is quite dim; there are quite a number of steps between the rooms and the main area. $ *Rooms from: $1280* ⊠ *Meru National Park* ☎ *0730/127–000 reservations* ⊕ *www.elewanacollection.com* ⌇ *10 rooms, 1 private house* ⦿ *All meals.*

LAKE NAIVASHA

One of the Rift Valley's few freshwater lakes, Lake Naivasha is a popular spot for day trips and weekends away from Nairobi. Although the lake is not part of a national park or game reserve, it has pleasant forested surroundings, which are a far cry from the congestion and noise of Nairobi and there is plentiful wildlife around. Keep an eye out for the fever trees, and the abundant populations of birds, giraffes, zebras, monkeys, and hippos. This is also Kenya's premier area for growing flowers for export—especially roses—and you'll see the farms all around the lake shore. Such an attractive location lured a group of British settlers to build their homes on its shores. Known collectively as "White Mischief," these settlers were internationally infamous for their decadent, hedonistic lifestyle. A 1987 movie of the same name, starring Greta Scacchi, was based on a notorious society murder set during this time in this location.

There are numerous things to do around Lake Naivasha and the lodges and camps on the grassy lake shore make perfect bases for a couple of days' exploration. Cross over by boat to Crescent Island Game Sanctuary where you can see (and walk with) giraffe, zebra, and other plains herbivores; there are no predators so it's quite safe. Visit Elsamere, the former home of George and Joy Adamson of *Born Free* fame, for afternoon tea on the lawns and a look at the small museum to learn about their lives and conservation work. Or hike or even cycle in Hell's Gate National Park, which is named after its magnificent red sandstone cliffs

The Kikuyu people account for almost 25% of Kenya's population, and most live around Mt. Kenya.

and is home to numerous plains game and fantastic birdlife including plenty of raptors such as the Rüppell's vulture and Verreaux's eagle.

GETTING HERE AND AROUND

Lake Naivasha is a one- to two-hour drive from Nairobi. There are two routes—a shorter but badly potholed route along the escarpment, or a longer but better maintained road, the A104 Uplands, which leads to Naivasha town. Hotels and lodges around the lake shore will arrange pickups from Nairobi, and taxis can transport you around the area.

EXPLORING

Crescent Island Game Sanctuary. Take a boat ride from one of the lakeshore hotels to Crescent Island Game Sanctuary, where you can see (and walk with) giraffe, zebra, and other plains herbivores; there are no predators so it's quite safe. **■ TIP→ On the way to the crater keep your eyes open for hippos as you are on the outer rim of a volcanic crater, which is also the deepest part of the lake.** ✉ *Naivasha* ☎ *0733/579–935* 🌐 *www.crescentisland.co* 🎟 *$30.*

WHERE TO STAY

$$ RESORT FAMILY 🏨 **Crater Lake Tented Camp.** About a half-hour drive from the town of Naivasha, Crater Lake Tented Camp is situated in the cauldron of a crater in the Crater Lake Game Sanctuary, on the edge of a lovely salt-water lake, which itself lies just off the southwestern shore of Lake Naivasha. **Pros:** the views are lovely; birding is excellent with birdbaths everywhere; it's the only camp in the Crater Lake Game Sanctuary. **Cons:** steep steps to access tents; the swimming pool is not always well-maintained; accommodation is rustic and basic, but has charm. [$] *Rooms from: $308* ✉ *Crater*

Lake Game Sanctuary, Moi North Lake Rd., Naivasha ☎ *050/202–0613* 🌐 *www.craterlakecamp.com* 🛏 *15 rooms* 🍴 *All meals.*

$ HOTEL FAMILY 🏨 **Lake Naivasha Country Club.** This resort sits on a large lakeside property and oozes historical character as it dates back to the 1930s when it served as a staging post for a flying boat service between Durban and Ireland and the planes landed on Lake Naivasha. **Pros:** lovely lakeside setting; top-quality buffet meals; large swimming pool. **Cons:** very small bathrooms; staff can be a little impersonal; can be busy with conference groups. [$] *Rooms from: $178* ✉ *Lake Naivasha, Moi South Lake Rd.* ☎ *0703/048–000 reservations* 🌐 *www.sunafricahotels.com* 🛏 *58 rooms* 🍴 *Breakfast.*

$$ RESORT FAMILY 🏨 **Lake Naivasha Sopa Resort.** In lovely forested grounds with huge established trees, very large rooms and loads of facilities, the comfortable and friendly Sopa offers everything you'll need for a couple of days at Lake Naivasha. **Pros:** kid-friendly with children's pool, menu, and babysitting; lovely forest environment; staff are warm and helpful. **Cons:** be careful after dark as hippos graze on the lawns; bedding is simple sheets and blankets, but they are warm; monkeys can be a nuisance around the pools. [$] *Rooms from: $347* ✉ *Mois South Lake Rd., Lake Naivasha* ☎ *020/375–0235 reservations* 🌐 *www.sopalodges.com* 🛏 *84 rooms* 🍴 *All meals.*

4

LAKE NAKURU NATIONAL PARK

This delightful and compact park covers around 188 square km (73 square miles) and completely surrounds Lake Nakuru on the floor of the Great Rift Valley. Until a few years ago it was most famous for the hundreds of thousands of flamingos that fed on the algae in the shallows. However because of rising lake levels, the water has lost much of its salinity. There are still some flamingos seen on the lake's edge but the mass flocks have gone elsewhere. Nevertheless this is still a very rewarding and easy park to visit. There are more than 400 other bird species, plus incredible game including leopard (often seen in daylight hours), good numbers of both black and white rhino, big herds of buffalo, and lots of plains game including Rothschild's giraffe, waterbuck, and eland. The beauty of game driving here is that many of the animals are used to vehicles on the small network of roads that encircle the lake, and it's possible they will allow you to get very close. The scenery is spectacular too and the lake is surrounded by escapements covered in thick acacia bush—don't miss stopping at the viewpoint at Baboon Cliffs for the expansive view down to the lake, but as the name suggests, keep an eye out for those mischievous baboons.

GETTING HERE AND AROUND

Lake Nakuru National Park is 166 km (103 miles) northwest of Nairobi, and the drive takes approximately 2½ to 3 hours along the main A104 road. You can drive around the park in just three hours, and this is one of the few parks that you can get around in a normal (not 4x4) car. Many taxi drivers in Nakuru town know the park well and can take you around, and for an extra fee you can take an expert Kenya Wildlife Service guide with you. A trip to Lake Nakuru can be arranged from Nairobi with a safari operator and is often combined with a stay at Lake Naivasha too, or is included on a longer safari to the Masai Mara.

Kenya Wildlife Service. ✉ *Nakuru National Park* ✣ *5 km (3.1 miles) south of Nakuru town* ☎ *0728/355–267* 🌐 *www.kws.go.ke.*

WHERE TO STAY

$$ RESORT FAMILY 🏨 **Lake Nakuru Sopa Lodge.** If you'd like to do an overnight in Lake Nakuru National Park, then this smart new mid-range Sopa lodge (opened in 2015) is a good choice thanks to its commanding position high up on a ridge in the quiet western area. **Pros:** amazing lake views from the rooms; easy game-viewing drives; wheelchair friendly. **Cons:** Wi-Fi only in the lobby; the swimming pool is not heated and it can be too cold to swim; the gardens are yet to fully mature. [$] *Rooms from: $310* ✉ *Lake Nakuru National Park* ☎ *020/375–0235 reservations* 🌐 *www.sopalodges.com* 🛏 *60 rooms* 🍴 *All meals.*

SAMBURU NATIONAL RESERVE

In the far northeast of the Laikipia Plateau, north of Mt. Kenya, is the remote Samburu National Reserve. Lying in the traditional homeland of the Samburu people in hot, arid, and relatively low country on the fringes of Kenya's vast northern deserts, this reserve is highly regarded by experienced travelers and old Africa hands alike. The drive from the foothills of Mt. Kenya into the semi-desert is awesome, and from the road that follows the Ewaso Nyiro River in the reserve, you'll be treated to the unusual spectacle of riverine bush and acacia and doum palm forest that provides a slash of greenery in the sandy plains. The Ewaso Nyiro flows north from Laikipia and is a life-giving resource to this parched region. There's game galore, and you're likely to see at least lion, cheetah, or leopard, or even all three—in addition to hippo, numerous antelope and elephant, and some dry-country species like gerenuk, Grevy's zebra, and reticulated giraffe. Look out for the particularly large Nile crocodiles in the river too. You might also see genuine traditional way of life such as the red-robed Samburu tribesmen bringing their cattle down to the river to drink. The lives of the Samburu, like the closely related Maasai, are centered round their livestock, their traditional source of wealth. Most visitors go to Samburu National Reserve itself as most of the lodges and camps are here on the north bank of the river. But Buffalo Springs National Reserve is on the south side of the river, and across the A2 highway is Shaba National Reserve—the 24-hour entrance ticket of US$70 to any one of these covers game drives in the others, too. Additionally there are private and community conservancies to the north and west of Samburu.

GETTING HERE AND AROUND

Samburu is often combined with visits to the Laikipia Plateau and/or Meru National Park as it's fairly easily accessed from the road that runs along the northern reaches of Mt. Kenya. The gates to Samburu (and Buffalo Springs and Shaba) are reached via the good tarred A2 road through Isiolo and Archer's Post, and it's approximately a five-hour drive from Nairobi. There are also daily scheduled flights to the reserve's airstrip.

WHERE TO STAY

$$ RESORT FAMILY **Samburu Intrepids.** Located in the western section of Samburu National Reserve, this mid-range and friendly tented camp offers a green oasis on the banks of the Ewaso Nyiro River. **Pros:** great for families with kids' activities; wonderful river views from all tents; newly refurbished to a high standard. **Cons:** the buffet meals can be a little mediocre; might not be intimate enough for some; activities and reserve fees cost extra. [$] *Rooms from: $334* ✉ *Samburu National Reserve* ☎ *020/444–7929 reservations* 🌐 *www.heritage-eastafrica.com* 🛏 *28 tents* 🍴 *All meals.*

$$$$ RESORT **Sarara Camp.** North of Samburu National Reserve, this small and remote tented camp lies below the peaks of the Mathews Mountains in the 850,000-acre Namunyak Wildlife Conservation Trust—a community conservancy that has been created between landowners and the local Samburu people. **Pros:** there's a wide range of activities available; staff are from the local community; wild and romantic and the only lodge in the conservancy. **Cons:** it's off the beaten track and is best reached by air; no power points in tents; Wi-Fi only in the lounge. [$] *Rooms from: $1800* ✉ *Namunyak Wildlife Conservation Trust* ☎ *216/433–025 satellite phone* 🌐 *www.sararacamp.com* ⏲ *Closed Apr., May, and mid-Oct.–mid-Dec.* 🛏 *6 tents* 🍴 *All-inclusive.*

$$$$ RESORT FAMILY Fodor's Choice ★ **Sasaab.** It's not just where Sasaab is located but how it's situated that makes it a wonderful place to stay in the Samburu region. **Pros:** sumptuous, spacious tents; guided walking safaris; beautifully designed common areas. **Cons:** some tents are far from the dining lodge; long, bumpy drive to and from local airstrip; about an hour's drive to Samburu National Reserve. [$] *Rooms from: $1900* ✉ *Westgate Community Conservancy* ☎ *0725/675–830 reservations* 🌐 *www.thesafaricollection.com* 🛏 *9 tents* 🍴 *All meals.*

GATEWAY CITIES

The starting point for safaris since the days of Teddy Roosevelt and Ernest Hemingway, Nairobi is still the first stop for many travelers heading to the wildlife parks of East Africa. With both Jomo Kenyatta International Airport and Wilson Airport, Kenya's capital city is the main hub for visitors, and it's very likely that you'll be spending at least an overnight here between flights.

NAIROBI

Nairobi's modern skyline often surprises first-time visitors, whose visions of the country are often shaped by stories of its colonial legacy or wildlife documentaries. With a population of around 3.5 million people, Nairobi is now one of the fastest developing cities in sub-Saharan Africa and is dominated by modern office, shopping, and residential towers. This isn't to say the city has lost all its charm though, and some early historical architecture survives here and there—the venerable Norfolk Hotel still recalls the elegant lifestyles of the city's early settlers, while the colonial farmhouse of *Out of Africa* author Karen Blixen (who wrote under the pen name Isak Dinesen) still sits at the foot of the Ngong Hills and is a reminder of Kenya's coffee heritage.

But Nairobi has had more than its share of urban problems. This city that grew too fast has paralyzing traffic jams, with many unsafe or overloaded vehicles on the road, and no hint of emissions control. Crime can be an issue and there are occasional incidents of muggings and carjackings. In addition, there's a growing disparity between rich and poor—private estates on the edge of Nairobi feature opulent mansions with stables, tennis courts, and swimming pools, while not far away you can glimpse vast mazes of tin shacks in slums, many with no electricity or running water.

But with booming economic growth and Nairobi being the preferred seat of many corporate institutions as well as the United Nations, Nairobi has done much to shake off its chaotic past in recent years. Neighborhoods have become more affluent, the middle class is expanding, crime is being reduced and infrastructure improves all the time—the sleek Nairobi Bypass was recently completed, for example, which has gone a long way to alleviate chronic traffic congestion. For the visitor, there's an interesting cross section of attractions, good shopping and restaurants, and many top-class hotels serving safari-bound tourists.

GETTING HERE AND AROUND

Nairobi National Park is to the south of the city, with Jomo Kenyatta International Airport (JKIA) and Wilson Airport on the park periphery. Karen and Langata, suburbs of Nairobi where there are hotels and sightseeing attractions, are southwest of the city center, while the Ngong Hills, on the edge the Great Rift Valley, are beyond them. The suburbs of Muthaiga, Gigiri, and Limuru are to the north of the city center.

International airlines and some domestic services fly into JKIA, Kenya's major airport, which is 16 km (10 miles) southeast of the city center. It has modern terminals with cafés, left luggage facilities, mobile phone stores, and ATM-equipped banks and Bureaux de Change. It usually takes about 40 minutes to drive from the airport to the city center by taxi (from US$25; always negotiate first), although it can take up to two hours in rush hour. Many hotels have comfortable shuttle services in a/c vehicles from about US$35 per person; be sure to organize this when you book your room.

Wilson Airport, 5.5 km (3.4 miles) southwest of the city center off Langata Road, is Nairobi's second airport. It's used for domestic, charter, and some regional flights. It has few facilities, but some of the airlines like Airkenya and Safarilink have lounges and cafés. A taxi into the city center from Wilson is about $15, and again, hotels can organize shuttle services. ■TIP→ When you book a local flight, make sure to note which airport it departs from.

You'll probably only be in Nairobi overnight or for a few hours, so you won't need to rent a car. Take a taxi to the attractions, but remember it's compulsory to buckle up, and *always* negotiate the price before setting out. Locals travel around on *matatus* (passenger minivans carrying up to 15 passengers), but the drivers are notoriously reckless and the vehicles not always roadworthy.

EMERGENCIES

Police in general are friendly and helpful to tourists. There are two private hospitals (avoid the government hospitals) with excellent staff and facilities, which have 24-hour pharmacies. There are plenty of pharmacies all over downtown Nairobi. Consult your concierge or host.

Emergency Contacts The Aga Khan University Hospital. ⊠ *3rd Parklands Ave., Parklands* ☎ *020/366–2000* ⊕ *www.agakhanhospitals.org/nairobi.* **Central Police Station.** ⊠ *University Way, Nairobi* ☎ *999 from a landline, 112 from a mobile* ⊕ *www.kenyapolice.go.ke.* **The Nairobi Hospital.** ⊠ *Argwings Kodhek Rd., Nairobi* ☎ *0703/082–000* ⊕ *www.thenairobihosp.org.*

DINING AND LODGING PRICES

WHAT IT COSTS IN U.S. DOLLARS			
$	**$$**	**$$$**	**$$$$**
Restaurants	under $12	$12–$20	$21–$30	over $30
Hotels	under $150	$150–$250	$251–$350	over $350

Restaurant prices are the average cost of a main course at dinner or, if dinner is not served, at lunch. Hotel prices are the lowest cost of a standard double room in high season.

EXPLORING

Nairobi is more than a gateway to your dream safari destination. It's a thriving city with restaurants, shopping malls, museums, and interesting wildlife attractions. If you only have a few hours in the morning, combine the David Sheldrick Wildlife Trust, where you can watch adorable baby elephants at the orphanage, and the Giraffe Centre, where you can hand feed Rothschild's giraffes from an elevated tower. If you have a bit more time, or days, check out the Big Five (minus elephants) on a game drive in the **Nairobi National Park.** It's just a 20-minute drive from downtown Nairobi (7 km/4 miles). You could also take in some history and culture at one of the museums, or go shopping for souvenirs in the many markets or curio stores—from carved wooden animals and batik art to Maasai beaded jewelry and leather sandals.

TOP ATTRACTIONS

FAMILY
Fodor's Choice
★

David Sheldrick Wildlife Trust. Take the morning excursion at 11 am, which you can book through your tour guide or hotel concierge, to this amazing elephant rescue center and orphanage on the edge of Nairobi National Park. It was set up by Dame Daphne Sheldrick after the death of her husband, David, who was famous for his anti-poaching activities in Tsavo East National Park. You'll be able to watch baby elephants at play or having a bath, knowing that one day when they're old enough they will be successfully reintroduced into the wild. It's an absolutely unmissable and heartwarming experience. Make a donation, however small, or go for gold and adopt your own baby elephant. ■ TIP➔ **The center is only open from 11 am–noon. If you miss the 11 am tour, you won't be able to visit until the following day.** ✉ *Nairobi National Park, entrance at maintenance gate off Magadi Rd., Nairobi* ✛ *16 km (10 miles) southwest of the city center* ☎ *020/230–1396* ⊕ *www.sheldrickwildlifetrust.org* ✉ *KSh500.*

FAMILY
Fodor's Choice
★

Giraffe Centre. Established by the African Fund for Endangered Wildlife (AFEW), this unique giraffe sanctuary is a wonderful excursion for children and adults alike. Located in Nairobi's western suburb of Langata, it has greatly contributed to boosting Kenya's population of rare Rothschild's giraffes—after being born and raised at this center, many have been relocated to the game parks and reserves. The original house of the founders is now the very impressive Giraffe Manor hotel. You can climb a giraffe-height tower for an eye-to-eye view and it's not unheard of for a giraffe to give a friendly and grateful lick as you feed

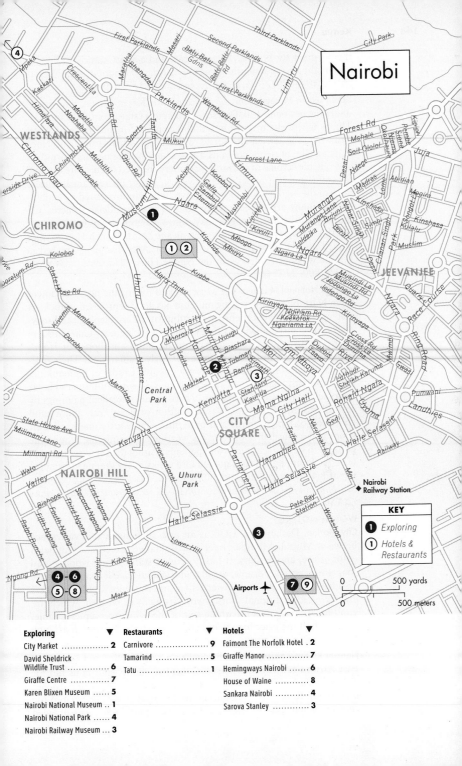

Nairobi

WESTLANDS

CHIROMO

JEEVANJEE

Central Park

University

CITY SQUARE

NAIROBI HILL

Uhuru Park

Nairobi Railway Station

Airports

KEY

① Exploring

① Hotels & Restaurants

500 yards

500 meters

them—great for photos. There's a café and a short nature trail where you might also spot warthogs. ⊠ *Duma Rd., off Koitobos Rd., Nairobi* ☎ *020/807–0804* ⊕ *www.giraffecenter.org* ⚑ *KSh1,000.*

Karen Blixen Museum. *Out of Africa* author Karen Blixen, who wrote under the pen name Isak Dinesen, lived at this estate from 1913 to 1931. This is where she threw a grand dinner party for the Prince of Wales and where she carried on a torrid relationship with aviator Denys Finch Hatton. The museum contains a few of her belongings and furniture, and outside is some of the farm machinery she used to cultivate the land for coffee and tea; guides will take you on a tour. There is a magnificent view of the Ngong Hills from her lawn, which is dominated by euphorbia, the many-armed plant widely known as the candelabra cactus. On the way to the museum you may notice a signpost reading "ndege." On this road, whose Swahili name means "bird," Finch Hatton once landed his plane for his visits with Blixen. After his plane crashed in Voi, he was buried nearby in the Ngong Hills. ⊠ *Karen Rd., Nairobi* ☎ *020/800–2139* ⊕ *www.museums.or.ke* ⚑ *KSh1,200.*

Nairobi National Museum. On Museum Hill just to the north of downtown Nairobi, this interesting museum has good reproduction rock art displays and excellent prehistory exhibits of the archaeological discoveries of Richard and Mary Leakey. When working near Lake Turkana in the 1960s, the Leakeys discovered the skull and bones of *Homo habilis,* believed to be the ancestor of early humankind. Their findings established the Rift Valley as the possible Cradle of Humankind, although both South Africa's Sterkfontein Caves and Ethiopia's Hadar region claim the same distinction. There are also excellent paintings by Joy Adamson, better known as the author of *Born Free,* and a good collection of Kenya's birds and butterflies. There are some good craft shops and a museum shop, and it's worthwhile wandering around the gardens to see the sculptures and perhaps visiting the small snake park. ■TIP→ **Nature Kenya runs guided bird walks every Wednesday morning at 8:45 from the museum (KSh200).** ⊠ *Museum Hill, off Chiromo St., Nairobi* ✛ *City Center* ☎ *020/816–4136* ⊕ *www.museums.or.ke* ⚑ *KSh1,200.*

WORTH NOTING

City Market. Designed in 1930 as an aircraft hangar, this vast space between Muindi Mbingu Street and Koinange Street is a jumble of color, noise, and activity. It has dozens of stalls selling wooden and soapstone carvings, drums, shields, and Maasai jewellery and there are also fruit, vegetable, and flower sellers and butchers. Look for *kikois* and *kangas,* traditional fabrics worn by Kenyan women, which are good for wearing over a bathing suit or throwing over a picnic table; they are half the price here than in the hotel shops. ⊠ *Muindi Mbingu St., City Center, Nairobi* ⚑ *Free.*

FAMILY **Nairobi Railway Museum.** Established to preserve relics and records of East African railways and harbors, this museum is enormous fun for rail enthusiasts and children of all ages. You can see the rhino catcher that Teddy Roosevelt rode during his 1908 safari and climb into the carriage where Charles Ryall, a British railroad builder, was dragged out a window by a hungry lion. There are great photos and posters, plus silver service from the more elegant days of the overnight train to Mombasa. You can clamber over the British-built locomotives in the old rail yard. ✉ *Station Rd., off Haile Sellasie Ave., Nairobi* ✥ *City Center* ☎ *020/204–9169* 🌐 *www.krc.co.ke* 🎫 *KSh600.*

WHERE TO EAT

$$$$ BARBECUE FAMILY 🍴 **Carnivore.** A firm fixture on the tourist trail, Carnivore became famous for serving wild game. Although this is no longer the case, you can still get crocodile and ostrich as well as beef, pork, and lamb. **Known for:** all-you-can eat meat; dawa cocktails; a Maasai barbecue pit. [$] *Average main: $45* ✉ *Carnivore Rd., off Langata Rd., Nairobi* ☎ *020/514–1300* 🌐 *www.tamarind.co.ke.*

4

$$$$ SEAFOOD 🍴 **Tamarind.** Hands-down the finest seafood restaurant in town, Tamarind is famous for its deep-fried crab claws, ginger crab, and *piri piri* (spicy, buttery prawns grilled over charcoal). Everything is flown up daily from the coast, including the Malindi sole and the Kilifi oysters, tiny but very flavorful and served either raw or as classic oysters Rockefeller. **Known for:** seafood; outside garden tables; refined atmosphere. [$] *Average main: $60* ✉ *Karen Rd., Nairobi* ☎ *0719/346–349* 🌐 *www.tamarind.co.ke* ☞ *Daily 5:30–10:30.*

$$$$ INTERNATIONAL 🍴 **Tatu.** The interior of Fairmont The Norfolk Hotel's fine-dining restaurant is minimalist and modern, with large black-and-white prints of tribespeople on the walls, an open-plan kitchen, leather tablecloths, and soft lighting in muted shades of orange, yellow, and green. The menu specializes in steaks, with some interesting sides, such as truffled Parmesan fries and mac-and-cheese. **Known for:** contemporary decor; historic venue; excellent service. [$] *Average main: $40* ✉ *Fairmont The Norfolk Hotel, Harry Thuku Rd., City Center, Nairobi* ☎ *020/226–5000* 🌐 *www.fairmont.com* ☞ *Daily 6 pm–10 pm.*

WHERE TO STAY

The two landmark lodgings in the capital, the Norfolk Hotel and the Sarova Stanley, have opened their doors to visitors for more than a century. Both have been renovated in recent years and now have everything from health clubs to business centers. However, newer luxury hotels, such as Sankara Nairobi, are giving them a run for their money and will appeal to those wanting a more contemporary experience.

$$ HOTEL 🏨 **Fairmont The Norfolk Hotel.** This grand old colonial lady will take you back to the heady early days when settlers, adventurers, colonial officers, and their ladies arrived in the capital to make their names and their fortunes. **Pros:** the breakfast buffet is the best in town; the terrace is a great place to watch the world go by; large heated swimming pool. **Cons:** lost a bit of its old-world charm in modern refurbishments; can be dominated by large conferences; very good but expensive restaurants. [$] *Rooms from: $248* ✉ *Harry Thuku Rd., Nairobi* ☎ *020/226–5000* 🌐 *www.fairmont.com* 🛏 *170 rooms* 🍽 *Breakfast.*

$$$$ HOTEL FAMILY 🏨 **Giraffe Manor.** Yes, giraffes really do pop their heads through the windows and bat their eyelashes at you at this stately old look-alike gabled Scottish hunting lodge. **Pros:** rates are full board and include most drinks; nonguests can book a table for lunch, subject to availability;

there's a vehicle available for local sightseeing tours. **Cons:** you need to book ahead as it's often fully booked; no pool; children need to be supervised in the garden because of the giraffes. [$] *Rooms from: $1190* ✉ *Gogo Falls Rd., Nairobi* ☎ *0725/675–830 reservations* 🌐 *www.thesafaricollection.com* 🛏 *12 rooms* 🍴 *All meals.*

$$$ HOTEL 🏨 **Hemingways Nairobi.** Named after writer Ernest Hemingway, this airy and elegant boutique hotel is in a peaceful location in Karen with views of the Ngong Hills. **Pros:** beautifully furnished with African artwork and contemporary touches; high level of service with butlers for every room; close to attractions in Karen. **Cons:** food and beverages are expensive; swimming pool is unheated; some rooms are a long walk from the main facilities. [$] *Rooms from: $325* ✉ *Mbagathi Ridge, Nairobi* ☎ *0711/032–204* 🌐 *www.hemingways-collection.com* 🛏 *45 rooms* 🍴 *Breakfast.*

$$$$ HOTEL 🏨 **House of Waine.** You'll find nostalgia, history, and romantic surroundings at this family-owned boutique hotel. **Pros:** you can choose to take your meal in your room, next to the pool, or in the dining room; the swimming pool is heated; the Karen Blixen Museum is just next door. **Cons:** the dining room feels too formal; the wooden floors can be noisy; some may feel it's overpriced. [$] *Rooms from: $640* ✉ *Masai La., off Bogani Rd., Nairobi* ☎ *020/260–1455* 🌐 *www.houseofwaine.com* ⏲ *Closed May* 🛏 *11 rooms* 🍴 *Breakfast.*

$$ HOTEL 🏨 **Sankara Nairobi.** This stylish city hotel is conveniently located in Westlands, close to a number of restaurants and shopping centers, although you will find all you need for a relaxing stay in the hotel itself. **Pros:** varied dining options; the hotel has been beautifully designed; great views of Nairobi's skyline from the rooftop. **Cons:** the pool is small; spa treatments are expensive; children are welcome but it's more business-orientated. [$] *Rooms from: $193* ✉ *5 Woodvale Grove, Westlands* ☎ *020/420–8000* 🌐 *www.sankara.com* 🛏 *156 rooms* 🍴 *No meals.*

$$ HOTEL 🏨 **Sarova Stanley.** Also one of Nairobi's oldest hotels, the Stanley was named after the journalist Henry Morton Stanley who immortalized himself by discovering a long-lost Scots explorer with one of the best sound-bites in history: "Dr. Livingstone, I presume?" **Pros:** security is good; the pool is heated; good choice of well-priced restaurants and bars. **Cons:** standard rooms are small; there's often heavy traffic around the hotel; service can be slow at busy times. [$] *Rooms from: $190* ✉ *Kenyatta Ave. at Kimati St., Nairobi* ☎ *0709/111–000* 🌐 *www.sarovahotels.com* 🛏 *217 rooms* 🍴 *No meals.*

4

BEACH ESCAPES

Intricately carved doorways studded with brass and white walls draped with bougainvillea distinguish the towns that dot Kenya's coastline. Arab traders who landed on these shores in the 9th century brought their own culture, creating a different style of dress and architecture from what you see in other parts of Kenya.

Men stroll the streets wearing traditional caps called *kofias* and billowing caftans known as *khanzus*, while women cover their faces with black veils called *bui-buis* that reveal only their eyes. The term "Swahili" comes from the Arabic words *sahil*, meaning "coast," and *i*, meaning "of the." The coastal communities of Lamu and Mombasa are strongholds of this language and culture that once dominated communities from Somalia to Mozambique.

Mombasa is the country's second-largest city and has a population of about two million. It's home to Kenya's only large seaport, and for centuries has been a hub of trade—from the early wooden dhows that crossed the Indian Ocean to the giant steel container ships that bring commodities to East Africa today. A hot, busy commercial city, Mombasa doesn't offer too much sightseeing, although the impressive Fort Jesus and atmospheric Old Town are on most visitors' itinerary.

The best-preserved Swahili town in Kenya, Lamu has streets hardly wide enough for a donkey cart. Winding alleyways are lined with houses set tight against one another. It's said that the beautifully carved doors found here are built first, then the house constructed around them.

The azure Indian Ocean waters from Lamu in the north to Wasini in the south are protected by the 240-km (150-mile) coral reef that runs parallel to the coast. The beautiful beaches are mostly white sand, are usually lined with shady coconut palms, and have calm and clear surf that hovers around 27°C (80°F).

GETTING HERE AND AROUND

Getting to the towns along the Kenya Coast is easier than ever. Mombasa has an international airport, but you can also fly directly to Lamu or the Ukunda airstrip at Diani Beach. Traveling by car around Mombasa is fairly safe and can be a good option if you want to stay at a few places along the coast.

ABOUT THE RESTAURANTS

The excellent cuisine reflects the region's rich history. Thanks to Italians, basil is everywhere, along with olive oil, garlic, and fresh lettuce. The Portuguese introduced tomatoes, corn, and cashews. Everything is combined with pungent spices such as coriander and ginger and the rich coconut milk often used as a cooking broth.

> ### THE BEACH BOYS
>
> Hawkers and hustlers known as "beach boys" prowl Kenya's coastline, although their numbers have reportedly dwindled. They sell everything from boat rides and souvenirs to drugs and sex, and their incessant pestering can ruin a beach walk (hotels employ guards to keep them off hotel grounds). A strategy may be to go on a boat trip or purchase something from one of them, and in theory, the rest should leave you alone. Otherwise, be firm and don't engage.

The Indian Ocean delivers some of the world's best fishing, so marlin, sailfish, red snapper, kingfish, and many other types of fish are on every menu. Not surprisingly, sashimi made from yellowtail tuna is favored by connoisseurs (and was listed on menus here as "fish tartare" before the rest of the world discovered Japanese cuisine). Prawns can be gargantuan, and wild oysters are small and sweet. You'll easily find boys who are happy to deliver fresh seafood to your door, and you can even place your order for the next day.

ABOUT THE HOTELS

Accommodations along the Kenya Coast range from sprawling resorts with several restaurants to small beach houses with kitchens where you can prepare your own meals. Most accommodations along the coast can arrange snorkeling, windsurfing, waterskiing, and deep-sea fishing.

For an alternative to a hotel stay, there's a large variety of cottages and houses for rent along the beach. Most come with a cook and housekeeper. You provide your own food—which is easy to do as there are nearby stores and supermarkets. Check out the following websites to start your search: ⊕ *www.kenyaholidayvillas.com*, ⊕ *www.dianibeach.com*, and ⊕ *www.lamu.org*.

WHAT IT COSTS IN U.S. DOLLARS				
	$	**$$**	**$$$**	**$$$$**
Dining	under $12	$12–$20	$21–$30	over $30
Hotels	under $150	$150–$250	$251–$350	over $350

Restaurant prices are the average cost of a main course at dinner or, if dinner is not served, at lunch. Hotel prices are the lowest cost of a standard double room in high season.

MOMBASA

You may well find yourself in Mombasa for a few hours or an overnight stop. The city (actually an island linked to the mainland by bridges and a ferry) is the second oldest trade center with Arabia and the Far East. Today it still plays an important role as the main port for Kenya. Although it lacks the beautiful beaches of the north and south, it has a rich, fascinating history. Visit the Old Town with its narrow streets lined with tiny shops and *souks* (markets). The Old Harbour, frequented by numerous dhows, is an ideal place to arrange a short cruise on one of these local boats that have plied the oceans for centuries. Fort Jesus, designed by an Italian and built by the Portuguese in the late 16th century, is a major visitor draw and well worth a visit. In summer there's an impressive sound-and-light show.

GETTING HERE AND AROUND

Between Kenya Airways, Fly540, and Jambojet, there are several daily flights between Nairobi and Mombasa, and from Mombasa you can fly to Lamu. The airport is located 10 km (6 miles) from the city center, on the mainland. Several taxi companies operate from the airport and have fixed rates to either the center of town or the beach resorts. You can also arrange for your hotel to pick you up. Taxis in Mombasa are inexpensive. The drivers are friendly and helpful and will wait or return to collect you if you ask.

Tired of flying? There's a daily train between Nairobi and Mombasa on a new line that was completed in 2017. The old overnight train on the original railway line built by the British in the late 19th century took 12–15 hours—the new service takes about 4½ hours. It departs both Nairobi and Mombasa at 9 am and arrives at 1:30 pm. To facilitate the new line, a new station has been built at Miritini on the mainland near the airport, 11 km (6.8 miles) from downtown Mombasa. In Nairobi a new station has been built at Syokimau, which is about 17 km (11 miles) southeast of the city center and is also near the airport. Fares are KSh700 in economy and KSh3,000 in first class. Tickets can only be booked up to four days before date of travel, either from the stations or through a local tour operator—ask your hotel to recommend one.

MONEY MATTERS

Most major banks have ATMs in Mombasa. If you want to change money, Forex Bureau has exchange shops on Digo Road near the Municipal Market and near the entrance of Fort Jesus.

SAFETY

The best way to see Mombasa is on foot, but you shouldn't walk around at night. If you take a taxi at night, make sure it delivers you all the way to the door of your destination. Purse snatchers are all too common. Beware of people who might approach you on Mombasa's Moi Avenue offering to become your guide. Tell them, "*Hapana, asante sana*" ("No, thank you"), and move on.

ESSENTIALS

Emergencies Mombasa Central Police Station. ☎ *041/225–501, 999 emergencies.*

Hospitals **The Aga Khan Hospital.** ✉ *Vanga Rd., Kizingo, Mombasa* ☏ *041/222–7710* ⊕ *www.agakhanhospitals.org/mombasa.*

Taxis **Kenatco Taxis Ltd.** ☏ *0720/108–222.*

Visitor Information **Kenya Coast.** ⊕ *www.kenya-coast.com.*

EXPLORING

To get a good insight into the daily life of downtown Mombasa, head to the narrow, cluttered streets of the Old Town north of Fort Jesus. Here ornately carved doors and balconies adorn the old buildings along the atmospheric alleys, and you can shop for souvenirs, antiques, fragrant oils and spices and stop for a glass of chai (tea) at one of the tiny cafés and watch the world go by. There are more than 20 historic mosques in the area, but keep your eyes peeled for the impressive Basheikh Mosque on Old Kilindini Road and the New Burhani Bohra Mosque off Ndia Kuu Road.

> **TIP**
>
> Safaris to Tsavo East and Tsavo West can be arranged from any of the beach resorts between Malindi in the north and Diani Beach in the south. Alternatively book ahead with a tour operator such as Diani Tours & Safaris ⊕ *www.dianisafaris-kenya.com*, Pollman's Tours & Safaris ⊕ *www.pollmans.com*, or Southern Cross Safaris ⊕ *www.southerncrosssafaris.com.*

In the northern part of the Old Town, Biashara (Swahili for "business") Street, which is just off Digo Road, you'll find all sorts of small shops that have been around for generations—selling everything from leather to textiles, live chickens, and food. While you're here, take a wander through the fruit, vegetable, and spice market, near where Biashara Street meets Digo Road. People are friendly and hospitable but, as in most poor backstreet areas, watch your belongings.

A.C.K. Mombasa Memorial Cathedral. Following Nkrumah Road from Fort Jesus will bring you to this impressive Anglican place of worship (A.C.K. stands for Anglican Church of Kenya). Built in 1903, the cathedral is a memorial to Archbishop James Hannington, a missionary who was executed in 1885. The influence of Middle Eastern Islamic architecture is clear in the frieze, the dome, and the tall, narrow windows. The paneling behind the high altar is reminiscent of the cathedral in Stone Town on Zanzibar. ✉ *Nkrumah Rd. at Cathedral Rd., Mombasa* ☏ *041/223–0502.*

Basheikh Mosque. Known locally as *Mskiti wa Mnara*, this was the first mosque in Mombasa with a minaret. Its purposeful square facade reflects the best in Islamic architecture, and the mosque dates back more than 800 years. It's really a place of worship rather than a tourist attraction. ✉ *Old Kilindini Rd. at Kibokoni Rd., Mombasa.*

Fort Jesus. Fort Jesus is a UNESCO World Heritage Site and one of Mombasa's top tourist attractions. This massive edifice was built in the late 16th century by the Portuguese, who were keen to control trade in the region. When the Omanis captured the fort at the end of the 17th century, they made some adjustments. The walls were raised to account for the improved trajectory of cannons mounted aboard attacking ships. By the end of the 18th century, turrets were erected. For water, the garrison relied on a pit cistern, which was used for bathing when the fort was a prison, between 1895 and 1958. The captain's house retains some traces of the Portuguese—note the outline of the old colonnade. The exhibits at the museum include an important display on ceramics of the coast and the remains of a Portuguese gunner, *San Antonio de Tanna*, which sank outside the fort at the end of the 17th century. Objects from the ship—shoes, glass bottles, a powder shovel, and cannon with its muzzle blown away—bring the period to life. There are also exhibits of finds from archaeological excavations at Gedi, Manda, Ungwana, and other sites. ⊠ *End of Nkrumah Rd., Mombasa* ☎ *041/222–0058* ⊕ *www.museums.or.ke* 🖃 *KSh1,200.*

New Burhani Bohra Mosque. The elaborate facade and soaring minaret of this mosque overlook the Old Harbor. Built in 1902, it's the third mosque to occupy this site. ⊠ *Off Ndia Kuu Rd., Mombasa.*

Tusks. A famous landmark in the city, the Tusks cross above Moi Avenue commemorating the 1952 visit of Britain's Princess Elizabeth, now Queen Elizabeth II. Designed to resemble pairs of intersecting elephant's tusks, and also forming the letter "M" for Mombasa, up close they can be somewhat disappointing as they are made of aluminum. But they do mark the entrance to the heart of town where visitors will find most of the banks, shops, and markets. ⊠ *Moi Ave. at Uhuru Gardens, Mombasa.*

WHERE TO EAT

$
INDIAN

✕ **Blue Room.** Serving the best samosas in Mombasa, this family-owned Indian restaurant has been in business for more than 50 years. It seats 140 people, making it one of the largest restaurants in the city and it's a good stop after a hot walk around the Old Town thanks to the whirring ceiling fans and clean restrooms. **Known for:** Indian snacks; delicious, homemade ice-cream; quick self-service. $ *Average main: $6* ⊠ *Haile Selassie Rd. at Digo Rd., Mombasa* ☎ *0721/786–868* ⊕ *www.blueroomonline.com.*

$$$$
SEAFOOD
Fodor's Choice
★

✕ **Tamarind.** What the Carnivore restaurant does for meat in Nairobi, this fine restaurant does for seafood in Mombasa. A 15-minute drive from downtown and a welcome house cocktail—a *dawa* made of lime, vodka, honey, and crushed ice—will introduce you to a memorable meal and unforgettable experience. **Known for:** seafood heaven; Swahili atmosphere; good service. $ *Average main: $60* ⊠ *Cement Silo Rd., Nyali* ☎ *041/447–4600* ⊕ *www.tamarind.co.ke.*

WHERE TO STAY

$
HOTEL

🏨 **Sentrim Castle Royal Hotel.** Originally built in 1919, this white old colonial building is in Mombasa's town center only a short distance away from the old town and Fort Jesus. **Pros:** the central location is unbeatable; rooms have fridges; only a 20-minute drive from the airport. **Cons:** some of the rooms are very noisy; hot water only available in the mornings and evenings; unless you want to stay in central Mombasa, there are better options on the beaches. $ *Rooms from: $90* ⊠ *Moi Ave.,*

Mombasa

KEY

- ① Exploring
- ① Hotels & Restaurants
- ⚓ Beaches

Exploring ▼

A.C.K. Mombasa
Memorial Cathedral **3**

Basheikh Mosque **5**

Fort Jesus **2**

New Burhani
Bohra Mosque **1**

Tusks **4**

Restaurants ▼

Blue Room **1**

Tamarind **3**

Hotels ▼

Sentrim Castle
Royal Hotel **2**

Serena Beach Hotel
and Spa **4**

Central Mombasa ☎ *041/222–8780* 🌐 *www.sentrimhotels.net* 🛏 *68 rooms* 🍴 *Breakfast.*

$$$ RESORT FAMILY 🏨 **Serena Beach Hotel and Spa.** This gorgeous resort at Shanzu Beach, about 30 km (19 miles) north of Mombasa, was built to resemble a 13th-century Arab town. **Pros:** high standard of service; the spa is excellent; family-friendly with babysitting, family rooms, and kids' menus. **Cons:** the resort has a serious monkey problem; rates hike over Christmas and New Year's; takes about an hour to drive to and from Mombasa. [$] *Rooms from: $285* ✉ *Shanzu Beach* ☎ *0732/125–000 hotel, 020/284–2333 reservations* 🌐 *www.serenahotels.com* 🛏 *164 rooms* 🍴 *Some meals.*

ARCHITECTURE

The region's architecture is characterized by arcaded balconies and red-tile roofs. One of the great concepts of coastal interiors is the *baraza*, an open sitting area with cushions perfect for parties or intimate conversations. Lamu furniture, with its deep brown color, provides a compelling contrast to the white walls. Local decorations can include fish traps made of palm rib or bamboo, and items made of old dhow wood.

DIANI BEACH

Kenya's coast south of Mombasa has some of the country's most beautiful beaches. From central Mombasa, access is via the Likoni Ferry, and beyond Likoni, the highway from Mombasa runs all the way to the Tanzania border, providing easy access to a string of resorts. Diani Beach is the most developed area along this stretch, but still fulfills most visitors' dreams of a turquoise ocean lapping broad sun-bleached sand backed by palm trees.

GETTING HERE AND AROUND

Many people fly into Mombasa's Moi International Airport and make their way down the south coast by taxi, rental car, or hotel shuttle. You must take the 24-hour Likoni Ferry to travel south of Mombasa. Two ferries run simultaneously, departing about 15 minutes apart, with fewer departures between 1 am and 4 am. The crossing takes about 10 minutes. Vehicles are charged by length, usually about KSh150 per car. Pedestrians ride free. To avoid the ferry crossing (and expensive taxi fares from Mombasa), a number of airlines are increasingly flying to the Ukunda airstrip at Diani Beach. Airkenya, Jambojet, and Safarilink offer services to Ukunda from Nairobi, while Mombasa Air Safari connects Ukunda with Amboseli, Tsavo West, and the Masai Mara.

SAFETY

If you take a taxi at night, make sure it delivers you all the way to your destination. Tourist Police officers patrol beaches, but don't tempt fate by bringing jewelry, cameras, or cash. Women shouldn't walk alone on the beach.

Drink plenty of bottled water and wear sunscreen. It's a good idea to wear a thick T-shirt to protect your back from sunburn when snorkeling.

EXPLORING

Kaya Kinondo Forest. If you're in the Diani Beach area, be sure to spend an hour or two exploring the Kaya Kinondo Forest. This UNESCO World Heritage Site has been sacred territory for the Digo people for centuries. You'll need to walk with a guide, who will tell you about the beliefs and ceremonies held here, as well as the medicinal and culinary uses of the plants growing in the forest which, although only 75 acres, is said to boast 187 species of trees. You'll also see black-and-white colobus and Sykes monkeys, as well as baboons. A walk here is highly recommended. If you have time, ask your guide to show you around the local Digo village, or even to introduce you to the spiritual healer. ✉ *Diani Beach* ✛ *4 km (2½ miles) south from the end of the tarmac at Diani Beach* ☎ *0722/446–916* ⊕ *www.kaya-kinondo-kenya.com* 🎫 *KSh1,000.*

Kisite Mpunguti Marine National Park and Wasini Island. Located on the south coast off Shimoni, and south of Wasini Island, this marine reserve is known for its beautiful coral gardens. More than 250 species of fish can be spotted feeding around the reef including barracuda, groupers, emperors, angelfish, parrotfish, lionfish, moray eels, and stingrays. Green and hawksbill turtles and humpback, bottlenose and spinner dolphins are a common sight. The shallow water can be easily reached by boat arranged from the jetty at Shimoni. However the easiest way to visit is on the popular Wasini Island day trip that can be organized at any of the south coast resorts—from US$135 including park fees. The day typically includes a transfer to Shimoni where you board a dhow to explore Kisite Mpunguti and go snorkeling. This is followed by a seafood lunch at one of the restaurants on the tiny Wasini Island with time to explore before the return dhow trip. Near Wasini village you'll find the ruins of 18th- and 19th-century houses and a Muslim pillar tomb inset with Chinese porcelain. ✉ *Shimoni* ✛ *40 km (25 miles) from Ukunda* ☎ *0722/674–183* ⊕ *www.kisite-mpungutimarinepark. info* 🎫 *$25.*

BEACHES

FAMILY

Fodor's Choice

★

Diani Beach. This 20-km (12-mile) stretch of picture-postcard-perfect white sand backed by coconut palms is 30 km (19 miles) south of Mombasa. It is the most developed part of the southern coast and where most holidaymakers head. Apart from the gorgeous location and climate, one reason that it's so popular is that the coral reef filters out the seaweed, so the beach is truly pristine, and it protects the swimming areas from offshore swells. There are numerous resorts, but fortunately most have been built sensitively in traditional style with low buildings and thatched roofs and are hidden in clumps of coastal forest. Much of this forest is home to vervet monkeys, troops of baboons, and endangered Angolan black-and-white colobus monkeys, as well as butterflies and birds. Diani Beach Road runs behind the beach and is dotted with good restaurants and shops, and if you stay in one of the private cottages, local fishermen will take your order and deliver lobsters and other delicacies of the deep to your door. All along Diani is a busy lineup of water sports on offer, such as windsurfing, parasailing, snorkeling, and scuba diving for some fun in the sun, or you could simply kick back with your feet in the sand at one of the beach bars. **Best for:** snorkeling, sunrise, walking, windsurfing. **Amenities:** food and drink, water sports. ✉ *Mombasa* ⊕ *www.dianibeach.com.*

WHERE TO EAT

$$$$
SEAFOOD
Fodor's Choice
★

✕**Ali Barbour's Cave Restaurant.** Considered the best restaurant at Diani Beach, this unique venue is in a naturally formed coral cave deep underground lit by candles and lanterns. It's definitely worth the splurge for the experience and ambience. **Known for:** unusual and romantic setting; superb food and service. $ *Average main: $50* ✉ *Ali Barbour's Rd., off Diani Beach Rd., Diani Beach* ☎ *0714/456–131* ⊕ *www.alibarbours. co* ⊗ *No lunch.*

$$
MODERN
EUROPEAN

✕**Forty Thieves Beach Bar.** This Diani institution is under the same ownership as Ali Barbour's but it's a much more casual affair with tables in the sand and a long wooden bar. Go for a leisurely breakfast or lunch followed by a swim, or dinner with live music and dancing on the floodlit beach. **Known for:** sand underfoot; lively and friendly vibe; late-night dining. $ *Average main: $15* ✉ *Forty Thieves Access Rd., off Diani Beach Rd., Diani Beach* ☎ *0712/294–873* ⊕ *www.fortythieves-beachbar.com.*

$$$
MODERN
EUROPEAN

✕**Nomad Beach Bar & Restaurant.** The perfect place to spend a few relaxing hours on a low-slung cushioned sofa with a tropical cocktail, Nomad's is a luxurious beach bar that overlooks the white sands of Diani. Open all day from breakfast right through to dinner, the menu features the usual popular snacks, sandwiches, pizzas, and pastas, but also has some dishes based on traditional Swahili cooking, plenty of seafood, and even Indian curries and Japanese sushi—there's something for everyone. **Known for:** Sunday lunch buffet; Japanese food; great ocean views. $ *Average main: $25* ✉ *The Sands at Nomad, Diani Beach Rd., Diani Beach* ☎ *0738/333–888* ⊕ *www.nomadbeachbar.com.*

WHERE TO STAY

Most of the hotels and resorts are on one or two roads running parallel to the beach. Often the properties aren't numbered, so landmarks are used to guide people instead. Everyone knows where all the places are, so you don't need to instruct a taxi driver with specific details.

$$$$
RESORT

⌂**AfroChic Diani Beach by Elewana.** This comfortable small villa-style boutique hotel, located to the north of the Ukunda junction on Diani Beach, is close to boutiques, craft markets, and restaurants, but still retains a quiet private beach frontage. **Pros:** smaller and quieter than the larger resorts; excellent food including Swahili specialities; easy access to the Ukunda airstrip. **Cons:** need to go off-site for activities like diving; not many facilities for children; drinks are not included, but are reasonably priced. $ *Rooms from: $568* ✉ *Golden Beach Rd., off Diani Beach Rd., Diani Beach* ☎ *0730/127–000 reservations* ⊕ *www.elewanacollection.com* ⇱ *9 rooms* ⦿| *All meals.*

$$$$
RESORT

⌂**Alfajiri Villas.** Built of stone and thatch, these luxurious double-story villas are elegantly furnished with the wit and style you would expect of owner and host Marika Molinaro, one of Kenya's top interior designers. **Pros:** daily menus are tailored to your preferences; villas have private pools; ideal for large families. **Cons:** the beach next to the hotel is not

4

great for swimming; you may find you don't use all the included activities, such as golf, gym, and yoga; even if there are only two of you, you need to book the entire villa. $ *Rooms from: $1600* ✉ *Diani Beach Rd., Diani Beach* ☎ *0733/630–491, 0722/727–876* ⊕ *www.alfajirivillas.com* ⌑ *3 villas* ⦿ *All meals.*

$$
RESORT
FAMILY

⊡ **Diani Reef Beach Resort & Spa.** This mid-range resort will make sure you get the best out of your beach break. **Pros:** the staff are extremely friendly; organized activities are excellent; good value family option. **Cons:** the buffet food is a little bland, but there are other restaurants; resident monkeys can be annoying; room decor is a little dated. $ *Rooms from: $215* ✉ *Diani Beach Rd., Diani Beach* ☎ *0709/481–000* ⊕ *www. dianireef.com* ⌑ *143 rooms* ⦿ *Some meals.*

$$$$
RESORT

⊡ **Kinondo Kwetu.** Owned by a Swedish family, the delightful Kinondo Kwetu was built in an idyllic location in a section of sacred forest on Galu Beach. **Pros:** dinner is served in a variety of romantically secluded locations; there's a good choice of activities; very professional and welcoming staff. **Cons:** the beach is only swimmable at high tide; no children under five; Wi-Fi only in reception. $ *Rooms from: $950* ✉ *Diani Beach Rd., Galu Beach, Kinondo* ☎ *0710/089–030* ⊕ *www. kinondo-kwetu.com* ⊘ *Closed May–June* ⌑ *11 rooms* ⦿ *All-inclusive.*

$$$$
RESORT
Fodor's Choice
★

⊡ **The Maji Beach Boutique Hotel.** One of the finest boutique resorts in Kenya, Maji means "water" in Swahili and the first thing you'll notice on arrival is the "lazy river" swimming pool that winds its way through the property, wrapping itself through palm trees and lounge areas, all in view of the beach. **Pros:** stunning design and architecture; easy access to Ukunda airstrip; superb gourmet food and impeccable service. **Cons:** beach boys can be a nuisance; monkeys can try to get into rooms; no children under 12. $ *Rooms from: $662* ✉ *Diani Beach Rd., Diani Beach* ☎ *0773/178–873* ⊕ *www.the-maji.com* ⌑ *15 rooms* ⦿ *All meals.*

$$$
RESORT
FAMILY

⊡ **The Sands at Chale Island.** Right at the southern end of Diani Beach Road, you'll find the access point to the only island resort in Kenya—Chale lies 600 meters off the mainland and is reached by boat at high tide, and quite delightfully by tractor at low tide. **Pros:** unique island location and fun to get to; stunning beach protected by a coral reef; daily program of water sports and other activities. **Cons:** the buffet food can be a little uninspiring; it's a long drive from both Ukunda and Mombasa; the rooms are simply furnished but comfortable. $ *Rooms from: $282* ✉ *Diani Beach Rd., Diani Beach* ☎ *0725/546–879* ⊕ *www. thesandsatchaleisland.com* ⌑ *45 rooms* ⦿ *Some meals.*

LAMU

Designated a UNESCO World Heritage Site in 2001, Lamu Old Town is the oldest and best-preserved Swahili settlement in East Africa. Some 260 km (162 miles) north of Mombasa—and just two degrees below the equator—Lamu is separated from the mainland by a narrow channel that's fringed with thick mangroves protected from the sea by coral reefs and huge sand dunes. Winding narrow alleyways lead past the ornate carved doorways and coral walls of magnificent merchant houses to the bustling waterfront. Life goes on much as it did when Lamu

Kenya's beautiful beaches are a great place to relax after a safari.

was a thriving port town in the 8th century; there are no cars (all transport and heavy lifting is by donkey), and more than 1,000 years of East African, Omani, Yemeni, Indian, and Portuguese influences have resulted in a unique mix of cultures, reflected in the faces of its inhabitants as well as in its architecture and cuisine. A stronghold of Islam for many centuries, you'll see men in *kofias* (traditional caps that Muslims wear) and *khanzus* (white caftanlike robes) and women in *bui-buis* (black veils). Some merchant houses have been converted into gorgeous boutique hotels, and rooftop restaurants offer abundant, fresh seafood for very little.

The island is roughly divided into two parts: Lamu Town, in the south, and Shela, a smaller, quieter village in the north and next to the beach. Some visitors split their holiday between staying on both sides of the island, or you could opt to stay on Manda Island or in farther flung hotels on the far northern or southern edges. You can walk between Lamu Town and Shela in about 45 minutes; a popular option is to walk one way and take a boat back. The beach offers 13 km (8 miles) of unspoiled coastline.

It's very easy to relax into the *pole-pole* ("slowly" in Swahili) pace of life in Lamu, spending hours on the beach or on your hotel terrace reading a book and sipping a delicious fresh fruit juice. There's also plenty for the energetic to do here—windsurfing, kayaking, fishing, and snorkeling. You can also take a dhow cruise to visit ruins on Pate and Manda islands.

Tourism hasn't made much of an impact on Lamu, and that's what makes it so special.

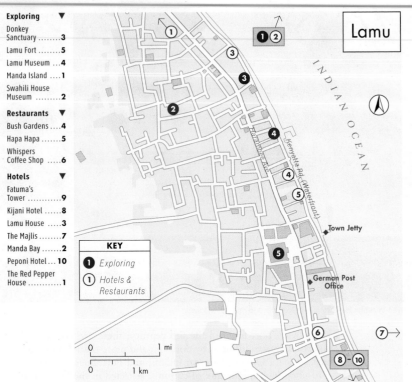

GETTING HERE AND AROUND

There are plenty of flights from Nairobi, some of which run in circuits to Malindi, too. Fly540 and Jammbojet fly from Jomo Kenyatta
International Airport, while Airkenya and Safarilink fly from Wilson
Airport. Flights land on Manda Island, and a speedboat takes about
10 minutes to get to Lamu (boat taxis meet the flights or your hotel
will pick you up). Getting to Lamu by road north from Malindi is not
recommended as there are only simple local buses and there have been
incidents of robbery on these.

Lamu is an easy town to get around because it's so small. The cobbled
streets are laid out in a grid fashion with the main street—Harambee
Ave—running parallel to the waterfront. Most hotels can arrange for a
trip by dhow between Lamu and Shela. Find out the going price from
your accommodation and confirm with the captain before setting out.

FESTIVALS AND SEASONAL EVENTS

The Maulidi festival, marking the birth of Muhammad, has been celebrated on Lamu for more than a century. Dhow races, poetry read-
ings, and other events take place around the town's main mosques.
Maulidi, which takes place in the spring, attracts pilgrims from all
over Kenya. The three-day Lamu Cultural Festival takes place each
November and offers a unique insight into island life. The event

showcases traditional dance, handicraft displays, and music and theater performances from both local and visiting artists.

EXPLORING

Ask at your lodging for a local guide. Agree on a price before you head out, and then let him introduce you to the history of this remarkable little town on a leisurely walking tour.

TOP ATTRACTIONS

Lamu Fort. This imposing edifice, which was completed in 1821, is set one street away from the seafront. It was used as a prison from 1910 to 1984, when it became part of the country's museum system. Today, it is a central part of the town as it hosts conferences, exhibitions, and theater productions. If you have a few moments, climb up to the battlements for some great views of Lamu, and pop into the vegetable and meat markets, which are just to the left of the fort. If you see a man pressing sugarcane, limes, and ginger to make juice, buy a glass—it's delicious. The entrance fee is a package and includes entry to Takwa, Pate, and Siyu Ruins, as well as Lamu Museum, Swahili House and the German Post Office. The latter was established in 1888 by the Germans and is now also a small museum on local history and is just across the street from the fort. ✉ *Harambee Ave., Lamu* ☎ *042/633–073* ⊕ *www. museums.or.ke* ✆ *KSh500.*

Lamu Museum. You enter this delightful museum through a brass-studded door that was imported from Zanzibar. Inside there are archaeological displays showing the Takwa Ruins excavations, some wonderful photos of Lamu taken by a French photographer from 1846 to 1849 (you'll be amazed at how little has changed in Lamu), some intricately carved Lamu headboards and throne chairs, and a library. In the Balcony Room upstairs is a fascinating display of musical instruments including the famed Siwa Horn, which is made of brass and resembles elephant tusks; the Pate Siwa horn, made of ivory, is now in the Nairobi National Museum. Dating from the 17th century, they're reputed to be the oldest surviving musical instruments in sub-Saharan Africa. ✉ *Waterfront, Lamu* ☎ *042/633–402* ⊕ *www.museums.or.ke* ✆ *KSh500.*

Manda Island. Just across the channel from Shela, the mostly uninhabited Manda Island once held one of the area's largest cities. The once-thriving community of Takwa was abandoned in the 17th century, and archaeologists have yet to discover why. The ruins can be explored and the Friday Mosque with a large pillar on top is among the most notable features. Reached by taking a dhow up a baobab tree-lined creek, this is a popular day trip from Lamu and Shela, perhaps with a picnic. ✉ *Lamu* ✈ *30 mins by boat from Lamu* ⊕ *www.museums.or.ke* ✆ *KSh500.*

Swahili House Museum. This beautifully restored 18th-century Swahili merchant's house has original period furniture. Notice the traditional beds with woven bases of rope, and the finely carved Kalinda screen in the main room. There's a garden full of flowering tropical shrubs and trees and the original well. ✉ *Off Harambee Ave., Lamu* ☎ *20/816–4134* ⊕ *www.museums.or.ke* ✆ *KSh500.*

4

WORTH NOTING

Donkey Sanctuary. Donkeys are the main transport in Lamu. The sanctuary was started in 1987 by Elisabeth Svendsen, a British doctor who founded The Donkey Sanctuary in the UK. Its main function is to protect and look after the working donkeys, and it's managed by the Kenyan branch of the charity. There's a treatment clinic where locals can get their donkeys wormed, a training center, and a resting place for a few of the old animals that can no longer work. The staff will show you around in the mornings, otherwise you can eyeball a few donkeys over the low wall in front of the yard. An annual prize is given to the Lamu donkey in the best physical condition. ✉ *Waterfront, Mkomani Location* 🌐 *www.thedonkeysanctuary.org.uk* 🎫 *Donations accepted.*

WHERE TO EAT

Most of the restaurants and hotels in Lamu town are along the waterfront or the road parallel to it, called Harambee Avenue.

$ SEAFOOD 🍴 **Bush Gardens.** Service isn't the fastest in the world at this lively waterfront eatery with colorful chairs and tables in primary colors, but it's worth waiting for the delicious seafood and fresh fish—definitely try the tuna, barracuda, or snapper. Entrées are served with coconut rice or french fries. **Known for:** Swahili-style seafood; filling breakfasts. [$] *Average main: $7* ✉ *Waterfront, south of the main jetty, Lamu* ☎ *0714/934–804* 💳 *No credit cards.*

$ SEAFOOD 🍴 **Hapa Hapa.** With a name that is Swahili for "Here, Here," Hapa Hapa is known for its outstanding seafood. Make sure to try the grilled barracuda with steamed coconut rice; sometimes there's lobster and crab. **Known for:** friendly service; views along the waterfront. [$] *Average main: $10* ✉ *Waterfront, south of the main jetty, Lamu* ☎ *0712/526–215* 💳 *No credit cards.*

$ CAFÉ 🍴 **Whispers Coffee Shop.** Located in the same building as the Baraka Gallery (which has a wonderful collection of African art, jewelry, and souvenirs for sale), this upscale café has a pretty, palm-fringed quiet courtyard where you can relax over a cappuccino. There's also a lunch and dinner menu, focusing on salads, pastas, and deli items, or you can order a packed lunch to take away. **Known for:** courtyard setting; excellent art gallery and shop. [$] *Average main: $8* ✉ *Harambee Ave., Lamu* ☎ *042/463–2024* 💳 *No credit cards* 🕒 *Closed May and June.*

WHERE TO STAY

$ HOTEL 🏨 **Fatuma's Tower.** Set against the dunes in little Shela village, Fatuma's Tower is a beautiful, cool, calm escape from the narrow alleys of the village. **Pros:** there's a cook who can do your food shopping and preparation of all meals; it's extremely peaceful and there's total serenity beyond the sound of motorboat engines; refreshing plunge pool in the garden. **Cons:** mosquitoes can occasionally be a nuisance; it's about a 10-minute walk through Shela to the beach; no air-conditioning but there are fans. [$] *Rooms from: $125* ✉ *Shela* ☎ *0722/277–138* 🛏 *10 rooms* 🍽 *Some meals.*

$$ HOTEL 🏨 **Kijani Hotel.** Located right on the waterfront in Shela, Kijani Hotel offers rooms in three converted Arab merchant houses grouped around a pretty central garden with swimming pool. **Pros:** rooms look out

onto the waterfront; the hotel is five minutes' walk from the beach; one of the few places that has a bar. **Cons:** can get hot at night; must preorder lunch and dinner; need to be appropriately dressed in Shela village on the way to and from the beach. $ *Rooms from: $188* ⊠ *Shela* ☎ *0733/545–264* ⊕ *www.kijani-lamu.com* ⊙ *Closed May and June* ⇗ *11 rooms* ⊙| *Breakfast.*

$ ⊞ **Lamu House.** The rooms in this boutique hotel, located next to the HOTEL Donkey Sanctuary on Lamu's waterfront, are all different, but each Fodor'sChoice one is superbly decorated in traditional Swahili style and has a separate ★ dressing room and a terrace looking out either onto the water or the town. **Pros:** each room has a fridge; there are free boats to shuttle you to Shela Beach; breakfast is available all day. **Cons:** it can be noisy as it's in the center of town; some staircases are narrow and steep; rooms downstairs are a little dark. $ *Rooms from: $145* ⊠ *Waterfront, Lamu* ☎ *0792/469–577* ⊕ *www.lamuhouse.com* ⇗ *10 rooms* ⊙| *Breakfast.*

$$$ ⊞ **The Majlis.** The rooms in this spectacular hotel are in three villas, and RESORT as each has a sitting room with white couches, antique Swahili furni- FAMILY ture, and African paintings and sculptures, you'll feel as though you're staying in an ultrastylish private beach house. **Pros:** unforgettable dhow sunset cruises; an excellent beach; rooms have air-conditioning. **Cons:** trips to Lamu aren't included; alcohol isn't included in the full-board option; not all rooms face the ocean. $ *Rooms from: $333* ⊠ *Manda Island, Lamu* ☎ *020/712–3301, 020/712–3300 reservations* ⊕ *www. themajlisresorts.com* ⇗ *25 rooms* ⊙| *All meals.*

$$$$ ⊞ **Manda Bay.** At high tide, you can dive right off your veranda into the RESORT ocean; at low tide, a lovely strand of beach appears in front of your room. **Pros:** truly a private island getaway; boutique-hotel amenities with laid-back feel; fantastic for both honeymooners and families. **Cons:** music from the bar can be heard in cottages near the main area; water in the showers is a little salty; Wi-Fi limited in the rooms. $ *Rooms from: $396* ⊠ *Manda Island, Lamu* ☎ *0712/579–999 reservations* ⊕ *www. mandabay.com* ⇗ *16 cottages* ⊙| *All meals.*

$$$ ⊞ **Peponi Hotel.** Peponi's is well-known for its beachfront location in HOTEL Shela, lovely accommodations, and superb food. **Pros:** only hotel guests get seating on the outside balcony at dinner; you can sleep with the sea-facing windows and doors open (guards are on duty all night); free boats to Lamu town. **Cons:** drinks are not included in the full-board option; the beach disappears at high tide; beach boys can be a nuisance. $ *Rooms from: $270* ⊠ *Waterfront, Shela* ☎ *0722/203–082* ⊕ *www. peponi-lamu.com* ⊙ *Closed May and June* ⇗ *28 rooms* ⊙| *Breakfast.*

$$$$ ⊞ **The Red Pepper House.** Guests here are practically doted on from the RESORT moment they cross the threshold of this architecturally stunning beach- Fodor'sChoice front property. **Pros:** flexible scheduling of meals and activities; impec- ★ cable personalized service; extensive outdoor and indoor space in each room. **Cons:** gift shop is small; no children under five; there are nicer beaches in the area, but the staff is willing to take you to the best spots at any time. $ *Rooms from: $360* ⊠ *Coconut Beach* ☎ *0721/230–521,* ⊕ *www.theredpepperhouse.com* ⇗ *9 rooms* ⊙| *All meals.*

4

TANZANIA

WELCOME TO TANZANIA

TOP REASONS TO GO

★ **The Great Migration:** This annual movement is one of the great natural wonders of the world.

★ **Big Game Adventures:** You'll be amazed at how close up and familiar you get not only with the Big Five, but with thousands of other animals as well.

★ **Sea, Sand, and Sun:** Tanzania's sun-spoiled but deserted beaches are lapped by the turquoise blue waters of the Indian Ocean. Swim, snorkel, scuba dive, sail, fish, or just chill on soft white sands under waving palm trees.

★ **Ancient Cultures:** From the traditional red-robed, bead-bedecked nomadic Maasai in the north to the exotic heady mix of Arab and African influences in Zanzibar, Pemba, and Mafia, you'll encounter unique peoples and cultures just about everywhere you go.

★ **Bird-Watching:** Stay glued to your binoculars in one of the finest bird-watching destinations in the world. You'll be able to watch hundreds of species in a variety of habitats.

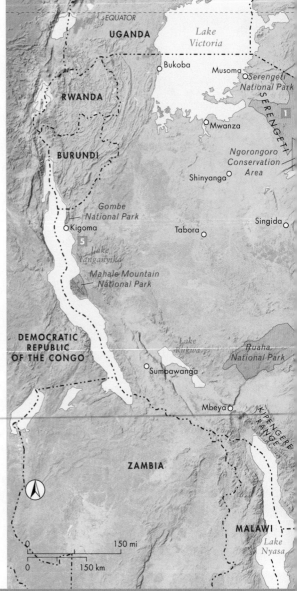

Tanzania is about twice the size of the state of California and is bordered by the Indian Ocean in the east, Kenya to the north, and Mozambique to the south. The country is home to some of the most coveted tourist destinations in the world.

1 **Serengeti National Park.** Endless plains of golden grass, teeming herds of game, stalking predators—you won't be disappointed.

2 **Ngorongoro Conservation Area.** The floor of the Ngorongoro Crater is home to the biggest concentration of predators on earth.

3 **Lake Manyara National Park.** This park is home to lions, baboons, giraffes, hippos, birds, ancient forest, lakeside plains, and towering cliffs.

4 **Selous Game Reserve.** Escape the crowds in the world's second-largest conservation area where you can view game on foot, by boat, or from your vehicle.

5 **Gombe Stream and Mahale Mountains National Parks.** Follow in the footsteps of world-famous primatologist Jane Goodall and come face-to-face with wild chimpanzees.

Updated
by Linda
Markovina

Tanzania is the quintessential, definitive Africa of your dreams. And who wouldn't want to visit a place where the names of its legendary travel destinations roll off the tongue like an incantation: Zanzibar, Serengeti, Mt. Kilimanjaro, Lake Tanganyika, Lake Victoria, the Rift Valley, the Ngorongoro Crater, and Olduvai Gorge, known as "the Cradle of Humankind."

Great plains abound with legions of game, snowcapped mountains soar above dusty valleys, rain forests teem with monkeys and birds, beaches are covered in sand as soft and white as talcum powder, and coral reefs host myriads of jewel-like tropical fish. Although Tanzania's economy—one of the poorest in the world—depends heavily on agriculture, which accounts for almost half of its GDP, it has more land (more than 25%) devoted to national parks and game reserves than any other wildlife destination in the world. Everything from pristine coral reefs to the Crater highlands, remote game reserves, and the famous national parks are protected by government law and placed in trust for future generations.

There are two circuits you can follow in Tanzania: the conventional northern tourist circuit, which includes the Serengeti and Ngorongoro Crater, or the lesser traveled southern tourist circuit of Selous Game Reserve and Ruaha, Mahale, and Gombe national parks among others. You'll be amply rewarded for the often lengthy traveling to these southern locations by having the places much more to yourself.

Serengeti *is* all it's cracked up to be with endless plains of golden grass (Serengeti means "endless plain" in the Maasai language), teeming game, abundant bird-life, and an awe-inspiring sense of space and timelessness. Ngorongoro Crater justly deserves its reputation as one of the natural wonders of the world. The ride down onto the crater floor is memorable enough as you pass through misty primeval forest with wild orchids, swinging vines, and chattering monkeys, but once on the floor you could well be in the middle of a *National Geographic* special. You can follow in the footsteps of legendary hunters and explorers when you visit Selous

FAST FACTS

Size 945,203 square km (364,898 square miles).

Capital Dar es Salaam, though legislative offices have been transferred to Dodoma, which is planned as the new national capital.

Number of National Parks 15, including the Serengeti, Tarangire, Lake Manyara, Gombe Stream, Ruaha, Selous, Katavi, and Mt. Kilimanjaro.

Number of Private Reserves Too many to count, but includes the Singita Grumeti Reserves.

Population Approximately 57 million.

Big Five All the Big Five, including black and white rhinos.

Language Official languages are Kiswahili and English.

Time Tanzania is on EAT (East Africa Time), which is three hours ahead of Greenwich mean time and eight hours ahead of Eastern Standard Time.

5

Game Reserve in the south. Although it's the second-largest conservation area in the world after Greenland National Park, only 5% of the northern part is open to tourists; but don't worry, you'll see all the game and birds you could wish for with the advantage of seeing it by boat and on foot. If it's chimpanzees you're after, then Gombe Stream and Mahale Mountains national parks are the places to head for. A lot of traveling (much of it by boat) is required, but the experience is well worth the effort, and you'll join only a small community of other privileged visitors who have had the unique experience of coming face-to-face with wild chimpanzees.

The animals aren't the only wonders Tanzania has to offer. There are the islands of Zanzibar, Pemba, and Mafia, as well as Mt. Kilimanjaro, Mt. Meru, and the three great lakes of Victoria, Tanganyika, and Malawi. Wherever you go, you're guaranteed travel experiences that you'll remember for the rest of your life.

PLANNING

WHEN TO GO

There are two rainy seasons: the short rains (*mvuli*) October through December and the long rains (*masika*) from late February to early May. Given the influence of global warming, these rains aren't as regular or as intense as they once were. It's best to avoid the two rainy seasons because many roads become impassable. Ngorongoro Crater is open all year, but the roads become extremely muddy and difficult to navigate during the wet seasons. High season is January through the end of September, but prices are much higher during this time. Make sure you find out in advance when the lodge or destination of your choice is closed as many are open only during the dry season. The coast is always pretty hot and humid, particularly during the rains, but is cooler and more pleasant the rest of the year. The hottest time is December just before the long rains. In high-altitude areas such as Ngorongoro Highlands and Mt. Kilimanjaro, temperatures can fall below freezing.

GETTING HERE AND AROUND
AIR TRAVEL

Most travelers arrive in Tanzania through Dar es Salaam airport. Many airlines fly directly to Dar es Salaam from Europe and the continent of Africa, but there are no direct flights from the United States.

KLM offers a daily flight to Dar es Salaam from Amsterdam's Schiphol airport as well as Emirates daily flights from Dubai. Other airlines that fly here frequently are Air Tanzania, Emirates, Ethiopian Airlines, Kenya Airways, Fast Jet, South African Airways, and Swiss Air. Turkish Airlines flies from Istanbul to Dar es Salaam and Kilimanjaro. Oman Air flies to Dar es Salaam via Muscat and then on to Zanzibar. Qatar Airways flies to Dar es Salaam and Zanzibar via Doha. British Airways flies to Dar es Salaam via Doha. Air Tanzania has daily flights to Dar es Salaam from destinations within East Africa.

> ### SERENGETI HIGHWAY
>
> Since 2014 there has been a continual battle for and against the construction of a paved and commercial highway through the Serengeti National Park. It is contended that the highway would cause irreparable damage to the Serengeti itself and increase wildlife poaching, and this was weighed up against the very real economic need for an improved transport system as local towns continue to grow. As of this writing the highway construction is on hold; the existing dirt road is upgraded but a highway of some sorts might be inevitable.

Airlines Air Tanzania. ⊠ *ATC House, Ohio St., 2nd fl., Dar es Salaam* ☎ *0800/110–045* ⊕ *www.airtanzania.co.tz.* **Emirates.** ⊠ *Haidry Plaza Complex, Ali Hassan Mwinyi Rd., Dar es Salaam* ☎ *22/2116–100* ⊕ *www.emirates.com.* **Ethiopian Airlines.** ⊠ *T.D.F.L Bldg., Upanga St., Dar es Salaam* ☎ *22/211–7063* ⊕ *www.ethiopianairlines.com.* **Fast Jet.** ⊠ *Samora Tower, Samora Ave., ground fl., Shop 1, Dar es Salaam* ☎ *784/108–900* ⊕ *www.fastjet.com.* **Kenya Airways.** ⊠ *Viva Towers, Ali Hassan Mwinyi Rd., 1st fl., Dar es Salaam* ☎ *22/216–3917* ⊕ *www.kenya-airways.com.* **KLM.** ⊠ *Viva Towers, Ali Hassan Mwinyi Rd., 1st fl., Dar es Salaam* ☎ *22/216–3914* ⊕ *www.klm.com.* **Mango Airlines.** ⊠ *OR Tambo International Airport, Johannesburg* ☎ *086/101–0217 South African contact* ⊕ *www.flymango.com.* **Oman Air.** ⊠ *Serena Hotel, 12 Ohio St., Dar es Salaam* ☎ *22/211–9426* ⊕ *www.omanair.com.* **Qatar Airways.** ⊠ *Diamond Plaza, 4th fl., Dar es Salaam* ☎ *22/2198–301* ⊕ *www.qatarairways.com/tz.* **South Africa Airways.** ⊠ *Raha Towers Bldg., Bibititi St. at Maktaba St., Dar es Salaam* ☎ *22/211–7045-7* ⊕ *www.flysaa.com.* **Swiss Air.** ⊠ *Acacia Estate, 84 Kinondoni Rd., Dar es Salaam* ☎ *22/551–0020* ⊕ *www.swiss.com.* **Turkish Airlines.** ⊠ *Maktaba Sq., Azikiwe St., Business Park, 4th fl., Dar es Salaam* ☎ *22/211–6681* ⊕ *www.turkishairlines.com.*

AIRPORTS AND TRANSFERS Julius Nyerere International Airport is about 13 km (8 miles) from the city center. There are a plethora of white-color taxis available at the airport that will cost you about Tsh40,000 (US$18) to the city center. There is a board detailing the standard rates, but this will be more expensive if you have not organized your own taxi; drivers often will take the price as high as they can, so agree before you get in. Most hotels will send drivers to meet your plane, if arranged in advance, although this will cost more. Taxis to Msasani Peninsula, a bay to the north of the city where many of the hotels listed in this guide are located, cost about Tsh50,000 (US$23). Prices can be, but are not usually, negotiated. Traffic into the city is notorious, especially during rush hours. ■TIP→ Don't get Uber from the airport until regulations are understood by everyone, as the taxi drivers tend to cause quite a bit of trouble for the Uber drivers at this stage.

Airport Contacts Abeid Amani Karume International Airport (Zanzibar, ZNZ). ⊠ *Nyerere Rd., Zanzibar Town, Zanzibar* ☎ *24/223–1336.* **Arusha Airport (ARK).** ⊠ *Dodoma Rd., Arusha* ☎ *27/250–5920* ⊕ *www.taa.go.tz.* **Julius Nyerere International Airport (DAR).** ⊠ *Julius Nyerere Rd., Dar es Salaam* ☎ *22/284–4371* ⊕ *www.taa.go.tz.* **Kilimanjaro International Airport (JRO).** ⊠ *Kilimanjaro Airport Rd.* ☎ *27/255–4252* ⊕ *www.kilimanjaroairport.co.tz.*

CHARTER FLIGHTS Affectionately known as the "sky donkeys" (due to the fact that they are the workhorses of the sky), there are a host of small charter companies that run daily flights from Dar es Salaam, Zanzibar, Pemba, and Mafia to all the popular tourism destinations, such as the Serengeti. From Cessna prop planes (a lucky person often gets to sit in the copilot's seat) to a slightly larger commuter plane, this is how most travelers move domestically across Tanzania. It's quick, fun, and makes for interesting photographs if you're lucky to be by the window. Low season has better prices ■TIP→ Those with a severe fear of small planes might consider road travel instead, although distances are far and the roads can be very bumpy.

Due to the limited space and size of the aircraft, charter carriers observe strict luggage regulations: luggage must be soft-sided and weigh between 15 and 20 kg (33 to 44 pounds) depending on the plane. ■TIP→ Seats can not be booked in advance on the prop planes.

Contacts Coastal Air. ⊠ *Slipway, Dar es Salaam* ☎ *222/602–430* ⊕ *www. coastal.co.tz.* **Flightlink.** ⊠ *Golden Tulip Hotel, Jamhuri St., 1st fl., Dar es Salaam* ☎ *782/354–4450* ⊕ *www.flightlinkaircharters.com.* **Precision Air.** ⊠ *Diamond Plaza, Mirambo St. at Samora Ave, 1st fl., Dar es Salaam* ☎ *022/2191–000* ⊕ *www.precisionairtz.com.* **ZanAir.** ⊠ *Julius Nyerere International Airport, Terminal 1, Dar es Salaam* ☎ *24/2233–670* ⊕ *www.zanair.com.*

ESSENTIALS

COMMUNICATIONS

PHONES **Calling within Tanzania:** The "0" in the regional code is used only for calls placed from other areas within the country.

Calling Tanzania from abroad: To call from abroad, dial the international access number 00, then the country code 255, then the area code, (e.g., 22 for Dar es Salaam), and then the telephone number, which should have six or seven digits.

Mobile Phones: Vodacom, Airtel Tanzania, and Zantel are the main service providers in Tanzania, but Airtel and Vodacom have the best reception coverage. The best option is to bring your own phone (if it's not locked to a particular network) or rent a phone and buy a SIM card on arrival. The starter packs for pay-as-you-go cell phones are very reasonable. You'll have to buy data or call credit for your phone, but this is easily done at shops or roadside vendors. Most places have free Wi-Fi.

Contacts Airtel. ⊕ www.africa.airtel.com. **Vodacom.** ☎ 082–111 ⊕ www. vodacom.co.za. **Zantel.** ⊠ Zanzibar Telecom Limited, Mwai Kibaki Rd. at Old Bagamoyo Rd., Dar es Salaam ⊕ www.zantel.co.tz.

CUSTOMS AND DUTIES

You can bring in a liter of spirits or wine and 200 cigarettes duty-fee. The import of zebra skin or other tourist products requires a CITES (Convention of International Trade in Endangered Species of Wild Fauna and Flora) permit. Although you can buy curios made from animal products in Tanzania, your home country may confiscate them on arrival. Don't buy shells. It is illegal to export elephant ivory, wildlife skins, and sea turtle products without permits.

■**TIP➜ As of 2017 there are strict rules to abide if you plan on bringing a drone into Tanzania and Zanzibar and flying it for commercial or recreation purposes.** A permit and license from the Tanzanian Civil Aviation Authority is required, without which your drone potentially could be impounded on arrival at the airport. Drones are not allowed to be flown in National Parks at all (due to concerns over poaching) and if the rangers catch you it will be a hefty fine. Visit the Tanzania Civil Aviation Authority website for up-to-date details.

Contacts Tanzania Civil Aviation Authority (*TCAA*). ⊕ www.tcaa.go.tz.

HEALTH AND SAFETY

Malaria is the biggest health threat in Tanzania, so be vigilant about taking antimalarials and applying bug spray. Consult with your doctor or travel clinic before leaving home for up-to-date antimalarial medication. At time of writing HIV/AIDS is less a risk than in some other African countries, but the golden rule is *never* have sex with a stranger. It's imperative to use strong sunscreen: remember you're just below the equator, where the sun is at its hottest. Stick to bottled water and ensure that the bottle seal is unbroken. Put your personal medications in your carry-on and bring copies of prescriptions.

SHOTS AND MEDICATIONS   Be up-to-date on yellow fever, polio, tetanus, typhoid, meningococcus, rabies, and Hepatitis A. It's not necessary to have a cholera jab, but if you're visiting Zanzibar it's sensible to get a cholera exception form from your GP or travel clinic. Visit a travel clinic 8 to 10 weeks before you travel to find out your requirements. If you're coming to Tanzania for a safari, chances are you're heading to a malarial game reserve. Millions of travelers take oral prophylactic drugs before, during, and after their safaris. It's up to you to weigh the risks and benefits of the type of antimalarial drug you choose to take. If you're pregnant or traveling with small children, consider a nonmalarial region for your safari.

Embassies U.S. Embassy. ⊠ 686 Old Bagamoyo Rd., Msasani, Msasani ☎ 22/229–4122 ⊕ tz.usembassy.gov.

Emergencies Police Hotline. ☎ 112, 22/211–7362.

Medical-Assistance Companies The Flying Doctors Service. ✉ *Summit Center, Sokoine Rd., West Wing, Block A, 2nd fl., Arusha* ☏ *20/699–2299 emergency, 71/988–1887 in Arusha* ⊕ *www.flydoc.org.*

MONEY MATTERS

The regulated currency is the Tanzanian shilling (Tsh). Notes are 500, 1,000, 2,000, 5,000, and 10,000. At this writing, the exchange rate was about Tsh2,246 to US$1. The V.A.T. in Tanzania is at 18% and is added to everything, except for restaurant and activity bills. Be sure to ask for the V.A.T. to be included in the price or your bill could add up unexpectedly.

To avoid administrative hassles, keep all foreign-exchange receipts until you leave the region, as you may need them as proof when changing any unspent local currency back into your own currency at the airport when you leave. Don't leave yourself with any shillings—you won't be able to change them outside of Tanzania unless you are traveling onward to other East African countries.

Bargaining, especially at marketplaces, is part of the shopping experience. But always be aware of the exchange rate and pay appropriately— you don't want to underpay, but you also don't want to be charged exorbitant "tourist" prices.

Most large hotels accept U.S. dollars and Tanzanian shillings and take all major credit cards but do be aware that using a credit card often comes with a surcharge of 3%–8% (sometimes as high as 10%). All budget hotels will accept Tanzanian shillings.

ATMS AND BANKS There are banks and ATMs in all major cities; you can draw cash directly from an ATM in Dar es Salaam, Arusha, Mwanza, Stone Town in Zanzibar, and Chake Chake on Pemba island; there is one ATM on Mafia island. Most ATMs accept Maestro, Visa Electron, Visa, and MasterCard. The best place to withdraw cash is at an indoor ATM, preferably one guarded by a security officer. Most machines won't let you withdraw more than the equivalent of about $300 at a time. Don't leave withdrawing money to the last minute or late on Friday when everyone gets paid their salaries.

TIPPING For a two- or three-night stay at a lodge or hotel, tip a couple of dollars for small services and US$5–US$8 per day for room steward and waiter. A good guide should get a tip of US$15–US$25 per day per person; if he's gone out of his way for you, then you may wish to give him more. It's a good idea to carry a number of small-denomination bills. U.S. dollars are acceptable almost everywhere, but if you're planning to go to more remote places, then shillings are preferred.

PASSPORTS AND VISAS

U.S. citizens require a visa to enter Tanzania; it's $100 and is valid for three months. Passports must be valid for six months after your planned departure date from Tanzania. You will need a valid yellow fever certificate to enter and exit Tanzania.

If you're not a U.S. citizen, check with your embassy as some countries are visa exempt. A multiple entry is $100 for everyone and you can get a transit visa for $30 valid for 14 days. You can buy a visa upon arrival, but you'll need cash and at least two passport pictures. Whenever possible, get your visa ahead of time to avoid long lines and headaches.

■TIP→ For all international travel to and from South Africa, new immigration regulations require that all children under the age of 18 carry a passport as well as an Unabridged Birth Certificate that shows the details of both parents.

ABOUT THE RESTAURANTS AND FOOD

Food in the lodges is plentiful and tasty, and if you head to the coast, you'll dine on superb seafood and fish with lots of fresh fruit and vegetables. Most places now cater for all food tastes and dietary requirements.

ABOUT THE HOTELS AND LODGES

You'll find the ultimate in luxury at many of the safari camps, lodges, and coastal resorts and hotels. It's highly recommended that you opt for a private camp or lodge if possible, because everything is usually included—lodging, transport to and from the lodge, meals, beverages (including excellent house wines), game drives, and other activities. Check in advance whether park fees are included in your rate, as these can get very expensive if you have to pay them daily. The southern safari circuit is cheaper in general, but you'll need to factor in the cost of transport and that can be quite pricey. Many lodges and hotels offer low-season rates. If you're opting for a private game lodge, find out whether they accept children (many specify only kids over 12), and stay a minimum of two nights, three if you can. If you're traveling to the more remote parks, allow for more time. ■TIP→ Most lodges offer a laundry service and will launder everything except underwear (it's against African culture). Remember to pack plenty of pairs or make sure you bring quick-dry ones so you can wash as you go. Most lodges will provide laundry detergent in your tent for this very purpose.

National park accommodations are few and very basic. Unless you're a hard-core camper, it's advised that you stick with another type of accommodation. It's essential to note that more often than not, there won't be an elevator in your lodge—which are usually one story—and because of the rustic locations, accommodations aren't wheelchair-friendly.

For information on plugging in while on safari, see Electricity, in the Planning Your Safari chapter. Restaurant and hotel reviews have been shortened. For full information, visit Fodors.com.

WHAT IT COSTS IN U.S. DOLLARS				
	$	**$$**	**$$$**	**$$$$**
Dining	under $12	$12–$20	$21–$30	over $30
Hotels	under $250	$250–$450	$451–$600	over $600

Hotel prices are for a standard double room in high season. All prices refer to an all-inclusive per-person, per-night rate including 12.5% tax. Restaurant prices are per person for a main course at dinner, a main course equivalent, or a prix-fixe meal.

It can be a battle of wills between a lion and a wildebeest and there's no guarentee on the victor.

ABOUT THE PARKS
You probably won't be able to see all of Tanzania in one trip, so we've broken it down by **Must-See Parks** (Serengeti National Park, Ngorongoro Conservation Area, Lake Manyara National Park, Mount Kilimanjaro, Selous Game Reserve, and Gombe Stream and Mahale Mountains National Parks) and **If You Have Time Parks** (Arusha National Park, Tarangire National Park, and Ruaha National Park) to help you better organize your time. We suggest, though, that you read about all of them and then choose for yourself.

VISITOR INFORMATION
The Tanzanian Tourist Board (TTB) has offices in Dar es Salaam and Arusha. The tourist board's website is a great online source for pretrip planning.

Contacts Tanzania National Parks. ☎ *272/970–408* ⊕ *www.tanzaniaparks. go.tz.* **Tanzanian Tourist Board.** ✉ *Utalii House, Laibon St. at Ali Hassan Mwinyi Rd., near French Embassy, Dar es Salaam* ☎ *22/266–4878/9* ⊕ *www.tanzania-tourism.go.tz.*

SERENGETI NATIONAL PARK

Game
★★★★★
Park Accessibility
★★★★★
Getting Around
★★★★★
Accommodations
★★★★★
Scenic Beauty
★★★★

The very name Serengeti is guaranteed to bring a glint to even the most jaded traveler's eye. It's up there in that wish list of legendary destinations alongside Machu Picchu, Angkor Wat, Kakadu, Killarney, and the Great Pyramid of Giza. But what distinguishes Serengeti from all its competitors is its sheer natural beauty.

It's 15,000 square km (5,791 square miles) of pristine wilderness and that's it. Its Maasai name *Serenget* means "Endless Plain." A primeval Eden par excellence, named a UNESCO World Heritage Site in 1978 and an International Biosphere Reserve in 1981, the Serengeti is incredibly popular and filled to the brim in high season. Despite its crowds, it's one of those iconic places in the world that manages to inspire a wild sense of adventure.

This ecosystem supports some of the most plentiful mammal populations left anywhere on earth, and the animals here seem bigger, stockier, stronger, and sturdier than elsewhere in Africa. Even the scrub hares are bigger than their southern neighbors, loping rather than scampering over the tussocks and grassy mounds. Hyenas are everywhere and raptors are in perpetual motion—tawny eagles, kestrels, harriers, kites, buzzards, and vultures. Expect to see at least one baby wildebeest that has fallen by the wayside lying alone encircled by patient, voracious vultures or prowling hyenas.

But let's put you right in the picture. You'll probably land at a busy landing strip, maybe near Ntuti, where a dozen open-sided vehicles wait to pick up the new arrivals. In your few days driving around the Serengeti you'll certainly see other vehicles, especially if there's a river crossing occurring (i.e. part of the migration). As you leave the airstrip, your vehicle will weave its way through herds of zebra and gazelle. Rufous-tailed weavers, endemic to northern Tanzania, flutter up from the sandy road. The plains stretch endlessly with misty mountains faint in the distance. At first the plains are ringed by trees, but then only an

During the Great Migration, some 750,000 zebra pass through the Serengeti.

occasional and solitary tree punctuates the golden grass. Wherever you stay, you'll be looked after royally, with comfortable accommodations, good food, a dawn chorus of bubbling birdsong, and an evening serenade of whooping hyenas with a backing group of softly calling lions.

What will you remember about the Serengeti? The unending horizons and limitless plains. The sheer space. The wildebeest. The oh-so-beautiful Thomson's and Grant's gazelles. The bat-eared foxes playing in the early morning sun. Lions galore, and in particular, the one that may wander past your tent one night and roar under the blazing stars. The hosts of water birds by the streams, lakes, and rivers. The flat-top acacia trees, ancient guardians of this windswept wilderness. The quiet. The Big Country. Knowing how small is your place in the interconnectedness of all things. And how privileged you are to be able to experience the wonder of it all.

WHEN TO GO
If you want to see the wildebeest migration and predators, visit June through October.

GETTING HERE AND AROUND
The drive from Arusha to Serengeti is about eight hours or 325 km (202 miles). Although there are places to refuel, breakdown facilities are virtually nonexistent. The roads outside of the cities are mostly dirt, and you'll have a lot of potholes to contend with on many of them; a 4x4 vehicle would be best if you're renting a car. Although you can drive to the Serengeti from Arusha, Lake Manyara, Tarangire, or Ngorongoro Crater, we suggest flying in, as it's quick, less of a headache, and gives you the sense of the scale of the landscape. There are scheduled

and charter flights to the Serengeti from Arusha, Lake Manyara, and Mwanza. The flights are daily. A flight from Arusha to Serengeti South is an hour long, the flight from Dar es Salaam to Arusha is two hours. Most tour operators will arrange the flights for you, and lodges will be sure to have someone pick you up at the airstrip.

Park fees are $60 per day per person, $20 for children between 5–15 years and this excludes V.A.T. Fees will also be added onto your activities prices, especially if you're planning on night or walking safaris.

TIMING

The route and timing of the wildebeest migration is unpredictable. With that said, you should allow at least three days to be assured of seeing the migration on your visit, longer if you'd like to see more interactions with predators.

WHERE TO STAY

$$$$ RESORT **Faru Faru River Lodge.** Sprawling but intimate, Faru Faru is built in a contemporary style with lots of stone, wood, and sand emphasizing the natural surroundings. **Pros:** the service and personal attention are outstanding; modern and earthy bush decor; relaxing in one of the two horizon swimming pools. **Cons:** check that the equestrian center is open if you are coming here for this reason; no mobile phone service; there can be a bit of a smell at the height of migration when, unfortunately, some animals perish in the river. [$] *Rooms from: $1670* ✉ *Serengeti National Park* ☎ *021/683–3424* 🌐 *www.singita.com* 🛏 *9 tented suites* 🍴 *All-inclusive.*

$$$$ RESORT FAMILY **Four Seasons Safari Lodge Serengeti.** Far from the traditional safari experience, at Four Seasons you'll find five-star amenities uncommon in the bush, such as white-glove service, multiple gourmet dining options, fitness center, flat-screen TVs, rain showers, Internet, and air-conditioning. **Pros:** breathtaking setting; good option for families and large groups; watch herds of elephants right from the pool. **Cons:** not for those wanting intimate, traditional safari luxury; views vary depending on room; game drives and airstrip transfers not included in all room rates. [$] *Rooms from: $1685* ✉ *Serengeti National Park* ☎ *768/981–981* 🌐 *www.fourseasons.com* 🛏 *77 rooms* 🍴 *All meals.*

$$$$ RESORT **Grumeti Serengeti Tented Camp.** Situated on the banks of a Grumeti River tributary, in the western corridor of the Serengeti Grumeti, is a hospitable, delightful camp that seamlessly mixes rustic safari tents with easy sophistication. **Pros:** hot air balloon experiences are a mere 15 minutes away; stellar service from staff and guides; great for hippo-viewing as the lodge overlooks the banks of the river. **Cons:** outdoor showers can be a bit chilly in the early mornings; river rooms will be close to the hippos and can be noisy during the night and early mornings; river does dry up during certain months of the year, plan accordingly. [$] *Rooms from: $1340* ✉ *Serengeti National Park* ☎ *11/809–4300* 🌐 *www.andbeyond.com* 🛏 *10 tented suites* 🍴 *All-inclusive.*

$$$$ RESORT **Klein's Camp.** Built on the crest of the Kuka Hills with 360-degree panoramic views over the Grumeti River valley, this lovely intimate camp prides itself on good service and quality game-viewing along the

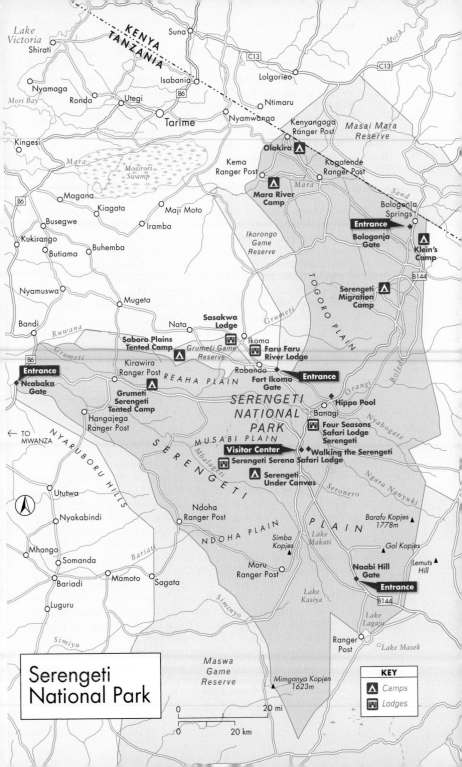

river. **Pros:** great service and attention to detail; stunning views from your cottage veranda; a more private and intimate atmosphere. **Cons:** Northern Serengeti is a good three hours' drive away; time the migration, which is tricky, if you want to see it from the concession; airstrip is an hour's drive, but some may love the additional "safari". [$] *Rooms from: $1340* ✉ *Serengeti National Park* ☎ *11/809–4300* 🌐 *www.andbeyond.com/kleins-camp* 🛏 *10 cottages* 🍴 *All-inclusive.*

$$$$ RESORT Fodor's Choice ★ 🏨 **Mara River Camp.** Considered one of the top properties in the Northern Serengeti, the luxurious Mara River Camp has spectacular views over its namesake river and a funky, bohemian, and oh-so-chic style. **Pros:** modern, African-inspired natural beauty of the camp; exquisite views; great food and fantastic, attentive service. **Cons:** very pricey; when the migration is in full swing there can be quite a smell emanating from the river due to the massive amounts of wildebeest in the area; not a traditional safari experience, but that's the allure for some. [$] *Rooms from: $1785* ✉ *Singita Lami, Serengeti National Park* ☎ *21/683–3424* 🌐 *www.singita.com* ⏲ *Closed Mar. and Apr.* 🛏 *6 tents* 🍴 *All-inclusive.*

$$$$ RESORT 🏨 **Olakira.** Light, delicate linens, fantastic dining, and touches of romantic Africa scattered all around the campsite make Olakira one of the finest mobile camps in the Serengeti. **Pros:** open-sided vehicles with exceptional guides; fantastic locations, including one near the river for crossings; spacious and stylish tents. **Cons:** there might be an odor when the migration crossing is at its peak; no credit card payments in the south camp; group dinners might not be for everyone. [$] *Rooms from: $859* ✉ *Serengeti National Park* ☎ *736/500–515* 🌐 *www.asiliaafrica.com* 🛏 *9 tents* 🍴 *All-inclusive.*

$$$$ RESORT 🏨 **Sabora Plains Tented Camp.** It's not often that you'll stay in a marquee-shaped tent elegantly furnished with silk curtains, antique furniture, stylish African artifacts, and a/c, but that's what you'll get at this ultraluxurious camp set among green lawns adjacent to the Great Migration route. **Pros:** wide, open spaces; gorgeous details in the tent furnishings; plenty of activities around the camp, like tennis. **Cons:** television in the main lodge, but it's only brought out upon request; not suited for families with children under 12; modern amenities, like a gym tent, which might deter those wanting only a bush experience. [$] *Rooms from: $1670* ✉ *Grumeti Game Reserve, Serengeti National Park* ☎ *021/683–3424* 🌐 *www.singita.com* 🛏 *9 tents* 🍴 *All-inclusive.*

$$$$ RESORT 🏨 **Sasakwa Lodge.** Located in the Grumeti Reserve, a 350,000-acre concession in Serengeti's Western Corridor, this superlative lodge is built in the style of a glamorous 1920s East African farm ranch. **Pros:** wonderful views of the Serengeti plains; your every need will be taken care of; being on a private reserve there are less crowds. **Cons:** the lodge is quite formal, but many may think that is a pro; luxury and privacy comes with a hefty price tag; the odd troupe of monkeys can come rather close to the rooms. [$] *Rooms from: $2045* ✉ *Grumeti Reserves* ☎ *21/683–3424 RSA phone number* 🌐 *www.singita.com* 🛏 *9 suites, 1 villa* 🍴 *All-inclusive.*

$$$$ RESORT 🏨 **Serengeti Migration Camp.** Found in northeast Serengeti among the rocky Ndasiata Hills, it's hard to believe that the accommodation is

Grumeti River Camp, Serengeti National Park

Grumeti Serengeti Camp

Klein's Camp

Klein's Camp, Serengeti National Park

actually tented because it looks so luxurious. **Pros:** 360-degree wooden deck veranda; walks along the Grumeti River; professional and attentive service. **Cons:** camp is about a three-hour trip from Central Serengeti; lots of steps may be a problem for people with mobility issues; slightly larger than other camps. [$] *Rooms from: $845* ✉ *Serengeti National Park* ☎ *754/250–630* 🌐 *www.elewanacollection.com* 🛏 *20 tented rooms* 🍴 *All meals.*

$$$ RESORT **Serengeti Serena Safari Lodge.** Situated high on a hill with superb views over the central Serengeti, the two-story thatch cottages are shaped like Masai huts and are set amongst indigenous trees. **Pros:** there are great views of the Serengeti from the lodge; the expanse of open plains make it ideal for hot air ballooning; wildlife often wanders around the lodge. **Cons:** larger hotel style and rooms are dated; all food is buffet-style so when the hotel is full you may have to wait in line; beware of tsetse flies. [$] *Rooms from: $467* ✉ *Serengeti National Park* ☎ *272/545–555* 🌐 *www.serenahotels.com* 🛏 *66 rooms* 🍴 *All meals.*

$$$$ RESORT **Serengeti Under Canvas.** This mobile camp, in the southern part of the Serengeti, follows the migration (usually in March) from an acacia-covered bluff that overlooks a small river. **Pros:** an authentic safari experience; up close wildlife experiences; friendly, attentive guides and staff. **Cons:** bucket showers might not be to everyone's taste, but it is part of the experience; "mobile" means no guarantee being in the thick of the migration; the proximity to wildlife might unnerve some people, especially at night. [$] *Rooms from: $1240* ✉ *Serengeti National Park* ☎ *11/809–4300* 🌐 *www.andbeyond.com* 💳 *No credit cards* 🛏 *9 tents* 🍴 *All-inclusive.*

NGORONGORO CONSERVATION AREA

Game
★★★★★
Park Accessibility
★★★★★
Getting Around
★★★
Accommodations
★★★★★
Scenic Beauty
★★★★★

Ngorongoro Crater ranks right up there among Africa's must-visit wildlife destinations: Serengeti, Masai Mara, Etosha, Kruger Park, and the Okavango Delta. One of only three UNESCO World Heritage Sites in Tanzania (together with the Serengeti and the Selous Game Reserve), the Crater is often called the Eighth Wonder of the World.

It lies in the Biosphere Reserve of the Ngorongoro Conservation Area, which covers 8,300 square km (3,204 square miles) in northern Tanzania. This reserve was specifically planned to accommodate both the traditional Maasai communities and tourists. You'll see Maasai villagers grazing their sheep and cattle all over.

The Ngorongoro Crater lies in a cluster of other volcanoes (sometimes seen rather ominously smoking) that borders the Serengeti National Park to the north and west. It's actually a collapsed volcano or caldera. The original volcano, which may have been higher than Kilimanjaro, collapsed in on itself over time and now forms a perfect basin. Once inside you'll feel like you're at the bottom of a deep soup bowl with very steep sides. The basin, measuring 18 km (11 miles) in diameter, lies 500 meters (1,640 feet) below the rim, which towers above it at about 2,200 meters (7,217 feet) above sea level.

Believed to have formed some 2 million years ago, the Crater harbors an astonishing variety of landscapes—forests, peaks, craters, valleys, rivers, lakes, and plains—including the world-famous Olduvai Gorge, where some of our earliest human ancestors once hunted and gathered. *See the Cradle of Humankind box, below.*

The very steep and bumpy drive into the Crater begins high up in the forest. The only downside you might face is the sheer number of safari vehicles that all clamber into the Crater at opening hours, creating often dusty drives through the Crater itself. But once you have left the masses behind, the charm of this site slowly leaves you in awe. Although this lush highland forest looks exactly like a rain forest, it's not. It's a *mist* forest, which depends on a regular and abundant amount of mist and drizzle. If you look closely enough, you'll see particles of mist swirling like raindrops among the ancient trees. The aptly named pillarwood trees stand sentinel over the stran-

gler figs, the croton trees, the highland *bersama* (a local evergreen), and purple wild tobacco flowers. The tree trunks and branches are home to thousands of epiphytes—specialized plants such as arboreal orchids and ferns—which cling to their hosts and absorb moisture with their own aerial roots. Look for the orchids among the curtains of Old Man's Beard, or hanging tree moss.

Monkeys, bushbuck, bush pigs, and elephants frequent the forest, although it's unlikely you'll see them. What you'll see if you're staying in one of the Crater lodges are well-mown lawns, which aren't the result of hardworking gardeners but that of zebras and buffaloes, which after dark seek sanctuary from predators here. It's not dogs you hear barking after sundown but the warning calls of vigilant zebras and baboons. The Crater floor, dominated by a huge flamingo-filled alkaline lake, holds the highest concentration of predators in the world—lions, hyenas, jackals, and leopards. Cheetahs can occasionally be seen but fall prey to lions and hyenas, which the nervous and fragile cheetah is no match for. Big herds of plains game such as Thomson's and Grant's gazelles, impalas, giraffes, zebras, and wildebeests are easy meat for the thoroughly spoiled predators that need to expend very little energy to score a megameal. You'll probably see at least one pride of bloated lions lying on their backs, paws in air, stuffed and totally damaging their noble image as the King of Beasts. Make sure to ask your guide to point out a black or white rhino if he spots one. This is also a great place to take a boat safari down one of the hippo-dense rivers.

Birdlife is also spectacular, with some endemic species: the Rufous-tailed weaver, Schalow's wheatear, and large flocks of the incredibly beautiful crowned cranes. Because this is a continuous killing ground, you'll quickly become a vulture expert. If you're a birder, ask for a guide who knows his birds well, because not all the guides do.

WHEN TO GO

Avoid April and May as these months are particularly wet in the Crater. Because there's no restriction on the number of vehicles, there can be far more than a hundred at one time in the high season (January to the end of September). It's amazing to have a close-up encounter with some of Africa's finest game, but not if you're surrounded by other vehicles and often very noisy, boisterous tourists. It's best to go down as early as possible (the gates open at 6 am) but be aware that many others might have the same plan. Regardless, the Crater is a once-in-a-lifetime experience so grit your teeth, ignore all the other tourists, and enjoy one of the world's most spectacular destinations.

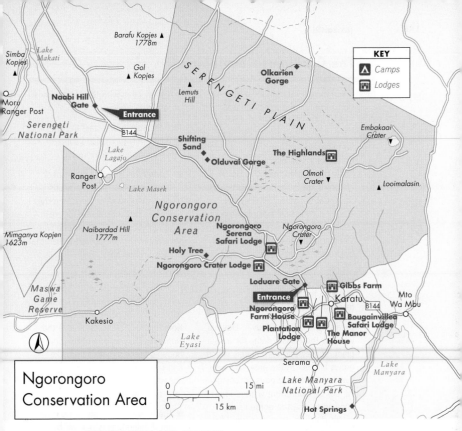

Ngorongoro Conservation Area

GETTING HERE AND AROUND

Ngorongoro is about 180 km (112 miles) from Arusha by road. You can also fly into the Crater rim airstrip or Ndutu Lodge airstrip. Tour operators can arrange your transfer in advance.

ESSENTIALS

Entrance fees It's US$60 per person, and US$250 for a car per 24-hour period, excluding V.A.T., to enter the Ngorongoro Conservation Area. These fees, as well as fees for activities inside the Crater—meals, walking safaris, etc.—should be included with your group tour or accommodation-arranged safari. If you're doing a self-drive, you'll need to pay for everything at either the tourism office in Ngorongoro, Lodare gate entrance, or at the tourism board office in Arusha. You will receive a Ngorongoro card, which you present as you enter the crater entrance. ■TIP→ You can pay in both USD and Tsh, but USD is preferred, and you will need to be accompanied by a licensed guide, for this and Oldupai Gorge.

Packing Be prepared for thick early-morning mist all year round, which makes it quite chilly. Be sure to pack warm clothes.

The Cradle of Humankind

If you have a great interest in evolution and human origins, Olduvai Gorge, a UNESCO World Heritage Site, is a definite must. It's about a 90-minute drive from the Ngorongoro Crater and is accessible only via a badly maintained road. The gorge, about 48 km (30 miles) long, is part of the Great Rift Valley, which stretches along East Africa. It has played a key role in palaeoanthropologists' understanding of the history of humanity by providing clues dating from about 2.5 million years ago. There's a small museum at the Gorge, but it doesn't really do justice to the magnitude of fossil discoveries made here.

Locals actually call Olduvai "Oldupai," which is the Maasai name for a sisal plant, *Sansevieria ehrenbergii,* which grows all over in the area. The view overlooking the gorge is spectacular, but be aware that visitors aren't allowed to visit the gorge itself. If you're short on time, it may not be worth your while. It's all a rather makeshift affair, and the guides aren't all fluent in English, so you may struggle to understand explanations

inevitably filled with the Latin names of fossils.

Archaeological rock stars like the Leakey family have made some of these important discoveries:

■ *Paranthropus boisei* dating back 2.5 million years. These hominids had massive jaws and large, thickly enameled molars suitable for crushing tough vegetation. Their bite was several times more powerful than that of modern humans.

■ The first specimens of *Homo habilis,* which lived about 2 million to 1.6 million years ago. This is the earliest known named species of the Homo genus. Scientists believe that *Homo habilis* was one of the first hominid species that could make and use stone tools, enhancing our ancestors' adaptability and chances of long-term survival.

■ The world's oldest stone tools date about 2 million years old, which are very primitive—basically just crude tools fashioned from pebbles.

WHERE TO STAY ON THE CRATER RIM

$$$$
RESORT
Fodor's Choice
★

Ngorongoro Crater Lodge. Imagine walking into a Hollywood film set where the spectacular setting is literally "Great Zimbabwe ruins meets SS *Titanic* baroque." Clusters of stilted rooms with woven conical banana-leaf domes and fancifully carved stone chimneys cling to the Crater's rim and somehow blend in with the natural surroundings. **Pros:** spectacular views over the Crater; unique rooms with views in every direction; expensive but service is exceptional. **Cons:** Crater can be jampacked with vehicles in peak season; high altitude means it's not easy to walk uphill; it gets incredibly cold here in the mornings, bring warm clothes. $ *Rooms from: $1775* ⊠ *Ngorongoro Crater* ☎ *011/809–4300 in Johannesburg* ⊕ *www.andbeyond.com* ⟿ *30 suites* ⏍ *All-inclusive.*

$$
RESORT
FAMILY

Ngorongoro Serena Safari Lodge. Emerging from the natural surroundings and indigenous vines of the western rim of the Ngorongoro Crater, the Serena Safari Lodge is home to one of the most famous views this side of the Mara River. **Pros:** amazing views of

Flying in unison over the Ngorongoro Crater, the large wingspan and bold colors of the crowned cranes provide a stark contrast to the natural browns and greens of the crater floor.

the Crater rim from each room; close to Crater entrance; free Wi-Fi. **Cons:** common areas can get crowded when the lodge is full; rooms are dated; there are a lot of stairs across the lodge. [$] *Rooms from: $434* ✉ *Ngorongoro Crater* ☎ *27/254–5555, 27/253–7053* 🌐 *www.serenahotels.com* 🛏 *75 rooms* 🍴 *All meals.*

WHERE TO STAY IN THE NGORONGORO CONSERVATION AREA

$ RESORT 🏨 **Bougainvillea Safari Lodge.** As a budget-friendly option either at the start or end of your safari, the Bougainvillea, halfway between Ngorongoro Crater and Lake Manyana, is a great option. **Pros:** fantastic budget option; big swimming pool; food is decent and plentiful. **Cons:** in Karatu Town with not much in the way of views; Wi-Fi is spotty; service can be a bit on the slow, glacial side. [$] *Rooms from: $231* ✉ *Karatu Town, Ngorongoro Conservation* ☎ *27/253–4083* 🌐 *www.bougainvilleasafarilodge.com* 🛏 *32 cottages* 🍴 *No meals.*

$$$$ RESORT 🏨 **Gibbs Farm.** With the feel of an English country house, this working organic coffee farm sits midway between Lake Manyara and the Ngorongoro Crater. **Pros:** locally produced food served up daily from their gardens; rooms are spacious and uniquely decorated; some of the prettiest outdoor showers around. **Cons:** a rather bumpy hour-long ride out to the Crater; you can end up paying for all the little extras; it is a working farm, so bear in mind there will be farm smells around some of the rooms. [$] *Rooms from: $903* ✉ *Ngorongoro Crater* ☎ *272/970–438* 🌐 *www.gibbsfarm.com* 🛏 *20 cottages* 🍴 *All-inclusive.*

Gibb's Farm

Gibb's Farm

Ngorongoro Serena Safari Lodge

$$$$ ⬚ **The Highlands.** North of the Ngorongoro Crater, situated along the
ALL-INCLUSIVE forested slopes of the Olmoti volcano, sits The Highlands, a low-impact
Fodor'sChoice high-luxury camp that overlooks the valley below. **Pros:** breathtaking
★ views in a unique, remote setting; rooms unlike anything on the safari
circuit; activities include guided walks, hikes up the summit, and cultural visits. **Cons:** rooms can get quite chilly in the early morning if
the fire goes out; might be an problem for those with mobility issues;
45-minute drive from the Crater. $ *Rooms from: $824* ⊠ *Ngorongoro
Conservation* ☎ *736/500–515* ⊕ *www.asiliaafrica.com* ⌕ *8 domed
suites* ¹⁰¹ *All-inclusive.*

$$$$ ⬚ **The Manor House.** A charming mix of Afro-European Architecture
RESORT from a bygone era greets you after a bumpy, dusty drive from the
FAMILY Crater. **Pros:** drawn baths after a long day of safari will make your
day; classical, stylish living and lounge areas; plenty of activities like
horse riding, billards, a movie theater, and hiking trails. **Cons:** 1-hour,
30-minute drive from the Crater on winding, bumpy roads; chilly in
the evenings, bring something warm; space and luxury comes at a price.
$ *Rooms from: $845* ⊠ *Ngorongoro Crater* ☎ *784/250–630* ⊕ *www.
elewanacollection.com* ⌕ *20 cottages* ¹⁰¹ *All meals.*

$$ ⬚ **Ngorongoro Farm House.** Scattered through the winding pathways of a
HOTEL 750-acre coffee plantation that was once owned by a 19th-century Ger-
man settler are a series of thatched cottages nestled around a generous
main farmhouse. **Pros:** working farm with walking tours and coffee-
making experience; garden-fresh produce used in the cooking; beauti-
ful, rustic setting with plenty of activities. **Cons:** rooms can be very
dim and dark; slightly large and impersonal dining and lounge areas;
some rooms are far distances from main lodge for those with mobility
issues. $ *Rooms from: $410* ⊠ *Ngorongoro Crater* ☎ *075/069–944*
⌕ *52 chalets* ¹⁰¹ *All meals.*

$$$$ ⬚ **Plantation Lodge.** Open spaces are at every turn here, from the hid-
RESORT den swimming pool to the stylish cottages with soft, earth-tone linens,
accents of rich African wood, and large en suite bathrooms. **Pros:** this
is a small lodge so you will have a bit of peace and quiet; pleasing views
over the countryside; staff are attentive and helpful. **Cons:** a bumpy
drive from the Crater; cold in the evenings, so bring warm clothes;
mainly used for private safari guests with private drivers. $ *Rooms
from: $643* ⊠ *Ngorongoro Crater* ☎ *27/253–4405* ⊕ *www.plantation-
lodge.com* ⌕ *24 rooms* ¹⁰¹ *All meals.*

5

LAKE MANYARA NATIONAL PARK

Game
★★★
Park Accessibility
★★★★★
Getting Around
★★★
Accommodations
★★★
Scenic Beauty
★★★★

In the Great Rift Valley south of Serengeti and the Ngorongoro Crater lies the Cinderella of Tanzania's parks—the once over-looked and underrated Lake Manyara National Park. When Ernest Hemingway faced the rust-red rocks of the almost 2,000-foot-high rift valley escarpment that dominates the park, he called it "the loveliest place I have seen in Africa."

The park may be small, but what it lacks in size it makes up for in diversity. Its range of ecosystems at different elevations makes for dramatic differences in scenery. At one moment you're traveling through a fairy-tale forest of tumbling, crystal-clear streams, waterfalls, rivers, and ancient trees; the next you're bumping over flat, grassy plains that edge the usually unruffled lake, pink with hundreds of flamingos. Situated near the park gate, Tanzania's first Tree Top Walkway ($47) opened in 2017. The 1,312-foot walkway takes guests through a series of suspension bridges that weave their way through the forest canopy (60 feet in the air) giving guests a bird's-eye view of the area's fauna and flora.

In the deep forest where old tuskers still roam, blue monkeys swing among huge fig and tamarind trees, giant baobabs, and mahoganies, using their long tail as an extra limb. They've got orange eyes, roman noses, and wistful expressions. In the evenings as motes of dusty sunlight dance in the setting sun, there's an excellent chance of spotting troops of more than 300 olive baboons (better looking and furrier than their chacma cousins) sitting in the road, grooming each other, chatting, and dozing, while dozens of naughty babies play around them and old granddaddies look on with knowing eyes.

The thick, tangled evergreen forest eventually gives way to woodlands with tall, flat-top acacias and fever trees, and finally to open plains where hundreds of elephants, buffalo, and antelope roam, accompanied by Masai giraffes so dark they look as if they've been dipped in chocolate. This is a great place to see hippos at close hand as they lie on the banks of the lake, or as they begin to forage as dusk approaches.

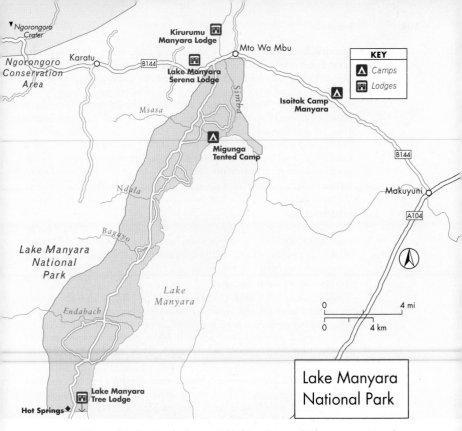

The park is known for its tree-climbing lions, which are rare to see, but you can be sure if one vehicle glimpses them then the "bush telegraph" (ranger walkie-talkie chatter) will quickly reach your truck, too. No one really knows why they climb and roost in trees, but it's been suggested by one former warden of the park that this unusual behavior probably started during a fly epidemic when the cats climbed high to escape the swarms of biting flies on the ground. He suggests that the present ongoing behavior is now part of their collective memory.

If you're a birder then put this park on your must-visit list. Because of the great variety of habitats, there's a great variety of birds; more than 400 species have been recorded. As you drive through the forest you'll hear the silvery-cheeked hornbills long before you see them flapping noisily in small groups among the massive trees, braying loudly as they fly. The edges of the lake as well as its placid surface attract all manner of water birds large and small. Along the reed-fringed lakeshore you'll see huge pink clouds drifting to and fro. These "clouds" are flocks of flamingos. White-backed pelicans paddle through the water as the ubiquitous African fish eagles soar overhead. Other water birds of all kinds congregate—waders, ducks, geese, storks, spoonbills, egrets, and herons. In the thickets at the base of the red escarpment overlooking the lake, which angles up dramatically at 90 degrees, watch out for Nubian woodpeckers, the very pretty and aptly named silver birds (flycatchers), superb, ashy, and Hildebrand's starlings, yellow wagtails, trilling cisticolas, red-cheeked cordon bleus, Peter's twinspots, bluenecked mousebirds, and every cuckoo imaginable. The red-and-yellow barbet is known as the "bed-and-breakfast bird" for its habit of living where it eats—in termite mounds. The park is also a raptor's paradise, where you can spot up to 51 daytime species, including dozens of augur buzzards, small hawks, and harriers. Deep in the forest you might be lucky enough to see Africa's most powerful eagle, the crowned eagle, which is strong enough to carry off young antelope, unwary baboons, and monkeys. At night listen for up to six different kinds of owls, including the giant eagle owl and the diminutive but very vocal African Scops owl.

WHEN TO GO

During the dry season (June–October), it's easier to see the larger mammals and track their movements because there's less foliage. The wet season (November–April) is a great time for bird-watching, glimpsing amazing waterfalls, and canoeing.

GETTING HERE AND AROUND

You can get here by road, charter, or scheduled flights from Arusha, or en route to Serengeti and Ngorongoro Crater. The entrance gate to Lake Manyara National Park lies 2 hours or 126 km (80 miles) west of Arusha along a good tar road. There are daily flights that are 20 minutes from Arusha. Your safari operator or lodge can help you organize your transfers.

ENTRY FEES

Entry fees for Lake Manyara National Park are US$45 per person You can get a decent map and a bird checklist at the park's headquarters at the gate as you drive in from Mto wa Mbu. **■TIP→ You can pay in both USD and Tsh, but USD is preferred.**

WHERE TO STAY

$ RESORT FAMILY Fodor's Choice ★

🏨 **Isoitok Camp Manyara.** In the morning when the Maasai head out of their bomas along the Losimingorti mountain range, you'll hear the gentle clanking of their cattle's bells from your accommodations at this very authentic camp. **Pros:** staff are wonderful and food is plentiful and excellent; well-positioned camp with beautiful views towards the Rift Valley; great community and ecologically sensitive camp policy. **Cons:** two older tents are positioned at the back of the camp with partial views; keep the tent zipped to avoid evening mosquitoes; an ever-so-slightly-bumpy ride from the main road. [$] *Rooms from: $215* ✉ *Lake Manyara National Park, Lake Manyara National Park* ☎ *739/503–700* 🌐 *www.isoitok.com* 💳 *No credit cards* 🛏 *8 tents* 🍴 *All-inclusive.*

$$ RESORT

🏨 **Kirurumu Manyara Lodge.** This intimate camp is set among indigenous bush high on the escarpment and will make you feel much closer to Africa than some of the bigger lodges. **Pros:** plenty of room for families; lovely view over the Rift Valley and Lake Manyara; coffee-making facilities in the rooms. **Cons:** can get incredibly hot in the tents and around the camp in summer; some tents have no views; drinks are expensive. [$] *Rooms from: $308* ✉ *Lake Manyara National Park, Lake Manyara National Park* ☎ *027/250–2417* 🌐 *www.kirurumu.net* 🛏 *31 tented rooms* 🍴 *All meals.*

$$ RESORT

🏨 **Lake Manyara Serena Lodge.** On the edge of an escarpment this lodge presents a cluster of clean, furnished, en suite, double-story rondavels with

More than 1 million wildebeest take part in the annual Great Migration and some 250,000 die during the journey.

breathtaking views over the lake. **Pros:** lovely infinity pool with views over the lake; gazebo bar by the pool is fantastic for sundowners; close to the air strip. **Cons:** the lodge can feel impersonal; not all rooms have been upgraded, nor do they all have views, and a request will not necessarily mean you will get a room with a view; mass dining. [$] *Rooms from: $320* ✉ *Lake Manyara National Park, Lake Manyara National Park* ☎ *27/253–9162, 27/253–9160* 🌐 *www.serenahotels.com* ⇨ *67 rooms* 🍴 *All meals.*

$$$$ RESORT Fodor's Choice ★ **Lake Manyara Tree Lodge.** The forest-floor-level entrance is flanked by an array of upturned wooden canoes that guests pass before climbing up to the main areas built under ancient branches heavy with flowers. **Pros:** charming, luxury rooms high in the trees; undisturbed, quiet southern location; the ride from (and to) the airstrip is treated as a game drive so keep your eyes open. **Cons:** located 35 km (22 miles) into the park, which requires a drive on very bumpy and dusty roads; rooms do not have views over the lake; not good for people with mobility issues. [$] *Rooms from: $1340* ✉ *Lake Manyara National Park* ☎ *11/809–4300 in Johannesburg* 🌐 *www.andbeyond.com* ⇨ *9 suites* 🍴 *All-inclusive.*

$$ RESORT **Migunga Tented Camp.** The main attraction of this secluded bush camp, apart from its reasonable price, is its location in an indigenous forest just 2 km (1.2 miles) from the town of Mto wa Mbu and only five minutes from the entrance of Lake Manyara National Park. **Pros:** secluded and quiet inside a beautiful acacia tree forest; close to the park entrance; camping is $15 per person. **Cons:** camp is near the village; views are only of the forest; monkeys can raid the tents if you leave them open. [$] *Rooms from: $350* ✉ *Lake Manyara National Park, Lake Manyara National Park* ☎ *027/250–6315* 🌐 *www.moivaro.com* ⇨ *21 tents* 🍴 *All meals.*

Lake Manyara Tree Lodge

Lake Manyara Tree Lodge

MOUNT KILIMANJARO

Game
★

Park Accessibility
★★★★

Getting Around
★★★★

Accommodations
N/A

Scenic Beauty
★★★★★

5

Kilimanjaro, a dormant volcano on the roof of Africa, is one of the closest points in the world to the sun (Chimborazo in the Andes is the closest). It's also the highest peak on the continent and the tallest freestanding mountain in the world. So great is her global attraction that approximately 12,000 people from around the world attempt to reach her mighty summit each year. Kili is also home to a variety of unique species found only along its slopes. Unfortunately, this biodiversity is under threat as the effects of climate change lead to the disappearance of the infamous snowcapped peaks, which scientists estimate could be gone by 2050.

Rising to an incredible height of 5,895 meters (19,336 feet) above sea level, Mt. Kilimanjaro is a continental icon. She towers over the surrounding Amboseli plains and covers an area of about 750 square km (290 square miles). On a clear day, she can be seen from 150 km (93 miles) away. Thousands attempt to reach Kilimanjaro's highest peak, but only about 64% will officially make the summit, known as Uhuru Peak. Many reach the lower Stella Point at 5,745 meters (18,848 feet) or Gilmans' Point, at 5,681 meters (18,638 feet), which earns them a certificate from the Kilimanjaro Parks Authority.

The origin of the name Kilimanjaro has varying interpretations. Some say it means "Mountain of Greatness," while others believe it to mean "Mountain of Caravans." There's a word in Swahili, *kilima*, which means "top of the hill." An additional claim is that it comes from the word *kilemakyaro*, which, in the Chagga language, means "impossible journey." Whatever the meaning, the visual image of Kilimanjaro is of a majestic peak.

A giraffe roams the plains below Mt. Kilimanjaro.

WHEN TO GO

The warmest, clearest trekking days run mid-December through February or September and October. June, July, and August are superb trekking months, too, but evening temperatures tend to be colder. The wettest months are November, early December, and March to the beginning of June, which brings some snow. Daytime temperatures range from 28°C (85°F) to 38°C (100°F) in the forest, but plummet to a frigid –2°C (28°F) to –16°C (3°F) at the summit. Generally, with every 200 meters ascended, the temperature drops one degree.

GETTING HERE

KLM, Turkish Airlines, and Qatar Airlines have direct flights to Kilimanjaro Airport (JRO); Kenya, Ethiopian, British, SAA and a number of other arlines have a number of daily flights from Nairobi; and local airlines have daily flights from Dar es Salaam. You can also fly direct to Zanzibar from here. Kilimanjaro Airport is located 45 km (28 miles) from Moshi and 50 km (31 miles) from Arusha, and it may be cheaper to fly to Arusha instead, so check before you book. Traveling overland is even cheaper but involves long journeys: a shuttle bus from Nairobi takes five or six hours, and from Dar es Salaam to Arusha or Moshi is seven to eight hours.

TREKKING KILI

Kilimanjaro is one of the few high peaks in the world that can be climbed without any technical gear. Most climbers head up her flanks with the aid of trekking poles, while others abandon their poles for a camera and a zoom lens. However, don't be fooled by the absence

KILIMANJARO TIPS

Choose an operator that's registered, has registered guides, has porters' interests at heart, and an environmental policy.

Communicate any health problems to your tour operator when you book.

Choose your route according to what you want: scenery, challenge, type of accommodation, and size of group.

Train before you leave—this also helps to "train your brain" that you're heading off for a challenge. Squats, lunges, and lots of hill walking with a pack are essential.

Read up on altitude sickness and symptoms and take the necessary medication with you. Add a day to get acclimated if possible or consider climbing Mt. Meru first.

Drink 3–5 liters of water a day. The rule is 1 liter per 1,000 meters (3,280 feet) ascent.

Take only photos; leave only footprints.

of technical gear. Oxygen levels near the summit decrease to about 60% of levels at the coast. The simple act of rolling up a sleeping bag can wear you out. Walking and ascending slowly will help your body adapt to these diminished oxygen levels. About 12,000 thrill seekers arrive on the mountain each year, each accompanied by an entourage of four to six people that include porters, guides, and a cook. Park fees will cost around $70 per person, with an additional $20 rescue fee, excluding V.A.T. Make sure these fees are included in your tour company's trekking fees.

WHERE TO START

Most treks head out from Moshi, a bustling town at the mountain's base whose streets are lined with tourist stalls, tailors, banks, and restaurants. Here you'll find registered guides and accredited trekking companies that will arrange your climb. We like Nomadic Adventure (⊕ *www.nomadicadventures.co.za*) because they offer great personal service, have climbed the mountain many times themselves, and get involved in the big Kilimanjaro Cleanup, a project that hauls thousands of pounds of waste off the mountain each year.

THE ROUTES

There are eight common routes to the summit: Marangu, Rongai, Shira, Lemosho, Machame, Umbwe, Mweka, and the Northern Circuit—all have long-drop toilets.

Marangu is the shortest (it takes a minimum of five days) and thus the most popular route, with accommodations in huts equipped with bunk beds, public dining areas, and flush toilets. Some even have solar-heated showers. The other routes, which take at least six days to trek, require camping.

Rongai (or Loitokitok) is the quietest as it heads out close to the Kenyan border, a fair distance from Moshi. Along with Marangu, Rongai is classified as an easier route.

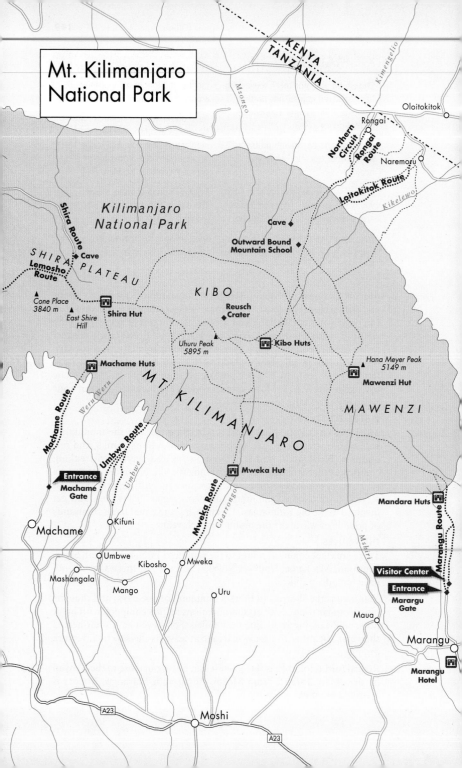

Shira, Lemosho, and Machame are steep and difficult, but also more scenic as they head through the distinct geographical zones: forest, shrub land, alpine desert, and snowfields.

Umbwe is the steepest, but also the most direct ascent to the summit. Mweka can only be used as a descending route from the western side.

The Northern Circuit takes eight or nine days through wilderness and there's little foot traffic. It's also the only route to cross the northern face.

GEOLOGY AND TERRAIN

Mount Kilimanjaro has five different types of terrain that you'll encounter while trying to reach the summit.

Cultivated Farmlands: Around the outskirts of Moshi near the base of the mountain are endless subsistence plantations of maize and bananas. Small villages line the routes up to the various starting points on Kilimanjaro, and small children play in the fields.

Forests: The forest zone spreads around the base of the mountain; it's hot, humid, and generally wet. Starting at about 1,798 meters (5,900 feet)—there's cultivated farmland below this—the forest reaches up to 2,800 meters (9,186 feet) and is home to a myriad of small creatures and primates, including the black-and-white colobus monkey. Tall trees reach for the sunlight, their feet firmly anchored into a maze of roots on which cling mosses and brightly colored flowers including the rare and exotic *impatiens kilimanjari* flower, unique to this mountain. Lichens hang in sheets and small birds dart to and fro.

Shrubland or Heath Zone: At the edge of the forest zone, the vegetation suddenly changes to shrubland that's full of flowers, shrubs like the 6-meter-high (20-feet-high) *Erica arborea,* and daisy bushes that grow as big as pompoms. This zone extends up to about 3,800 meters (12,467 feet) where the landscape turns into alpine desert.

Alpine Desert: As the shrubs of the heath zone diminish in size, one enters the alpine desert, full of gnarled volcanic lava rock. Small burrows shelter the hyrax and field mice that eke out a living in this desert moonscape. Large white-naped ravens scavenge among the sand and stone.

Glaciers and Summit: As the desert rises to 5,000 meters (16,404 feet), the summit of the mountain looms above, her flanks covered in ashen scree. Massive age-old glaciers, hanging as though suspended in time, are slowly receding as the planet warms. Here among these towering blocks of ice at 5,895 meters (19,340 feet), is Uhuru Peak, the summit of Kilimanjaro.

SELOUS GAME RESERVE

Game
★★★
Park Accessibility
★★★★
Getting Around
★★★★
Accommodations
★★★
Scenic Beauty
★★★★

Most visitors come away from Selous (sel-oo) Game Reserve acknowledging that this is Africa as it is—not as tourism has made it. The reserve is one of seven UNESCO World Heritage Sites in Tanzania. A true untamed wilderness, the reserve covers 50,000 square km (19,305 square miles) and comprises 5% of Tanzania. Selous Game Reserve is the largest national park in Africa and the second largest in the world.

Only Greenland National Park at 972,000 square km (375,398 square miles), which is larger than England and France combined, beats Selous. This is still arguably the biggest area of protected pristine wilderness left in Africa, but keep in mind that most of it is off-limits to tourists. The reserve is bisected from west to east by Tanzania's biggest river, the Rufiji, and only the area north of the river is open to visitors. So although it's teeming with game, it forms only about 5% of the total park.

The other 95% is mainly leased to hunting concessions. Hunting is still a very contentious issue, and although both sides passionately argue a plausible case, it's hard for many people to accept that shooting some of Africa's most beautiful and precious animals just for fun is ethically acceptable. However, hunting is under strict government control, and half of each substantial hunting fee is put back into the management and conservation of the reserve. It's possible that without this money the Selous would not exist, and rampant poaching would take over.

The visitor area of Selous north of the Rufiji River stretches for about 1,000 square km (386 square miles) and has great game-viewing and bird-watching opportunities. The fact that there are fewer lodges than the other bigger parks adds to the area's exclusivity. Most lodges are along and beside the Rufiji River, which rises in Tanzania's highlands, then flows 250 km (155 miles) to the Indian Ocean. The Rufiji boasts the highest water-catchment area in East Africa. A string of five small lakes—Tagalala, Manze, Nzerekea, Siwando, and Mzizimia—interlinked by meandering waterways, gives the area the feel of Botswana's Okavango Delta. The birdlife—more than 400 recorded species—is prolific, as are the huge crocodiles and lumbering hippos.

There are major advantages to visiting this park. First, although tourist numbers are now creeping up, there's little chance that you'll be game-viewing in the middle of a bunch of noisy vehicles.

Another major draw is that game-viewing and bird-watching can be done from the water. Because Selous is a game reserve, not a national park, a larger range of activities is permitted (at an extra cost), so you can walk, camp, and go on a boat safari.

SELOUS'S NAMESAKE

Captain Frederick Courtneney Selous was a famous English explorer and Great White Hunter who roamed the area in the late 1800s. Considered by many to be the greatest hunter of all time, he recounted his adventures in best-selling books of the day, and his safari clients included none other than Teddy Roosevelt. He was killed by a German sniper at Beho Beho in 1917 while scouting for the British against the German *Schutztruppe* (a mixed force of German troops and local Africans) during World War I. His grave lies where he fell.

There's nothing quite like watching a herd of elephants showering, playing, and generally having fun as you sit in a boat in the middle of a lake or river. As you watch, lots of other game including buffalo and giraffes will also amble down to the banks to quench their thirst. If giraffes are your favorite animals, Selous will delight you because it's one of the few places in Africa where you can see big herds of up to 50.

Selous is the only natural World Heritage Site in southern Tanzania and it's on UNESCO'S list of World Heritage Sites under threat. Rampant poaching has decimated the elephant and rhino populations with numbers dropping by as much as 90% since 1982. Because of the increased demand for ivory, particularly from countries in the Far East, only some 15,000 elephants remain. Conservation efforts in Selous are desperately trying to stem the tide of poaching; it's estimated that Selous could loose all of its elephants within the next six years. There are also ongoing projects to try to protect and bolster the rhino population inside the park, which sits below 100, perhaps even as low as 30 individuals. You will have a good chance of spotting the endangered African wild dog from June to August when they're denning and stay put for a few months north of the Rufiji. Selous has up to 1,300 individuals in several wide-ranging packs: double that of any other African reserve. Selous is a birder's mecca with more than 400 species. Along the river with its attendant baobab trees and borassus palms, expect to see different species of herons from the aptly named greenback heron to the Malagasy squacco heron, which winters here. Storks, skimmers, and little waders of all kinds dig in the mud and shallow water, while at dusk you may get a glimpse of the rare orange-color Pel's fishing owl, which screeches like a soul in torment. In summer, flocks of hundreds of brightly colored Carmine bee-eaters flash crimson along the banks where they nest in holes, and kingfishers of all kinds dart to and fro.

WHEN TO GO

June to October is the best time to visit, as it's the driest. During the long rains from February to May most of the camps aren't accessible, and many roads are impassable.

GETTING HERE AND AROUND

The best way to get to Selous is by charter or scheduled flight from Dar es Salaam or Arusha. Arusha to Selous is a three-hour flight, Dar es Salaam to Arusha is a two-hour flight. There's also the option of getting there by road from Dar es Salaam, which will take four-and-a-half hours. However, it's recommended that you fly, especially between February and April, when the road conditions can become very bad because of the rainy season. Your operator or lodge should be able to help you arrange your transportation.

WHERE TO STAY

$$$$
ALL-INCLUSIVE
Fodor'sChoice
★

Azura Selous. Found on the far western corner Selous Reserve, Azura has created a luxurious camp along the curve of the Ruaha River. **Pros:** fantastic location right on the river's edge; private and spacious rooms with fantastic outdoor areas; the bush sundowners are wonderfully romantic. **Cons:** small main area can feel crowded if at full capacity; game concentration is not as high as the opposite end of the park; you may have to spend time tracking animals to view them. $ *Rooms from: $700* ⊠ *Selous Game Reserve, Selous Game Reserve* ☎ *11/467–0907 in South Africa* ⊕ *www.azura-retreats.com* ↪ *12 tented villas* ᛏᴑᛁ *All-inclusive.*

$$$$
RESORT
Fodor'sChoice
★

Beho Beho. Many safari aficionados consider Beho Beho to be one of the best accommodations in East Africa. **Pros:** private waterhole where wildlife abounds; elegant accommodations and fantastic service; breathtaking elevated and expansive views. **Cons:** privacy and exclusivity comes at a cost; vehicles have to be back in the camp at dusk; no riverbank or lake views. $ *Rooms from: $1060* ⊠ *Selous Game Reserve* ☎ *01/932–260618 in U.K.* ⊕ *www.behobeho.com* ⊘ *Closed mid-Mar.–May* ↪ *8 chalets, 1 tree house* ᛏᴑᛁ *All-inclusive.*

$$$$
RESORT

Lake Manze. Manze camp is found in the far eastern section of the reserve in a bountiful game-viewing area—just follow the well-worn elephant trail from the river to a large thatch roof spreading out over the sand floor. **Pros:** great lake-side location; tents are spacious and positioned to make the most of the cooling breeze; boat cruises on the lake are a must. **Cons:** not a luxury camp; you have to pay for extras with cash; no electricity in the tents, but that is part of the eco charm. $ *Rooms from: $675* ⊠ *Selous Game Reserve* ☎ *222/601–747* ⊕ *www.ed.co.tz* ⊘ *Closed Apr.–May* ↪ *12 tents* ᛏᴑᛁ *All meals.*

$$
RESORT

Rufiji River Camp. This camp—the oldest in the reserve—has a great location on a wide bend on the Rufiji at the end of the eastern sector of the reserve. **Pros:** family units have their own private plunge pool; variety of game-viewing options gives you a different perspective of the wildlife and allows you to see a wide variety of animals, large and small; great views from the front of the lodge. **Cons:** monkeys can be a problem in camp as they try to steal food from tables—don't feed them; simpler style than other camps in the area; activities are at set

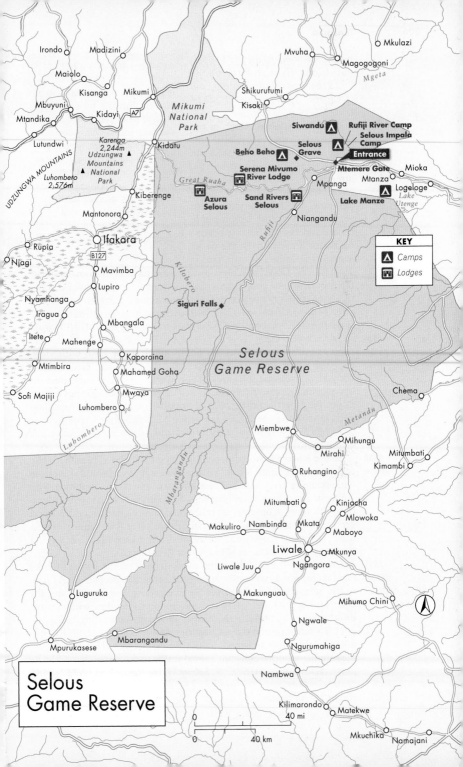

Selous
Game Reserve

times. [$] *Rooms from: $425* ✉ *Selous Game Reserve* ☎ *078/423–7422* ⊕ *www.rufijirivercamp.com* ⊗ *Closed April 1–June 1* ⇲ *14 tents* ⦿ *All-inclusive.*

$$$$
RESORT
Fodor'sChoice
★

⌗ **Sand Rivers Selous.** Deep in the southwest corner of Selous, this lodge is just about as isolated and exclusive as you can get, but the attentive service and home-away-from-home atmosphere is unlike any other lodge in the park. **Pros:** some of the most comfortable rooms and beds in Selous; beautiful riverside views from the decks around the lodge; fly camping is a must here. **Cons:** mischievous monkeys have been known to raid the rooms, so put your belongings safely away; limited mobile phone reception; the very open rooms might make some nervous, but it's very safe. [$] *Rooms from: $1070* ✉ *Selous Game Reserve* ☎ *763/333–383* ⊕ *www.nomad-tanzania.com* ⇲ *8 chalets, 1 family house* ⦿ *All meals.*

$$$$
RESORT
FAMILY

⌗ **Selous Impala Camp.** This attractive small camp on Lake Mzizimia's shores nestles among borassus palms and riverine bush with views over the Rufiji. **Pros:** river cruises and the game and prolific bird-life you will see; the staff are delightful and very knowledgeable; the overwhelming "secret surprise sunset". **Cons:** animal sightings are not as prolific as in the north; tents are smaller than in other camps; limited views of the river. [$] *Rooms from: $739* ✉ *Selous Game Reserve* ☎ *753/115–908* ⊕ *www.selousimpalacamp.com* ▭ *No credit cards* ⇲ *8 tents* ⦿ *All meals.*

$$$$
RESORT

⌗ **Serena Mivumo River Lodge.** Set high on a bluff above Tanzania's biggest river, the mighty Rufiji, Mivumo lodge hosts a beautiful location with relaxing river views. **Pros:** fantastic amenities combined with authentic bush experience; boat trips down Rufiji River; incredible location with views. **Cons:** not the traditional luxury safari tent experience; very rough, bumpy roads; abundant game but it does require quite a drive. [$] *Rooms from: $652* ✉ *Selous Game Reserve* ☎ *27/254–5555* ⊕ *www.serenahotels.com* ⇲ *12 rooms* ⦿ *All meals.*

$$$$
RESORT
Fodor'sChoice
★

⌗ **Siwandu.** In the middle of the riverine bush on the banks of Lake Nzerakera, this luxuriously appointed camp has become a real gem in the Selous reserve. **Pros:** service goes above and beyond and the details make it a standout; beautifully appointed lounges with viewing decks to relax and take in the surroundings; divine boating safari and gourmet lunch on the river. **Cons:** the boat trip up the Rufiji River is not available all year round; Selous Reserve is incredibly hot during the summer months; constant animal traffic to the water source can be noisy. [$] *Rooms from: $783* ✉ *Selous Game Reserve* ☎ *22/212–8485* ⊕ *www.selous.com* ⊗ *Closed end of Mar.–early June* ⇲ *13 tented rooms* ⦿ *All meals.*

Sand Rivers Selous

Beho Beho Safari Lodge

Siwandu

GOMBE STREAM AND MAHALE MOUNTAINS NATIONAL PARKS

Game
★★
Park Accessibility
★★
Getting Around
★
Accommodations
★★
Scenic Beauty
★★★★★

If your heart is set on tracking our nearest animal relatives—the intriguing, beguiling, and oh-so-human chimpanzees—then take the time and effort to get to one or both of these rarely visited but dramatically beautiful parks. You'll meet very few other visitors, and very few other people on earth will share your experience.

The best time to see chimps is the last two months of the dry season, September and October, when they come out of the forest and move lower down the slopes—sometimes even to the beach.

Don't go trekking if you have a cold, flu, or any other infectious diseases. Chimps are highly susceptible to human diseases, and you certainly wouldn't wish to reduce the chimp population even further.

GOMBE STREAM NATIONAL PARK

Bordering Burundi to the west, Tanzania's smallest national park—only 52 square km (20 square miles)—is easily one of the country's loveliest. It's tucked away on the shores of Africa's longest and deepest lake, Lake Tanganyika, 676 km (420 miles) long and 48 km (30 miles) wide. The lake is a veritable inland sea, the second deepest lake in the world after Russia's Lake Baikal. This small gem of a park 3.5 km (2 miles) wide and only 15 km (9½ miles) long stretches from the white sandy beaches of the blue lake up into the thick forest and the mountains of the rift escarpment behind.

Though the area is famous for its primates, don't expect Tarzan-like rain forest because the area is mainly covered with thick Brachystegia woodland. There are also strips of riverine bush alongside the many streams that gouge out steep valleys as they make their way from the highlands to flow down into the lake.

Gombe isn't as easy to get to as other parks, and it's going to cost you, but you'll be amply rewarded with one of the most excitingly close animal encounters still possible on our planet. You'll hear the chimps long before you see them. A series of hoots and shrieks rising to a crescendo of piercing whoops sounds like a major primate battle is about to begin. But it's only the members of the clan identifying one another, recognizing one another, and finally greeting one another.

Gombe became famous when Jane Goodall came to the area in 1960 to study the chimpanzee population. At the time she wasn't known or recognized as the world-renowned primatologist she would later become. Sponsored by the legendary paleontologist Louis Leakey of Olduvai Gorge, Goodall came to Gombe as an eager but unqualified student of chimpanzees. At first many of her amazing unique studies of chimp behavior were discounted because she was a young, unknown scientist. How could a chimpanzee be a hunter and meat-eater? How could a chimpanzee possibly use grass stalks and sticks as tools? Whoever had heard of inter-troop warfare? Today her groundbreaking work is universally acknowledged. Read more about her and her experiences at Gombe in her best-selling book *In the Shadow of Man*. You'll also be able to meet descendants of those chimpanzees she studied and made famous. Fifi, who was only three when Goodall arrived at Gombe in 1960, survived until 2004. Her youngest surviving son, Ferdinand, was alpha male in 2010.

But be warned—to follow in Jane or Fifi's footsteps you need to be fairly fit. Keeping up with a group of feeding and moving chimpanzees as they climb hills and forage in deep valleys can be very strenuous work. But the effort will be worth it—there's nothing on earth quite like coming face-to-face with a chimpanzee or accompanying a group as they make their way through the forest.

WHEN TO GO

Trekking can be done throughout the year, but the wet season (November–mid-May) is the best time to see the chimps as they don't roam very far. Dry season (May–October) does allow for better photography and usually better vantage points, but no matter the season, there's never a guarantee that you will spot the chimps.

GETTING HERE AND AROUND

Kigoma is connected to Dar es Salaam, Mwanza, and Arusha by scheduled flights, and to Mwanza, Dar es Salaam, Arusha and Mbeya by rough dirt roads. Kigoma to Dar es Salaam is a three-hour flight; from Kigoma to Arusha is roughly a two-hour flight. The drive from Kigoma to Mwanza is roughly 575 km (357 miles), and the roads are bad. If you go by bus it'll take two days. To get into the park from Kigoma you can arrange a boat transfer (1–2 hours), which can be done with your lodge or with the parks authority; local taxi transfer is possible but it can be a three-hour adventure. The lodge can arrange your travel to and from your destination; talk to your safari operator about getting to and from the camps.

TIMING

Strict rules are in place to safeguard you and the chimps. Allow at least two days to see them—they're in a wild state, so there are no guarantees where they'll be each day. Trekking is done between 6 am and 6:30 pm.

ESSENTIALS

Entry fees for Gombe are US$100 per person per day for a 24-hour period, the highest of any park in Tanzania. Guided walks on Lake Tanganyika will cost US$20 per person. Your guide will cost an additional US$20 per day for both activities. **■TIP→ You can pay in both USD and Tsh, but USD is preferred.** Kids under seven aren't permitted to enter either park. Because of the traveling time it's suggested that you spend at least two nights in either or both of the parks to get the most out of the experience.

WHERE TO STAY

$$$ ALL-INCLUSIVE **Gombe Forest Lodge.** The only accommodation inside of Gombe National Park, the cozy and intimate Forest Lodge sits amidst the mopane trees as a series of stand-alone canvas tents raised up off the ground on wooden platforms. **Pros:** being in the midst of the park at night; right on the lake shore, this is a birder's paradise; beach-side campfires after a day of chimp trekking. **Cons:** it will cost you; you need to be fit to do any activities in this lodge; no Wi-Fi. [$] *Rooms from: $527* ✉ *Gombe National Park* 🛏 *7 tents* 🍴 *All meals* 💳 *No credit cards.*

$ HOTEL **Kigoma Hilltop Hotel.** On a hill overlooking the lake about 2 km (1.2 miles) from Kigoma's town center, this hotel makes an ideal base for your chimpanzee trekking. **Pros:** lovely view of Lake Tanganyika from your balcony; a large pool to cool off after trekking; day trips to the park from the hotel. **Cons:** limited menu and quite pricy; Wi-Fi is very expensive; boat hire to Gombe Island will be more expensive here than if you go to the Tanap office directly. [$] *Rooms from: $91* ✉ *Kigoma* ☎ *737/206–420, 732/978–879* 🌐 *www.mbalimbali.com* 🛏 *30 cottages* 🍴 *Breakfast.*

MAHALE MOUNTAINS NATIONAL PARK

Just south of Gombe on the shores of Lake Tanganyika lies Tanzania's most remote, and most astonishingly beautiful, national park. Thirty times bigger than Gombe, Mahale is a stunningly beautiful park with crystal clear streams, soaring forested mountains, and deserted, white sandy beaches. Mt. Nkungwe at 2,460 meters (8,070 feet) dominates the landscape. This is the premier place to spot chimpanzees, with hundreds living in the area; they are more accessible and more regularly seen here than at Gombe.

In 1965 the University of Kyoto in Japan established a permanent chimpanzee research station in Mahale at Kisoge, about a kilometer from the beach. It's still going strong and remains highly respected.

There are no roads in Gombe or Mahale: all your game-viewing and chimpanzee tracking is done on foot. If you're a couch potato, stick with the National Geographic TV channel. What will you see other than chimpanzees? You'll almost certainly see olive baboons, vervet

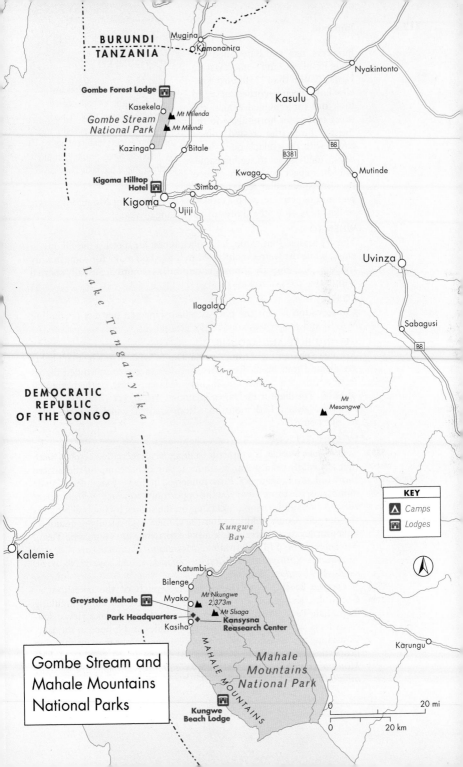

BURUNDI
TANZANIA

Mugina

Kamonanira

Nyakintonto

Gombe Forest Lodge

Kasulu

Kasekela

*Gombe Stream
National Park*

▲ *Mt Milenda*

▲ *Mt Milundi*

Kazinga

Bitale

Kwaga

B381

B8

Mutinde

**Kigoma Hilltop
Hotel**

Simbo

Kigoma

Ujiji

L a k e   T a n g a n y i k a

Ilagala

Uvinza

Sabagusi

B8

**DEMOCRATIC
REPUBLIC
OF THE CONGO**

▲ *Mt
Mesangwe*

KEY

▲ *Camps*

🏠 *Lodges*

*Kungwe
Bay*

Kalemie

Katumbi

Bilenge

Greystoke Mahale

Myako

▲ *Mt Nkungwe
2,373m*

Park Headquarters

▲ *Mt Sisaga*

**Kansysna
Reasearch Center**

Kasiha

M A H A L E   M O U N T A I N S

*Mahale
Mountains
National Park*

Karungu

Gombe Stream and
Mahale Mountains
National Parks

**Kungwe
Beach Lodge**

20 mi

0

0

20 km

monkeys, red- and blue-tailed colobus monkeys, and some exciting
birds. More than 230 bird species have been recorded here, so
look out for crowned eagles, the
noisy trumpeter hornbills, and the
"rasta" birds (the crested guinea
fowls with their black punk hair-
dos). Don't expect to see big game,
but do expect to be surrounded
by some spectacular scenery and a

> **DID YOU KNOW?**
>
> Illegal trafficking is the greatest
> threat to Tanzania's endangered
> chimpanzee population. Highly
> coveted for medical research,
> zoos, and as pets, baby chimps
> are taken by force, resulting in the
> death of many protective adults.

plethora of activities such as trekking to the peak of Mount Nkungwe
or kayaking along the shores of Lake Tanganyika.

WHEN TO GO

The dry season, June through October, is best for spotting the chimps up
close, while the wetter months (March to May) make for some muddy
trekking. Sightings are almost guaranteed, as chimps are usually spotted
within two days of trekking.

COST

Conservation fee for the park is $80 per person per day (excluding
V.A.T.) and ranger fees are $20 per group

GETTING HERE AND AROUND

Arrange a charter flight from Arusha, Dar es Salaam, or Kigoma. Flights
are around four hours from Arusha; there are two scheduled flights
from Arusha every week (no flights in March, April, or the beginning
of May). The flight from Dar es Salaam to Arusha is two hours. There's
also the National Park motorboat from Kigoma, which will take three
to four hours.

WHERE TO STAY

$$$$
RESORT
Fodor's Choice
★

Greystoke Mahale. It's difficult to imagine almost anywhere on earth
that's as wildly beautiful and remote as this exotic camp on the eastern
shore of Lake Tanganyika. **Pros:** immersed in the very secluded Mahale
mountains; the camp gives you the opportunity to watch wild chimpanzees up close and personal; relaxing on the shores by the beach bar as
the sun sets. **Cons:** trekking after the chimps is physically demanding;
long journey to get there; this kind of experience does not come cheap.
$ *Rooms from: $1365* ⊠ *Mahale Mountains National Park, Mahale
Mountains National Park* ⊕ *www.nomad-tanzania.com* ⊟ *No credit
cards* ⇄ *6 bandas* ‖○‖ *All meals.*

$$$$
RESORT

Kungwe Beach Lodge. On the same stretch of the lakeshore as
Greystoke, Kungwe is the only other alternative for chimp trekking
in Mahale Park. **Pros:** cheaper prices with fantastic lake views; spacious tents with Wi-Fi; kayak with crocodiles and hippos in the lake.
Cons: long travel distances; simpler accommodations than neighboring
properties; cost to get here is high. $ *Rooms from: $667* ⊠ *Mahale
Mountains National Park, Mahale Mountains National Park* ⊕ *www.
mbalimbali.com* ⊟ *No credit cards* ⇄ *10 tents* ‖○‖ *All-inclusive.*

IF YOU HAVE TIME

If you still have time after you've explored our picks for Must-See Parks, put the following national parks on your list, too: Arusha, Tarangire, and Ruaha.

ARUSHA NATIONAL PARK

Don't overlook the tiny Arusha National Park. Though it covers only 137 square km (58 square miles), it has more to see than many much larger reserves. You'll find three distinct areas within the park: the forests that surround the Ngurdoto Crater, the brightly colored pools of the Momella Lakes, and the soaring peaks of Mt. Meru. And with the city of Arusha only a 32-km (20-mile) drive to the northeast, it's easy to see the park in a day.

Established in 1960, the park was originally called Ngurdoto Crater National Park, but after the mountain was annexed in 1967 it became known as Mt. Meru National Park. Today it's named for the Warusha people who once lived in this area. The Maasai also lived here, which is why many of the names for sights within the park are Swahili.

WHEN TO GO

To climb Mt. Meru, the best time is between June and February, although it may rain in November. The best views of Kilimanjaro are December through February.

GETTING HERE AND AROUND

Arusha National Park/Mt. Meru/Ngurdoto Crater is a 40-minute drive from Kilimanjaro International Airport. The lakes, forest, and Ngurdoto Crater can all be visited in the course of a half-day visit.

Park fees are $45, and there are a few campsites and huts inside the park as well as some charming accommodations if you want to spend the night, including the homey Kiota Nest, the quirky and stylish Hatari Lodge, and for something truly unique, the Bedouin-styled camps with a Swahili out-of-Africa twist at Shu'mata Camp.

EXPLORING

Momella Lakes. Northeast of the Ngurdoto Crater, this series of seven lakes was formed by lava flow from the nearby Mt. Meru. Each body of water has its own distinct color thanks to varying mineral content, which attracts different types of birds—more than 400 species of birds have been spotted in the area. Reedbuck and waterbuck are also common sights near the dirt road and there are numerous observation points along the way for getting a closer look at the flora and fauna. You can also arrange through your safari company to go on a canoe around the smaller portion of the lake. Keep an eye out for the thousands of flamingos that feed on the algae that cover the lake in a pink hue at certain times of the year. ⊠ *Momella Lake, Arusha.*

Mt. Meru. Because it is not as well-known, the slopes of Mt. Meru are blissfully uncrowded. ⚠ Although Meru looks diminutive alongside Kilimanjaro, do not underestimate what it takes to climb to the top. You must be in good shape, and you need to allow time to acclimatize.

Climbing Mt. Meru itself takes at least four days when it is dry; during the wet season the tracks can be very slippery and it can take more than four days. Huts along the way sleep 24–48 people, but inquire beforehand whether beds are available. You can arrange for no-frills journeys up the mountain through the park service, or book a luxury package through a travel company that includes porters to carry all your supplies. Either way you'll be accompanied by an armed guard to protect you from unfriendly encounters with elephant or buffalo. The rim of Meru Crater has a breathtaking view of the sheer cliffs rising to the summit. Keep an eye out for a diminutive antelope called the klipspringer. ⊠ *Mt. Meru.*

Ngurdoto Forest and Crater. After entering the park through the Ngurdoto Gate, you'll pass through the fig, olive, and wild mango trees of the Ngurdoto Forest. Farther along is the Ngurdoto Crater, which is actually a caldera, or collapsed crater. Unlike the nearby Ngorongoro Crater, this caldera appears to have had two cones. There are no roads into the crater itself, so the buffalo and other animals that make their homes in the swampy habitat remain protected. You can do a day safari around the rim, where you'll find a misty landscape covered with date palms, orchids, and lichens. The grasslands to the west are known as Serengeti Ndogo ("Little Serengeti") and boast a herd of Burchell's zebras, thriving because there are no lions nearby. ■ TIP→ Expect traffic during peak season.

WHERE TO EAT

Arusha might just be a stopover city for some, but there is a lot of great food on offer in the town that goes beyond packed safari lunchboxes. If you are looking for some fine dining, **Machewo** and **Arusha Coffee House** have two of the top restaurants in town. Fancy a decent drink and some good hearty food? **Blues and Chutney** has a wonderful restaurant and bar area serving up great home-cooked meals. **Abyssinia** is a favorite if you like Ethiopian food. A good quick-bites option is **Alpha Choice** on Sokine Road. But, if you have 24 hours before your safari you will not go wrong if you phone up **Damascus** (⊠ *off Perfect Printers Road* ☎ 255–76–587–8453) and ask for their homemade safari lunchboxes to take on your trip; they have some of the best homemade tapas around. While other safari goers are munching on sandwiches and peanuts, you'll have the option of dining on chicken satay, pita bread with coriander tomato and onion mix, meat falafels, and some divine dips to go with your cold wine and sweet puddings. ⇨ *For restaurant reviews, see the dining section in Arusha below.*

TARANGIRE NATIONAL PARK

Although this lovely 2,600-square-km (1,004-square-mile) park is an easy drive from Arusha—just 118 km (71 miles) southwest—and adjacent to Lake Manyara, it's continued to be something of a well-kept secret. During the dry season it's part of the migratory movement and is second only to Ngorongoro Crater in concentration of wildlife. Not only does it have the highest concentration of elephants in Tanzania, as well as some of the more spectacular places to photograph baobab trees, but it's also home to the Big Five. The best time to visit is July through October, when thousands of parched animals flock to the waterholes and thousands more make their long way to the permanent water of the Tarangire River.

Park fees are around $45 and night game drives, which have just opened up in the park, will cost $50. Staying within the park is quite an experience, especially in the plush safari-chic surrounds of Sanctuary Swala Camp or in the authentically styled Oliver Camp. But at the top of the pack is by far the treetop experience of Tarangire Treetops, with its expansive rooms and wraparound balconies with views out over the park.

Visit the UNESCO World Heritage Site of Kondo, near Kolo, just south of the park. From the last Stone Age, the illustrations of hunting scenes painted on the cave walls have been suggested to date back some 29,000 years and are still considered to have ritual associations with the local Hadza and Sandawe peoples who live nearby.

WHEN TO GO

You can visit year-round, but the dry season (June–October) is the best for its sheer number of animals.

GETTING HERE AND AROUND

It's an easy drive from Arusha or Lake Manyara following a surfaced road to within 7 km (4 miles) of the main entrance gate. Charter flights from Arusha and the Serengeti are also possible. The flight from Arusha to southern Serengeti is roughly 1½ hours; the drive is 335 km (208 miles), which will take around eight hours.

GAME-VIEWING

During the dry season, huge herds of elephant, eland, oryx, zebra, buffalo, wildebeest, giraffe, and impala roam the park. Hippos are plentiful and pythons can sometimes be seen in trees near the swamps. If you want to spot waterbuck or the gerenuk, head for the Mkungero Pools. Tarangire is much more densely wooded than Serengeti with acacia, mixed woodland, and the ubiquitous baobab trees, although you'll find grasslands on the southern plains where cheetahs hunt.

There are more than 500 species of birds in Tarangire National Park, including martial and bateleur eagles. Especially good bird-watching can be done along the wetlands of the Silale Swamp and around the Tarangire River. Yellow-collared lovebirds, hammerkops, helmeted guinea fowl, long-toed lapwings, brown parrots, white-bellied go-away birds, and a variety of kingfishers, weavers, owls, plovers, and sandpipers make their homes here. A shallow alkaline lake attracts flamingos and pelicans in the rainy season. Raptors are plentiful, including the palm-nut vulture and lots of eagles. You may hear a cry that sounds quite similar to the American bald eagle but is in fact its look-alike cousin, the African fish eagle.

RUAHA NATIONAL PARK

Remote and rarely visited, Ruaha is Tanzania's second-largest park—10,300 square km (3,980 square miles). Oddly enough, it attracts only a fraction of the visitors that go to Serengeti, which could be because it's less well-known and difficult to access. But East Africa safari aficionados claim it to be the country's best-kept secret. There are huge concentrations of buffalos, elephants, antelope, and more than 400 bird species.

POACHING

Poaching continues throughout the Ruaha-Rungwa ecosystem. However, because of the devastating poaching in Selous, Ruaha now holds some of the largest elephant populations on record in East Africa. This population is also under threat as reports of increased elephant poaching in the park surface each day.

Classified as a national park in 1964, it was once part of the Sabia River Game Reserve, which the German colonial government established in 1911. Ruaha is derived from the word "great" in the Hehe language and refers to the mighty Ruaha River, which flows around the park's borders, and it's only around the river that the park is developed for tourism with a 400-km (249-mile) road circuit. The main portion of the park sits on top of a 1,800-meter (5,900-foot) plateau with spectacular views of valleys, hills, and plains—a wonderful backdrop for game-viewing. Habitats include riverine forest, savanna, swamps, and acacia woodland.

WHEN TO GO

The best time to visit is May through November because, although even in the wet season the all-weather roads are passable, it's incredibly difficult to spot game at that time because of the lush, tall vegetation. If you're into bird-watching, lush scenery, and wildflowers, you'll like the wet season (December–March).

GETTING HERE AND AROUND

Most visitors arrive by charter flight from Dar es Salaam, Selous, the Serengeti, or Arusha. The flight is 2½ hours to Ruaha from Arusha or Dar es Salaam, and one hour from Selous. It's possible to drive to Ruaha but it takes longer. Visitors often drive from Dar es Salaam, but not many drive from Arusha. The drive to Ruaha from Dar es Salaam is roughly 10 hours through Iringa. The roads do get a bit bumpy as you near the park. Safari companies will arrange road transfers if you so wish. If time is of the essence, fly; if it's interaction and experience (atmosphere) of the various places en route to Ruaha you'd like, drive.

ESSENTIALS

There's a conservation fee of US$30 per person (excluding V.A.T.), per 24-hour visit and $40 per vehicle (if you're driving). ■TIP→ **You can pay in both USD and Tsh.** Ask at your lodge for a copy of the Ruaha booklet, which has maps, checklists, and hints on where to look for particular species.

TIMING

Four nights will give you the chance to fully experience the varied areas of the park.

GAME-VIEWING

There are elephant, buffalo, lion, spotted hyena, gazelle, zebra, greater and lesser kudu, and giraffe roaming this park. If you're lucky, you might even see roan and sable antelope or witness a cheetah hunt on the open plains in the Lundu area. Lion are well habituated to vehicles, so you'd be very unlucky not to spot at least one pride, and if you've set your heart on seeing wild dogs, then try to come in June or July when they're denning; this makes them easier to spot than at other times because they stay in one place for a couple of months. There are also lots of crocs and hippos in the river areas. Bird "specials" include the lovely little Eleonora's falcon (December through January is the best time to spot one), Pel's fishing owl, and the pale-billed hornbill.

DID YOU KNOW?

Tanzania is one of the world's largest producers of cashews, exporting more than 200,000 tons of raw nuts each year, a big source of income for small-scale farmers.

WHERE TO STAY

$$$$ ALL-INCLUSIVE **Jabali Ridge.** Contemporary in style amongst the rocky outcrops, Jabali blends seamlessly into the impressive natural beauty at the heart of Ruaha. **Pros:** incredible views from the rooms; expert safari guides; panoramic views from the infinity pool. **Cons:** you are right among the wildlife, so be prepared for close encounters; Ruaha, in peak summer, is incredibly hot; not the traditional tented camp experience. [$] *Rooms from: $914* ✉ *Ruaha National Park* ☎ *736/500–515* 🌐 *www.asiliaafrica.com* 🛏 *8 rooms* 🍴 *All-inclusive.*

$$$$ RESORT Fodor's Choice ★ **Jongomero Tented Camp.** The only camp in the southwest corner of Ruaha National Park, Jongomero exudes a laid-back bush atmosphere with stellar service amid luxurious trimmings. **Pros:** enthusiastic staff and excellent food; fly camping is a must; the special little surprises and deft, thoughtful touches make this a unique experience. **Cons:** tsetse flies are in the area and around the camp; rhinos, sadly due to poaching, are a very rare sight; thicker bush during wet seasons make it harder to spot certain animals. [$] *Rooms from: $701* ✉ *Ruaha National Park, Ruaha National Park* ☎ *22/212–8485* 🌐 *www.selous.com* 🕓 *Closed Apr.–May* 🛏 *8 tents* 🍴 *All-inclusive.*

$$$$ RESORT **Kigelia Camp.** Set in a forest of baobabs and sausage trees along the Ifaguru sand river, Kigelia has a prime location in Ruaha. **Pros:** classic tented safari camp feel with a few modern twists; watching the fire under the stars at night; wildlife frequently move through the camp itself. **Cons:** the camp is an hour's drive from the airstrip; Wi-Fi is intermittent to nonexistent; time the weather to avoid the rainier seasons (camp is closed during peak wet season). [$] *Rooms from: $765* ✉ *Ruaha National Park, Ruaha National Park* ☎ *784/208–343* 🌐 *www.nomad-tanzania.com* 💳 *No credit cards* 🕓 *Closed Apr.–May* 🛏 *6 tents* 🍴 *All meals.*

$$$ RESORT **Mwagusi Safari Camp.** This well-established camp is situated on the shady banks of the Mwagusi River, giving it a prime position in Ruaha for game-viewing. **Pros:** delicious food; excellent guides and bush knowledge; superb location for wildlife viewing. **Cons:** bandas

WORD OF MOUTH

Known to be great warriors, the Maasai are mainly found in southern Kenya and Tanzania.

are rustic-looking from the outside; charging cameras and batteries is difficult in this remote location; some bandas can be a bit of a distance from the main tent. [$] *Rooms from: $565* ✉ *Ruaha National Park* ☎ *75 /2517–0940 in U.K.* 🌐 *www.mwagusicamp.com* 💳 *No credit cards* 🕒 *Closed late Mar.–late May* 🛏 *13 tents* 🍴 *All meals.*

$ RESORT 🏨 **Tandala Camp.** Because Tandala is in a private conservancy 5 km (3 miles) outside the entrance gate, guests can take early morning game walks and game drives, engage in bird-viewing or experience authentic cultural visits to the Maasai bomas, local village, and market. **Pros:** great views from your tent's raised deck; elephants often frequent the nearby waterhole; children of all ages welcome. **Cons:** very bumpy road to the Ruaha park entrance (10 minutes); outside of the main park; can only accept smaller amounts of money in camp for payments of extras. [$] *Rooms from: $165* ✉ *Ruaha National Park, Ruaha National Park* ☎ *755/680–220* 🌐 *www.tandalacamp.com* 💳 *No credit cards* 🛏 *11 tents* 🍴 *All-inclusive.*

GATEWAY CITIES

Many visitors to Tanzania will find themselves with a layover in Dar es Salaam or Arusha before or after their safari. Dar es Salaam is often dismissed as a mere transition point, but it's a city on the rise and a wonderful expression of the changing landscape of modern Tanzania beyond the beach and safaris. For some ideas and suggestions to help determine where you should stay, eat, and, if you have time, sightsee, read on.

DAR ES SALAAM

Graceful triangular-sail dhows share the harbor with mammoth tankers, as the once sleepy village of Dar es Salaam, which means "haven of peace" in Arabic, has been transformed into one of East Africa's busiest ports, second only to Kenya's Mombasa. The country's major commercial center, Dar es Salaam has also become its largest city, home to more than 3.5 million inhabitants. The city also serves as the seat of government during the very slow move to Dodoma, which was named the official capital in 1973. The legislature resides in Dodoma, but most government offices are still found in Dar es Salaam.

In the early 1860s, Sultan Seyyid Majid of Zanzibar visited what was then the isolated fishing village of Mzizima on the Tanzanian coast. Eager to have a protected port on the mainland, Majid began constructing a palace here in 1865. The city, poised to compete with neighboring ports such as Bagamoyo and Kilwa, suffered a setback after the sultan died in 1870. His successor, his half-brother Seyyid Barghash, had little interest in the city, and its royal buildings fell into ruins. Only the Old Boma, which once housed royal guests, still survives.

The city remained a small port until Germany moved its colonial capital here in 1891 and began constructing roads, offices, and many of the public buildings still in use today. The Treaty of Versailles granted Great Britain control of the region in 1916, but that country added comparatively little to the city's infrastructure during its 45-year rule.

Tanzania gained its independence in 1961. During the years that followed, President Julius Nyerere, who focused on issues such as education and health care, allowed the capital city to fall into a decline that lasted into the 1980s. When Benjamin William Mkapa took office in 1985, his market-oriented reforms helped to revitalize the city. The city continues to evolve—those who visited only a few years ago will be startled by the changes—as new hotels and restaurants have appeared almost overnight. There are a few sights to detain visitors, but the only one really worth a visit is the National Museum, which contains the famous fossil discoveries by Richard and Mary Leakey, including the 1.7-million-year-old hominid skull discovered by Mary Leakey in the Olduvai Gorge in 1959. What Dar es Salaam has in blossoming abundance are exciting restaurants, beautiful hotels, and some of the best nightlife around.

GETTING HERE AND AROUND

To find your way around central Dar es Salaam, use the Askari Monument, at the intersection of Samora Avenue and Azikiwe Street, as a compass. Most sights are within walking distance. Four blocks northeast on Samora Avenue you'll find the National Museum and Botanical Gardens; about seven blocks southwest stands the Clock Tower, another good landmark. One block southeast is Sokoine Drive, which empties into Kivukoni Front as it follows the harbor. Farther along, Kivukoni Front becomes Ocean Road.

Along Samora Avenue and Sokoine Drive you'll find banks, pharmacies, grocery stores, and shops selling everything from clothing to curios. Northwest of Samora Avenue, around India, Jamhuri, and Libya streets, is the busy Swahili neighborhood where merchants sell all kinds of items, including Tanzania's best *kangas* (sarongs or wraps). Farther west you'll find the large Kariakoo Market.

■TIP➔ Don't buy tickets for transport, especially on ferries, trains, or buses, from anyone other than an accredited ticket seller.

Julius Nyerere International Airport is about 13 km (8 miles) from the city center. Plenty of white-color taxis are available at the airport and cost about Tsh50,000 (US$23) to the city center. This is not often negotiable as the airport taxi drivers are notorious for taking advantage of tourists. Most hotels will send drivers to meet your plane if arranged in advance, although this will cost more. While Uber is available in Dar Es Salaam, do not order one from the airport as the local taxis will kick up a fuss for your driver. (This will hopefully change in the next few years.)

Ferries depart to Zanzibar daily, starting at 7 am from the Zanzibar Ferry Terminal. The two-hour journey costs about Tsh63,000 (US$40). Although thousands of locals and tourists use the service every year, two ferries capsized in 2011 and 2012 due to overcrowding (note that this was not Azam, which has not had an incident to date). If you prefer to fly to Zanzibar the cost, on average, is between US$40 and US$80 depending on time and day of the week. ■TIP➔ Tourists aren't

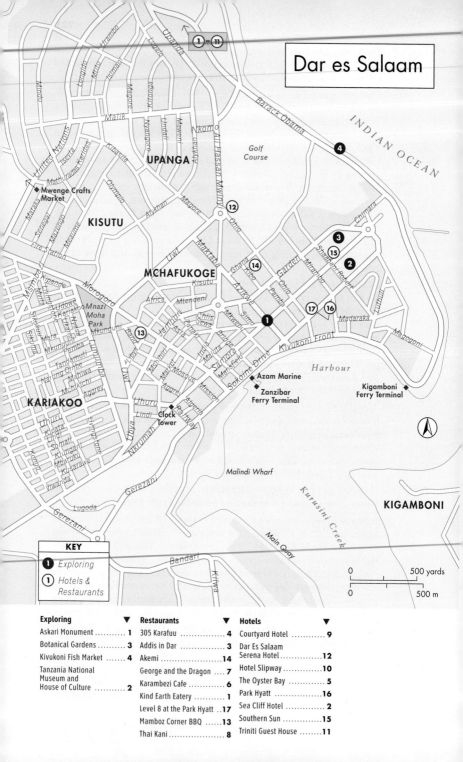

Dar es Salaam

KEY

🅰 Exploring

① Hotels & Restaurants

Exploring ▼

Askari Monument **1**
Botanical Gardens **3**
Kivukoni Fish Market **4**
Tanzania National Museum and House of Culture **2**

Restaurants ▼

305 Karafuu **4**
Addis in Dar **3**
Akemi **14**
George and the Dragon ... **7**
Karambezi Cafe **6**
Kind Earth Eatery **1**
Level 8 at the Park Hyatt .. **17**
Mamboz Corner BBQ **13**
Thai Kani **8**

Hotels ▼

Courtyard Hotel **9**
Dar Es Salaam Serena Hotel **12**
Hotel Slipway **10**
The Oyster Bay **5**
Park Hyatt **16**
Sea Cliff Hotel **2**
Southern Sun **15**
Triniti Guest House **11**

thought to be at risk from pirates from Somalia. The Kigamboni ferry to the southern beaches runs continuously throughout the day and departs from the southern tip of the city center, where Kivukoni Front meets Ocean Road. The five-minute ride costs about Tsh200 (US$2) one-way per person, but you can end up waiting half an hour. You buy your ticket as you walk in. By far, Azam is the safest and best ferry operator to Zanzibar. Tickets are booked online and reserved up to 48 hours before you depart; you pay for and receive the tickets at the terminal or at the Azam office (cash only) in Dar Es Slaam or Zanzibar.

Taxis are the most efficient way to get around town. During the day they're easy to find outside hotels

5

and at major intersections, but at night they're often scarce. Ask someone to call one for you. Taxis don't have meters, so you must agree on the fare before getting in. Fares run about Tsh5,000 within the city and Tsh15,000 from the city to Msisani Peninsula. Uber is available, and a lot cheaper, around the city but the drivers do sometimes get a bit lost. Make sure they close the trip when you exit the car, so that you are not overcharged.

MONEY MATTERS

You can pay in both USD and Tsh, but USD is preferred.

SAFETY

Dar es Salaam is fine to wander around by yourself during the day, but after dark it's best to take a taxi. The area with the most street crime is along the harbor, especially Kivukoni Front and Ocean Road.

Foreign women tend to feel safe in Dar es Salaam. But remember, women in Dar es Salaam never wear clothing that exposes their shoulders or legs. You should do the same. You'll feel more comfortable in modest dress.

VISITOR INFORMATION

The Tanzania Tourist Board's head office is in Dar es Salaam. It has maps and information on travel to dozens of points of interest around Tanzania and is very helpful. The staff will discuss hotel options with you and assist you in making reservations. *See Health and Safety in the chapter's Planning section for information on the U.S. Embassy.*

ESSENTIALS

Ferries Azam Marine. ⊠ *Zanzibar ferry terminal, Dar es Salaam* ☎ *22/212–3324* ⊕ *www.azammarine.com.* **Kigamboni Ferry.** ⊠ *Kivukoni Rd., Dar es Salaam* ⊹ *The mainland port is located at Magogoni near the main fish market*

past the Park Hyatt Dar Es Salaam ☎.
Zanzibar Ferry Terminal. ⊠ *Sokoine
Dr., Dar es Salaam.*

**Visitor Information Tanzania Tourist
Board** (*TTB*). ⊠ *Utalii House, Laibon
St. at Ali Hassan Mwinyi Rd., opposite
French Embassy, Dar es Salaam*
☎ *022/266–4873 tourism services, 022/
266–4878/9 general* ⊕ *www.tanzania-
touristboard.go.tz.*

EXPLORING

Askari Monument. This bronze statue
was erected by the British in 1927
in memory of African troops who
died during World War I. (The
word *askari* means "soldier" in
Swahili.) It stands on the site of a
monument erected by Germany to
celebrate its victory here in 1888.
That monument stood only five
years before being demolished in
1916. ⊠ *Samora Ave. at Azikiwe
St., Dar es Salaam.*

> ### A REAL GEM
>
> Looking for that one-of-a-kind
> gift or keepsake? How about
> jewelry with tanzanite in it? Given
> by Maasai fathers to mothers
> upon the birth of their child,
> this deep-blue stone, discovered
> in 1967, is unique to Tanzania.
> And though you can purchase
> the gems just about anywhere
> these days, you can't beat the
> prices or the bargaining you'll
> find in the shops of Arusha and
> Dar es Salaam—you'll be able to
> purchase loose stones, existing
> pieces, or customize your own
> design. ■ TIP→ Don't buy any
> tanzanite from street vendors.
> Nine times out of 10 it'll be a
> fake stone.

Botanical Gardens. If you are heading to the National Museum it's well
worth a quiet stroll through the indigenous plants in the botanical gardens. It provides respite from the city underneath purple bougainvilleas
and blue jacarandas. ⊠ *Samora Ave., Dar es Salaam* ☎.

Kivukoni Fish Market. If you are feeling brave and interested in experiencing Dar's fish market at its nosiest and fishiest then wake up early and
head down to Kivukoni. There is no charge to walk around. Be prepared
for quite a smell, but the sight of hundreds of weathered fishermen haul-
ing in their catch and the thrumming sounds of commerce—bargaining
and haggling, prepping the seafood—is a fun experience. Please don't
purchase any of the seashells or turtle products on sale. ■ TIP→ If you
prefer to be accompanied by a guide, take part in a city tour, which
will include a stop at the market. ⊠ *Barak Obama Dr., Dar es Salaam.*

Tanzania National Museum and House of Culture. Apart from the Leakey
fossil discoveries, which are some of the most important in the world,
there are also good displays of colonial exploration and German occupation. This is also a spot to learn about Tanzania's tribal heritage and
the impact of the slave trade. ⊠ *Between Samora Ave. and Sokoine
Dr., near Botanical Gardens, Dar es Salaam* ☎ *022/211–7508* ⊒ *US$3.*

BEACHES

The islands may have some exquisite beaches, but don't discount the
sandy shores a few hours' drive around Dar Es Salaam. North is Mbezi
beach, right across the bay from Hotel Slipway and the small harbour
where you can find boat trips to the infamous sandbank parties. Kigamboni, in the south, is a wonderful stretch of beach ideal for families and

anyone seeking respite from the city. You can stay at the barefoot chic Ras Kutani or Marriott Amani Beach hotel. ■ **TIP→ Roads are very good south, while north has more potholed terrain, but it's nothing a little rental car won't get through.**

WHERE TO EAT

Recent years have seen a flourish of imaginative and exciting restaurants opening up across Dar Es Salaam. From rooftop bars to hearty vegan and even Korean barbecue joints the city has something for everyone and every taste. You can spend as much or as little as you like, just bring your appetite, because if it's local street food fare or high-end Continental, the portion sizes are not for the picky. One thing is guaranteed, you are going to want to get out of your hotel and explore as much as you can. Be sure to watch out for the ever-present happy hour from 5 pm that runs across most restaurants and bars; the specials help with those looking to keep the budget amenable. Typical *chakula* (food) for an East African meal includes *wali* (rice) or *ugali* (a damp mound of breadlike ground corn) served with a meat, fish, or vegetable stew. A common side dish found on most menus is *kachumbari,* a fresh mixture of chopped tomatoes, onions, and cucumbers. Street-side snacks not to miss are chicken and beef kebabs, roast corn on the cob, and samosas. Breakfast isn't the same without trying the doughnut-like *mandazi.* Wash it all down with a local beer—Kilimanjaro, Tusker, or Safari—or with a fragrant and delicious hot chai.

Most tourists frequent the more well-known restaurants, which can be quite expensive; entrées can set you back $10 to $15. Even at the smallest of restaurants, reservations are rarely required. Restaurants in hotels generally are open until at least 10:30 pm, even on Sunday, although hours of local restaurants vary.

$$ ETHIOPIAN Fodor's Choice ★

🍴 **Addis in Dar.** It might look unassuming from the outside, but as soon as you climb the stairs of this popular Ethiopian restaurant, you'll be welcomed into a space that has been a long-standing go-to in the city. Seating is around a small table with low chairs on an outside terrace overlooking a tranquil leafy garden (bring insect repellent) amid traditional umbrellas. **Known for:** as authentically Ethiopian as you can get; atmospheric patio dining under the stars; consistently good service. [$] *Average main: $15* ✉ *35 Ursino St., Dar es Salaam* ☎ *713/266–299* 🌐 *www.addisindar.com* 🕒 *Closed Sun.*

$$ INTERNATIONAL

🍴 **Akemi.** On the rooftop of one of the tallest buildings in downtown Dar es Salaam, Akemi sits as a popular dining establishment for the well-heeled for special occasions. With spectacular 360-degree views of the city and harbor, the cuisine is of a standard Continental fare. **Known for:** Tanzania's only revolving restaurant; a decent happy hour special at the bar; the romantic city views at night. [$] *Average main: $20* ✉ *Golden Jubilee Towers, Ohio St., 21st fl., Dar es Salaam* ✣ *Next to PPF Bldg.* ☎ *75/3360–360* 🌐 *www.akemidining.com.*

$ AMERICAN

🍴 **George and the Dragon.** Known locally as The George, sports fans and those seeking a good old-fashioned burger and fries head to this classic British pub. Big screen TVs, buckets of icy cold beers, an expansive barbecue list, and a dedicated area called the sports arena keep punters, expats, and locals satisfied and jovial. **Known for:** large, juicy cheeseburgers with plenty of fries; huge sports area with pool and pub games galore; a lively outdoor beer garden with a resident DJ. [$] *Average main: $10* ✉ *Haile Selassie Rd., Kinondoni* ☎ *717/800–002* ⏲ *Closed Mon.*

$$ CONTEMPORARY 🍴 **Karambezi Cafe.** This popular double-story open-air restaurant in the Sea Cliff Hotel is right next to the crashing sea, providing the best views in town. The café-style restaurant features a decent array of Continental foods like battered fish-and-chips, hamburgers, and juicy steaks, while the lunch buffet has a wonderful spread of local seafood. **Known for:** 180-degree views over the Indian Ocean; live entertainment on weekends; homemade pastry and cakes for teatime treats. [$] *Average main: $12* ✉ *Sea Cliff Hotel, Toure Dr., Dar es Salaam* ☎ *784/342–500* 🌐 *www.hotelseacliff.com.*

$$ VEGETARIAN 🍴 **Kind Earth Eatery.** With creative and delicious food combinations that utilize fresh, local ingredients, owner and chef Betty Delfosse-Ingleton has created a real standout vegan and vegetarian dining option in Dar. Jamaican influences are found in the raw, vegan, and vegetarian haute cuisine that's served in the little outside courtyard decorated with bright art murals. Try raw vegan sushi with tasty Jamaican peanut dipping sauce, or the popular vegetarian "meat" balls made of dates, assorted vegetables, and a voluminous side of black rice slathered in mouthwatering coconut sauce. **Known for:** fresh and vibrant flavor combinations; very generous portions; delicious all-natural-ingredient cocktails. [$] *Average main: $12* ✉ *11 Kahama Rd., Dar es Salaam* ✥ *Opposite Tuk Tuk Thai* ☎ *076–339–1456* ⏲ *Closed Sun.*

$$ INTERNATIONAL Fodor's Choice ★ 🍴 **Level 8 at the Park Hyatt.** The Park Hyatt's Brassiere and Oriental restaurants are both equally fantastic, but by far the hotel's real gem is the spectacular rooftop bar, Level 8. Commanding views of both the city and the working port extend out on either side of the striking, sweeping architecture and high glass walls. **Known for:** delicious snacks and light meals; wonderful views over the city; Friday sunset live acoustic music and cocktails. [$] *Average main: $8* ✉ *24 Kivukoni Rd., Dar es Salaam* ☎ *764/701–234* 🌐 *daressalaamkilimanjaro.regency.hyatt.com/en/hotel/dining/level-8.html.*

$ INDIAN 🍴 **Mamboz Corner BBQ.** Nearly every major African city has a local joint where you can mingle, chat, eat hearty grilled street food, and absorb the city life. Mamboz, and its sister restaurant Mamboz SizGrill, are just this kind of place for Dar es Salaam. **Known for:** hearty plates of delicious grilled meats; takeaway available; simple, but filled with local atmosphere. [$] *Average main: $10* ✉ *Morongoro Rd. at Lybia St., Kinondoni* ✥ *Mind the street directions if coming by taxi—there are a few one-ways that can get you lost* ☎ *785/243–735* 💳 *No credit cards* ⏲ *Closed Tues.*

$ ASIAN 🍴 **Thai Kani.** Overlooking Slipway Beach, this may be the priciest Thai food in town, but Thai Kani still has a reputation for being tasty and deliciously authentic. The outside patio views, accompanied by one of their champagne and sushi platter specials, is a very atmospheric way to while away the evening. **Known for:** vibrant Thai-style salads; delicious and well-made sushi; great views over the bay with happy

Vervet monkeys are found throughout East and Southern Africa.

hour specials. $ *Average main: $11* ✉ *Slipway Beach, Yacht Club Rd., Msasani Peninsula* ☎ *715/486–014* ⊕ *www.thaikani.com.*

$$
CONTEMPORARY

✕ **305 Karafuu.** Tucked away in a small neighborhood, this is a favorite with people who have been coming to Dar es Salaam for a while. Unpretentious, family-run and with some exceptionally tasty food, 305 Karafuu is all local atmosphere and good times. **Known for:** cozy and relaxed atmosphere; the must-try chef's special steak; local neighborhood vibe. $ *Average main: $13* ✉ *Plot 305, Karafuu St., Kinondoni* ☎ *754/277–188* ⊕ *www.305karafuu.co.tz* ☽ *Closed Mon.*

WHERE TO STAY

$
HOTEL

▣ **Courtyard Hotel.** With traditional Arabic wooden balconies, glass-stained windows, and a lush courtyard, this hotel has the feel of a welcoming riad. **Pros:** beautiful architecture and more intimate than the larger chain hotels; a quite, leafy courtyard away from the rush hour street; general manager who is attentive to your every need. **Cons:** traffic outside of the hotel is often at a standstill in peak hours; gym is rather small; service outside can be slow at times. $ *Rooms from: $150* ✉ *Seaview Ocean Rd., Oyster Bay* ☎ *22/213–0130* ⊕ *www.marriot.com* ⤳ *41 rooms* ❑❘ *Breakfast.*

$
HOTEL

▣ **Dar Es Salaam Serena Hotel.** A towering feature of the cityscape for many years, the Serena stands in the center of Dar es Salaam. **Pros:** surrounded by large, pleasant gardens; an expansive pool with outdoor gazebo; central location in the city. **Cons:** very large and caters to big groups and conferences; slightly dated decor in older rooms; small snack café is out of the way. $ *Rooms from: $231* ✉ *Ohio St., Dar es Salaam* ☎ *022/211–2416* ⊕ *www.serenahotels.com* ⤳ *230 rooms* ❑❘ *Breakfast.*

$ HOTEL **Hotel Slipway.** Located in the Slipway, a shopping-and-leisure complex in a converted boatyard, this hotel of the same name is a great place for an overnight or home base in Dar. The large, modern block rises three stories above the shopping complex providing views of Msasani Bay. The simple, but comfortable rooms—a welcome respite from the craziness of the city in calming shades of blue and white—have balconies, free Wi-Fi, satellite TV, and air-conditioning. **Pros:** convenient for restaurants and shopping; bright and modern sea-facing rooms; suites have ample space and an extra lounge area. **Cons:** occasional loud pool parties can change the atmosphere; restaurant and pool seperated from main rooms; older rooms facing the street are dated. *Rooms from: $180 ✉ The Slipway, Chole Rd., Masani Bay, Dar es Salaam ☎ 22/260–0893 ⊕ www.hotelslipway.com 72 rooms Breakfast.*

$$ HOTEL **The Oyster Bay.** This stylish, contemporary boutique hotel has been created as a tranquil haven for guests to recuperate in before or after a flight or safari, and it certainly more than fits the bill. **Pros:** all the rooms have sea views; incredibly stylish and well put together; there are no hidden fees—everything is inclusive. **Cons:** it's expensive, especially if you stay more than one night; there's no elevator; far from the airport. *Rooms from: $450 ✉ 344 Toure Dr., Oyster Bay ☎ 193/226–0618 ⊕ www.theoysterbayhotel.com 8 rooms All-inclusive.*

$$ HOTEL Fodor's Choice ★ **Park Hyatt.** Once known as the Kilimanjaro, the Park Hyatt has carved out a niche for itself as the premier hotel in Dar Es Salaam in both unique style and service; even the Obamas stayed here in 2013. **Pros:** beautiful design and charming outside bistro under a giant tree; relaxing spa and pool on the upper floors; incredibly well-equipped gym. **Cons:** traffic jams can be quite intense during rush hours around the hotel; every now and then you get noise from the nearby rooftop clubs; some distance from popular restaurants in Dar. *Rooms from: $250 ✉ 24 Kivukoni, Dar es Salaam ✣ On the way to the ferry terminal ☎ 076/470–1234 ⊕ www.hyatt.com 180 rooms Breakfast.*

$ HOTEL **Sea Cliff Hotel.** Only 15 minutes from downtown on the edge of the Msasani Peninsula, this classy hotel has commanding views of the sea and good-size, comfortable rooms (insist on one with a sea view). **Pros:** views over the sea; on-site ATM and good facilities; the popular resturant, Karambezi, is on your doorstep. **Cons:** one floor is a smoking floor, check beforehand; gym is basic; cheaper rooms have no views. *Rooms from: $180 ✉ 10 Toure Dr., Msasani Peninsula ☎ 764/700–600 ⊕ www.hotelseacliff.com 114 rooms Breakfast.*

$ HOTEL **Southern Sun.** The Southern Sun may be on the small side, but it packs a delightful punch in terms of charm and service. **Pros:** the earliest, and most bountiful breakfast buffet in Dar—it starts at 4 am; close to all the embassies; 24-hour gym. **Cons:** outside space is small and limited; city-facing rooms are noisy; bathrooms are a bit dated. *Rooms from: $201 ✉ Garden Ave., Dar es Salaam ☎ 75/770–0000 ⊕ www.tsogosun.com 152 rooms Breakfast.*

$ B&B/INN **Triniti Guest House.** Many people will tell you that Dar es Salaam is not made for budget travel, but after spending a night at Triniti Guest House you will change your mind. **Pros:** best budget accommodations in Dar; safe for solo travelers; food is fantastic, plentiful, and well priced.

Cons: Friday night disco at the main bar; bring mosquito repellent; not for families. $ *Rooms from: $65* ✉ *8 Msasani Rd., Dar es Salaam* ☎ *079/628–328* ⊕ *www.triniti.co.tz* ⤷ *12 rooms* ¶⊙¶ *Breakfast.*

SHOPPING

You might want to pick up some amazing Tanzanian fabric, especially the colorful kanga, kitenge, and batik material. Vendors in Mnazi Mmoja on Uhuru Street or inside the Kariakoo cloth market (Congo Street) are some of your best spots to find material and cloth. Sometimes the prices are set, sometimes it's possible to haggle.

Mwenge Craft Market. If you're looking to take home hand-crafted items like bowls, Tinga Tinga paintings, wooden carvings, jewelery, and antique masks then this market is the place to find treasures of varying shapes and sizes and watch the local artists at work. ■ **TIP→ Just down the road, visit the Mwenge Woodcarvers Market for more crafts.** ✉ *Sam Nujoma Rd., Dar es Salaam.*

ARUSHA

Arusha may be the gateway to all of the Serengeti Safari but on a clear day, you can see Mt. Meru, Africa's fifth highest mountain at 4,556 meters (14,947 feet), looming in the distance. There are some wonderful accommodation options on the outskirts of Arusha that are well worth a day or two pre- or post-safari, just to recharge, relax, and be pampered while experiencing some Northern Tanzanian hospitality.

The town is bisected by the Nauru River. The more modern part is to the east of the river where most of the hotels, safari companies, and banks are located; west of the river are the bus station and main market. Most people spend an overnight here either coming or going.

GETTING HERE AND AROUND

There are no direct flights from the United States to Arusha. Generally you need to connect through a city on the mainland, the easiest being Dar es Salaam.

You'll be approached immediately after you land by taxi drivers. Be sure to agree on a price before getting in, as taxis don't have meters. The fare to downtown Arusha is approximately US$30.

SAFETY

It's unlikely that you'd want to explore Arusha at night, but if you do, take a taxi. As in any city, muggings and purse-snatching are common.

VISITOR INFORMATION

The Tanzanian Tourist Board (TTB) has an Arusha office where you can pick up maps and brochures for the area, as well as book cultural excursions. Tanzania National Parks also has an office here that can help you book accommodations or answer any of your safari questions.

CONTACTS

Airports Arusha Airport (*ARK*). ✉ *A 104, Arusha* ☎ *27/741–530, 27/744–317* ⊕ *www.taa.go.tz.*

Hospitals AICC Hospital. ✉ *Old Moshi Rd., Arusha* ☎ *27/254–4113* ⊕ *www.aicc.co.tz.*

Restaurants ▼

- Abyssinia **6**
- Alpha Choice **11**
- Blue Heron **5**
- Blues and Chutney **1**
- Damascus Tapas and Meze **7**
- Fifi's **10**
- The Grill Room **13**
- Machewo **2**

Hotels ▼

- The African Tulip **8**
- Arusha Coffee Lodge **12**
- The Arusha Hotel **9**
- Ngare Sero Mountain Lodge **3**
- Onsea House and Machweo Retreat **4**

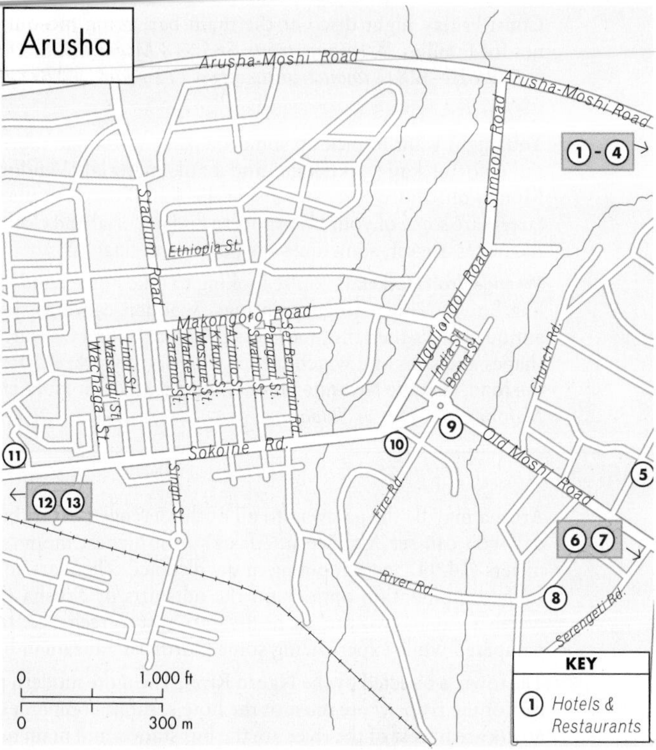

Visitor Information Tanzania Tourist Board (*TTB*). ✉ *E 47 Bldg., Boma Rd., Arusha* ☎ *27/254–8628* 🌐 *www.tanzaniatouristboard.com.*

WHERE TO EAT

Arusha might just be a stopover city for some, but there's a lot of great food on offer in the town that goes beyond packed safari lunchboxes.

$ ETHIOPIAN 🍴 **Abyssinia.** If you like Ethiopian food, the dishes at Abyssinia are prepared as if you were a guest in someone's home, or in this case, a peaceful garden. Large shared plates of *injere* (traditional sourdough flat bread) are served with well-known staples like *wot* (hearty stews) or kitfo (minced, raw seasoned beef). **Known for:** vegan and vegetarian friendly; the Tej wine is a must-try; run family-style, the food quality reflects the time gone into its making. [$] *Average main: $8* ✉ *Njiro Rd., Arusha* ✣ *Next to Alliance Franceaise, after Impala roundabout* ☎ *685/652–222* ▬ *No credit cards.*

$ BURGER 🍴 **Alpha Choice.** A good quick-bites option, Alpha Choice offers simple fare like burgers and seafood with all the accompaniments. The service can be slow, but the quality is always dependable and the food is always filling. **Known for:** great burgers; an unpretentious dining atmosphere; an actual sushi menu with decent sushi. [$] *Average main: $7* ✉ *Nakumatt Plaza, Sokine Rd., Arusha* ☎ *688/ 813–954* ▬ *No credit cards.*

$ ✗ **Blue Heron.** A popular hangout for the ex-pat community, the Blue
ITALIAN   Heron has long been the go-to spot for alfresco dining in Arusha. It's
also the place to go if you're looking for Western-styled food like burgers, pizza, and generous salads. **Known for:** a lovely garden to have
a coffee; wood-fired pizzas; tasty teatime treats. $ *Average main: $8*
✉ *Haile Sellassie Rd., Arusha* ☎ *555–127* ⊘ *Closed Sun.*

$ ✗ **Blues and Chutney.** Fancy a decent drink and some good, hearty food?
INTERNATIONAL   Blues and Chutney has a wonderful restaurant and bar area where great
home-cooked meals are served; there's also seating in a lovely garden.
Known for: fantastic home cooking; homemade soups and generous
salad portions; unfussy meals in a quiet atmosphere. $ *Average main:*
$8 ✉ *Leganga Rd., next to Ngare Sero Lodge, Arusha* ☎ *732/971–668*
⊕ *www.bluesandchutney.com.*

$ ✗ **Damascus Tapas and Meze.** The on-site restaurant for the aptly named
MIDDLE EASTERN   Bed 'ou Inn B&B, Damascus Tapas is a simple affair in a quiet neighborhood. If you have 24 hours before your safari, ask for their homemade
lunchboxes to take on your trip. **Known for:** laid-back atmosphere;
hearty-sized meals; meze platters that are perfect for sharing. $ *Average*
main: $8 ✉ *Off Perfect Printers Rd., Arusha* ☎ *765/878–453* ⊕ *www.*
escapetz.com ▭ *No credit cards.*

$ ✗ **Fifi's.** If you're looking for a quick escape in between flights or safaris,
INTERNATIONAL   Fifi's is a firm favorite for those looking for simple fare in a relaxed,
casual dining atmosphere. The menu is a lovely fusion of Tanzanian
favorites—*mishkaki* (spicy, cubes of grilled beef) and *mtori* soup (aka
banana soup)—and international fare like burgers and homemade pancakes. **Known for:** freshly brewed coffee and tea; the friendly staff and
laid-back atmosphere; milkshakes. $ *Average main: $8* ✉ *Themi Rd.,*
Arusha ⊹ *Next door to the Tanesco office building* ☎ *789/666–518*
⊕ *www.fifistanzania.com.*

$$ ✗ **The Grill Room.** If you're looking for fresh and well-prepared dishes
INTERNATIONAL   in a fine dining setting, Arusha Coffee Lodge's Grill Room is a star
in the local fine-dining scene. The eclectic and modern à la carte and
three-course tasting menus feature dishes like grilled steaks with Swa-
hili spices and generously sized lobsters and prawns delicately seared
alongside a fresh citrus-infused salad. **Known for:** picturesque and luxu-
riously homey main dining area; an extensive, quality wine list; superb,
quality meals. $ *Average main: $12* ✉ *A 104, Arusha* ☎ *783/509–279*
⊕ *www.elewanacollection.com.*

$$ ✗ **Machewo.** A fusion of French and Swahili cuisine, the hallmark of
FUSION   one of Arusha's top restaurants is its inventive five-course tasting menus
Fodor's Choice   that feature dishes like Swahili-style grilled calamari and the trio of
★   sweet melon, beef samosa, and avocado and crab amuses-bouche. The
outdoor dining terrace has magnificent views over the valley towards
Arusha town, making it a popular spot for those seeking some quiet
and comfort in classic style. **Known for:** the fantastic views at sunset;
Chef Axel's salads; seasonal, local produce-inspired lunch menu with
Swahili influences. $ *Average main: $12* ✉ *Onsea Guest House, Arusha*
☎ *787/112–498* ⊕ *www.onseahouse.com.*

WHERE TO STAY

$ 🏨 **The African Tulip.** If you are in need of a short stay with some mod-
HOTEL   ern hotel amenities before heading off into the savanna, the safari-
themed Tulip is a good option outside the bustle of Arusha. **Pros:** an
intimate hotel outside of the main city; can arrange to leave behind
extra luggage if necessary; service is stellar. **Cons:** no elevator; Wi-Fi
is expensive; not all rooms have balconies. $ *Rooms from: $190* ✉ *44
Serengeti Rd., Arusha* ☎ *27/254–3004* ⊕ *www.theafricantulip.com*
↪ *29 rooms* ❍| *Breakfast.*

$$ 🏨 **Arusha Coffee Lodge.** Just 5 km (3 miles) from town, and five min-
HOTEL   utes from Arusha Airport, the lodge is a great option for pre- or post-
FAMILY   safari layovers. **Pros:** beautiful setting; easy access to the airport; large
comfortable rooms. **Cons:** near the highway so you can hear traffic;
many non–hotel guests at the restaurants; some rooms don't have
views. $ *Rooms from: $385* ✉ *Serengeti Rd., airport vicinity, Arusha*
☎ *754/250–630* ⊕ *www.elewana.com* ↪ *30 rooms* ❍| *Breakfast.*

$ 🏨 **The Arusha Hotel.** Bang in the middle of town, opposite the clock
HOTEL   tower, this historic hotel was built in 1894. **Pros:** walking distance from
banks and shops; spacious rooms; you can store luggage. **Cons:** food is
average; location means traffic can take a while to get to airport; large
conference hotel which can get very crowded with business meetings
and socializing. $ *Rooms from: $223* ✉ *Main Rd., Arusha* ☎ *027/250–
7777* ⊕ *www.thearushahotel.com* ↪ *86 rooms* ❍| *Breakfast.*

$ 🏨 **Ngare Sero Mountain Lodge.** Located on the outskirts of a forest, this
B&B/INN   1905 farmhouse is now home to this intimate, family-run mountain
FAMILY   lodge. **Pros:** spectacular scenery with an exquisite lake and multiple activi-
Fodor'sChoice   ties; a quiet retreat after a safari; main lounge area with fireplace is warm
★   and welcoming. **Cons:** outside rooms don't receive much natural light; far
from town but for some that is a worthwhile aspect; tricky to find with-
out a driver. $ *Rooms from: $190* ✉ *Off A23, east of Arusha, Arusha*
☎ *764/305–435* ⊕ *www.ngare-sero-lodge.com* ↪ *13 rooms* ❍| *All meals.*

$$ 🏨 **Onsea House and Machweo Retreat.** On a small, winding dirt road just
B&B/INN   off the main highway heading toward Moshi sits conjoined properties
Fodor'sChoice   with some of the most spectacular views in the area, overlooking Aru-
★   sha and Mt. Merua. **Pros:** spectacular location; beautiful outdoor deck
and pool; excellent food. **Cons:** you can encounter traffic between the
house and the airport; you are amid village life so you might be woken
early by chickens and cattle; many stairs, so not ideal for people with
mobility issues. $ *Rooms from: $280* ✉ *Onsea Moivaro Rd., Arusha*
☎ *689/103–552* ⊕ *www.onseahouse.com* ↪ *14 suites* ❍| *Breakfast.*

SHOPPING

Cultural Heritage Centre. If you haven't yet picked up your gifts and
curios, then stop by Arusha's Cultural Heritage Centre. It's one of the
largest curio shops in Tanzania and is only 3 km (2 miles) out of town.
You can buy carvings, jewelry, including the gemstone tanzanite, colorful African clothing, local music, and much more. It's a bit pricey so
take advantage of the museum that is part of the complex to get your
money's worth. The king and queen of Norway and Bill Clinton and
daughter Chelsea have all stopped here to pick up last-minute gifts and
souvenirs. ✉ *A 104, Arusha* ⊕ *www.culturalheritage.co.tz.*

BEACH ESCAPES

Looking for a little R&R after your safari? Tanzania has 1,424 km (883 miles) of beautiful pristine coastline to explore. Looking for an island getaway? Tanzania has those, too. Zanzibar is the larger, louder, and more party-oriented island, unless you opt for more secluded resorts and hotels, while Mafia is home to some of the best diving in Tanzania and Pemba sits quietly in the Northern corners with its picture-perfect beaches and limited number of tourists.

ZANZIBAR

This ancient isle once ruled by sultans and slave traders served as the stepping stone into the African continent for missionaries and explorers. Once known as the Spice Island for its export of cloves, Zanzibar—the name Zanzibar also includes the islands of Unguja (the main island) and Pemba—has become one of the most exotic flavors in travel, better than Bali or Mali when it comes to beauty that'll make your jaw drop. Today, this tiny archipelago attracts visitors intent on discovering sandy beaches, rain forests, or blue water snorkeling; it's the perfect post-safari spot.

WHEN TO GO

June through October is the best time to visit Zanzibar because the temperature averages 26°C (79°F). Spice tours are best during harvest time, July and October, when cloves (unopened flower buds) are picked and laid out to dry. Zanzibar experiences a short rainy season in November, but heavy rains can fall from March until the end of May. Temperatures soar during this period, often reaching over 30°C (90°F). Most travelers come between June and August and from mid-November to early January. During these periods many hotels add a surcharge.

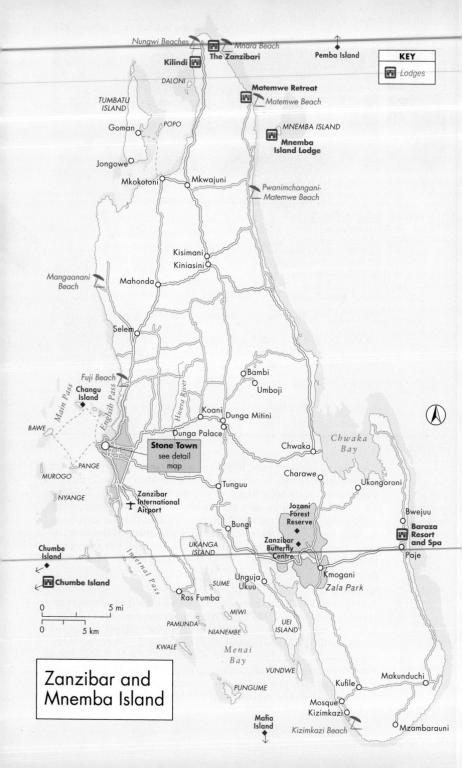

Zanzibar and Mnemba Island

Zanzibar observes Ramadan for a month every year. During this period Muslims are forbidden to eat, drink, or smoke between sunrise and sunset. Although hotels catering to tourists aren't affected, many small shops and restaurants are closed during the day. If you plan to arrive during Ramadan, aim

DID YOU KNOW?

Freddie Mercury, lead singer of Queen, was born Farouk Bulsara in Stone Town on September 5, 1946.

for the end, when a huge feast called the Eid al-Fitr (which means "end of the fast") brings everyone out to the streets.

GETTING HERE AND AROUND

There are no direct flights from the United States. Generally you need to connect through a city on the mainland, the easiest being Dar es Salaam. From Dar es Salaam to Stone Town, there are regular flights in small twin-engine aircraft operated by numerous companies including Precision Air and Coastal Aviation. The flight takes around 20 minutes. From Nairobi and Mombasa, you can fly to Stone Town on Kenya Airways. Mango Airlines does not offer direct flights from South Africa. At this writing the airport is undergoing some major renovations so you may have to be bused across the runways or have to wait under shaded tarpaulins before flights arrive and depart.

Visitors from the United States and Europe require visas to enter Tanzania. Zanzibar is a semiautonomous state within Tanzania, so you don't need a separate visa to visit, but you do need to show your passport, fill in an arrival form, and go through the baggage scanners.

Bikes can be rented from shops near Darajani Market. Mopeds and motorcycles are another great way to get about the island, although nothing is signposted so you could get lost frequently.

Hydrofoil ferries travel between Dar es Salaam and Stone Town. The trip takes about two hours on catamarans owned by Azam Marine, the most reliable operator. Departures leave from Dar es Salaam at 7 am, 9:30 am, 12:30 pm, and 3:45 pm. Tickets can be purchased on the spot or online, but you will need to go to the offices—next to the port in Dar es Salaam or in their Zanzibar offices a short walk from the ferry terminal—to pay by cash or card 48 hours before departure. Timetables and prices are displayed on boards outside each office. Tickets for nonresidents range from $40 (Tsh90,000) for business class to $35 (Tsh78,224) for economy. The harbor is quite busy so keep an eye on your possessions. And if you don't want help from a porter, be firm. Note that two ferries sank in 2011 and 2012, thought to be due to overcrowding, but they were the local goods and transport ferries, which may be the cheapest way to get to Zanzibar, but by far not the safest. Whether you arrive by plane or ferry, you'll be approached by taxi drivers. Be sure to agree on a price before getting in, as taxis don't have meters. The fare to Stone Town should be around Tsh40,000 (around $15–$20). Your driver may let you out several blocks before you reach your hotel because the streets are too narrow. Ask the driver to walk you to the hotel. Alternately arrange to be picked up by your accommodation, as they will guide you into Stone Town without much fuss. Be sure to tip anyone that carries your luggage.

DAY TOURS

Spice tours are a popular way to see Zanzibar. Guides take you to farms in Kizimbani or Kindichi and teach you to identify plants that produce cinnamon, turmeric, nutmeg, and vanilla. A curry luncheon will undoubtedly use some of the local spices. Any tour company can arrange a spice tour, with the average price for a spice tour ranging from $20 to $50, depending on the number of people, including lunch. Most depart around 9 am from Stone Town.

Various tour operators and most hotels offer tour options that include visits to Prison Island, Jozani Forest, and the Zanzibar Butterfly Centre. One Ocean is able to take you diving from their offices opposite the NBC bank outside of the tunnel. Unwind at Mrembo Spa with some of their signature Swahili Frangipani massages or take a tour with a difference tailored by Zanzibar Different or Amo Zanzibar—both have good reputations on the island for offering more than just your standard spice and island tour.

HEALTH AND SAFETY

Visitors to Zanzibar are required to have a yellow-fever vaccination certificate; some websites also recommend polio, hepatitis A, and typhoid vaccinations. You should also talk with your doctor about a malaria prophylactic. The best way to avoid malaria is to avoid being bitten by mosquitoes, so make sure your arms and legs are covered and that you wear plenty of mosquito repellent, especially after dusk. Antihistamine cream is also quite useful to stop the itch of mosquito bites. Always sleep under a mosquito net; most hotels and guesthouses provide them. The sun can be very strong here, so make sure to slather yourself with sunscreen as well. Drink bottled water, and plenty of it—it'll help you avoid dehydration. Avoid raw fruits and vegetables that may have been washed in untreated water.

Although the best way to experience Stone Town is to wander around its labyrinthine streets, you should always be on your guard. Don't wear jewelry or watches that might attract attention, and keep a firm grasp on purses and camera bags. Leave valuables in the safe at your hotel.

Muggings have been reported at Nungwi and other coastal resorts, so never carry valuables onto the beach. Nungwi is known as the party side of Zanzibar; if you want a quiet retreat free from beach boys and loud beach parties then head elsewhere.

As Zanzibar is a largely conservative, Muslim state, it's advisable for women to dress modestly. This means a long dress or skirt. Uncovered shoulders and heads are fine, but never cleavage or torsos. Many tourists often ignore this advice, and although locals are too polite to say anything, it's not appreciated and it does not put tourists in good standing among locals. It does not take much effort to cover up, and if it is not your home country, it is respectful to adhere to basic social customs, even if you might not feel like it. Holding hands is fine, but overly intimate displays of affection should be avoided. With that being

said, homosexuality is frowned on in Zanzibar, and displays of public affection can be prosecutable.

■TIP→ **Always ask permission before taking photographs, and be prepared to pay a small tip in return, particularly from the Maasai.**

MONEY MATTERS

There are handy currency exchange booths in Stone Town that offer good rates. The best rates are at Forex Bureau around the corner from Mazson's Hotel on Kenyatta Road, and the Malindi Exchange across from Cine Afrique. Most people will except U.S. dollars, but be aware of the exchange rate and make sure you're not being overcharged.

■TIP→ **Be very careful when using ATMs. Make sure you use one at a reputable bank, and check to make sure the bank is open—cards get swallowed all the time.**

TELEPHONES

The regional code for Zanzibar is 024. ■TIP→ **Telephone numbers seem to lack consistency, so they're listed as they appear in promotional materials.**

VISITOR INFORMATION

The free tourist magazine, *Swahili Coast,* found in hotels, shops, and on most of the flights, lists cultural events, as well as tide tables that are very useful for divers. There's a tourist information center north of Stone Town. Although not very useful for information about the city, it does book rooms at inns in other parts of the island.

CONTACTS

Airlines Coastal Aviation. ☎ 242/233–112 ⊕ www.coastal.co.tz. **Kenya Airways.** ✉ Peugeot House, Upanga Rd., Dar es Salaam ☎ 22/211–9377 ⊕ www.kenya-airways.com. **Mango Airlines.** ☎ 101/0217 ⊕ www.flymango. com. **Precision Air.** ✉ Diamond Plaza, Mirambo St., 1st fl., Dar es Salaam ⊕ www.precisionairtz.com. **ZanAir.** ✉ Muzammil Center, Stone Town ⊕ www. zanair.com.

Airports Abeid Amani Karume International Airport. ⊕ www.zaa.go.tz.

Day Tours Amo Zanzibar Tours. ✉ Mkunazini Street, Stone Town ☎ 744/590–020 ⊕ www.amozanzibartours.com. **Eco & Culture Tours.** ✉ Hurumizi St., House 272, Stone Town ☎ 242/233–731 ⊕ www.ecoculture-zanzibar.org. **Mrembo Spa.** ✉ Cathedral St., Stone Town, Zanzibar ☎ 242/230–004. **Neno Tours.** ☎ 767/708–026 ⊕ www.nenotoursntravels.co.tz. **One Ocean Diving and Water Sports.** ✉ Kenyatta Rd., Stone Town, Zanzibar ☎ 774/310–003 ⊕ www.zanzibaroneocean.com. **The Original Dhow Safaris.** ✉ Stone Town ☎ 772/007–090 ⊕ www.dhowsafaris.net. **Vanora Zanzibar.** ✉ Stone Town, Bwejuu ⊕ www. vanorazanzibar.com. **Zanzibar Different Tours.** ✉ Soko Muhogo St., Stone Town, Zanzibar ☎ 777/430–117 ⊕ www.zanzibardifferent.com.

Ferries Azam Marine. ✉ Zanzibar Terminal, Bwejuu ☎ 22/212–3324 in Dar es Salaam, 24/223–1655 in Zanzibar ⊕ www.azammarine.com.

Visitor Information Zanzibar Tourist Corporation. ✉ Aamani, Bwejuu ☎ 24/223–3485/6 ⊕ www.zanzibartourism.go.tz.

STONE TOWN

Stone Town, the archipelago's major metropolis, is a maze of narrow streets lined with houses featuring magnificently carved doors studded with brass. There are 51 mosques, six Hindu temples, and two Christian churches. Minarets punctuate the town's skyline, where more than 90% of the residents are Muslim. In the harbor you'll see dhows, the Arabian boats with triangular sails. Islamic women covered by black boubou veils scurry down alleyways so narrow their outstretched arms could touch buildings on both sides.

It's also regarded as a mini fashion mecca for East Africa. Don't miss visiting the famous Doreen Mashinka or the delightful Upendo Means Love and Mago for unique fashion items.

EXPLORING

The sights in Stone Town are all minutes from one another so you'll see them all as you walk. However, the old part of town is very compact and maze-like and can be a bit disconcerting. Hiring a guide is a great way to see the city without stress, and a guide can provide information about the sights you'll see. Many tour operators offer a guided walking tour for approximately US$20–US$25. Ask your hotel for guide suggestions, or see Day Tours *above* for tour guide recommendations. That said, getting lost is part of the experience of Stone Town; it is a small, compact area and you can easily ask a vendor to point you in the general direction of the Fort, an easy landmark. Take your time around the streets, don't panic if you don't know exactly where you are—the joy of traveling is chatting to people and discovering quiet corners, intimate exchanges of daily life and, yes, the shopping.

Beit el-Ajaib. Known as the House of Wonders because it was the first building in Zanzibar to use electric lights, this four-story palace is still one of the largest buildings in the city. Built in the late 1800s for Sultan Barghash, it was bombarded by the British in 1886, forcing the sultan to abdicate his throne. Today you'll find cannons guarding the beautifully carved doors at the entrance, which leads to marble-floored rooms that house exhibits that detail the country's battle for independence. Unfortunately, the building was under renovation at the time of writing, so visitors will have to gaze at the building. ⊠ *North of Old Fort, Zanzibar.*

Christ Church Cathedral and Slave Museum. A must-see in Stone town, this was the first Anglican cathedral in East Africa and its crucifix was carved from the tree under which explorer David Livingstone's heart was buried in the village of Chitambo. Built in 1887 to mark the end of the slave trade, the cathedral's high altar was constructed on the site of a whipping post. The moving and contemplative slave memorial and slave trade exhibit are sobering reminders of the ravages of slavery across East Africa and on the island. Nearby are underground chambers in which slaves were forced to crouch on stone shelves less than 2 feet high. It is recommended to take a guide with you as with such a poignant space you would want to get as much information as possible. ⊠ *Off Creek Rd., Zanzibar* ⊠ *Tsh12,000 (US$5).*

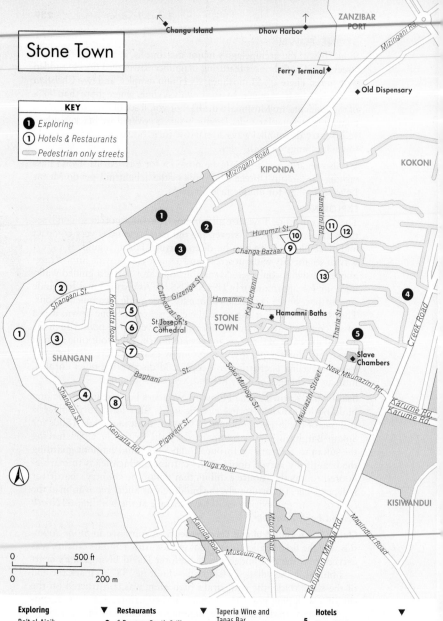

Stone Town

KEY
- **1** Exploring
- (1) Hotels & Restaurants
- Pedestrian only streets

ZANZIBAR PORT

Changu Island
Dhow Harbor
Ferry Terminal
Old Dispensary

Mizingani Rd.

KIPONDA
KOKONI

Mizingani Road

Hurumzi St.
Changa Bazaar
Jamatini Rd.

Shangani St.
Kenyatta Road
Gizenga St.
Cathedral St.
Hamamni St.
Kajificheni St.
Tharia St.
Creek Road

St Joseph's Cathedral
STONE TOWN
Hamamni Baths

SHANGANI
Slave Chambers

Baghani St.
Soko Muhogo St.
Mkunazini Street
New Mkunazini Rd.
Karume Rd.
Karume Rd.

Shangani St.
Kenyatta Rd.
Pigawadi St.

Vuga Road

Mtoro Road
KISIWANDUI

Kaunda Road
Museum Rd.
Benjamin Mkapa Rd.
Mapindizi Road

0   500 ft
0   200 m

Darajani Market. This gable-roofed structure built in 1904 and also known as Estella Market, houses a sprawling fruit, fish, meat, and vegetable market. Goods of all sorts—colorful fabrics, wooden chests, and all types of jewelry—are sold in the shops that line the surrounding streets. To the east of the main building you'll find spices laid out in colorful displays of beige, yellow, and red. On Wednesday and Saturday there's an antiques fair. The market is most active in the morning between 9 and 11. ⊠ *Creek Rd., north of New Mkunazini St., Zanzibar* 🎫 *Free.*

Forodhani Gardens. This pleasant waterfront park is a favorite spot for an evening stroll both for locals and tourists. Dozens of venders sell grilled fish under the light of gas lanterns—not all the food is great, but the atmosphere is fantastic for a visit, especially during the evening hours. ■TIP→ **Always try to smell the seafood before you eat it as some of it can be old, and don't be pressured by any of the vendors. You should look at everything before making your decisions.** ⊠ *Mizingani St., Zanzibar.*

Old Fort. Built by the Portuguese in 1560, this bastioned fortress is the oldest structure in Stone Town. It withstood an attack from Arabs in 1754. It was later used as a jail, and prisoners who were sentenced to death met their ends here. It has undergone extensive renovation and today is headquarters for many cultural organizations, including the Zanzibar International Film Festival and the Jahazi Literary and Jazz Festival. There is also a small craft market inside. Performances of traditional dance and music are sometimes staged here during the week. Check the office and posters outside for details. ⊠ *Creek Rd. at Malawi Rd., Zanzibar* 🎫 *Free.*

WHERE TO EAT

Zanzibar was the legendary Spice Island, so it's no surprise the cuisine here is flavored with lemongrass, cumin, and garlic. Cinnamon enlivens tea and coffee, while ginger flavors a refreshing soft drink called Tangawizi. More than 20 types of mangos, as well as bananas, papayas, pineapples, and passion fruit grow on the island. When it comes to dinner, seafood reigns supreme. Stone Town's fish market sells skewers of kingfish and tuna. Stop by in the early evening, when the catch of the day is hauled in and cleaned. Try the prawn kebabs, roasted peanuts, and corn on the cob at the outdoor market at Forodhani Gardens (but not if you have a sensitive tummy). Try the vegetarian Zanzibar pizza for breakfast; it's more like an omelet.

Gratuities are often included in the bill, so ask the staff before adding the usual 10% tip. Credit cards aren't widely accepted, so make sure you have enough cash. Lunch hours are generally 12:30 to 2:30, dinner 7 to 10:30. Dress is casual for all but upscale restaurants, where you should avoid T-shirts, shorts, and trainers.

$$$$ ╳ **Emerson Spice Teahouse Restaurant.** One of those dining experiences that seems to be a rite of passage for visitors to Stone Town, guests ascend **AFRICAN** a mammoth series of stairs that lead to the rooftop dining area and an expansive view over Stone Town. A seasonal five course degustation menu of tasty Swahili-inspired cuisine ranges from prawns and grilled fish to slivers of seared beef in traditional spices. **Known for:** upmarket

5

dining with one of the most popular rooftop views in town; the ability to adjust the menu for a variety of dietary requirements; a downstairs secret garden filled with atmosphere that is well worth the visit for lunch. $ *Average main: $40* ⊠ *Tharia St., Kiponda* ☎ *24/223–2776* ⊕ *www.emersonspice.com* ⊘ *Closed Thurs.*

$
INTERNATIONAL
Fodor's Choice
★

✕ **Lazuli.** This quaint restaurant serves up healthy, utterly delicious homemade food. Large wraps, the special dish of the day, and some inventive smoothies are all prepared with fresh, local ingredients. **Known for:** some of the best and most generously sized smoothies in town; share if you don't have a big appetite; wonderfully well priced for the great quality. $ *Average main: $6* ⊠ *Stone Town* ⊹ *Head past all the main tourist shops, look out for the bank on the corner—it's right there.*

$
ASIAN FUSION

✕ **Masa.** Sitting on a small terrace that overlooks the colorful and lively streets of downtown Stone Town, this Japanese restaurant—the only one on the island—offers up small share plates of Asian-inspired fusion food. The wide selection of freshly prepared seafood dishes and good service make this a good bet for any occasion. **Known for:** great views of the passing nightlife; tasty sushi and tempura; a larger vegetarian menu than other restaurants; open until 11 pm nightly. $ *Average main: $9* ⊠ *Shangani Post Office, 1st fl., Stone Town* ⊹ *Entrance is behind the building; follow the signs to "Tapas Bar," up some flights of stairs* ☎ *776/885–049* ⊕ *www.masalimited.com.*

$$
CONTEMPORARY

✕ **6 Degrees South Grill and Wine Bar.** If you're looking for a sunset cock-tail with views of the Zanzibar ocean, then head on over to 6 Degrees on Shangani Street. Fresh, modern Afro-Continental cuisine such as generously sized burgers and steaks grilled on the flame are served in a relaxed, breezy atmosphere under a large double-story terrace that's decked out with modern, white loungers. **Known for:** refreshing Madafu-coconut water; great views from the upper floor; floor-to-ceiling wine vault offers the perfect chilled glass of vino. $ *Average main: $12* ⊠ *Shangani St., Zanzibar* ⊕ *www.6degreessouth.co.tz.*

$
MEDITERRANEAN

✕ **Taperia Wine and Tapas Bar.** Sharing the same balcony space at Masa Japanese, the Taperia has one of the most extensive Italian-inspired tapas menus in town. The central location, jovial atmosphere, and group dining means that many people stop in for an evening snack and a glass of wine before heading out for the evening. **Known for:** generous tapas, perfect for sharing; takeaway deli good for picnic pro-visions; Mediterranean flavors with fresh local food. $ *Average main: $10* ⊠ *Shangani St., Bwejuu.*

$$$
SEAFOOD
Fodor's Choice
★

✕ **Tea House Restaurant.** With stunning views past the city's minarets to the harbor where dhows are setting out to sea, this rooftop restaurant is a wonderful homage to Stone Towns' rich and varied past. Din-ing is done in the traditional Arabic manner with low wooden tables, plush patterned cushions, and billowing fabric and hanging lanterns. **Known for:** stunning views in a luxuriant and atmospheric setting; traditional Persian and Asian dishes; sunset serenading by the talented Dhow Music Academy. $ *Average main: $30* ⊠ *236 Hurumzi St., Stone Town* ☎ *242/232–784* ⊘ *Closed Mon.*

$
CAFÉ

✕ **Zanzibar Coffee House Cafe.** If there is one place to get a good cup of locally brewed African coffee it's the unassuming Zanzibar Coffee house, a sweet paradise tucked in amid the houses to the alleyways. There might not be any Wi-Fi thanks to the thick walls common in a traditional Arabic house, but it is a cool and deliciously simple café. **Known for:** coffee and cakes; lovely rooftop coffee experience; a small, cozy space. $ *Average main: $9* ✉ *Mkunazini St., Stone Town* 📞 *24/2239–319* ⊕ *www.zanzibar-cafe.com.*

WHERE TO STAY

$

B&B/INN

Beyt al Salaam. This former teahouse is now an intimate hotel with a whole lot of character and great service. **Pros:** authentic property; excellent location just outside of the main town; beautiful resturant dining area that oozes old-world Zanzibar charm. **Cons:** if overbooked you get bumped to the sister hotel, which is not as lovely; plenty of stairs for those with mobility issues; some rooms are small, so if you need space get the deluxe rooms. $ *Rooms from: $90* ✉ *Kele Sq., Kilele Square* 📞 *773/000–086* ⊕ *www.beytalsaalam.com* 🛏 *6 rooms* ⦿| *Breakfast.*

$

B&B/INN

Fodor's Choice

★

Emerson on Hurumzi. Tucked away in Stone Town, this small hotel, once the home of one of the richest men in Zanzibar, was the brainchild of two New Yorkers. **Pros:** unique room designs in keeping with the Emerson Spice brand; historic ambience; wonderfully authentic rooftop teahouse is a must (booking essential). **Cons:** lots and lots of wooden stairs; some rooms have no sea views; no TV or radio in the rooms, but for some that is a bonus. $ *Rooms from: $185* ✉ *236 Hurumzi St., Stone Town* 📞 *24/32–784* ⊕ *www.emersononhurumzi. com* 🛏 *10 rooms* ⦿| *Breakfast.*

$

B&B/INN

Emerson Spice Hotel. Two gorgeous historic buildings right in the center of the maze of alleyways that make up Stone Town have been converted into a hotel with whimsically wonderful rooms, each with a different theme. **Pros:** delightful teahouse on the roof; enormous rooms; authentic, quirky ambience—bring your camera!; hidden garden makes for fantastic dining ambience (booking is essential). **Cons:** lots and lots of stairs; rooms are getting a little tired; rooms facing into other buildings might be a bit dark. $ *Rooms from: $225* ✉ *Tharia St., Kipondo, Kiponda* 📞 *24/223–2776* ⊕ *www.emersonspice.com* 🛏 *11 suites* ⦿| *Breakfast.*

$

HOTEL

Fodor's Choice

★

Kisiwa House. This stylish boutique hotel, housed in a beautifully restored 19th-century Zanzibari town house, manages to combine old-fashioned authenticity—steep wooden staircases, high ceilings, an inner courtyard, and pretty rooftop restaurant—with modern touches, such as the contemporary art on the walls, flat-screen TVs, and large, modern, luxurious bathrooms that have bathtubs as well as showers. **Pros:** rates are very reasonable considering the amenities; great location; rooms are incredibly large. **Cons:** lots of steep stairs; no views from the rooms; sparse public areas to lounge around in. $ *Rooms from: $230* ✉ *572 Baghani St., Stone Town* 📞 *24/223–0685* ⊕ *www.kisiwahouse. com* 🛏 *10 rooms* ⦿| *Breakfast.*

$$

HOTEL

Park Hyatt Zanzibar. Once the home of a 17th-century businessman, the Park Hyatt occupies the desirable beachside location near the winding streets of central Stone Town. **Pros:** high-end, classy luxury in an exquisite setting; attention to detail pays homage to the building's history; views of the sunset from the beautiful outdoor areas. **Cons:** a very small pool area can get crowded during peak season; modern luxury comes at a price; it

5

does not have the darker, traditional furnishings, but for some that is not an issue. [$] *Rooms from: $449* ✉ *Shangani St.* ☎ *24/550–1234* 🌐 *zanzibar.park.hyatt.com/en/hotel/home.html* 🛏 *67 rooms* 🍴 *Breakfast.*

$$ HOTEL
🏨 **Serena Inn.** On one side of Shangani Square, on the fringe of Stone Town, this beautiful hotel is the result of the restoration of two of Zanzibar's historic buildings: the old Telekoms building, an original colonial-era building, and the Chinese doctors' residence. **Pros:** location on the outside of town with beach views; stunning, spacious swimming pool; modern rooms on upper floors have large balconies with views. **Cons:** rather large hotel, where service suffers in peak season; no elevator for the upper floors; cheaper-priced rooms are quite small. [$] *Rooms from: $414* ✉ *Shangani St., Stone Town* ☎ *24/223–3051* 🌐 *www.serenahotels.com* 🛏 *51 rooms* 🍴 *Breakfast.*

BEYOND STONE TOWN

Zanzibar Island, locally known as Unguja, has amazing beaches and resorts, warm-water diving, and acres of spice plantations. Much of the western part of the larger island is a slumbering paradise where cloves, as well as rice and coconuts, still grow.

Smaller islands in the Zanzibar Archipelago range from mere sandbanks to Chumbe Island, the country's first marine national park; Mnemba, a private retreat for guests who pay hundreds of dollars per day to get away from it all; and Changu, once a prison island, it's now home to the giant Aldabra tortoise.

EXPLORING

Changuu Island (*Prison Island*). This tiny island, just a 20-minute boat ride from Stone Town, was once a prison and a quarantine location. Now it's a tropical paradise that's home to the giant Aldabra tortoise (you can visit the tortoises for a small fee), the duiker antelope, and a variety of birds and butterflies. There's also decent swimming and snorkeling, and a hotel and restaurant. Note that 70% of the island is private property and thus inaccessible. **■ TIP→ You can visit Changuu Island on a tour, or arrange transport with the myriad of little boats that line the beach outside Archipelago. There's no entry fee for the island itself.** ✉ *Zanzibar* ✧ *5.6 km (3.5 miles) northwest of the main island of Zanzibar* 🎟 *US$4 for tortoise visit.*

Fodor's Choice ★
Chumbe Island. Between the Tanzanian coast and the islands of Zanzibar, Chumbe Island is the country's first marine national park. It's home to 400 species of coral and 200 species of fish. There's scuba diving, snorkeling, island hikes, and outrigger boat rides. **■ TIP→ The island can only be visited on an organized day trip. Price includes boat transfers, lunch, snorkeling, forest walk, and V.A.T.** ✉ *Chumbe Island, Zanzibar* ☎ *24/223–1040* 🌐 *www.chumbeisland.com* 🎟 *$90.*

Jozani Forest Reserve. Jozani Chakwa Bay National Park, Zanzibar's only national park, is home to this reserve where you'll find the rare Kirk's red colobus monkey, which is named after Sir John Kirk, the British consul in Zanzibar from 1866 to 1887. The species is known for its white whiskers and rusty coat. Many of the other animals that call this reserve home—including the blue duiker, a diminutive antelope whose coat is a dusty bluish-gray—are endangered because 95% of the original forests of the archipelago have been destroyed. There are also more than 50 species of butterfly and 40 bird species. The entry fee includes entrance to the forest and a circular boardwalk walk through mangrove swamps, plus the services of a guide (tip him if he's good). **TIP→ Early morning and evenings are the best time to visit.** ✉ *Zanzibar* ✣ *38 km (27 miles) southeast of Stone Town* 🎫 *US$8.*

Zanzibar Butterfly Centre. This center is well worth a half-hour visit. It's a community development project, and your entry fee pays for local farmers to bring in cocoons (most of which are sent to museums overseas) and helps preserve the forest. Guided tours end in a visit to an enclosure filled with hundreds of colorful butterflies. ✉ *1 km (½ mile) from Jozani Forest, Zanzibar* 🌐 *www.zanzibarbutterflies.com* 🎫 *Tsh 8,000 (US$5).*

5

BEACHES

Although Zanzibar offers quintessential powdery white sand and calm, warm turquoise waters, traveling from one beach to another by taxi can get quite expensive (and local taxis, or *daladalas,* are uncomfortable). Most tourists opt instead to enjoy the beach in front of their resort *(See Where to Stay, below).* Doing so offers you a measure of protection from "beach boys," or touts, who frequent the beaches looking for customers. Young backpackers and those wanting some nightlife usually head to Nungwi, or Kendwa on the north coast, which have good beaches that aren't greatly affected by the tides; it's near impossible to swim during low tide. You can, however, take this opportunity to explore rock pools. Just be sure to wear reef shoes—sea urchins are painful to step on.

Nakupenda Beach. Grab some snacks and plenty of bottled water and head to this charming sandbank that's about a 30-minute boat ride from Stone Town. A lovely, sandy beach and place to snorkel make it a great day trip. You can hire a boat from the harbor to take you there on a negotiated fee for a few hours or, if you prefer to be fully catered to, go with a tour company who will provide the shade and the beach picnic with seafood and drinks as part of their price. **TIP→ There is no shade on the island, so make sure you bring a hat and umbrella.** **Amenities:** none. **Best for:** snorkeling; swimming; walking.

WHERE TO STAY

$$$$ RESORT FAMILY

🏨 **Baraza Resort & Spa.** While there's nothing authentic about the Arabian decor at this award-winning hotel, there's a "wow" factor that extends from the opulent reception and lounging areas, complete with carved wooden furnishings, copper urns, and billowing drapes, to the beautifully appointed individual villas. **Pros:** large spa with lavish arabesque chill rooms; spacious two-bedroom villas are ideal for families; fantastic swimming pool with romantic, curtained daybeds. **Cons:** the decor might be a bit much for some; the pool area gets crowded in season; the beach is very tide-dependent. [$] *Rooms from: $1117* ✉ *Bwejuu* ☎ *472/053–8148* 🌐 *www.baraza-zanzibar.com* 🛏 *30 villas* 🍴 *All-inclusive.*

$$ RESORT Fodor's Choice ★

🏨 **Chumbe Island.** The island's ecotourism concept was the brainstorm of a German conservationist who, since the early 1990s, has succeeded in developing it as one of the world's foremost marine sanctuaries. **Pros:** excellent food and involved staff; some of the best snorkeling in

Zanzibar; quaint stretch of beach that is pure magic. **Cons:** the boat trip from Stone Town takes 45 minutes, and there's only one departure a day (later departures cost extra); it's expensive for the level of rusticity but some will like this; low tide means exposed coral on the beach. $ *Rooms from: $280* ✉ *Chumbe Island, Coral Park, Zanzibar* ⊕ *www.chumbeisland.com* ↪ *7 bungalows* ⊠ *All-inclusive.*

$$$$
RESORT
Fodor's Choice
★

Kilindi. Kilindi whisks you away to a private, luxury resort on the northernmost part of the island with a combination of barefoot luxury and excellent service. **Pros:** wonderfully romantic on-site spa; your own butler to cater to your needs; remote location with a beautiful beach. **Cons:** location might be too remote for some; the rooms are open, which means insect sightings are possible; bathrooms are separate from rooms. $ *Rooms from: $650* ✉ *Kendwa, Zanzibar* ☎ *272/500–630* ⊕ *www.elewanacollection.com* ↪ *15 suites* ⊠ *All meals.*

$$$$
ALL-INCLUSIVE

Matemwe Retreat. Overlooking Mnemba Atoll on the more secluded stretch of Matemwe beach in Northern Zanzibar, the four self-contained double-story villas of Matemwe retreat are nestled amid the island palms. **Pros:** a quiet stretch of beach, away from the crowds of the north; plenty of on-site ocean activities worth venturing out of your villa for; an on-site spa for extra pampering. **Cons:** not the place if you want to party; tides on the beach are very shallow for swimming; main areas are quite a walk from the villas. $ *Rooms from: $700* ✉ *Matemwe* ☎ *21/418–0468* ⊕ *www.asiliaafrica.com* ↪ *4 villas* ⊠ *All-inclusive.*

$$$$
HOTEL

Mnemba Island Lodge. For the ultimate beach escape where time stands still, where sand, sea, and horizon melt into each other, where there's exclusivity, total relaxation, and impeccable food and service, it would be hard to find anywhere in the world as alluring as Mnemba Island Lodge. **Pros:** an on-site PADI diver center caters for all water lovers; evenings on the beach on a private island watching the sunset are pure heaven; gorgeous communal lounge and dining spaces on the sand. **Cons:** large flocks of doves that come over from mainland can be noisy; ride to the lodge is through bumpy village roads; hordes of divers and tourists arrive twice a day even though the island is private (there is a hefty fine). $ *Rooms from: $1760* ✉ *Mnemba Island, Mnemba Island* ☎ *11/809–4300 in Johannesburg* ⊕ *www.andbeyond.com* ↪ *11 bungalows* ⊠ *All-inclusive.*

$
RESORT

The Zanzibari. Although the standard rooms are somewhat plain and located in a two-story block, they all have balconies overlooking the beautiful gardens and, on the upper level, the turquoise sea beyond. **Pros:** quite an out-of-the-way little hotel; tours and snorkeling can be arranged; three delightful little man-made rock pools sit out overlooking the shoreline. **Cons:** basic rooms inside the main lodge; ocean swimming is very much tide-dependent; Wi-Fi is very slow. $ *Rooms from: $225* ✉ *Nungwi Peninsula, Nungwi, Zanzibar* ☎ *772 /222–919* ⊕ *www.thezanzibari.com* ↪ *11 rooms* ⊠ *Some meals.*

MAFIA ISLAND

Just 160 km (99 miles) south of Zanzibar is an archipelago of inland bays and lagoons, towering palm groves dotted with ancient 8th-century ruins, and one of the most interesting marine ecosystems and coral reefs in

Tanzania. With a population of only 50,000 people, what was once a safe haven for ships searching for supplies now offers up a far more intimate island escape with a bounty of wildlife above and below the waters without the hordes of tourists that descend on Zanzibar. The Marine Park was one of the first established in Tanzania, spanning 821 km (510 miles) and bordered by a barrier reef teeming with marine life. Whale sharks are the big attraction here and they normally frequent the waters around Mafia from November to February. Choose your operator carefully as some are only out to make a buck and put the animals' lives at risk. Walk through the ancient ruins at Kisimani Mafia, Kanga, Kua on Juani Island, and Chole Island, visit some of the most famous boat builders in East Africa, or join a sunset cruise to spot the giant flying fox (pteropus).

GETTING HERE AND AROUND

There are daily flights from Dar es Salaam and Zanzibar to Mafia Island via the many local airlines. Generally there are taxis at the airport, but it is best to arrange transport with your accommodation. If you are feeling brave you can take a bajaj (a tiny vehicle with three wheels), which will cost around Tsh20,000, but make sure you don't have a lot of luggage in tow. All snorkeling and diving activities inside Chole Bay are tide-dependent. It's better to book your diving as you arrive on the island and not through tour operators, unless you are an experienced diver. Take advantage of any good offers, but do so through the dive centers directly. The entry fee into the marine park is US$23 per day, to be paid in cash at the offices on the way into the park. There is one international ATM on the island and you can change foreign currency at the bank in Kilondoni.

WHERE TO STAY

Options for budget accommodations on Mafia Island are fairly limited, and most of them will be either outside of the Marine Park or buried deep in the villages and in varying degrees of maintenance.

$
RESORT
Big Blue Divers. If you are in Mafia to dive but also are watching the wallet then Big Blue is a great option, with a selection of affordable tents and bungalows. **Pros:** budget friendly; great for diving and snorkeling; lovely location near the water. **Cons:** rather Spartan accommodation, but worth it if coupled with diving packages; tents can be hot during peak summer; Mafia island prices in general are quite expensive. $ *Rooms from: $72* ✉ *Utende Beach, Mafia Island* ☎ *787/474–108* ⊕ *www.bigblumafia.com* ⤣ *7 bungalows, 7 tents* ⏀ *No meals.*

$
RESORT
FAMILY
Butiama Beach. Situated to the southwest of the island Butiama Beach is one of the best accommodations outside of the marine park, with well-appointed, colorful bungalows that have wide outdoor verandas equipped with loungers and inviting hammocks. **Pros:** best place for fishing or water sports and whale shark sightings; large, open dining and relaxation spaces with a swimming pool; decent on-site spa. **Cons:** outside of the Marine Park so you travel some distance to get to dive sites; next to main port area so beach is not always private; some bungalows have limited sea views. $ *Rooms from: $150* ✉ *Butiama Beach, Mafia Island* ☎ *787/474–084* ⊕ *www.butiamabeach.com* ⤣ *15 bungalows* ⏀ *All-inclusive.*

$ RESORT Fodor's Choice ★ 🏨 **Chole Mjini.** Climbing up the winding steps rotating around the trunk of a baobab tree, the tree houses of Chole Mjini will fulfill anyone with an island castaway fantasy. **Pros:** sleeping in one of East Africa's unique settings; dinner by candlelight in an ancient ruin; the best place to see whale sharks in an ethical manner. **Cons:** no toilets in the tree house, so you have to walk down stairs to get to the bathroom at night; no swimming beach; open tree house means there will be a few night critters. [$] *Rooms from: $200* ✉ *Chole Island, Mafia Island* ☎ *784/712–427* 🌐 *www.cholemjini.com* 🛏 *6 houses* 🍴 *All-inclusive.*

$$ RESORT 🏨 **Kinasi Lodge.** Nestled on a hillside between an old cashew nut and coconut plantation, Kinasi has beautiful views over the mangroves towards the bay on Mafia Island. **Pros:** gorgeous views over the bay; plenty of water sports or lounging in the sun; rooms are spread out enough to offer privacy. **Cons:** beach disappears at high tide; not all rooms have views of the sea; very hilly to get to lower rooms. [$] *Rooms from: $280* ✉ *Mafia Island, Utende* ☎ *71/566–9145* 🌐 *www.kinasi-lodge.com* 🕒 *Closed Apr.–May* 🛏 *14 rooms* 🍴 *All-inclusive.*

$$ RESORT Fodor's Choice ★ 🏨 **Pole Pole Bungalows.** In Swahili, *pole pole* means to go slowly, and at this intimate little resort this is very much encouraged. **Pros:** barefoot luxury and seclusion; lovely swimming pool; complimentary sunset cruises in traditional dhows. **Cons:** there is no air-conditioning, but the bungalows are constructed to direct the breeze inside; dive shop is only accessible at low tide; beach is tidal. [$] *Rooms from: $295* ✉ *Mafia Island, Utende* ☎ 🌐 *www.polepole.com* 🛏 *7 bungalows* 🍴 *All-inclusive.*

PEMBA ISLAND

With a population around 300,000 people and only a small amount of visiting tourists every year this relatively pristine island is dotted with mangroves and ancient forests, lush lagoons, spectacular diving, delicate white-sand beaches, and a coastline that is rugged, with large stretches relatively untouched by tourism activities. Out here the monsoons set the pace of life—the only constant that has survived Portuguese occupation, Omani Arab rule, and British administration are the Arab dhows that sail in and out through the lagoons bound by the old trade winds and the rising and ebbing tides. Pemba draws its name for the Arabic for "Green Island" and it produces about 70% of the world's cloves. The population here is a mix of Arab and original Swahili inhabitants, and because it has not been open to tourists until recently, it is a completely different experience to Zanzibar and Mafia, so it is advised to be culturally sensitive and respect local customs and beliefs by dressing and acting accordingly: no shorts or mini dresses in villages. This is an island that might be one of the best-kept secrets in Tanzania. The people of the island are some of the friendliest and most welcoming around, curious without any pretense. The limited amount of tourism development enables it to maintain a spectacular diving and island culture.

GETTING HERE AND AROUND

The best way to get to Pemba is to use one of the local internal flight companies like Coastal Air or Zanair that have daily flights out of Zanzibar and Dar es Salaam. Most resorts will arrange a boat transfer. Because distances are similar no matter which resort you choose, it's roughly between $45 and $50 for a taxi and boat ride from Chake Chake airport to your accommodations on the north and south sides. Moving around the island can be expensive, and local buses do take a while and will not be able to get you directly to the lodges, so best to arrange transportation with your accommodations beforehand. There are ATMs in Chake Chake only; if you need money withdraw it before you get to your lodge as driving distances can be from 40 to 50 minutes.

WHERE TO STAY

$$
RESORT
Fodor's Choice
★

Fundu Lagoon. Fundu is the type of place that begs you to just kick off your shoes and indulge in some restful jungle lounging—but from the balcony of your private luxury tent. **Pros:** jungle setting is exquisite and unique; the jetty bar is the perfect sundowner spot for romantics; superior rooms are on another level and have their own private plunge pools. **Cons:** mosquitoes are in abundance; a 15-minute boat ride to the nearest bathing beach; not all drinks are included. $ *Rooms from: $440* ✉ *Fundu Lagoon, Pemba Island* ☎ *75/6136–6593* ⊕ *www.fundulagoon.com* ⤳ *18 bungalows* ❑ *All-inclusive.*

$$
ALL-INCLUSIVE
Fodor's Choice
★

The Manta Resort. Hidden in the ancient Ngezi Forest, home to the endemic Pemba Flying Fox, Manta Resort sits on a hillside that rolls down to tranquil turquoise waters with a beautiful 180-degree sea-view open dining area. **Pros:** friendly, attentive staff, who go above and beyond; great diving and snorkeling is easily accessible; spectacular beach with large swimming pool above. **Cons:** the drive to get there is an hour and a half with bumpy terrain at the end; standard garden rooms are quite pricey for the size; no Wi-Fi in the rooms (could be a bonus). $ *Rooms from: $272* ✉ *Pemba Island* ☎ *77/671–8852* ⊕ *www.themantaresort.com* ⤳ *18 rooms* ❑ *All-inclusive.*

$
RESORT

Pemba Eco Lodge. On the more remote Shaminiani Island, a short boat ride from a small village, a series of bandas are built facing out over a bay. **Pros:** intimate resort; neat and impeccably clean rooms; lovely beach with just you and the local fishermen. **Cons:** alcoholic beverages are prohibitively expensive; food is of average standard; compost toilet might not be to everyone's taste. $ *Rooms from: $120* ✉ *Shamiani Island, Pemba Island* ☎ *24/224–0494* ⊕ *www.pembalodge.com* ⤳ *5 bungalows* ❑ *All-inclusive.*

SOUTH AFRICA

WELCOME TO SOUTH AFRICA

TOP REASONS TO GO

★ **Big Game.** You're guaranteed to see big game—including the Big Five—both in national parks and at many private lodges.

★ **Escape the Crowds.** South Africa's game parks are rarely crowded. You'll see more game with fewer other visitors than almost anywhere else in Africa.

★ **Luxury Escapes.** Few other sub-Saharan countries can offer South Africa's high standards of accommodation, service, and food amid gorgeous surroundings of bush, beach, mountains, and desert.

★ **Take the Family.** All the national parks accept children (choose a malaria-free one if your kids are small), and many private lodges have fantastic children's programs.

★ **Beyond the Parks.** Visit Cape Town, one of the most beautiful and stylish cities in the world; the nearby stunning Winelands; the inspiring scenery of the Garden Route; and glorious, soft white-sand beaches.

South Africa lies at the very foot of the continent. Not only geographically and scenically diverse, it's a nation of more than 47 million people of varied origins, cultures, languages, and beliefs.

1 **Kruger National Park.** A visit to Kruger, one of the world's great game parks, may rank among the best experiences of your life.

2 **Sabi Sand Game Reserve.** The most famous and exclusive of South Africa's private reserves, this 153,000-acre park is home to dozens of private lodges, including the world-famous MalaMala and Londolozi.

3 **KwaZulu-Natal Parks.** Zululand's Hluhluwe-Imfolozi is tiny—less than 6% of Kruger's size—but delivers the Big Five plus all the plains game. Mkuze and Itala are even smaller, but worth a visit, and if you're looking for the ultimate in luxury, stay at Phinda or Thanda private reserves.

4 **Kgalagadi Transfrontier Park.** Together with its neighbor, Botswana's Gemsbok National Park, this park covers more than 38,000 square km (14,670 square miles)—one of very few conservation areas of this magnitude left in the world.

6

Updated by Mary Holland, Lee Middleton, and Barbara Noe Kennedy

Since 1994, when Nelson Mandela spearheaded its peaceful transition to democracy, South Africa has been one of the greatest tourist destinations in the world. The country is stable and affordable, with an excellent infrastructure; friendly, interesting, amazingly diverse people; and enough stunning sights, sounds, scenery, and attractions to make even the most jaded traveler sit up and take notice. And nearly everybody speaks English—a huge bonus for international visitors.

South Africa has always teemed with game. That's what drew the early European explorers, who aimed to bring something exotic home with them. After all, as Pliny the Elder, one of Africa's earliest explorers, wrote almost 2,000 years ago, *"ex Africa semper aliquid novi"* (translated, "Out of Africa always comes something new"). Sometimes it was a giraffe, a rhinoceros, a strange bird, or an unheard-of plant.

In the latter half of the 19th century, Dr. Livingstone, Scotland's most famous Christian missionary, opened up much of the interior on his evangelizing expeditions, as did the piratical Englishman Cecil John Rhodes, who famously made his fortune on the Kimberley diamond mines and planned an unsuccessful Cape-to-Cairo railway line. About the same time, lured by the rumors of gold and instant fortunes, hundreds of hunters came to the lowveld to lay their hands on much-sought-after skins, horns, and ivory. Trophy hunters followed, vying with one another to see how many animals they could shoot in one day—often more than 100 each.

Paul Kruger, president of the Transvaal Republic (a 19th-century Boer country that occupied a portion of present-day South Africa), took the unprecedented visionary step of establishing a protected area for the wildlife in the lowveld region; in 1898 Kruger National Park was born.

South Africa has 22 national parks covering deserts, wetland and marine areas, forests, mountains, scrub, and savanna. Hunting safaris

FAST FACTS

Size 1,221,037 square km (471,442 square miles).

Capital Pretoria (administrative capital); Cape Town (legislative capital); Bloemfontein (judicial capital).

Number of National Parks 22: Addo Elephant, Agulhas, Augrabies Falls, Bontebok, Camdeboo, Golden Gate Highlands, Karoo, Kruger, Mapungubwe, Marakele, Mokala, Mountain Zebra, Namaqua, Table Mountain, Tankwa Karoo, Tsitsikamma, West Coast, and Wilderness National Parks; Ais/Richtersveld and Kgalagadi Transfrontier Parks; Knysna

National Lake Area; uKhahlamba/Drakensberg Park.

Number of Private Reserves Hundreds, including Sabi Sands and KwaZulu-Natal's Phinda and Thanda.

Population Approximately 48 million.

Big Five The gang's all here.

Language South Africa has 11 official languages: Afrikaans, English, Ndebele, North and South Sotho, Swati, Tsonga, Tswana, Venda, Xhosa, and Zulu. English is widely spoken.

Time SAST (South African Standard Time), seven hours ahead of North American Eastern Standard Time.

6

are still popular but are strictly controlled by the government, and licenses are compulsory. Although hunting is a controversial issue, the revenue is substantial and can be ploughed into sustainable conservation, and the impact on the environment is minimal. Increasingly, wildlife conservation is linked with community development; many conservation areas have integrated local communities, the wildlife, and the environment, with benefits for all. Londolozi, MalaMala, and Phinda are internationally acclaimed role models for linking tourism with community-development projects.

PLANNING

WHEN TO GO

In the north, summers are sunny and hot (never humid), with short afternoon thunderstorms. Winter days are bright and sunny, but nights can be frosty. Although November through January is Cape Town's most popular time, with glorious sunshine and long, light evenings, the best weather is in February and March. Cape winters (May–August) are unpredictable with cold, windy, rainy days interspersed with glorious sun. The coastal areas of KwaZulu-Natal are warm year-round, but summers are steamy and hot. The ocean water is warmest in February, but it seldom dips below 17°C (65°F).

GETTING HERE AND AROUND

Countless cities, towns, streets, parks, and more have gotten or will get new monikers, both to rid the country of names that recall the apartheid era and to honor the previously unsung. The names in this book were accurate at time of writing but may still change.

AIR TRAVEL

At this writing, only South African Airways and Delta provide direct service from the United States to South Africa, but flights routed through Europe may be preferable since they allow you a stop en route.

In peak season (midsummer, which is from December to the end of February, and South African school vacations), give yourself at least a half hour extra at the airport for domestic flights, as the check-in lines can be endless—particularly on flights to the coast at the start of vacations and back to Johannesburg's O. R. Tambo International Airport at the end.

If you are visiting a game lodge deep in the bush, you will be arriving by light plane—and you will be restricted in what you can bring. Excess luggage can usually be stored with the operator until your return. Don't just gloss over this: charter operators take weight very seriously, and some will charge you for an extra ticket if you insist on bringing excess baggage.

AIRPORTS Most international flights arrive at and depart from Johannesburg's O. R. Tambo International Airport, 19 km (12 miles) from the city. The country's other major airports are in Cape Town and Durban, but international flights departing from Cape Town often stop in Johannesburg. O. R. Tambo has a tourist information desk, a V.A.T. refund office, several ATMs, and a computerized accommodations service. If you're leaving O. R. Tambo's international terminal (Terminal A), the domestic terminal (Terminal B) is connected by a busy and fairly long walkway. ■TIP➔ **Allow 10–15 minutes' walking time between international and domestic terminals.**

Cape Town International is 19 km (12 miles) southeast of the city, and Durban International is 16 km (10 miles) north of the city. If you are traveling to or from either Johannesburg or Cape Town airport (and, to a lesser extent, Durban) be aware of the time of day. Traffic can be horrendous between 7 and 9 in the morning and between about 3:30 and 6 in the evening.

The other major cities are served by small airports that are really easy to navigate. Port Elizabeth is the main airport for the Eastern Cape, George serves the Garden Route, and the closest airports to Kruger National Park are the small airports at Nelspruit, Hoedspruit, and Phalaborwa. Most airports are managed by the Airports Company of South Africa.

International Airports Cape Town International Airport (*CPT*). ⊠ *Matroosfontein, Cape Town* ☎ *021/937–1200* ⊕ *www.capetown-airport.com.* **King Shaka International Airport** (*DUR*). ⊠ *King Shaka Dr., La Mercy* ☎ *032/436–6000* ⊕ *www.kingshakainternational.co.za.* **O. R. Tambo International Airport** (*JNB*). ⊠ *O. R. Tambo Airport Rd., Johannesburg* ☎ *011/921–6262* ⊕ *www.johannesburg-airport.com.*

FLIGHTS South Africa's international airline is South African Airways (SAA), which offers nonstop service between Johannesburg and New York–JFK (JFK) and Washington–Dulles (IAD), though some flights from Dulles make a stopover in Dakar, Senegal. Delta also offers nonstop service from the United States to South Africa. Flight times from the U.S. East Coast range from 15 hours (from Atlanta to Johannesburg on Delta) to almost 20 hours (on Delta via Amsterdam). When booking flights, check the routing carefully; some involve stopovers of an hour or two, which may change from day to day. European airlines serving South Africa are British Airways, KLM, Virgin Atlantic, Lufthansa, and Air France.

Three major domestic airlines have flights connecting South Africa's principal airports. SA Airlink and SA Express are subsidiaries of SAA, and Comair is a subsidiary of British Airways. Comair and SAA serve Livingstone, Zambia (for Victoria Falls); Air Zimbabwe and SAA serve Victoria Falls airport in Zimbabwe.

Recent years have seen an explosion of low-cost carriers serving popular domestic routes in South Africa with regularly scheduled flights. Kulula. com and Mango provide reasonably priced domestic air tickets if you book in advance. Phakalane Airways provides service to airports in the Northern Cape. The only downside is that they have fewer flights per day and aren't always cheaper than SAA.

Airlines Air France. ☎ 0861/340–340 in South Africa, 800/237–2747 in U.S. ⊕ www.airfrance.co.za. **British Airways.** ☎ 011/920–7525 in South Africa, 800/247–9297 in U.S. ⊕ www.britishairways.com. **Delta.** ☎ 011/408–8200 in South Africa, 800/241–4141 in U.S. ⊕ www.delta.com. **KLM.** ☎ 0860/247–747 in South Africa, 866/434–0320 in U.S. ⊕ www.klm.com. **Lufthansa.** ☎ 0861/842–538 in South Africa, 800/645–3880 in U.S. ⊕ www.lufthansa.com. **South African Airways.** ☎ 0860/003–146 in South Africa, 800/722–9675 in U.S. ⊕ www.flysaa. com. **United.** ☎ 011/463–1170 in South Africa, 800/864–8331 in U.S. ⊕ www. united.com. **Virgin Atlantic.** ☎ 011/340–3400 in South Africa, 800/862–8621 in U.S. ⊕ www.virginatlantic.com.

Domestic Airlines Air Zimbabwe. ☎ 263/457–5021 ⊕ www.airzimbabwe. aero. **British Airways Comair.** ☎ 011/921–0222 in South Africa, 0860/435–922 toll-free in South Africa, 800/247–9297 in U.S. ⊕ www.britishairways. com. **Kulula.** ☎ 086/158–5852 in South Africa ⊕ www.kulula.com. **Mango.** ☎ 011/086–6100 in Johannesburg, 021/815–4100 in Cape Town, 086/101–0002 toll-free in South Africa ⊕ www.flymango.com. **SA Airlink.** ☎ 011/451–7300 in South Africa, 010/590–3170 in South Africa ⊕ www.flyairlink.com. **SA Express.** ☎ 011/978–1111 toll-free in South Africa ⊕ www.flyexpress.aero.

CHARTER
FLIGHTS
Charters are common for getting to safari lodges and remote destinations throughout Southern Africa. These aircraft are well maintained and are almost always booked by your lodge or travel agent. The major charter companies run daily shuttles from O. R. Tambo to destinations such as Kruger Park. On-demand flights are very expensive for independent travelers, as they require minimum passenger loads. If it's just two passengers, you will be charged for the vacant seats. Keep in mind that you probably won't get to choose the charter company you fly with. The aircraft you get depends on the number of passengers flying and can vary from very small (you will sit in the copilot's seat) to a much more comfortable commuter plane.

Because of the limited space and size of the aircraft, charter carriers observe strict luggage regulations: luggage must be soft-sided and weigh no more than 57 pounds (and often less); on many charter flights the weight cannot exceed 33 pounds.

Charter Companies African Ramble. ☎ 083/375–6514, 083/375–6514 ⊕ www.aframble.co.za. **Federal Air.** ☎ 011/395–9000 ⊕ www.fedair.com. **Wilderness Air.** ⊕ www.wilderness-air.com.

CAR TRAVEL

South Africa has a superb network of multilane roads and highways. Distances are vast, so guard against fatigue (a definite factor for jet-lagged drivers), which is an even bigger killer than alcohol. Toll roads, scattered among the main routes, charge anything from R10 to R60.

You can drive in South Africa for up to six months on any English-language license. South Africa's Automobile Association publishes a range of maps, atlases, and travel guides, available for purchase on its website (⊕ www.aa.co.za). The commercial website Drive South Africa (⊕ www.drivesouthafrica.co.za) has everything you need to know about driving in the country, including road safety and driving distances. ■TIP→ Carjackings can and do occur with such frequency that certain high-risk areas are marked by permanent carjacking signs.

GASOLINE Service stations (open 24 hours) are positioned at regular intervals along all major highways in South Africa. There are no self-service stations. In return, tip the attendant R2–R5 (more if you've filled the tank). South Africa has a choice of unleaded or leaded gasoline, and many vehicles operate on diesel—be sure you get the right fuel. Gasoline is measured in liters, and the cost is higher than in the United States. When driving long distances, check your routes carefully, as the distances between towns—and hence gas stations—can be more than 100 miles.

PARKING In the countryside, parking is mostly free, but you will almost certainly need to pay for parking in cities, which will probably run you about R5–R8 per hour. Many towns have an official attendant (who should be wearing a vest of some sort) who will log the number of the spot you park in; you're asked to pay up front for the amount of time you expect to park. If the guard is unofficial, acknowledge them on arrival, ask them to look after your car, and pay a few rand when you return (they depend on these tips). At pay-and-display parking lots you pay in advance; other garages expect payment at the exit. Many (such as those at shopping malls and airports) require that you pay for your parking before you return to your car (at kiosks near the exits to the parking areas). Your receipt ticket allows you to exit. Just read the signs carefully.

RENTAL CARS Rates are similar to those in the United States. Some companies charge more on weekends, so it's best to get a range of quotes before booking your car.

For a car with automatic transmission and air-conditioning, you'll pay slightly less for a car that doesn't have unlimited mileage. When comparing prices, make sure you're getting the same thing. Some companies quote prices without insurance, some include 80% or 90% coverage, and some quote with 100% protection. Get all terms in writing before you leave on your trip.

There's no need to rent a 4x4 vehicle, as all roads are paved, including those in Kruger National Park.

You can often save some money by booking a car through a broker, who will access the car from one of the main agencies. Smaller, local agencies often give a much better price, but the car must be returned in the same city. This is pretty popular in Cape Town but not so much in other centers.

To rent a car you need to be 23 years or older and have held a driver's license for three years. Younger international drivers can rent from some companies but will pay a penalty. You need to get special permission to take rental cars into neighboring countries (including Lesotho and Swaziland). Most companies allow additional drivers, but some charge.

CAR-RENTAL INSURANCE In South Africa it's necessary to buy special insurance if you plan to cross borders into neighboring countries, but CDW and TDW (collision-damage waiver and theft-damage waiver) are optional on domestic rentals. Any time you are considering crossing a border with your rental vehicle, you must inform the rental company ahead of time to fulfill any paperwork requirements and pay additional fees.

Emergency Services General emergency number. ☎ *112 from mobile phone, 10111 from landline, 107 in Cape Town only.*

Local Agencies Car Mania. ☎ *021/447–3001* ⊕ *www.carmania.co.za.* **Value Car Hire.** ☎ *021/386–7699* ⊕ *www.valuerentalcar.com.*

Major Agencies Avis. ☎ *0861/021–111, 011/387–8431* ⊕ *www.avis.co.za.* **Budget.** ☎ *011/387–8432* ⊕ *www.budget.co.za.* **Europcar.** ☎ *0861/131–000, 011/479–4000* ⊕ *www.europcar.co.za.* **Hertz.** ☎ *021/935–4800, 0861/600136* ⊕ *www.hertz.co.za.*

6

ABOUT THE RESTAURANTS

South Africa's cities and towns are full of dining options, from chain restaurants like the popular Nando's to chic cafés. Indian food and Cape Malay dishes are regional favorites in Cape Town, while traditional smoked meats and sausages are available countrywide. In South Africa dinner is eaten at night and lunch at noon. Restaurants serve breakfast until about 11:30; a few serve breakfast all day. If you're staying at a game lodge, your mealtimes will revolve around the game drives—usually coffee and *rusks* (similar to biscotti) early in the morning, more coffee and probably muffins on the first game drive, a huge brunch in the late morning, no lunch, tea and something sweet in the late afternoon before the evening game drive, cocktails and snacks on the drive, and a substantial supper, or dinner, at about 8 or 8:30.

Many restaurants accustomed to serving tourists accept credit cards, usually Visa and American Express, with MasterCard increasingly accepted.

Most restaurants welcome casual dress, including jeans and sneakers, but draw the line at shorts and a halter top at dinner, except for restaurants on the beach.

ABOUT THE LODGES AND HOTELS

Be warned that lodging terminology in South Africa can be misleading. The term *lodge* is a particularly tricky one. A guest lodge or a game lodge is almost always an upmarket, full-service facility with loads of extra attractions. But the term *lodge* when applied to city hotels often indicates a minimum-service hotel, like the City and Town Lodges and Holiday Inn Garden Courts. A backpacker lodge, however, is essentially a hostel.

A *rondavel* can be a small cabin, often in a rounded shape, and its cousin, the *banda,* can be anything from a basic stand-alone structure to a Quonset hut. Think very rustic.

Be sure you understand the hotel's cancellation policy. Some places allow you to cancel without any kind of penalty—even if you prepaid to secure a discounted rate—if you cancel at least 24 hours in advance. Others require you to cancel a week in advance or penalize you the cost of one night. Small inns and B&Bs are most likely to require you to cancel far in advance. Always have written confirmation of your booking when you check in. ■TIP➔ **Most hotels allow children under a certain age to stay in their parents' room at no extra charge, but others charge for them as extra adults, and some don't allow children under 12 at all.** Ask about the policy on children before checking in, and make sure you find out the cutoff age for discounts.

In South Africa, most accommodations from hotels to guesthouses do include breakfast in the rate. Most game lodges include all meals, or they may be all-inclusive (including alcohol as well). All hotels listed have private bath unless otherwise noted.

Restaurant and hotel reviews have been shortened. For full information, visit Fodors.com.

WHAT IT COSTS IN SOUTH AFRICAN RAND

	$	$$	$$$	$$$$
Restaurants	under R100	R100–R150	R151–R200	over R200
Hotels	under R1,500	R1,500–R2,500	R2,501–R3,500	over R3,500

Restaurant prices are the average cost of a main course at dinner or, if dinner is not served, at lunch. Hotel prices are the lowest cost of a standard double room in high season.

COMMUNICATIONS
INTERNET
Most hotels have Wi-Fi. Stores such as Woolworths, restaurants such as Wimpy, and most airports offer a countrywide Wi-Fi service called AlwaysOn (*www.alwayson.co.za*) that allows you 30 minutes of free Wi-Fi per day. If you need more time, you can pay for it.

PHONES
The country code for South Africa is 27. When dialing from abroad, drop the initial 0 from local area codes.

CALLING WITHIN SOUTH AFRICA When making a phone call in South Africa, always use the full 10-digit number, including the area code, even if you're in the same area. For directory assistance, call 1023. For operator-assisted national long-distance calls, call 1025. For international operator assistance, dial 10903#. These numbers are free if dialed from a Telkom (landline) phone but are charged at normal cell-phone rates from a mobile—and they're busy call centers. Directory inquiry numbers are different for each cell-phone network. Vodacom is 111, MTN is 200, and Cell C is 146. These calls are charged at normal rates, but the call is timed only from when it is actually answered.

CALLING
OUTSIDE
SOUTH AFRICA

When dialing out from South Africa, dial 00 before the international code. So, for example, you would dial 001 for the United States, since the country code for the United States is 1.

Internet calling like Skype also works well from the United States, but it's not always functional in South Africa, unless you're on a reliable high-speed Internet connection, which isn't available everywhere. However, if you have a South African "free" cell phone (meaning you can receive calls for free; all phones using an SA SIM card do this), someone in the United States can call you from their Skype account, for reasonable per-minute charges, and you won't be charged.

Access Codes AT&T Direct. ☎ *314/925–6925 in South Africa* ⊕ *www.att.com.* **MCI Worldwide Access.** ☎ *0800/990–011 in South Africa.* **Sprint International Access.** ☎ *0800/990–001 in South Africa.*

MOBILE
PHONES

Cell phones are ubiquitous and have quite extensive coverage. There are four cell-phone service providers in South Africa—Cell C, MTN, Virgin Mobile, and Vodacom—and you can buy these SIM cards, as well as airtime, in supermarkets for as little as R10 for the SIM card. (If you purchase SIM cards at the airport, you will be charged much more.) Bear in mind that your U.S. cell phone may not work with the local GSM system and/or that your phone may be blocked from using SIM cards outside of your plan if your phone is not unlocked. Basic but functional GSM cell phones start at R100, and are available at the mobile carrier shops as well as major department stores like Woolworths.

Cellular Abroad rents and sells GMS phones and sells SIM cards that work in many countries, but they cost a lot more than local solutions. Mobal rents mobiles and sells GSM phones (starting at $49) that will operate in 150 countries. Per-call rates vary throughout the world. Vodacom is the country's leading cellular network.

The least complicated way to make and receive phone calls is to obtain international roaming service from your cell-phone service provider before you leave home, but this can be expensive. Any phone that you take abroad must be unlocked by your company for you to be able to use it.

Contacts Cell C. ☎ *084/140* ⊕ *www.cellc.co.za.* **Mobal.** ☎ *888/888–9162 in U.S.* ⊕ *www.mobal.com.* **MTN.** ☎ *083/173* ⊕ *www.mtn.co.za.* **Virgin Mobile.** ☎ *0741/000–123* ⊕ *www.virginmobile.co.za.* **Vodacom.** ☎ *082–111* ⊕ *www.vodacom.co.za.*

EMERGENCIES

If you specifically need an ambulance, you can get one by calling the special ambulance number or through the general emergency number. If you intend to scuba dive in South Africa, make sure you have DAN membership, which will be honored by Divers Alert Network South Africa (DANSA).

Emergency Contacts DANSA. ☎ *0800/020–111 emergency hotline, 27/828–106010 outside South Africa* ⊕ *www.dansa.org.* **General emergency.** ☎ *10111 from landline, 112 from mobile phone, 107 for Cape Town only.*

HEALTH AND SAFETY

The drinking water in South Africa is treated and, except in rural areas, is safe to drink. Many people filter it, though, to get rid of the chlorine, as that aseptic status does not come free. You can eat fresh fruits and salads and have ice in your drinks.

It is always wise for travelers to have medical insurance for travel that will also help with emergency evacuation (most safari operators require emergency evacuation coverage and may ask you to pay for it along with your tour payments). If you don't want general travel insurance, many companies offer medical-only policies.

Although the majority of visitors experience a crime-free trip to South Africa, it's essential to practice vigilance and extreme care. Do not walk alone at night, and exercise caution even during the day. Avoid wearing jewelry (even costume jewelry), don't invite attention by wearing an expensive camera around your neck, and don't flash a large wad of cash. If you are toting a handbag, wear the strap across your body; even better, wear a money belt, preferably hidden from view under your clothing. When sitting at airports or at restaurants, especially outdoor cafés, make sure to keep your bag on your lap or between your legs. Even better, loop the strap around your leg, or clip the strap around the table or chair.

Carjacking is another problem, with armed bandits often forcing drivers out of their vehicles at traffic lights, in driveways, or during a fake accident. Always drive with your windows closed and doors locked, don't stop for hitchhikers, and park in well-lighted places. At traffic lights, leave enough space between you and the vehicle in front so you can pull into another lane if necessary. In the unlikely event you are carjacked, don't argue, and don't look at the carjacker's face. Just get out of the car, or ask to be let out of the car. Do not try to keep any of your belongings—they are all replaceable, even that laptop with all that data on it. If you aren't given the opportunity to leave the car, try to stay calm, ostentatiously look away from the hijackers so they can be sure you can't identify them, and follow all instructions. Ask again, calmly, to be let out of the car.

Many places that are unsafe in South Africa will not bear obvious signs of danger. Purchase a good map and obtain comprehensive directions from your hotel or rental-car agent. Taking the wrong exit off a highway into a township could lead you straight to troubles. Many cities are ringed by "no go" areas. Learn from your hotel or the locals which areas to avoid. If you sense you have taken a wrong turn, drive toward a public area, such as a gas station, or building with an armed guard, before attempting to correct your mistake, which could just compound the problem. When parking, don't leave anything visible in the car; stow it all in the trunk—this includes clothing or shoes. As an added measure, leave the glove box open, to show there's nothing of value inside (take the rental agreement with you).

Before setting out on foot, ask your hotel concierge which route to take and how far you can safely go. Walk with a purposeful stride so you look like you know where you're going, and duck into a shop or café if you need to check a map or speak on your mobile phone. ■TIP→ **Don't walk while speaking on a cell phone.**

Lone women travelers need to be particularly vigilant about walking alone and locking their rooms. South Africa has one of the world's highest rates of rape. If you do encounter someone who won't take a firm but polite "*No*" for an answer, appeal immediately to the hotel manager, bartender, or someone else who seems to be in charge. If you have to walk a short distance alone at night, such as from the hotel reception to your room in a dark motel compound or back from a café along a main street, have a plan, carry a whistle, and know what you'll do if you are grabbed.

MONEY MATTERS

Rand is the South African currency: 100 cents equal 1 rand. Dollar/rand exchange rate varies from day to day, but for the past couple years has hovered around a trading rate of US$1 to R8. Credit cards are widely accepted in shops, restaurants, and hotels, and there are plenty of ATMs at banks, service stations, and shopping malls.

ABOUT THE PARKS

We've broken the chapter down into **Must-See Parks** (Kruger National Park, Sabi Sand Game Reserve, KwaZulu-Natal Parks, Kgalagadi Transfrontier Park) and **If You Have Time Parks** (Tswalu Kalahari Reserve, Madikwe, Kwandwe, Addo Elephant Park, Pilanesberg Game Reserve) to help you better organize your time.

VISITOR INFO

The official South Africa Tourism website and SouthAfrica.info are full of general country information.

For Cape Town and Johannesburg visitor information, see Visitor Info in each city's section below.

Visitor Info SouthAfrica.info. ⊕ *www.southafrica.info.* **South African Tourism.** ☏⊕ *www.southafrica.net.*

KRUGER NATIONAL PARK

Game
★★★★★
Park Accessibility
★★★★★
Getting Around
★★★★★
Accommodations
★★★★★
Scenic Beauty
★★★★

Visiting Kruger is likely to be one of the greatest experiences of your life, truly providing ultimate "Wow!" moments. You'll be amazed at the diversity of life forms—the tallest (the giraffe), the biggest (the elephant), the funkiest (the dung beetle), the toothiest (the crocodile), and the glitziest (the lilac-breasted roller).

But it's not all game and safari. If you're into ancient human history, there are also major archaeological sites and fascinating San (Bushman) rock paintings. (There is ample evidence that prehistoric humans (*Homo erectus*) roamed the area between 500,000 and 100,000 years ago.) Founded in 1898 by Paul Kruger, president of what was then the Transvaal Republic, the park is a place to safari at your own pace, choosing between upscale private camps or simple campsites.

Kruger lies in the hot lowveld, a subtropical section of Mpumalanga and Limpopo provinces that abuts Mozambique. The park cuts a swath 80 km (50 miles) wide and 320 km (200 miles) long from Zimbabwe and the Limpopo River in the north to the Crocodile River in the south. It is divided into 16 macro eco-zones, each supporting a great variety of plants, birds, and animals, including 145 mammal species and almost 500 species of birds, some of which are not found elsewhere in South Africa. In 2002 a treaty was signed between South Africa, Zimbabwe, and Mozambique to form a giant conservation area, the Great Limpopo Transfrontier Park. It's a complex ongoing process, but once all the fences between Kruger, the Gonarezhou National Park in Mozambique, and the Limpopo National Park in Zimbabwe are finally removed, the Peace Park will be the largest conservation area in the world.

WHEN TO GO

Kruger National Park is hellishly hot in midsummer (November–March), but the bush is green, the animals are sleek and glossy, and the birdlife is prolific, even though high grass and dense foliage make spotting animals more difficult. Winter (May–September) is the high season. The bush is at its dullest, driest, and most colorless, but the game is much easier to spot, as many trees are bare, the grass is low, and animals congregate around the few available permanent water sources. However, temperatures can drop to almost freezing at night and in the very early morning. The shoulder months of April and October are also good, and less crowded.

GETTING HERE AND AROUND

You can fly to Kruger Mpumalanga International Airport (KMIA), at Mbombela (Nelspruit); Skukuza Airport in Kruger itself; Hoedspruit Airport, close to Kruger's Orpen Gate; or Phalaborwa Airport (if you're going to the north of Kruger) from either Johannesburg or Cape Town. You can also drive to Kruger from Johannesburg in about six hours; if you drive, a 4x4 isn't necessary since all roads are paved.

Airports Hoedspruit Airport (*HDS*). ✉ *Eastgate Airport, Hoedspruit* ☎ *015/793-3681* ⊕ *www.eastgateairport.co.za.* **Kruger Mpumalanga International Airport (KMIA).** ☎ *013/753-7500* ⊕ *www.kmiairport.co.za.* **Phalaborwa Airport** (*PHW, Hendrik Van Eck Airport*). ✉ *Off R71, near Phalaborwa Gate, Access Rd., Phalaborwa* ☎ *015/781-5823.* **Skukuza Airport** (*SZK*). ☎ *013/735-5074* ⊕ *www.skukuzaairport.com.*

MONEY MATTERS

Kruger accepts credit cards, which are also useful for big purchases, but you should always have some small change for staff tips (tip your cleaning person R20 per hut per day) and for drinks and snacks at the camp shops, although camp shops also accept credit cards.

PLANNING YOUR TIME

How and where you tackle Kruger will depend on your time frame. With excellent roads and accommodations, it's a great place to drive yourself. If you don't feel up to driving or self-catering, you can choose a private lodge in Kruger itself or just outside the park and take the guided drives—although it's not quite the same as lying in bed and hearing the hyenas prowling around the camp fence or a lion roaring under the stars.

If you can spend a week here, start in the north at the very top of the park at the Punda Maria Camp, then make your way leisurely south to the very bottom at Crocodile Bridge Gate or Malelane Gate. With only three days or fewer, reserve one of the southern camps such as Berg-en-Dal or Lower Sabie and just plan to explore these areas. No matter where you go in Kruger, be sure to plan your route and accommodations (advance booking is essential). Game-viewing isn't an exact science: you might see all the Big Five plus hundreds of other animals, but you could see much less. Try to plan your route to include waterholes and rivers, which afford your best opportunity to see game. Old Africa hands claim that the very early morning, when the camp gates open, is the best time for game-viewing, but it's all quite random—you could see a leopard drinking at noon, a breeding herd of elephants midmorning, or a lion pride dozing under a tree in the middle of the afternoon. You could also head out at dawn and find very little wildlife. Be sure to take at least one guided sunset drive; you won't likely forget the thrill of catching a nocturnal animal in the spotlight.

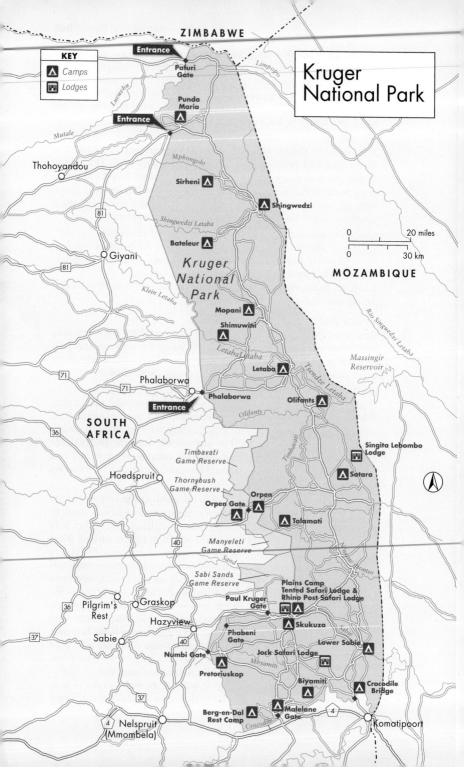

WALKING KRUGER

Kruger's seven wilderness trails accommodate eight hikers each. On three-day, two-night hikes, led by an armed ranger and local tracker, you walk in the mornings and evenings, with an afternoon siesta. You can generally get closer to animals in a vehicle, but many hikers can recount face-to-face encounters with everything from rhinos to lions.

Be prepared to walk up to 19 km (12 miles) a day. No one under 12 is allowed; those over 60 must have a doctor's certificate. Hikers sleep in rustic two-bed huts and share a reed-wall bathroom (flush toilets, bucket showers). Meals are simple (stews and barbecues); you bring your own drinks. In summer, walking is uncomfortably hot (and trails are cheaper); in winter, nights can be freezing—bring warm clothes and an extra blanket. Reserve 13 months ahead, when bookings open. The cost is about R3,430 per person per trail.

Bushman Trail. In the southwestern corner of the park, this trail takes its name from the San rock paintings and sites found in the area. The trail camp lies in a secluded valley dominated by granite hills and cliffs. Watch for white rhinos, elephants, and buffalo. Check in at Berg-en-Dal.

Metsi Metsi Trail. The permanent water of the nearby N'waswitsontso River makes this one of the best trails for winter game-viewing. Midway between Skukuza and Satara, the trail camp is in the lee of a mountain in an area of gorges, cliffs, and rolling savanna. Check in at Skukuza.

Napi Trail. White rhino sightings are common on this trail, which runs through mixed bushveld between Pretoriuskop and Skukuza. Other possibilities are black rhinos, cheetahs, leopards, elephants, and, if you're lucky, nomadic wild dogs. The camp is tucked into dense riverine forest at the confluence of the Napi and Biyamiti rivers. Check in at Pretoriuskop.

Nyalaland Trail. In the far north of the park, this trail camp sits among ancient baobab trees near the Luvuvhu River. Walk at the foot of huge rocky gorges and in dense forest. Look for highly sought-after birds: Böhm's spinetail, crowned eagle, and Pel's fishing owl. Hippos, crocs, elephants, buffalo, and the nyala antelope are almost a sure thing. Check in at Punda Maria.

Olifants Trail. This spectacularly sited camp sits on a high bluff overlooking the Olifants River and affords regular sightings of elephants, lions, buffalo, and hippos. The landscape varies from riverine forest to the rocky foothills of the Lebombo Mountains. Check in at Letaba.

Sweni Trail. East of Satara, this trail camp overlooks the Sweni Spruit and savanna. The area attracts large herds of zebras, wildebeests, and buffalo with their attendant predators: lions, spotted hyenas, and wild dogs. Check in at Satara.

Wolhuter Trail. You just might come face-to-face with a white rhino on this trail through undulating bushveld, interspersed with rocky kopjes, midway between Berg-en-Dal and Pretoriuskop. Elephants, buffalo, and lions are also likely. Check in at Berg-en-Dal.

6

If a female elephant feels threatened, she will charge, like this elephant in Kruger National Park.

Visitor Information **South African National Parks.** ☎ 012/428–9111 *Pretoria* ⊕ *www.sanparks.org.*

WHERE TO STAY

It's impossible to recommend just one camp in Kruger. One person might prefer the intimacy of Kruger's oldest camp, Punda Maria, with its whitewashed thatch cottages; another might favor big, bustling Skukuza. A great way to experience the park is to stay in as many of the camps as possible. The SANParks website (*www.sanparks.org*) has a comprehensive overview of the different camps. The bushveld camps are more expensive than the regular camps, but offer much more privacy and exclusivity—but no shops, restaurants, or pools. If you seek the ultimate in luxury, stay at one of the private luxury lodges in the concession areas, some of which also have walking trails.

Reservations for park-operated accommodations should be made through **South African National Parks.** If air-conditioning is a must for you, be sure to check the website to confirm its availability in the accommodation of your choice. ■TIP→ **Book your guided game drives and walks when you check in. Opt for the sunset drive. You'll get to see the animals coming to drink plus a thrilling night drive.**

$$
RESORT
Bateleur. Hidden in the northern reaches of the park, this tiny camp, the oldest of the bushveld camps, is one of Kruger's most remote destinations. **Pros:** private and intimate; guests see a lot at the camp's hide; no traffic jams. **Cons:** long distance to travel; there's a TV, which can be a pro or a con depending on your point of view. $ *Rooms from:*

R1930 ✉ Kruger National Park ☎ 012/428–9111 reservations 🌐 www.sanparks.org 🛏 7 rooms 🍴 No meals.

$ RESORT FAMILY Fodor's Choice ★ **Berg-en-Dal Rest Camp.** This rest camp lies at the southern tip of the park, in a basin surrounded by rocky hills. **Pros:** you can sit on benches at the perimeter fence and watch game come and go all day; leopard and wild dog regularly seen. **Cons:** always crowded (although chalets are well spaced out). [$] *Rooms from: R1150 ✉ Kruger National Park ☎ 012/428–9111 reservations 🌐 www.sanparks.org 🛏 166 rooms 🍴 No meals.*

$ RESORT **Biyamiti.** Close to the park gate at Crocodile Bridge, this larger-than-average, beautiful, sought-after bush camp overlooks the normally dry sands of the Biyamiti River. **Pros:** easily accessible; lots of game; variety of drives in area. **Cons:** difficult to book because of its popularity. [$] *Rooms from: R1375 ✉ Biyamiti Camp Rd., Kruger National Park ☎ 012/428–9111 reservations 🌐 www.sanparks.org 🛏 15 rooms 🍴 No meals.*

$ RESORT FAMILY **Crocodile Bridge.** Situated in Kruger's southeastern corner, this award-winning small rest camp sits on the scenic Crocodile River and doubles as an entrance gate, which makes it a convenient stopover if you arrive near the park's closing time and are too late to make it to another camp. **Pros:** adjacent to one of best game roads in park; ideal for guests looking for self-catering bushveld experience; sunrise and night drives are offered. **Cons:** close proximity to the outside world of roads and farms. [$] *Rooms from: R1350 ✉ Kruger National Park ☎ 012/428–9111 reservations 🌐 www.sanparks.org 🛏 46 rooms 🍴 No meals.*

$$$$ RESORT Fodor's Choice ★ **Jock Safari Lodge.** This lodge, one of South Africa's loveliest, is set among 14,826 acres of private concession in southwest Kruger. **Pros:** authentic safari experience. **Cons:** busy in season. [$] *Rooms from: R15444 ✉ Kruger National Park ☎ 041/509–3000 reservations, 041/509–3001 reservations 🌐 www.jocksafarilodge.com 🛏 12 rooms 🍴 All meals.*

$ RESORT FAMILY **Letaba.** Overlooking the frequently dry Letaba River, this lovely old camp sits in the middle of elephant country in the park's central section. **Pros:** camp has a real bush feel. **Cons:** far from southern entrance gates, so you'll need more traveling time. [$] *Rooms from: R1120 ✉ Kruger National Park ☎ 012/428–9111 reservations 🌐 www.sanparks.org 🛏 183 rooms 🍴 No meals.*

$ RESORT FAMILY **Lower Sabie.** One of the most popular camps in Kruger, Lower Sabie has tremendous views over a broad sweep of the Sabie River and sits in one of the best game-viewing areas of the park (along with Skukuza and Satara). **Pros:** great location; superb game in vicinity. **Cons:** camp and restaurant always crowded. [$] *Rooms from: R1310 ✉ Kruger National Park ☎ 012/428–9111 reservations 🌐 www.sanparks.org 🛏 150 rooms 🍴 No meals.*

$ RESORT **Mopani.** Built in the lee of a rocky kopje overlooking a dam, amid surrounding mopane woodlands, this camp in the northern section is one of Kruger's biggest. **Pros:** attractive accommodations in landscaped camp overlooking big hippo dam. **Cons:** thick mopane bush around camp and beyond not great for game-viewing although elephants love

Singita Lebombo Lodge, Kruger National Park

Rhino Post Plains Camp, Kruger National Park

it. [$] *Rooms from: R1100* ✉ *Kruger National Park* ☎ *012/428–9111 reservations* 🌐 *www.sanparks.org* 🛏 *103 rooms* 🍴 *No meals.*

$ RESORT 🏨 **Olifants.** In the center of Kruger, Olifants has the best setting of all the camps: high atop cliffs on a rocky ridge with panoramic views of the distant hills and the Olifants River below. **Pros:** stunning location. **Cons:** huts in the middle of the camp have no privacy; high malaria area. [$] *Rooms from: R1120* ✉ *Olifants Camp Rd., Kruger National Park* ☎ *012/428–9111 reservations* 🌐 *www.sanparks.org* 🛏 *109 rooms* 🍴 *No meals.*

$ RESORT 🏨 **Orpen.** Don't dismiss this tiny, underappreciated rest camp on Kruger's western border in the center of the park because of its proximity to the Orpen Gate. **Pros:** great game; quiet. **Cons:** close to main gate; not the most attractive camp; rustic. [$] *Rooms from: R1270* ✉ *Kruger National Park* ☎ *012/428–9111 reservations* 🌐 *www.sanparks.org* 🛏 *9 rooms* 🍴 *No meals.*

$ RESORT FAMILY 🏨 **Pretoriuskop.** This large, nostalgically old-fashioned camp, close to the Numbi Gate in southwest Kruger, makes a good overnight stop or touring base. **Pros:** good restaurant for snacks and toasted sandwiches; ideal habitat for mountain reedbuck and klipspringers; great swimming pool. **Cons:** bleak and bare in winter; barracks-style feel; lack of privacy. [$] *Rooms from: R1125* ✉ *Kruger National Park* ☎ *012/428–9111 reservations* 🌐 *www.sanparks.org* 🛏 *180 rooms* 🍴 *No meals.*

$$$$ RESORT 🏨 **Plains Camp Tented Safari Lodge.** Overlooking a waterhole amid an acacia knobthorn thicket deep in the heart of the Timbitene Plain, Plains Camp has four comfortably furnished tents with wooden decks and great views of the plains. **Pros:** right in the middle of Kruger; great game; fabulous night drives when everyone else in the Kruger camps is confined to barracks. **Cons:** surroundings a bit bleak, especially in winter; not much privacy between tents. [$] *Rooms from: R8500* ✉ *Off Marula Loop, Kruger National Park* ☎ *035/474–1473* 🌐 *www.isibindi.co.za* 🛏 *4 rooms* 🍴 *All meals.*

$ RESORT 🏨 **Punda Maria.** It's worth visiting this lovely little camp in Kruger's far north, because it offers one of the park's best bush experiences. **Pros:** very attractive camp; Kruger's best birding area. **Cons:** very far north; game less abundant than the south. [$] *Rooms from: R880* ✉ *Punda Maria Camp Rd., Kruger National Park* ☎ *012/428–9111 reservations* 🌐 *www.sanparks.org* 🛏 *31 rooms* 🍴 *No meals.*

$$$$ RESORT 🏨 **Rhino Post Safari Lodge.** Rhino Post Safari Lodge is located within the 30,000-acre Rhino Plains Concession, with eight spacious suites on stilts overlooking the Mutlumuvi riverbed. **Pros:** right in the middle of Kruger National Park. **Cons:** canvas makes the suites very hot in summer and very cold in winter; you need to be walking-fit for this camp. [$] *Rooms from: R8400* ✉ *Kruger National Park* ☎ *035/474–1473* 🌐 *www.isibindiafrica.co.za* 🛏 *8 rooms* 🍴 *All meals.*

$ RESORT FAMILY 🏨 **Satara.** With some of the best guaranteed game-viewing in Kruger (especially on the N'wanetsi River Road, also known as S100), this large camp sits in the park's central section. **Pros:** good shop, restaurant, pool; great guided sunset drives; probably the most productive guided game tours in park. **Cons:** early booking essential. [$] *Rooms from:*

R1355 ✉ Kruger National Park ☎ 012/428–9111 reservations 🌐 www.sanparks.org 🛏 255 rooms 🍴 No meals.

$ RESORT 🏨 **Shimuwini.** Birders descend in droves on this peaceful bushveld camp set on a lovely dam on the Letaba River. **Pros:** lovely situation overlooking permanent lake. **Cons:** only one access road, so coming and going gets monotonous; game can be sparse. [$] *Rooms from: R1200 ✉ Shimuwini Camp Rd., Kruger National Park ☎ 012/428–9111 reservations 🌐 www.sanparks.org 🛏 15 rooms 🍴 No meals.*

$ RESORT FAMILY 🏨 **Shingwedzi.** This attractive thatch-and-stone camp sits in northern Kruger beside the Shingwedzi River and near the Kanniedood (Never Die) Dam. Consequently there's more game around this camp than anywhere else in the region—especially when you drive the Shingwedzi River Road early in the morning or just before the camp closes at night. **Pros:** game-busy river road; in winter, gorgeous bright pink impala lilies. **Cons:** some accommodations are grouped in a circle around a big bare open space that affords little individual privacy; more rustic than most; lack of modern technology (which some might consider a good thing). [$] *Rooms from: R880 ✉ Kruger National Park ☎ 012/428–9111 reservations 🌐 www.sanparks.org 🛏 130 rooms 🍴 No meals.*

$$$$ RESORT 🏨 **Singita Lebombo Lodge.** Named for the nearby Lebombo mountain range, the breathtakingly beautiful Singita Lebombo—winner of numerous international accolades and eco-driven in concept—is Bauhaus in the bush, with a uniquely African feel. **Pros:** stunning avant-garde architecture; excellent game; great curio shop and spa; lovely riverside bush breakfasts. **Cons:** avoid if you prefer a traditional safari lodge; very pricey. [$] *Rooms from: R45500 ✉ Kruger National Park ☎ 021/683–3424 reservations 🌐 www.singita.co.za 🛏 14 rooms 🍴 All-inclusive.*

$ RESORT 🏨 **Sirheni.** Remote and lovely, Sirheni lies on the edge of the Sirheni Dam in an isolated wilderness area in Kruger's far north. **Pros:** permanent waterhole; superb bird-watching. **Cons:** high malaria area; no electrical plug points; no cell-phone reception (which can be a pro or con). [$] *Rooms from: R1150 ✉ Sirheni Camp Rd., Kruger National Park ☎ 012/428–9111 reservations 🌐 www.sanparks.org 🛏 15 cottages 🍴 No meals.*

$ RESORT FAMILY 🏨 **Skukuza.** Skukuza is highly popular because it lies in an area teeming with game, including lions, cheetahs, and hyenas, and sits on a bank of the crocodile-filled Sabie River, with good views of dozing hippos, elephants, and grazing waterbuck. **Pros:** in middle of the park's best game areas; great river location. **Cons:** usually crowded with regular visitors and busloads of day-trippers. [$] *Rooms from: R1135 ✉ Kruger National Park ☎ 012/428–9111 reservations 🌐 www.sanparks.org 🛏 309 rooms 🍴 No meals.*

$ RESORT 🏨 **Talamati.** On the banks of the normally dry N'waswitsontso River in Kruger's central section, this peaceful camp in the middle of a wide, open valley has excellent game-viewing. **Pros:** peaceful; good plains game; couple of good picnic spots in vicinity; bigger camps near enough to stock up on supplies. **Cons:** a bit bland. [$] *Rooms from: R1200 ✉ Talamati-camp Rd., Kruger National Park ☎ 012/428–9111 reservations 🌐 www.sanparks.org 🛏 15 rooms 🍴 No meals.*

SABI SAND GAME RESERVE

Game	★★★★★
Park Accessibility	★★★★★
Getting Around	★★★★★
Accommodations	★★★★★
Scenic Beauty	★★★

This is the most famous and exclusive of South Africa's private reserves. Collectively owned and managed, the 153,000-acre reserve near Kruger is home to dozens of private lodges, including the world-famous MalaMala and Londolozi. Sabi Sand fully deserves its exalted reputation, boasting perhaps the highest game density of any private reserve in southern Africa.

Although not all lodges own vast tracts of land, the majority have traversing rights over most of the reserve. With an average of 20 vehicles watching for game and communicating by radio, you're bound to see an enormous amount of game and almost certainly the Big Five, and since only three vehicles are allowed at a sighting at a time, you can be assured of a grandstand seat. Sabi Sand is the best area for leopard sightings. It's a memorable experience to see this beautiful, powerful, and often elusive cat padding purposefully through the bush at night, illuminated in your ranger's spotlight. There are many lion prides, and occasionally the increasingly rare wild dogs will migrate from Kruger to den in Sabi Sand. You'll also see white and black rhinos, zebras, giraffes, wildebeests, and most of the antelope species, plus birds galore.

The daily program at each lodge rarely deviates from a pattern, starting with tea, coffee, and muffins or rusks before an early-morning game drive (usually starting at dawn, later in winter). You return to the lodge around 10 am, at which point you dine on an extensive hot breakfast or brunch. You can then choose to go on a bush walk with an armed ranger, where you learn about some of the minutiae of the bush (including the Little Five), although you could also happen on giraffes, antelopes, or any one of the Big Five. But don't worry—you'll be well briefed in advance on what you should do if you come face-to-face with, say, a lion. The rest of the day, until the late-afternoon game drive, is spent at leisure—reading up on the bush in the camp library, snoozing, swimming,

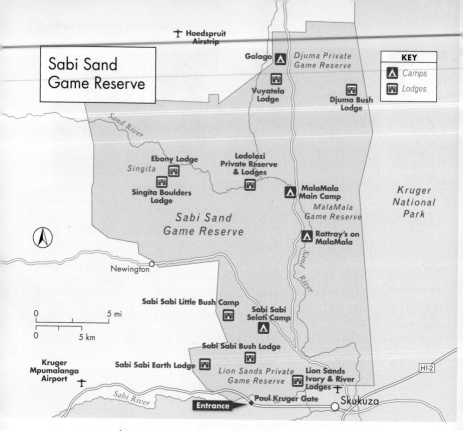

or having a spa treatment. A sumptuous afternoon tea is served at 3:30 or 4 before you head back into the bush for your night drive. During the drive, your ranger will find a peaceful spot for sundowners, and you can sip the drink of your choice and nibble snacks as you watch one of Africa's spectacular sunsets. As darkness falls, your ranger will switch on the spotlight so you can spy nocturnal animals: lions, leopards, jackals, porcupines, servals (small spotted cats like bonsai leopards), civets, and the enchanting little bush babies. You'll return to the lodge around 7:30, in time to freshen up before a three- or five-course dinner, with at least one dinner in a *boma* (open-air dining area) around a blazing fire. Often the camp staff entertains after dinner with local songs and dances—an unforgettable experience. Children under 12 aren't allowed at some of the camps; others have great kids' programs.

GETTING HERE AND AROUND

Kruger Mpumalanga International Airport (KMIA), at Nelspruit, and Hoedspruit airport, close to Kruger's Orpen Gate, serve Sabi Sand Reserve. You can also drive yourself to the reserve and park at your lodge.

Airports Hoedspruit Airport (*HDS*). ⊠ *Eastgate Airport, Hoedspruit* 🕾 015/793–3681 ⊕ www.eastgateairport.co.za. **Kruger Mpumalanga International Airport (KMIA).** 🕾 013/753–7500 ⊕ www.kmiairport.co.za.

Visitor Info Sabi Sand Game Reserve. 🕾 013/735–5102 ⊕ www.sabisand.co.za.

DJUMA PRIVATE GAME RESERVE

This 17,297-acre reserve sits right up against Kruger in the northeast corner of the world-famous Sabi Sand Reserve. Expect classic bush-veld terrain—dams, rivers, ancient riverine trees, grassland, and plains. There are no fences separating Kruger from Sabi Sand, so game wanders freely back and forth, and no matter where you are in the Sabi Sand Reserve, you'll be treated to some of South Africa's best game-viewing. Djuma is no exception. The Big Five are all here, plus hundreds of birds. The reserve's rangers are famous for their dedication and knowledge, which they share in a friendly, very informal way.

WHERE TO STAY

$$$$
RESORT

Galago. A delightful and affordable alternative to other upscale lodges, Galago, which means "lesser bush baby" in Shangaan, is a converted U-shaped farmhouse whose five rooms form an arc around a central fireplace. **Pros:** exclusive experience; luxurious. **Cons:** hire a cook or you'll spend your time working. *$ Rooms from: R12300 ⊠ Djuma Private Game Reserve ☎ 013/735–5555 reservations ⊕ www. djuma.com ⟿ 5 rooms ⦿ No meals.*

$$$$
RESORT
FAMILY

Vuyatela Lodge. Djuma's vibey, most upscale camp mixes contemporary African township culture with modern Shangaan culture, making it very different from most of the other private camps. **Pros:** amazing African art; legendary hosts; ideal for extended family or group of friends. **Cons:** funky township style (corrugated iron, recycled metals, in-your-face glitzy township feel) may not be to everyone's taste. *$ Rooms from: R16900 ⊠ Djuma Private Game Reserve ☎ 013/735–5555 reservations, 013/735–5118 lodge ⊕ www.djuma.com ⟿ 5 rooms ⦿ No meals ⟲ Rate is for entire house.*

LION SANDS PRIVATE GAME RESERVE

Situated along the Sabie River, this reserve has one of the best locations in the Sabi Sand Game Reserve. All of the lodges overlook the river, which is a magnet for all kinds of game. You'll be able to peer into Kruger Park, on the other side of the river, and watch game meander along the riverbanks among big riverine trees. You may never want to leave your personal deck, or the big viewing decks even for an exciting game drive or guided walk, because you're bound to spot animals, birds, and crocs from camp.

WHERE TO STAY

$$$$
RESORT
Fodor's Choice
★

Lion Sands Ivory Lodge. Ivory Lodge offers the ultimate in luxury, privacy, and relaxation. **Pros:** exclusivity; great views; brilliant game-viewing. **Cons:** the temptation of abundant great food—it's so decadent, you might forget to leave. *$ Rooms from: R50900 ⊠ Lion Sands Private Game Reserve ☎ 031/735–5000 lodge, 011/880–9992 head office and reservations ⊕ www.lionsands.com ⟿ 9 rooms ⦿ All meals ⟲ No children under 10 years old.*

$$$$
RESORT

Lion Sands River Lodge. Set on one of the longest and best stretches of river frontage in Sabi Sand, you can watch the passing animal and bird show from your deck or from the huge, tree-shaded, wooden viewing area that juts out over the riverbank facing Kruger National Park. **Pros:** fabulous river frontage; well managed. **Cons:** some chalets quite close together so not much privacy. $ *Rooms from: R22540* ⊠ *Lion Sands Private Game Reserve* ☎ *013/735–5000 lodge, 011/880–9992 head office and reservations* ⊕ *www.lionsands.com* ⇨ *20 rooms* |◉| *All meals* ☞ *No children under 10 years old.*

LONDOLOZI RESERVE

Since its inception in 1974 (it was a family farm and retreat before that), Londolozi has become synonymous with South Africa's finest game lodges and game experiences. (*Londolozi* is the Zulu word for "protector of all living things.") Brother-and-sister Bronwyn and Boyd Varty, the third generation of the Varty family, are now in charge with a mission to reconnect the human spirit with the wilderness and to carry on their family's quest to honor the animal kingdom. The Big Five are all here, as are the world-famous leopards of Londolozi. (You are guaranteed to see at least one.) There are five camps, each representing a different element in nature: Pioneer Camp (water), Tree Camp (wood), Granite Suites (rock), Varty Camp (fire), and Founders Camp (earth). Each is totally private, hidden in dense riverine forest on the banks of the Sand River. The Varty family live on the property, and their friendliness and personal attention, along with the many staff who have been here for decades, will make you feel part of the family immediately. The central reception and curio shop are at Varty Camp.

WHERE TO STAY

$$$$ | RESORT | FAMILY — **Founders Camp.** This inviting camp has 10 stone-and-thatch suites in individual chalets set amid thick riverine bush; some chalets are linked by interconnecting skywalks, which is great for families or groups traveling together (children six years and older are welcome). **Pros:** quick, safe access between family rooms; children over four welcome. **Cons:** lodges are in quite close proximity to one another. $ *Rooms from: R31475* ⊠ *Londolozi Reserve* ☎ *011/280–6655 reservations, 013/735–5653 lodge* ⊕ *www.londolozi.com* ⇨ *10 rooms* |◉| *All-inclusive.*

$$$$ | RESORT — **Pioneer Camp.** The most secluded of all of Londolozi's camps, Pioneer's three private suites overlook the river and are perfect for getting away from others. **Pros:** authentic romantic-safari atmosphere; only three suites; intimate atmosphere. **Cons:** with only three suites it's best if you know all other guests. $ *Rooms from: R45400* ⊠ *Londolozi Reserve* ☎ *011/280–6655 reservations, 013/735–5653 lodge* ⊕ *www.londolozi.com* ⇨ *3 rooms* |◉| *All-inclusive* ☞ *No children under 6 years old.*

$$$$ | RESORT | Fodor's Choice ★ — **Tree Camp.** The first Relais & Chateaux game lodge in the world, this gorgeous camp (think leopards, lanterns, leadwoods, and leopard orchids) is tucked into the riverbank overlooking indigenous forest. **Pros:** the viewing deck; state-of-the-art designer interiors. **Cons:** stylishness nudges out coziness. $ *Rooms from: R45400* ⊠ *Londolozi Reserve* ☎ *011/280–6655 reservations, 013/735–5653 lodge* ⊕ *www.londolozi.com* ⇨ *6 rooms* |◉| *All-inclusive* ☞ *Children under 16 not allowed.*

$$$$ 🏕 **Varty Camp.** This camp's fire has been burning for more than nine
RESORT decades, making Varty Camp the very soul and center of Londolozi.
FAMILY **Pros:** friendly atmosphere; great game; all chalets are interleading. **Cons:**
lots of kids might not be for you. $ *Rooms from: R25900* ⊠ *Londolozi
Reserve* ☎ *011/280–6655 reservations, 013/735–5653 lodge* ⊕ *www.
londolozi.com* ⤳ *10 rooms* ¶○¶ *All-inclusive.*

MALAMALA GAME RESERVE

This legendary game reserve (designated as such in 1929) is tops in
its field. The first and only community-owned game reserve in Sabi
Sand, it continues to be managed by the legendary Rattray family in
partnership with the N'wandlamharhi Community. It's the largest
privately owned Big Five game area in South Africa, and includes
an unfenced 30-km (19-mile) boundary with Kruger National Park,
across which game cross continuously. The variety of habitats range
from riverine bush, favorite hiding place of the leopard, to open
grasslands, where cheetahs hunt.

You'll be delighted with incomparable personal service, superb food,
and discreetly elegant, comfortable accommodations, where you'll rub
shoulders with statesmen and stateswomen, aristocrats, celebrities, and
returning visitors alike. Mike Rattray, a legend in his own time in South
Africa's game-lodge industry, describes MalaMala as "a camp in the
bush," but it's certainly more than that, although it still retains that
genuine bushveld feel of bygone days. Both the outstanding hospitality
and the game-viewing experience keep guests coming back.

MalaMala's animal-viewing statistics are impressive: the Big Five are
spotted almost every day. At one moment your well-educated, friendly,
articulate ranger will fascinate you with the description of the sex life
of a dung beetle, as you watch the sturdy male battling his way along
the road pushing his perfectly round ball of dung with wife-to-be
perched perilously on top; at another, your adrenaline will flow as
you follow a leopard stalking impala in the gathering gloom. Along
with the local Shangaan trackers, whose eyesight rivals that of the
animals they are tracking, the top-class rangers ensure that your game
experience is unforgettable.

WHERE TO STAY

$$$$ 🏕 **MalaMala Main Camp.** Stone and thatch air-conditioned rondavels
RESORT with separate his-and-her bathrooms are decorated in creams and
FAMILY browns and furnished with cane armchairs, colorful handwoven tapes-
tries and rugs, terra-cotta floors, and original artwork. **Pros:** authentic;
sweeping wilderness views; amazing game-viewing. **Cons:** rondavels are
a bit old-fashioned, but that goes with the ambience. $ *Rooms from:
R21418* ⊠ *Mala Mala Game Reserve* ☎ *011/442–2267 reservations,
013/735–9200 MalaMala Main Camp* ⊕ *www.malamala.com* ⤳ *17
rooms* ¶○¶ *All-inclusive.*

$$$$ 🏕 **Rattray's on MalaMala.** The breathtakingly beautiful Rattray's merges
RESORT original bushveld style with daring contemporary ideas. **Pros:** superb
Fodor'sChoice game-viewing; tantalizing views over the river. **Cons:** Tuscan villas in
★ the bush may not be your idea of Africa; though this may be a pro for

some, no children under 16. *[$] Rooms from: R15018 ✉ Mala Mala Game Reserve ☎ 011/442–2267 reservations, 013/735–3000 Rattray's on MalaMala 🌐 www.malamala.com 🛏 8 rooms 🍴 All-inclusive.*

SABI SABI PRIVATE GAME RESERVE

Founded in 1978 at the southern end of Sabi Sand, the multi-award-winning Sabi Sabi Private Game Reserve was one of the first reserves to offer photo safaris and to link ecotourism, conservation, and community. Superb accommodations and abundant game lure guests back to Sabi Sabi in large numbers.

WHERE TO STAY

$$$$ RESORT FAMILY **Sabi Sabi Bush Lodge.** Bush Lodge overlooks a busy waterhole (lions are frequent visitors) and the dry course of the Msuthlu River. **Pros:** always prolific game around the lodge; roomy chalets. **Cons:** big and busy might not be your idea of a relaxing getaway. *[$] Rooms from: R21800 ✉ Sabi Sand Game Reserve ☎ 013/735–5656 reservations, 013/735–5080 lodge 🌐 www.sabisabi.com 🛏 24 rooms 🍴 All meals.*

$$$$ RESORT **Sabi Sabi Earth Lodge.** This avant-garde, eco-friendly lodge was the first to break away from the traditional safari style and strive for a contemporary theme. **Pros:** stunning architecture and design. **Cons:** if you favor traditonal safari accommodations, this is not for you. *[$] Rooms from: R34500 ✉ Sabi Sand Game Reserve ☎ 013/735–5261 lodge, 011/447–7172 reservations 🌐 www.sabisabi.com 🛏 14 rooms 🍴 All-inclusive.*

$$$$ RESORT FAMILY **Sabi Sabi Little Bush Camp.** Sabi Sabi's delightful little camp is tucked away in the bushveld on the banks of the Msuthlu River and combines spaciousness with a sense of intimacy. **Pros:** perfect for families. **Cons:** there may be other families. *[$] Rooms from: R21800 ✉ Sabi Sand Game Reserve ☎ 011/447–7172 reservations, 013/735–5080 lodge 🌐 www.sabisabi.com 🛏 6 rooms 🍴 All meals.*

$$$$ RESORT Fodor's Choice ★ **Sabi Sabi Selati Camp.** For an *Out of Africa* experience and great game, you can't beat Selati, an intimate, stylish, colonial-style camp that was formerly the private hunting lodge of a famous South African opera singer. **Pros:** unique atmosphere; Ivory Presidential Suite superb value for money; secluded and intimate. **Cons:** some old-timers preferred the camp when it was just lantern-lit with no electricity. *[$] Rooms from: R21800 ✉ Sabi Sand Game Reserve ☎ 011/447–7172 reservations, 013/735–5771 lodge, 013/735–5236 lodge 🌐 www.sabisabi.com 🛏 8 rooms 🍴 All meals.*

SINGITA

Although Singita (Shangaan for "the miracle") offers much the same thrilling Sabi Sand bush and game experiences as other lodges, superb service really puts it head and shoulders above many of the rest of the herd.

Did you know? Rhinos have poor eyesight, but excellent hearing.

WHERE TO STAY

$$$$
RESORT
FAMILY

⌂ **Ebony Lodge.** If Ernest Hemingway had built his ideal home in the African bush, this would be it. **Pros:** the mother lodge of all the Singita properties; cozy library. **Cons:** the beds are very high off the ground—if you have short legs or creak a bit, ask for a stool. $ *Rooms from: R43268 ⊠ Singita Sabi Sand ☎ 021/683–3424 reservations, 013/735–9800 lodge ⊕ www.singita.co.za ➫ 12 rooms ⓘ All-inclusive.*

$$$$
RESORT
Fodor's Choice
★

⌂ **Singita Boulders Lodge.** Overlooking the beautiful Sand River, Singita Boulders Lodge intermingles the wildness of its setting among boulders with traditional Africa decor at its most luxurious. **Pros:** spacious accommodations; superb food. **Cons:** a bit of a walk from the suites to the main lodge; refuse the crackling log fire if you're at all congested. $ *Rooms from: R43268 ⊠ Singita Sabi Sand ☎ 021/683–3424 reservations, 013/735–9800 lodge ⊕ www.singita.co.za ➫ 12 rooms ⓘ All-inclusive.*

KWAZULU-NATAL PARKS

Game
★★★★
Park Accessibility
★★★★★
Getting Around
★★★★★
Accommodations
★★★★★
Scenic Beauty
★★★★

The province of KwaZulu-Natal is a premier vacation destination for South Africans, with some of the finest game reserves in the country, including the Hluhluwe-Imfolozi Game Reserve. The reserve is small compared to Kruger, but here you'll see the Big Five and plenty of plains game, plus an incredibly biologically diverse mix of plants and trees. The nearby Mkuze and Ithala game reserves are even smaller but are still worth a visit for their numerous bird species and game.

KwaZulu-Natal's best private lodges lie in northern Zululand and Maputaland, a remote region close to Mozambique. These lodges are sufficiently close to one another and Hluhluwe-Imfolozi Game Reserve to allow you to put together a bush experience that delivers the Big Five and a great deal more, including superb bird-watching opportunities and an unrivaled beach paradise.

WHEN TO GO

Summers are hot, hot, hot. If you can't take heat and humidity, then autumn, winter, and early summer are probably the best times to visit.

GETTING HERE AND AROUND

The Richards Bay airport is the closest to the Hluhluwe-Imfolozi area—about 100 km (60 miles) south of Hluhluwe-Imfolozi and about 224 km (140 miles) south of Ithala.

There are daily flights from Johannesburg to Richards Bay; flight time is about an hour. Private lodges will arrange your transfers for you.

If you're traveling to Hluhluwe-Imfolozi from Durban, drive north on the N2 to Mtubatuba, then cut west on the R618 to Mambeni Gate. Otherwise, continue up the N2 to the Hluhluwe exit and follow the signs to the park and Memorial Gate. The whole trip takes about three hours, but watch out for potholes.

If you're headed to Ithala from Durban, drive north on the N2 to Empangeni, and then head west on the R34 to Vryheid. From here cut east on the R69 to Louwsburg. The reserve is immediately northwest of the village, from which there are clear signs. The journey from Durban takes around 5 hours and from Hluhluwe-Imfolozi about 2½ hours. Roads are good, and there are plenty of gas stations along the way.

Airport Richards Bay Airport. ✉ *30 Fish Eagle Flight, Birdswood, Richards Bay* ☎ *035/789–9630.*

HLUHLUWE-IMFOLOZI PARK

Renowned for its conservation successes—most notably with white rhinos—this park is a wonderful place to view the Big Five and many other species. Until 1989 it consisted of two separate reserves, Hluhluwe in the north and Imfolozi in the south, separated by a fenced corridor. Although a road (R618) still runs through this corridor, the fences have been removed, and the reserves—now known as Hluhluwe-Imfolozi Park or HIP—operate as a single entity.

In an area of just 906 square km (350 square miles), Hluhluwe-Imfolozi delivers the Big Five plus all the plains game and species like nyala and red duiker that are rare in other parts of the country. Equally important, it encompasses one of the most biologically diverse habitats on the planet, with a unique mix of forest, woodland, savanna, and grassland. You'll find about 1,250 species of plants and trees here—more than in some entire countries.

The park is administered by Ezemvelo KZN Wildlife, the province's official conservation organization, which looks after all the large game reserves and parks as well as many nature reserves. Thanks to its conservation efforts and those of its predecessor, the highly regarded Natal Parks Board, the park can take credit for saving the white rhino from extinction. So successful was the park at increasing white rhino numbers that in 1960 it established its now famous Rhino Capture Unit to relocate rhinos to other reserves in Africa. The park is currently trying to do for the black rhino what it did for its white cousins. Poaching in the past nearly decimated Africa's black rhino population, but as a result of the park's remarkable conservation program, 20% of Africa's remaining black rhinos now live in this reserve—and you won't get a better chance of seeing them in the wild than here.

GETTING HERE AND AROUND

If you're traveling to Hluhluwe-Imfolozi from Durban, drive north on the N2 to Mtubatuba, then cut west on the R618 to Mambeni Gate. Otherwise, continue up the N2 to the Hluhluwe exit and follow the signs to the park and Memorial Gate. The whole trip takes about three hours, but watch out for potholes.

TIMING

Compared to Kruger, Hluhluwe-Imfolozi is tiny—less than 6% of Kruger's size—but such comparisons can be misleading. You can spend days driving around this park and still not see everything, or feel like you're going in circles. Probably the biggest advantage Hluhluwe has over Kruger is that game-viewing is good year-round, whereas Kruger has seasonal peaks and valleys. Another bonus is its proximity to Mkuze Game Reserve and the spectacular coastal reserves of iSimangaliso Greater St. Lucia Wetland Park. The park is also close enough to Durban to make it a worthwhile one- or two-day excursion.

ACTIVITIES

BUSH WALKS

Armed rangers lead groups of eight on two- to three-hour bush walks departing from Hilltop or Mpila Camp. You may not spot much game on these walks, but you do see plenty of birds, and you learn a great deal about the area's ecology and tips on how to recognize the signs of the bush, including animal spoor. Walks depart daily at 5:30 am and 3:30 pm (6 and 3 in winter) and cost R250. Reserve a few days in advance at **Hilltop Camp** reception (☎ 035/562–0848).

GAME DRIVES

A great way to see the park is on game drives led by rangers. These drives (R300 per person) hold several advantages over driving through the park yourself: you sit high up in an open-air vehicle with a good view and the wind in your face, a ranger explains the finer points of animal behavior and ecology, and your guide has a good idea where to find animals like leopards, cheetahs, and lions. Game drives leave daily at 5:30 am in summer, 6:30 am in winter. The park also offers three-hour night drives, during which you search with powerful spotlights for nocturnal animals. These three-hour drives depart at 7, and you should make advance reservations at **Hilltop Camp reception** (☎ 035/562–0848).

WILDERNESS TRAILS

The park's **Wilderness Trails** are every bit as popular as Kruger's, but they tend to be tougher and more rustic. You should be fit enough to walk up to 16 km (10 miles) a day for a period of three days and four nights. An armed ranger leads the hikes, and all equipment, food, and baggage are carried by donkeys. The first and last nights are spent at Mndindini, a permanent tented camp. The other two are spent under canvas in the bush. While in the bush, hikers bathe in the Imfolozi River or have a hot bucket shower; toilet facilities consist of a spade and toilet-paper roll. Trails, open March through October, are limited to eight people and should be reserved a year in advance (R3,450 per person per trail).

Fully catered two- or three-night **Short Wilderness Trails** (R2,250 per person) involve stays at a satellite camp in the wilderness area. You'll sleep in a dome tent, and although there's hot water from a bucket shower, your toilet is a spade.

If that sounds too easy, you can always opt for the four-night **Primitive Trail.** On this trek hikers carry their own packs and sleep out under the stars, although there are lightweight tents for inclement weather. A campfire burns all night to scare off animals, and each participant is expected to sit a 90-minute watch. A ranger acts as guide. The cost is R2,400 per person.

A less rugged wilderness experience can be had on the **Base Camp Trail,** based out of the tented Mndindini camp, where you're guaranteed a bed and some creature comforts. The idea behind these trails is to instill in the participants an appreciation for the beauty of the untamed bush. You can also join the Mpila night drive if you wish. Participation is limited to eight people and costs about R3,900 per person.

The **Explorer Trail,** two nights and three days, combines the most comfortable Base Camp trail with the Primitive Trail. On this trail you sleep out under the stars at a different spot each night. The cost is R2,350 per person.

WHERE TO STAY

Hluhluwe-Imfolozi offers a range of accommodations in government-run rest camps, with an emphasis on self-catering (only Hilltop has a restaurant). The park also has secluded bush lodges and camps, but most foreign visitors can't avail themselves of these lodgings, as each must be reserved in a block, and the smallest accommodates at least eight people. Conservation levies are R80 per person.

$$
RESORT
FAMILY
Hilltop Camp. This delightful lodge in the Hluhluwe half of the park matches some of South Africa's best private lodges. **Pros:** floodlit waterhole; warm, friendly staff; incredible views. **Cons:** watch out for marauding monkeys; outdoor grill area not covered and is dimly lit at night; bathrooms can smell a little moldy. $ *Rooms from: R2188* ✉ *Hluhluwe* ☎ *031/208-3684* ⊕ *www.hilltopcamp.co.za* ⤴ *70 rooms* ⊙*Breakfast.*

$$
RENTAL
FAMILY
Mpila Camp. In the central Imfolozi section of the park, Mpila is reminiscent of some of Kruger's older camps. **Pros:** free-roaming game; lovely location; good value for money compared to other parks up north. **Cons:** needs a refurb; watch out for hyenas stealing your braai meat; little privacy. $ *Rooms from: R1640* ✉ *Hluhluwe iMfolozi* ☎ *033/845-1000, 031/208-3684* ⊕ *www.mpilacamp.co.za* ⤴ *40 rooms* ⊙ *No meals.*

$$
HOTEL
FAMILY
Ubizane Zululand Tree Lodge. About 16 km (10 miles) from Hluhluwe-Imfolozi Park, this lodge lies in a forest of fever trees on the 3,700-acre Ubizane Game Reserve and makes a great base from which to explore Hluhluwe, Mkuze, and St. Lucia. **Pros:** bird's-eye views over lovely surroundings; friendly staff; mosquito nets on all beds. **Cons:** crocodiles in pool near dining area are off-putting; bathrooms need attention; dinner buffet a little expensive for what you get. $ *Rooms from: R2234* ✉ *1020 Main Rd., Hluhluwe* ☎ *035/562-1020* ⊕ *www.ubizane.co.za* ⤴ *49 rooms* ⊙ *Breakfast.*

UMKHUZE KZN PARK

Wildlife—and amazing birdlife—abounds in this 400-square-km (154-square-mile) reserve in the shadow of the Ubombo Mountains. Lying between the uMkhuze and Msunduzi rivers, it makes up the northwestern spur of the iSimangaliso Wetland Park, a UNESCO World Heritage Site. It has been a protected area since 1912.

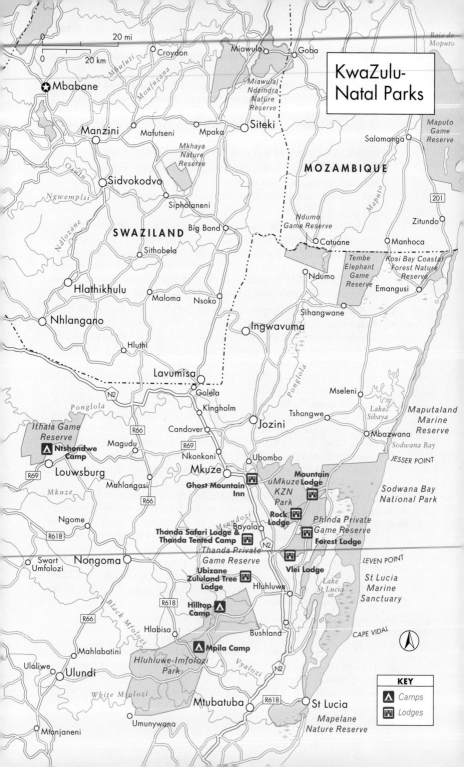

WHERE TO STAY

$$ B&B/INN **Ghost Mountain Inn.** Swaths of scarlet bougainvillea run riot in the lush gardens of this family-owned country inn with tastefully furnished rooms that each have a small veranda. **Pros:** good value for money; generous buffet; spa on-site. **Cons:** hotel-like atmosphere; tour buses overnight here; can get noisy in peak season. [$] *Rooms from: R1675* ✉ *Fish Eagle Rd., uMkhuze* ☎ *035/573–1025* 🌐 *www.ghostmountain-inn.co.za* 🛏 *50 rooms* 🍴 *Breakfast.*

ITHALA GAME RESERVE

The topography of this reserve, from mountaintop to deep river valleys, incorporates varied terrain and plant life, and makes for superior game-viewing in relation to its relatively small size. Thousands of years of human habitation have also provided archaeological and historical interest.

WHERE TO STAY

Although Ithala has several exclusive bush camps, these are booked up months in advance by South Africans, making the chalets at its main camp the only practical accommodations for foreign visitors.

$ RENTAL **Ntshondwe Camp.** Arriving at the award-winning Ntshondwe Camp is nothing short of dramatic. **Pros:** tarred road access; game drives; self-guided walks. **Cons:** busy conference and wedding venue; you can't tick the Big Five off your list here; roads are in bad condition. [$] *Rooms from: R1360* ✉ *Ithala Game Reserve* ☎ *033/845–1000* 🌐 *www.ithala.info* 🛏 *68 rooms* 🍴 *No meals.*

6

PHINDA PRIVATE GAME RESERVE

Where Phinda excels is in the superb quality of its rangers, who can provide fascinating commentary on everything from local birds to frogs. It's amazing just how enthralling the love life of a dung beetle can be! There are also Phinda adventures (optional extras) down the Mzinene River for a close-up look at crocodiles, hippos, and birds; big-game fishing or scuba diving off the deserted, wildly beautiful Maputaland coast; and sightseeing flights over Phinda and the highest vegetated dunes in the world.

WHERE TO STAY

$$$$ RESORT Fodor's Choice ★ **Forest Lodge.** Hidden in a rare sand forest, this fabulous lodge overlooks a small waterhole where nyalas, warthogs, and baboons frequently come to drink. **Pros:** magical feeling of oneness with the surrounding bush; modern conveniences; lovely views from the pool. **Cons:** being in a glass box could make some visitors nervous; not for traditional tastes; cell phone reception can be iffy. [$] *Rooms from: R16970* ✉ *Phinda Game Reserve* ☎ *011/809–4300 reservations* 🌐 *andbeyond.com* 🛏 *16 rooms* 🍴 *All-inclusive.*

$$$$ RESORT FAMILY **Mountain Lodge.** This attractive thatch lodge sits on a rocky hill overlooking miles of bushveld plains and the Ubombo Mountains. **Pros:** great mountain views; very family-friendly; guaranteed a warm welcome. **Cons:** rather bland interiors; pricey if you take the kids (pricey

Hilltop Camp, Hluhluwe Game Reserve

Mpila Camp, Hluhluwe Game Reserve

Hilltop Camp Chalet, Hluhluwe GR

Rock Lodge, Phinda Game Reserve   Mountain Lodge, Phinda Private Game Reserve

Forest Lodge, Phinda Game Reserve

even if you don't take the kids); not the best choice for couples seeking solitude. [$] *Rooms from: R15600* ✉ *Phinda Game Reserve, off R22, Hluhluwe* ☎ *011/809–4300 reservations* 🌐 *andbeyond.com* 🛏 *25 rooms* 🍴 *All-inclusive.*

$$$$ RESORT 🏨 **Rock Lodge.** If you get tired of the eagle's-eye view of the deep valley below from your private veranda, you can write in your journal in your luxurious sitting room or take a late-night dip in your own plunge pool. **Pros:** personal plunge pools; amazing views; luxurious sitting rooms. **Cons:** stay away if you suffer from vertigo; not suitable for families (also, no kids under 12 allowed); not the place for a lively atmosphere. [$] *Rooms from: R19500* ✉ *Phinda Game Reserve* ☎ *011/809–4300 reservations* 🌐 *andbeyond.com* 🛏 *6 rooms* 🍴 *All-inclusive.*

$$$$ RESORT Fodor's Choice ★ 🏨 **Vlei Lodge.** Your suite at this comfortable lodge, tucked into the shade of a sand forest, is so private it's hard to believe there are other guests. **Pros:** superb views over the floodplains; intimate; Wi-Fi en suite. **Cons:** lots of mosquitoes and other flying insects; no children under 12; expensive. [$] *Rooms from: R19500* ✉ *Phinda Game Reserve* ☎ *011/809–4300* 🌐 *andbeyond.com* 🛏 *6 rooms* 🍴 *All-inclusive.*

SELF-GUIDED TRAILS

An unusual feature of Ithala is its self-guided walking trails, in the mountainside above Ntshondwe Camp. The trails give you a chance to stretch your limbs if you've just spent hours cooped up in a car. They also let you get really close to the euphorbias, acacias, and other fascinating indigenous vegetation that festoon the hills. Ask at the camp reception for further information.

THANDA PRIVATE GAME RESERVE

One of KwaZulu-Natal's newer game reserves, Thanda offers a more intimate nature experience than some. Game may sometimes be elusive, but the highly experienced and enthusiastic rangers work hard to find the Big Five and other wildlife. Enjoyable cultural interactions with local people are a highlight of any visit.

WHERE TO STAY

$$$$ RESORT FAMILY 🏨 **Thanda Safari Lodge.** This exquisite lodge blends elements of royal Zulu with an eclectic pan-African feel. **Pros:** luxurious; private plunge pool; unique dwelling in Zulu beehive hut. **Cons:** some might say it's Hollywood in the bush; wild animals do roam close; furniture could do with a refurb. [$] *Rooms from: R15400* ✉ *Off N2 and D242, Hluhluwe* ☎ *032/586–0149 reservations* 🌐 *www.thanda.com* 🛏 *9 rooms* 🍴 *All-inclusive.*

$$$$ RESORT FAMILY 🏨 **Thanda Tented Camp.** Perfect for a family or friends' reunion (although it's great for individual travelers, too), this intimate and luxurious eco-forward camp deep in the bush brings you into close contact with your surroundings. **Pros:** five-star luxury; eco-friendly. **Cons:** not for the nervous type; no air-conditioning; no children under eight. [$] *Rooms from: R8080* ✉ *Off N2 and D242, Hluhluwe* ☎ *032/586–0149 reservations* 🌐 *www.thanda.co.za* 🛏 *15 rooms* 🍴 *All-inclusive.*

KGALAGADI TRANSFRONTIER PARK

Game
★★★★
Park Accessibility
★★★
Getting Around
★★★★★
Accommodations
★★★★
Scenic Beauty
★★★★★

If you're looking for true wilderness, remoteness, and stark, almost surreal landscapes and you're not averse to forgoing luxury and getting sand in your hair, then this uniquely beautiful park within the Kalahari Desert is for you.

In an odd little finger of the country jutting north between Botswana in the east and Namibia in the west lies South Africa's second-largest park after Kruger. The "reborn" Kgalagadi was officially launched in 2000 as the first transfrontier, or "peace park," in southern Africa by merging South Africa's vast Kalahari Gemsbok National Park with the even larger Gemsbok National Park in Botswana. The name Kgalagadi (pronounced "kala-*hardy*") is derived from the San language and means "place of thirst." It's now one of the largest protected wilderness areas in the world—an area of more than 38,000 square km (14,670 square miles). Of this awesome area, 9,600 square km (3,700 square miles) fall in South Africa, and the rest fall in Botswana.

Passing through the Twee Rivieren Gate, you'll encounter a vast desert under enormous, usually cloudless skies and a sense of space and openness that few other places can offer. With the rest camp to the left, just a little farther down the dirt road to the right is the dry Nossob River, lined by camel-thorn trees, which winds its way to Botswana, into which the park continues.

The Kgalagadi Transfrontier is less commercialized and developed than Kruger. The roads aren't paved, and you'll come across far fewer people and cars. There's less game on the whole than in Kruger, but because there's also less vegetation, the animals are much more visible. Also, because the game and large carnivores are concentrated in two riverbeds (the route that two roads follow), the park offers unsurpassed game-viewing and photographic opportunities. Perhaps the key to really appreciating this barren place is in understanding how its creatures have adapted to their harsh surroundings to survive—like the gemsbok, which has a sophisticated cooling system allowing it to tolerate extreme changes in body temperature. There are also insects in the park that inhale only every half hour or so to preserve the moisture that breathing expends.

The landscape—endless dunes punctuated with blond grass and the odd thorn tree—is dominated by two *wadis* (dry riverbeds): the Nossob (which forms the border between South Africa and Botswana) and its tributary, the Auob. The Nossob flows only a few times a century, and the Auob flows only once every couple of decades or so. A single road runs beside each riverbed, along which windmills pump water into man-made waterholes, which help the animals to survive and provide good viewing stations for visitors. There are 82 waterholes, 49 of which are along tourist roads. Park management struggles to keep up their maintenance; it's a constant battle against the elements, with the elements often winning. Similarly, the park constantly maintains and improves tourist roads, but again it's a never-ending struggle. A third road traverses the park's interior to join the other two. The scenery and vegetation on this road change dramatically from two river valleys dominated by sandy banks to a grassy escarpment. Two more dune roads have been added, and several 4x4 routes have been developed. From Nossob camp a road leads to Union's End, the country's northernmost tip, where South Africa, Namibia, and Botswana meet. Allow a full day for the long and dusty drive, which is 124 km (77 miles) one way. It's possible to enter Botswana from the South African side, but you'll need a 4x4. The park infrastructure in Botswana is very basic, with just three campsites and mostly 4x4 terrain.

The park is famous for its gemsbok, the desert-adapted springbok, and its legendary, huge, black-maned Kalahari lions. It also has leopards, cheetahs, eland, blue wildebeests, jackals, and giraffes, as well as meerkats and mongooses. Rarer desert species, such as the elusive aardvark and the pretty Cape fox, also make their home here. Among birders, the park is known as one of Africa's raptor meccas; it's filled with bateleurs, lappet-faced vultures, pygmy falcons, and the cooperatively hunting red-necked falcons and gabar goshawks.

The park's legendary night drives (approximately R200 per person) depart most evenings around 5:30 in summer, earlier in winter (check when you get to your camp), from Twee Rivieren Camp and Nossob. The drives set out just as the park gate closes to everyone else. You'll have a chance to see rare nocturnal animals like the brown hyena and the bat-eared fox by spotlight. The guided morning walks—during which you see the sun rise over the Kalahari and could bump into a lion—are also a must. Reservations are essential and can be made when you book your accommodations.

WHEN TO GO

The park can be superhot in summer and freezing at night in winter (literally below zero, with frost on the ground). Autumn—from late February to mid-April—is perhaps the best time to visit. It's cool after the rains, and many of the migratory birds are still around. The winter months of June and July are also a good time. It's best to make reservations as far in advance as possible, even up to 11 months if you want to visit at Easter or in June or July, when there are school vacations.

Giraffes are the world's tallest mammals and can grow to be 18 feet tall!

GETTING HERE AND AROUND

Upington International Airport is 260 km (162 miles) south of Kgalagadi Transfrontier Park; many lodgings provide shuttle service, or you can rent a car at the airport. If you reserve a car through an agency in Upington, you can pick it up from the Twee Rivieren Camp. If you drive from Johannesburg, you have a choice of two routes: either via Upington (with the last stretch a 60-km [37-mile] gravel road) or via Kuruman, Hotazel, and Vanzylrus (with about 340 km [211 miles] of gravel road). The gravel sections on both routes are badly corrugated, so don't speed.

Airport Information Upington International Airport. ⊠ *Diedricks St., Upington* ☎ *054/337–7900.*

VISITOR INFORMATION

There's a daily conservation fee, but Wild Cards, available at the gates or online, are more economical for stays of more than a few days. Reservations for all accommodations, bush drives, wilderness trails, and other park activities must be made through South African National Parks.

WHERE TO STAY

Accommodations within the park are in three traditional rest camps and several highly sought-after wilderness camps (try to reserve these if possible) that are spread around the park. All of the traditional rest camps have shops selling food, curios, and some basic equipment, but Twee Rivieren has the best variety of fresh fruit, vegetables, milk, and meat,

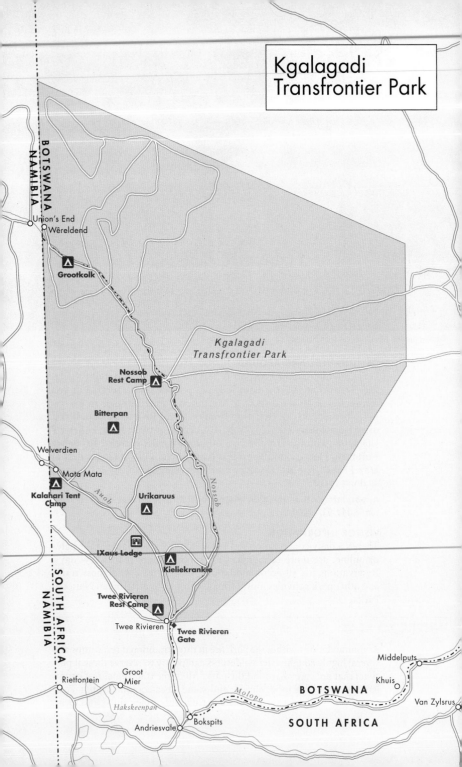

and is the only camp with a restaurant. Twee Rivieren is also the only camp with telephone and cell-phone reception (although cell-phone reception quickly disappears as you head into the dunes) and 24-hour electricity; the other camps have gas and electricity, but the electricity runs only part of the day, at different times in each camp.

For all national park accommodations, contact South African National Parks (reservation@sanparks.org), or you can reserve directly through the park if you happen to be there and would like to stay a night or add another night onto your stay.

For a private luxury lodge, !Xaus, owned by the Khomani San community, is deep in the west of the park. Because it's roughly 50 km (32 miles) in from the gate, guests are met by a vehicle at the Kumqwa rest area, where they park their car. From there it is exactly 91 dunes to the lodge in a 4x4—and well worth it.

BOOKING

South African National Parks. It's usually safest and quickest to book through the central booking office in Pretoria, although oftentimes when that office says "full," the camp itself has vacancies. ☎ *012/428–9111 Pretoria ⊕ www.sanparks.org.*

A limited number of campsites (R195) are available at Nossob (20) and Twee Rivieren (24). All campsites have a *braai* and access to electricity and water, and there are communal bathroom facilities and a basic communal kitchen. Before you arrive, be sure to arm yourself with the "blue camping plug"—available from any camping–RV shop—to plug into the electrical system and a long extension cord. Try to find a shady spot.

LODGES AND CAMPS

$ | Bitterpan. This elevated camp overlooks an enormous expanse of sand
RENTAL and a waterhole, where you can watch game come and go from your deck or from the communal areas. **Pros:** spectacular game-viewing from your accommodations; beautiful desert scenery; only four cabins. **Cons:** 4x4s only; no children under 12; it's a long drive to get here from any starting point. ⓢ *Rooms from: R1495 ⊠ Kgalagadi Transfrontier Park ☎ 012/428–9111 reservations ⊕ www.sanparks.org ⟿ 4 rooms ⫶◯⫶ No meals.*

$$ | Grootkolk. Surrounded by camel-thorn trees and close to the Nossob
RENTAL River bed, this lovely camp has good game-viewing, with lions, cheetahs, hyenas, and lots of antelope, including oryx and springbok, and it can book up months in advance. **Pros:** spotlighted waterhole; sublime wilderness; ceiling fans in the cabins. **Cons:** a long drive from other camps; no children under 12; the cabins are not the prettiest. ⓢ *Rooms from: R1630 ⊠ Kgalagadi Transfrontier Park ☎ 012/428–9111 reservations ⊕ www.sanparks.org ⟿ 4 rooms ⫶◯⫶ No meals.*

$$ | Kalahari Tent Camp. Many visitors say that this good game-viewing camp
RENTAL overlooking the Auob River bed and waterhole is one of the most beautiful
FAMILY places in the park, so try to stay for more than one night. **Pros:** near Mata Mata, which has a shop and gas; excellent game; family-friendly. **Cons:** guests must bring their own drinking water and firewood; not as intimate as some of the other wilderness camps; camp kitchen not the best equipped. ⓢ *Rooms from: R1600 ⊠ Kgalagadi Transfrontier Park ☎ 012/428–9111 reservations ⊕ www.sanparks.org ⟿ 15 rooms ⫶◯⫶ No meals.*

$$ RENTAL **Kieliekrankie.** Perched high on a big sand dune only 8 km (5 miles) from the game-rich Auob River road, this small camp overlooks seemingly infinite red Kalahari sands, creating an amazing sense of space and isolation. **Pros:** easily accessible with a sedan; you can start your game drives before residents of the other camps reach the area so you have the game to yourself for awhile; the red Kalahari sands are unforgettable. **Cons:** no children under 12; guests must bring their own drinking water and firewood; no double beds. [$] *Rooms from: R1630* ✉ *Kgalagadi Transfrontier Park* ☎ *012/428–9111 reservations* 🌐 *www.sanparks.org* 🛏 *4 rooms* 🍴 *No meals.*

$ RESORT **Nossob Rest Camp.** In the central section of the park, this camp is on the Botswana border, 166 km (103 miles) from Twee Rivieren. **Pros:** riverbed location in a desert landscape makes it a great place to see predators, particularly lions; there's a predator information center; it's right in the thick of the action. **Cons:** barren, unattractive camp; no phone reception; perpetually in need of a spruce-up. [$] *Rooms from: R995* ✉ *Kgalagadi Transfrontier Park* ☎ *012/428–9111 reservations* 🌐 *www.sanparks.org* 🛏 *18 rooms* 🍴 *No meals.*

$ RESORT FAMILY **Twee Rivieren Rest Camp.** On the Kgalagadi's southern boundary, this camp is home to the park's headquarters. **Pros:** modern, well-equipped chalets; on-site grocery store selling basics; not-to-be-missed guided morning and night drives. **Cons:** the biggest and noisiest camp in the park; not particularly attractive; a fair drive from the park's best wildlife hot spots. [$] *Rooms from: R1110* ✉ *Kgalagadi Transfrontier Park* ☎ *012/428–9111 reservations* 🌐 *www.sanparks.org* 🛏 *31 rooms* 🍴 *No meals.*

$$ RENTAL **Urikaruus.** Four cabins with kitchens, bedrooms, and bathrooms are built on stilts among camel-thorn trees with beautiful vistas overlooking the Auob River. **Pros:** accessible with a sedan; stunning location; game to yourself on early-morning and late-afternoon drives. **Cons:** no children under 12; guests must bring their own drinking water and firewood; only single beds available. [$] *Rooms from: R1630* ✉ *Kgalagadi Transfrontier Park* ☎ *012/428–9111 reservations* 🌐 *www.sanparks.org* 🛏 *4 rooms* 🍴 *No meals.*

$$$$ RESORT Fodor's Choice ★ **!Xaus Lodge** If you want to experience one of South Africa's most beautiful and isolated parks without hassle, then this luxury lodge owned by the Khomani San and Mier communities and jointly managed with Transfrontier Parks Destinations is the place for you. **Pros:** unique wilderness setting; only private lodge in area; opportunities to interact with the local indigenous people. **Cons:** it doesn't get much more remote than this; not a Big Five destination; chalets in need of a spruce-up. [$] *Rooms from: R4390* ✉ *Dune 92 Kgalagadi, Kgalagadi Transfrontier Park* ☎ *021/701–7860* 🌐 *www.xauslodge.co.za* 🛏 *12 rooms* 🍴 *All-inclusive.*

IF YOU HAVE TIME

Although this chapter goes into great detail about the must-see parks in South Africa, there are many others to explore if you have time. Here are a few good ones to consider.

NORTHERN CAPE

TSWALU KALAHARI RESERVE

250 km (155 miles) southeast of Kgalagadi Transfrontier Park; 262 km (163 miles) northeast of Upington; 145 km (90 miles) northwest of Kuruman.

Near the Kgalagadi Transfrontier Park is the malaria-free Tswalu Kalahari Reserve, at 1,000 square km (386 square miles) the largest privately owned game reserve in Africa; it's the perfect place to photograph a gemsbok against a red dune and big blue sky. Initially founded as a conservation project by the late millionaire Stephen Boler (how he made his money is a story in itself), primarily to protect and breed the endangered desert rhino, he left it to the Oppenheimer family (of De Beers diamonds fame) in his will. Today it spreads over endless Kalahari dunes covered with tufts of golden veld and over much of the Northern Cape's Korannaberg mountain range. Its initial population of 7,000 animals has grown, and it's now home to lions, cheetahs, buffalo, giraffes, and a range of antelope species—including rare species such as roan and sable antelope, black wildebeests, and mountain zebras. For (sadly) financial reasons a fence keeps the lion and the sable antelope separate in this massive reserve. There's not as much game as in some of Mpumalanga's private reserves because the land has a lower carrying capacity (the annual rainfall is only about 9¾ inches). But when you do see the animals, the lack of vegetation makes sightings spectacular.

6

GETTING HERE AND AROUND

The lodge operates a direct flight between its Johannesburg airport hangar and Tswalu (this has to be booked directly through the reserve). It's also easy (and cheaper) to fly to Kimberley or Upington and be picked up from there by the lodge. Daily charter flights are available from Johannesburg, Durban, and Cape Town with Airlink and Federal Air. Road transfers from Kimberley or Upington can be arranged, or you can book a charter flight from Johannesburg.

WHERE TO STAY

$$$$ RESORT FAMILY 🏨 **The Motse.** Tswalu's main lodge is made up of freestanding thatch-and-stone suites clustered around a large main building with a heated natural-color pool and a floodlighted waterhole. **Pros:** special children's room and babysitting services and nannies available; unique desert landscape; wonderful library with rare books. **Cons:** no elephants; sable antelopes kept separate from the lions, making the experience feel a little manufactured; if being waited on hand and foot isn't your thing, this may not be the place for you. [$] *Rooms from: R17000* ✉ *Tswalu Kalahari Reserve* 🌐 *www.tswalu.com* 🛏 *8 rooms* 🍴 *All meals.*

The 400,000-acre Addo Elephant National Park is home to 700 elephants.

$$$$ RENTAL FAMILY **Tswalu Tarkuni Lodge.** In a private section of Tswalu, Tarkuni is an exclusive, self-contained house decorated similarly to The Motse and offering a comparable level of luxury. **Pros:** this is excellent value for money if you're a group who can fill the house; a children's paradise; black-maned Kalahari lions, occasional wild dogs, cheetahs, and one-third of South Africa's endangered desert black rhino population. **Cons:** no elephants; not for couples or small groups; no chance to mingle with guests outside your group. [$] *Rooms from: R18000* ✉ *Tswalu Kalahari Reserve* 🌐 *www.tswalu.com* 🛏 *5 rooms* 🍴 *All meals.*

EASTERN CAPE

ADDO ELEPHANT NATIONAL PARK

72 km (45 miles) north of Port Elizabeth.

Smack in the middle of a citrus-growing and horse-breeding area, Addo Elephant National Park is home to a staggering 700 elephants not to mention plenty of buffalo, black rhino, leopards, spotted hyena, hundreds of kudu and other antelopes, and lions. At present the park has about 400,000 acres, but it's expanding all the time and is intended to reach a total of about 600,000 acres, including a fully incorporated marine section. The most accessible parts of the park are the original, main section and the Colchester, Kabouga, Woody Cape, and Zuurberg sections. The original section of Addo still holds most of the game and is served by Addo Main Camp. The Colchester section, in the south, which has one SANParks camp, is contiguous with the main area. The scenic Nyati section is separated from the main section by a road and railway line. Just north of Nyati is the mountainous Zuurberg section, which doesn't have a large variety of game but is particularly scenic, with fabulous hiking trails and horse trails.

GETTING HERE AND AROUND

The closest airport to Addo Elephant Park is Port Elizabeth (PLZ) airport. Flights arrive daily from all of South Africa's main cities via South African Airways, SA Express, SA Airlink, British Airways, and the budget airlines Mango and Kulula. Flights from Cape Town take roughly 1 hour and from Johannesburg 1½ hours.

Traveling by car is the easiest and best way to tour this area, as public transport is limited. Some roads are unpaved but in decent condition. Most lodges will organize airport transfers for their guests.

WHERE TO STAY

$

RESORT

FAMILY

Addo Elephant National Park Main Camp. One of the best SANParks rest camps, this location has a range of self-catering accommodations, such as safari tents, forest cabins, rondavels, cottages, and chalets, and a shop that sells basic supplies as well as souvenirs. **Pros:** great value; you get to enter the game area before the main gates open and go on night drives; good amenities. **Cons:** the shop has only basic supplies; the rondavels have shared cooking facilities; can feel crowded. $ *Rooms from: R1300* ⊠ *Addo Elephant National Park* ☎ *012/428–9111* ⊕ *www.addoelephant.com* ⌁ *65 rooms* ⏣ *No meals.*

$$$$

RESORT

Gorah Elephant Camp. On a private concession within the main section of Addo, this picturesque colonial-themed camp has accommodations in spacious, luxurious safari tents with thick thatch canopies and furnished in fine antiques from the colonial era. **Pros:** the food and service are top-notch; guests are not required to sit together at meals; the location and colonial style recall a bygone era. **Cons:** rooms don't have bathtubs; rooms can get cold at night in winter; you often have to leave the private concession area to find the best game. $ *Rooms from: R11000* ⊠ *Addo Elephant National Park* ☎ *044/501–1111* ⊕ *www.gorahelephantcamp.com* ⌁ *11 rooms* ⏣ *All-inclusive.*

$$$

B&B/INN

Fodor's Choice

★

Hitgeheim Country Lodge. This lovely lodge is set on a steep cliff overlooking the Sundays River and the town of Addo. **Pros:** attentive personal touches; friendly and helpful owners; excellent facilities. **Cons:** not for independent travelers, as the owners like to arrange your activities for you; the restaurant is not open to nonguests; a bit of a drive from the main gate into the national park. $ *Rooms from: R3325* ⊠ *Addo Elephant National Park* ⟁ *18 km (11 miles) from Addo Main Gate on R335, then follow R336 to Kirkwood* ☎ *042/234–0778* ⊕ *www.hitgeheim.com* ⌁ *16 rooms* ⏣ *Breakfast.*

$$$$

B&B/INN

FAMILY

River Bend Lodge. Situated on a 34,594-acre private concession within the Nyati section of Addo, River Bend perfectly balances the feel of a sophisticated, comfortable country house with all the facilities of a game lodge. **Pros:** kids are welcome, and there's an enclosed playground; the food is excellent, especially the seven-course dinner menu; all food and drinks are included in the rack rates. **Cons:** decor is more English colonial than African; only the honeymoon suite has a plunge pool; it's not the most exciting section of the park in terms of game. $ *Rooms from: R12000* ⊠ *Zuurberg, Addo Elephant National Park* ☎ *042/233–8000* ⊕ *www.riverbendlodge.co.za* ⌁ *8 rooms* ⏣ *All-inclusive.*

KWANDWE PRIVATE GAME RESERVE
38 km (24 miles) northeast of Grahamstown.

Tucked away in the Eastern Cape, near the quaint, historic cathedral city of Grahamstown, Kwandwe is a conservation triumph, as its more than 55,000 reclaimed acres of various vegetation types and scenic diversity—rocky outcrops, great plains, thorn thickets, forests, desert scrub, and the Great Fish River—are home to more than 7,000 mammals, including the Big Five. Your chances of seeing the elusive black rhino are very good, and it's likely you'll see fauna you don't always see elsewhere, such as black wildebeest and the endangered blue crane (*Kwandwe* means "place of the blue crane" in Xhosa). If you come in winter, you'll see one of nature's finest floral displays, when thousands of scarlet, orange, and fiery-red aloes are in bloom, attended by colorful sunbirds. The reserve also has a strong focus on community development, as evinced by the Community Centre and village within the reserve, both of which are worth a visit.

GETTING HERE AND AROUND
Kwandwe is a 30-minute drive from Grahamstown, and air and road shuttles are available from Port Elizabeth, which is a 1½-hour drive.

WHERE TO STAY
There are four great places to stay within the reserve; guests can choose between classic colonial or modern chic. You'll be cosseted, pampered, well fed, and taken on some memorable wildlife adventures. Kwandwe is a member of the prestigious Relais & Châteaux group. All the lodges listed here have cable TV in a communal area as well as a safari shop, and massages are available upon request. The child-friendly lodges have movies and games. In the single-use lodges, these are hidden away in a cupboard, so you can keep their existence a secret from your brood unless a rainy day makes them essential.

$$$$
RESORT
Ecca Lodge. This classy lodge combines understated modern elegance with vibrant African colors. **Pros:** superb food; an extensive self-service bar; magnificent open outdoor and indoor showers. **Cons:** some guides are young and slightly inexperienced; service can be a little disorganized; the lounge can feel big and impersonal. $ *Rooms from: R11850* ⌧ *Kwandwe Private Game Reserve* ☎ *046/603–3400* ⊕ *www. kwandwe.com* ⊗ *Closed June* ⏆ *6 rooms* ⦿ *All meals.*

$$$$
RESORT
Fodor's Choice
★
Great Fish River Lodge. If you have an artistic eye, you'll immediately notice how the curving thatch roof of the main buildings echoes the mountain skyline opposite. **Pros:** spectacular river views; unusual habitats (it's not often you find lions clambering up and down rocky outcrops); ultrafriendly staff. **Cons:** avoid if you're a bit unsteady as there are lots of tricky steps; also avoid if you don't like unfenced camps and predators potentially wandering around the lodge at night; not the most family-friendly lodge. $ *Rooms from: R11850* ⌧ *Kwandwe Private Game Reserve* ☎ *046/603–3400* ⊕ *www.kwandwe.com* ⊗ *Closed June* ⏆ *9 rooms* ⦿ *All meals.*

$$$$
RESORT
Melton Manor. Slightly bigger than Uplands Homestead, the Manor accommodates up to eight guests and offers the same superb service and exclusivity. **Pros:** great food; great service. **Cons:** as you're in your

own group you miss out on the opportunity to meet other lodge guests; unlike other Kwandwe lodges, there are no private plunge pools and decks; you can only book for a minimum of four people. $ *Rooms from: R10000* ✉ *Kwandwe Private Game Reserve* ☎ *046/603–3400* ⊕ *www.kwandwe.com* ☉ *Closed June* ⌇4 *rooms* ❍| *All meals.*

$$$$ 🔲 **Uplands Homestead.** If you're a small family or a bunch of friends and
RESORT want to have a genuine, very exclusive, out-of-Africa experience, then stay at this restored 1905 colonial farmhouse. **Pros:** perfect for that special family occasion or friends' reunion; great food and service; steeped in history. **Cons:** can only be booked for families or parties of up to six; the colonial nostalgia might be a little overwhelming for some; not a good option if you want to meet other guests. $ *Rooms from: R10000* ✉ *Kwandwe Private Game Reserve* ⊕ *www.kwandwe.com* ☉ *Closed June* ⌇3 *rooms* ❍| *All meals.*

NORTH WEST

PILANESBERG GAME RESERVE
200 km (124 miles) northwest of Johannesburg.

The 150,000-acre Pilanesberg Game Reserve is often called the Pilanesberg National Park. It isn't actually a South African national park these days, though it was one in the days when Bophutatswana was independent Bantustan. The game reserve is centered on the caldera of an extinct volcano dating back 1.3 billion years that may well have once been Africa's highest peak. Concentric rings of mountains surround a lake filled with crocodiles and hippos. Open grassland, rocky crags, and densely forested gorges provide ideal habitats for a wide range of plains and woodland game, including rare brown hyenas and cheetahs, and wildebeests and zebras, which are abundant in this reserve. Since the introduction of lions in 1993, Pilanesberg (pronounced "pee- *luns*-berg") can boast the Big Five. One of the best places in the country to see rhinos, it's also a bird-watcher's paradise, with a vast range of grassland species, waterbirds, and birds of prey. It's also malaria-free and an excellent choice for game-viewing if you're short on time and can't make it all the way to Kruger National Park, for instance. You can drive around the park in your own vehicle or join guided safaris with Pilanesberg Mankwe Safaris. The entertainment and resort complex of Sun City is nearby.

GETTING HERE AND AROUND
To get to the Pilanesberg from Johannesburg, get on the N4 highway to Krugersdorp and take the R556 off-ramp and follow the signs. The drive is about 2½ to 3 hours. There is a shuttle from Johannesburg to Sun City, just outside the park, but public transportation in and around the park is limited, so you'll need to rent a car or hire a transfer company.

WHERE TO STAY
$$$$ 🔲 **Bakubung Bush Lodge.** Abutting Pilanesberg, this lodge sits at the head
HOTEL of a long valley with terrific views of a hippo pool that forms the lodge's central attraction—it's not unusual to have hippos grazing 100 feet from the terrace restaurant. **Pros:** malaria-free; resident hippos; cheerful

atmosphere. **Cons:** close to a main gate; always crowded; feels vaguely institutional. [$] *Rooms from: R4380* ✉ *Bakubung, Pilanesberg Game Reserve* ☎ *014/552–6000 lodge, 014/552–4006 reservations* 🌐 *www.legacyhotels.co.za* 🛏 *142 rooms* 🍴 *Some meals.*

$$$$ HOTEL FAMILY 🏨 **Kwa Maritane Bush Lodge.** The greatest asset of this hotel, primarily a time-share resort, is its location: in a bowl of rocky hills on the edge of the national park. **Pros:** malaria-free; you've got the best of both worlds—bushveld on your doorstep and Sun City only 20 minutes away by free shuttle bus; lovely swimming pools. **Cons:** you can't get away from the hotel feel; busy during school holidays; it gets noisy around reception, pool, and dining areas. [$] *Rooms from: R5316* ✉ *Kwa Maritane, Pilanesberg Game Reserve* ☎ *014/552–5100* 🌐 *www.legacyhotels.co.za* 🛏 *90 rooms* 🍴 *Some meals.*

$$ RESORT 🏨 **Manyane.** In a thinly wooded savanna east of Pilanesberg's volcanic ridges, this resort offers affordable accommodations in the Sun City area for those travelers who want to experience the region but can't pay five-star prices. **Pros:** accommodations are very basic but a good value; there is a good restaurant if you want a break from self-catering; lovely pool, which is a delight on a hot day. **Cons:** more down-market than other options in the area; can be full of noisy campers and late-night revelers; there's a lot of dust. [$] *Rooms from: R1800* ✉ *Manyane, Pilanesberg Game Reserve* ☎ *014/555–1000 reservations, 072/746–9013 reception* 🌐 *www.manyaneresort-pilanesberg.com* 🛏 *24 rooms* 🍴 *No meals.*

$$$$ HOTEL 🏨 **Tshukudu Bush Lodge.** Tshukudu Bush Lodge is built into the side of a steep, rocky hill and overlooks open grassland and a large waterhole where elephants bathe. **Pros:** malaria-free; luxurious and secluded accommodations; high on a hill with great views. **Cons:** it's a 132-step climb to the main lodge from the parking area, so may not be suitable for guests with disabilities or who get winded easily; game good, but not as abundant as Kruger; no children under 12 permitted. [$] *Rooms from: R9960* ✉ *Tshukudu, Pilanesberg Game Reserve* ☎ *014/552–6255* 🌐 *www.legacyhotels.co.za* 🛏 *10 rooms* 🍴 *All-inclusive.*

MADIKWE GAME RESERVE

300 km (186 miles) northwest of Johannesburg (or farther, depending on which gate you enter).

Just as leopards and Sabi Sand Game Reserve are synonymous, think of Madikwe Game Reserve and wild dogs in the same way. This is probably your best chance in South Africa to have an almost guaranteed sighting of the "painted wolves."

More than two decades ago the 765-square-km (475-square-mile) area bordering Botswana was a wasteland of abandoned cattle farms, overgrown bush, and rusting fences. A brilliant and unique collaboration between the North West Parks Board, private enterprise, and local communities changed all that when Operation Phoenix—one of the most ambitious game relocation programs in the world—relocated more than 8,000 animals of 27 different species to Madikwe. Soon after, it became one of the fastest-growing safari destinations in South Africa.

Madikwe today is teeming with game. Spot the Big Five, plus resident breeding packs of the endangered painted wolves—the wild dogs of Africa. On your morning, evening, or night game drive, you also might spot cheetahs, hippos, lions, elephants, and buffalos, but you'll certainly see zebras, wildebeests, and several kinds of antelope (South Africans refer to all antelope generically as "buck," whether they're male or female). Birders can spot more than 350 birds. Be dazzled by the crimson-breasted shrike, the lilac-breasted roller, yellow- and red-billed hornbills, blue waxbills, and many more.

Madikwe can't claim the great rivers, giant riverine trees, and range of habitats that Kruger or Sabi Sand have, but it has a diverse landscape including wide plains, thick bushveld, an area steeped in history, and a background of low purple mountains. The reserve also has three advantages over many of the others: it's only 3½ hours from Johannesburg on good roads, it's malaria-free, and it doesn't allow day visitors. Choose between more than 20 top-class lodges, get your binoculars ready, and off you go.

GETTING HERE AND AROUND

Madikwe is an easy drive on good roads from Johannesburg. Go to Sun City via Hartbeespoort Dam and follow the signs to Madikwe, which is about an hour's drive from Sun City (though your trip could be an hour longer if your lodge is in the north of the park). Ask at your lodge for detailed instructions. You'll be driven around in an open game vehicle by a staff member of your lodge; guided bush walks are also available. No day visitors are allowed.

WHERE TO STAY

In the south, choose between the ultraluxurious Tuningi Lodge, where a 300-year-old fig tree stands sentinel over a busy waterhole, or either of Jaci's delightful lodges. Madikwe Safari Lodge, managed by the More family of Mpumalanga's Lion Sands, is another example of this company's high standards of luxury, service, and game-viewing.

Tau Lodge in the north of the reserve is more like a small resort than a private safari lodge, but the accommodations are excellent, the food is good, and the game drives are well done. Always check for special offers at any of the Madikwe lodges. You can often get very affordable rates, especially off-season.

$$$$ — **Jaci's Lodges.** The two lodges that make up Jaci's Lodges are family owned and have a longstanding reputation for friendliness, superb game drives, and comfortable accommodations that has made them synonymous with the name Madikwe Game Reserve. **Pros:** friendly, welcoming atmosphere; great children's activities and facilities; great game-viewing. **Cons:** if children aren't your thing, stay away from Jaci's Safari Lodge; pricey. $ *Rooms from: R16990* ⊠ *Madikwe Game Reserve* ☎ *083/700–2071 reservations, 083/303–0885 Jaci's Safari Lodge manager, 083/276–2387 Jaci's Tree Lodge manager* ⊕ *www.jacislodges.co.za* ⊋ *10 rooms* ⎟⊙⎟ *All meals.*

$$$$ — **Madikwe Safari Lodge.** This stunning five-star lodge in the central eastern region of the park is managed by the More family of Lion Sands, and their attention to detail, reputation for fine food and excellent

ALL-INCLUSIVE
FAMILY

RESORT
FAMILY

6

service, and thrilling game drives are readily apparent. **Pros:** malaria-free; superb accommodations; great food; excellent game-viewing. **Cons:** not as scenically beautiful as the Mpumalanga and KwaZulu-Natal reserves; long walks between suites. $ *Rooms from: R9010* ✉ *Madikwe Game Reserve* ☎ *018/350–9902* ⊕ *www.madikwesafarilodge.co.za* ➴ *20 suites* ⦿ *All meals.*

$$$$ ⊡ **Tuningi Safari Lodge.** A 300-year-old fig tree dominates the ultraluxu-
RESORT rious Tuningi Lodge overlooking a busy waterhole that will keep you entranced all day. **Pros:** superb accommodations; excellent Big Five game-viewing; designed with families in mind, including a children's program. **Cons:** pricey, but watch for special offers particularly in the off-season; additional fee per child per night. $ *Rooms from: R7000* ✉ *Madikwe Game Reserve* ☎ *011/781–5384* ⊕ *www.tuningi.com* ➴ *6 rooms* ⦿ *All meals* ⌁ *Rate includes accommodations, 3 meals daily, 2 game drives daily, tea/coffee.*

GATEWAY CITIES

South Africa's two hub cities are Johannesburg and Cape Town. It's almost certain that you'll arrive and leave the country from one of these two cities. Make the most of your time in transit—there's a lot you can do in 24 hours.

6

JOHANNESBURG

Johannesburg is South Africa's most-visited city by far, and it's well worth a stopover of at least two or three days. There's plenty to see here, including the Apartheid Museum and Constitution Hill in the city, not to mention the nearby city of Soweto, and the Cradle of Humankind UNESCO World Heritage Site about 90 minutes away.

Ask a *jol* (lively party) of Jo'burgers what they love about their home-town, and they may point to its high-paced energy; its opportunity; afternoon thunderstorms in the summer; the Pirates versus Chiefs derby (the Orlando Pirates and Kaizer Chiefs are South Africa's most loved—and hated—soccer teams); spectacular sunsets; jacaranda blooms carpeting the city in purple in October and November; a great climate; the dog walks around Emmarentia Dam; the fast-paced lifestyle; the can-do attitude; the down-to-earth nature of its people; and the city's rich history. For many, Johannesburg is the gateway to the rest of Africa, and it may very well be the continent's most cosmopolitan city.

Johannesburg's origins lie in the discovery of gold. The city sits at the center of a vast urban industrial complex that covers most of the province of Gauteng (the *g* is pronounced like the *ch* in Chanukah), which means "Place Where the Gold Is" in the Sotho language and is home to the world's deepest gold mines (more than 3.9 km [2.4 miles] deep). More than 100 years ago it was just a rocky piece of unwanted Highveld land. But in 1886 an Australian, George Harrison, officially discovered gold, catapulting Johannesburg into a modern metropolis that still helps to power the country's economy (though gold mining has been winding down in recent years).

Despite its industrial past, Jozi remains a green city, with more than 10 million trees and many beautiful parks and nature reserves, which is all the more exceptional considering it is the largest city in the world not built on a river or near a significant water source.

Local government has invested in an extensive new public transportation system that serves the local working population and tourists alike. This includes the Gautrain rapid rail system that connects Johannesburg with Pretoria and the O. R. Tambo International Airport, moving Jo'burg steadily toward its goal of being—as the city's government is eager to brand it—"a world-class African city."

WHEN TO GO

Jo'burgers boast that they enjoy the best climate in the world: not too hot in summer (mid-September–mid-April), not too cold in winter (mid-April–mid-September), and not prone to sudden temperature changes. Summer (especially during December and January) may have the edge, though: it's when the gardens and open spaces are at their most beautiful.

GETTING HERE AND AROUND

It's difficult but not impossible to see the Johannesburg area without a car. A good bet is to rent one, decide what you want to see, and get a good road map or rent a GPS navigator. If you're reluctant to drive yourself, book a couple of full-day or half-day tours that will pick you up from your hotel or a central landmark. The City Sightseeing bus can give you an excellent overview of the city and enable you to hop on and off at most of Johannesburg's attractions. Spend a half day or a full day doing this.

O. R. Tambo International Airport is about 19 km (12 miles) from the Johannesburg city center and is linked to the city by a fast highway, which is always busy but especially so before 9 am and between 4 and 7 pm. The best way to travel to and from it is via the Gautrain, a high-speed train that connects Sandton, Johannesburg, and Pretoria directly with O. R. Tambo. It takes about 30 minutes to travel from the airport to Sandton. The train runs from between 5 or 5:30 am and 9 or 9:30 pm every day, depending on the station.

Alternatively, Magic Bus offers private transfers to all major Sandton hotels (R575 per vehicle for one or two people, R630 for three people, R670 for four to seven people). The journey takes 30 minutes to an hour. Getthere Transfers and Tours charges R450 from the airport to anywhere in Johannesburg for the first rider and R30 for each additional person (R500 to Pretoria and R50 for each additional person). Airport Link will ferry you anywhere in the central Johannesburg area for R490 per person.

Wilro Tours runs from the airport to Sandton (R835 for one to three people, R1,230 for four to seven).

In addition, scores of licensed taxis line up outside the airport terminal. By law they must have a working meter. Expect to pay about R500 for a trip to Sandton. Negotiate a price before you get into a taxi.

Lines at the airport can be long: plan to arrive two to three hours before an international departure and at least an hour before domestic departures. The airport has its own police station, but luggage theft has still been a problem in recent years. Keep your belongings close to you at all times.

If your hotel or guesthouse does not have a shuttle, ask a staff member to arrange for your transportation with a reliable company. Most lodgings have a regular service they use, so you should have no problem arranging this in advance.

Prices vary, depending on where you are staying, but plan on R400–R500 for a ride from your hotel or guesthouse in Sandton, Rosebank, or the city center to the airport. Some companies charge per head, whereas others charge per trip, so be sure to check that in advance. The Gautrain is less expensive, quick, and safe, but you'll have to handle your own luggage. Most guesthouses or hotels will be able to drop you at the closest Gautrain station.

Airport Contacts O. R. Tambo International Airport. ☎ 086/727–7888, 011/921–6262 *information desk* ⊕ www.acsa.co.za.

Airport Transfers Airport Link. ☎ 011/794–8300, 083/625–5090 ⊕ www.airportlink.co.za. **Gautrain.** ☎ 0800/428–87246 ⊕ www.gautrain.co.za. **Legend Tours and Transfers.** ☎ 021/704–9140 ⊕ www.legendtours.co.za. **Magic Transfers.** ☎ 011/548–0800 ⊕ www.magictransfers.co.za/us.

Traveling by car is the easiest way to get around Johannesburg, as the city's public transportation is not that reliable or extensive, though this is changing (the Gautrain, for example, is incredibly reliable). The general speed limit for city streets is 60 kph (37 mph); for main streets it's often 80 kph (50 mph), and for highways it's 100 kph or 120 kph (62 mph or 75 mph). But be warned that Johannesburg drivers are known as the most aggressive in the country, and minibus taxis are famous for ignoring the rules of the road, often stopping for passengers with little or no warning. Most city roads and main countryside roads are in good condition, with plenty of signage. City street names are sometimes visible only on the curb, however. Avoid driving in rush hours, 7 to 8:30 am and 4 to 6:30 pm, as the main roads become terribly congested. Gas stations are plentiful in most areas. (Don't pump your own gas, though; stations employ operators to do that for you.)

If you plan to drive yourself around, get a *good* map of the city center and northern suburbs or buy or rent a GPS (available at the airport and most car-rental agencies). MapStudio prints excellent street guides, available at bookstores and many gas stations and convenience stores.

Rental agencies have offices in the northern suburbs and at the airport.

Minibus taxis form the backbone of Jo'burg's transportation for ordinary commuters, but you should avoid using them since they're often not roadworthy, drivers can be irresponsible, and it's difficult to know where they're going without consulting a local. Car taxis, though more expensive, are easier to use. They have stands at the airport and the train stations, but otherwise you must phone for one (be sure to ask how long it will take the taxi to get to you). Taxis should be licensed and have a working meter. Meters usually start at R50 (includes first 3 km [2 miles]) and are about R13 per kilometer (½ mile) thereafter. Expect to pay about R500 to the airport from town or Sandton and about R300 to the city center from Sandton. Uber is a popular, safe, and inexpensive taxi service, but it can be accessed only from a smartphone app.

Contacts Maxi Taxi. ☎ 011/648–1111, 011/648–1112 ⊕ *www.maxi-taxisa. co.za.* **Rose Taxis.** ☎ 011/403–0000, 083/255–0933 ⊕ *www.rosetaxis.com.* **Uber.** ⊕ *www.uber.com/cities/johannesburg.*

For information on airlines or roadside assistance or car-rental companies, see the Planning section at the beginning of the chapter.

TIMING

If you have only one day in Jo'burg, take a tour of Soweto and visit the Apartheid Museum, then stop by Constitution Hill if you have a chance. Spend the evening having dinner at an African-style restaurant, such as Moyo. If you have a second day, focus on what interests you most: perhaps a trip to the Cradle of Humankind, where you can explore the sites of some of the world's most significant paleontological discoveries; a trip to Cullinan, where you can visit a working diamond mine; or a fun day or two at Sun City.

TOURS

Township tours (to Soweto in particular) are offered by a number of local operators. One of the best options is to do a Soweto tour with the City Sightseeing bus, which partners with local operators for tours of Soweto. For more recommendations of reputable tour operators, inquire at Johannesburg Tourism.

Fodor's Choice ★ **City Sightseeing Bus.** The City Sightseeing bus is a great and very safe way to see the Johannesburg city center and all its main attractions. The bus departs from nine locations every 30 minutes from 9 to 5 every day, but the best places to catch it are either at Gold Reef City or Park station (accessible via the Gautrain). Adults and kids alike will love the experience; there's a special children's soundtrack, and the adult commentary is available in 15 languages. The total trip takes about 1½ hours if you don't get off (though you should consider at least getting off at the Apartheid Museum and Constitution Hill); you can get a one- or two-day pass. There is also an option to pair it with a Soweto tour, also highly recommended. You can buy your tickets at The Zone @ Rosebank (stop 1) or you can wait and buy tickets on any City Sightseeing bus, but there's a discount for purchasing them online. ⊠ *Johannesburg* ☎ *0861/733–287* ⊕ *www.citysightseeing.co.za* 🎫 *From R170.*

SAFETY

Johannesburg is notorious for being a dangerous city—it's quite common to hear about serious crimes such as armed robbery and murder. That said, it's safe for visitors who avoid dangerous areas and take reasonable precautions. Do not leave bags or valuables visible in a car, and keep the doors locked, even while driving (to minimize the risk of smash-and-grab robberies or carjackings); don't wear flashy jewelry or carry large wads of cash or expensive equipment. ■ TIP→ **Don't visit a township or squatter camp on your own.** ■ TIP→ **Unemployment is rife, and foreigners are easy pickings. If you wish to see a township, check** with reputable companies, which run excellent tours and know which areas to avoid. The Apartheid Museum and Constitution Hill within the city and the Cradle of Humankind just outside are perfectly safe to visit on your own.

■TIP➜ If you drive yourself around the city, it's safest to keep your doors locked and windows up, and to not leave valuables such as bags, cameras, or phones on the seat or visible.

VISITOR INFORMATION

The helpful Gauteng Tourism Authority has information on the whole province, but more detailed information is often available from local tourism associations—for example, the Soweto Accommodation Association lists more than 20 lodgings. Joburg Tourism has a good website, with information about Johannesburg and up-to-date listings of events happening around the city.

Contacts Joburg Tourism. ☎ 011/883–3525 ⊕ www.joburgtourism.com. **Soweto.co.za.** ☎ 083/535–4553, 071/204–5594 ⊕ www.soweto.co.za.

EXPLORING

The Greater Johannesburg metropolitan area is massive—more than 1,600 square km (618 square miles)—incorporating the large municipalities of Randburg and Sandton to the north. Most of the sights are just north of the city center, which degenerated badly in the 1990s but is now being revamped.

To the south, in Ormonde, are the Apartheid Museum and Gold Reef City; the sprawling township of Soweto is just a little farther to the southwest. Johannesburg's northern suburbs are its most affluent. On the way to the shopping meccas of Rosebank and Sandton, you can find the superb Johannesburg Zoo and the South African Museum of Military History, in the leafy suburb of Saxonwold.

TOP ATTRACTIONS

Fodor's Choice ★ **Apartheid Museum.** The Apartheid Museum, in Ormonde, takes you on a journey through South African apartheid history—from the entrance, where you pass through a turnstile according to your assigned skin color (black or white), to the myriad historical, brutally honest, and sometimes shocking photographs, video displays, films, documents, and other exhibits. It's an emotional, multilayered journey. As you walk chronologically through the apartheid years and eventually reach the country's first steps to freedom, with democratic elections in 1994, you experience a taste of the pain and suffering with which so many South Africans had to live. A room with 121 ropes with hangman's knots hanging from the ceiling—one rope for each political prisoner executed in the apartheid era—is especially chilling. ⊠ *Northern Pkwy. at Gold Reef Rd., Ormonde* ☎ *011/309–4700* ⊕ *www.apartheidmuseum.org* ☑ *R85.*

Fodor's Choice ★ **Constitution Hill.** Overlooking Jo'burg's inner city and suburbs, Constitution Hill houses the **Constitutional Court,** set up in 1994 with the birth of democracy, as well as the austere **Old Fort Prison Complex** (also called Number Four), where thousands of political prisoners were incarcerated, including South African Nobel Peace Prize laureates Albert Luthuli and Nelson Mandela, and iconic Indian leader Mahatma Gandhi. The court decides on the most important cases relating to human rights, much like the Supreme Court in the United States. Exhibits in the visitor center portray the country's journey to democracy. You can walk along the prison ramparts (built in the 1890s), read messages on the We the People Wall (and add your own), or view the court itself, in which large, slanting columns represent the trees under which African villagers traditionally met to discuss matters of importance. If the court isn't in session, you can walk right into the courtroom, where many of the country's landmark legal decisions have been made in recent years and where the 11 chairs of the justices are each covered in a different cowhide, representing their individuality. Group tours of the Old Fort Prison Complex are given every hour on the hour from 9 to 4 and include a visit to the Women's Jail, where there are photographs and exhibits of how women were treated in the prison system and how they contributed to the struggle against apartheid. ⊠ *Joubert St. at Kotze St., entrance on Joubert St., Braamfontein, City Center* ☎ *011/381–3100* ⊕ *www.constitutionhill.org.za* ✉ *Court free; Constitution Hill tour R65.*

Fodor's Choice
★

Hector Pieterson Memorial and Museum. Opposite Holy Cross Church, a stone's throw from the former homes of Nelson Mandela and Archbishop Desmond Tutu on Vilakazi Street, the Hector Pieterson Memorial and Museum is a crucial landmark. Pieterson, a 12-year-old student, was one of the first victims of police fire on June 16, 1976, when schoolchildren rose up to protest their second-rate Bantu (black) education system. The memorial is a paved area with benches for reflection, an inscribed stone, and simple water feature; inside the museum are grainy photographs and films that bring that fateful day to life and put it into the context of the broader apartheid struggle. A total of 562 small granite blocks in the museum courtyard are a tribute to the children who died in the Soweto uprisings. ⊠ *Khumalo St. at Phela St., Orlando West* ☎ *011/536–0611* ⊕ *www.joburg.org.za* ✉ *R30.*

WHERE TO EAT

Jo'burgers love eating out, and there are hundreds of restaurants throughout the city to satisfy them. Some notable destinations for food include Melrose Arch, Parkhurst, Sandton, and Greenside. Smart-casual dress is a good bet. Many establishments are closed on Sunday night and Monday.

There's no way to do justice to the sheer scope and variety of Johannesburg's restaurants in a few examples. What follows is a (necessarily subjective) list of some of the best. Try asking locals what they recommend; eating out is the most popular form of entertainment in Johannesburg, and everyone has a list of favorite spots, which changes often.

$$$
AFRICAN
Fodor's Choice
★

✕ **Moyo.** The rich and varied menu at Moyo is pan-African, incorporating tandoori cookery from northern Africa, Cape Malay influences such as lentil bobotie, Moroccan-influenced tasty *tagines*, and ostrich burgers and other dishes representing South Africa. Diners are often entertained by storytellers, face painters, and musicians. **Known for:** live entertainment; African food, music, and decor. ⓢ *Average main: R180* ⊠ *Melrose Arch, High St., Shop 5, Melrose Arch* ☎ *011/684–1477* ⊕ *www.moyo.co.za.*

$$ ITALIAN Fodor's Choice ★ 🍴 **Tortellino d'Oro.** This small and unpretentious restaurant and deli has legendary food, especially the pasta. Try the Parma ham and melon as an antipasto, and then get a pasta for your main course, such as the tortellini, which is filled with a mixture of ham, mortadella sausage, chicken, and Parmesan cheese, then served with mushroom cream, or butter and sage sauce. **Known for:** outstanding service; excellent wine list; authentic pasta. [$] *Average main: R150* ✉ *Oaklands Shopping Centre, Pretoria St. at Victoria St., Oaklands* ☎ *011/483–1249* 🌐 *www.tortellino.co.za* 🕘 *No dinner Sun.*

$$ AFRICAN 🍴 **Wandie's Place.** Wandie's Place isn't the only good township restaurant, but it's the best known and one of the most popular spots in Jo'burg. The waiters are smartly dressed in ties, and the food is truly African, with meat stews, sweet potatoes, beans, corn porridge, traditionally cooked pumpkin, chicken, and tripe laid out in a buffet of pots and containers. **Known for:** eclectic decor; tour groups. [$] *Average main: R150* ✉ *618 Makhalamele St., Dube* ☎ *081/420–6051* 🌐 *www.wandiesplace.co.za.*

WHERE TO STAY

Most, if not all, of the good hotels are in the northern suburbs. Many of them are linked to nearby malls and are well policed. Boutique hotels have sprung up everywhere, as have bed-and-breakfasts from Melville to Soweto. Hotels are quieter in December and January, when many locals take their annual vacations and rates are often cheaper. But beware: if there's a major conference, some of the smaller hotels can be booked months in advance.

All the hotels we list offer no-smoking rooms, and many have no-smoking floors.

$$ HOTEL 🏨 **Clico Boutique Hotel.** This small, upmarket boutique hotel in central Rosebank is a renovated Cape Dutch house with a gracious garden that offers good value in an area known for expensive accommodations. **Pros:** 24-hour manned security and CCTV cameras; free Wi-Fi throughout the hotel; central location near Rosebank Mall. **Cons:** neighborhood not safe to walk at night; noise from the pool activity can travel to the suites; stairs might be difficult to navigate. [$] *Rooms from: R1685* ✉ *27 Sturdee Ave., at Jellicoe Ave., Rosebank* ☎ *011/252–3300* 🌐 *www.clicohotel.com* 🛏 *9 suites* 🍽 *Breakfast.*

$$$$ HOTEL Fodor's Choice ★ 🏨 **Four Seasons The Westcliff.** The iconic Westcliff, now under the Four Seasons banner and with a $56-million revamp, has been transformed into the paragon of a luxurious urban resort. **Pros:** great location; spectacular views over Johannesburg; impeccable service. **Cons:** all this luxury and service comes at a high cost; rather formal atmosphere, which may not be to everyone's liking; rooms spread out along a steep hill, sometimes requiring a shuttle. [$] *Rooms from: R3600* ✉ *67 Jan Smuts Ave., Westcliff* ☎ *011/481–6000* 🌐 *www.fourseasons.com/johannesburg* 🛏 *153 rooms* 🍽 *Breakfast.*

$$$$ HOTEL Fodor's Choice ★ 🏨 **The Saxon Hotel, Village & Spa.** In the exclusive suburb of Sandhurst, the luxurious, exclusive, and impeccably designed Saxon Hotel has repeatedly received awards for its excellence. **Pros:** possibly the most exclusive address in Gauteng; exceptional spa on-site; good for business

travelers or high-profile folk who'd rather not see anyone else in the corridors. **Cons:** some might find the atmosphere a bit snooty; children under 14 not welcome in restaurant; pricey. $ *Rooms from: R6600* ✉ *36 Saxon Rd., Sandhurst* ☎ *011/292–6000* ⊕ *www.saxon.co.za* ⤴ *53 rooms* ❘◯❘ *Breakfast.*

SHOPPING

Whether you're after designer clothes, high-quality African art, or glamorous gifts, Johannesburg offers outstanding shopping opportunities. At the city's several markets, bargaining can get you a great price.

Fodor's Choice
★

Rosebank Art and Craft Market. The Rosebank Art and Craft Market, between the Rosebank Mall and the Zone, has a huge variety of African crafts from Cape to Cairo, all displayed to the background beat of traditional African music. Drive a hard bargain here—the vendors expect you to! If you want to save your shopping until the end of your trip, then this should be your destination. It's the best place in Jo'burg to buy African crafts, and it's an entertaining place to visit as well. ✉ *Mall of Rosebank, Cradock Ave., Rosebank* ☎ *072/614–5506* ⊕ *www.rosebankartandcraftmarket.co.za.*

SIDE TRIP FROM JOHANNESBURG

CRADLE OF HUMANKIND

72 km (45 miles) northwest of Johannesburg.

This UNESCO World Heritage Site stretches over an area of about 470 square km (181 square miles), with about 300 caves. Inside these caves, paleoanthropologists have discovered thousands of fossils of hominids and other animals, dating back some 4 million years. The most famous of these fossils are Mrs. Ples, a skull more than 2 million years old, and Little Foot, a skeleton more than 3 million years old. Although the Cradle does not have the world's oldest hominid fossils, it has the most complete fossil record of human evolution anywhere on earth, has produced more hominid fossils than anywhere else, and has been designated a UNESCO World Heritage Site.

Archaeological finds at the Cradle of Humankind include 1.7-million-year-old stone tools, the oldest recorded in Southern Africa. At Swartkrans, near Sterkfontein, a collection of burned bones tells us that our ancestors could manage fire more than a million years ago.

Not all the fossil sites in the Cradle are open to the public, but a tour of the Sterkfontein Caves and the visitor center provides an excellent overview of the paleontological work in progress, and a trip to Maropeng, a much larger visitor center 10 km (6 miles) from the Sterkfontein Caves, provides even more background. Special tours to fossil sites with expert guides can be booked via tour operator Palaeo-Tours.

GETTING HERE AND AROUND

Public transportation to the Cradle of Humankind area is limited, so using a rental car or taking an organized tour is best. Some hotels in the area will arrange transportation on request. The Cradle of Humankind is about a 90-minute drive from Johannesburg or Pretoria, but isn't

Maropeng is the official visitor center at the Cradle of Humankind, which is one of eight World Heritage Sites in South Africa.

well signposted, so use a GPS or download instructions on how to get there from the Maropeng website if you don't visit on a guided tour.

EXPLORING

FAMILY
Fodor's Choice
★

Maropeng Visitor Centre. Maropeng is the official visitor center of the Cradle of Humankind World Heritage Site and offers much more than information about the region: it's a modern, interactive museum dedicated to the history of humanity. It provides information about the various fossil sites in the area. About a 90-minute drive from either Johannesburg or Pretoria, it's one of the area's top attractions. It's best visited in parallel with the nearby fossil site of Sterkfontein Caves (about 5 km/3 miles away), but to visit both you'll need to set aside at least half a day. ⊠ *Off R563 (Hekpoort Rd.), Sterkfontein* ☎ *014/577–9000* ⊕ *www.maropeng.co.za* ✉ *R120 (combo ticket with Sterkfontein Caves for R190).*

CAPE TOWN

A favorite South African topic of debate is whether Cape Town really is part of Africa. That's how different it is, both from the rest of the country and the rest of the continent. And therein lies its attraction. South Africa's most urbane, sophisticated city sits in stark contrast to the South Africa north of the Hex River Valley. Here, the traffic lights work pretty much consistently and good restaurants are commonplace. In fact, dining establishments in the so-called Mother City always dominate the country's "best of" lists.

What also distinguishes this city is its deep sense of history. Nowhere else in the country will you find structures dating back to the 17th century. South Africa as it is known today began here.

A visit to Cape Town is synonymous with a visit to the peninsula south of the city, and for good reason. With pristine white-sand beaches, hundreds of mountain trails, and numerous activities from surfing to paragliding to mountain biking, the accessibility, variety, and pure beauty of the great outdoors will keep nature lovers and outdoor adventurers occupied for hours, if not days. A week exploring just the city and peninsula is barely enough.

Often likened to San Francisco, Cape Town has two things that the former doesn't: Table Mountain and Africa. The mountain, or tabletop, is vital to Cape Town's identity. It dominates the city in a way that's difficult to comprehend until you visit. In the afternoon, when creeping fingers of clouds spill over Table Mountain and reach toward the city, the whole town seems to hold its breath—because in summer it brings frequent strong southeasterly winds. Meanwhile, for all of its bon-vivant European vibe, Cape Town also reflects the diversity, vitality, and spirit of Africa, with many West and Central Africans and Zimbabweans—many of them having fled from conflicts elsewhere—calling this city home.

WHEN TO GO

Whatever activities you hope to accomplish in Cape Town, head up Table Mountain as soon as the wind isn't blowing. Cape Town wind is notorious, and the mountain can be shut for days on end when there are gales. Summer (October–March) is the windiest time of the year, and from December to April winds can reach 60 km (37 miles) an hour. But they will often happen in the winter months, too—just less frequently. If you're planning to visit Robben Island during peak season, it's also wise to book well in advance. One of the best months to visit is April, when the heat and wind have abated and the Cape is bathed in warm autumnal hues. Winter rains can put off visitors, but this time of the year holds its own surprises: the countryside is a brilliant green, and without fail the best sunny and temperate days come between the rainy spells. Whales are seen in False Bay in spring (late August to early September), when wildflowers are also in bloom.

GETTING HERE AND AROUND

Cape Town International Airport is about 19 km (12 miles) from the city center. It should take about 20 minutes to get from the airport to the city; during rush hour it can easily be double that. Private airport-transfer operators abound, and there is now public bus service to and from the airport. All major car-rental companies have counters at Cape Town International, and driving to the City Bowl or V&A Waterfront is straightforward in daylight. If your flight arrives after dark, consider prearranging transportation through your hotel. There are tourist information desks in both the domestic and international terminals. *For information about airlines that fly to Cape Town, see Air Travel in Travel Smart.*

Contacts Cape Town International Airport. ✉ *Matroosfontein, Cape Town* ☎ *021/937–1200, 086/727–7888 flight information* ⊕ *capetown-airport.co.za.*

Metered taxis and shuttle services (usually minivans) are based inside the domestic baggage hall and outside the international and domestic terminals and can also be phoned for airport drop-offs. Rates vary depending on the operator, number of passengers, destination, and time of arrival. The fare for one person to the city center is R300 in a metered taxi; a group of up to four will usually pay the same rate. A surcharge of up to R50 is sometimes levied from 10 pm until early morning, and some services charge more for arrivals than for departures to cover waiting time. For single travelers, a prearranged shared shuttle is the most economical, costing about R150–R180 per person; however, there may be numerous drop-offs, so this can be slow. MyCiti, a public bus, also serves the airport, and for R90 it's the cheapest way to or from the airport and City Centre. ■TIP→ **Reports of overcharging are common, so discuss the fare before entering any taxi.**

Rikkis provides inexpensive, unmetered fares (R220 to City Centre, for example) from the airport. *For contact information, see Taxi Travel.*

Recommended shared-van services include Legend Tours and Transfers or Magic Bus Airport. Citi Hopper provides both shared-van transfers and private-car transfers.

Airport Transfers Citi Hopper. ☎ *021/936–3460/1, 082/773–7678* ⊕ *www. citihopper.co.za.* **Legend Tours and Transfers.** ☎ *021/704–9140* ⊕ *www. legendtours.co.za.* **Magic Bus Airport Transfers.** ☎ *021/505–6300* ⊕ *www. magicbus.co.za.*

Although many locals drive, tourists may find public transportation (MyCiti buses) or taxis a better option; save the rental car for when you are getting out of town. Cape Town's roads are excellent, but getting around can be a bit confusing. Signposting is inconsistent, switching between Afrikaans and English, between different names for the same road (especially highways), and between different destinations on the same route. Sometimes the signs simply vanish. ■TIP→ **Cape Town is also littered with signs indicating "Cape Town" instead of "City Centre," as well as "Kaapstad," which is Afrikaans for Cape Town.** A good one-page map is essential and available from car-rental agencies and tourism information desks. Among the hazards are pedestrians running across highways, speeding vehicles, and minibus taxis. Roadblocks for document and DWI checks are also becoming more frequent.

Parking in the city center is a nightmare. There are simply not enough parking garages, longer-stay parking spaces are scarce, and most hotels charge a small fortune for parking. There are numerous pay-and-display (i.e., put a ticket in your windshield) and pay-on-exit parking lots around the city, but parking is strictly enforced. Prices range from R6 to R12 per half hour. For central attractions like Greenmarket Square, the Company's Garden, the South African National Gallery, and the Castle of Good Hope, look for a lot around the Grand Parade on Darling Street. The Sanlam Golden Acre Parking Garage on Adderley Street offers covered parking, as does the Parkade on Strand Street, but Queen

Victoria Street alongside the South African Museum (and Company's Garden) is always bound to have a few spaces.

The main arteries leading out of the city are the N1, which bypasses the city's Northern Suburbs en route to Paarl and, ultimately, Johannesburg; and the N2, which heads out past Khayelitsha and through Somerset West to the Overberg and the Garden Route before continuing on through the Eastern Cape to Durban and beyond. Branching off the N1, the N7 goes to Namibia. The M3 splits off from the N2 near Observatory, leading to the False Bay side of the peninsula via Claremont and Constantia; it's the main and quickest route to the beaches of Muizenberg, Kalk Bay, St. James, and Simon's Town. Rush hour sees bumper-to-bumper traffic on all major arteries into the city from 6 to 9, and out of the city from 4 to 6:30.

Taxis are expensive compared with other forms of transportation, but offer a quick way to get around the city center. Don't expect to see the throngs of cabs you find in London or New York, as most people in Cape Town use public transportation or their own cars. You'll be lucky to hail one on the street. Your best bet is to summon a taxi by phone or head to one of the major taxi stands, such as those at Greenmarket Square or either end of Adderley Street. Expect to pay R50–R70 for a trip from the City Centre to the Waterfront. For lower rates at night, try prebooking the Backpacker Bus, a shuttle service on Adderley Street. Lodging establishments often have a relationship with particular companies and/or drivers, and this way you may be assured of safe, reliable service.

To the airport from the City Bowl will cost R220, with the cost rising the farther out you are.

Contacts Backpacker Bus. ☎ 082/809–9185 ⊕ www.backpackerbus.co.za. **Excite Taxis.** ☎ 021/448–4444 ⊕ www.excitetaxis.co.za. **Unicab.** ☎ 021/486–1600 ⊕ www.unicab.co.za.

SAFETY

Women and couples are strongly advised not to walk in isolated places after dark.

Watch your valuables closely or leave them at the hotel. Windows will be smashed to snatch cell phones lying on car seats, and phones may even be pulled out of people's hands while in use. Watch your pockets at busy transportation hubs and on trains. It's better to sit in a crowded car; if you suddenly find yourself alone, move to another one. Public transportation collapses after dark. Unless you're at the Waterfront or in a large group, use metered taxis.

Despite thousands of safe visits every year, Lion's Head—the peak below Table Mountain—and the running trails around Newlands Forest have been the sites of several knifepoint robberies around sunrise or sunset.

As in other major cities, drug use is a problem in Cape Town, including both IV drugs and ingestibles. You will undoubtedly come across many people begging in Cape Town, including kids. Please do not give cash directly to children, as this often supports either a glue habit or adults lurking in the background.

TOUR OPTIONS

Numerous companies offer guided tours of the city center, the peninsula, the Winelands, and any place else in the Cape (or beyond) that you might wish to visit. They differ in type of transportation used, focus, and size. For comprehensive information on touring companies, head to one of the Cape Town Tourism offices or ask for recommendations at your hotel.

Wanderlust – Cape Town on Foot Walking Tour. Owner Ursula Stevens leads walks through Cape Town, around the Cape of Good Hope, and up the West Coast—all guided by the seven books she has written on the areas full of interesting historical information. City walking tours last about 2½ hours and cover major historical attractions, architecture, and highlights of modern-day Cape Town. ☎ *021/462–4252* ⊕ *www. wanderlust.co.za.*

City Sightseeing. The hop-on/hop-off red City Sightseeing bus is a great way to familiarize yourself with Cape Town; a day ticket costs R170, and there are two routes to choose from. The Red Route runs through the city, and you can get on and off at major museums, the V&A Waterfront, Table Mountain Cableway, Two Oceans Aquarium, and other attractions. The Blue Route takes you farther afield—to Kirstenbosch National Botanic Gardens, Hout Bay, and Camps Bay, to name a few destinations. Tickets are available at the Waterfront outside the aquarium or on the bus. The newer Cape Explorer options offer full-day tours of Cape Point or the Winelands, and at R550 are an economical way to visit these popular destinations. ⊕ *www.citysightseeing.co.za.*

VISITOR INFORMATION

From October to March, the office in City Centre is open weekdays 8–6, Saturday 8:30–2, and Sunday 9–1; from April to September, it's open weekdays 8–5:30, Saturday 8:30–1, and Sunday 9–1. The branch at the Waterfront is open daily 9–7.

Contact Cape Town Tourism. ✉ *The Pinnacle Bldg., Burg St. at Castle St., Cape Town Central* ☎ *021/487–6800* ⊕ *www.capetown.travel.*

EXPLORING

TOP ATTRACTIONS

FAMILY

Fodor's Choice

★

Kirstenbosch National Botanical Gardens. Spectacular in each season, this renowned botanical garden was established in 1913, and was the first in the world to conserve and showcase a country's indigenous flora. With its magnificent setting extending up the eastern slopes of Table Mountain and overlooking the city and distant Hottentots Holland Mountains, these gardens are truly a national treasure. In addition to thousands of out-of-town visitors, Capetonians flock here on weekends to laze on the grassy lawns, picnicking and reading newspapers while the kids run riot. Walking trails meander through the plantings, which are limited to species indigenous to Southern Africa. Naturally the fynbos biome—the hardy, thin-leaved plants that proliferate in the Cape—is heavily featured, and you will find plenty of proteas, ericas, and restios (reeds). Garden highlights include the Tree Canopy Walkway, a large cycad garden, the Bird Bath (a beautiful stone pool built around a crystal-clear spring), the fragrance garden (which is wheelchair-friendly and has a tapping rail), and the Sculpture Garden. Free 90-minute guided tours take place daily except Sunday. Those who have difficulty walking can enjoy a comprehensive tour lasting one hour (R70, hourly 9–3) in seven-person (excluding the driver) golf carts. Concerts featuring the best of South African entertainment—from classical music to township jazz to indie rock—are held on summer Sundays at 5 (be sure to arrive early to get a spot), and the Galileo Outdoor Cinema screens movies on Wednesdays an hour after sunset. A visitor center by the nursery houses a restaurant, bookstore, and coffee shop. There are also several trails taking you to the top of Table Mountain, from which point you can hike to the cable car station. Unfortunately, muggings have become increasingly more common in the gardens' isolated areas, and women are advised not to walk alone in the upper reaches of the park far from general activity. ⊠ *Rhodes Dr., Newlands* ☎ *021/799–8783* ⊕ *www.sanbi.org* ⊠ *R60.*

Fodor's Choice
★
Robben Island. Made famous by its most illustrious inhabitant, Nelson Mandela, this island, whose name is Dutch for "seals," has a long and sad history. At various times a prison, leper colony, mental institution, and military base, it is finally filling a positive, enlightening, and empowering role in its latest incarnation as a museum.

Declared a World Heritage site on December 1, 1997, Robben Island has become a symbol of the triumph of the human spirit. In 1997 around 90,000 made the pilgrimage; in 2006 more than 300,000 crossed the water to see where some of the greatest South Africans spent decades of their lives. Visiting the island is a sobering experience. The approximately four-hour tour begins at the Nelson Mandela Gateway to Robben Island, an impressive embarkation center that doubles as a conference center. Changing exhibits display historic photos of prisoners and prison life. Next make the 45-minute journey across the water, remembering to watch Table Mountain recede in the distance and imagine what it must have been like to have just received a 20-year jail sentence. Boats leave three or four times a day, depending on season and weather.

Tours are organized by the Robben Island Museum (other operators that advertise Robben Island tours only take visitors on a boat trip *around* the island.) Most guides are former political prisoners, and during the two-hour tour, they will take you through the prison where you will see the cells where Mandela and other leaders were imprisoned. The tour also takes you to the lime quarry, Robert Sobukwe's place of confinement, and the leper church. Due to increased demand for tickets during peak season (December and January), make bookings at least three weeks in advance. Take sunglasses and a hat in summer. ■ TIP→ **You are advised to tip your guide only if you feel that the tour has been informative.** ⊠ *Nelson Mandela Gateway, Victoria and Alfred Waterfront* ☎ *021/413–4200* ⊕ *www.robben-island.org.za* ⊠ *R320.*

Fodor's Choice
★
Table Mountain. Table Mountain truly is one of Southern Africa's most beautiful and impressive natural wonders. The views from its summit are awe-inspiring. The mountain rises more than 3,500 feet above the city, and its distinctive flat top is visible to sailors 65 km (40 miles) out

You can see African penguins, most commonly known as Jackass Penguins, at the beaches in Simon's Town. You can also see African penguins at Cape Town's Two Oceans Aquarium.

to sea. Climbing up the step-like Plattekloof Gorge—the most popular route up—will take two to three hours, depending on your fitness level. There is no water along the route; you *must* take at least 2 liters (½ gallon) of water per person. Table Mountain can be dangerous if you're not familiar with the terrain. Many paths that look like good routes down the mountain end in treacherous cliffs. ⚠ **Do not underestimate this mountain: every year local and foreign visitors to the mountain get lost, some falling off ledges, with fatal consequences.** It may be in the middle of a city, but it is not a genteel town park. Because of occasional muggings near the Rhodes Memorial (east) of the mountain, it's unwise to walk alone on that side. It's recommended that you travel in a group or, better yet, with a guide. If you want to do the climb on your own, wear sturdy shoes or hiking boots; always take warm clothes, including a windbreaker or fleece; travel with a mobile phone; and let someone know of your plans. Consult the staff at a Cape Town Tourism office for more guidelines. Another (much easier) way to reach the summit is to take the cable car, which affords fantastic views. Cable cars (R135 one way) depart from the Lower Cable Station, which lies on the slope of Table Mountain near its western end; the station is a long way from the city on foot, so save your hiking energy for the mountain, and take a taxi or the MyCiti bus to get here. ⊠ *Tafelberg Rd., Table Mountain National Park* ☎ *021/712–0527* ⊕ *www.sanparks. org/parks/table_mountain.*

FAMILY
Fodor's Choice
★

Two Oceans Aquarium. This aquarium is widely considered one of the finest in the world. Stunning displays reveal the regional marine life of the warmer Indian Ocean and the icy Atlantic. It's a hands-on place, with a touch pool for children, opportunities to interact with penguins, and (for certified divers only) to dive in the vast, five-story ocean exhibit with shoals of fish, huge turtles, and sting rays, or the new shark exhibit, where you might share the water with large ragged-tooth sharks (*Carcharias taurus*) and enjoy a legal adrenaline rush (for an additional fee, of course). If you don't fancy getting wet, you can still watch daily feedings in either the ocean, penguin, or shark exhibits. But there's more to the aquarium than just snapping jaws. Look for the trippy jellyfish display, the Knysna seahorses, and the alien-like spider crabs. ⊠ *Dock Rd., Victoria and Alfred Waterfront* ☎ *021/418–3823* ⊕ *www.aquarium.co.za* ✉ *R160.*

Fodor's Choice
★
Woodstock Galleries and Art Tours. Most of Cape Town's best-known galleries are clustered along a few blocks of Sir Lowry Road (*Main Rad.*) and a slightly longer stretch of Albert Road (*Lower Main Rd.*) in Woodstock. In fact, along with the renovation of **The Old Biscuit Mill** (*375 Albert Rd.*) and its celebrated Saturday market, the relocation of galleries like **Stevenson** (*160 Sir Lowry Rd.*) and **The Goodman Cape Town** (*176 Sir Lowry Rd.*) from the CBD in the early aughts were integral to the revitalization of this semi-industrial neighborhood. While wandering from gallery to gallery (**Whatiftheworld, blank projects,** and **Art It Is** are also worthwhile), art lovers can also enjoy the plethora of cafés and boutiques that have sprung up on Sir Lowry Road, and on the stretch of Albert Road between The Biscuit Mill and **The Woodstock Exchange** (*66 Albert Rd.*). While in the area keep an eye out for the remarkable street art—mostly in the form of graffiti murals—much of which predates the gallery invasion. To fully appreciate the latter, take a tour like those offered by **Juma Mkwela** (⊕ *www.townshiptours. co.za/woodstock-creative*). ⊠ *Sir Lowry Rd. at Albert Rd., Woodstock.*

Fodor's Choice
★
Zeitz Museum of Contemporary Art Africa. Opened in September 2017, this museum is the first major museum dedicated to contemporary art from Africa and its diaspora on the African continent. Inhabiting the massively renovated historic Grain Silo in what is now called the Silo District of the V&A Waterfront, the museum itself is a work of art, reimagined by designer Thomas Heatherwick. ⊠ *Silo District, Victoria and Alfred Waterfront* ⊕ *www.zeitzmocaa.museum* ✉ *R180* ⊘ *Closed Tues.*

WHERE TO EAT

Cape Town is the culinary capital of South Africa and quite possibly the continent. It certainly has the best restaurants in southern Africa. Nowhere else in the country is the populace so discerning about food, and nowhere else is there such a wide selection of high-quality restaurants. Western culinary history here dates back to the 17th century—Cape Town was founded specifically to grow food—and that heritage is reflected in the city's cuisine and the fact that a number of restaurants operate in historic townhouses and 18th-century wine estates.

$$
ECLECTIC
Fodor's Choice
★
✕ **Hemelhuijs.** Super-stylish Hemelhuijs is both a showcase for a range of exquisite and fanciful ceramicware, and a centrally located restaurant serving equally fanciful and exquisite food. Though a little pricey for lunch, the owner-chef's inventive seasonal dishes burst with freshness and flavor (think pear-and-celeriac salad with hazelnuts and trout, or a crispy panfried veal of sublime flavor and texture) are well worth

it. **Known for:** supercreative and seasonal menu; constantly evolving designer interior; intimate friendly service. $ *Average main: R140* ⊠ *71 Waterkant St., Cape Town Central* ☎ *021/418–2042* ⊕ *hemelhuijs.co.za* ☉ *Closed Sun. No dinner.*

$$$$ ╳ **La Colombe.** Rightfully known as one of South Africa's most lauded
ECLECTIC fine-dining establishments and listed in the world's top 100 restaurants,
Fodor'sChoice La Colombe's sublime French-Asian inspired tasting menus are served
★ in a delightful minimalist setting overlooking the bucolic green of the Constantia wine valley. The menu changes regularly, but the best option is to order the full eight-course gourmand menu, as there is not a false note to be found. **Known for:** stellar French-Asian fusion haute cuisine; excellent, knowledgeable service; fantastic wine pairings. $ *Average main: R990* ⊠ *Silvermist Mountain Lodge, Main Rd., Constantia Nek, Constantia* ☎ *021/795–0125* ⊕ *www.lacolombe.co.za.*

$$$ ╳ **La Tête.** Although the chef-owner at this small French-influenced bistro
BISTRO would rather people see his menu as "sensibly sustainable" versus "nose-
Fodor'sChoice to-tail," whatever you call it, the dishes served (all in tapas portions at
★ lunch) make fantastic use of the freshest local ingredients, resulting in food that is both uniformly excellent and refreshingly simple. Naturally the menu changes regularly, but favorites include an octopus, cucumber, and mint salad and a mind-blowing pig-cheek, watercress, and radish dish. **Known for:** delightful, experimental food that, in addition to offering lovely fresh produce, employs less commonly favored animal parts; perfect freshly baked madeleines; minimalist ambience. $ *Average main: R170* ⊠ *17 Bree St., Foreshore* ☎ *021/418–1299* ⊕ *latete. co.za* ☉ *Closed Sun. and Mon. No lunch Sat.*

$$$$ ╳ **mulberry & prince.** Exceptionally delicious things are happening in
CONTEMPORARY this dinner-only designer space of exposed brick, funky lighting, and
Fodor'sChoice leather seats. Having adopted the sharing plates concept to great effect,
★ the chef-owners are serving an inventive and changing selection of high-quality "small" dishes that leave a big impression: think buffalo stracciatella on a glaze of strawberry gazpacho with toasted puffed rice, or oysters with a shaved-ice kick of yuzu and grapefruit. **Known for:** kitchen stays open late; understated designer interior; extremely creative small "sharing" plates. $ *Average main: R250* ⊠ *12 Pepper St., Cape Town Central* ☎ *021/422–3301* ⊕ *www.mulberryandprince.co.za* ☉ *Closed Sun. and Mon. No lunch.*

$$$$ ╳ **Nobu.** If you've always wanted to try Nobuyuki "Nobu" Mat-
JAPANESE suhisa's famous Japanese cuisine, but were put off by the potential
FUSION bill in New York or London, Nobu Cape Town offers a chance to sample what may not constitute exactly the same level of cuisine, but will nonetheless make for a highly enjoyable experience. A vast modern space in the Waterfront's One&Only resort provides a fitting backdrop for the splurge of the Omakase multicourse tasting menu, which will likely include dishes such as the signature Alaskan black cod with miso. **Known for:** branch of the famous Nobu chain; glitzy, bold atmosphere. $ *Average main: R475* ⊠ *One&Only Cape Town, Dock Rd., Victoria and Alfred Waterfront* ☎ *021/431–4511* ⊕ *www. oneandonlyresorts.com* ☉ *No lunch.*

6

DID YOU KNOW?

This aerial shot of Cape Town includes the city's most well-known attraction, Table Mountain (background), as well as Signal Hill, Devil's Peak, Lions Head, and the neighborhood of Greenpoint.

$$$$ ECLECTIC Fodor's Choice ★ 🍴 **The Pot Luck Club.** A meal at this playful and inventive tapas-style venture from Cape Town star-chef Luke Dale Roberts always promises fabulous fun. With great harbor and mountain views from its position on the sixth floor of a renovated silo, this hip eatery serves an eclectic but clearly Asian-influenced array of fine-dining nibbles. **Known for:** super-creative and umami-packed dishes with distinct Asian flair; simultaneously hip, elegant, and casual ambience; two seatings for dinner—don't expect to linger if you choose the early one. [$] *Average main: R250* ✉ *Old Biscuit Mill, 375 Albert Rd., Silo top fl., Woodstock* ☎ *021/447–0804* 🌐 *www.thepotluckclub.co.za* 🕓 *Brunch only on Sun.*

$$$$ MODERN EUROPEAN 🍴 **The Roundhouse.** Known for its exceptional natural beauty, Cape Town is surprisingly short on restaurants with killer views; The Roundhouse, serving modern South African cuisine, is helping close that gap. Converted from its origins as an 18th-century Table Mountain–side hunting lodge, this unique fine-dining restaurant overlooking Camps Bay specializes in applying creative flavor combinations to local ingredients—think Karoo ostrich with a fennel seed glaze or hake with carrot and cashew puree. **Known for:** excellent and exceptionally suave team of waiters; gorgeous views over Camps Bay. [$] *Average main: R665* ✉ *The Glen, Round House Rd., Table Mountain National Park* ☎ *021/438–4347* 🌐 *www.theroundhouserestaurant.com* 🕓 *Closed Mon. No dinner Sun. No lunch May–Sept.*

$$$$ ECLECTIC Fodor's Choice ★ 🍴 **The Test Kitchen.** Consistently rated South Africa's top restaurant and on the top 50 restaurants in the world list, this industrial-elegant boutique eatery in Cape Town's trendy Woodstock neighborhood is a struggle to get a table at, but the fantastical sensory and culinary journey that awaits you is a worthy and potentially life-changing reward. Since opening in 2009, TTK, as it's known, has led fine-dining trends in foodie-mecca Cape Town. **Known for:** sensory-culinary food-theater experience; intense flavors from all over the globe presented in unexpected and thrilling ways; great cocktails (served from a delightful trolley), amazing wine pairings; bevy of excellent servers. [$] *Average main: R1600* ✉ *The Old Biscuit Mill, 375 Albert Rd., Shop 104A, Woodstock* ☎ *021/447–2337* 🌐 *www.thetestkitchen.co.za* 🕓 *Closed Sun. and Mon.*

WHERE TO STAY

Finding lodging in Cape Town can be a nightmare during peak travel season (December–January), as many of the more reasonable accommodations are booked up. It's worth traveling between April and August, if you can, to take advantage of the "secret season" discounts that are sometimes half the high-season rate. Other reduced rates can be scored by booking directly online, checking the "Best Available Rate" at large hotels, or simply asking if any specials or discounts are available.

First-time, short-term, or business visitors will want to locate themselves centrally. The historic city center is a vibrant and pedestrian-friendly place by day, but at night can feel a bit deserted and edgy, depending on where you are. Night owls may prefer to stay amid the nonstop action of Long Street or Kloof Street, or at the V&A Waterfront, with its plethora of pedestrian-friendly shopping and dining options (though be aware that locals don't consider the Waterfront the "real" Cape Town). Boutique hotels and bed-and-breakfasts in Gardens are often within walking distance of attractions and dining but will be quieter and often enjoy lovely views. Options along the Atlantic Seaboard are also close to the action and (mostly) pedestrian-friendly, with the added advantage of sea and sunset views. Staying farther out on the Cape Peninsula, whether the False Bay or Atlantic side, provides the closest thing in Cape Town to a beach-vacation atmosphere despite the cold ocean waters. The Southern Suburbs, especially around Constantia or Tokai, can make a good base from which to explore the area's wine estates as well as the peninsula, but you'll be dependent on a car for everything, and should plan on 25 to 45 minutes to get into town.

LODGING ALTERNATIVES

When South Africans travel, they often stay in guesthouses or B&Bs. Among them you will find some of the most elegant and professionally run establishments available, offering everything a hotel does but on a smaller, more personal scale. If you prefer a bit more anonymity or want to save money, consider renting a fully furnished apartment, especially if you're staying two or more weeks. Airbnb has listings in Cape Town, and several agencies can help you make bookings.

Cape Stay. Cape Stay offers a huge selection of accommodations to suit different needs, from very simple and affordable apartments to luxurious villas to special rates at well-known hotels, covering both Cape Town and popular Western Cape destinations. ⊠ *Cape Town* ⊕ *www.capestay.co.za.*

CAPSOL Property & Tourism Solutions. CAPSOL has more than 2,000 high-quality, furnished, fully stocked luxury villas and apartments along the Atlantic seaboard from Cape Town to Bakoven, including Clifton, Bantry Bay, and Camps Bay. Apartments range from R3,000 to R40,000 per night, most with a minimum three-night stay depending on season. ⊠ *The Penthouse, 13 Totnes Ave., Camps Bay* ☎ *021/438–9644* ⊕ *www.capsol.co.za.*

HOTELS AND RESORTS

$$$ **Cape Heritage Hotel.** Built as a private home in 1771, this centrally
HOTEL located boutique hotel's spacious rooms are individually decorated, melding the best of South Africa's dynamic contemporary art scene with colonial elegance, and making the most of the building's teak-beamed ceilings, foot-wide yellowwood floorboards, and numerous other details that recall its gracious past. **Pros:** excellent eateries in adjoining Heritage Square and Bree Street; beautiful old building and quirky style; great location in Cape Town's historic district. **Cons:** bordered by one busy road; parking isn't free; lighting in some rooms is too dark. $ *Rooms from: R3135* ⊠ *90 Bree St., Cape Town Central* ☎ *021/424–4646* ⊕ *www.capeheritage.co.za* ⌂ *20 rooms* ‖⊙‖ *Breakfast.*

$$$$ **Cellars-Hohenort Hotel & Spa.** With acres of gardens and spectacular
HOTEL views across the Constantia Valley, this idyllic old-school getaway in two historic buildings makes the world beyond disappear. **Pros:** beautiful gardens; two pools (one for children); fantastic breakfast in lovely Conservatory Restaurant. **Cons:** need a car to get around; more modern rooms on Cellars side are starting to feel old-fashioned; a lot of stairs to access best rooms. $ *Rooms from: R5700* ⊠ *93 Brommersvlei Rd., Constantia* ☎ *021/794–2137* ⊕ *www.collectionmcgrath.com/hotels/the-cellars-hohenort* ⌂ *53 rooms* ‖⊙‖ *Breakfast.*

$$$$ HOTEL Fodor's Choice ★ **Ellerman House.** Built in 1906 for shipping magnate Sir John Ellerman, what may be Cape Town's finest hotel sits high on a hill up from Sea Point in Bantry Bay, graced with stupendous views of the sea, and an art collection that puts the National Gallery to shame. **Pros:** amazing sense of intimacy and privacy to enjoy this spectacular environment; lovely treats like canapés and cocktails at sunset; fully stocked complimentary guest pantry available 24 hours. **Cons:** Kloof Road is busy (though noise not audible from hotel); often booked a year in advance. [$] *Rooms from: R10000* ✉ *180 Kloof Rd., Bantry Bay, Sea Point* ☎ *021/430–3200* 🌐 *www.ellerman.co.za* 🛏 *15 rooms* 🍴 *Breakfast.*

$$ B&B/INN FAMILY Fodor's Choice ★ **La Grenadine Petit Hotel.** Built around a verdant courtyard shaded by pomegranate, guava, and avocado trees, the five gorgeous rooms at this well-located and good-value hotel are all Gallic-charm-meets-South-African-vintage-hipster: hand-embroidered bed linens, badminton paddles repurposed as mirrors, and art deco light fittings. **Pros:** great bustling location in walking distance to dozens of restaurants and attractions; excellent Continental breakfast filled with homemade treats; wonderful fusion of French and South African vintage style. **Cons:** no TVs in rooms and Wi-Fi can be slow; limited off-street parking; some rooms have bathrooms that are not fully closed off. [$] *Rooms from: R1860* ✉ *15 Park Rd., Gardens* ☎ *021/424–1358* 🌐 *www.lagrenadine.co.za* 🛏 *10 rooms* 🍴 *Breakfast.*

$$$$ HOTEL **Pod.** This compact designer boutique hotel that blends modern sleekness with accents of stone, rough wood, and slate to create a sexy Zen ambience enjoys a great location on a quiet corner just a block from Camps Bay's main drag. **Pros:** excellent breakfast; wellness room with shower for use by late check-outs; eco-friendly additions like door sensor to switch air-conditioning off and tree planting for guests of three nights or more. **Cons:** classic rooms are small, and open-plan bathrooms might be too much sharing; no on-site restaurant after breakfast; eyesore apartment block across the street from some rooms. [$] *Rooms from: R6400* ✉ *3 Argyle Rd., Camps Bay* ☎ *021/438–8550* 🌐 *www.pod.co.za* 🛏 *17 rooms* 🍴 *Breakfast.*

$$$$ HOTEL **The Silo Hotel.** Brilliantly melding industrial grit and sumptuous glamour, Cape Town's hottest new luxury hotel rises out of the old grain silo in the working harbor section of the Waterfront. **Pros:** surprisingly child-friendly; mind-blowing decor and artwork; incredible views from rooftop bar. **Cons:** policy towards nonresidents still being worked out, resulting in guests potentially being treated as strangers; starting category rooms are small; extremely pricey. [$] *Rooms from: R20300* ✉ *Silo Sq., Victoria and Alfred Waterfront* ☎ *021/670–0500* 🌐 *www.theroyalportfolio.com/the-silo/overview* 🛏 *28 rooms* 🍴 *Breakfast.*

$$$$ RESORT Fodor's Choice ★ **Tintswalo Atlantic.** Visitors attracted to the Cape Peninsula for its natural grandeur will think they've died and gone to heaven when arriving at this discreetly luxurious boutique hotel. **Pros:** unique mind-blowing location; attentive service and setup creates a bit of a "safari by the sea" ambience; fantastic breakfast in one of the most beautiful spots imaginable. **Cons:** must drive to all activities and sights; building requirements in the national park mean exteriors of buildings have a prefab look; about a 35- to 40-minute drive from Cape Town Central. [$] *Rooms*

from: R12250 ✉ *Chapman's Peak Dr., Km 2, Hout Bay* ☎ *021/201–0025* 🌐 *www.tintswalo.com/atlantic* 🛏 *11 rooms* 🍴 *Breakfast.*

$$$$ HOTEL Fodor's Choice ★ 🏨 **Twelve Apostles Hotel & Spa.** If you fancy taking a helicopter to the airport or lazing in a bubble bath while looking out floor-to-ceiling windows at breathtaking sea and mountain views, then this award-winning, luxurious hotel and spa that is the only such property within Table Mountain National Park may be for you. **Pros:** wonderfully attentive staff; stunning and unique location in Table Mountain National Park; great breakfast in Azure restaurant with insane sea views. **Cons:** overlooks a road that gets busy; nearest off-site restaurant is at least 10 minutes by car; views and room size are extremely varied. [$] *Rooms from: R7855* ✉ *Victoria Rd., Camps Bay* ☎ *021/437–9000* 🌐 *www.12apostleshotel.com* 🛏 *70 rooms* 🍴 *Breakfast.*

SIDE TRIP FROM CAPE TOWN

THE CAPE WINELANDS

Although the Cape Winelands region is largely thought of as the wine centers of Stellenbosch, Franschhoek, and Paarl, today these areas make up only about 33% of all the land in the Cape under vine. This wine-growing region is now so vast, you can trek to the fringes of the Karoo Desert, in the northeast, and still find a grape. There are around 18 wine routes in the Western Cape, ranging from the Olifants River, in the north, to the coastal mountains of the Overberg and beyond. There's also a well-established Winelands brandy route, and an annual port festival is held in Calitzdorp, in the Little Karoo.

The secret to touring the Cape Winelands is not to hurry. Dally over lunch on a vine-shaded veranda at a 300-year-old estate, enjoy an afternoon nap under a spreading oak, or sip wine while savoring the impossible views. Of the scores of wineries and estates in the Cape Winelands, the ones listed here are chosen for their great wine, their beauty, or their historic significance. It would be a mistake to try to cover them all in less than a week. You have nothing to gain from hightailing it around the Cape Winelands other than a headache. If your interest is more aesthetic and cultural than wine-driven, you would do well to focus on the historic estates of Stellenbosch and Franschhoek. Most Paarl wineries stand out more for the quality of their wine than for their beauty.

GETTING HERE AND AROUND

Driving yourself is undoubtedly the best way to appreciate the area. Each wine route is clearly marked with attractive road signs, and there are complimentary maps available at the tourism bureaus and at most wine farms. Roads in the area are good, and even the dirt roads leading up to a couple of the farms are nothing to worry about.

The best way to get to the Cape Winelands is to take the N2 out of Cape Town and then the R310 to Stellenbosch. Outside of rush hour, this will take you around 45 minutes. Expect some delays during the harvest months (generally late January through late March), when tractors ferry grapes from farms to cellars on the narrower secondary roads. On your way back to Cape Town, stick to the R310 and the N2. Avoid taking the M12, as it gets very confusing, and you'll end up in suburbs that aren't on tourist maps.

The major car-rental agencies have offices in the smaller towns, but it's best to deal with the Cape Town offices. Besides, you'll probably want to pick up a car at the airport. Since driving yourself around limits the amount of wine you can taste, unless you have a designated driver, it's best to join a tour, take a taxi, or—do it in style—rent a limo from Cape Limousine Services. Limos cost about R1,500 for the first hour and R600 per hour thereafter, so they're relatively cost-effective if you have a group of four or five.

Paarl Radio Taxis will transport up to three people at about R10 per kilometer (half mile). Waiting time is around R60 per hour. Larger groups can arrange transportation by minibus. Daksi Cab, based in Stellenbosch, works on a trip rate rather than a per-kilometer basis. A trip to a local restaurant costs around R90 regardless of the number of people. Daksi also provides shuttle service to the airport.

There's no regular bus service to the Cape Winelands suitable for tourists. If you are based in Stellenbosch, however, and don't want to drive to the wineries, you can make use of the Vine Hopper, a minibus that follows a fixed route to six wine farms. Tickets cost around R240 for a one-day ticket and R420 for a two-day ticket, and you'll be given a timetable so that you can get on and off as you please.

We do not recommend Cape Metro trains to Stellenbosch and Paarl because of an increase in violent muggings.

Contacts Paarl Radio Taxis. ☎ *021/872–5671.* **Vine Hopper.** ✉ *Black Horse Centre, Dorp St. at Mark Rd., Stellenbosch* ☎ *021/882–8112* ⊕ *www.vinehopper.co.za.*

TOURS

Most tours of the Cape Winelands are operated by companies based in Cape Town; most have half- or full-day tours, but they vary by company and might include a cheese tasting or cellar tour in addition to wine tasting. Expect to pay around R580 for a half day and R800 for a full day, including all tasting fees. Though you stop for lunch, it is not included in the cost.

EXPLORING

Delaire Graff Estate. This has to be one of the most spectacular settings of any winery in the country. Sit on the terrace of the tasting room or restaurant and look past a screen of pin oaks to the valley below and the majestic crags of the Groot Drakenstein and Simonsberg Mountains. It's an ideal place to stop for lunch, and you'll need at least three hours to do your meal and the wines justice. The wine lounge has an upmarket, clubby feel, and the staff are slick and on top of their game. So are the crew in the vineyard and cellar. Within just three years the estate has gone from so-so to stellar, and now it's regarded as one of the country's top 10 wine producers. Although the Botmaskop Red Blend is the farm's flagship wine, do try the Cabernet Franc Rose. It's a new release and a lovely take on a varietal that usually gets added to the Bordeaux Blend. The Coastal Cuvée Sauvignon Blanc is exceptional and is reeling in the awards. The Chardonnay is very elegant with fresh

CLOSE UP

South African Wine

The South African wine industry is booming. Buried by sanctions during apartheid, South African wines were largely unknown internationally. But today there's enormous interest in South African reds *and* whites. Although South Africa has a reputation for delivering good quality at the bottom end of the market, more and more ultrapremium wines are emerging. Good-quality wines at varied prices are readily available—even in supermarkets.

Currently white wine production outstrips red, but the quality continually improves for both, and they regularly win international awards. Particularly notable is Pinotage, South Africa's own grape variety, a cross between Pinot Noir and Cinsaut (formerly Hermitage). Chenin Blanc is the country's most widely planted variety and is used in everything from blends to bubbly (known in South Africa as Méthode Cap Classique).

The industry is transforming itself slowly. The illegal *dop* (drink) or tot system, in which farmers pay some of laborers' wages in wine, is finally on its way out, and there's a concerted effort among producers to uplift their laborers' quality of life. Many international companies refuse to import wine from farms that don't secure their workers' rights, and many farms are working at black empowerment. Tukulu, Riebeek Cellars, Thandi Wines, Ses'Fikile (which translated means "we have arrived"), M'hudi, and Freedom Road are just some of the pioneers. Three farms that deserve a special mention when it comes to transformation are Bosman Family Vineyard (Wellington), Solms-Delta wine estate (Franschhoek), and Van Loveren Family Cellar (Robertson). Tragically, South Africa has one of the highest incidences of fetal alcohol syndrome, a legacy left over from the dop system.

If you're serious about wine, arm yourself with *John Platter's Wine Guide* or visit 🌐 *www.winemag.co.za* (the new digital form of *Wine* magazine), featuring local wineries. For an in-depth read and fantastic photos, pick up *Wines and Vineyards of South Africa* by Wendy Torein or *New World of Wine from the Cape of Good Hope: The Definitive Guide to the South African Wine Industry* by Phyllis Hands, David Hughes, and Keith Phillips. *Wines of the New South Africa: Tradition and Revolution* by Tim James is also recommended reading.

6

lime and creamy butterscotch flavors. ✉ *Helshoogte Pass Rd., between Stellenbosch and Franschhoek, Stellenbosch* ☎ *021/885–8160* 🌐 *www.delaire.co.za* 🎫 *Tastings R70 for 5 wines.*

WHERE TO EAT

$$$$ ECLECTIC Fodor's Choice ★

🍴 **Tokara.** At the top of the Helshoogte Pass with absolutely amazing views of the valley and mountains, Tokara is a Winelands must-visit, known for innovation and playful twists. The adventurous menu changes seasonally but could include dishes like beef tartare with Parmesan custard, cured egg, and anchovy and pepper vinaigrette or tempura line fish with sushi rice, avocado, sesame, and wasabi mayonnaise. **Known for:** chef Richard Carstens; surprising flavors; child-friendly fine dining. [$] *Average main: R205* ✉ *Helshoogte Pass Rd. (R310), Stellenbosch* ☎ *021/885–2550* 🌐 *www.tokara.co.za* 🕘 *Closed Mon. No dinner Sun.*

RWANDA AND UGANDA

WELCOME TO RWANDA AND UGANDA

TOP REASONS TO GO

★ **Gorilla Trekking.** The sheer size and eerily humanlike interactions of the world's largest living primates will leave you spellbound.

★ **Volcanoes National Park.** This slice of the Virunga Mountains may be synonymous with gorilla trekking, but its active volcanoes, caves, and grasslands offer stunning views, rewarding hikes, and the chance to see buffalo, hyena, golden monkeys, and some 200 bird species.

★ **Kigali.** Arguably East Africa's safest and most future-focused city, Rwanda's capital is a patchwork of palm tree–lined boulevards, artisan coffee shops, and international restaurants.

★ **Off the Beaten Path.** Uganda is home to the Big Five, but not the tourist hordes and inflated rates that plague the more well-known safari parks in Kenya, Tanzania, and South Africa.

★ **Kampala.** Uganda's capital city is regionally renowned for its dancing-till-dawn nightlife, bustling markets, and white-knuckle motorbike taxi rides.

At 26,338 square km (10,169 square miles), Rwanda encompasses 5 volcanoes, 23 lakes, and a spectacular assortment of wildlife. Biological diversity is concentrated in three national parks: Nyungwe National Park, which has the largest mountain rain forest in Africa; Volcanoes National Park, home to the critically endangered mountain gorillas; and Akagera National Park, the largest protected wetland in Central Africa.

Uganda, Rwanda's larger northern neighbor, spans 236,040 square km (146,675 square miles), with Kenya to the east, the Democratic Republic of the Congo to the west, and South Sudan to the north. "The Pearl of Africa" has 10 national parks, more than 1,000 species of birds, and 13 types of primates, including mountain gorillas.

1 Rwanda. Trekking mountain gorillas in this landlocked country of undulating hills, terraced farmlands, volcanic mountain chains, and dense rain forests is an experience unlike any other. You'll witness awe-inspiring panoramas, a plethora of primates, friendly local people, and one of Africa's most promising capitals.

2 Uganda. Uganda's dramatically diverse landscapes, from the snow-capped Rwenzori Mountains to the mist-cloaked hillsides of Bwindi Impenetrable National Park, make it an award-winning destination among travelers.

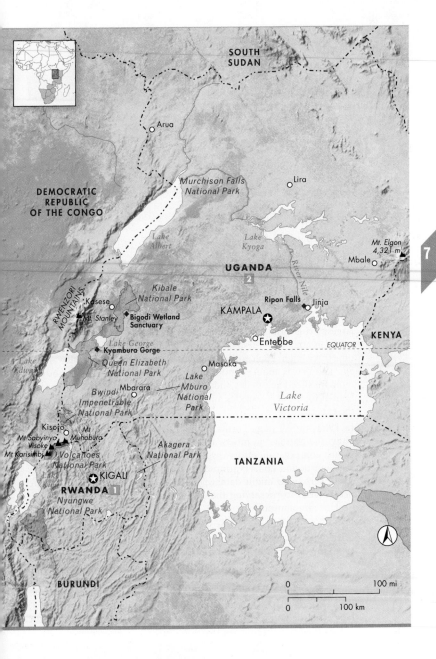

SOUTH
SUDAN

Arua

Murchison Falls
National Park

Lira

DEMOCRATIC
REPUBLIC
OF THE CONGO

Lake
Albert

Lake
Kyoga

Mt. Elgon
4,321 m

7

UGANDA

Mbale

RWENZORI MOUNTAINS

Kibale
National Park

Ripon Falls

Jinja

Kasese

KAMPALA

Mt. Stanley

Bigodi Wetland
Sanctuary

KENYA

Lake George

Entebbe

EQUATOR

Kyambura Gorge

Lake
Edward

Queen Elizabeth
National Park

Masaka

Lake
Mburo
National
Park

Bwindi

Mbarara

Impenetrable
National Park

Lake
Victoria

Kisoro

Mt
Muhabura

Akagera
National Park

Mt Sabyinyo

Visoke

Mt Karisimbi

Volcanoes
National Park

TANZANIA

KIGALI

RWANDA

Nyungwe
National Park

BURUNDI

0   100 mi

0   100 km

Updated by
Leah Feiger
and Charlotte
Beauvoisin

Looking into the eyes of a mountain gorilla, trekkers will experience a profound sense of recognition that no lion or elephant encounter, however thrilling, can match. Experiencing the exchange in the lush landscapes of this magnificent animal's own territory can humble even the most seasoned traveler.

Fewer than 900 mountain gorillas remain, and more than half of them live in the Virunga Moutains, a string of volcanoes that straddles Uganda, Rwanda, and the Democratic Republic of the Congo. The rest reside in Uganda's Bwindi Impenetrable National Park. Instability in the Congo makes Rwanda and Uganda the best places to behold the world's largest living primates. Though the required permit seems expensive, a golden hour with these fascinating animals will likely rank as an all-time travel high. Each gorilla group offers a new experience: Rwanda's Susa group was famously studied by primatologist Dian Fossey and has multiple silverback males and several sets of twins. Other groups are known for power struggles and female snatching. Some trekkers find the experience so exhilarating they go back for a second day.

In 1981, the Virunga gorilla population dipped to 254 individuals. Now, the gorillas' numbers are on the rise, thanks in large part to robust conservation efforts by both countries. Those include attracting high-dollar, conservation-conscious visitors rather than hordes of viewers, who might damage the environment. Revenue from the permit goes to preserving the endangered primates and supporting nearby communities.

Picking a country for your trek will depend on your priorities. Rwanda's pricier permits, US$1,500, are offset by the close proximity of the gorillas to the country's main airport, a two-hour drive on excellent roads. The Rwandan trek is generally gentler, and the less dense foliage is more photo-friendly. Meanwhile, Uganda offers two gorilla-spotting locations and a bargain off-season permit price of US$450 (normally US$600). Both Uganda parks are a solid seven-hour drive from the main airport. However, the journey presents excellent sightseeing opportunities for travelers with flexible itineraries. The upshot: If you're pressed for time and prefer easier gorilla access, pick Rwanda. If you've got a few days for exploring the surrounding countryside or prefer to go during the off-season, Uganda is your best bet.

Regardless of which country you choose for your gorilla trek, it's a heady experience you'll never find in a zoo, as mountain gorillas don't survive in captivity. All told, you'll witness one of mankind's closest relatives in its natural habitat and contribute to its preservation.

WHEN TO GO

Gorilla trekking occurs year-round, but the optimal time is during the two dry seasons: June through September (the long dry season) and December through February (the short dry season). Travelers willing to brave a wet and muddy hike in October and November or between March and May will be rewarded by lower lodging prices, fewer crowds, and often shorter treks as gorillas keep to the lower slopes during the rainy seasons. Uganda slashes its gorilla permits from US$600 to US$450 from April to May, as well as in November. Rwanda does not, but lodges in both countries offer low-season rates. Rest assured, whenever you go, your gorilla encounter will not disappoint.

TOUR OPERATORS

The complex logistics of planning a gorilla-tracking safari means all but the hardiest of independent travelers would be advised to rely on the services of a reputable tour operator with local expertise. The following list includes a selection of established, high-end operators with local offices in both Uganda or Rwanda. ■TIP→ See the specific country section for country-specific tour operators. All offer tailor-made tours; some also provide scheduled group departures as a more affordable alternative.

Journeys Discovering Africa. One of the few upmarket East Africa operators with fully owned operations in both Rwanda and Uganda, Journeys Discovering Africa receive glowing feedback for their customized private tours and affordable group safaris. ⊠ *51 Elmwood Ave., Harrow* ☎ *0800/088–5470 toll-free in U.K., 888/428–2772 toll-free in U.S.* ⊕ *www.journeysdiscoveringafrica.com.*

Volcanoes Safaris. This established safari operator, with sales offices in the United Kingdom and the United States, offers luxury gorilla and chimp tracking safaris of Uganda and Rwanda. Their itineraries focus largely on their own lodges, but they are well-regarded upmarket properties in stunning locations. ⊠ *27 Lumumba Ave., Kampala* ☎ *0414/346–464, 0772/741–718* ⊕ *www.volcanoessafaris.com.*

RWANDA

Rwanda has made massive strides in security and national development in the two decades since the infamous 1994 genocide and is now internationally recognized as one of the safest countries in Africa. A sense of order prevails: violent crime is nearly nonexistent, and police can be spotted at most major intersections. New roads and tidy villages characterize the countryside. Citizens are required to participate in a monthly day of community service, and you'll be hard-pressed to find litter on the streets, particularly plastic bags, which are banned. You'll find new businesses, homes, and roadways under construction in every corner of the country.

It's worth noting that Rwanda offers more than just gorillas: The primeval forests of Nyungwe National Park are inhabited by more than 75 different mammals, including hundreds of chimpanzees and nearly 300 bird species. Akagera National Park in the northeast offers the Big Five and a savanna safari experience without the usual khaki-clad crowds.

PLANNING
GETTING HERE AND AROUND

Kigali International Airport, previously known as Gregoire Kayibanda Airport, is approximately 10 km (6 miles) or a 20-minute drive from central Kigali. It serves as the primary gateway for Rwanda's gorilla safaris. There are no direct flights from the United States, but many carriers offer one-stop options. Brussels Airlines departs from Washington, D.C., with a stopover in Brussels. Ethiopian Airlines also flies from Washington, D.C., to Kigali by way of Addis Ababa. Lufthansa offers a flight from Chicago to Kigali via

Rwanda's Nyungwe National Park has East Africa's only Canopy Walkway, which hangs 60 meters (196 feet) above the forest floor providing stunning views of the park.

Brussels. Other airlines that fly to Kigali include Air France, KLM, South African Airways, and Turkish Airlines.

Uniformed taxi drivers are in abundance around the airport and will zip you downtown for a negotiable fee of around Rwf15,000 (US$18). Be warned that pricier hotels like the Kigali Serena Hotel draw higher fare quotes.

Airport Kigali International Airport. ⊠ *KN5 Rd., Kanombe.*

ESSENTIALS

Wi-Fi in Rwanda, though often spotty, can be commonly found at most restaurants, cafés, and hotels. Outside of Kigali, however, Wi-Fi becomes much more unreliable. If you think you might be in need of consistent Internet or phone access, bring an unlocked cell phone and get a SIM card upon arrival; MTN and Tigo are considered to be the most consistent providers.

Visitors to Rwanda are required to present proof of yellow fever vaccination upon arrival at the airport. Hepatitis A and B vaccinations are recommended. Adventurous eaters and travelers to rural areas should also consider the typhoid vaccine. Malaria is a risk, so consult with your doctor on antimalarial tablet options. At the very least, sleep under a mosquito net at night and wear insect repellent during the day. Avoid tap water and opt for bottled instead. Petty theft and muggings do occur, so don't wander around alone at night, particularly in urban areas.

Rwanda's official currency is the Rwandan franc (Rwf). At this writing the exchange rate is approximately Rwf840 to US$1. Although larger

RWANDA FAST FACTS

Size 26,338 square km (10,169 square miles) and roughly the size of Switzerland.

Population Approximately 12 million.

Capital Kigali.

Number of National Parks Four: Volcanoes National Park, Nyunwe National Forest, Akagera National Park, Gishwati Forest National Park.

Number of Private Reserves There are no private reserves.

Big Five All here, with lions reintroduced in 2015 and rhinos following soon after in 2017 due to efforts of the Rwandan government and African Parks.

Language The national language is Kinyarwanda, and English, French, and Swahili are also official languages.

Time Rwanda is on CAST (Central African Standard Time), which is two hours ahead of Greenwich mean time and seven hours ahead of North American Eastern Standard Time.

Drives on the right

Currency Rwandan franc (RWF)

hotels and tour companies may accept U.S. dollars and credit cards, expect to pay in francs at local shops and restaurants. You can withdraw the local currency at ATMs, found in large cities, or exchange your U.S. dollars at the airport and local banks. US$50 and US$100 bills will fetch better exchange rates, as will newer notes. Bills printed before 2005 may not be accepted.

Tourist visas are required in Rwanda, and 30-day visas can be obtained upon arrival for certain passports, including those from the United States. Check with your embassy or consulate at least a month before your flight to see if rules and regulations have changed. Your passport must be valid for six months from the date of intended travel and contain at least one blank page.

ABOUT THE RESTAURANTS

Rwanda's culinary scene is on the rise. Local and international restaurants can be found all over the country. In addition to international offerings, try some of Rwanda's traditional dishes; brochettes (grilled meat or fish on a stick), *akabenz* (roasted and marinated pork), and *misuzu* (fried sweet plantains) are delicious and available throughout the country. Unfortunately, food poisoning is common, and avoiding raw vegetables can go a long way. Tipping is considered to be largely unnecessary, though if service is exemplary feel free to leave a few small notes.

ABOUT THE LODGES AND HOTELS

The quality of hotels and lodges in Rwanda has improved in leaps and bounds over the past several years. Expect good food; excellent, personalized service; and a few special touches—like a hot water bottle under your sheets—from Rwanda's best. Bring travel necessities, such as toothbrushes and shampoo, but don't be surprised if those items are already awaiting your arrival. Most lodges will supply rooms with mosquito bed nets, although some properties seal the rooms well enough to do without.

TOP REASONS TO GO TO RWANDA

Gorilla Trekking. Navigate your way through emerald foliage, bamboo forests, and gauzelike mists to behold the world's largest living primates on their own turf. Their sheer size and eerily humanlike interactions will leave you spellbound, and Rwanda's focus on their conservation is impressive.

Volcanoes National Park. This slice of the Virunga Mountains may be synonymous with gorilla trekking, but its active volcanoes, lakes, and grasslands offer stunning views and rewarding hikes. You can spot buffalo, hyena, golden monkeys, and some 200 bird species in its environs.

Kigali. Arguably East Africa's safest and most future-focused city, Rwanda's capital is a patchwork of palm tree–lined boulevards, artisan coffee shops, international restaurants, and a downtown dotted with new buildings.

Nyunge National Forest Home to roving families of chimpanzees, colobus monkeys, and almost 300 colorful bird species, this mountainous rain forest is located in the southwest of the country and offers travelers canopy walks, bird spotting, primate trekking, waterfall hikes, and tea field visits.

Akagera National Park: With newly imported lions and rhinos, Rwanda's main safari park is once again home to Africa's Big Five. Akagera is just two hours east of Kigali, and the spectacular northern plains cannot be missed.

Restaurant and hotel reviews have been shortened. For full information, visit Fodors.com.

WHAT IT COSTS IN U.S. DOLLARS

	$	$$	$$$	$$$$
Restaurants	under $12	$12–$20	$21–$30	over $30
Hotels	under $250	$250–450	$451–$600	over $600

Most safari prices refer to an all-inclusive per-person rate excluding tax (a few only operate on a half-board rate), assuming double occupancy. Hotel rates refer to double occupancy excluding tax.

TOUR OPERATORS
Contacts Thousand Hills Expeditions. ✉ *1000 Rue de L'Akanyaru, Kiyovu* ☎ *0280/311–000, 0788/351–000* ⊕ *www.thousandhillsexpeditions.com.*

VISITOR INFORMATION
Rwanda's Tourism and Conservation Department, Remarkable Rwanda, has a decent website that will give you a helpful overview of possible destinations and activities, but don't expect a timely response to personal inquiries. For more candid and thorough reviews, your best bet is Living in Kigali, a blog that has restaurant and site suggestions and tips for traveling outside the city.

Contacts Living in Kigali. ⊕ *www.livinginkigali.com.* **Rwanda's Tourism and Conservation Department.** ⊕ *www.rwandatourism.com.*

VOLCANOES NATIONAL PARK

Game
★★★★★
Park Accessibility
★★★
Getting Around
★★★
Accommodations
★★★★★
Scenic Beauty
★★★★★

Volcanoes National Park is one of only four places on earth where visitors can commune with the critically endangered mountain gorillas. The park encompasses a 160-square-km (62-square-mile) slice of the Virunga Mountains, including a string of nine volcanoes that extends into neighboring Uganda and the Democratic Republic of the Congo. The ecologically rich Virunga region is home to more than half of the world's mountain gorillas, which number fewer than 900.

Volcanoes was gazetted in 1925, making it the first national park in Rwanda. Tourism activities were suspended during the Rwanda Civil War but resumed in 1999. Now travelers can visit one of 10 habituated gorilla groups by purchasing a permit for US$750. A maximum of eight people are allowed to visit each group daily.

Gorillas may be the headline act, but there's plenty more to see and do in the park. Hiking enthusiasts can navigate a network of trails through the Virunga Mountains, including summiting the 3,711-meter (12,175-foot) Mount Bisoke, with its crater lake and rewarding cross-border views of the Democratic Republic of the Congo. History and mammal buffs can visit the grave and research center of prominent primatologist Dian Fossey, whose life and work inspired the movie *Gorillas in the Mist*.

A visit with the park's population of golden monkeys is worth the US$100 permit. These hyper, cherub-cheeked primates swing through the bamboo forests, occasionally swooping down to the forest floor for a particularly choice bamboo shoot. Be warned that catching them on camera can prove tricky. Volcanoes is also home to forest elephants, buffalo, spotted hyenas, and nearly 200 bird species.

WHEN TO GO

The best time for gorilla trekking is during Rwanda's two dry seasons: from December to early February and from June to September. The drier months make for a more pleasant (and less muddy) hike. Note that this is high season, so secure your gorilla permit well in advance and prepare to pay more for lodging. The temperate climate can be fickle regardless of when you go, so pack a jacket for cool evenings and a rain poncho.

GETTING HERE AND AROUND

Most tour operators will provide transport for the two-hour trip from Kigali to Musanze, the country's bustling gorilla tourism hub. Independent travelers can catch a public bus from Kigali's Nyabugogo bus station to Musanze for less than US$5. ■TIP➔ **All gorilla trekkers are required to secure gorilla permits in advance. Less than 100 permits are available each day, so visitors are advised to purchase them early from tour operators or by emailing the Rwanda Development Board.** All trekkers must arrive at the park's headquarters in the nearby village of Kinigi at 7 am, where they're assigned to a gorilla group. Transportation for the trek is required. Tour operators will generally provide a vehicle, or trekkers can rent a 4x4 and driver in Musanze from US$80.

WHERE TO STAY

$$$$
HOTEL
Fodor's Choice
★
 Bisate Lodge. Located in the foothills of Mt. Bisoke, this stunning lodge offers an eco-luxury experience accompanied by unique insights into rural Rwanda. **Pros:** warm and attentive staff; breathtaking views from every well-designed and large suite; excellent food made primarily with local ingredients. **Cons:** lodge access for elderly and disabled guests is limited; 40-minute drive to gorilla trekking. $ *Rooms from: US$2200* ✉ *Kinigi* ☎ *27/11–807–1800* ⊕ *www.wilderness-safaris.com/camps/bisate-lodge* ➪ *6 suites* ⦿*All-inclusive.*

$
B&B/INN
 Villa Gorilla. This Rwandan-owned boutique hotel is a top pick for ape trekkers looking for local flavor without scrimping on comfort. **Pros:** five-minute drive to park headquarters; welcoming and responsive staff; meals included with room. **Cons:** noise from the lobby filters into the rooms; only one wine choice. $ *Rooms from: US$212* ✉ *Kinigi* ☎ *250/788–592–924* ⊕ *www.villagorillarwanda.com* ➪ *4 rooms, 3 cottages* ⦿*All meals.*

$$$$
HOTEL
 Virunga Lodge. Perched on a 2,300-meter (7,500-foot) ridge between Lake Ruhondo and Lake Bulera, this remote lodge offers a bush-chic experience and breathtaking views. **Pros:** massive bathrooms with lake-and-mountain views; secluded and spacious patios; well-appointed common area with communal dinner. **Cons:** staff can be scarce; food quality is inconsistent; 45-minute drive to gorilla trekking. $ *Rooms from: US$1652* ✉ *Mwiko Village* ☎ *250/782–574–363* ⊕ *www.volcanoessafaris.com* ➪ *10 rooms* ⦿*All-inclusive.*

$
B&B/INN
 Waterfront Resort Lake Kivu. This intimate inn on the shores of Lake Kivu is well worth the hour drive from Volcanoes National Park for a post–gorilla trek chill-out; the gentle shush of waves and the chants of local fisherman can be heard from the botanical-garden-worthy grounds. **Pros:** stunning grounds with palm trees, tropical flowers, and thatched-roof lounge areas; spacious rooms with comfortable beds; private beach. **Cons:** mediocre food; Wi-Fi only in lobby; noise at night can permeate into the rooms. $ *Rooms from: US$100* ✉ *Gisenyi* ☎ *250/789–528–772* ➪ *7 rooms, 3 cottages* ⦿*Breakfast.*

DID YOU KNOW?

Rwanda's Volcanoes National Park encompasses six active and three extinct volcanoes including Mount Sabyinyo, which is home to mountain gorillas.

NYUNGWE NATIONAL PARK

Game
★★★
Park Accessibility
★★★
Getting Around
★★★
Accommodations
★★
Scenic Beauty
★★★★★

Nyungwe National Park may be most famous for chimpanzee trekking, but this stretch of 1,020 square km (394 square miles) in southwestern Rwanda teams with a dazzling array of flora and fauna and an impressive spread of hiking trails. Meander though and you'll feel as though you've wandered onto the set of Jurassic Park. You'll spot 100-year-old trees, fern-fringed waterfalls, and oversize driver ants to the accompaniment of a cacophony of bird calls.

Nestled in the Albertine Rift, a biodiversity-rich area of East Africa, Nyungwe is home to nearly 300 bird species, more than 75 different mammals, and some 1,000 plant types. It was recognized as a national park in 2005 and remains Africa's largest protected mountain rain forest. Trails cut through the park's closed-canopy forests, bamboo thickets, and orchid-filled swamps. Be warned that the weather can be wet—it is a rain forest after all. The park receives more than 2,000 mm (79 inches) of precipitation annually and provides water to approximately 70% of the county. In 2006, an exploring team claimed to find the furthest source of the Nile River in Nyungwe.

Most visitors come to witness the park's 500-some-odd chimpanzees or its "super group" of several hundred black-and-white colobus monkeys, whose clever antics and aerial acrobatics will keep your camera clicking. But chimps and giant troupes aren't the only show in town. With 13 species, the park has one of the highest primate diversity concentrations in the world. You'll see L'Hoest's monkeys frolicking around the roads, and, if you're really lucky, the reclusive owl-faced monkey.

Primate trekking can be costly (a chimpanzee pass is US$90 for foreigners), but visitors can also opt for a reasonably priced guided hike for US$40. The 13 trails range from the 2-km (1.2-mile) Karamba Trail (an excellent choice for birders) to the rigorous Mount Bigugu Trail that leads to the park's highest point. Hardy trekkers can also take in an impressive waterfall on the four-hour Isumo Trail or spend three days camping along the Congo Nile Trail.

WHEN TO GO

Late June through early September is dry season and high season at Nyungwe for good reason: the rain forest receives a reprieve from daily downpours, meaning you can explore all day. But even during the wet season, from March to May, showers generally arrive in the afternoon, leaving plenty of time for morning hiking and an outdoor lunch. Plus, you'll enjoy less competition for tours and discounted rates at some hotels.

GETTING HERE AND AROUND

Nyungwe National Park is approximately 225 km (140 miles), or four to five hours driving, from Kigali. Many visitors choose to hire a car and driver. Budget travelers can take one of three bus lines from Kigali's central bus station, Nyabugogo, to the park for Rwf5,000 (US$7), though quarters are cramped, and drivers can be reckless. Alternately, you can fly into Kamembe Airport, a half-hour drive from the park's western edge, and arrange for pickup with your lodge. For transport inside the park, your best bet is to hire a car from Kigali or ask for recommended drivers at your accommodation. Most activities depart from the park's Uwinka Reception Center. To get there from nearby Gisakura village, the location of our lodging suggestions, you'll need to use a private car or a public bus. Note that chimpanzee trekking requires a 4x4.

EXPLORING

FAMILY **Canopy Walkway.** In 2010, Nyungwe National Park opened East Africa's only Canopy Walkway, a 200-meter (656-foot) wood bridge suspended 60 meters (196 feet) above the ground. The "hanging trail" affords magnificent views of the treetop canopy and up-close bird encounters. Nyungwe is a little-known birders' paradise, though spotting them typically requires the help of a trained guide, who can be secured at one of the park's three reception centers. ■ TIP→ Rain is a frequent occurrence in Nyungwe so a raincoat is essential. If you don't have a raincoat, one can be rented, as can walking boots and walking sticks. ⊕ *www.rwandatourism.com* ✉ *US$60*.

WHERE TO STAY

$$$$ **Nyungwe House.** You'll forget you're next to a rain forest in this lavish retreat—until you slide back the glass balcony doors to let in forest breezes and birdsong. **Pros:** rooms are practically suites with private balconies; close proximity to the park; included meal plan is wideranging and good. **Cons:** short and expensive wine list; in-room Wi-Fi is spotty at best. $ *Rooms from: US$1360* ⊠ *Gisakura* ☎ *971/4426–1099 reservations* ⊕ *www.oneandonlyresorts.com/one-and-only-nyungwe-house-rwanda* ✑ *24 rooms* ☉ *All meals.*

HOTEL

Fodor'sChoice
★

$ **Nyungwe Top View Hill Hotel.** Stunning views of mist-veiled mountains, excellent service, and convenient access to Nyungwe National Park, all for US$220, make this hilltop hotel a best-value option. **Pros:** spacious cottages; helpful staff; stunning balcony views from every room. **Cons:** hotel can be drafty; rooms show some wear; entrance road is steep and rocky. $ *Rooms from: US$220* ⊠ *Gisakura* ☎ *250/787–109–335* ⊕ *www.nyungwehotel.com* ✑ *12 cottages* ☉ *Breakfast.*

HOTEL

7

IF YOU HAVE TIME IN RWANDA

AKAGERA NATIONAL PARK

This 1,122-square-km (433-square-mile) park along Rwanda's northeastern border with Tanzania is the safari scene's best-kept secret. You can experience prime safari lands without the Land Rover wagon circles that surround wildlife in Kenya and Tanzania. The borders encompass a labyrinth of lakes and papyrus swamps teeming with hippos and crocodiles, plus savannas dotted by giraffes, zebras, elephants, and nearly a dozen varieties of antelope.

Originally established in 1934, Akagera has weathered a tumultuous history. The park lost half its territory and all of its lions in the wake of the 1994 genocide. Now, however, the park has experienced a rebirth. Nonprofit African Parks partnered with the Rwandan government to spend approximately US$10 million on restoring the country's only protected savanna environment. Animals that once roamed Akagera have since been reintroduced to the park, with lions brought back in 2015; rhinoceroses returned in 2017. Akagera National Park is now home to Africa's Big Five once more, and the park has a new thatch-roof reception center, a café, and a luxury tented lodge. It also offers camping facilities, guided game drives, boat cruises, and fishing trips. For now, Akagera is still off the main tourist circuit, though this will likely change in the coming years. Currently, if you're seeking solitude and a one-on-one experience with nature, it doesn't get better than this.

GETTING HERE AND AROUND

The park is self-drive, so your best option is to rent a 4x4 in Kigali. Akagera is 2½ hours from the capital city. Rental fees are at least US$200 per day and typically include gas and a driver-guide. If you're comfortable driving yourself, you can find 4x4s starting from US$65 per day. Park entrance fees are US$40 per day. Visitors are encouraged to hire a guide for a daily fee of US$30. Should you opt to forego the guide, pick up the helpful guidebook for US$3 from the reception center just inside the Kiyonza Entrance Gate. It takes approximately six hours to drive from the park's southern entrance to the northernmost exit gate, so plan for a long day trip from Kigali or an overnight at one of the campsites.

WHERE TO STAY

$$ HOTEL **Ruzizi Tented Lodge.** Akagera visitors flock to this solar-powered tented lodge on the shores of Lake Ihema to commune with nature without foregoing warm showers, three-course meals, and a fully stocked bar. **Pros:** camping without the hassle; excellent showers; beautiful communal deck with lakeside views. **Cons:** no Wi-Fi; drinking water gets expensive; wildlife may keep you up at night. $ *Rooms from: US$390* ✉ *Akagera National Park* ☎ *250/787–113–300* 🌐 *www.ruzizilodge.com* 🕓 *Closes 2 wks in Nov.* 🛏 *9 tents* 🍴 *All meals.*

GATEWAY CITY

Kigali's location in the center of Rwanda makes it the logical, and convenient, place to start or finish any Rwandan adventure. It's clean, safe, and home to some great cultural and dining options.

7

KIGALI

Kigali is a fascinating example of a future-focused African city. Once known for civil war and genocide, Rwanda's capital has transformed itself into a model of urban development. In the two decades after the genocide, exiles have flocked to the city flush with education, investment dollars, and entrepreneurial ideas. Foreigners have jumped in the mix, opening sushi joints, yoga studios, bakeries, artisan coffee shops, and even a co-working space for start-ups. The nightlife is also picking up, and you'll find dance clubs, sports bars, and live music.

With a population of approximately 1 million people, the city is the commercial and governmental hub for the rest of the country. Its trash-free boulevards, smooth roads, LED streetlights, and meticulously manicured medians are a closer approximation of Europe than East Africa. It's an image the country is keen to expand. The new and ultramodern Kigali Convention Centre and many new hotels have ushered in a wave of international conferences and meetings, as the slick master plan calls for an overhaul of the business district and more urban housing.

Even without gleaming new buildings, the city is something to behold. The undulating skyline of red-roofed houses, terraced farm plots, and brilliant green foliage is stunning. Kigali is also safe: violent crime is rare, particularly against foreigners, and police do their job, including handing out speeding tickets. You'll rarely find yourself hassled, and negotiating traffic will be your biggest obstacle. Some expatriates say that they feel safer raising their kids in Kigali than in U.S. cities.

GETTING HERE AND AROUND

Kigali is relatively easy to navigate. The ubiquitous motorbike taxis, called "motos," are a cheap and convenient mode of transport and a ride from the airport to the city center costs less than US$3. Note that moto fares are negotiable, and their safety record is questionable. Professionally run taxis are marked and metered, though they are generally the most expensive option. An airport transfer to town can run upward of US$15. Unmarked private taxis are also available, but be prepared to negotiate the fare in advance. If you plan to stay in Kigali for several days, you may want to rent a car from US$65 per day. The roads are generally in excellent condition, but be warned that other drivers, pedestrians, and motos can make driving a stressful experience.

EXPLORING

Kigali Genocide Memorial Centre. Visitors should not miss this well-conceived tribute to the victims of the 1994 genocide, which saw an estimated 1 million people killed in the span of 100 days. Outside, a terraced series of mass graves entombs some 250,000 victims. Inside, an informative exhibition walks visitors through the historical lead-up to the Rwandan genocide and the global community's faltering response. A display of skulls and bones alongside personal effects personifies the tragedy. A second section explores mankind's capacity for cruelty with a display on genocides from around the world. The exhibition ends with enlarged black-and-white photos of child genocide victims, ranging from 8 months to 17 years. Each picture is accompanied by a placard listing the child's favorite foods and activities and his or her final moments. There is no entrance fee, but donations are encouraged. The audio guide is worthwhile for US$15. ⊠ *KG 14 Ave., Gisozi* ⊕ *www.kgm.rw* ☑ *Free.*

Presidential Palace Museum. Former Rwandan President Juvenal Habyarimana's home offers an intimate look at the actors and spaces that gave rise to the 1994 genocide. The president's assassination is said to have sparked the killing spree. The remains of his private plane, which was shot down over his home, are still on display outside the museum walls. The sunroom where the president's wife and her infamous coterie, the *akuzu*, plotted the genocide still has the original furniture and carpet. A tour guide will point out artifacts of the president's paranoia: censors on the stairs, a secret escape route, and a bathroom safe once stuffed with cash. Other highlights include a Rwanda-shape pool for the president's 8-meter (26-foot) pet python and a witchcraft consultation room next to the house's Catholic chapel. Much of the furniture was looted during the genocide but pieces such as Habyarimana's imposing desk, an elephant-foot table, and the still-working German refrigerator illustrate the leader's extravagant tastes. The full tour takes one hour and costs US$12. ⊠ *Kanombe.*

WHERE TO EAT

$$
ECLECTIC

✕ **Heaven.** Founded by American couple Alissa and Josh Ruxin, this oasis of gourmet cuisine is a favorite among foreign residents and affluent Rwandans for weekend brunch, evening cocktails, and special-occasion dinners. The wooden terrace with thatched-roof and recessed lighting affords spectacular hillside views, while art from the adjoining gallery bedecks the brick walls. **Known for:** weekend brunch; terrace view. [$] *Average main: US$15* ⊠ *No. 7 KN 29 St., Kiyovu* ☎ *250/788–486–581* ⊕ *www.heavenrwanda.com.*

$$
BELGIAN
Fodor'sChoice
★

✕ **Poivre Noir.** This intimate and quiet setting in Kimihurura, one of the Kigali neighborhoods most known for restaurants and nightlife, is a welcome reprieve. With a French and Belgian focus, Poivre Noir masterfully crafts some of Kigali's best meals. **Known for:** upscale cuisine; intimate setting. [$] *Average main: US$15* ⊠ *2 KG 670 St., Kigali* ☎ *250/735–823–282* ⊗ *Closed Sun.*

$
AFRICAN
Fodor'sChoice
★

✕ **Repub Lounge.** Kigali's fickle social scene finally found a staple in this hilltop African fusion restaurant that has been in business for more than a decade, a true feat in this city. Americans, Europeans, and Kigali's elite flock to the brother-and-sister-run Republ Lounge for happy hour, late-night drinks, and a belt-loosening menu. **Known for:** quality food and service; happy hour specials. [$] *Average main: US$11* ⊠ *16 KG 674 St., Kigali* ⊹ *Next door to the buzzing Papyrus bar and restaurant* ☎ *250/788–303–030* ⊗ *Closed Sun.*

WHERE TO STAY

$
HOTEL

🏨 **Golf Hills Residence.** More American McMansion than African accommodation, this boutique hotel with golf course views and bend-over-backward service is a convenient base for safari-goers. **Pros:** great value; quiet and clean rooms for a restful night; accommodating staff. **Cons:** 10-minute ride to town and top tourist destinations; few restaurants and nightspots in immediate area. [$] *Rooms from: US$100* ⊠ *KG 415 St., Nyarutarama* ☎ *250/787–113–300* ⊕ *www.golfhillsresidence.com* ↪ *17 rooms* ⦿*Breakfast.*

$$
HOTEL

🏨 **Kigali Marriott Hotel.** One of Kigali's new hot spots, the Marriott has quickly become a see-and-be-seen destination among locals. **Pros:** great bar and event offerings; comfortable beds and sophisticated bathrooms; tasty breakfast spread. **Cons:** Wi-Fi is not included; service is lacking; food options can be inconsistent and overpriced. [$] *Rooms from: US$350* ⊠ *Kn 3 Ave., Nyarugenge* ☎ *250/222–111–111* ⊕ *www.marriott.com/hotels/travel/kglmc-kigali-marriott-hotel* ↪ *265 rooms* ⦿*Breakfast.*

$$
HOTEL

🏨 **Kigali Serena Hotel.** One of the city's only five-star hotels, the Serena draws an elite crowd with its open-air restaurants, heliconia-and-palm-fringed pool, up-to-date business center, and fully equipped gym. **Pros:** central location; wide array of amenities; excellent on-site dining options. **Cons:** spotty service; atmosphere can feel stifled; small standard rooms. [$] *Rooms from: US$400* ⊠ *KN 3 Ave., Nyarugenge* ☎ *250/788–184–500* ⊕ *www.serenahotels.com* ↪ *148 rooms* ⦿*Breakfast.*

UGANDA

Uganda has earned a tourism reputation as the "Pearl of Africa." The country has 10 national parks and a dazzling array of landscapes, which range from dry savannas to dense forests and snowcapped mountains. Visitors can observe lions prowling the grasslands one day and go white-water rafting down the Nile the next. Ugandans are also famously friendly, and English is widely spoken.

PLANNING
GETTING HERE AND AROUND

Most visitors arrive in Uganda via Entebbe International Airport, which has more than a dozen international carriers including: Turkish Airlines, Qatar Airways, Emirates, Brussels Airlines, Ethiopian Airlines, South African Airways, RwandAir, Egyptair, Kenya Airways, and Etihad. There are no direct flights from the U.S. nor is there currently a direct flight from the U.K. Emirates and Qatar offer one-stop itineraries from Washington, D.C., to Entebbe via Dubai and Doha, respectively. By 2018, airport expansion works should be complete.

Two popular operators offer internal air transfers around Uganda. The Entebbe-based company, Aerolink Uganda Limited, is known for its affordable daily scheduled service plying a circuit that includes many of the national parks. Kampala Executive Aviation (KEA), operating from their private hub at Kajjansi Airfield (roughly halfway between Kampala and Entebbe), offer private charter flights in a fleet of various aircraft, serving airstrips around the country. ■TIP→ For a special treat, ask about their scenic flights over Kampala or the Source of the Nile at Jinja, a great way to take in this area.

Contacts AeroLink Uganda Limited. ✉ *Entebbe International Airport, Entebbe* ☎ *317/333–000, 776/882–205* ⊕ *www.aerolinkuganda.com.* **Entebbe International Airport (EBB).** ✉ *5536 Kampala Rd., Entebbe.* **Kampala Executive Aviation (KEA).** ☎ *0772/712–554, 0776/333–114* ⊕ *www.flykea.com.*

TOP REASONS TO GO TO UGANDA

Kampala. Uganda's capital city is regionally renowned for its dancing-till-dawn nightlife, bustling markets, and white-knuckle "boda boda" motorbike taxi rides. Arts and music festivals and booming café culture add to the buzz of this popular city.

Gorilla Trekking. Climb through 25,000-year-old rain forest via misty tea plantations to encounter the world's largest living primates on their own turf. Their sheer size and beguiling humanlike interactions will leave you spellbound. Uganda has the largest mountain gorilla population and is cheaper than Rwanda. Primate-lovers can also trek chimpanzees and golden monkeys.

Adventure Abounds. Thrill-seekers can't get enough of Uganda's white-water rafting, kayaking, quad biking, and volcano climbing.

Bird lovers Paradise. The Pearl of Africa is home to more than 1,030 species of bird species. That's 49% of Africa's total bird population!

Community tourism. There are ample opportunities for visitors to experience Uganda beyond the gorillas. From watching traditional dance and learning about bee-keeping to visiting herb gardens or taking a community cooperative coffee tour, there's something for everyone.

ESSENTIALS

Entebbe, Kampala, large towns, and tourist areas are covered by numerous phone networks, although signals may be on and off. Local SIM cards are cheap and international calling bundles make calling home easy. Ideally, have your mobile phone unlocked before you arrive. Phone unlocking is possible in Kampala but may delay your safari. Wi-Fi, of variable quality, is provided free in all lodges and hotels listed in this guide.

Kampala has the best Wi-Fi coverage, including 4G. Google has recently completed installation of an 800-km fiber ring around Kampala.

Visitors to Uganda are required to present proof of yellow fever vaccination upon arrival at the airport. Hepatitis A and B vaccinations are recommended. Adventurous eaters and travelers to rural areas should also consider the typhoid vaccine. Malaria is a risk in Uganda, so consult with your doctor on antimalarial tablet options. At the very least, sleep under a mosquito net at night and wear insect repellent during the day. Drink bottled or filtered water. Petty theft and muggings do occur, so don't wander around alone at night, particularly in urban areas.

Ugandans are generally tolerant people, but most hold traditional beliefs so public displays of affection (even between a man and a woman) are frowned upon. With that being said, there is also a government-supported anti-homosexuality stance, so LGBTQ+ travelers should travel with caution.

Uganda's shilling (UGX) has an exchange rate of Ush3,500 to US$1. Although larger hotels and tour companies may accept U.S. dollars and credit cards, expect to pay in shillings at local shops and restaurants. You can withdraw local currency at ATMs, in large towns, or exchange your U.S. dollars at the airport, foreign exchange branch (known locally as forex), and local banks. ■TIP→ US$50 and US$100 bills fetch better exchange rates. Bills printed before 2006 may not be accepted. Later bills get better exchange rates.

A single-entry, three-month tourist visa costs US$50. In theory, visa applications should be made via the Uganda immigration online system but can also be obtained from the Uganda Embassy in Washington, D.C., or the Uganda Mission to the U.N. in New York City. You'll need a completed application form, two passport-size photos, and the correct visa fee two months before travel. Although not recommended, visas can also be secured at Entebbe International Airport, where you must pay in U.S. dollars cash. ■TIP→ Your passport must be valid for six months from the date of intended travel and contain at least one blank page.

ABOUT THE RESTAURANTS

Kampala has a thriving restaurant scene offering a diversity of cuisines, from *nyama choma* (roasted meat) and farmed game meats from South Africa, to authentic Indian (best for vegetarians), Korean, and Italian. Ugandans are incredibly sociable every day of the week. Uganda produces excellent beers such as Nile Special, Club, and Bell. Triple-distilled Uganda Waragi gin is also universally popular.

Ugandans are big eaters and always eat a cooked lunch, sometimes mid-afternoon; traditional African food is heavy on carbs and light on vegetables. Street foods are mainly fried; a trip to Uganda is not complete without the universally popular rolex—think an omelette wrapped in a chapati. ■TIP→ If you're visiting in November, keep an eye out for fresh grasshoppers. They are considered a local delicacy.

Tipping is at your discretion in restaurants.

International lodges and restaurants cater well for vegetarians.

ABOUT THE LODGES

Upcountry lodges favored by international tourists generally have a traditional African feel to them but with the modern conveniences of hot water, power (sometimes solar), and Wi-Fi (often slow). Many lodges provide massages; some are even complimentary. Upmarket lodges provide turn-down and other housekeeping services as well as a daily maid service. Cuisine is international in style and generally offered on full board basis; at upmarket lodges, this often includes local beers and spirits. ■TIP→ Read the terms and conditions of your safari itinerary carefully so you know what's included and what isn't.

Restaurant and hotel reviews have been shortened. For full information, visit Fodors.com.

WHAT IT COSTS IN U.S. DOLLARS			
$	$$	$$$	$$$$
Hotels	under $250	$250–450	$451–$600	over $600
Restaurants	under $12	$12–$20	$21–$30	over $30

Most safari prices refer to an all-inclusive per person rate excluding tax (a few only operate on a half-board rate), assuming double occupancy. Hotel rates refer to double occupancy excluding tax.

UGANDA FAST FACTS

Size 241,038 square km (93,065 square miles), approximately the same size as the state of Oregon

Population roughly 41 million

Capital Kampala.

Number of National Parks Ten. Bwindi Impenetrable Forest, Kibale Forest, Kidepo Valley, Lake Mburo, Mgahinga Gorilla, Mount Elgon, Murchison Falls, Queen Elizabeth, Rwenzori Mountains, Semliki. Uganda also has numerous Wildlife and Forest Reserves.

Number of Private Reserves Private reserves and concessions are rare in Uganda. The best-known are Ngamba Island Chimapnzee Sanctuary and Ziwa Rhino Sanctuary.

Big Five Uganda boasts of the Big Seven: the Big Five plus mountain gorillas and chimpanzees. Rhinos have only been reintroduced (to a private sanctuary) in 2005.

Language The official language is English; the second language is Swahili (although rarely spoken).

Time Uganda is on EAT (East African Standard Time), which is two hours ahead of Greenwich mean time and eight hours ahead of North American Eastern Standard Time.

Drives on the left

Currency Ugandan shilling (UGX)

TOUR OPERATORS

Classic Africa Safaris. This Uganda-based safari operator (with strong representation in the United States) has some of the best vehicles and guides in the country. Offering customized tours of Uganda and Rwanda, they also boast carbon neutral status. ⊠ *Plot 26, Eric Magala Rd., Entebbe* ☎ *0414/320–121* ⊕ *classicuganda.com.*

Wild Frontiers. This experienced safari outfitter offers personalized and set departure safaris of Uganda from its base in Entebbe, Uganda. The company operates its own network of upmarket lodges, can set up private mobile camps, and runs an equally tight ship with their Murchison Falls National Park and Lake Victoria–based boat operations, providing well-guided launch cruises and sport fishing in both locations. They also offer day trips to Ngamba Island Chimpanzee Sanctuary and the Uganda Wildlife Education Centre in Entebbe. ⊠ *Nsamizi Rd., Entebbe* ☎ *0414/321–479, 0772/502–155* ⊕ *wildfrontiers.co.ug.*

VISITOR INFORMATION

The Uganda Tourism Board website has a helpful FAQ, directories, and activity suggestions. Many safari operators and high-end lodges provide comprehensive information for guests on their websites and will answer individual concerns.

The Uganda Wildlife Authority (UWA) is in charge of managing Uganda's national parks and wildlife reserves. They issue various primate tracking permits.

Contacts Uganda Tourism Board. ⊕ *www.visituganda.com.* **Uganda Wildlife Authority.** ⊠ *Plot 7 Kira Rd., Kamwokya* ☎ *0414/355–400* ⊕ *www. ugandawildlife.org.*

BWINDI IMPENETRABLE NATIONAL PARK

Game
★★★★★
Park Accessibility
★★★
Getting Around
★★★
Accommodations
★★★★
Scenic Beauty
★★★★★

Home to over half the world's remaining population of critically endangered mountain gorillas, Bwindi is one of only four places in the world where one can spend a magical hour in the company of these gentle giants.

Once part of a much larger forest stretching as far as Rwanda and beyond, the park is now an oasis of 128 square miles of pristine rain forest in southwest Uganda. Designated a UNESCO World Heritage Site, Bwindi is one of the largest African forests encompassing both lowland and montane species. It has an incredibly rich ecosystem: more diversity of tree and fern species than anywhere else in the region, around 202 species of butterfly, 120 mammal species, and the only place one can find gorillas and chimpanzees in the same forest.

Since the first group was habituated for tourism nearly a quarter of a century ago, a total of 11 gorilla families (out of an estimated 408 individuals) are now used for tourism. Small groups of tourists set off on bracing hikes every morning for a bucket list encounter with a Silverback and his clan. Permits—$600 per permit through 2019—are strictly controlled to minimize contact between gorillas and the outside world (their DNA makes them susceptible to human ailments—so you won't be allowed to track if you're ill) and the funds raised go toward conservation activities in Bwindi, and all over Uganda. ■ TIP→ When trekking the gorillas (or chimpanzees), it's highly recommended that you hire a porter who will carry your bag (for a small fee) and help you climb muddy slopes. A tip of $5–10 is appreciated. Ranger guides also appreciate a tip of $5–15, but at your discretion, of course.

A percentage of tracking fees also supports nearby communities, and many local people now work in tourism: from serving as porters on gorilla-tracking expeditions to guiding visitors on other local tourism initiatives: forest hikes, community walks, and living history encounters with the Batwa, the ancient forest tribe. In some areas, the relationship between community and conservation is even more symbiotic, with local people donating land for use as wildlife buffer zones in exchange for collecting "bed night" fees from lodges. Bwindi today is a leading example of ecotourism done well.

WHEN TO GO

Bwindi experiences rainfall year-round (it is a rain forest, after all). The wettest months are March through May and October through November, with comparatively drier weather from June to August and from December to February. Daytime temperatures are fairly constant, hovering around 75°F (24°C), but nights can be chilly, with lows of around 50°F (10°C). Low-season discounts are occasionally available at some lodges. Permit availability can be tricky in peak months of July through September.

GETTING HERE AND AROUND

Lying about 500 km (300 miles; 10-hour drive) from Kampala, Bwindi is served by scheduled/charter flights via airstrips around the park. There are four distinct sectors for tracking: Buhoma, Ruhija, Rushaga, and Nkuringo. ■ TIP→ **Securing your permit in advance from Uganda Wildlife Authority is vital, as this dictates where you track, and therefore where you stay. And, with Rwanda's doubling of gorilla permit prices, Uganda's permits are in high demand throughout the year, so book early.** Some of the best accommodations are at Buhoma and Nkuringo, but don't rule out tracking elsewhere if you plan carefully: Ruhija tracking is viable from Buhoma; Rushaga can be reached from Nkuringo. If driving, you'll need a 4x4 because roads can be difficult, especially in the wettest months. Because of this, and the permit permutations, most people travel with a tour operator.

7

WHERE TO STAY

$$$ HOTEL **Buhoma Lodge.** The cottages at Buhoma Lodge, located within Bwindi Impenetrable National Park, rise up on stilts out of the hillside, ensuring that views from the highest rooms—long, sweeping vistas down the mist-clad valley—are some of the best this side of the forest. **Pros:** two-minute walk from the briefing point for gorilla tracking; smiling staff and professional management; in good weather the Wi-Fi reaches up to bedrooms; in-room USB charging. **Cons:** admirable eco-credentials means hair dryers can only be used by arrangement; close to park offices so occasional passing traffic; book your complementary massage at the spa in advance to avoid disappointment. [$] *Rooms from: US$500* ✉ *Bwindi Impenetrable National Park, Buhoma* ✢ *400 meters on right after park gate* ☎ *0414/321–479, 0772/721–155* 🌐 *ugandaexclusivecamps.com* ⇨ *10 rooms* 🍴 *All meals.*

$$$ ALL-INCLUSIVE Fodor's Choice ★ **Chameleon Hill.** Set on a tiny promontory of land high above Lake Mutanda, Chameleon Hill's windmill-like towers and individually color-themed rooms look across to majestic volcanic peaks that wouldn't look amiss in a Disney movie. **Pros:** unique setting with unforgettable view; food is excellent and plentiful; a multitude of innovative adventure activities. **Cons:** one-hour drive to starting point for gorilla tracking; perhaps not for you if you are allergic to dogs; remote location means public transport access can be difficult. [$] *Rooms from: US$500* ✢ *As you enter Kisoro town look out for "Kindly Petrol Station" where you*

turn right. From here the lodge is clearly signposted ☎ *0772/721–818* 🌐 *www.chameleonhill.com* 🛏 *10 rooms* 🍴 *All-inclusive.*

$$$$ HOTEL FAMILY 🏨 **Clouds Mountain Gorilla Lodge.** Regarded by many as the most exclusive lodge in Bwindi, Clouds also has one of the greatest views in Uganda: high on a ridge, verdant hills tumble away to a valley below, under distant volcanic peaks. **Pros:** a "welcome hand massage" and personal butler at your beck and call; lodge has own helipad on Top of the World; excellent meals full of fresh produce grown on-site. **Cons:** rates are pricey; not all cottages have the view, so ask for Safari or Rafiki if this is important to you; dark pathways to and from the cottages. [$] *Rooms from: US$1280* ✉ *Bwindi Impenetrable National Park* ✥ *Entrance on left, opposite UWA ranger post at northern end of Nkuringo village* ☎ *0414/251–182* 🌐 *www.wildplacesafrica.com* 🛏 *8 rooms* 🍴 *All-inclusive.*

$ HOTEL 🏨 **Nkuringo Gorilla Lodge.** This eco-friendly lodge has graduated from humble beginnings to become an award-winning property offering exceptional value for this area. **Pros:** impeccable green credentials; excellent value low- and high-season rates; great for walkers and adventurers. **Cons:** remote gorilla trekking destination; the high altitude (7,090 feet/2,161 meters) means it can be chilly at night; drinks are an extra charge. [$] *Rooms from: US$190* ✉ *Bwindi Impenetrable National Park* ✥ *On right-hand side on bend in road, just before Nkuringo village* ☎ *0774/805–580, 0792/805–580, 0702/805–580* 🌐 *mountaingorillalodge.com* 🛏 *12 rooms, honeymoon cottage under construction* 🍴 *All meals.*

$$$$ HOTEL 🏨 **Sanctuary Gorilla Forest Camp.** A standout property in northern Bwindi, Sanctuary Gorilla Forest Camp delivers impeccable service in a classic forest setting. **Pros:** supersmooth service from award-winning operator; forest location occasionally visited by gorillas; invests in community projects. **Cons:** closeness of forest to tents obscures views and invites the occasional creepy-crawly; massages are charged extra; fireplace in dining area (not cottages). [$] *Rooms from: US$760* ✉ *Bwindi Impenetrable National Park, Buhoma* ✥ *500 meters on right after park gate* ☎ *0414/340–290, 0776/340–290* 🌐 *www.sanctuaryretreats.com* 🛏 *8 luxury tents* 🍴 *All-inclusive.*

$$$$ HOTEL 🏨 **Volcanoes Bwindi Lodge.** This quirkily decorated eco-lodge has the grandest vantage point of Bwindi in its own reserve of secondary forest, creating a 50-acre gorilla-friendly buffer zone. **Pros:** extensive veranda and living area look straight into the forest; friendly, well-trained staff with great attention to detail; innovative food menus, superbly prepared. **Cons:** a bit expensive for some; lots of steps in and out of the lodge; gorilla sightings in lodge grounds can't be guaranteed. [$] *Rooms from: US$700* ✉ *Buhoma* ✥ *Look for lodge sign on left as you enter Buhoma village* ☎ *0414/346–464, 0772/741–720* 🌐 *www.volcanoessafaris.com* 🛏 *8 rooms* 🍴 *All-inclusive.*

SPORTS AND THE OUTDOORS

CANOEING

If visiting Southern Bwindi (Rushaga or Nkuringo sectors), nearby Lake Mutanda beckons for a rather special experience: paddling across its waters in a traditional dug-out canoe. The backdrop is stunning. The island-studded lake is overlooked by distant volcanic peaks and the Virunga Massif that straddles the Uganda/Rwanda border. Canoeing can be combined with a guided hike from nearby Rubuguri to the lakeshore. A peaceful diversion from the hectic pace of safari itineraries, canoeing offers far more insight into the charms and challenges of daily life than driving by in your 4x4 vehicle.

FAMILY
Fodor'sChoice
★
Edirisa Canoe Trekking and Batwa Today. A social enterprise with a sense of adventure, Edirisa offers their unique blend of hiking, paddling, and community on canoe-trekking expeditions (using dug-outs, naturally). This Lake Bunyonyi-based nonprofit allows visitors to experience authentic Uganda, while providing employment and promoting local culture. Enthusiastic young guides accompany guests, with assistance from *Bakiga* and *Batwa* elders along the way. Single- or multiday options are available, including the epic week-long Ultimate Hike from Lake Bunyonyi to Mgahinga to Buhoma along one of the **Gorilla Highlands Trails**. Accommodation can be basic—you camp in tents (upgrade options usually available) but many visitors love the authenticity of the village experience. The popular Batwa Today tour gives access to the Batwa community like no other, and the "Batwa Kids" tour is a special program for those under 15. ⊠ *Bufuka Village, Lake Bunyonyi, Kabale* ☎ *0752/558–558, 0752/558–222* ⊕ *www.edirisa.org.*

HIKING

Various trails exist at Bwindi, through the forest and nearby scenery. Shorter hikes of three hours with park rangers are available: in Buhoma and Rushaga we recommend the different (but similarly monikered) Waterfall Trails; birders can head to Ruhija for the ornithologically rewarding Mubwindi Swamp hike. Longer forays—arranged by private outfitters—include the four- to five-hour Ivy River Trail from Buhoma to Nkuringo (or vice versa, for a more gentle gradient). From Nkuringo, the Kashasha River Trail offers a strenuous seven- to eight-hour loop, or you can strike out on the multiday Gorilla Highlands Trail to scenic Lake Bunyonyi.

FAMILY
Nkuringo Walking Safaris. This pioneering trekking company, with offices in Entebbe and a base at Nkuringo on the south side of Bwindi Impenetrable National Park, offers various guided day and multiday hikes through Bwindi and surrounding farmland, alongside dug-out canoe trips on Lake Mutanda. Their professional guides are trained to identify local flora and fauna, and will also share insights into history, culture, local everyday life, and farming practices. Their hiking packages are an excellent value and can be combined with your choice of accommodation (so you can scale the comfort factor up or down as required). ⊠ *Nkuringo Gorilla Lodge, Bwindi Impenetrable National Park* ☎ *0774/805–580, 39/217–66327* ⊕ *www.nkuringowalkingsafaris.com.*

KIBALE NATIONAL PARK

Game
★★★★★
Park Accessibility
★★★★
Getting Around
★★★★
Accommodations
★★★★
Scenic Beauty
★★★★★

This 296-square-mile tract of forest is home to one of the greatest variety and concentration of primates on the continent, and its population of nearly 1,500 chimpanzees makes it a great place to track these endangered apes.

Kibale weaves a rich tapestry of rain forest life: 13 primate species reside here; around 335 bird species are found, including six that are endemic to the region; and nearly 230 different species of tree create a varied canopy, some towering more than 130 feet (50 meters).

Chimpanzee-tracking excursions set out from the Kanyanchu Tourist Centre twice a day. Accompanied by a forest ranger you will hike along forest trails in search of man's closest relatives (chimps share 98.7% of our DNA). Once located, the group spends a maximum of one hour with these fascinating great apes. You can watch them feed, groom, play, and sometimes even hunt together. There is no guarantee of a sighting, but chances are generally high, with a success rate of more than 90%.

Those with a real passion for primates (and the stamina to match) can join a "chimpanzee habituation" experience. This unique opportunity to observe chimpanzees from dawn until dusk allows visitors to gather deeper insight into their behavior. Nocturnal primates may also be seen, with varying degrees of success, on the guided walk that departs Kanyanchu every evening at nightfall. Birders will love exploring Kibale, and neighboring Bigodi Wetland Sanctuary, in search of prized species as green-breasted pitta, brown-chested alethe, and little greenbul.

Outside the park, rolling panoramas of tea plantations and ancient volcanic craters dominate the landscape between Kibale and Fort Portal, with plenty of informal hiking and biking opportunities offering a pleasant way to pass an afternoon. Ask your lodge or guide for details of local routes; many are self-guided and offer the chance to witness everyday rural life in one of the prettiest regions of Uganda.

WHEN TO GO

Kibale is a rain forest, with the chance of wet weather year-round. If you avoid March through May and September through November you will miss the worst of it, though dry-season months can make the chimp tracking more arduous, as the apes travel farther in search of fruiting trees. Temperatures are fairly constant, with average daytime highs around 80°F (27°C) and nights dropping to about 59°F (15°C). Be sure to secure chimp permits well in advance at any time of year.

GETTING HERE AND AROUND

Located in western Uganda, Kibale lies about 16 miles (26 km) southeast of the town of Fort Portal on the Kamwenge Road. The park is about a five-hour drive from Kampala or Entebbe respectively, and three hours from northern Queen Elizabeth National Park. Drive times have improved thanks to better roads. If you prefer to fly, you can choose from a small charter to Fort Portal airstrip (its limited length excludes all but the tiniest light aircraft), or charter to Kasese, two hours south, in a wider choice of planes. Chimp tracking or habituation permits should be secured in advance from the Uganda Wildlife Authority.

EXPLORING

FAMILY **Bigodi Wetland Sanctuary.** This community-run conservation project managed by the Kibale Association for Rural and Environmental Development (KAFRED) offers a popular guided nature trail through Magombe Wetland, near Bigodi. Its more open terrain frequently delivers better bird-watching and monkey-spotting than neighboring Kibale Forest. Here, red colobus are common, with the chance of seeing black and white colobus, grey-cheeked mangabey, and L'Hoest's and red-tailed monkeys. Serious birders will enjoy the knowledgeable guides, who can identify the wetland's 200-odd species with ease. The 3-mile/5-km trail takes three to four hours, and if you don't have waterproof boots KAFRED can lend you a pair for free. Porters can be booked in advance. Traditional lunches, village walks, and Tinka's Homestay (voted Best Homestay 2016) are also on offer. ✉ *KAFRED Office, Fort Portal-Kamwenge Rd., near Kibale National Park, Bigodi* ✥ *From Kanyanchu HQ in Kibale Forest, head southeast on Kamwenge Rd. After a couple of miles, you reach village of Bigodi. KAFRED office is on right at start of trading center* ☎ *0772/468–113,* 🌐 *bigoditourism.com* 🎫 *$15.*

WHERE TO EAT

$ INTERNATIONAL FAMILY 🍴 **The Bee Hive Bar & Bistro, Bigodi.** The unmissable yellow two-story building is home to the Bee Hive Bar & Bistro, which opened in 2017. Stop for a cappuccino or a cold Nile Special beer on the upstairs veranda and watch the world go by. **Known for:** cold beers; satellite TV and pool table; coffee. [$] *Average main: US$10* ✉ *Bigodi Trading Center, On the main Fort Portal–Kamwenge Rd., Bigodi* ✥ *Opposite the turning to KAFRED Office. Follow directions to Bigodi Wetland Sanctuary* ☎ *0787/357–717,* ⏲ *Off-road parking. Service may be slow when there are groups* 💳 *No credit cards.*

WHERE TO STAY

$$$$
HOTEL
🛏 **Kyaninga Lodge.** Overlooking a cobalt-blue crater lake, the design of this fairy-tale property provides serious wow factor: Kyaninga took 130 men, six years, and more than 1,000 hand-carved logs to build this masterpiece. **Pros:** stunning property; friendly staff; much of their tasty food grown on-site. **Cons:** farther from Kibale Forest than most; lots of steps to climb; quickly booked up by expats during charity events. $ *Rooms from: US$770* ⊠ *Lake Kyaninga near Fort Portal, Fort Portal* ⊹ *Turn north at Mpanga Bridge, about 1.25 miles/2 km outside Fort Portal town on Kampala Road (signed for lodge). Follow road 1.1 miles/1.8 km and turn left at Kyaninga Lodge signpost. Follow road for another 3.7 miles (6 km) until you reach lodge* ☎ *0794/304–211, 0772/999–750* ⊕ *www.kyaningalodge.com* ⊟ *No credit cards* ⇗ *9 rooms* ⦿ *All meals.*

$$$$
HOTEL
FAMILY
🛏 **Ndali Lodge.** A Ugandan Downton Abbey, Ndali is a bit of an institution; offering a charming blend of warm hospitality and colonial history. **Pros:** the home-away-from-home feel; fantastic walking and biking country; massages available; great for kids. **Cons:** hair dryers can only be used on request; spotty Wi-Fi; if dogs aren't your thing, forget it; alcohol costs extra. $ *Rooms from: US$770* ⊠ *Lake Nyinambuga, Kabata, Bigodi* ⊹ *Take Kamwenge Road (also for Kibale National Park) and fork right at cluster of signs at Kasiisi (after just under 7.5 miles/12 km). After about the same distance again, having passed through scruffy Rwaihamba trading center, you reach turn-off for Ndali on right-hand side, by small school* ☎ *0772/221–309, 0772/487–673* ⊕ *www.ndalilodge.com* ⊟ *No credit cards* ⇗ *8 cottages* ⦿ *All meals.*

$$$
ALL-INCLUSIVE
🛏 **Papaya Lake Lodge.** Built overlooking a crater lake, the latest lodge in the Fort Portal area offers high levels of personal service in another stunning location. **Pros:** personal service from lodge owners; the only lodge in Uganda to have a tennis wall; best food in the region: imaginative and beautifully cooked. **Cons:** pricey; lots of steps between living area and lower cottages; meal plan excludes drinks. $ *Rooms from: US$550* ⊠ *Fort Portal* ☎ *793 /388–277* ⊕ *papayalakelodge.com* ⇗ *11 rooms* ⦿ *All meals.*

$
HOTEL
🛏 **Primate Lodge Kibale.** Right behind the Park Headquarters, Primate Lodge Kibale is convenient for those early mornings when tracking chimps or birding. **Pros:** location next to trailhead; impressive refurbishment and beautiful hardwood interiors; great location for birders. **Cons:** better value can be found elsewhere; Wi-Fi available only when generator on; service is too relaxed for some. $ *Rooms from: US$198* ⊠ *Kanyanchu, Kibale National Park, Fort Portal* ⊹ *Take Kamwenge Road from Fort Portal toward Kibale National Park. Pass through park, and look for turn on left just before leaving forest. The lodge is by Kanyanchu Park HQ* ☎ *0393 /267–153, 0701/426–368, 0772/426–368* ⊕ *ugandalodges.com* ⇗ *17 rooms* ⦿ *All meals.*

QUEEN ELIZABETH NATIONAL PARK

Game
★★★
Park Accessibility
★★★★
Getting Around
★★★★
Accommodations
★★★★
Scenic Beauty
★★★★★

Serving up a rich diversity of game and scenery, Queen Elizabeth National Park (QENP) is a rewarding safari stop-over between the primate hubs of Kibale and Bwindi.

For the purposes of safari planning, the park is divided into two sectors. The northern sector, Mweya, straddles the equator, the euphorbia-studded valley framed by the Rwenzoris, and the Kichwamba Escarpment to the north and south, with Lakes George and Edward to the east and west.

Despite the lack of wildlife volumes of parks like the Serengeti in Tanzania, the variety of habitat in QENP provides a wealth of activities: popular launch cruises ply the bird-lined Kazinga Channel (the park has more than 600 species, more than any other national park in Africa); the geologically intriguing Explosion Crater Drive offers panoramic views; guided hikes in Kyambura Gorge, though no substitute for Kibale, provide the chance of spotting chimpanzees; and the Uganda kob breeding grounds of Kasenyi Plains, which attract lions, hyenas, and leopards, offer more traditional wildlife-viewing. Cat-crazed visitors can ask about Lion Monitoring at Mweya Visitor Centre. This researcher-accompanied activity uses radio technology to get you up close, though availability is weather- (and researcher-) dependent.

To the south, the Ishasha sector is a wilder, more remote destination. Far from the crowds, there are no gimmicks, just plain, old-fashioned wilderness. Rolling plains are home to herds of elephants, kob, and topi, and local lion prides are known for climbing the giant fig trees. These show-stealing cats are usually given top billing for any foray into this sector, but Ishasha's beauty is best savored slowly. Spend time appreciating the full abundance of life on the savanna, and the discovery of telltale feline tails dangling from a tree will not be the only reward.

Nearby, communities have developed several worthwhile tourism activities. Visit a working salt lake at Katwe or participate in a craft workshop with Kikorongo Community Group in the north, or tour Agartha's Taste of Uganda near Ishasha for insight into the challenges of farming near wildlife. Such community interactions offer a welcome change of pace, as well as a fascinating contrast to the wealth of wildlife in this beautiful park.

WHEN TO GO

Located in the Albertine rift at a lower altitude than most of Uganda, the climate in QENP is warm and constant, with mean annual temperatures of 59°F to 84°F (15°C to 29°C). Biannual wet seasons March through May and August through November are better for photography, with (generally short) storms producing interesting light and clearer skies. Drier periods in January and February and June and July are dusty and hot, with controlled burning by park authorities toward the end of these seasons making wildlife-viewing feel positively postapocalyptic.

GETTING HERE AND AROUND

Around 400 km (250 miles) from Entebbe, Mweya is a seven-hour drive on tarmac roads. Ishasha lies two hours (100 km [60 miles]) farther south on murram. Kibale is three hours (160 km [100 miles]) north; and Ishasha is two hours (60 km [40 miles]) from northern Bwindi. Aero-Link will drop off at Mweya airstrip at no extra charge, and their scheduled stop at Kihihi serves Ishasha. Private charters are also available. Mweya Visitor Centre (at the tip of the peninsula) is a good resource. Head here to book UWA boat cruises or lion monitoring. Rangers for game drives on Kasenyi Plains are collected from Kasenyi gate, and in Ishasha from the UWA bandas near the start of the southern circuit.

EXPLORING

Fodor's Choice ★ **Explosion Crater Drive.** A stunning three-hour diversion along rocky tracks in northern Queen Elizabeth National Park, the Explosion Crater Drive runs between the Queen's Pavillion (turn off the Kikorongo-Katunguru highway at the Equator Markers) and the Kabatoro Gate (aka the Main Gate) on the Katwe public road. There is no need to prebook, or take a ranger, but a competent 4x4 driver and vehicle is most definitely required. Known for its scenic vistas rather than wildlife-viewing potential (though elephants are relatively common, lions are not unheard of, and the crater environment is great for spotting birds of prey), the drive traverses the Katwe crater field. This area of the park is littered with steep-sided volcanic craters, each containing its own microhabitat, from ancient rain forest to a sulfurous lake. It's enough to make geologists of us all. ✉ *Explosion Crater Dr., Queen Elizabeth National Park* ☎ *0414/355–400, 0414/355–403* ⊕ *www.ugandawildlife.org* ✉ *Included in park entry fee.*

Kyambura Gorge. The forested ridges of Kyambura Gorge form a deep cleft in the savanna landscape between Maramagambo Forest and Lake George, creating a natural boundary between Queen Elizabeth National Park and neighboring Kyambura Wildlife Reserve. Offering the chance to spot chimps on guided forest walks, the chimpanzee tracking in Kyambura Gorge is more active than most; you may have to cross the river by fallen log (slippery when wet!) and the steep sides of the gorge can be difficult at best. But it's a mysterious, primeval place (made famous by the BBC's *Chimps of the Lost Gorge*) and worth the 1.6 mile (2.5 km) drive from the Katunguru highway just for the view alone.

Chimp permits (USD$50) can be arranged with the UWA locally, but limited availability means it's best to secure them in advance from their HQ in Kampala. Visiting the viewing platform is free, provided one has paid park entry fees. ✉ *Fig Tree Camp, Kyambura Gorge, Queen Elizabeth National Park* ☎ *0414/355–400* 🌐 *www.ugandawildlife.org.*

WHERE TO STAY

$$$$ HOTEL Fodor's Choice ★ 🏨 **Ishasha Wilderness Camp.** Steeped in classic safari style, this intimate eco-friendly camp will make you feel as if you have stumbled onto the set of *Out of Africa*. **Pros:** remote wilderness location; sundowners and bush breakfasts can be arranged; Wi-Fi throughout lodge plus in-room charging. **Cons:** too cut-off for some tastes; no hot running water (bush showers); admirable eco-credentials means hair dryers can only be used by arrangement. [$] *Rooms from: US$720* ✉ *Ishasha Sector, Queen Elizabeth National Park* ☎ *0414/321–479, 0772/721–155* 🌐 *ugandaexclusivecamps.com* 🛏 *10 en suite tented rooms* 🍴 *All meals.*

$$ HOTEL 🏨 **Mazike Valley Lodge.** Phoenix-like, this lodge (formerly Kyambura Game Lodge) has *literally* risen from the ashes, having been restored after a 2012 bushfire destroyed most of its structures. **Pros:** great service and rooms for the price; excellent food; ideal location for chimp tracking. **Cons:** frequent call-to-prayer from nearby mosque and road noise can disturb light sleepers; Wi-Fi in communal areas only; a/c electricity with generator backup. [$] *Rooms from: US$364* ✉ *Bushenyi* ✥ *Turn off main Bushenyi-Katunguru road at Kyambura trading center (cluster of signs on corner, including one for Volcanoes lodge). After about 100 meters, turn left at sign for Mazike Valley Lodge* ☎ *0414/322–789, 0777/251–093, 0414/322–789* 🌐 *www.mazikelodge.com* 🛏 *8 rooms* 🍴 *All meals.*

$$ RESORT FAMILY 🏨 **Mweya Safari Lodge.** Big groups love the location of this "hotel-in-the-bush," situated on the Mweya peninsula overlooking Kazinga Channel (a popular watering hole for big game), in the heart of Queen Elizabeth National Park. **Pros:** located in the park; rooms to suit all budgets/styles; great views in every direction. **Cons:** with 46 rooms, 4 tents, and 4 cottages, it can feel big and impersonal; restaurant switches to buffet meals in busy periods; can be very busy during peak seasons. [$] *Rooms from: US$402* ✉ *Mweya Peninsula, Queen Elizabeth National Park* ✥ *Gate on left after passing through UWA checkpoint on Mweya peninsula, inside Queen Elizabeth National Park* ☎ *0392/796–773, 0752/798–882* 🌐 *www.mweyalodge.com* 🛏 *54 rooms* 🍴 *All meals.*

$$$$ ALL-INCLUSIVE FAMILY Fodor's Choice ★ 🏨 **Volcanoes Kyambura Gorge Lodge.** This masterpiece of design, converted from an old coffee station, sometimes feels more like a hip New York loft than a safari lodge; but the combination of whimsical upcycling chic with local building materials is part of its eclectic charm. **Pros:** stylish contemporary design; impressive commitment to community and conservation; your own personal butler—staff are eager to please. **Cons:** for those who prefer traditional lodge design, it may feel a little too modern; a steep walk from lower cottages to dining area. [$] *Rooms from: US$620* ✉ *Bushenyi* ✥ *Turn off (at lodge sign) at Kyambura trading center on Bushenyi-Katunguru Rd. Continue through village and*

7

then turn left at lodge sign ☎ *0414/346–464, 0772/741–720* ⊕ *www. volcanoessafaris.com* ⌁ *8 cottages* ♯○♯ *All-inclusive.*

SPORTS AND THE OUTDOORS

BOATING

In the northern sector of Queen Elizabeth National Park, the Kazinga Channel attracts all manner of game. Herds of elephants and buffalo throng the banks; smaller herbivores such as warthog and kob are also present; pods of hippo and solitary crocs bask in the shallows; and a significant proportion of the park's staggering 610 bird species can be seen here. With such natural bounty, it's no wonder the two-hour boat cruise along its banks is far and away the highlight activity in this sector of the park. The Uganda Wildlife Authority and Mweya Safari Lodge both operate boats for this purpose from the jetty below the lodge.

Fodor's Choice ★ **Mweya Safari Lodge Boats.** With a variety of comfortable, modern craft, the slick river operations from Mweya Safari Lodge offer several scheduled or private Kazinga Channel cruises a day, leaving at 9, 11, 2, and 4:15 pm subject to demand. Choose from the 38-seater *Hippo* or 10-seater *Sunbird*. Both are thoughtfully equipped with a cash bar, or book yourself on the luxury 12-seater *Kingfisher* boat, where the price includes drinks and nibbles. ✉ *Mweya Jetty, Mweya Peninsula, Queen Elizabeth National Park* ☎ *312/260–263, 0752/798–882* ⊕ *www. mweyalodge.com* ⌁ *From $30 USD.*

UWA Mweya Boats. The Uganda Wildlife Authority operate their own boat cruises along the Kazinga Channel. Two-hour trips depart daily at 9 and 11 am and 3 and 5 pm from the UWA jetty below Mweya Safari Lodge. There is a relatively large minimum number requirement of 10 passengers; some of their craft are older than the lodge boats but a new 45-seater boat joined the fleet in 2017. The guides certainly know their stuff and departures are often fully booked during peak season. Book ahead at their offices in Kampala, or take your chances locally at the Katunguru HQ and Mweya Visitor Centre. ✉ *Plot 7 Kira Rd., Kampala* ☎ *0414/355–400* ⊕ *www.ugandawildlife.org* ⌁ *US$30* ⊙ *Kampala reservations office closed Sat. afternoon and Sun. The boats and park offices operate daily.*

IF YOU HAVE TIME IN UGANDA

Although the must-see parks in Uganda are described in detail above, there are still other places worth exploring if you have time.

LAKE MBURO NATIONAL PARK

Roughly halfway between Kampala and Bwindi, Lake Mburo National Park is underrated; its unique variety of game and birdlife, plenty of opportunities to get out of the car, and excellent lodges means it offers far more than just a convenient stopover en route to the gorillas. The park's also home to endangered Rothschild's giraffes, which were reintroduced from Murchison Falls National Park by the Uganda Wildlife Authority in 2015. Only a few hundred Rothschild's giraffes are left in the wild. It is believed that disease and poaching caused giraffes to disappear from Lake Mburo in the last century.

This little park is made up of wetlands (including the eponymous lake itself), open savanna, and acacia woodland, studded with rocky outcrops. Its range of habitats supports around 315 bird species, including certain southern varieties for whom the park is the most northerly part of their range. Bird-watchers will appreciate the Lake Mburo boat cruise, a shoe-in for the elusive African finfoot.

For wildlife-lovers, the park delivers a wealth of smaller herbivores: large gatherings of impala not found anywhere else in Uganda mingle with zebra, topi, oribi, and bushbuck; herds of the largest living antelope, the eland, take up seasonal residence; and dainty klipspringers hide out on rocky *koppies*. Local leopard and hyena populations are on the increase, with plenty of smaller predators, such as genet and white-tailed mongoose, also present. This makes for interesting nocturnal viewing, as the park is one of the few places allowing such game drives. Other novel activities include horseback safaris and nature walks that offer a different perspective on wildlife-viewing and allow you to appreciate the peaceful serenity of the bush.

GETTING HERE AND AROUND

City traffic allowing, this park is less than a four-hour drive (230 km [140 miles]) from Kampala, with newly resurfaced highways making the journey relatively pleasant. A handy café/crafts pit stop can be made at the equator (75 km/47 miles south of Kampala). The Nshara gate is reached by turning off the Masaka-Mbarara highway about 20 km (12 miles) past Lyantonde; turn off for the more westerly Sanga gate 37 km (23 miles) shy of Mbarara, at the town of the same name. No public transport exists beyond the main highway, and a 4x4 is recommended for navigating the park and approach roads. If you prefer to fly in, charters to nearby Mbarara airstrip are available, just more than an hour from the park.

WHERE TO STAY

$$$
HOTEL
FAMILY
Fodor's Choice
★

Mihingo Lodge. High up on a *kopje* (rocky outcrop), the cottages at this superb boutique lodge blend seamlessly into the landscape, each offering a different view of the surrounding bush. **Pros:** a true eco-lodge; delicious buffet meals from 100% organic garden; vast array of activities to satisfy young and old. **Cons:** often overlooked as off the mainstream safari trail; limited Wi-Fi; holiday weekends can see it filled with expats. $ *Rooms from: US$520 ⊠ Lake Mburo National Park ✢ From Nshara gate of Lake Mburo NP, drive 3 miles/5 km and then turn left onto Ruroko track. Follow for around 4 miles (6 km) until you see right turn signed for Mihingo* ☎ *0752/410–509* ⊕ *www.mihingolodge.com* ↬ *12 luxury tented rooms* ⧉ *All meals.*

$$
HOTEL
FAMILY
Fodor's Choice
★

Rwakobo Rock. A gem of a budget lodge, Rwakobo Rock is deservedly popular with the adventure crowd. **Pros:** relaxed, informal style offering great value; climbers will love bouldering on the rock; pay no park fees by taking a walking safari outside the park. **Cons:** poorly lit paths to the rooms; watch your step—occasionally herds of cattle come through the lodge, with slippery consequences; small swimming pool. $ *Rooms from: US$250 ⊠ Near Nshara Gate, Lake Mburo National Park ✢ Turn off main Masaka-Mbarara Hwy. following signs for Nshara gate of Lake Mburo National Park. The lodge is on right after 8 km (5 miles), just 1.5 km (1 mile) from Nshara Gate* ☎ *0755/211–771* ⊕ *www.rwakoborock.com* ↬ *16 rooms* ⧉ *All meals.*

MURCHISON FALLS NATIONAL PARK

Historically a highlight of the East African safari circuit, at 1,483 square miles Murchison Falls National Park is the largest of Uganda's reserves, offering an abundance of wildlife against a superbly scenic backdrop.

Bisected by the Nile River, many of the activities are centred around the water. Delta cruises offer peaceful contemplation of papyrus-lined channels (and a good chance of spotting Shoebill); half- and full-day sport-fishing trips can be arranged; and the most popular activity is the launch cruise to Murchison Falls. Here, 300 cubic meters of water per second explodes through a narrow gorge, creating the most powerful stretch of water in the world. Active adventurers can prearrange to be dropped by boat at the base of the Falls, known as the Devil's Cauldron, for a steep hike up to the Top of the Falls where dramatic vistas await. The viewpoints can also be accessed by vehicle, from the south and north banks.

North-bank game tracks promise rewarding wildlife-viewing: herds of elephant, buffalo, and critically endangered Rothschild's giraffe; smaller herbivores include Uganda kob, Jackson's hartebeest, oribi and warthog; elusive predators such as spotted hyena, lion, leopard, and jackal; and an impressive bird list of more than 450 species. Lion monitoring, in which visitors accompany researchers to locate local prides, is also available here. Most activities are centered on Paraa in the heart of the park, but the southerly Budongo Forest provides a worthy diversion for excellent chimpanzee tracking and bird-watching.

GETTING HERE AND AROUND

The park lies five- to six-hours' drive (320 km/185 miles) northwest of Kampala. Schedule and charter flights fly in from Entebbe airport or Kajjansi airfield, landing at Bugungu, Pakuba, or Chobe airstrips as required. Kichumbanyobo gate in the south, just north of Masindi town, is best for access to Budongo Forest, and can also be used for the most efficient access to south bank lodges, along with the westerly Bugungu gate. From Paraa, a car ferry crosses the Nile in both directions, so those heading to north bank lodges may prefer to enter from Wangkwar or Tangi gates, both accessed from the main Karuma-Pakwach highway, and enjoy game drives en route to their accommodations.

WHERE TO STAY

$$ HOTEL Fodor's Choice ★ **Baker's Lodge.** Located in a grove of Kigelia (aka sausage trees) at the water's edge, Baker's Lodge has 180-degree views of the Nile. **Pros:** beautiful riverfront location delivers understated luxury with a light environmental footprint; swimming pool, deck, poolhouse, and outdoor bar; boat cruises depart two minutes from your tent. **Cons:** Wi-Fi and phone networks can be poor; hair dryers can only be used by arrangement at this solar lodge; lodge is inside park, meaning park fees must be paid. [$] *Rooms from: US$440* ✉ *Near Murchison Falls National Park, Paraa* ✣ *Head south from ferry crossing in Murchison Falls National Park and take exit road to Mubako gate (on right after UWA offices up hill from jetty). After passing primary school look for lodge sign on right-hand side of road* ☎ *0772/721–155, 0414/321–479* 🌐 *www.ugandaexclusivecamps.com* 🛏 *10 en suite tented rooms* 🍴 *All meals.*

$ HOTEL FAMILY Fodor's Choice ★ **Murchison River Lodge.** This budget boutique lodge has found its niche; local expats and price-conscious tourists love its laid-back, unpretentious style. **Pros:** simple pleasures, done well; great value for money; a warm and welcoming staff. **Cons:** no Wi-Fi and poor phone reception; due to environmental considerations the three tents with river views have chemical toilets (the rest have flush); sells out quickly. [$] *Rooms from: US$200* ✉ *Near Murchison Falls National Park, Paraa* ✣ *From Paraa, head south and take first right turn (signed for Murchison River Lodge) after leaving the river. Continue along road, through Mubako gate, until you see lodge on right. From Bulisa, turn east toward park and Bugungu gate. Turn left after 10 km/6 miles (signed for lodge). Follow this track, and signs, through fields until you reach lodge* ☎ *0714/000–085, 0782/007–552* 🌐 *murchisonriverlodge.com* 🛏 *10 rooms* 🍴 *All meals.*

SPORTS AND THE OUTDOORS

BOATING

The undisputed highlight of Murchison Falls National Park are the many ways visitors can "mess about on the river": cruises to the Falls, exploring the Nile delta, sundowner trips with chilled drinks onboard, and even sportfishing expeditions for keen anglers. Watching the sun set (or rise) over this ancient river, to a backing track of hippo snorts and birdcalls, is stirring stuff. Three different outfitters—the park authorities and two private operators with lodges in the area—offer boat cruises from Paraa with varying degrees of choice. Book a scheduled departure for the best value, or ask about private cruising rates for an exclusive experience tailored to your interests.

Paraa Safari Lodge Boats. Sleek new boats are the hallmark of the Paraa Safari Lodge river operations; their variously sized watercrafts include the double-decker *African Queen*, the 14-seater *Paraa Voyager*, or the 10-seater *Jewel of the Nile*. Their scheduled trips head upstream to the Falls from their jetty on the north bank, with regular departures at 8:30 am and 2:30 pm, subject to demand. In addition, they also offer launch cruises to the Nile delta area. ⊠ *North bank, Murchison Falls National Park* ☎ *0772/788–880, 0752/788–880* ⊕ *www.paraalodge.com.*

FAMILY **UWA Murchison Boats.** Operating from their south bank jetty at Paraa, the Uganda Wildlife Authority offers daily cruises upstream to Murchison Falls, departing at 8 am and 2 pm. Although some of their large boats are somewhat older than those of the area's private outfitters, UWA introduced a new 45-seater boat in 2017. A minimum of 10 passengers are required for a cruise to depart, but their seasoned guides and this remarkable stretch of river ensure the excursion is excellent value. You can secure your place on one of their cruises by visiting UWA's central reservations office in Kampala, or the local park offices at Paraa. ⊠ *South Bank, Murchison Falls National Park* ☎ *0414/355–400, 0414/355–405* ⊕ *www.ugandawildlife.org* ⊠ *US$30* ☉ *Closed Sat. afternoon and Sun.*

Fodor's Choice **Wild Frontiers Murchison Boats.** This established safari outfitter, and ★ operator of nearby Baker's Lodge, provides scenic wildlife cruises and sportfishing trips with their fleet of boats stationed at the Paraa jetty. Scheduled and private departures include trips to the Falls and the fabulous Nile delta—the latter providing many a Shoebill stork sighting. ■TIP➔ When booking your Falls cruise, ask about their Falls & Sundowner option. The later departure time of 3:30 pm generally means better wildlife sightings and a more peaceful river setting. They have a variety of comfortable craft; offer the most flexibility for customized trips; and their skippers and guides are well-trained, with a knack for knowing just when to turn off the engines and glide silently past the riverbanks, enjoying the natural sounds of the bush. ⊠ *South Bank, Murchison Falls National Park* ☎ *0772/721–155* ⊕ *wildfrontiers.co.ug* ⊠ *From US$20 per person (short sunset cruise) to over US$1,000 per day for a private group (up to 40 guests).*

JINJA AND THE RIVER NILE

The age-old quest to locate the source of the Nile finally ended at Jinja, now the self-appointed adventure capital of East Africa where today's modern explorers avail themselves of a veritable smorgasbord of white-knuckle activities.

Back in 1862, John Hanning Speke declared Ripon Falls to be the source of the Nile. Today, the laid-back town of Jinja overlooks this mighty river as it flows out of Lake Victoria, at the start of its 6,800-km (4,200-mile) journey to the Mediterranean. Thanks to a 1950s hydropower dam, Ripon Falls are now completely submerged; visitors can still view the official "source" in a 30-minute boat trip, but all that remains is a suggestive ripple on the water's surface, so it can be rather an anticlimax.

The river remains the reason behind why people come, but for a cluster of adventure activities rather than a history lesson. An industry fueled by sheer adrenaline has sprung up around the Nile's greatest asset: a series of dramatically churning white-water rapids that mark its course. White-water rafting is the main attraction, but visitors can choose from a mind-boggling variety of other thrills (and possible spills): kayaking, riverboarding, bungee jumping, quad bike safaris, horseback riding, and mountain biking. For fans of more serene outdoor pursuits, the "lake" of flat water at Bujagali, created by the second hydropower dam, offers stand-up paddleboarding, sit-on kayak trips, birding, and sunset cruises. Golf, sports fishing, and sailing on Lake Victoria are all on offer, too.

GETTING HERE AND AROUND

A two- to three-hour drive (80 km/50 miles) east of Kampala, Jinja can be reached by the more direct (but juggernaut-choked) Jinja Road through Mabira Forest, or the more peaceful Gayaza Road route. The final approach to Jinja for both routes involves crossing the Nile over the Owen Falls Dam. Enjoy the views but don't take any pictures—cameras can be confiscated because this is an important government installation. Bujagali, with its community of adventure companies and budget camps, lies 12 km (7 miles) north of Jinja on the east bank. Kampala Executive Aviation (KEA) offer charter flights to nearby Jinja Airstrip.

WHERE TO STAY

$$$ **Wildwaters Lodge.** If this world-class lodge, part of the respected
HOTEL Lemala group, does not enchant you with its magical location, it will
Fodor'sChoice win you over with its winning service and superb cuisine. **Pros:** one
★ of the best lodges in Uganda, Wildwaters is a destination in itself; an excellent spot to wind down after a safari; a great base for adrenaline adventures. **Cons:** not on the main safari trail; some people find the roar of the rapids too noisy; occasional tsetse flies can be annoying. $\boxed{\$}$ *Rooms from: US$510* ⊠ *Kalagala Falls, River Nile, Jinja* ⊹ *From Jinja Road turn north at Nile Breweries and continue for 26 km/16 miles till you get to Kangulamira town. Turn right here just before Petrocity fuel station. Travel 3 km.2 miles until you reach lodge parking area. The lodge guard will then radio lodge to send a boat. Alternatively, take Gayaza Road northeast from Kampala. At Kayunga town, turn right toward Jinja. Turn left in Kangulamira town just after Petrocity fuel station, then follow directions as above* ☎ *039/277–6669, 0772/237–400* ⊕ *www.wildwaterslodge.com* ⊷ *10 rooms* ⦿ *All meals.*

SPORTS AND THE OUTDOORS

WHITE-WATER RAFTING

None of Jinja's activities is more popular than rafting the Nile. Trips tackle a sequence of white-water rapids, graded between 3 and 5, with names such as Vengeance and the ominous-sounding Bad Place. At local beauty spot Itanda Falls, a Class VI rapid necessitates a portage via surrounding rocks that fall within a nature reserve. Three established, reputable companies offer similarly priced half- and one-day packages, including transport from Kampala if required, lunch on the river, and beers afterward to toast the excitements of the day. Two-day or longer expeditions are also available.

FAMILY   **Adrift East Africa.** Adrift was established in 1981 and has pioneered rafting on the Nile in Uganda and on the Zambezi in Zimbabwe. The team is made up of smart professionals, managing bookings for white-water rafting, kayaking, and Wildwaters Lodge from their offices in Arusha, Tanzania, and Jinja, Uganda. Adrift's client list includes royals, actors, and TV celebrities. They also operate the Nile High Bungee from their riverside camp off the Bujagali Road. Full-moon jumps and tandem jumps also available. If staying at Wildwaters Lodge, they will collect you from, and drop you back at the lodge. ⊠ *Riverbase, Kimaka Rd., Jinja* ✢ *At the end of Jinja Nile Resort's road* ☎ *0755 /225–587* ⊕ *www.adrift.ug* ✉ *Full-day rafting package, $140 per person. Bungee jump $115 per person.*

FAMILY   **Nalubale Rafting.** The folks at Nalubale Rafting are a friendly and enthusiastic bunch, with a laid-back base in Jinja town and the cheap and cheerful Nile River Camp at Bujagali. Groups of volunteers, students, and independent travelers paddle confidently under supervision from their professional river guides; families are well catered for on their "Fish'n'Flip" trips; and they conjure up an impressive riverside lunch spread for hungry rafters. If you hunger for something worthy of a modern-day explorer, they occasionally run six-day Jinja-Karuma rafting expeditions. ⊠ *Plot 38, Kiira Rd., Eastern Region, Jinja* ☎ *782/638–938 mobile* ⊕ *www.nalubalerafting.com* ✉ *From USD$125 per person; Fish'n'flips from $30.*

Fodor's Choice ★   **Nile River Explorers.** The bustling NRE camp at Bujagali, high above the Nile, is a hip hangout for backpackers and the de facto center point for Jinja's adventure tourism activities. Their typical clientele like to raft hard and party harder, and the company's enduring popularity ensures there is rarely a day when they are not on the river. They offer high standards of professionalism and, in addition to rafting, have a great network of connections. ■TIP→ **Raft with Nile River Explorers to get vouchers for discounts on other adventure activities and accommodations in the area.** The NRE office in Jinja is affiliated to Jinja Base Camp, which offers very reasonably priced accommodations, food, and drink at the same Wilson Avenue address. ⊠ *Plot 30, Wilson Ave., Eastern Region, Jinja* ☎ *772/422–373* ⊕ *www.raftafrica.com* ✉ *Full-day rafting $140.*

GATEWAY CITIES

Visitors to Uganda looking for a base as the start or end of their gorilla safari have a choice between two very different destinations: the bustling sprawl of the country's capital Kampala, or the simple serenity of Entebbe, its international airport hub.

Whatever you choose, a Chinese company has almost finished construction of a tolled superhighway between Kampala and Entebbe. Estimates suggest it should be open early 2018; once completed, the new toll road should significantly reduce the time it takes to get between the two destinations. Until then, your overnight stop of choice will probably be based on a trade-off between personal preferences, traffic jams, and flight times.

ENTEBBE

Entebbe is a peaceful, sleepy town, situated at the tip of a peninsula extending south of Kampala into Lake Victoria. Just a couple of miles from the country's only international airport, overnighting here is definitely convenient for anyone with early or late flight arrival/departure times. Entebbe's proximity to the airport, and Kajjansi Airfield a few miles up the road, also makes it handy for the domestic air services to the national parks. Charming, boutique guesthouses or mediocre business hotels typify the accommodations here. If these are not your style they become significantly more appealing when you realize that the 40-km (25-mile) journey between Kampala and Entebbe can take more than 90 minutes to complete.

GETTING HERE AND AROUND
Entebbe International Airport (EBB) serves Entebbe (5 km/3 miles) and Kampala (40 km/25 miles). Regional services from RwandAir, Precision Air, and Kenya Airways serve destinations in Rwanda, Tanzania, and Kenya respectively. From Entebbe, licensed airport taxis are available at all hours from the stand just outside arrivals, though it's less stressful to prebook a hotel or tour company driver to meet your flight. Most Entebbe properties include this in their rates.

EXPLORING

FAMILY
Fodor's Choice ★

Ngamba Island Chimpanzee Sanctuary. Delivering a different experience to tracking wild chimps, this island sanctuary in Lake Victoria offers the chance for visitors to observe its population of rescued chimps, and the opportunity to get up close and personal with our primate cousins. Lying 23 km (14 miles) southeast of Entebbe, the sanctuary was established in 1998 by the Chimpanzee Sanctuary and Wildlife Conservation Trust (now known as Chimpanzee Trust). Its mission is to care for chimps rescued from captivity; each has its own sad story. A small corner of its 50 hectares is fenced off for day-trippers to observe feeding sessions from a viewing platform—an excellent photographic opportunity in itself. The real appeal, however, lies in getting behind-the-scenes: overnight visitors (the island has a small tented camp) can opt for the Caregiver Experience. Be prepared for extensive medical requirements, but the chance to care for our closest relatives will melt your heart. Volunteering programs are also available. ✉ *Chimpanzee Trust, Plot 1, Bank Close, Entebbe* ☎ *0414/320–662, 0758/221–880* 🌐 *www.ngambaisland.org* 🎟 *Half-day speedboat trips from US$145 per person; Caregiver Experience US$200 per person (plus transfers, entry fee, and accommodation).*

FAMILY

Uganda Wildlife Education Centre. On the lakeshore in Entebbe, the Uganda Wildlife Education Centre plays a multifaceted role: it's an animal rescue center, veterinary institution, and tourist attraction all rolled into one—but perhaps its most significant role is as an education facility for the country's schoolchildren, who roll up in busloads daily. UWEC (pronounced *Ooh-Eck*), is home to an array of Ugandan species. Facilities for the animals may feel a little cramped, but the team places great importance on putting conservation first, making it a pleasant place to while away a spare morning or afternoon in Entebbe. Kids love the camel and donkey camel rides, the children's play center, and beach games. **■ TIP→ To get the most out of your visit, book the Behind-the-Scenes tour ($70) for a chance to enter some of the enclosures and meet the animals, or the Chimpanzee Close-up ($260) for a grooming session courtesy of one of UWEC's orphaned chimpanzees.** There's also an interactive Keeper for the Day program ($150), and traditional banda (cottages) are available to rent on the property. ✉ *Plot 56/57, Lugard Ave., Entebbe* ☎ *0414/320–520, 0706/505–722* 🎟 *US$15 adults, US$8 children.*

WHERE TO EAT

$
ECLECTIC

🍴 **Faze 3.** A lively choice for Entebbe nights out, and handy for diners en route to the airport for late-night flights, Faze 3 boasts a mind-boggling menu that encompasses a wide range of cuisines. The choices include starters and snacks, light salads, pita pockets, and sandwiches. **Known for:** meaty feasts served sizzlingly hot on cast-iron skillets; authentic curries. [$] *Average main: US$10* ✉ *106 Circular Rd., Entebbe* ✣ *Last turn on the left before the airport* ☎ *0778/609–595, 0393/671–345, 0778/609–595* 🌐 *faze3ug.com.*

$
PIZZA
FAMILY
Fodor's Choice ★

🍴 **Goretti's Beachside Pizzeria and Grill.** A cold beer, crisp pizza, and curling your toes in the sand are a few of life's simple pleasures. Enjoy all three simultaneously at Goretti's Beachside Pizzeria, a popular haunt for tourists and locals alike. **Known for:** crisp, wood-fired pizza; grilled fish and meat. [$] *Average main: US$10* ✉ *Anderita Beach,*

Nambi Rd., Entebbe ☎ 0772/308–887 🌐 www.gorettisafarisuganda.com 💳 No credit cards.

$$ 🍴 **Mediterraneo.** Restauranteur Stefano Ginnetti has created a stylish addition to his similarly monikered Nairobi eateries: from its location within the grounds of Villa Kololo (a quirky boutique hotel), Kampala's Mediterraneo serves up world-class Italian food to a fashionable crowd. Tiered hardwood decks encircle a leafy courtyard, creating intimate spaces decorated with vintage bric-a-brac. **Known for:** genuine Italian cooking; romantic atmosphere; excellent desserts. [$] *Average main: US$20 ✉ Villa Kololo, 31 Acacia Ave., Kampala ☎ 0414/500–533, 0701/098–732 🌐 villakololo.com.*

ITALIAN
Fodor's Choice ★

WHERE TO STAY

$ 🏨 **The Boma.** This popular boutique hotel with a reputation for great service is tucked away on a leafy residential street in Entebbe, a few minutes' drive from the airport. **Pros:** colonial style and professional service at an affordable price; rate includes airport transfers if required; superb service. **Cons:** can get booked up quickly; incoming/outgoing guests can make it noisy at night. [$] *Rooms from: US$165 ✉ Plot 20A, Gowers Rd., Entebbe ✣ Turn off airport road at AAR Victoria Medical Centre (and Boma sign) ☎ 0772/467–929 🌐 www.boma.co.ug 💳 No credit cards 🛏 16 rooms 🍽 Breakfast.*

B&B/INN
Fodor's Choice ★

$ 🏨 **Karibu Guesthouse.** An unprententious guesthouse in a peaceful area of Entebbe, Karibu lives up to its name (it means "you're welcome" in Swahili) with friendly, well-trained staff and some of the best food this side of Kampala. **Pros:** 10 minutes from airport; lovers of French cuisine will appreciate the food; swimming pool; rate includes airport transfer. **Cons:** some airport/guest noise at night. [$] *Rooms from: US$145 ✉ 84 Nsamizi Rd., Entebbe ✣ From Entebbe airport, take main highway to Kampala. After 5 km (3 miles) the road bends to right and you see Lake Victoria Hotel on right. Turn left here (signed Karibu) and then turn right, up hill, at T-junction. At next T-junction, turn left. Karibu is signed on left side after 800 meters ☎ 0777/044–984, 0788/714–587 🌐 karibuguesthouse.com 🛏 7 rooms 🍽 Breakfast.*

B&B/INN

$$ 🏨 **Protea Hotel Entebbe.** Part of an established network of business hotels, the Protea Entebbe is just off the main approach road to the airport, offering a practical base to stay. **Pros:** super-convenient for the airport; beautiful beach location; international brand. **Cons:** service can be slow; generic business style; food gets mixed reviews. [$] *Rooms from: US$275 ✉ 36-40 Sebugwawo Dr., Entebbe ☎ 0414/323–132 🛏 70 rooms 🍽 Breakfast.*

HOTEL

KAMPALA

If the bright lights of Kampala beckon—and if time is not a precious commodity—then Uganda's dynamic capital offers an impressive roll call of positive qualities: a far wider range of fashionable eateries dot the city, it delivers a better quality of high-end hotels, the nightlife is buzzing, the city is host to a growing arts and festival scene, and shopping mavens will love the craft markets. Buildings of historical interest include sub-Saharan Africa's only Baha'i Temple, the dated (but still worth a visit) Uganda

Museum, the Uganda National Mosque (East Africa's biggest mosque, a gift from Muamar Gaddafi of Libya, and a great vantage point to survey the city), and the Uganda Martyrs Shrines in Namugongo. Sadly the magnificent Kasubi Tombs—a burial ground for members of the Buganda royal family, are still under reconstruction after a fire gutted the main structures in 2010. For many visitors, however, Kampala's own brand of vibrant urban chaos is a sight in itself. This really is a tale of two cities.

GETTING HERE AND AROUND

Entebbe International Airport (EBB) serves Kampala (40 km/25 miles). Regional services from RwandAir, Precision Air, and Kenya Airways serve destinations in Rwanda, Tanzania, and Kenya, respectively.

WHERE TO EAT

Kampala's Industrial Area has undergone a major shake-up in 2017 with the conversion of traditional industrial units into happening places. Seventh Street is home to the cutting-edge Ember's cocktail bar and Afri-art Gallery on Seventh, a grand exhibition space unlike anything else in Kampala. Converted industrial spaces elsewhere include Design Hub, a European-inspired co-working space, and The Square, a rooftop bar that regularly hosts Kampala's best DJs. Conveniently, Uber's Uganda office is on the floor below.

$$
ECLECTIC
Fodor's Choice
★

✕ **The Bistro.** This stylish, modern restaurant in the heart of buzzing Kisementi delivers accomplished fusion cuisine with considerable flair, transforming effortlessly from convivial café by day to happening eaterie by night. Customers love the laid-back atmosphere of the Bistro's shaded terrace. **Known for:** café by day, eaterie by night; "Gin o'clock" every Monday–Thursday, 4–7 pm; live music Friday night. $ *Average main: US$15* ✉ *15 Cooper Rd., Kisementi* ☎ *0757/247–876* ⊕ *facebook.com/thebistrokampala.*

$$
INDIAN

✕ **Khazana: The Verandah.** The Verandah, the stylish southside sister of the popular Khana Khazana restaurant in Kololo, serves up classic Indian cuisine in a white-stucco loggia overlooking a fountain. Petal-strewn water features, ornately decorated wall alcoves, and Nehru-collared waiting staff add to the subcontinental style of this high-caliber curry house. **Known for:** Indian food. $ *Average main: US$18* ✉ *Khazana: The Verandah, Plot 7921/7922, Tank Hill Rd., Muyenga* ☎ *0752/224–003, 0752/224–004.*

$$
AFRICAN

✕ **The Lawns.** The only restaurant in Kampala with a license to serve game—the meat is sourced legally from registered South African game ranches—the Lawns unashamedly celebrates the wildest cuts of meat, with dishes like ostrich burgers, smoked kudu steak, or whole crocodile tail (preorder 2–3 hours). Manicured gardens and a beautiful wooden deck overlooking the perennially verdant golf course adds to the charm of the place. **Known for:** legally sourced game meat; award-winning presentation; excellent service. $ *Average main: US$20* ✉ *Plot 3A, Lower Kololo Terr., Kololo* ⟡ *On Acacia Avenue, next to Golf Course* ☎ *0414/250–337, 0312/515–373* ⊕ *www.thelawns.co.ug.*

WHERE TO STAY

$$
HOTEL

🛏 **Kampala Serena Hotel.** Towering above sculpted water features and landscaped gardens like a modern-day Moorish palace, the 5-star Kampala Serena sets *the* standard for hotel service in Uganda. **Pros:** international standards; central location; extremely professional. **Cons:** too large and impersonal for some tastes; long lines at security when president visits; the building has a macabre history—before it was extensively renovated by the Serena chain the property was the infamous Nile Hotel, associated with state-sanctioned torture that took place under the bloody regimes of Obote and Amin. $ *Rooms from: US$325* ✉ *Kintu Rd., Kampala* ☎ *0312/309–000,* ⊕ *www.serenahotels.com/serenakampala* ⏎ *122 rooms* ❙◎❙ *Breakfast.*

$$
RESORT
FAMILY

🛏 **Lake Victoria Serena Golf Resort and Spa.** Despite its neither-here-nor-there location, visitors to this pastel-hue citadel on Lake Victoria happily trade off the plush comfort of the rooms and extensive facilities for its remote position. **Pros:** well-appointed rooms with lake views; comfortable spot to wind down post-safari; Presidential Suite voted Uganda's Leading Hotel Suite, World Travel Awards 2017. **Cons:** a long way from anywhere; guests complain of poor Wi-Fi in some rooms; corporate, business-style. $ *Rooms from: US$322* ✉ *Lweza-Kigo Rd., off Entebbe Rd., Kampala* ⚓ *From Entebbe, turn right off Entebbe Road in Kajjansi trading center (after footbridge). At T-junction, turn left, and continue until you pass turn-off for Lweza estate. After this, turn right onto Kigo Road. Continue along this road until you reach property. From Kampala, turn left off Entebbe Road in Kajjansi trading center (before footbridge). Then follow the directions as above* ☎ *0417/121–000* ⊕ *www.serenahotels.com/serenalakevictoria* ⏎ *124 rooms* ❙◎❙ *Breakfast.*

$$
HOTEL

🛏 **Sheraton Kampala Hotel.** Located in Kampala's Central Business District, among mature palm-tree filled gardens, the Sheraton Kampala Hotel celebrated its 50th anniversary in 2017. **Pros:** central Kampala location; global brand with international service standards; regular themed evening events. **Cons:** majority of guests are there on business; security lines at main entrance gate; popular gym can get very busy. $ *Rooms from: US$297* ✉ *Ternan Ave., Kampala* ☎ *0312/322–499* ⊕ *www.sheratonkampala.com* ⏎ *236 rooms* ❙◎❙ *Breakfast.*

SPORTS AND OUTDOORS

Lake Victoria Serena Golf Resort. Uganda has a sprinkling of small golf courses across the country but this is East Africa's first 9-hole island green (playing as 18 holes). Constructed to full USGA specifications, with a principal architect from San Francisco and golfing expertise from South Africa, Serena Hotels has created a championship golf course with a clubhouse that has locker rooms with showers and a steam room, two restaurants, a bar, and pro shop. Golf equipment can be rented on-site and individual and group golf lessons are available with the resident pro. Caddies are on hand, too. ✉ *Lweza-Kigo Rd., off Entebbe Rd., Kajjansi* ☎ *417/121–000, 312/322–1000* ⊕ *www.serenahotels.com* ⛳ *18 holes, par 70* 🏌 *Serena Hotel guests: $15 for 9 holes, $25 for 18 holes.*

7

BOTSWANA

WELCOME TO BOTSWANA

TOP REASONS TO GO

★ **The Okavango Delta:**
Whether you're drifting dreamily in a *mokoro* (canoe) through crystal clear, papyrus-fringed channels or walking among ancient trees on one of the many islands, your everyday world is guaranteed to fade from your consciousness.

★ **Big Game:** You won't find huge herds as in the Serengeti, but you'll come face-to-face with more critters than you ever knew existed. And there won't be hordes of other visitors blocking your view or diluting the experience.

★ **Birding:** Marvel at more than 900 species—many endemic—that crowd the game reserves. A sighting of a Pel's fishing owl, one of the world's rarest birds, will have Audubon twitching in his grave.

★ **Walking with the Bushmen:** Far from being lifeless, deserts are miracles of plenty, you just have to be in the right company—that of the Kalahari Bushmen. Listen to their dissonant music and watch them dance a dance as old as time.

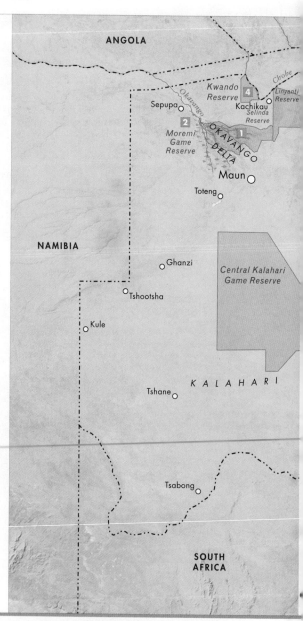

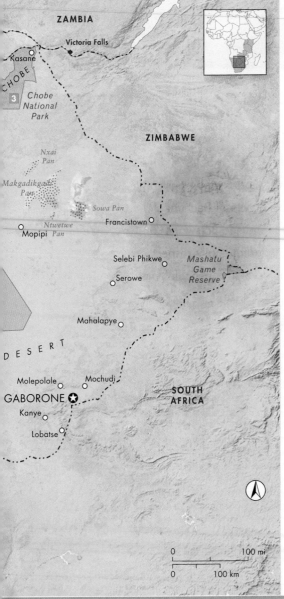

ZAMBIA

Victoria Falls

Kasane

CHOBE

3 Chobe
National
Park

ZIMBABWE

Nxai
Pan

Makgadikgadi
Pan

Sowa Pan

Ntwetwe   Francistown
Mopipi Pan

Selebi Phikwe   Mashatu
Game
Serowe   Reserve

Mahalapye

D E S E R T

Molepolole   Mochudi

GABORONE ✪   SOUTH
AFRICA
Kanye

Lobatse

0   100 mi

0   100 km

Botswana is roughly the
size of France, and nearly
18% is reserved for con-
servation and tourism.

1 The Okavango Delta.
The Okavango Delta is
formed by the Okavango
River, which descends from
the Angolan highlands and
then fans out over north-
western Botswana. The
magical scenery of this
recently declared UNESCO
World Heritage Site is
impressive.

2 Moremi Game Reserve.
In the southeastern sector
of the Okavango lies this
spectacular reserve where
the life-giving waters of the
Okavango meet the vast
Kalahari.

3 Chobe National Park.
Huge herds of elephants
roam this 11,700-square-km
(4,500-square-mile) park
that borders the Chobe
River in northeast Botswana.

4 Kwando, Selinda, and
Linyanti Reserves. These
three neighboring private
concessions lie on Botswana's northern border tracking the Kwando River until it
becomes the Linyanti and
finally the Chobe River.

8

Updated by
James Gifford

More than half a century ago Botswana was a Cinderella among nations. Then the Fairy Godmother visited and bestowed upon her the gift of diamonds. The resulting economic boom transformed Botswana into one of Africa's richest countries (as measured by per capita income). In 1966 the British Protectorate of Bechuanaland was granted independence and renamed Botswana, and the first democratic president, the internationally respected Sir Seretse Khama, guided his country into a peaceful future.

Where other nations' celebrations quickly turned sour, Botswana's independence brought an enduring tide of optimism. The country sidestepped the scourge of tribalism and factional fighting that cursed much of the continent and is considered one of Africa's most stable democracies. The infrastructure is excellent, and the country is extremely safe. Another big bonus is that nearly everybody speaks English—a legacy from when Botswana was a British protectorate.

Although cities such as Gaborone (pronounced "*ha*-bo-ronee"), the capital, have been modernized, Botswana has little in the way of urban excitement. But outside the cities it's a land of amazing variety: the Kalahari Desert lies in stark contrast to the lush beauty of the Okavango Delta, one of Botswana's most magnificent and best-known regions. Botswana is passionate about conservation, and its legendary big game goes hand-in-hand with its admirable conservation record. Once a hunting mecca for the so-called Great White Hunters (i.e., Ernest Hemingway), shooting now is with cameras, not rifles. The government effectively banned all commercial hunting on non–privately owned land in 2014.

Botswana's policy of low-impact, high-cost tourism ensures the wilderness remains pristine and exclusive. The great rivers—the Chobe, the Linyanti, and the Kwando—are teeming with herds of elephants and packs of wild dogs, otherwise known as the elusive "painted wolves" of

FAST FACTS

Size At 581,730 square km (224,607 square miles), it's roughly the size of France or Texas.

Number of National Parks Seven. Chobe National Park (including the Savuti and Linyanti areas); Moremi Game Reserve; Central Kalahari Game Reserve; Khutse Game Reserve; Kgalagadi Transfrontier Park; Magkadikgadi Pans National Park; Nxai Pan National Park.

Number of Private Reserves As new private reserves or concessions are established regularly, it's difficult to estimate. Outside of Moremi Game Reserve, the Okavango Delta is made up of a large number of private concessions and this system of leased land allocation is used throughout the country, mostly as buffer zones surrounding the national parks.

Big Five All here, although rhinos have only been reintroduced relatively recently through the collaborative efforts of the government, Wilderness Safaris, Sanctuary Retreats, &Beyond, Great Plains, and Desert & Delta Safaris.

Africa. The Savuti Channel, which flowed for a brief period from 2012 to 2015, may now have been reduced to a river of sand but the nearby hills and golden grass of the Savuti plains are still home to prowling leopards and huge prides of lions that hunt under skies pulsing with brilliant stars. Then there are the vast white pie-crust surfaces of the Makgadikgadi Pans (the nearest thing on earth to the surface of the moon), once a mega inland lake where flamingos still flock to breed and strange prehistoric islands of rock rise dramatically from the flaky, arid surface.

If you'd like to meet some of the most fascinating people in existence, the stark wilderness of the Central Kalahari Game Reserve is home to the fastest disappearing indigenous population on earth, the Kalahari San Bushmen, as well as majestic black-maned lions.

PLANNING

WHEN TO GO

The best time to visit Botswana is in the autumn and winter months (April–September), the dry season; however, it's also the most expensive time. In the Delta during the winter months the water comes in from the Angolan highlands, and the floodplains, channels, lakes, and inland waterways are literally brimming with sparkling, fresh water. Elsewhere, because it's the dry season, the grass and vegetation are sparse, and it's much easier to see game, which often have no choice but to drink at available waterholes or rivers. But be warned: it can be bitterly cold, particularly early in the morning and at night. Dress in layers, which you can discard or add to as the sun goes up or down.

During the green season (November–February), aptly named since it's when the bush is at its most lush and is populated with lots of baby animals, you'll find great economy deals offered by most of the lodges, but it can be very hot, especially in October and early November when temperatures can reach up to 35°C (95°F) or more. The rains tend to arrive from November onwards and can continue until late March or early April, which helps to cool things down but can impact your activities. If you're a birder (Botswana has more than 400 species of birds), this is the best time to visit because all the migratory birds have returned; the green vegetation also provides an attractive backdrop for keen photographers. Generally speaking, though, unless you can stand great heat, don't mind getting wet, or are a devoted bird-watcher, stick with fall and winter.

GETTING HERE AND AROUND

AIR TRAVEL

AIRPORTS In this huge, often inaccessible country, air travel is the easiest way to get around. Sir Seretse Khama Airport, 15 km (9½ miles) from Gaborone's city center, is Botswana's main point of entry. Kasane International Airport is 3 km (2 miles) from the entrance to Chobe National Park, and small but very busy Maun Airport, the gateway to the Okavango Delta, is 1 km (½ mile) from the city center of this northern safari capital. All three are easy to find your way around in and rarely crowded.

Airports Kasane International Airport. ⊠ *Upper Rd., Kasane* ☎ *625–5000.* **Maun Airport.** ⊠ *Mathiba I St., Maun* ☎ *686–0238.* **Sir Seretse Khama Airport.** ⊠ *Airport Rd., Phakalane, Gaborone* ☎ *369–2504.*

FLIGHTS Air Botswana has scheduled flights from Johannesburg to Gaborone and Maun on a daily basis. The airline also flies Johannesburg to Kasane on Tuesday and from Cape Town to Gaborone and Maun on Thursday and Sunday. SA Airlink also has daily flights from Johannesburg to Gaborone, Maun, and Kasane.

Mack Air, Wilderness Air, and Delta Air fly directly between Johannesburg's Lanseria airport and Maun on private charters.

Airlines Air Botswana. ⊠ *Dalale House, Queens Rd., Main Mall, Gaborone* ✛ *Behind South African Embassy* ☎ *368–0900* ⊕ *www.airbotswana.co.bw.* **Delta Air.** ⊠ *Mathiba I St., Maun* ✛ *Inside airport, opposite terminal* ☎ *686–0044.* **Mack Air.** ⊠ *Mathiba I St., Maun* ✛ *Opposite airport* ☎ *686–0675* ⊕ *www. mackair.co.bw.* **SA Airlink.** ☎ *11/451–7300 in South Africa, 395–1820* ⊕ *www. flyairlink.com.* **Wilderness Air.** ⊠ *Mathiba I St., Maun* ☎ *686–0778* ⊕ *www. wilderness-air.com.*

CHARTER FLIGHTS Air charter companies operate small planes from Kasane and Maun to all the camps. Flown by some of the youngest-looking pilots in the world, these flights, which your travel agent will arrange, are reliable, reasonably cheap, and average between 25 and 50 minutes. Maximum baggage allowance is 12 kilograms (26 pounds) in a soft sports/duffel bag (no hard cases allowed), excluding the weight of camera equipment (within reason). Because of the thermal air currents over Botswana, and because most flights are around midday, when thermals are at their strongest, flights can sometimes be very bumpy. Take air-sickness pills if you're susceptible to motion sickness; then sit back and enjoy the fabulous bird's-eye views. You're sure to spot elephants and hippos from the air.

CAR TRAVEL

All the main access roads from neighboring countries are paved, and cross-border formalities are user-friendly. Maun is easy to reach from South Africa, Namibia, and Zimbabwe, but the distances are long and not very scenic. Gaborone is 360 km (225 miles) from Johannesburg via Rustenburg, Zeerust, and the Tlokweng border post. Driving in Botswana is on the left-hand side of the road. The "Shell Tourist Map of Botswana" is the best available map. Find it at Botswana airports or in airport bookstores.

Forget about a car in the Okavango Delta unless it's amphibious. Only the western and eastern sides of the Delta panhandle and the Moremi Game Reserve are accessible by car; but it's wisest to always take a 4x4 vehicle. The road from Maun to Moremi North Gate is paved for the first 47 km (29 miles) up to Shorobe, where it becomes gravel for 11 km (7 miles) and then a dirt road.

A 4x4 vehicle is also essential in Chobe National Park. The roads are sandy and/or very muddy, depending on the season.

ESSENTIALS

COMMUNICATIONS

Botswana phone numbers begin with the 267 country code, which you don't dial within the country. (There are no internal area codes in Botswana.)

HEALTH AND SAFETY

There are high standards of hygiene in all the private lodges, and most hotels are usually up to international health standards. But malaria is present, so don't forget to take those antimalarials. Botswana has one of the highest AIDS rates in Africa, but it also has one of Africa's most progressive and comprehensive programs for dealing with the disease. All the private lodges and camps have excellent staff medical programs; you're in no danger of contracting the disease unless you have sex with a stranger. As in most cities, crime is prevalent in Gaborone, but simple safety precautions such as locking up your documents and valuables and not walking alone at night will keep you safe. On safari, there's always potential danger from wild animals, but your ranger will brief you thoroughly on the dos and don'ts of encountering big game.

The American embassy is in Gaborone, the country's capital city.

Most safari companies include emergency medical evacuation insurance for public liability to the nearest hospital, but you must have your own travel and medical insurance as well. There are two 24-hour emergency rescue companies: Medical Rescue International, which will require confirmation with your insurance company before evacuation, and Okavango Air Rescue, which will liaise with your insurance after your safe evacuation.

Embassies U.S. Embassy. ⊠ *Embassy Dr., Government Enclave, Gaborone* ☎ *395–3982, 395–7111 after hours* ⊕ *bw.usembassy.gov.*

Emergencies Ambulance. ☎ *997.* **Police.** ☎ *999.*

8

Emergency Services **Medical Rescue International.** ☎ *390–1601, 992 Emergency toll-free.* **Okavango Air Rescue.** ☎ *686–1616, 995 emergency toll-free.*

MONEY MATTERS

The pula and the thebe constitute the country's currency; one pula equals 100 thebe. You'll need to change your money into pula, as this is the only legally accepted currency. However, most camp prices are quoted in U.S. dollars.

There are no restrictions on foreign currency notes brought into the country as long as they're declared. Travelers can carry up to P10,000 (about US$1,000), or the equivalent in foreign currency, out of the country without declaring it. Banking hours are weekdays 9–3:30, Saturday 8:30–12:30. Hours at Barclays Bank at Sir Seretse Khama International Airport are Monday–Saturday 6 am–10 pm.

■ TIP→ Though the national currency is the pula, you can use U.S. dollars or euros as tips. Your information folder at each lodge will give helpful suggestions on whom and what to tip.

PASSPORTS AND VISAS

All visitors, including infants, need a valid passport to enter Botswana for visits of up to 90 days.

ABOUT THE HOTELS AND LODGES

Most camps accommodate 12 to 20 people, so the only traffic you'll encounter among the Delta's waterways in the private concessions is that of grazing hippos and dozing crocodiles. In the national parks and particularly in the northern part of Chobe, where most vehicles are, the roads and river are noticeably busier but it's still significantly quieter than most of the continent's parks. Many lodges now have family units although most operators have a minimum age requirement of at least six. An increasing number also offer in-room massages and helicopter flights (sometimes called flips) for a surcharge. Room prices are highest June through October. Check with individual camps for special offers.

A word about terminology: "Land camps" are in game reserves or concessions and offer morning and evening game drives. If you're not in a national park, you'll be able to go out for night drives off-road with a powerful spotlight to pick out nocturnal animals. "Water camps" are deep in the Okavango Delta and often accessible only by air or water. Many camps offer both a land and a true water experience, so you get the best of both worlds.

There's limited local cuisine in Botswana, so the food is designed to appeal to an international palate. Nevertheless, it's very tasty. Most camps bake their own excellent bread, muffins, and cakes and often make desserts such as meringues, éclairs, and homemade ice cream. And you'll find plenty of tasty South African wine and beer. Don't expect TVs or elevators, even at very expensive camps.

For information on converters and electricity while on Safari, see Electricity, in the Planning Your Safari chapter.

The Bayei people live along the tributaries of the Okanvago and Chobe Rivers.

MOBILE SAFARIS

Often incorrectly viewed only as a cost-cutting measure, the range of mobile safari options in Botswana is staggering. At the top end, your large walk-in en suite tent will have Persian rugs, antique furniture and flush toilets; at the other extreme, you will help with the cooking and even setting up camp. The most popular option lies somewhere in the middle—a nonparticipatory safari with en suite tents, hot-water bucket showers, and a talented chef who can create delicious three-course meals that would rival many lodges, all on an open fire. As well as feeling closer to nature (lions can easily walk through your camp at night), mobile safari guides tend to be the most knowledgeable in the country, and spending 10 days with the same guide as you move through different habitats gives you a greater depth of understanding. It also gives the guide the opportunity to tailor the focus of game drives to your specific interests, helped by the inherent flexible nature of mobiles. The one downside is that although you will have your own private campsite, you will probably be in the national parks so will see other vehicles during the day.

DINING AND LODGING PRICES

Most lodging prices are quoted in U.S. dollars, and you can use dollars, euros, or South African rand as tips wherever you stay. The average price per person per night at private lodges is US$500–US$1,000, which includes accommodations, all game activities, all meals, soft drinks, and good South African wine. Camps arrange transfers from the nearest airport or airstrip.

■ TIP→ It's important to note that there are few budget lodging options available in Botswana, and most of the camps we write about fall into the "luxury" category.

Restaurant and hotel reviews have been shortened. For full information, visit Fodors.com.

WHAT IT COSTS IN U.S. DOLLARS			
$	**$$**	**$$$**	**$$$$**
Restaurants	under $12	$12–$20	$21–$30	over $30
Hotels	under $250	$250–$450	$451–$600	over $600

Prices in the restaurant reviews are the average cost of a main course at dinner or, if dinner isn't served, at lunch; taxes and service charges are generally included. Prices in the lodging reviews are the lowest cost of a standard double room in high season.

GOING GREEN

In such a pristine, finely balanced environment, it's vital to limit the impact on the flora and fauna, and many safari companies are now installing ecologically sound practices. Gone are the days of camps accruing mountains of empty, plastic water bottles—almost all lodges (and some mobile operators) will give you metal water bottles to fill and reuse with filtered drinking water from their reverse osmosis plants. Solar power is also taking over from noisy, diesel-guzzling generators. In addition, the major companies run a range of community initiatives aimed at ensuring the local Batswana population see the benefits from the unique habitat and its wildlife, creating a framework for long-term sustainable tourism.

ABOUT THE PARKS

This chapter has been broken down by **Must-See Parks** (Okavango Delta, Moremi Game Reserve, Chobe National Park, Kwando Reserve, Linyanti Reserve, and Selinda Reserve) and **If You Have Time Parks** (Central Kalahari Game Reserve, Makgadikgadi Pans, and Tuli Block) to help you bettter organize your time.

VISITOR INFORMATION

Visit Botswana Tourism's website for tour operator and travel agency information. To be listed on the website, these organizations must satisfy and adhere to the high standards demanded by Botswana Tourism.

Contacts Botswana Tourism Organization. ⊕ *www.botswanatourism.co.bw.*

THE OKAVANGO DELTA

Game
★★★★★
Park Accessibility
★★★
Getting Around
★★★★
Accommodations
★★★★★
Scenic Beauty
★★★★★

There's no place on earth like the Okavango. The world's largest inland delta, the Okavango was formed by the Okavango River, which floods down from the Angolan highlands once a year and fans out into northwestern Botswana in a meandering complex network of papyrus-lined channels, deep, still pools (where crocodiles and hippos lurk), secret waterways (where reeds and grass almost meet over your head), palm-fringed islands, and natural lagoons.

This watery network covers an area of more than 15,000 square km (5,791 square miles). This vast area is sometimes referred to as the Swamps, but this gives a false impression because there are no murky mangroves or sinister everglades here. It's just open, crystal clear waters where you'll discover an unparalleled experience of being in one of the world's last great wilderness areas. Often, the only way to get around this network of waterways is by boat.

The *mokoro*, a canoelike boat synonymous with the Okavango, was introduced to the Delta in the mid-18th century, when the Bayei people moved down from the Zambezi. The Bayei invented the mokoro as a controllable craft that could be maneuvered up- or downstream. These boats were traditionally made from the trunks of the great jackalberry, morula, and sausage trees. Today, because of the need to protect the trees, you may find yourself in the modern equivalent: a fiberglass canoe. Either way, a skilled poler (think gondolier) will stand or sit at the rear of the narrow craft guiding you through the Delta's waterways—he'll be on full alert for the ubiquitous and unpredictable hippos but may be a bit more laid-back when it comes to the mighty crocs that lie in the sun. (Powerboats are an option in deeper waters.) Bird-watching from these boats is a special thrill: the annual return of thousands of gorgeous carmine bee-eaters to the northern Delta and Linyanti in September and October is a dazzling sight, as is a glimpse of the huge orange-color

8

Pel's fishing owl. ■ TIP→ **Don't miss the chance to go on a guided walk on one of the many islands.**

Although most camps are now both land- and water-based, in a water camp—usually an island surrounded by water—you'll almost certainly see elephants, hippos, crocs, and red *lechwes* (beautiful antelope endemic to the Swamps), and you may catch a glimpse of the rare, aquatic sitatunga antelope. You'll almost certainly hear lions but may not always see them; if you're very lucky, you may see a pride swimming between islands. On the other hand, if you're in a land-and-water camp, you'll see lots of game. Remember that you'll see plenty of animals elsewhere in Botswana. You're in the Delta to experience the unforgettable beauty.

GETTING HERE AND AROUND

You'll fly into Maun and then be transferred by your tour operator to a small plane that'll bring you to an airstrip in the Delta. Distance from the airstrip to camps varies, but normally won't be much longer than 20–25 minutes, and this is often an exciting game drive through the bush. Roads are bumpy—but you're in a game vehicle.

WHERE TO STAY

$$$$
RESORT

Abu Camp. You will want for nothing at this lavish camp where the main draw is its opportunity for immersion into a resident elephant herd—from walking among their towering tree-trunk legs to drifting alongside their splashing feet in a mokoro, to sharing a mud-bath. **Pros:** a once-in-a-lifetime opportunity to get up close to elephants; break from the typical safari mold; great food. **Cons:** one of the country's most expensive camps; lion sightings can be sporadic; separate dining tables results in less safari camaraderie. $ *Rooms from: US$2985* ✉ *Okavango Delta* ☎ *11/257–5000 in South Africa* ⊕ *www.abucamp. com* ☞ *6 tents* ⊙| *All-inclusive.*

$$$$
RESORT
FAMILY

&Beyond Nxabega Okavango Safari Camp. Renowned for its beauty, Nxabega (pronounced *na*-becka) is in the very heart of the Delta and offers both a water and a land experience. **Pros:** true land and water camp; children's program; chance to see Pel's fishing owl. **Cons:** no sweeping views of the Delta; game can be less spectacular than elsewhere; no private plunge pools. $ *Rooms from: US$1750* ✉ *Okavango Delta* ☎ *11/809–4300 in South Africa* ⊕ *www.nxabega.com* ☞ *9 tents* ⊙| *All-inclusive.*

$$$$
RESORT
FAMILY

&Beyond Sandibe Okavango Safari Lodge. Sandibe clings to the edge of a pristine channel of the Santantadibe River and has the reputation for being &Beyond's best camp for wildlife viewing in the Delta. **Pros:** beautiful, stylish accommodations; great game; helicopter flights available at extra cost. **Cons:** might be too modern for some; no water activities; universal child policy may not suit everyone. $ *Rooms from: US$2350* ✉ *Okavango Delta* ☎ *11/809–4300 in South Africa* ⊕ *www. sandibe.com* ☞ *12 cottages* ⊙| *All-inclusive.*

$$$$
RESORT
FAMILY

&Beyond Xaranna Okavango Delta Camp. In 2008 she was the brash new princess on the block, dazzling the eye with bright pink, sage green, and white canvas decor; today, however, Xaranna is indisputably the Queen of the Delta. **Pros:** luxurious rooms; great food; private concession.

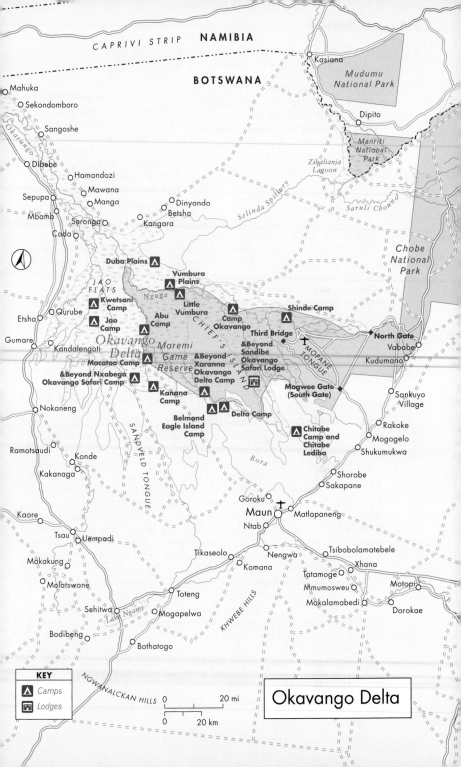

Okavango Delta

Cons: not renowned for big game; water activities are seasonal; not cheap. $ *Rooms from: US$1820* ✉ *Okavango Delta* ☎ *11/809–4300 in South Africa* ⊕ *www.xaranna. com* ➦ *9 tents* ⁣†⊙⁣ *All-inclusive.*

$$$$ ⊡ **Belmond Eagle Island Camp.** Sur-
RESORT rounded by pristine waterways, tall palm trees, and vast floodplains, this predominantly solar-powered camp was imaginatively designed to mimic its surroundings. **Pros:** gorgeous views of the Delta; genuine Delta water experience; helicopter on-site for scenic flights. **Cons:** less chance of seeing predators; usually no game drives; it's not cheap. $ *Rooms from: US$2470* ✉ *Okavango Delta* ☎ *21/483–1600 in South Africa* ⊕ *www.belmondsafaris.com* ➦ *12 tents* ⁣†⊙⁣ *All-inclusive.*

$$$$ ⊡ **Camp Okavango.** Unrecognizable from its former, humbler self, the
RESORT now solar-powered Camp Okavango was rebuilt in 2016 on a grand scale that included multi-layered decks and curved walkways that link the thatched dining, library, and lounge areas set among a forest of palm, knobthorn, and jackalberry trees. **Pros:** a truly authentic water camp; great views; eco-friendly. **Cons:** no game-viewing by road; unlikely to see much big game other than elephants and hippos; lots of long walkways. $ *Rooms from: US$995* ✉ *Shinde Concession* ☎ *11/394–3873 in South Africa* ⊕ *www.desertdelta.com* ☾ *Closed Feb.* ➦ *12 rooms* ⁣†⊙⁣ *All-inclusive.*

$$$$ ⊡ **Chitabe Camp and Chitabe Lediba.** Be sure to have your camera at the
RESORT ready in this exclusive concession that borders the Moremi Wildlife Reserve; you'll want to take pictures of everything. **Pros:** very good chance to see wild dogs; great reputation for predators; unpretentious. **Cons:** no water activities; not ultraluxurious; no Wi-Fi. $ *Rooms from: US$1690* ✉ *Chitabe Concession* ☎ *11/257–5000 in South Africa* ⊕ *www.wilderness-safaris.com* ➦ *13 tents* ⁣†⊙⁣ *All meals.*

$$$$ ⊡ **Delta Camp.** Family-owned for many years, this enchanting camp is
RESORT set deep on an island in the Okavango and the goal here is to experience
FAMILY the tranquility of the environment. **Pros:** splendid isolation; no noise from boats or vehicles; accepts children of all ages. **Cons:** less likely to see big game; comfortable but not luxurious accommodations; no game drives. $ *Rooms from: US$885* ✉ *Okavango Delta* ☎ *686–1154* ⊕ *www.deltacampbotswana.com* ➦ *7 chalets* ⁣†⊙⁣ *All-inclusive.*

$$$$ ⊡ **Duba Plains.** Completely rebuilt in 2017, Duba Plains has been pro-
RESORT pelled from the ranks of simple comfort into the echelons of luxury with
Fodor's Choice five giant, safari-style rooms bursting with character. **Pros:** some of the
★ Delta's best game-viewing with lions hunting by day; luxurious rooms; can boat as well as drive. **Cons:** very pricey; no wild dogs; leopards and cheetahs seen infrequently. $ *Rooms from: US$2800* ✉ *Okavango Delta* ☎ *87/354–6591 in South Africa* ⊕ *greatplainsconservation.com* ➦ *6 tents* ⁣†⊙⁣ *All-inclusive.*

A HAZARDOUS HERBIVORE

They may look cute and harmless, but hippos are responsible for more human fatalities than any other large animal in Africa. Though they're not threatening creatures by nature and quickly retreat to water at any sign of danger, the trouble occurs when people get between a hippo and its water.

The elephants at Vumbura camp can be quite friendly and curious.

$$$$
RESORT

Jao Camp. Spectacular Jao (as in "now"), a pure Hollywood-meets-Africa fantasy, is on a densely wooded island in a private concession bordering the Moremi Wildlife Reserve. **Pros:** African fantasy deluxe; superb service; gorgeous views; separate spa. **Cons:** lots of steps; game not always on tap; not cheap. $ *Rooms from: US$2425* ⊠ *Jao Concession* ☎ *11/257–5000 in South Africa* ⊕ *www.wilderness-safaris.com* ↪ *9 tents* ⦿ *All-inclusive.*

$$$$
RESORT

Kanana Camp. The simple, natural charm of solar-powered Kanana makes you feel part of the Delta, not cocooned away from it. **Pros:** superb birding in the nearby heronry; private sleep-out deck; authentic safari atmosphere. **Cons:** no Wi-Fi; predators not always on tap; no spa. $ *Rooms from: US$1010* ⊠ *Kanana Private Concession* ☎ *686–1226* ⊕ *www.kerdowneybotswana.com* ⊗ *Closed most of Jan. and Feb.* ↪ *8 tents* ⦿ *All-inclusive.*

$$$$
RESORT

Kwetsani Camp. Perched on high wooden stilts amid a forest canopy on a small island surrounded by enormous open plains, Kwetsani is one of the loveliest of the Delta camps. **Pros:** gorgeous views; genuine Delta feel; good all-round safari experience. **Cons:** predators may be less common in the wet season; water activities can be seasonal; there are cheaper camps. $ *Rooms from: US$1690* ⊠ *Jao Concession, Jao Concession* ☎ *11/257–5000 in South Africa* ⊕ *www.kwetsani.com* ↪ *5 tents* ⦿ *All-inclusive.*

$$$$
RESORT
Fodor's Choice
★

Little Vumbura. Situated on its own tiny, private island, Little Vumbura has a genuine water camp feel, yet just a short boat drive away lies the predator-packed Vumbura concession. **Pros:** best of both land and water activities; tranquil, relaxed ambience. **Cons:** rooms not as big as some of the other camps; can get booked up a long way in advance.

Vumbura Plains

Kwetsani

Jao

$ *Rooms from: US$1830* ✉ *Vumbura Concession* ☎ *11/257–5000 in South Africa* 🌐 *www.littlevumbura.com* 🛏 *6 tents* 🍴 *All-inclusive.*

$$$$ RESORT 🏨 **Macatoo Camp.** Be prepared to get wet as you gallop through knee-deep, crystal clear floodwaters among herds of giraffe on your chosen steed at Macatoo Camp. **Pros:** an alternative safari perspective; stable of 50 horses ensures a match for your riding style; can cater for non-riders. **Cons:** riders must be experienced; no electrical sockets in rooms; rooms are comfortable rather than luxurious. $ *Rooms from: US$885* ✉ *Okavango Delta* ☎ *686–1523* 🌐 *www.africanhorseback.com* 🛏 *8 tents* 🍴 *All-inclusive.*

$$$$ RESORT Fodor's Choice ★ 🏨 **Shinde Camp.** Ker & Downey's oldest camp, and possibly its loveliest, lies in a vast palm-dotted area in the heart of the northern Delta. **Pros:** perfect for those looking for the out-of-Africa experience; great predators and birdlife; fabulous bush dinners. **Cons:** lots of steps; no spa; no children under 10 in main lodge. $ *Rooms from: US$1130* ✉ *Shinde Concession* ☎ *686–1226* 🌐 *www.kerdowneybotswana.com* ⏲ *Closed most of Jan. and Feb.* 🛏 *8 tents* 🍴 *All-inclusive.*

$$$$ RESORT 🏨 **Vumbura Plains.** If it's old-style African safari ambience you're looking for, then this camp is not for you. **Pros:** uniquely modern design; awesome game; helicopter trips and hot air balloon rides. **Cons:** not for the traditionalist; rooms have an open floor plan; pretty pricey. $ *Rooms from: US$2520* ✉ *Vumbura Concession* ☎ *11/257–5000 in South Africa* 🌐 *www.wilderness-safaris.com* 🛏 *14 rooms* 🍴 *All-inclusive.*

MOREMI GAME RESERVE

Game
★★★★★
Park Accessibility
★★★
Getting Around
★★★★
Accommodations
★★★★★
Scenic Beauty
★★★★

Prolific wildlife and an astonishing variety of birdlife characterize this reserve, which has become well-known because it's the first in southern Africa to be proclaimed by the local people (the Batswana) themselves. As there are no fences, the big game—and there's lots of it—can migrate to and from the rest of the country.

Sometimes it seems as if a large proportion of Botswana's 150,000 elephants have made their way here, particularly in the dry winter season. Be prepared to check off on your game list lions, cheetahs, leopards, hyenas, wild dogs, buffalo, hippos, dozens of different antelopes, zebras, giraffes, monkeys, baboons, and more than 400 kinds of birds.

WHEN TO GO

If you're a birder, choose the hot summer months (November–March) because dozens of returning migrants flock here in the thousands. The return of the Carmine bee-eaters and Woodland kingfishers is a dazzling sight, as are the hosts of wading water birds, from storks of all kinds to elegant little sandpipers. Although during the South African school vacations (July and December) there are more vehicles than normal, traffic is mostly light, and in the Moremi, unlike many of Africa's other great reserves, you'll often be the only ones watching the game. The dry season (May–October) is the best game-viewing time as the vegetation is sparse and it's easier to spot game. Also, because there's little or no surface water, animals are forced to drink at the rivers or permanent waterholes. However, during the other months—known as the green season or rainy season—you'll often get fantastic offers by individual lodges, with greatly reduced rates. But be warned, summer temperatures can soar to 100°F and higher, so make sure your lodge of choice has a pool and at least a fan.

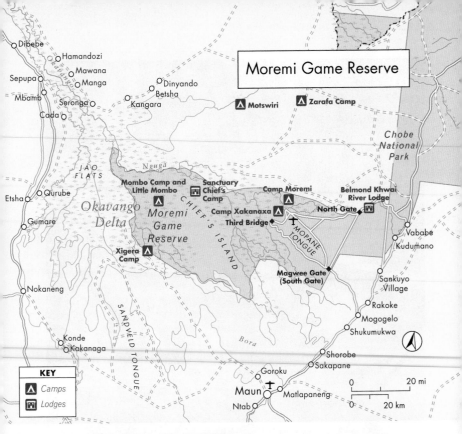

Moremi Game Reserve

Dibebe
Hamandozi
Mawana
Sepupa
Manga
Mbamb
Seronga
Cada
Dinyando
Betsha
Kangara

▲ Motswiri   ▲ Zarafa Camp

Chobe
National
Park

JAO
FLATS
Nguga

Okavango
Delta

Mombo Camp and
Little Mombo
▲
Sanctuary
Chief's
Camp
▣
▲
Camp Moremi
▲
Belmond Khwai
River Lodge
▲

Moremi
Game
Reserve
Camp Xakanaxa ▲
Third Bridge ◆
North Gate ◆ ▣

Etsha
Qurube
Gumare
Xigera
Camp ▲

C H I E F ' S   I S L A N D

M O P A N E
T O N G U E

Vabebe
Kudumano

Nokaneng
Magwee Gate
(South Gate) ◆
Sankuyo
Village

S A N D V E L D   T O N G U E
Rakoke
Mogogelo
Shukumukwa

Konde
Kakanaga
Bora
Shorobe
Sakapane

Goroku
Maun ✝
Matlapaneng
Ntab

0   20 mi
0   20 km

KEY
▲ *Camps*
▣ *Lodges*

GETTING HERE AND AROUND

Self-driving is possible in the Moremi, but a 4x4 is essential because road conditions are poor (sometimes impassable in the rainy season) and distances from cities are long. Unless you have lots of time, are a really experienced 4x4 driver and camper, and are prepared for only limited camping facilities, it's recommended that you stick to an all-inclusive fly-in package.

WHERE TO STAY

$$$$
RESORT

▣ **Belmond Khwai River Lodge.** As you sit on the wooden deck jutting out over the narrow Khwai river, eating brunch or chilling out, you may just forget the outside world. **Pros:** romantic bar with fabulous sunset views; great game especially in dry season; a/c in rooms. **Cons:** the concession is not private; the area can get busy in peak season; not as eco-friendly as some other camps. ⓢ *Rooms from: US$1970* ✉ *Moremi Game Reserve* ☎ *21/483–1600 in South Africa* ⊕ *www.belmondsafaris. com* ⤷ *15 tents* ⦿ *All-inclusive.*

$$$$
RESORT
FAMILY

▣ **Camp Moremi.** You get the best of both water and land at Camp Moremi. **Pros:** excellent location in great game area; great vistas from the main area; Pel's fishing owl known to frequent camp. **Cons:** tents are comfortable but not ultraluxurious; located inside a national park,

Mombo Camp

Mombo

Xigera

so no exclusivity; no guided walks. $ *Rooms from: US$995* ✉ *Moremi Game Reserve* ☎ *11/394–3873 in South Africa* ⊕ *www.desertdelta.com* ⊘ *Closed in Feb.* ↝ *12 tents* ⦿ *All-inclusive.*

$$$$ ⛺ **Camp Xakanaxa.** For a genuine bush-camp experience—no unneces-
RESORT sary frills—it would be hard to beat this old-fashioned camp (pro-
Fodor's Choice nounced ka- *kan*-ah-ka). **Pros:** authentic, unpretentious, out-of-Africa
★ experience; heaps of return guests; generally good game. **Cons:** it's
not drop-dead luxury; not in a private concession; no guided walks.
$ *Rooms from: US$995* ✉ *Moremi Game Reserve* ☎ *11/394–3873
in South Africa* ⊕ *www.desertdelta.com* ⊘ *Closed Feb.* ↝ *12 tents*
⦿ *All-inclusive.*

$$$$ ⛺ **Mombo Camp and Little Mombo.** On Mombo Island, off the northwest
RESORT tip of Chief's Island, this legendary camp is surrounded by wall-to-wall
Fodor's Choice game. **Pros:** brilliant Big Five game-viewing; one of the best safari lodges
★ in Botswana ; 100% solar-powered. **Cons:** very, very pricey; often fully
booked; no water activities. $ *Rooms from: US$2955* ✉ *Chief's Island,
Moremi Game Reserve* ☎ *11/257–5000 in South Africa* ⊕ *www.wilder-
ness-safaris.com* ↝ *12 rooms* ⦿ *All-inclusive.*

$$$$ ⛺ **Sanctuary Chief's Camp.** Ultraluxurious Chief's Camp is set on its
RESORT eponymous island, with some of the greatest predator and wildlife viewing on the continent including both (reintroduced) rhino species. **Pros:**
extensive spa treatments; uber-luxurious rooms; fantastic game, including chance to see rhinos. **Cons:** have to book a long way in advance;
might feel too formal for some; very pricey. $ *Rooms from: US$2815*
✉ *Chief's Island, Moremi Game Reserve* ☎ *11/438–4650 in South
Africa* ⊕ *www.sanctuaryretreats.com* ↝ *11 pavilions* ⦿ *All-inclusive.*

$$$$ ⛺ **Xigera Camp.** The cry of the fish eagle permeates this delightfully
RESORT laid-back and predominantly solar-powered camp (pronounced *kee*-jer-
FAMILY ah), which is set on the aptly named Paradise Island in a picturesque
corner of Moremi Game Reserve. **Pros:** lovely setting; relaxed, con-
vivial atmosphere; outstanding food. **Cons:** less luxurious than some
other camps; predators not on tap; no night drives. $ *Rooms from:
US$1120* ✉ *Moremi Game Reserve* ☎ *11/257–5000 in South Africa*
⊕ *www.wilderness-safaris.com* ↝ *10 rooms* ⦿ *All-inclusive.*

8

CHOBE NATIONAL PARK

Game
★★★★
Park Accessibility
★★★★
Getting Around
★★★★
Accommodations
★★★★★
Scenic Beauty
★★★★

This 12,000-square-km (4,500-square-mile) reserve is the second largest national park in Botswana, and it has four very different ecosystems: Serondela in the extreme northeast with fertile plains and thick forests; the Savuti Channel in the west, which very occasionally spills its contents into Savuti marsh; the Linyanti Swamps in the northwest; and the arid hinterland in between.

The whole area, however, is home to a shifting migratory population of more than 50,000 elephants. In addition to spotting Chobe's great pachyderm herds, you should see lions, leopards, hyenas, wild dogs, impalas, waterbucks, kudus, zebras, wildebeests (gnus), giraffes, and warthogs. Watch closely at the waterholes when prey species come down to drink and are most vulnerable—they are so palpably nervous that you'll feel jumpy, too. Lions in this area are often specialized killers; one pride might target giraffes, another zebras, another buffalo, or even young elephants. But lions are also opportunistic, and you could see them pounce on anything from a porcupine to a lowly scrub hare. Bird life along the river is awesome and the major must-sees are the slaty egrets, rock pratincoles, pink-throated longclaws, and lesser gallinules.

The northern section of the park comprises riverine bush devastated by the hordes of elephants coming down to the perennial Chobe River to drink in winter. Fortunately, the wide sweep of the Caprivi floodplains, where hundreds of buffalo and elephants graze silhouetted against almost psychedelic sunsets, softens this harsh, featureless landscape where it faces neighboring Namibia.

Chobe can be crowded, unlike the rest of Botswana, because there are simply too many vehicles on too few roads, particularly in the dry season. One of the quieter parts of the park is around the Ngwezumba River, an area of forests and pans in the more remote middle of the park; the drawback here is that game is harder to find.

A baby baboon takes a rest under the watchful eye of mommy baboon.

In the southwestern part of the park lies the fabled Savuti area, famous for its predators. Savuti offers a sweeping expanse of savanna brooded over by seven rocky outcrops that guard a lush marsh, courtesy of the occasionally flowing Savuti Channel. Savuti is dramatically different from elsewhere in Botswana; there are open spaces, limitless horizons, wide skies, and unending miles of waving tall grass punctuated by starkly beautiful dead trees—the legacy of the relentless drought. After exceptional rains and an above-average flood in 2010, the Savuti Channel started flowing again, attracting thousands of plains animals and attendant predators. It dried up again in 2015, but your chances of seeing one or more of wild dogs, lions, and leopards are still good. Like Chobe National Park overall, Savuti is famed for its elephants, but breeding herds are only there for a two- to three-month period before the first rains. The rest of the year, Savuti is the domain of the bull elephants: old grandfathers, middle-aged males, and feisty young teenagers. The old ones gaze at you with imperturbable dignity, but it's the youngsters who'll make your adrenaline run riot when they kick up the dust and bellow belligerently as they make a mock charge in your direction.

And while you're in the Savuti area looking for leopards and the tiny acrobatic klipspringer antelopes, be sure to pay a visit to the striking rock paintings, early humans' attempts to represent the wildlife all around. In summertime thousands of migrating zebras and wildebeests provide the equivalent of fast food for the lion prides, hungry hyenas, and cheetahs that follow the herds. The Cape buffalo herds also arrive in summer along with thousands of returning bird migrants. The raptors

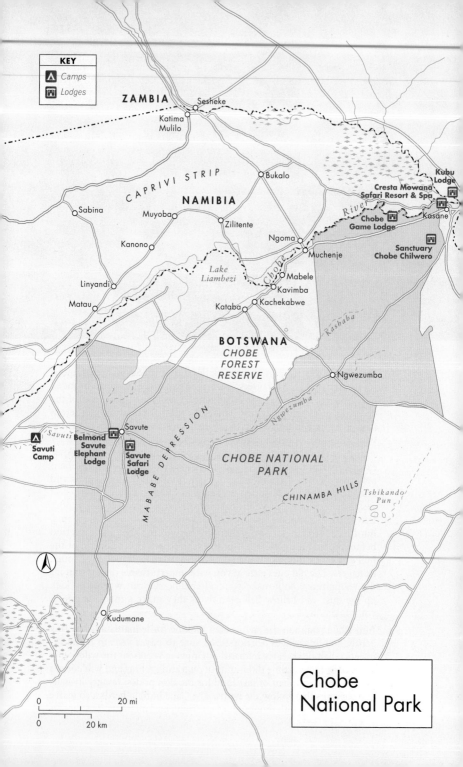

Chobe
National Park

are spectacular. You'll see falcons, eagles, kestrels, goshawks, ospreys, and sparrow hawks. In the northwest of the park are the Linyanti Swamps, also famous for their game concentrations, and in particular wild dogs. ■TIP→ **Early morning and late afternoon are the best game-spotting times.**

WHEN TO GO
In the rainy season, roughly October through April, much of the game moves away from the permanent water provided by the rivers so you should visit May through September to find out why this place is unique.

GETTING HERE AND AROUND
You can fly straight to Kasane from Johannesburg where your lodge will meet and transfer you. Most lodges are 10 minutes from the airport.

WHERE TO STAY

$$$$
RESORT

Belmond Savute Elephant Lodge. In the thriving Savuti region, splendid, spacious, air-conditioned, twin-bedded rooms are elegantly furnished with cane and dark wood furniture, an impressive bed canopy with mosquito net, and a roomy bathroom with his-and-her sinks. **Pros:** great location; good predators all year round; cheaper than the other Belmond camps. **Cons:** no night drives; glass-enclosed rooms can feel isolated from the bush; no exclusivity as not in a private concession. $ *Rooms from: US$1470* ⊠ *Chobe National Park* ☎ *21/483–1600 in South Africa* ⊕ *www.belmondsafaris.com* ⤴ *12 rooms* ⃝ *All-inclusive.*

$$$$
RESORT
FAMILY

Chobe Game Lodge. The only permanent lodge in Chobe National Park, this grand old dame—Liz Taylor and Richard Burton got married for the second time here in the '70s—still offers one of Botswana's most sophisticated stays, while maintaining a lodge feel despite its size. **Pros:** Botswana's first electric game-viewers and boats; excellent boardwalk and viewing decks; its location means you are ahead of the crowds. **Cons:** bigger than most lodges; concrete rooms mean you are segregated from nature; Chobe National Park can get busy. $ *Rooms from: US$995* ⊠ *Chobe National Park* ☎ *11/394–3873* ⊕ *www.chobegamelodge.com* ⤴ *44 rooms* ⃝ *All-inclusive.*

$
RESORT
FAMILY

Cresta Mowana Safari Resort & Spa. Built round an 800-year-old baobab tree situated among lovely private gardens on the banks of the Chobe River, you'll find this lodge just 8 km (5 miles) from the entrance to Chobe National Park. **Pros:** great location; excellent excursions; golf course. **Cons:** big and bustling; lacks the flexibility of smaller operators; more like a hotel than a lodge. $ *Rooms from: US$240* ⊠ *President Ave., Kasane* ☎ *625–0300* ⊕ *www.crestamowana.com* ⤴ *108 rooms* ⃝ *Breakfast.*

$$
RESORT
FAMILY

Kubu Lodge. If you want to escape the real world for a while, then this small, quiet, attractive lodge on the banks of the Chobe, which prides itself on its seclusion, is right for you; it has no phones, radios, or TV in its rooms. **Pros:** very affordable; located outside Kasane; comfortable rooms. **Cons:** 14 km (9 miles) from Chobe National Park; activities are additional costs; not as luxurious as other lodges. $ *Rooms from: US$365* ⊠ *Kubu Rd., Kazungula, Kasane* ☎ *625–0312* ⊕ *www.*

8

Savuti Camp

Savuti Camp

Savuti Camp

kubulodge.net ⏲ *Closed Feb.* 🛏 *11 chalets* 🍴 *Breakfast* ☞ *Rates are per room based on 2 people sharing.*

$$$$ RESORT FAMILY 🏨 **Sanctuary Chobe Chilwero.** Easily accessible from both the Zimbabwe and Zambian side of Vic Falls, this lodge is perched on a small hill on the border of Chobe National Park (Chilwero means "high view" in Setswana, the national language). **Pros:** lovely views; intimate atmosphere; great spa. **Cons:** situated near the town, which means you are not in the bush; Chobe National Park can get busy; might feel too tame for some. [$] *Rooms from: US$1020* ✉ *Kasane* ☎ *11/438–4650 in South Africa* 🌐 *www.sanctuaryretreats.com* 🛏 *15 cottages* 🍴 *All-inclusive.*

$$$$ RESORT 🏨 **Savute Safari Lodge.** As your small plane flies over this attractive lodge, you can see the wide meanders of the occasionally-flowing Savuti Channel before it melts into the Savuti marsh. **Pros:** elephants galore; great predator sightings; good wilderness feel. **Cons:** if you've an elephant phobia stay away; inside a national park, so no exclusivity; no night drives or walks. [$] *Rooms from: US$995* ✉ *Savuti, Chobe National Park* ☎ *11/394–3873 in South Africa* 🌐 *www.desertdelta.com* ⏲ *Closed Feb.* 🛏 *12 rooms* 🍴 *All-inclusive.*

$$$$ RESORT 🏨 **Savuti Camp.** This intimate friendly camp has only seven thatched chalets, which are raised on stilts above the seasonal Savuti Channel. **Pros:** good animal variety; opportunity to sleep under the stars; photographic hides. **Cons:** very dry and hot in summer; no boating; no a/c. [$] *Rooms from: US$1545* ✉ *Linyanti Reserve* ☎ *11/257–5000 in South Africa* 🌐 *www.wilderness-safaris.com* 🛏 *8 tents* 🍴 *All-inclusive.*

KWANDO RESERVE

Game
★★★★★
Park Accessibility
★★★
Getting Around
★★★★
Accommodations
★★★
Scenic Beauty
★★★

The Kwando Reserve is a 2,300-square-km (900-square-mile) private concession that has more than 80 km (50 miles) of river frontage. It stretches south from the banks of the Kwando River, through open plains and mopane forests to the Okavango Delta.

It's an area crisscrossed by thousands of ancient game trails traversed by wildlife that move freely between the Okavango Delta, Chobe, and the open Namibian wilderness to the north. As you fly in to the reserve, you'll see this web of thousands of interlacing natural game trails—from hippo highways to the tiny paths of smaller animals. This should clue you in to Kwando's diverse animal life: elephants, crowds of buffalo, zebras, antelope of all kinds, wild dogs, lions, and wildebeests. Participants on one night drive came upon a running battle between a pack of 14 wild dogs and two hyenas who had stolen the dogs' fresh kill. The noisy battle ended when a loudly trumpeting elephant, fed up with the commotion, charged the wild dogs and drove them off. There's a sheer joy in knowing you are one of very few vehicles in a half-million acres of wilderness.

If you have children older than six years, Kwando is a good option (for under-12s, you will need to book a private vehicle). The safari starts with a safety briefing, and kids get their own tents next to mom and dad (or you can share). Kids learn to track and take plaster casts of spoor, sit up in the tracker's seat on the vehicle to follow game, cook marshmallows over the boma fire, and make bush jewelry. Kids can eat on their own or with you, and if you want an afternoon snooze, they'll be supervised in a fun activity. The program's available at both Kwando camps; the price is the same per night as for an adult.

WHEN TO GO
Visit May through September. You'll see loads of game, especially predators, and fewer than 40 other guests in the whole reserve.

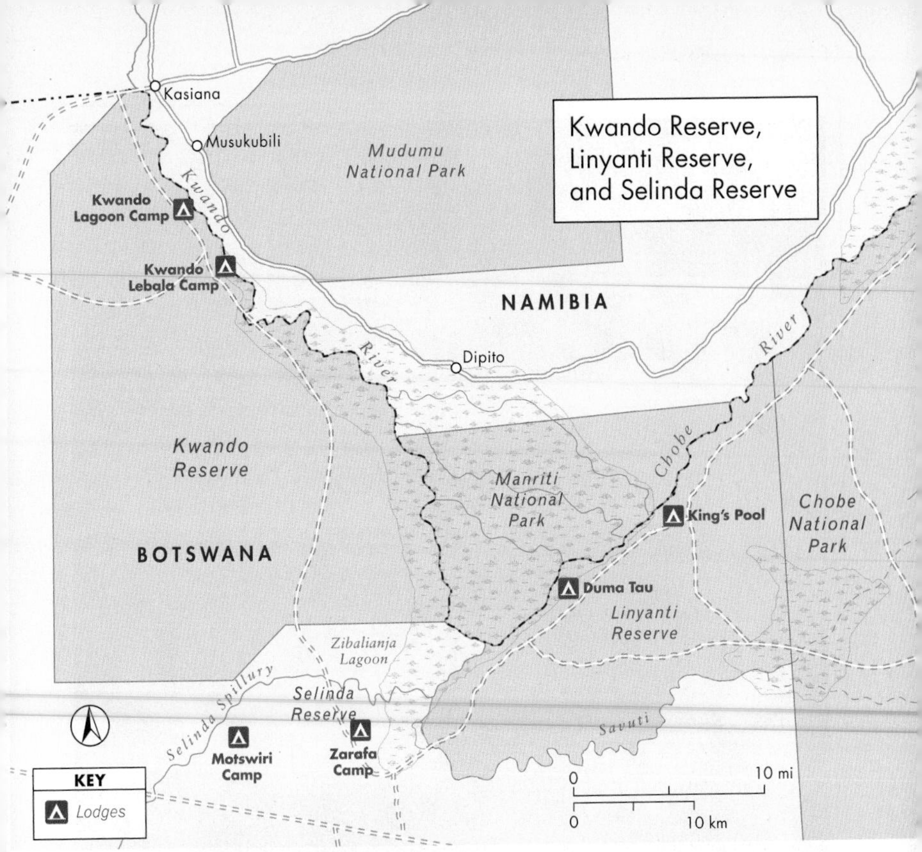

GETTING HERE AND AROUND

Guests fly directly into Kwando Reserve from Maun; the flight takes about 35–40 minutes. Transfer to lodges will take between 10 and 30 minutes.

VISITOR INFO

Contacts Kwando Safaris. ☎ *686–1449* 🌐 *www.kwando.co.za.*

WHERE TO STAY

$$$$ RESORT FAMILY Fodor's Choice ★ **Kwando Lagoon Camp.** The camp perches on the banks of a tributary of the fast-flowing Kwando River, quite literally in the middle of nowhere. **Pros:** private concession; solar-powered; good chance to see predators including wild dogs. **Cons:** single-minded focus on predators may not suit all; no spa; no a/c. [$] *Rooms from: US$1343* ✉ *Kwando Reserve* ☎ *686–1449* 🌐 *www.kwando.co.bw* 🛏 *8 tents* 🍴 *All-inclusive.*

$$$$ RESORT FAMILY **Kwando Lebala Camp.** Lebala Camp is 30 km (18 miles) south of Lagoon Camp and looks out over the Linyanti wetlands. **Pros:** superb predator viewing; private concession means you can go off-road; night drives. **Cons:** no water activites; single pursuit of predators may not suit all; can get hot in open-top vehicles. [$] *Rooms from: US$1343* ✉ *Kwando Reserve* ☎ *686–1449* 🌐 *www.kwando.co.bw* 🛏 *8 tents* 🍴 *All-inclusive.*

Kwando Lebala Camp

Kwando Lebala Camp

Kwando Lagoon Camp

LINYANTI RESERVE

Game
★★★★
Park Accessibility
★★★
Getting Around
★★★★
Accommodations
★★★★★
Scenic Beauty
★★★

The Linyanti Reserve, which borders Chobe National Park, is one of the huge concession areas leased to different companies by the Department of Wildlife and National Parks and the Tawana Land Board.

Concessions can be leased for up to 15 years. It's a spectacular wildlife area comprising the Linyanti marshes, open floodplains, rolling savanna, and the Savuti Channel. Because it's a private concession, open vehicles can drive where and when they like, which means superb game-viewing at all hours of the day.

Your choices for viewing wildlife include game drives (including thrilling night drives with spotlights), boat trips, and walks with friendly and knowledgeable Motswana guides. Even in peak season there's a maximum of only six game vehicles driving around at one time, allowing you to see Africa as the early hunters and explorers might have first seen it. The Savuti Channel is a 100 km (62 miles) long river that has appeared in several *National Geographic* documentaries. Take lots of pictures, and for once you won't bore your friends with the results: hundreds of elephants drinking from pools at sunset, hippos and hyenas nonchalantly strolling past a pride of lions preparing to hunt under moonlight, and thousands of water and land birds everywhere.

WHEN TO GO

Summers are very hot and winters can be cold. The shoulder seasons (April and September) are the best.

GETTING HERE AND AROUND

Flights from Maun take about 40 minutes; don't be shocked when you land on a dirt airstrip in the middle of the bush. Your transportation to and from the lodge and on all game drives will be in an open-sided vehicle.

8

WHERE TO STAY

$$$$
RESORT

🏕 **Duma Tau.** This welcoming camp, imaginatively decorated and furnished, is in raised tent chalets with a spectacular view over Osprey Lagoon. **Pros:** great predator viewing; solar-powered; sleep-out deck. **Cons:** public areas can be cold in winter; no mokoros; no Wi-Fi. $ *Rooms from: US$1780* ⊠ *Linyanti Reserve* ☎ *11/257–5000 in South Africa* ⊕ *www.dumatau.com* ⇱ *10 chalets* ⦿ *All-inclusive.*

$$$$
RESORT

🏕 **King's Pool.** Despite its traditional thatched roof and African artifact adornments, there is a modern feel to this camp's main area, overlooking the Linyanti River. **Pros:** classy, comfortable; 100% solar-powered; private concession. **Cons:** very grand—you may prefer something simpler; game less reliable in the wet season; no mokoros. $ *Rooms from: US$2425* ⊠ *Linyanti Reserve* ☎ *11/257–5000 in South Africa* ⊕ *www.wilderness-safaris.com* ⇱ *9 chalets* ⦿ *All-inclusive.*

SELINDA RESERVE

Sandwiched between the Kwando and Linyanti concessions, this 1,300-square-km (500-square-mile) reserve trades the river frontage of its neighbors for the Zibadianja Lagoon, a sprawling, permanent body of water fed by the Kwando River and presided over by towering African mangosteen and jackalberry trees. It is also the location for the seasonal and intriguing Selinda Spillway. After a multidecade arid period the spillway sprang to life in 2009 as water from the Kwando River flooded the Linyanti Swamps, filling this narrow, west-flowing channel until it eventually joined up with the Okavango River. The Okavango, which tends to flood a couple of months before the Linyanti Swamps, flows in the opposite direction, leading to the remarkable phenomenon that the Selinda Spillway can flow in both directions at the same time.

Game-viewing is on a par with the Kwando and Linyanti reserves: lions, leopards and wild dogs are all sighted regularly in the dry season, along with the usual plains game.

WHEN TO GO

The dry season (May–October) has the best game viewing, but be aware October can get very hot.

GETTING HERE AND AROUND

Flights from Maun take about 45 minutes; the transfer time to the lodges varies depending on the camp.

WHERE TO STAY

$$$$
RESORT

Motswiri Camp. If you are looking for a more active safari wrapped up in some good, old-fashioned hospitality, then you'll love this camp, operated by Ride and Walk Botswana. **Pros:** lots of laughter; limitless range of different walks and rides; can cater to wheelchair-bound guests. **Cons:** rooms are comfortable rather than luxurious; focus is not on big game; riders must be experienced. $ *Rooms from: US$895* ✉ *Selinda Reserve* ☎ 686–0243 ⊕ *www.rawbotswana.com* 🛏 *5 tents* ⦿ *All-inclusive.*

$$$$
RESORT
Fodor'sChoice
★

Zarafa Camp. There is a welcome air of authenticity surrounding this intimate, luxury tented camp set on the banks of Zibadianja Lagoon. **Pros:** understated luxury; flexible timetables; reliable game. **Cons:** rooms can be a bit hot in summer; very pricey; no mokoros. $ *Rooms from: US$2430* ✉ *Selinda Reserve* ☎ 686–4001 ⊕ *www.greatplainsconservation.com* 🛏 *4 tents, 1 villa* ⦿ *All-inclusive.*

IF YOU HAVE TIME

By all means, do your Big Five, big-park thing, but if you can make the time, explore the following parks and areas.

THE CENTRAL KALAHARI GAME RESERVE

The second largest national park in Africa has its own unique beauty that's only enhanced by its vastness, emptiness, grandeur, and desolation. You won't see the prolific game of Chobe or Moremi, but there's unusual wildlife, such as the elusive brown hyena, stately gemsbok, pronking springbok, bat-eared foxes, African wild cats, cheetahs, leopards, and porcupines. And if you're very lucky, you may spot the huge, black-maned Kalahari lions, which dwarf their bush counterparts. Deception Valley—so-called because from a distance a dry riverbed appears to run deep and full—lies on the northern border of the reserve.

WHEN TO GO

Summers are very hot and winters very cold. Temperatures are most comfortable in the shoulder seasons (April and September). Game-viewing is best just after the rains (around April) when large herds of gemsbok and springbok converge on the pans.

GETTING HERE AND AROUND

Although self-drives are possible here, it's not advised. Instead, fly in from Maun. Your lodge can and will arrange all your transportation to and from the airstrip for you in an open-sided game vehicle.

WHERE TO STAY

$$$$
RESORT
Fodor'sChoice
★

Deception Valley Lodge. Situated on private land bordering the Central Kalahari Game Reserve, this striking wood-and-thatch lodge was the first to be built in the Central Kalahari and is arguably still the best. **Pros:** if you're looking for solitude, this is the place; great curio shop; great bushman experience. **Cons:** there's game here, but it's not always easy to find; landscape not as scenic as inside the park; can get very dry and hot in summer. $ *Rooms from: US$635* ✉ *Central Kalahari Game Reserve* ⊕ *www.dvl.co.za* ➳ *8 chalets* ⊚ *All-inclusive.*

$$$$
RESORT
FAMILY

Kalahari Plains Camp. Situated in the desolate northern part of the Central Kalahari Game Reserve—one of the largest game reserves in the world and bigger than Switzerland—this solar-powered camp overlooks a huge pan, with eight en suite, innovatively insulated canvas tents designed to keep you cool in summer and warm in winter. **Pros:** stunning desert scenery all year round; abundant game in season; interpretive walks with the local San Bushmen. **Cons:** tents get very hot in summer, even with the insulation; water is quite salty; game not as abundant as in the Delta. $ *Rooms from: US$965* ✉ *Central Kalahari Game Reserve* ☎ *11/257–5000 in South Africa* ⊕ *www.wilderness-safaris.com* ➳ *8 tents* ⊚ *All-inclusive.*

$$$$
ALL-INCLUSIVE
FAMILY
Fodor'sChoice
★

The Lodge. From the moment you arrive at this remote, independently owned, Kalahari oasis it's clear that The Lodge represents a welcome break from the safari mold. **Pros:** refreshingly different ambience; extensive range of activities; great place to relax at the end of a safari. **Cons:** not a place for big game; no water activities; style may not suit traditionalists. $ *Rooms from: US$890* ☎ *686–5756* ⊕ *www.felinefields.com* ➳ *6 suites* ⊚ *All-inclusive.*

THE MAKGADIKGADI PANS

These immense salt pans in the eastern Kalahari—once the bed of an African superlake—provide some of Botswana's most dramatic scenery. Two of these pans, Ntetwe and Sowa, the largest of their kind in the world, have a flaky, pastrylike surface that might be the nearest thing on earth to the surface of the moon. In winter (May–September) these huge bone-dry surfaces, punctuated by islands of grass and lines of fantastic palm trees, dazzle and shimmer into hundreds of dancing mirages under the midday sun. In summer months (October–April) the last great migration in Southern Africa takes place here: more than 20,000 zebras and wildebeests with predators on their heels come seeking the fresh young grass of the rainwater-flooded pans. Waterbirds also flock here from all over the continent; the flamingos are particularly spectacular.

WHEN TO GO

May through September you will experience the surreal, dry winter landscapes, but there tends to be less game. October through February are the months of the migration with game galore.

GETTING HERE AND AROUND

Just like the Central Kalahari Game Reserve, self-drives are possible here but not advised. Instead, have your lodge arrange your transportation. Flights from Maun take about 40 minutes, and don't be shocked when you land on a dirt airstrip in the middle of the bush. Your transportation to and from the lodge and on all game drives will be in an open-sided vehicle.

WHERE TO STAY

$$$$
RESORT
FAMILY
Camp Kalahari. Offering all the Makgadikgadi activities, Camp Kalahari represents a more down-to-earth and affordable option in this area and is ideally suited to families. **Pros:** 100% solar; accepts children of all ages; horse-riding options. **Cons:** not fancy; no power in rooms; can be hot and dusty in summer. $ *Rooms from: US$830* ⊠ *Makgadikgadi Pans* ☎ *21/001–1574 in South Africa* ⊕ *www.unchartedafrica.com* ⤳ *10 tents* ⓞ| *All-inclusive.*

$$$$
RESORT
Jack's Camp. If you're bold-spirited, reasonably fit, and have kept your childlike sense of wonder, then Jack's is for you. **Pros:** exclusivity and isolation; unique, alternative safari experience; good chance to see meerkats. **Cons:** no shaded walkways; the desert locale can be dusty; summer days are blisteringly hot, winter nights can be freezing. $ *Rooms from: US$1750* ⊠ *Makgadikgadi Pans* ☎ *21/001–1574* ⊕ *www.unchartedafrica.com* ⤳ *10 tents* ⓞ| *All-inclusive.*

$$$$
RESORT
Fodor's Choice
★
San Camp. It's all about the view from this collection of snow-white tents looking out over the surreal, stark landscape of Botswana's Makgadikgadi salt pans. **Pros:** friendly, knowledgeable staff; more intimate than its neighbors; stunningly surreal setting. **Cons:** no power in tents; game not as prolific as elsewhere in the country; can get very hot and dusty in October. $ *Rooms from: US$1485* ⊠ *Makgadikgadi Pans* ☎ *21/001–1574 in South Africa* ⊕ *www.unchartedafrica.com* ⊗ *Closed during rainy season (Oct. 15–Apr. 16)* ⤳ *7 tents* ⓞ| *All-inclusive.*

Continued on page 413

(top) Weaving pandanu vegetal carpets. (bottom) Botswana basket.

AFRICAN ARTS & CULTURE

African art is as diverse as its peoples. If you're a collector, an artist, or just an admirer, you'll find everything from masks and carvings to world famous rock art, hand-painted batiks, and hand-woven cloths.

African art is centered on meaning. Its sculptures, carvings, and masks symbolize the powerful spirit world that underpins most African societies. Christianity and the Westernization of many African communities has stifled much of the traditional craftsmanship by imposing new themes and, in the past, denigrating traditional religions. Fortunately, wooden masks—some genuine, some not, some beautiful, some seriously scary—wire and bead tribal necklaces, beadwork, woven baskets, and much, much more continue to be big sellers all over Southern and East Africa.

If you're looking for something a little funky or unique, check out the handmade bead-and-wire animals, birds, cars, and mobiles for sale along South Africa's roads and in Tanzania's markets.

TYPES OF CRAFTS AND ART

High-quality crafts abound, from handwoven cloths in East Africa, to stunning soapstone and wood carvings at Victoria Falls, handwoven baskets in Botswana and Zululand, leatherwork, pottery and embroidery in Namibia, and jewelry just about everywhere.

BOTSWANA BASKETS

Once used for storage purposes, these baskets are now sought-after works of art that incorporate many traditional designs and patterns. Known for the intricately woven geometric designs, it can take up to six weeks to make a basket. Zulu baskets, from South Africa's KwaZulu province, can be made of brightly colored wire or grass and palm coils. For either type, expect to pay anywhere from US$20 to US$300.

MASKS

Masks were often worn by tribal elders in rites of passage (birth, initiation, weddings, and funerals) and can range from frightening depictions of devils and evil spirits, to more gentle and benign expressions. A few dollars will buy you a readily available tourist mask; an authentic piece could run you hundreds, sometimes thousands of U.S. dollars.

BEADWORK

Each color and pattern has meaning. Green is for grass or a baby, red is for blood or young women, and white is for purity. By looking at a women's beadwork you can tell how many children she has (and what sex), how old she is or how long she's been married. Beading is used in headdresses, necklaces, rings, earrings, wedding aprons, barrettes, and baskets. Expect to pay US$10 for a Zulu bracelet or US$200 for a Masai wedding necklace.

WEAVING

The striking red handmade robes of East Africa's Masai people are a fine example of a centuries-old African weaving tradition. Fabrics, like kekois and Masai cloaks, are usually made of cotton. Handpainted or batik cloths are more expensive than factory printed ones. A cotton kekoi will cost you US$15, a red Masai cloth US$20, a batik US$30.

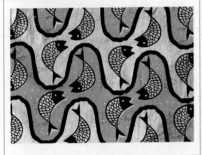

ROCK ART

Engravings (made by scratching into a rock's surface), paintings, and finger paintings are found all over sub-Saharan Africa, particularly in South Africa. The rock paintings in the Drakensburg Mountains in Kwa-Zulu Natal, are regarded as the world's finest. Central Namibia has the world's largest open-air art gallery at Twyfelfontein where thousands of paintings and engravings line the sides of the rocks and mountain. Materials came from the immediate environment: ocher (red iron-oxide clay) for red, charcoal for black, and white clay for white. Many images illustrate the activities and experiences of the African shamans. The shamans believed that when an image was drawn, power was transferred to the people and the land.

WIRECRAFT FIGURES

Wire-and-bead animals and all kinds of previously unimagined subjects are now contemporary works of art. First made and sold in South Africa, you can now buy them just about anywhere. A palm-sized critter usually sells for US$10, but a nearly-life-sized animal can cost up to US$450; you'd pay three times more in a European or U.S. gallery. Tip: Beaded key rings (US$5) make great easy-to-pack gifts.

PAINTING

Painting in acrylics is a fairly recent medium in Africa. Keep an eye out for Tinga Tinga paintings (above) at curio shops or stalls in Kenya and Tanzania. Prices range from $10 to $50; you can expect to pay upwards of $100 online. The semi-impressionistic wildlife paintings of Keith Joubert are particularly sought-after. Consult his website (⊕ www.keith-joubert.com) for locations of his exhibitions.

SMART SHOPPING TIPS

So where should you buy all of this amazing handiwork? And what do you do when you've found that piece you want to take home? Read on for helpful tips and locations across our Safari coverage.

■ Local markets, roadside stalls, and cooperatives often offer the cheapest, most authentic crafts.

■ Safari lodge shops can be pricey, but stock really classy souvenirs (often from all over Africa) and cool safari gear.

■ A universal rule for bargaining is to divide the seller's first price by half, then up it a bit.

■ If possible, carry your purchases with you. Try to get breakables bubble-wrapped and pack securely in the middle of your main suitcase. Pack smaller purchases in your carry-on.

■ Mail your dirty clothes home or donate them to a local charity so you'll have more room for purchases.

■ Only ship home if you've bought something very big, very fragile, or very expensive.

AFRICAN BEADS

Small discs, dating from 10,000 B.C., made from ostrich eggshells are the earliest known African beads. The introduction of glass beads came with the trade from around 200 B.C. Subsequently, European and Arab traders bartered beads for ivory, gold, and slaves. In many African societies, beads are still highly prized for both everyday and ceremonial ornamentation.

TULI BLOCK

This ruggedly beautiful corner of northeastern Botswana is easily accessible from South Africa and well worth a visit. Huge, striking red-rock formations, unlike anywhere else in Botswana, mingle with acacia woodlands, riverine bush, hills, wooded valleys, and open grassy plains. Be sure to visit the Motloutse ruins, where ancient baobabs stand sentinel over Stone Age ruins that have existed here for more than 30,000 years, as majestic black eagles soar overhead.

Still relatively unknown to foreign travelers, the Tuli Block is home to huge elephant herds, the *eland*—Africa's largest and highest-jumping antelope—zebras, wildebeests, leopards, and prolific bird life. Try to catch a glimpse of the elusive and diminutive klipspringer antelope perching on top of a rock zealously guarding his mountain home. If the Limpopo River is full, you'll be winched into Botswana over the river in a small cage—a unique way of getting from one country to another. If the river is dry, you'll be driven over in an open-sided game vehicle.

MASHATU GAME RESERVE

Mashatu offers a genuine wilderness experience on 90,000 acres that seem to stretch to infinity on all sides. There are wall-to-wall elephants—breeding herds often with tiny babies in tow—as well as aardvarks, aardwolves (a relative of the hyena), lots of leopards, wandering lions, cheetahs, and hundreds of birds. All the superb rangers are Batswana—most were born in the area and some have been here for more than 15 years. They have a bottomless reservoir of local knowledge.

GETTING HERE AND AROUND

Mashatu is an easy six- to seven-hour drive from Johannesburg and Gaborone. You'll be met at Pont Drift, the South African–Botswana border post, where you leave your car under huge jackalberry trees at the South African police station before crossing the Limpopo River by 4x4 vehicle or cable car—depending on whether the river is flooded.

If you'd rather fly, South African Airlink flies daily from O.R. Tambo International Airport, Johannesburg, to Polokwane, where you can pick up a self-drive or chauffeur-driven car from Budget Rent a Car for the just-under-two-hour drive to Pont Drift. You can also fly by direct charter from Mala Mala in South Africa.

Airlines South African Airlink. ☎ 11/451–7300 in South Africa ⊕ www.flyairlink.com.

Car Rentals Budget. ⊠ Natlee Centre, Mathiba Rd., Maun Airport, Maun ☎ 686–0039 ⊕ www.budget.co.za.

WHERE TO STAY

$$$
RESORT
FAMILY
Fodor's Choice
★

🏠 Mashatu Lodge. A sister camp to South Africa's world-famous Mala Mala Camp, Mashatu's game-viewing lives up to its billing with a deserved reputation for prolific predators. **Pros:** game galore, particularly lions and leopards; superb service and guiding; amazing photographic opportunities from low-level hides. **Cons:** atmosphere feels more South Africa than Botswana; no wild dogs; lacks some of the charm of the camps in the north. $ *Rooms from: US$560* ⊠ *Mashatu*

8

Also known as "painted dogs," African Wild Dogs are an endangered species found only in Zimbabwe, Tanzania, Botswana, and South Africa.

Game Reserve ☎ *31/761–3440 in South Africa* 🌐 *www.mashatu.com* 🛏 *14 suites* 🍴 *All meals.*

$$ RESORT 🏨 **Mashatu Tent Camp.** This small and intimate camp offers the same excellent service as Mashatu Lodge but with a firsthand bush experience. **Pros:** true wilderness experience; splendid isolation; great game, especially predators. **Cons:** very close to nature; don't come here if you are fearful of critters big or small; not uber-luxurious. [$] *Rooms from: US$415* ✉ *Mashatu Game Reserve* ☎ *31/761–3440 in South Africa* 🌐 *www.mashatu.com* 🛏 *8 tents* 🍴 *All meals.*

GATEWAY CITY

The little town of Maun serves as the gateway to the Okavango Delta and the Moremi Game Reserve. The city itself is by no means a tourist destination—at best you'd probably stay a night or even two before setting off farther afield.

MAUN

Despite the city's rapid development in the last decade, Maun has kept the feel of a pioneer border town. The name comes from the San word *maung*, which means the "place of short reeds," and Maun became the capital of the Tawana people in 1915; it's now Botswana's fifth-largest town. Although there are now shopping centers and a paved road to Gaborone, Botswana's capital, cement block houses and mud huts still give Maun a rural feel, especially as goats and donkeys litter the roads.

The town spreads along the banks of the Thamalakane River, and it's possible to take mokoro trips into the Delta directly from Maun. It's also a good base from which to explore the Tsolido hills and the Makgadikgadi Pans by road.

GETTING HERE AND AROUND

Many visitors to Botswana will find themselves with a layover in Johannesburg before or after their safari. It's a massive metropolitan area—more than 1,300 square km (800 square miles)—that epitomizes South Africa's paradoxical makeup: it's rich, poor, innovative, and historical all rolled into one. Most of the sights and many of the city's good hotels and major malls are in the northern suburbs (Greenside, Parkhurst, Sandton, and Rosebank, among many others). Some notable destinations for food include Melrose Arch, Parkhurst, Sandton, the South (for its Portuguese cuisine), Melville, and Chinatown in the CBD (Central Business District).

If you don't fly to Gaborone, your first entry into Botswana will probably be by air into Maun, the gateway to the Delta. At best, you'd spend only a night here, though most visitors are picked up at Maun airport immediately on arrival by their respective tour operators and whisked away to their lodges by charter planes.

8

A local taxi is your best bet for getting around, as there's no public transportation. Taxis are usually available outside Maun airport. It's possible to hire a fully equipped 4x4 for camping, but generally speaking, you're better off and safer (the roads in the Delta are sometimes impassable) to fly between Maun and the tourist camps. Make sure your tour package includes all local flights.

SAFETY AND PRECAUTIONS

Crime has increased in recent years, so take good care of your belongings and utilize your hotel's safe. Don't walk alone at night. If you must leave the hotel, have the concierge or front desk call a taxi for you.

TIMING

Most people will be here only a night, if not just a few hours, so use the time to relax or stock up on supplies at one of the local grocery stores if you're self-driving.

ESSENTIALS

Banks Barclays Bank. ✉ *Old Mall, Tsheko-Tsheko Rd., Maun* ☎ *686–0210.* **First National Bank.** ✉ *1-2 Ngami Centre, Koro St., Maun* ☎ *686–0919.* **Standard Chartered Bank.** ✉ *Sethunya Complex, Old Mall, Tsaro St., Maun* ☎ *686–0209.*

Medical Assistance Doctors Inn. ✉ *Moeti Rd., Maun* ☎ *686–5115, 7123–3329 emergency.* **General Emergency Number.** ☎ *911.* **Medi-Help Clinic.** ✉ *New Mall, Sir Seretse Khama Rd., Maun* ☎ *686–4084.*

MRI Prime Health. ✉ *Old Mall, Tsheko Tsheko Rd., Maun* ☎ *686–4564, 992 emergency* 🌐 *www.mri.co.bw.*

Rental Cars Avis. ✉ *Mathiba I Rd., Maun* ☎ *686–0039, 7583–6018* 🌐 *www.avis.com.* **Maun Self Drive 4x4.** ✉ *16–17 Nkwe Rd., Maun* ☎ *686–1875, 7130–3788* 🌐 *www.maunselfdrive4x4.com.*

EXPLORING

Nhabe Museum. Housed in a former British military building, Nhabe Museum has a few permanent displays of Ngamiland's history and artifacts, including musical instruments and hunting tools. More interesting are the rotating exhibitions featuring the work of local Botswana painters, photographers, sculptors, woodworkers, and weavers. ✉ *Sir Seretse Kharma Rd., Town Center, Maun* ☎ *686–1346* 🎫 *Free* 🕒 *Closed Sun.*

WHERE TO EAT

$ FRENCH 🍴 **French Connection.** This alfresco restaurant adds a refreshing French twist to its dishes, distinguishing it from the steak-and-burger menus of its rivals. Generous portions and imaginative specials attract locals and tourists alike for lunch; they are open in the evening on request. **Known for:** flavorsome French food; intimate atmosphere. [$] *Average main: US$10* ✉ *Mophane St., Maun* ☎ *680–0625* 🌐 *www.frenchconnection.co.bw* 🕒 *Closed Sun. No dinner Sat.*

$ CAFÉ 🍴 **Hilary's Coffee Shop.** If you've time for a cup of coffee and a quick snack in between flights or before you set out on safari, leave the airport and turn right. You'll find the coffee shop behind the offices of Okavango Wilderness Safaris. **Known for:** reliable service; great homemade lemonade. [$] *Average main: US$8* ✉ *The Studio Complex, Mathiba Rd., next to the Studio gym, Maun* ☎ *686–1610* 🌐 *www.hilaryscoffeeshop.wordpress.com* 🕒 *Closed Sun. No lunch Sat.*

$ **× Il Pomodoro.** This authentic Italian establishment serves the best piz-
ITALIAN zas in town and some excellent homemade pasta. At this writing, the
restaurant is due to move to larger premises close to the airport. **Known
for:** fantastic Italian-style pizzas; homemade pasta. $ *Average main:
US$10* ⊠ *Nkwe Rd., Maun* ☏ *7438–7590* ✆ *Closed Sun. No lunch Sat.*

$ **× Motsana.** The café at the Gothic-looking Motsana center serves tasty
CAFÉ sandwiches, delicious pancakes, lip-smacking milkshakes, and a hand-
FAMILY ful of simple main courses. Wander round the curio shops while you
wait for your food or make use of the free Wi-Fi. **Known for:** tasty
milkshakes; good coffee; good brunch options. $ *Average main: US$10*
⊠ *Shorobe Rd. to Moremi, Maun* ☏ *684–0405.*

$ **× Tandurei.** Of the batch of Indian restaurants that's recently opened in
INDIAN Maun, this is the most reliable, serving up a wide range of classic curries and tandoori dishes as well as some Chinese staples. The alfresco
ambience is relaxed and the service is consistently good. **Known for:**
good service; reliable food. $ *Average main: US$8* ⊠ *Moeti Rd., Maun*
☏ *680–0227* ⊕ *www.tandurei.com.*

$ **× The Tshilli Farmstall Café.** This welcoming alfresco newcomer to Maun's
ECLECTIC eatery scene has quickly become its most popular, with a diverse, imagi-
Fodor's Choice native menu spanning pizzas and quesadillas to hoisin pulled duck and
★ succulent meatballs. It also serves the best coffee in town, delicious
fresh juice concoctions, and homemade ice cream. **Known for:** excellent,
reasonably priced food; relaxed atmosphere; good vegetarian options.
$ *Average main: US$8* ⊠ *Maun* ☏ *684–0490.*

WHERE TO STAY

$ **⌂ Audi Camp.** This lively tented camp offers a budget option for the Oka-
RESORT vango Delta. **Pros:** affordable lodging; excellent service and staff; good value
FAMILY excursions. **Cons:** not much privacy; only four en suite tents; all activities
extra. $ *Rooms from: US$75* ⊠ *Shorobe Rd., Maun* ✛ *12 km (7½ miles)
from Maun* ☏ *686–0599* ⇆ *14 tents, 1 self-catered house* ⦿| *Breakfast.*

$ **⌂ Cresta Maun.** Situated on the banks of the Thamalakane River, Cresta
HOTEL Maun, which opened its doors in 2017, is one of Maun's largest and
most modern hotels. **Pros:** good location; all mod-cons. **Cons:** lacks
intimacy and safari ambience; service can be hit-and-miss; pool is a bit
small. $ *Rooms from: US$130* ⊠ *Maun* ✛ *Situated off the Shorobe
road to Moremi, 100 meters from Audi Camp* ☏ *686–3455* ⊕ *www.
crestahotels.com* ⇆ *83 rooms* ⦿| *Breakfast.*

$ **⌂ Riley's Hotel.** A Maun institution, this comfortable modern hotel, on
HOTEL the banks of the Thamalakane River, is a far cry from the seven dusty
rooms built by the legendary Harry Riley in the middle 1930s. **Pros:** central location; clean and comfortable; nice gardens. **Cons:** bland hotel-
like rooms; indifferent service; in the busy center of town. $ *Rooms
from: US$120* ⊠ *Tsheko Tsheko Rd., Maun* ☏ *686–0204* ⊕ *www.cres-
tahotels.com* ⇆ *51 rooms* ⦿| *Breakfast.*

$ **⌂ Thamalakane River Lodge.** Situated en route to Moremi Game Reserve,
B&B/INN this lovely lodge sits on the bank of the Thamalakane River. **Pros:** lodge
FAMILY feel; closest accommodation in Maun to Moremi Game Reserve; good
atmosphere. **Cons:** if you're not en route to Moremi it's a bit out of the
way; limited food choice at dinner; quite expensive for what it is. $ *Rooms
from: US$204* ⊠ *Shorobe Rd., Maun* ☏ *680–0217* ⊕ *www.thamalakane.
com* ⇆ *20 chalets* ⦿| *Breakfast.*

8

NAMIBIA

9

WELCOME TO NAMIBIA

TOP REASONS TO GO

★ **The world's oldest living desert:** The Namib is everything you might imagine a "real" desert to be.

★ **A memorable drive:** The road from Swakopmund to Walvis Bay is one of the most beautiful and unusual routes in the world.

★ **Waterhole wonders:** Arm yourself with binoculars, drinks, a picnic, and patience. Open your car windows and wait for the game to come. You won't be disappointed.

★ **Ride the Desert Express:** During this two-day train journey between Windhoek and Swakopmund, you'll stop to walk in the desert, visit the world's biggest outdoor rock-art gallery, watch lions being fed, and view a spectacular desert sunset (or sunrise).

★ **Etosha National Park:** One of Africa's largest and most spectacular game parks, Etosha has cheap and cheerful self-catering accommodations, an excellent road network, and superb game-viewing.

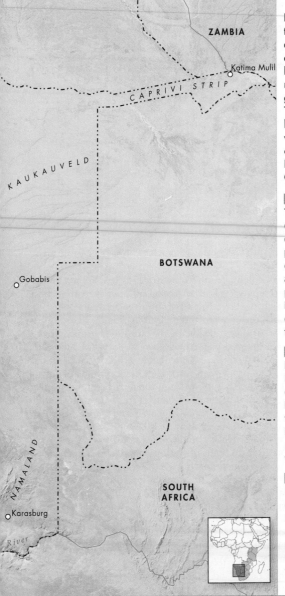

ZAMBIA

Katima Mulil

CAPRIVI STRIP

KAUKAUVELD

BOTSWANA

Gobabis

NAMALAND

SOUTH
AFRICA

Karasburg

River

Namibia is a big country, four times as large as the United Kingdom and bigger than Texas, but its excellent road network means you can get around very easily. The country is bordered by the icy Atlantic on the west, the Kalahari Desert on the east, the Kunene River to the north, and the Orange River to the south.

1 Namib-Naukluft Park. This park, which harbors the oldest desert in the world, is one of the largest national parks in Africa. Expect classic desert scenery but also windswept gravel plains, rocky outcrops and inselbergs, and some of the earth's strangest living things.

2 Damaraland. Situated in northwest Namibia, Damaraland is a different desert from Namib. It's barren and inhospitable, but there's life and plenty of it, including *Welwitschia mirabilis*, reputed to be the world's longest-living plant.

3 Etosha National Park. Regarded as one of Africa's great national parks, Etosha is dominated by Etosha Pan: a landscape of white, salty plains. The numerous waterholes make this park ideal for game-viewing.

9

Updated by
Colleen Blaine

Many countries in Africa boast teeming wildlife and gorgeous scenery, but few, if any, can claim such limitless horizons; such untamed wilderness; such a pleasant climate; so few people (fewer than two per square mile); the oldest desert in the world; a wild, beautiful coastline; one of Africa's greatest game parks; plus—and this is a big bonus—a well-developed infrastructure and tourist facilities that are among the best in Africa. Welcome to Namibia.

A former German colony, South West Africa, as it was then known, was a pawn in the power games of European politics. Although the Portuguese navigators were the first Europeans to arrive, in 1485, they quickly abandoned the desolate and dangerous Atlantic shores of the "Coast of Death," as they called it. By the late 1700s British, French, and American whalers were using the deepwater ports of Lüderitz and Walvis (Whalefish) Bay, which the Dutch, now settled in the Cape, then claimed as their own. A few years later, after France invaded Holland, England seized the opportunity to claim the territory, together with the Cape Colony. Then it became Germany's turn to throw its hat into the ring. In the wake of its early missionaries and traders, Germany claimed the entire country as a colony in 1884, only to surrender it to the South African forces fighting on the Allied side during World War I. South Africa was given a League of Nations mandate to administer the territory after the war, and despite a 1978 UN resolution to revoke that mandate, South Africa held on to Namibia for 10 years. A bitter and bloody bush war with SWAPO (South West African People's Organization) freedom fighters raged until Namibia finally won its independence on March 21, 1990, after 106 years of foreign rule. Although most of the earlier colonial influences have now vanished, everywhere you go in Namibia today you'll find traces of the German past—forts and castles, place names, cuisine, and even German efficiency.

Often called the "Land God Made in Anger" because of its stark landscapes, untamed wilderness, harsh environment, and rare beauty,

FAST FACTS

Size Namibia covers 824,292 square km (318,259 square miles)

Capital Windhoek

Number of National Parks 20: Etosha, Kaudom, Mamili, Mudumu, Namib-Naukluft, and Waterberg National Parks, Ai-Ais & Fish River Canyon, and Skeleton Coast Park are among the most visited.

Number of Private Reserves There are more than 400 privately owned game reserves.

Population Slightly more than 2 million

Big Five In Etosha you can see all of the Big Five.

Language English is the official language, but it's usually spoken as a second language. Afrikaans is spoken by many residents of various races, and there's a large population of German-speaking people. The most widely spoken indigenous languages are Kwanyama (a dialect of Owambo), Herero, and a number of Nama (San) dialects.

Time Namibia, like Botswana, is on CAST (Central African Standard Time), which is two hours ahead of Greenwich mean time and seven hours ahead of North American Eastern Standard Time (six hours during eastern daylight saving time).

Namibia was carved out by the forces of nature. The same continuous geological movements produced not only spectacular beauty but also considerable mineral wealth: alluvial diamonds, uranium, gold, lead, zinc, silver, copper, tungsten, and tin—still the cornerstone of Namibia's economy. In addition it is also a significant resource of semiprecious stones (tourmaline, citrine, amethyst, topaz, and aquamarine) and mineral specimens to buyers and collectors alike. Humans have lived here for thousands of years; the San (Bushmen) are the earliest known residents, although their hunting-gathering way of life is now almost extinct. Today most Namibians work in agriculture, from subsistence farms to huge cattle ranches and game farms.

Namibia prides itself on its conservation policies and vision. In many conservation areas, local communities, the wildlife, and the environment have been successfully integrated. Wilderness Damaraland Camp, for example, is an internationally acclaimed role model in linking tourism with community development projects. Hunting, a controversial issue for many people, is carefully controlled so that the impact on the environment is minimal and the revenue earned is substantial and can often be ploughed back into sustainable conservation.

PLANNING

WHEN TO GO

Namibia has a subtropical desert climate with nonstop sunshine throughout the year. It's classified as arid to non-arid, and, generally speaking, it gets wet only in the northwest and then only during the rainy season (October–April), which is the hottest season. The south is warm and dry, although temperatures vary dramatically between night and day, particularly in the desert, where the air is sparkling, and pollution practically unheard of. Days are crystal clear and perfect for traveling. Elsewhere the weather is clear, dry, crisp, and nearly perfect, averaging 25°C (77°F) during the day, but in the desert areas it can drop to freezing at night, especially in winter. (Bring warm clothes for after the sun goes down.)

The climate can be breathtakingly varied along the Skeleton Coast because of the Atlantic and its cold Benguela current, which makes the night cool and damp and brings thick morning coastal fog. Days are usually bright and sunny, and in summer, extremely hot, so dress in layers.

Etosha's best season is winter (May–September), when the weather is cooler, the grass shorter, and game easier to see. But if you can stand the heat, consider a summer visit to see the return of thousands of waterbirds, as well as tens of thousands of animals, to the lush feeding grounds around Okuakuejo.

GETTING HERE AND AROUND

AIR TRAVEL

Namibia's main point of entry is Hosea Kutako International Airport, near Windhoek. The smaller Eros Airport handles local flights and charters. Once in the country you can make use of scheduled flights or charter flights that service all domestic destinations. Walvis Bay—the nearest airport for Namib-Naukluft and the Skeleton Coast—now has a small international airport with flights to and from Windhoek, Johannesburg, and Cape Town.

The national carrier is Air Namibia, which operates international flights between Windhoek and Frankfurt, Johannesburg, and Cape Town, and internal flights to most of Namibia's major tourist destinations. South African Airways (SAA) and British Airways (BA) operate links to Johannesburg and Cape Town. SA Express Airways flies between Johannesburg or Cape Town and Walvis Bay.

Airlines Air Namibia. ☎ 61/299–6333 ⊕ www.airnamibia.com. **SA Express Airways.** ☎ 11/978–1111 in South Africa ⊕ www.flyexpress.aero. **South African Airways.** ☎ 11/978–1111 in South Africa ⊕ www.flysaa.com.

CAR TRAVEL

FROM SOUTH AFRICA Driving to Namibia from South Africa is possible, and there's an excellent road network for all in-country tourist attractions, but be warned that the trip is tiring and time-consuming because of the huge distances involved. The Trans-Kalahari Highway links Johannesburg to Windhoek and Gaborone. From Johannesburg to Windhoek on this road it's 1,426 km (884 miles). To allow free access to game, there are no fences in the Kalahari, so don't speed, and look out for antelope as well as donkeys and cows on the road. You can also drive from Johannesburg to Windhoek (1,791 km [1,110 miles]) via Upington, going through the Narochas (Nakop) border post (open 24 hours). This is a good route if you want to visit the Augrabies Falls and Kgalagadi Transfrontier Park in South Africa first. You can also drive from Cape Town to Namibia along the N7, an excellent road that becomes the B1 as you cross into Namibia at the Noordoewer border post (open 24 hours). It's 763 km (473 miles) from Cape Town to Noordoewer, 795 km (493 miles) from

Noordoewer to Windhoek. Border posts are efficient and friendly. Make sure you have all your paperwork to hand over—you'll need a current international driver's license.

FROM BOTSWANA Coming from Botswana, Namibia is entered at the Buitepos on the Trans-Kalahari Highway if coming from Gabarone, or through Ngoma on the Caprivi Strip if coming from the Okavango Delta. Border posts aren't open 24 hours, and opening times should be confirmed before traveling. Cross-border charges (CBCs) must be paid by all foreign-registered vehicles entering Namibia, and cost about N$280 per vehicle (more for buses and motor homes). Tourists driving a rental car must also pay the CBC and will receive a CBC certificate for every entry into Namibia.

TO ETOSHA NATIONAL PARK You can drive from Windhoek, via Otjiwarongo and Tsumeb, and arrive at the park on its eastern side by the Von Lindequist Gate, 106 km (66 miles) from Tsumeb and 550 km (341 miles) north of Windhoek. Alternatively, you can drive from Windhoek via Otjiwarongo and Outjo and come in the Anderson Gate, south of Okaukuejo, 120 km (74½ miles) from Outjo, 450 km (279 miles) north of Windhoek. The latter is the more popular route. The newest option is to drive through Kamanjab to access the park's recently opened western side through the Galton Gate, 476 km (296 miles) north of Windhoek. All three drives are long, hot, and dusty, so you might want to fly to your camp's landing strip if you're short on time. Travel time will depend on your driving and choice of vehicle, so check with your car-rental company.

DRIVING TIPS If you're not staying at a private lodge in Etosha that provides transportation, you'll need to rent a vehicle. Air-conditioning is a must at any time of the year, as are spare tires in good condition. You can pick up rental cars at the town nearest whichever park you're visiting or at Etosha itself, but it's better to book them before you leave home. For driving on the main roads, a two-wheel-drive vehicle is fine. In some areas, though, including parts of the Namib-Naukluft Park and Damaraland, four-wheel drive is essential. In Etosha a two-wheel-drive car is fine; don't exceed the speed limit of 60 kph (37 mph). Always check the state of the roads with the nearest tourist office before you set off, and never underestimate the long distances involved. Don't drive at night unless you absolutely have to. Roads are unlit, and animals like to bed down on the warm surfaces. If you hit an animal, even a small one, it could be the end of you and your vehicle, not to mention the critter. Don't speed on gravel roads. It's very easy to skid or roll your vehicle—at least one tourist per year dies this way. Don't drive off marked roads: Namibia's "empty" landscapes are incredible fragile habitats that cars can scar for hundreds of years. Make sure you have plenty of water and *padkos*, Afrikaans for "road food." Try out the ubiquitous *biltong*, Namibia's upgraded version of jerky. Finally, keep in mind that gas stations sometimes only accept cash and can be few and far between.

Automobile Associations Automobile Association of Namibia (AAN). ☎ 61/224-201 ⊕ www.aa-namibia.com.

9

TRAIN TRAVEL

The Desert Express travels between Windhoek, the capital of Namibia, and Swakopmund, the country's premier coastal resort. The train departs from Windhoek on Friday and from Swakopmund on Saturday. Longer journeys to Etosha are also available.

Train Information Desert Express. ✉ *Windhoek Railway Station, Bahnhof St., Windhoek* ☎ *11/913–2442* ⊕ *www.jbtours.co.za.*

ESSENTIALS
COMMUNICATIONS

The country code for Namibia is 264. When dialing from abroad, drop the initial 0 from local area codes.

CALLING WITHIN NAMIBIA
Namibian telephone numbers vary and are constantly changing; many have six digits (not including the area and country code), but some have fewer or more digits.

CALLING OUT-SIDE NAMIBIA
You can use public phones for direct international calls. Buy Telecards in different denominations from post offices and telecom offices.

MOBILE PHONES
There's cell-phone reception in all major towns. Enable your own for international roaming before you leave home, or buy a local SIM card when you arrive (a much cheaper option, and very easy to do). The two major cell networks are MTC, and the newer (government-owned) TN Mobile. A SIM card will cost around N$10–N$20, and the prepaid rate varies from about N$1–N$3 per minute. Airtime is available in most supermarkets, convenience stores, and some bookshops.

HEALTH AND SAFETY

Malaria is endemic in the east, north, and northeast, so antimalarials are essential. Never venture into the desert without water, a sun hat, and sunblock. AIDS is a major problem, as elsewhere in Africa; sex with a stranger puts you at risk. In towns, don't walk alone at night, and lock your valuables, documents, and cash in the hotel or lodge safe. In game areas, never walk after dark unless accompanied by an armed guide. Because there's comparatively little traffic, self-driving visitors are often tempted to speed. Don't. Gravel roads can be treacherous.

Be sure you have comprehensive medical insurance before you leave home. There's a high standard of medical care in Namibia. Consult your hotel or the white pages of the telephone directory under medical practitioners. If you get sick, go to a private clinic rather than a government-run one.

Embassies U.S. Embassy. ✉ *14 Lossen St., Windhoek* ☎ *61/295–8500* ⊕ *na. usembassy.gov.*

Emergency Services International SOS. ☎ *112 from mobile phone, 61/289–0999 in Windhoek* ⊕ *www.internationalsos.com.* **Netcare 911.** ☎ *61/223–330.*

Hospitals Medi-Clinic. ✉ *Heliodoor St. at Eros St., Eros Park* ☎ *61/433–1000* ✉ *Franziska van Neel St., Swakopmund* ☎ *64/441–220* ✉ *Sonn St., Otjiwarongo* ☎ *65/130–3734.* **Roman Catholic Hospital.** ✉ *92 Werner List St., Windhoek* ☎ *61/270–2004.*

The stark beauty of the Namibian desert and the Deadvlei trees, which have stood for almost a thousand years, can leave you speechless.

MONEY MATTERS

Namibia's currency is the Namibian dollar (N$), which is linked to the South African rand. (Namibia's currency can't be used in South Africa except unofficially at border towns.) At this writing, the Namibian dollar was trading at about N$13 to US$1. *Bureau de change* offices at the airports often stay open until late.

There are main branches of major banks near or in the city center of Windhoek, Swakopmund, and Walvis Bay, plus several easy-to-find ATMs. Ask at your accommodation for more information. Major credit cards are accepted everywhere but at street markets, with Visa being the preferred card. South African rand are accepted everywhere. In more rural or remote areas, carry Namibian dollars or South African rand. Note that some gas stations take only cash.

Tipping: Tipping is tricky and depends on where you're staying and what services you've received. Your in-room lodge-information package often makes tipping suggestions. Tips can be given in U.S. or Namibian dollars or South African rand. Most lodges suggest US$10 per person per day for your guide and US$5 per person per day for your tracker.

PASSPORTS AND VISAS

All non-nationals, including infants, need a valid passport to enter Namibia for visits of up to 90 days. Business visitors need visas.

ABOUT THE RESTAURANTS

You won't find much truly Namibian food (although local venison, seafood, and Namibian oysters are superb); the cuisine is mainly European, often German, though international variety and standards increasingly are found in the larger towns. Lodges usually serve good homestyle cooking—pies, pastries, fresh vegetables, lots of red meat, mouthwatering desserts, and the traditional *braai* (barbecue). Because of its past as a German colony, Namibia is known for its lager. South African wine, which is excellent, is readily available.

ABOUT THE HOTELS AND LODGES

Namibia's private camps, lodges, and other accommodations are often up to high international standards. Even deep at tented camps, there are en-suite bathrooms and private verandas, but don't expect TVs. Most private lodges are all-inclusive (Full American Plan), including transfers, meals, activities, and usually drinks. Camps offer at least two activities a day.

In Windhoek and Swakopmund, a large array of lodgings, from large upmarket hotels to intimate boutique hotels and family-run bed-and-breakfasts, are yours to choose from. All urban lodging rates include breakfast, but rarely any other meals.

Restaurant and hotel reviews have been shortened. For full information, visit Fodors.com.

WHAT IT COSTS			
$	**$$**	**$$$**	**$$$$**
Restaurants under $12	$12–$20	$21–$30	over $30
Hotels under $250	$250–$450	$451–$600	over $600

Prices in the restaurant reviews are the average cost of a main course at dinner or, if dinner isn't served, at lunch. Prices in the lodging reviews are the lowest cost of a standard double room in high season.

ABOUT THE PARKS

We've broken down this chapter by **Must-See Parks** (Namin-Naukluft Park, Damaraland, and Etosha National Park) amd **If You Have Time Parks** (the Skeleton Coast, Caprivi Strip, and Waterberg Plateau Park) to help you organize your time.

VISITOR INFORMATION

The Namibia Tourism Board (NTB) can provide a free map and a free copy of *Welcome to Namibia—Official Visitors' Guide,* which gives useful information plus accommodation lists, but doesn't provide detailed personalized advice. It's open weekdays 8–5. For more hands-on assistance, check out the tourist information centers (all run by different agencies, from the City of Windhoek to private companies) located in Windhoek and Swakopmund. Namibia Wildlife Resorts (NWR) offers information on accommodations in the national parks, which you can also book through them.

Contacts City Tourism Office. ⊠ 39 Post St. Mall, Windhoek ☎ 61/290–2092, 61/290–2401 ⊕ www.windhoekcc.org.na. **Namibia Tourism Board** (NTB). ⊠ Haddy St. and Sam Nujoma Dr., Windhoek ☎ 61/290–6000 ⊕ www.namibia-tourism.com.na. **Namibia Wildlife Resorts** (NWR). ⊠ Independence Ave., 181 Gathemann Bldg., Windhoek ☎ 61/285–7200 ⊕ www.nwr.com.na.

NAMIB-NAUKLUFT PARK

Game	★★
Park Accessibility	★★★★
Getting Around	★★★★
Accommodations	★★★★★
Scenic Beauty	★★★★★

Namib-Naukluft Park, south of Walvis Bay, is the fourth-largest national park in the world and is renowned for its beauty, isolation, tranquility, romantic desert landscapes, and rare desert-adapted plants and creatures.

Covering an area of 12.1 million acres, it stretches 400 km (248 miles) long and 150 km (93 miles) wide, along the southern part of Namibia's coastline from Walvis Bay to Lüderitz, and accounts for a tenth of Namibia's surface area. The Namib Desert is considered the world's most ancient desert, at more than 55 million years old. To examine the park properly, it's best to think of it as five distinct areas: the northern section—between the Kuiseb and Swakops rivers—synonymous with rocky stone surfaces, *inselbergs* (granite islands), and dry riverbeds; the middle section, the 80-million-year-old heart of the desert and home of Sesriem Canyon and Sossusvlei, the highest sand dunes in the world; Naukluft (meaning "narrow gorge"), some 120 km (74½ miles) northwest of Sesriem, which has wall-to-wall game and birds and is the home of the Kuiseb Canyon; the western section, with its lichen-covered plains, prehistoric plants, and bird sanctuaries of Walvis Bay and Sandwich Harbour; and the southern section, where, if you're traveling up from South Africa by road, it's worth having a look at Duwisib Castle, 72 km (45 miles) southwest of Maltahöhe beside the D286—an anachronistic stone castle built in 1909 by a German army officer who was later killed at the Somme. The park's southern border ends at the charming little town of Lüderitz, which is a good base for exploring Kolmanskop, the deserted mining town.

The kind of wildlife you'll encounter will depend on which area of the park you visit. In the north look out for the staggeringly beautiful *gemsbok* (oryx), the quintessential desert antelope, believed by some to be the animal behind the unicorn myth. Well-adapted for the desert, they obtain moisture from roots, tubers, and wild melons when water is scarce, and adapt their body temperatures and brains through specialized nasal blood vessels. Also found in the park are more than

9

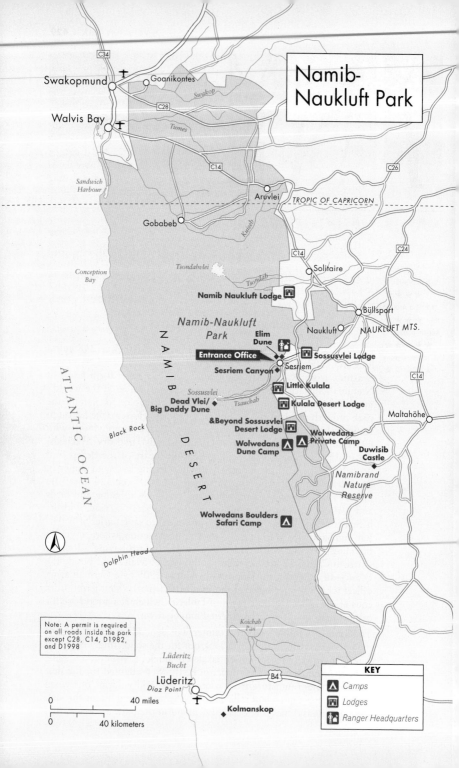

Namib-Naukluft Park

Swakopmund
C34
Goanikontes
Swakop
C28
Walvis Bay
Tumes
C14
Sandwich Harbour
Aruvlei
TROPIC OF CAPRICORN
C26
Gobabeb
Kuiseb
C14
Tsondabvlei
Tsondab
Solitaire
C24
Conception Bay
Namib Naukluft Lodge
Büllsport
Namib-Naukluft Park
Naukluft
NAUKLUFT MTS.
Elim Dune
Entrance Office
Sossusvlei Lodge
Sesriem
Sesriem Canyon
C14
Little Kulala
Sossusvlei
Kulala Desert Lodge
Dead Vlei/ Big Daddy Dune
Tsauchab
Maltahöhe
&Beyond Sossusvlei Desert Lodge
Wolwedans Private Camp
Black Rock
Wolwedans Dune Camp
Duwisib Castle
Namibrand Nature Reserve
Wolwedans Boulders Safari Camp

ATLANTIC OCEAN

N A M I B   D E S E R T

Dolphin Head

Note: A permit is required on all roads inside the park except C28, C14, D1982, and D1998

Lüderitz Bucht
Koichab Pan
Lüderitz
Diaz Point
B4
Kolmanskop

0   40 miles
0   40 kilometers

KEY	
▲	Camps
🏠	Lodges
👥	Ranger Headquarters

50 species of mammals, including springboks, zebras, leopards, caracals, Cape and bat-eared foxes, aardwolves, and klipspringers as well as cheetahs, spotted hyenas, black-backed jackals, and the awesome lappet-face vultures, the biggest in Africa.

WHEN TO GO

Temperatures can be extremely variable, with days generally hot (sometimes exceeding 104°F [40°C]) and nights that can descend to freezing. Given these extremes, the dunes are best visited early in the morning, especially in the summer (September–March). The park is open throughout the year, and in winter you can visit the dunes during the day, though note that it can still get warm, especially when you're climbing the dunes.

GETTING HERE AND AROUND

At its closest, the Namib-Naukluft is approximately 200 km (124 miles) from Windhoek and can be accessed by many roads, both major and minor. Entry permits for the park, including Sossusvlei and Sandwich Harbour, are required, and can be obtained from the Ministry of Environment Tourism offices in Windhoek, Swakopmund, or Sesriem. The park is officially split into four sections: Sesriem and Sossusvlei; Namib; Naukluft; and Sandwich Harbour. Entrance is between sunrise and sunset only. The distance between Sesriem and Sossusvlei is 65 km (40 miles), the last 5 km (3 miles) of which require a 4x4. The dunes are easily accessible by foot from the sedan car park. Sandwich Harbour is accessible only with a 4x4, and an experienced guide is highly recommended.

SAFETY AND PRECAUTIONS

Stay on existing roads and tracks, and always have plenty of water available (at least a liter per person in case the car breaks down and it takes time for help to arrive). The lichen and gravel plains are extremely fragile and tire tracks can last for hundreds of years. Avoid disturbing nesting raptors if mountain climbing. Campsites, which are mostly concentrated in the northern section of the park, have very limited facilities. You must be fully independent when camping. Bring firewood, water, and food. Always carry water, sunblock, and a hat, regardless of the season. If traveling in an open vehicle, always take a thick jacket (i.e., a windbreaker) as the wind while driving can be freezing (even in summer in the early morning before sunrise). At Sesriem Canyon there are ablution blocks with potable water. Private campsites at guest farms or lodges also often have water. Always be sure to inquire ahead of time and make use of dedicated campsites. Community campsites may not always have water, so if you plan to visit these, bring water for washing up and cooking as well as for drinking.

TIMING

Those only intending to visit Sossusvlei should plan on at least two nights so as to have an entire day to climb the dunes and visit Dead Vlei. Climbing the dunes should be done very early in the morning to avoid the heat. If you're planning to hike the Namib-Naukluft Trail as well, five days total should suffice.

In the early 20th Century, Kolmanskop was the heart of diamond mining, but by the 1950s it was a ghost town.

EXPLORING

Even if you're not a romantic, the Sossusvlei's huge, star-shape desert dunes, which rise dramatically 1,000 feet above the surrounding plains and sprawl like massive pieces of abstract sculpture, are guaranteed to stir your soul and imagination. The landscape has continuously shifting colors—from yellow-gold and ocher to rose, purple, and deep red—that grow paler or darker according to the time of day. The dunes have their own distinctive features, ranging from the crescent-shape barchan dunes—which migrate up to 2 or 3 yards a year, covering and uncovering whatever crosses their path—to the spectacular, stationary star-shape dunes, formed by the multidirectional winds that tease and tumble the sands back and forth. Park gates open an hour before sunrise, so if you can, try to be among the dunes as the sun comes up—it's a spectacular sight.

TOP ATTRACTIONS

Big Daddy Dune. If you're in good shape, you can hike to the top of Big Daddy, the highest sand dune in the world at 360 meters (1,181 feet). But it's tough going: more than an hour of very hot trudging and wading through ankle- and sometimes knee-deep sand to climb along the ridge that overlooks the famous Dead Vlei (where ghostly skeletons of ancient trees jut up from a flat, sandy, dried-up lake). If you don't feel up to any physical exertion at all, then sit in the shade of camelthorn trees at the bottom of the dunes and watch the birdlife, or focus your binoculars on the distant climbers. ⊠ *Namib Naukluft Park* ⊕ *70 km (43 miles) from the Sesriem gate.*

KOLMANSKOP: NAMIBIA'S GHOST TOWN

This dilapidated ghost town found in the very south of the Namib Desert, near the little coastal town of Luderitz, was once home to hundreds of miners during the diamond boom over 100 years ago. It is now a collection of once-glorious homes filled to the windowsills with the desert sand, a famous spot for capturing emotive photographs of the peeling walls and the soft dunes that fill the rooms and doorways.

A permit (N85) is required to enter Kolmanskop. The pass allows entrance between 9 am to 1 pm and includes a guided tour (Monday–Saturday, 9:30 am or 11 am and Sunday, 10 am). There are a restaurant and a museum (Monday–Saturday, 9 am–1 pm) on the premises.

Dead Vlei. If you're not up to trudging up the steep edges of sand dunes, head to Sossusvlei and take the shorter hike from the parking lot to the much photographed Dead Vlei. This stark white dried pan is dotted with dead, black camelthorn trees, thought to be almost 900 years old, and surrounded by red sand dunes. The image of Dead Vlei is almost synonymous with Namibia and is as picturesque as it is remarkable. ■ TIP→ If you're not traveling by 4x4 you can park at the 2x4 parking and catch the shuttle (it runs all day long) that covers the 5 km (3 miles) to Sossusvlei. ⊠ *Namib Naukluft Park ⊕ 1 km (0.6 mile) from Sossusvlei 4x4 parking.*

Elim Dune. If you're fairly fit, it's well worth climbing the towering Elim Dune, the nearest sand dune to Sesriem, about 5 km (3 miles) away; it will take you more than an hour, but the superb views of the surrounding desert and gravel plains are infinitely rewarding. Be warned: dune climbing is exhausting, so make discretion the better part of valor. This is an excellent place to photograph the early morning or late afternoon light as it's a lot closer to the park's entrance gate. ⊠ *Namib Naukluft Park ⊕ 5 km (3 miles) from Sesriem.*

Sesriem Canyon. About 4 km (2½ miles) from Sesriem Gate, your entry point to Sossusvlei, is Sesriem Canyon, named after the six *rieme* (thongs) that were tied to the buckets of the early Dutch settlers when they drew up water from the canyon. A narrow gorge of about 1 km in length, the Sesriem Canyon is the product of centuries of erosion. Plunging down 30–40 meters at its end are a series of pools that fill with water during the rains, which only happens during the wetter months and not very often. If you are lucky you will get to cool off in the pools, otherwise climbing down into the canyon offers you a wonderful escape from the desert heat as you wander along in the deep shade. ⊠ *Near entry to Sossusvlei, Namib Naukluft Park.*

9

WHERE TO STAY

$$$$
ALL-INCLUSIVE
Fodor's Choice
★

&Beyond Sossusvlei Desert Lodge. This gorgeous glass and stone lodge has a spectacular setting in the NamibRand Nature Reserve. **Pros:** fantastic, personal service; lodge observatory with resident astronomers; more than the usual activities available, including guided or unguided nature walks, a game drive to a petrified dune, expeditions to San caves to view paintings, the highly recommended quad biking tour to see the thousands of mysterious, unexplained fairy circles as the sun sets, and even a day trip to visit the famous Sossusvlei. **Cons:** the dressing room/area is in the hallway of the suites; the road to the lodge from Sesriem is not in great condition if you are self-driving. $ *Rooms from: US$863* ✉ *Namib Naukluft Park* ☎ *2711/809–4300* ⊕ *www.andbeyond.com* ⌁ *10 villas* ⦿ *All-inclusive.*

$$$
HOTEL

Kulala Desert Lodge. In the heart of the Namib and set on a 91,000-acre wilderness reserve that borders the Namib Naukluft Park, this lodge offers magnificent views of the famous red dunes of Sossusvlei, superb mountain scenery, and vast open plains. **Pros:** this is the lodge closest to the dune belt at Namib Naukluft Park and has its own private entrance to the Sossusvlei area; great staff with genuine energy; staff sings for guests at dinner. **Cons:** decor can seem stark to some; if you choose the half-board option you must pay for activities and extras like bottled water. $ *Rooms from: US$470* ✉ *Namib Naukluft Park* ☎ *2711/257–5000 in Johannesburg, 2721/702–7500 in Cape Town* ⊕ *www.wilderness-safaris.com* ⌁ *23 chalets* ⦿ *All-inclusive.*

$$$$
HOTEL

Little Kulala. In the private Kulala Wilderness Reserve this smaller and more intimate lodge gives guests a real sense of a cool inviting oasis in the desert. **Pros:** each room has its own plunge pool and they serve lunch to you around your pool if requested; the reserve has its own private entrance to the red dunes of the Namib Naukluft park. **Cons:** although the reserve is beautiful do not expect to see a great deal of wildlife on game drives; if not on an all-inclusive package the activities are at an extra cost. $ *Rooms from: US$866* ✉ *Namib Naukluft Park* ☎ *2711/257–5000* ⊕ *www.wilderness-safaris.com* ⌁ *11 suites* ⦿ *All-inclusive.*

$
B&B/INN

Namib Naukluft Lodge. Resembling children's building blocks set down by a giant hand in the middle of nowhere, this pinkish-brown desert-toned lodge sits in the midst of a wide plain of desert, backed by gorgeous granite hills. **Pros:** shuttle available from Windhoek and Swakopmund to the lodge; friendly service; stunning location. **Cons:** relatively long drive to Sossusvlei; no-frills accommodations; some expected activities are at extra cost. $ *Rooms from: US$90* ✉ *Namib Naukluft Park* ☎ *061/372–100* ⊕ *www.namib-naukluft-lodge.com* ⌁ *16 rooms* ⦿ *All meals.*

$
HOTEL

Sossusvlei Lodge. If you want to be on the spot when the park gates open at first light, then this hotel right at the Sesriem entrance is the right choice for you. **Pros:** great, convenient location for early-morning drives; many of the rooms have a good view of the waterhole; excellent buffet. **Cons:** Wi-Fi only available in the bar and reception and is very inconsistent; lacks the personal touch of a smaller, more

Continued on page 440

The Sossusvlei salt pans.

THE NAMIBIA DUNES

Be prepared for sand like you've never seen it before: in dunes that roar, rumble, and ramble. We guarantee the sight will stir your soul and imagination.

Namibia's dunes, which rise dramatically more than 1,000 meters (3,281 feet) above the surrounding plains, are said to be the world's highest. But don't think that if you've seen one sandy ridge you've seen them all. Expect great variety here. There are crescent-shaped dunes that migrate up to 2 or 3 meters (7 to 10 feet) a year, covering and uncovering whatever's in their path. There are also fossil dunes made of ancient sand that solidified millions of years ago, and star-shaped dunes formed by multidirectional winds teasing and tumbling the sand.

Amid this unique landscape live some of the world's strangest, most well-adapted creatures. The golden mole, for instance, spends its life "swimming" under the sand, popping up to the surface to grab unwary insects. Certain types of beetles collect condensed droplets of water on their backs and then roll the liquid down to their mouths; still other beetles dig trenches to collect moisture. As its name suggests, the side-winding adder moves itself from side to side over the sand, while, contrary to its name, the sand-diving lizard stands motionless, one foot raised, as if in some ancient ritual dance. And then there's the quintessential desert antelope: the beautiful gemsbok (oryx), which is believed by some to be the animal behind the unicorn myth.

WHERE DID THE DUNES COME FROM?

The formation and structure of sand dunes is extremely complex, but basically there are three prerequisites for dunes: plenty of loose sand, plenty of wind, and a flat surface with no obstacles like trees or mountains to prevent dunes building up. Namibia has these three things in abundance.

EXPLORING THE DUNES

SKELETON
COAST

NAMIBIA

**Big Daddy Dune
Dead Vlei Vally**

Walvis Bay

Sossusvlei *NAMIB
NAUKLUFT
PARK*

Luderitz

Gemsbok in the desert dunes of Namib-Naukluft Park.

WHERE ARE THE DUNES?

Enormous Namib-Naukluft Park—renowned for its isolated, romantic desert scapes—stretches 400 km (250 miles) along the southern part of Namibia's coastline, from Walvis Bay to Lüderitz, and accounts for a tenth of the country's surface area. Sossusvlei, the 80-million-year-old heart of the desert, is in the middle section of the park. It's a great entry point from which you can start your adventures. This desert is thought to be the oldest desert in the world. Although its geological base area is relatively stable, the dunes themselves are continuously sculpted by the desert winds.

DUNE EXPLORER

Sure, you could explore the dunes on your own, but you really can't beat the know-how of an experienced guide; ask your lodge to arrange this. Look to climb "Big Daddy," a dune that's as tall as a seven-story building, or Dune 7 (about 1,256 feet) or Dune 45 (557 feet). You could also just climb to the halfway point of Big Daddy or simply sit in the shade at the bottom of a dune and watch the distant climbers exert themselves.

WHEN TO GO

Sunset and sunrise are the best times to visit (be at the gates of Sesriem when it opens at 5 am or camp in the park), because the colors of the dunes change in spectacular fashion from yellow-gold and ocher to rose, purple, and deep red. Keep in mind that midday temperatures can peak at over 40°C (104°F) in summer.

THE SLOW PACE

Sip sundowners as the sun sinks, go hot-air ballooning at dawn, or simply marvel at the life that is found in this harsh environment. You won't see big game, but you will see a wealth of unique birds, insects, plants, and geological formations. Whatever you do, make sure you take a moment to appreciate the soul-searing and soul-searching silence.

ADRENALINE JUNKIES WELCOME

(top) Preparing to sandboard. (bottom) Sandboarding.

Looking for some excitement? Adrenaline junkies can try their hand (or feet) at skydiving, dune-buggying, paragliding, sandboarding, or dune-boarding (for the more advanced). The less adventurous (but romantic) can take day, moonlight, sunrise, or sunset horseback or camel rides through the riverbeds and up into the moonlike landscape.

If you have time for just one thing, make it sandboarding because it will certainly get your heart pumping. Once you are ferried up the dunes by quad bike, your operator will arm you with the necessary equipment: a sandboard—a flat piece of hardboard, a safety hat, gloves, and elbow guards. It's also a good idea to wear long pants and long sleeves to avoid a sandburn. Beginners should head to the smaller dunes to practice (i.e. sliding down on your stomach) to get the feel of it. As you get better and more adventurous, head to the top of a high dune, but be advised, you can reach speeds of up to

80 kph (50 mph). Once you get the hang of this, try standing up. Hey, if Cameron Diaz survived, so will you.

If you get really advanced, there's always dune-boarding. You use all the same gear as sandboarding, except your board is similar to a regular surfboard on which you stand up and "surf" down the dunes.

Kulala Desert Lodge

Sossusvlei Wilderness

Sossusvlei Desert Lodge

intimate lodge. [$] *Rooms from: US$160* ✉ *Namib Naukluft Park* ☎ *63/293–636 lodge, 21/930–4564 reservations* 🌐 *www.sossusvleilodge.com* 🛏 *44 rooms* 🍴 *All meals.*

$$$$ ALL-INCLUSIVE 🏨 **Wolwedans Boulders Safari Camp.** The Namibrand Reserve is just about as remote as it can get, but here in the middle of the Namib Desert you'll find this elegant canvas and wood camp hidden amongst giant granite boulders. **Pros:** magnificent scenery and remote location; excellent cuisine; well-thought-out itineraries that allow you to experience everything at the reserve. **Cons:** long drive to reach the camp after arrival at reception; can be extremely hot in the summer months (which is why they are closed in peak summer); minimum three-night stay booked with fixed arrival dates. [$] *Rooms from: US$664* ✉ *Namib Naukluft Park* ☎ *061/230–616* 🌐 *www.wolwedans.com* ⏲ *Closed Dec. and Jan. (except the week between Christmas and New Year's Eve)* 🛏 *5 rooms* 🍴 *All-inclusive.*

$$$ ALL-INCLUSIVE 🏨 **Wolwedans Dune Camp.** For seclusion and green, conscience-free travel in a ridiculously pretty setting, Wolwedans Dune Camp is unbeatable. **Pros:** privacy or company as you want it; excellent service; a clean conscience thanks to Wolwedans's in-depth greening efforts; outstanding lunch and dinner menus. **Cons:** there's only one honeymoon table for couples who aren't in the mood to socialize over dinner; if your time is limited a trip to the Sossusvlei Dunes takes the better part of a day; minimum two-night stay. [$] *Rooms from: US$579* ✉ *Namib Naukluft Park* ☎ *61/230–616* 🌐 *www.wolwedans.com* ⏲ *Closed Dec.–Feb. (except the week between Christmas and New Year's Eve)* 🛏 *6 tents* 🍴 *All-inclusive.*

$$$$ ALL-INCLUSIVE 🏨 **Wolwedans Private Camp.** This simple wood and canvas camp, in the serene and secluded NamibRand Nature Reserve, gives its guests up-close access to the surrounding desert habitat. **Pros:** beautiful, private, and intimate location with outdoor salas and decks to enjoy the views; fully equipped kitchen and open-plan design; guided activities include drives, flights, walks, and hot-air ballooning. **Cons:** you won't meet any other guests; some activities are at extra charge. [$] *Rooms from: US$710* ✉ *Namib Naukluft Park* ☎ *061/230–616* 🌐 *www.wolwedans.com* 🛏 *3 rooms* 🍴 *All meals* ☞ *Minimum two-night stay.*

DAMARALAND

Game	★★★
Park Accessibility	★
Getting Around	★★
Accommodations	★★
Scenic Beauty	★★★★★

Stretching 600 km (370 miles) from just south of Etosha to Usakos in the south and 200 km (125 miles) from east to west, this stark, mountainous area is inland from Skeleton Coast National Park.

You can drive into Damaraland from the park via the Springbokwater Gate or drive from Swakopmund to Uis, where you can visit the Daureb Craft Centre and watch the craftspeople at work, or make it part of your customized safari. A good base for touring southern Damaraland is the little town of Khorixas. From here you can visit the Organ Pipes, hundreds of angular rock formations, or watch the rising or setting sun bathe the slopes of Burnt Mountain in fiery splendor. You'll find yourself surrounded by a dramatic landscape of steep valleys; rugged cliffs of red, gray, black, and brown; and towering mountains, including Spitzkoppe (Namibia's Matterhorn, which towers nearly 610 meters/2,000 feet above the plains), where Damara guides will show you the Golden Snake and the Bridge—an interesting rock formation—and the San paintings at Bushman's Paradise. There are more spectacular rock paintings at Brandberg Mountain, especially the famous White Lady of Brandberg at Tsisab Gorge, whose depiction and origin have teased the minds of scholars for decades. (Is she of Mediterranean origin? Is "she" really a "he" covered in white initiation paint?)

Other stops of interest are the Petrified Forest, 42 km (25 miles) west of Khorixas, where the corpses of dead trees lie forever frozen in a bed of sandstone. The first UNESCO World Heritage Site in Namibia, Twyfelfontein, 90 km (56 miles) west of Khorixas, is also the biggest outdoor art gallery in the world, where thousands of rock paintings and ancient rock engravings are open to the sky. It's extremely rare for this many paintings and engravings to be found at the same site. As you approach, you'll see scattered boulders everywhere—a closer examination will reveal thousands of rock paintings and engravings. Get yourself a local, knowledgeable guide when you arrive, and try to give yourself a full day here. Start early (it's hard to pick out some of the

art in full sunshine), bring binoculars, wear sturdy shoes, and bring
water (at least a gallon) and a hat.

Northern Damaraland consists of
concession areas that have been set
aside for tourism, with many tourist operators working hand in hand
with the local communities. This is
a desert of a different kind from the
classic sand dunes of the Namib.
It's a landscape of almost unsurpassed rugged beauty formed by
millions of years of unending geological movement. Vivid brick-red
sediments complement gray lava

slopes punctuated by black fingers of "frozen" basaltic rock creeping
down from the jagged rocky horizons. Millions of stones, interspersed
with clumps of silvery-gray shrubs and pioneer grass, litter the unending slopes, hillsides, and mountain faces. There seem to be as many
rocks, huge and small, as there are grains of sand on the beaches of the
windswept, treacherous Skeleton Coast, some 90 km (56 miles) to the
west. But there's life, and plenty of it, in this seemingly inhospitable
landscape, including dozens of *Welwitschia mirabilis*—plants that can
live for up to 1,000 years. Stop at a 500-year-old "youngster" and
consider that when this plant was a newborn, Columbus was sailing
for the New World and the Portuguese to Namibia.

The landscape is also dotted with colorful lichen fields, dark-green
umbrella-shape camelthorn trees, candelabra euphorbias raising their
prickly fleshy arms to the cloudless sky, saltbushes, and the ubiquitous
shepherd's tree. Also here is the *moringa* tree—the "enchanted" tree,
so-called because according to San legend, the god of thunder, not wanting moringa trees in heaven, pulled them all up and threw them out.
They fell upside down into the earth, looking like miniature baobab
trees. In the middle of this rocky desert rubble is Slangpost, a small,
verdant oasis in the middle of what seems to be nowhere (not even the
mountains have a name in this part of the world; they're referred to
simply as the "no-name mountains"). Look out for traces of the amazing desert elephants (sometimes called the desert-adapted elephants),
their huge footprints trodden over by the healthy herds of goats and
sheep belonging to the local Damara farmers. Your best chance of seeing the elephants is along the surprisingly green and fertile dry Huab
River bed, where they browse on the large seedpods of the Ana tree
and whatever else they find edible. The great gray shapes silhouetted
against the dry river's sandy mounds ringed by mountains and sand
dunes are an incredible sight.

The Kaokoveld, north of Damaraland, although enticing because it's
pristine and rarely visited, is also inhospitably rugged. Self-drives are
for the really intrepid, do-it-yourself explorer.

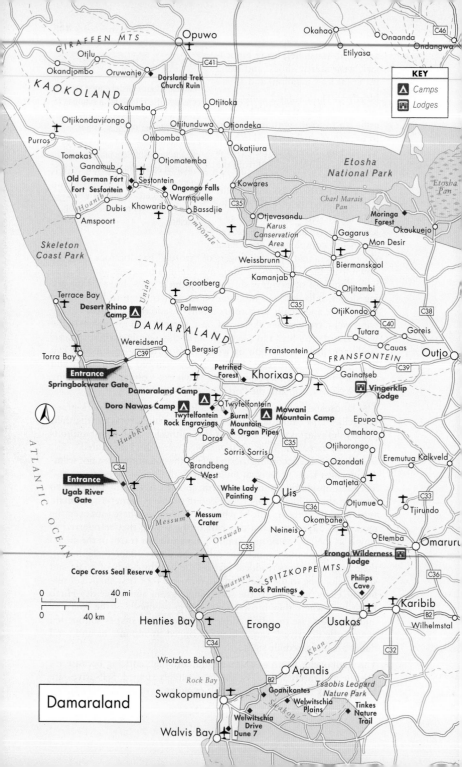

WHEN TO GO

The area can be visited throughout the year. However, during the rainy season (January–April), roads and tracks may be difficult to negotiate, or not accessible at all due to flooding. Come May the area has a special splendor with waves of green grass growing on the plains and hills. From May to September the days will be cooler and more bearable, but nights can be very cold, especially for the camper. From October to December nights can be cool and days very hot.

GETTING HERE AND AROUND

One can access Damaraland from the coast (Swakopmund and Walvis Bay) by traveling via Henties Bay and Uis on the C35, or farther up the coast, accessing the park from Springbokwater on the C39. Coming from Windhoek, drive via Omaruru (C33) and Uis (C36) to Damaraland. From the north, travel via Kamanjab (C35) and Outjo (C39) to Khorixas. Good gravel roads can be traveled between attractions. The area is extremely fragile, and vehicles must always stay on existing roads and tracks. It's not advised to travel on to smaller tracks without the company of an experienced Namibian guide, as tourists frequently lose their way in these parts.

SAFETY AND PRECAUTIONS

Don't travel faster than 80 kph (50 mph) on gravel roads. Always fill up your tank when a gas station is available (e.g., Kamanjab, Outjo, Khorixas, and Uis). Smaller towns such as Palmwag and Sesfontein may not have gas available, so it's also advisable to take additional gas in a can if you plan to travel long stretches between places where gas isn't available. Always bring sufficient water.

TIMING

Four days is a suggested minimum, especially if you plan to visit Burnt Mountain, the Organ Pipes, Twyfelfontein, and the Petrified Forest, which can easily take a full day or a day and a half to explore. A half-day or full-day drive to view the desert-adapted elephant and other wildlife in the Huab River is also a highlight. Additionally, a day trip to the Welwitschia plains and Messum Crater is worthwhile.

WHERE TO STAY

$$$ HOTEL ★ **Damaraland Camp.** A joint community venture with the Torra Conservancy (the local community), this desolate camp is on the Huab River in central Damaraland, midway between Khorixas and the coast. **Pros:** one of Namibia's most pristine wilderness areas; solar powered and using eco-building techniques; impressive community-based responsible tourism model. **Cons:** game drives are additional for those on half-board basis; rough entrance road means leaving your 2x4 vehicle in a parking area about 45 minutes away on arrival. [$] *Rooms from: US$547* ✉ *Damaraland* ☎ *11/257–5000 in South Africa* 🌐 *www.wilderness-safaris.com* 🛏 *10 tents* 🍴 *All-inclusive.*

$$$$ ALL-INCLUSIVE ★ **Desert Rhino Camp.** If it's rhinos you're after, especially the rare black rhino, then this remote tented camp in the heart of the private 1-million-acre Palmwag Reserve is a must. **Pros:** amazing educational experience on rhinos and their ecology; evening meals taken together

Doro Nawas

Vingerklip Lodge

Damaraland Camp

by the fire pit allow guests to mingle. **Cons:** some visitors could find this experience overly rustic. $ *Rooms from: US$710* ⊠ *Damaraland* ☎ *11/257–5000 in South Africa* ⊕ *www.wilderness-safaris.com* ⇌ *8 tents* ❙○❙ *All-inclusive.*

$$
HOTEL
🏠 **Doro Nawas Camp.** Blending into the backdrop and set amid stony slopes, rugged boulders, the distant Entendeka Mountains, and the pink and russet sandstone cliffs of Twyfelfontein to the south (where you can visit some of the most famous San rock paintings and engravings in the world), this is classic Damaraland. **Pros:** guided walking trails; great community-based responsible tourism model; amazing location close to rock art at Twyfelfontein. **Cons:** half-board clients must pay for guided trips to see the elephants. $ *Rooms from: US$341* ⊠ *Damaraland* ☎ *11/257–5000 in South Africa,* ⊕ *www.wilderness-safaris.com* ⇌ *17 chalets* ❙○❙ *All-inclusive.*

$
HOTEL
🏠 **Erongo Wilderness Lodge.** Discover an absolute closeness to nature at this tranquil lodge completely surrounded by colossal granite boulders. **Pros:** incredibly peaceful; attentive and warm staff; spectacular views. **Cons:** some chalets are far from main lodge with many steps to navigate; not everyone will appreciate the open-air bathroom. $ *Rooms from: US$206* ⊠ *Omaruru Conservancy, Swakopmund* ☎ *61/239–199* ⊕ *www.erongowilderness-namibia.com* ⇌ *10 chalets* ❙○❙ *Some meals.*

$$
HOTEL
🏠 **Mowani Mountain Camp.** A scenic, centrally located locale from which to explore Damaraland's desolate attractions, Mowani Mountain Camp is perched on a pile of giant round boulders in sight of the impressive Brandberg Mountain. **Pros:** the sundowner rock; convenient to local attractions; excellent campsites with private bathrooms should you prefer a collapsible tent to a permanent camp. **Cons:** very small swimming pool; activities are extra if you're not on fully inclusive plan. $ *Rooms from: US$318* ⊠ *Damaraland* ☎ *61/232–009* ⊕ *www.mowani.com* ⇌ *15 rooms* ❙○❙ *All meals.*

$
HOTEL
🏠 **Vingerklip Lodge.** In a dramatic locale in Damaraland's Valley of the Ugab Terraces, this lodge is set against the backdrop of a mighty stone finger pointing toward the sky. **Pros:** drop-dead gorgeous views; great food. **Cons:** rooms are not large; service can vary; bit too far to use as a base to explore Damaraland attractions. $ *Rooms from: US$102* ⊠ *Damaraland* ☎ *61/255–344 reservations, 67/290–319 lodge* ✉ *reservations@vingerklip.com.na* ⊕ *www.vingerklip.com.na* ⇌ *24 bungalows* ❙○❙ *Some meals.*

9

ETOSHA NATIONAL PARK

Game
★★★★★
Park Accessibility
★★★★★
Getting Around
★★★★
Accommodations
★★★★★
Scenic Beauty
★★★★★

This photogenic, startlingly beautiful park takes its name—meaning Great White Place—from a vast flat depression that was a deep inland lake 12 million years ago. The white clay pan, also known as the Place of Mirages, covers nearly 25% of the park's surface.

Although it's usually dry, in a good rainy season it floods and becomes home to many waterbirds, including tens of thousands of flamingos that feed on the blue-green algae of the pan. Although the park is never crowded with visitors like some of the East African game parks, the scenery here is no less spectacular: huge herds that dot the plains and gather at the many and varied waterholes. The dust devils, mirages, and terrain that changes from densely wooded thickets to wide-open spaces, and from white salt-encrusted pans to blond grasslands, will keep you captivated for hours.

The game's all here—the Big Five—large and small, fierce and gentle, beautiful and ugly. But one of Etosha's main attractions isn't the numbers of animals that you can see (more than 114 species), but how easily you can see them. The game depend on the natural springs that are found all along the edges of the pan, and as the animals have grown used to drinking at these waterholes for decades, they're not put off by vehicles or game-seeking visitors. On the road from the Von Lindequist Gate, the eastern entrance to Etosha, look out for the smallest of all African antelope, the Damara dik-dik. If you see a diminutive "Bambi" sheltering under a roadside bush, that's it. The Namutoni area and the two Okevi waterholes—Klein Namutoni and Kalkheuwel—probably provide the best chances to see leopards. Don't miss the blackface impala, native to Etosha, and one of the rarest of antelope and an endangered species. Bigger and more boldly marked than its smaller cousin, the impala, you'll find it drinking in small herds at waterholes all over the park.

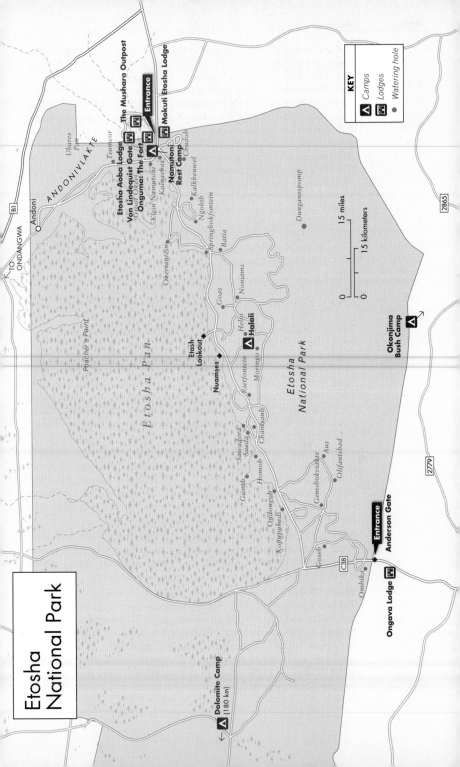

Etosha National Park

KEY
- 🔺 Camps
- 🅿 Lodges
- • Watering hole

Dolomite Camp (180 km)

TO ONDANGWA

ONDANGWA

B1

ANDONIVLAKTE

Uhares Pan

Andoni

Poacher's Point

Etosha Pan

ANDONIVLAKTE

Tsumcor

Etosha Aoba Lodge
Von Lindequist Gate
Onguma: The Fort
Groot Okevi

The Mushara Outpost
Entrance
Mokuti Etosha Lodge

Klein Namutoni
Namutoni
Rest Camp
Koinachas
Kalkheuwel
Chudob

Ngobib
Springbokfontein
Batia
Okerfontein

Goas
Noniams

Helio
Halali
Rietfontein
Moringo

Etash
Lookout
Nuamses

Dunganespomp

15 miles
15 kilometers
0   15 miles
0   15 kilometers

Etosha National Park

Okonjima Bush Camp

2865

2779

Salvadora
Sueda
Charitsaub

Gemsboknabte
Aus
Olifantsbad

Genab
Homob
Ozonjuitji
Kapupuhedi

Goseb

Ombika

C38

Entrance
Anderson Gate

Ongava Lodge

The real secret of game-watching in the park is to settle in at one of the many waterholes, most of which are on the southern edges of the pan, and wait. And wait. Each waterhole has its own unique personality and characteristics. Even if the hole is small and deep, like Ombika, on the western side, you'll be amazed at what may arrive. Old Africa hands maintain that you should be up at dawn for the best sightings, but you can see marvelous game at all times of day. The plains, where you'll likely spot cheetahs, are also home to huge herds of zebras and wildebeests, and you may see the silhouettes of giraffes as they cross the skyline in stately procession. Watch out for herds of springbok "pronking"—an activity wherein these lovely little antelope bounce and bound high into the air as they run. Zoologists argue over the reason for this behavior. Some say it's to avoid predators, others that it's to demonstrate agility, strength, and stamina; most visitors like to believe that pronking is just for fun. Salvadora, a constant spring on the fringe of Etosha Pan near Halali, is a favorite watering point for some of these big herds. Watch out also for the stately eland, Africa's largest antelope. As big as a cow, although more streamlined and elegant, this antelope can jump higher than any other African antelope—amazing when you consider its huge size. And where there's water, there's always game. Predators, especially lions, lurk around most of the waterholes looking for a meal. Plan to spend at least half a night sitting on a bench at the floodlighted Okaukuejo waterhole. You really are within spitting distance of the game. Bring a book, write in your journal, or just sit while you wait. You may be amazed at the variety of animals that come down to drink: black and white rhinos, lions, jackals, and even the occasional leopard. This is a particularly good place to look out for black rhinos, which trot purposefully up to drink and in so doing scare all but the bravest of other game away. Groot Okevi waterhole, close to Namutoni, is also good for black rhinos.

Don't overlook the more than 340 dazzling varieties of bird—the crimson-breasted shrike is particularly gorgeous—and watch for ostriches running over the plains or raptors hunting silently overhead. There are many endemics, including the black-faced and bare-cheeked babblers, violet wood-hoopoe (look for them in Halali camp), Rüppell's parrot, Bradfield's swift, and the white-tailed shrike.

Be aware of the trees, shrubs, and plants as well. Just east of Okaukuejo is the legendary Haunted or Ghost Forest, where moringa trees have morphed into twisted, strange, and grotesque shapes: you may feel as if you're in Snow White's forest or deep in Middle Earth.

WHEN TO GO

The best time to visit is from April to September, when the temperatures are cooler, and the increasingly thirsty animals gather at waterholes, making it easiest to see them (the driest time of year when this will be the case is August to September). May to August is the coolest time of year, and nights can be downright freezing—be sure to bring adequate warm clothes for night drives. Bird-watchers will want to visit in the summer (November to March) when the migratory birds (both intra-African and Palaearctic) flock in the park's many habitats after the

Namibia's Herero women are known for their colorful gowns and wide-brimmed hats.

summer rains. The main Etosha Pan can become a huge expanse of shallow water filled with flamingos, wildfowl, and waders.

GETTING HERE AND AROUND

Tourists coming from the Oshakati area via the B1 can access the park through King Nehale Gate (northeast); coming from Tsumeb also via the B1 through the Von Lindequist Gate (east); coming from Outjo via the C38 through the Anderson Gate (south) from sunrise to sunset; and coming from Kamanjab via the C35 through the Galton Gate (west) (but note that if you are heading east to Okaukuejo, it is almost a five-hour drive through the park). Tourists may not drive in the park after sunset or before sunrise, and thus need to allow time to arrive at their respective rest camps if moving around close to these times. Namibia Wildlife Resorts (NWR) also offers guided night drives, which can be booked directly at the camps. If you're staying at Onkoshi, you need to report to reception at Namutoni to be transferred to Onkoshi, as only guests with 4x4 vehicles are able to travel along this section of road (at this writing the road is being prepared for all-vehicle access in the near future).

ADMISSION

The park gates are open from sunrise to sunset, and the daily entrance fee is N$80 for foreign visitors and N$10 for a passenger vehicle with fewer than 10 seats. You pay for your vehicle entry permit and for any balance remaining on your prebooked accommodations (which include personal entry fees) at the reception of the rest camp closest to the gate through which you enter.

SAFETY AND PRECAUTIONS

Motorists aren't allowed to travel faster than 60 kph (37 mph) inside the park, nor are they allowed to exit their vehicles unless they're at the rest camps or toilets. Always be on the lookout for animals, which can cross the road at random, and often are concealed by bushes before emerging. Refrain from making noise and getting too close to any animals, especially elephants, as they could panic and charge your car.

TIMING AND TOURING TIPS

Two to three days will allow you to visit the eastern and central parts of the park, as well as Okaukuejo. Taking in the "newer" western part of the park properly will require at least two days due to its relative isolation from the rest of the park—it's only 180 km (112 miles) to the next camp, but the speed limit is 60 kph (37 mph). Throughout most of the park there are numerous waterholes to visit, but that's best done in the early morning and late afternoon when the animals are more active and temperatures are cooler.

The park is huge—22,270 square km (8,598 square miles), 300 km (186 miles) wide, and 110 km (68 miles) long. The western part, which makes up a third of the overall park, is open to the public through the Galton Gate, but if you plan to drive through to Okaukeujo you need to arrive by 1 pm otherwise they will not allow access (unless you have a booking at the NWR's Dolomite Camp in the west). If you prefer to visit the park on one of the many safaris offered by various tour companies, make sure you choose one with an open vehicle or pop-top with few passengers—you probably don't want to find yourself in an air-conditioned 75-seater bus. That said, the best way to see the park is to drive yourself so you can stop at your leisure (don't exceed the 60 kph speed limit, and stick to marked roads). A two-wheel-drive car is fine, as the roads are good, but the higher up you sit, the better your view, so opt for the more expensive *combis* (vans) or 4x4s if possible. In addition to patience, you'll need drinks, snacks, field guides to the animals and birds, binoculars, and your camera. There are more than 40 waterholes, with Rietfontein, Okaukuejo, Goas, Halali, Klein Namutoni, and Chudob regarded as the best for game-watching and taking pictures, but nothing is certain in the bush. Keep your eyes and ears open, and you may come across game at any time, in any place. Arm yourself with the MET map of Etosha (available in the camps), which shows the names and locations of the waterholes and indicates which roads are open.

WHERE TO STAY

If you wish to stay inside Etosha itself you can lodge at one of the NWR rest camps (book months in advance, especially for the peak periods of July to September and around Christmas and Easter, though you may want to avoid the crowds at these times). The rest camps of Halali, Onkoshi, Dolomite, Namutoni, and Okaukuejo have pools, grocery-curio-liquor stores, gas stations, and restaurants serving breakfast, lunch, and dinner. There are also numerous full-service private lodges and guest farms near the park.

Ongava Lodge

Halali

Namutoni

$ Dolomite Camp. This is the place for those looking for something
HOTEL   unique and far from the maddening crowds. **Pros:** no crowds; a newer, better-designed camp than the other NWR offerings; more personal service than any other NWR camp. **Cons:** far from the rest of the park and the Etosha Pan; long uneven pathways from chalets to lodge could be off-putting for some. $ *Rooms from: US$148* ⊠ *Etosha National Park* ☎ *61/285–7200* ⊕ *www.nwr.com.na* ⇴ *20 chalets* ⦿ *Some meals.*

$ **Etosha Aoba Lodge.** This small, family-owned, ultrafriendly lodge is
HOTEL   10 km (6 miles) east of the Von Lindequist Gate—about a 30-minute drive from the park. **Pros:** lodge is set in a beautiful natural forest; great night drive with bush stargazing for budding astronomers; fabulous food and wine tastings every night. **Cons:** rooms are on the small side. $ *Rooms from: US$138* ⊠ *Etosha National Park* ☎ *61/237–055 bookings, 67/229–100 lodge* ⊕ *www.etosha-aoba-lodge.com* ⇴ *11 bungalows* ⦿ *Some meals.*

$ **Halali.** Etosha's smallest NWR camp with self-catering and non-self-
B&B/INN   catering chalets as well as a campsite has undergone a renovation that has vastly improved most of the chalets (though the cheapest category is still very small). **Pros:** prime location in the middle of Etosha; one of the quieter and less trafficked camps; lovely big swimming pool with shady grass and loungers. **Cons:** mosquito nets are not all in great shape; only offers an expensive buffet option for dinners; service can be disappointing. $ *Rooms from: US$84* ⊠ *Etosha National Park* ☎ *61/285–7200* ⊕ *www.nwr.com.na* ⇴ *70 chalets* ⦿ *Breakfast.*

$ **Mokuti Etosha Lodge.** Since this lodge is in its own park, a stone's throw
HOTEL   from the Von Lindequist Gate, you may well wake up and find an antelope
FAMILY   or warthog munching the grass outside your room. **Pros:** stone's throw from Etosha gate; all the amenities of a big hotel, including tennis and an in-house spa. **Cons:** rooms lack views and the character of a smaller lodge; dinners feel rather chaotic and busy when the lodge is full. $ *Rooms from: US$151* ⊠ *Etosha National Park* ☎ *61/431–8001 reservations, 67/229–084 lodge* ⊕ *www.mokutietoshalodge.com* ⇴ *106 rooms* ⦿ *Some meals.*

$$ **The Mushara Outpost.** If you're a fan of old-fashioned luxury, warm
HOTEL   service, and accommodations that combine the authenticity of the bush with a stylish and comfortable interior, then this is an excellent option. **Pros:** rooms are bright and comfortable; indoor and outdoor showers; excellent service. **Cons:** laundry services are an additional charge; no children under 12. $ *Rooms from: US$338* ⊠ *Etosha National Park* ☎ *61/241–880 reservations, 67/229–106 lodge* ⊕ *www.mushara-lodge.com* ⇴ *8 tents* ⦿ *All-inclusive.*

$ **Namutoni Rest Camp.** On the eastern edge of the park and resem-
B&B/INN   bling something out of the novel and films *Beau Geste,* this restored colonial fort with its flying flag and graceful palm trees is the most picturesque of the national-park camps. **Pros:** great location with access to the northeast section of the park where the flamingo colony at Fischer's Pan is found; prettier than the other camps; daily game drives available. **Cons:** service unpredictable; camp water hole not one of the best in the area; only campsites are self-catering. $ *Rooms from: US$89* ⊠ *Etosha National Park* ☎ *61/285–7200* ⊕ *www.nwr.com.na* ⇴ *44 chalets* ⦿ *Breakfast.*

$$$ HOTEL **Okonjima Bush Camp.** Located about halfway between Windhoek and Etosha, this camp is an excellent stopover point on your way to the park. **Pros:** numerous activities including cheetah/leopard-tracking, self-guided walking trails, and bird-watching; great service; kitchen facilities are available. **Cons:** some of the garden rooms—in the Plains Camp—are small and dark; sometimes there is a bit of herding of guests for activities; too far from Etosha to make it a base for exploration. [$] *Rooms from: US$491* ✉ *Otjiwarongo* ☎ *67/314–000 reservations* 🌐 *www.okonjima.com* 🛏 *10 rooms* 🍴 *Some meals.*

$$$$ ALL-INCLUSIVE **Ongava Lodge.** On the southern boundary of Etosha close to the Anderson Gate, this lodge has its own surrounding game reserve. **Pros:** great location by the entrance of Etosha; large luxurious rooms; great wildlife viewing from the lodge waterhole; guided walks include white rhino tracking. **Cons:** pool on the small side; there are many stairs to the lodge. [$] *Rooms from: US$734* ✉ *Etosha National Park* ☎ *83/330–3920 reservations* 🌐 *www.ongava.com* 🛏 *23 rooms* 🍴 *All-inclusive.*

$$ ALL-INCLUSIVE Fodor's Choice ★ **Onguma: The Fort.** This flagship lodge in the Onguma Game Reserve on the eastern border of Etosha National Park's Fischer Pan is the epitomy of luxury and style. **Pros:** arresting view of the pan; stunning swimming pool and sundowner area; extensive wine cellar and first-class food. **Cons:** no walking around after dark or between room and lodge (but they provide a golf cart transport). [$] *Rooms from: US$375* ✉ *Etosha National Park* ☎ *61/237–055* 🌐 *www.onguma.com* 🛏 *13 suites* 🍴 *Some meals.*

IF YOU HAVE TIME

Although the must-see parks in Namibia are described in great detail above, there are still other places worth exploring if you have time.

THE SKELETON COAST

This wildly beautiful but dangerous shore, a third of Namibia's coastline, stretches from the Ugab River in the south to the Kunene River, the border with Angola, in the north. The Portuguese seafarers who explored this area in the 15th century called this treacherous coast with its cold Benguela current and deadly crosscurrents the "Coast of Death." Its newer, no-less-sinister name, the Skeleton Coast, testifies to innumerable shipwrecks, lives lost, bleached whale bones, and the insignificant, transient nature of humans in the face of the raw power of nature. Still comparatively unknown to tourists, this region has a stark beauty and an awesomely diverse landscape—gray gravel plains, rugged wilderness, rusting shipwrecks, desert wastes, meandering barchan dunes, distant mountains, towering walls of sand and granite, and crashing seas. You'll rarely see more than a handful of visitors in this inaccessible and rugged coastal area. This isn't an easy ride, as distances are vast, amenities scarce or nonexistent, and the roads demanding. Don't exceed 80 kph (50 mph) on the gravel roads, and never drive off the road onto the ecologically vulnerable salt pans and lichen fields: the scars left by vehicles can last for hundreds of years and do irreparable damage.

Skeleton Coast National Park extends along this rugged Atlantic coast and about 40 km (25 miles) inland; the 200-km (125-mile) stretch of coast from Swakopmund to the Ugab River is the National West Coast Tourist Recreational Area. You can drive along a coastal road right up to Terrace Bay, and for the first 250 km (155 miles) from Swakopmund north to Terrace Bay you'll find not sand dunes but glinting gravel plains and scattered rocks. Stop and sift a handful of gravel: you may well find garnets and crystals among the tiny stones. In other places the plains are carpeted with lichens—yellow, red, orange, and many shades of green. In the early morning these lichen fields look lushly attractive, but during the heat of midday they seem dried up and insignificant. But don't whiz by. Stop and pour a drop of water on the lichens and watch a small miracle as they unfurl and come alive. If you're a birder, the salt pans on the way from Swakopmund to Henties Bay are worth a visit; you might spot a rare migrant wader there. The famous Namibian oysters are farmed here in sea ponds—don't leave Namibia without tasting these. The surreal little seaside holiday town of Henties Bay is like a deserted Hollywood back lot in winter, but in summer is full of holidaying Namibian fisherfolk from Swakopmund, Windhoek, and Tsumeb.

You'll smell the hundreds of thousands of Cape fur seals (*Arctocephalus pusillus pusillus*) at the Cape Cross seal colony, north of Henties Bay, long before you get there, but stifle your gags and go goggle at the seething mass on land and in the water. If you visit in late November or early December, you can "ooh" and "aah" at the furry baby seal pups, as well as the marauding jackals looking for a fast-food snack. Farther north the dunes begin, ending in the north at the Kunene River, Namibia's border with Angola. This northern stretch of coast from the Ugab River to the Kunene River is managed by the government as a wilderness area and accounts for a third of Namibia's coastline. But if it's lush green pastures and abundance of game you want, then this raw, rugged, harsh, and uncompromising landscape isn't for you. What you'll find are dramatically different scenery—big skies and unending horizons—an absence of tourists ("crowds" around here means one or two vehicles), and some wildlife: brown hyenas, springbok, oryx, jackals, and, if you're really lucky, a cheetah or rhino. The sight of a majestic oryx silhouetted against towering sand dunes or a cheeky jackal scavenging seal pups on the beaches is extremely rewarding. The best activity, however, is just concentrating on the freedom, beauty, and strange solitude of the area.

PARK ESSENTIALS

Limited facilities exist in the park. Gas and water are available at Terrace Bay and camping with basic ablutions is found at Torra Bay. Booking is essential.

WHEN TO GO

The northern Skeleton Coast experiences the same weather year-round: moderate temperatures with mist, wind, and hardly any rain. For anglers, the best time to visit is November to March. For the inland Kaokoveld, the dry winter season from May to August is best. The rainy summer months of January to March can bring extremely high temperatures and flash floods.

GETTING HERE AND AROUND

You can drive (a 4x4 gives you more flexibility) from Swakopmund north through Henties Bay via the Ugab Gate, with its eerie painted skulls and crossbones on the gates, or from the more northerly Springbokwater Gate. You must reach your gate of entry before 3 pm. Always stick to the marked roads and avoid driving on treacherous salt pans. Look out for an abandoned 1960s oil rig lying next to the road between the Ugab River and Terrace Bay.

The Uniab River valley, between Torra Bay and Terrace Bay, is your best chance of spotting big game such as rhinos and occasionally elephants. Once you get to Terrace Bay, 287 km (178 miles) north of Henties Bay, that's the end of your car trip: it's the last outpost. If you want to explore further, then a fly-in safari is your only option.

Many parts of the Skeleton Coast can be visited only with a dedicated operator, and the lengths of tours vary. If you intend to spend time only in Torra Bay or Terrace Bay, two to three days will suffice. Bear in mind that this coastline doesn't conform to the usual "beach holiday" image: Namibia's beaches are wild and desolate, offering a welcome respite from the hot inland areas during summer months and a wonderful destination for fishermen.

The C34 road runs parallel to the coast, and then a rough track continues up past Torra Bay to the ranger station (Ministry of Environment and Tourism). Driving the C34 is straightforward, although fog can

CLOSE UP

From Portugal to the Skeleton Coast

More than 500 years ago, a daring little band of Portuguese sailors, inspired by the vision of their charismatic leader, Prince Henry the Navigator—who, contrary to what you might expect from his name, never left his native land—set sail from the School of Navigation at Sagres, the farthest western point of Europe, to find fame, fortune, and new lands for the Crown. Facing unknown dangers and terra incognita—the maps of the time were little more than fanciful sketchbooks filled with dragons and warnings that "here be monsters"—the intrepid sailors pushed back the edges of the known world nautical mile by nautical mile until they entered the waters of the southwest coastline of Africa on tiny, frail caravels. In 1485, Captain Diego Cão and his battered crew finally dropped anchor off a desolate beach thousands of miles from home and safety. There, on the lonely windswept sands, they erected a cross both in honor of their heavenly king, whom they credited with protecting and directing them during their arduous journey, as well as to King John I, their earthly monarch. North of Swakopmund, as you marvel at thousands upon thousands of the Cape fur seals at Cape Cross, you can see a replica of that cross (the original is in the Berlin Oceanographic Museum). Sadly, the courageous Captain Cão never made it home: he's buried nearby on a rocky outcrop.

make the surface slick and the road is mostly gravel, so keep speeds below 80 kph (49 mph). You can purchase your entry permit either at the Ugab or Springbokwasser Gates. There are several short detours to points of interest, but off-road driving is strictly prohibited.

WHERE TO STAY

$$$$ ALL-INCLUSIVE **Hoanib Skeleton Coast Camp.** This luxurious and completely solar-powered camp is located in the remote, broad valley of the Hoanib River. **Pros:** absolute luxury in a totally remote setting; game drives and guides that are some of the best in the country; a chance to see the rare desert-adapted elephants. **Cons:** only accessible by fly-in; the camp is not fenced so you have to be escorted to your tent at night. [$] *Rooms from: US$1130* ☎ *11/257–5000* 🌐 *www.wilderness-safaris.com* 🛏 *8 tents* 🍴 *All-inclusive.*

$$$$ ALL-INCLUSIVE Fodor's Choice ★ **Serra Cafema.** This astonishingly different and dramatically sited camp in the extreme northwest of Namibia on the Angolan border is the most remote camp in southern Africa. **Pros:** surreal remote wilderness area (malaria-free zone); gorgeous camp and rooms with views of Kunene River; a wealth of activities beyond game drives; outstanding service. **Cons:** you may find yourself torn between activities and relaxing in your lovely tent; not a lot of wildlife; arduous travel to get here. [$] *Rooms from: US$1038* ☎ *11/257–5000 in South Africa* 🌐 *www.wilderness-safaris.com* 🛏 *8 tents* 🍴 *All-inclusive.*

CAPRIVI STRIP

This lovely unspoiled area—one of Namibia's best-kept secrets—lies in northeast Namibia (and is sometimes simply referred to as "northeast Namibia") at the confluence of the Zambezi and Chobe rivers, and serves as a gateway to Zimbabwe's Victoria Falls and Botswana's Chobe National Park. Because it's relatively unknown as a tourist area, you'll get the feeling here that you're truly alone with nature.

Think of the Caprivi Strip as a long finger of land at the top of the country pointing eastward for 450 km (280 miles) toward Zimbabwe and Zambia; in many ways, because of its rivers, marshes, and forests, the area is much more like those countries than the rest of Namibia. This part of Namibia is the closest thing to Botswana's Okavango Delta, and it shelters much of the same game: elephants, the aquatic lechwe and the rare sitatunga antelope, the uncommon roan and sable antelope, and, hardly ever seen in Namibia, big buffalo herds. However, you're unlikely to see predators.

This corridor of land became strategically important when Germany annexed South West Africa (now Namibia) in 1884. The British, concerned about further German colonial expansion up into Africa, struck a deal with Khama, a local Bechuana king, and formed the British Protectorate of Bechuanaland (now Botswana). The Caprivi Strip was part of the deal. It was then shuttled back and forth between Britain and Germany until it finally passed into the hands of South Africa at the end of World War II. However, its troubles were far from over, and during the Namibian struggle for independence, the area became the scene of bitter fighting between Sam Nujoma's freedom fighters (Sam Nujoma became the first president of Namibia in 1990) and the South African Defence Force (SADF). Today, the game that was scared away is back, the area is once again peaceful, and it's a relatively little-known and little-visited destination by overseas tourists. If you've seen your Big Five, had your classic desert experience, and are looking for somewhere offbeat, then this is a great destination.

You've got to be fairly determined to get here because the journey can be circuitous, to say the least. You can fly in to Katima Mulilo, the vibey little main town (which is closer to Gaborone, Botswana, or Lusaka, Zambia, than it is to Windhoek), pick up a vehicle, and drive. Visit the Caprivi Art Centre near the African market, where you'll find beautifully crafted baskets, carvings, and handmade pottery. There's a main road across the strip, the B8, but it's relatively busy with commercial traffic to and from Zambia and Botswana. Or you can fly into Livingstone in Zambia, cross the Sesheke border (over the Zambezi River), and continue by road and river to your chosen lodge. (To give you some idea: to get to Susuwe Island Lodge, you fly from Johannesburg into Livingstone, then take a small plane to the Namibian immigration post at Katima Mulilo, then fly to the Immelman airstrip nearby, the once infamous Doppies SADF forward base, and travel by road and river to the lodge.) However you get here, the destination is well worth every last mile for a remote, water-wilderness experience. Your best bet is to choose a lodge and then let it make all your travel arrangements for you.

9

Neither the Caprivi Strip's Mudumu National Park or Mahango National Park is easily accessible—particularly in the wet season—but if you're a do-it-yourself adventure type, you might enjoy a visit to either park. You'll see plenty of game, including hippos, elephants, buffalo, roan and sable antelope, kudu, zebras, and maybe even wild dogs. Mahango is great for bird-watching, with more species than any other Namibian park.

WHEN TO GO

For bird-watchers the best time to visit is summer (December–February), but be forewarned that the heat and humidity can be unbearable. Toward the end of summer, the Zambezi, Chobe, and Linyanti rivers usually flood, making access to Lake Liambezi and the Mamili National Park difficult. Access will be by 4x4, and will require negotiating completely submerged roads. Otherwise, the Caprivi can be visited for most of the year, but inquire at the lodge you're interested in how negotiable their roads are during the rainy season (November–April/May). The winter months of April to October are great for game-viewing, and far more pleasant what with the cooler temperatures and lack of rainfall.

GETTING HERE AND AROUND

The B8 road from Katima Mulilo to Kasane is paved, and the Namibia/Kasane Bridge has been renovated. The immigration office in Kasane is open from 7:30 to 4. Roads from Katima Mulilo to Victoria Falls and through Gaborone to Johannesburg are all paved and in good condition. The Sesheke Bridge between Namibia and Zambia opened in 2004, completing the TransCaprivi Highway, and linking the port of Walvis Bay with Zambia's capital, Lusaka. The Wenela Border Post is open from 6 to 6. Immigration and customs facilities are also available at Lianshulu Lodge, open from 8 to 5. The Ngoma border is open from 7 to 6. Day trips can be taken across the border in Chobe National Park.

■TIP➔ **A 4x4 vehicle is required for some of the parks. One can travel on the main roads by sedan car.**

TIMING

To explore Caprivi from east to west and to enjoy its peace and quiet, at least a week should be set aside.

WHERE TO STAY

$$$$
ALL-INCLUSIVE

Chobe Water Villas. Sitting on the banks of the famous Chobe River, right where it meets the mighty Zambezi River, this elegant lodge gives you a taste of effortless luxury. **Pros:** unrivaled views of Sedudu Island and the wildlife dense river; luxurious rooms with well-stocked mini-bars (all-inclusive); game drives and boat cruises included in room rate. **Cons:** at some times of the year there can be a lot of irritating insects (due to the water and heat); some hassles getting across to the National Park as it crosses into Botswana. *$ Rooms from: US$630 ⊠ Caprivi Strip* ☎ *66/253–602 lodge, 61/431–8008 reservations* ⊕ *www.chobe-watervillas.com* ⬎ *16 villas* ⦿ *All-inclusive.*

$$$
HOTEL

Nambwa Tented Camp. Situated in a tall shady forest, this lodge stands on its tiptoes high up off the ground overlooking the lush floodplain below. **Pros:** the treetop setting is especially unusual and exciting; location allows for close encounters with game such as elephants; warm personal service. **Cons:** access road only passable by 4x4; Wi-Fi only available in the main area. $\boxed{\text{S}}$ *Rooms from: US$496* ⊠ *Caprivi Strip* ☎ *61/400–510* ⊕ *www.africanmonarchlodges.com* ↻ *9 tents* ◯ *Some meals.*

WATERBERG PLATEAU PARK

This lovely game reserve, established in 1972 when several rare and endangered species were introduced from other areas of Namibia and South Africa, is one of the most peaceful and relatively unknown wilderness areas in Namibia. About 91 km (56 miles) east of Otjiwarongo, it's also an ideal stopover on the way from Windhoek to Etosha. The plateau is a huge, flat-top massif rising abruptly from the surrounding plain and offering superb views of the park, the outstanding rock formations, and the magnitude of the plateau itself. Edged with steep-sided, rugged, reddish-brown cliffs, the plateau is covered with red Kalahari sand that supports a range of dry woodland vegetation, from the red syringa trees and Kalahari apple leaf to the kudu bush. You're not allowed to drive yourself, but game-viewing tours operate every morning and evening from the beautifully landscaped Waterberg Camp (book in advance through the NWR; you can join a tour even if you're not a guest of the camp). Although you won't see the big numbers of game that you'll find in Etosha, you could spot the rare roan and sable antelope, Cape buffalo, white and black rhinos, giraffes, hyenas, leopards, and cheetahs. But game-spotting isn't an exact science, so there are no guarantees. The park is a wonderful place to hike, whether on the much-sought-after, three-day, accompanied Waterberg Wilderness Trail (book through the NWR at the Waterberg Camp [formerly the Bernabé de la Bat Rest Camp] in advance) or on a short 3-km (2-mile) walk around camp.

WHEN TO GO
The park can be visited throughout the year. During the rainy season (December–April) the last stretch of road (which is gravel) must be negotiated very carefully as the surface can be slippery when wet.

GETTING HERE AND AROUND
The park is located about 300 km (186 miles) northeast of Windhoek. Visitors can't drive up onto the plateau in their own vehicles but can explore by foot on self-guided wilderness trails. Daily guided game drives (about four hours) include visits to fantastic hides on the plateau that offer excellent views of waterhole life. Daily game drives can be booked at the Waterberg Camp.

SAFETY AND PRECAUTIONS
Don't feed the animals, and keep your belongings safely away from inquisitive baboons. Lock your bungalow when leaving, as baboons may try to enter an unlocked room. Bring warm clothing for winter weather: game drives in the early morning or late afternoon can be very chilly—even in summer, and especially when it's rained.

TIMING
There are hikes of differing lengths, so inquire how much time you'll need for your chosen route from NWR. If not hiking, then a minimum stay of two nights is recommended so you'll have one whole day to

climb the mountain, go on a game drive, relax at the pool, and explore the walking trails around the camp.

WHERE TO STAY

$ HOTEL **Waterberg Plateau Lodge.** Located on the magnificent rock terrace of the geological phenomenon known as the Waterberg Plateau, the chalets of this lodge are hidden from one another by bush and red sandstone boulders. **Pros:** genuine warm and friendly staff; opportunity to see rhinos on the game drive is almost guaranteed. **Cons:** not as luxurious as other lodges but they make up for it with the views; sometimes the baboons can be a little pesky trying to enter the rooms. [$] *Rooms from: US$127* ✉ *Waterberg Plateau Park* ☎ *67/687–018* 🌐 *www.waterberg-wilderness.com* 🛏 *8 chalets* 🍴 *Some meals.*

GATEWAY CITY

If you're going on safari in Namibia, it's very likely that you'll have to take a connecting flight through Windhoek en route to your safari destination, so you'll likely spend at least one overnight here.

WINDHOEK

The pleasant if provincial little capital city of Windhoek lies almost exactly in the center of the country and is surrounded by the Khomas Highland and the Auas and Eros mountains. With its colonial architecture, sidewalk cafés, shopping centers, and shady parks, it's by no means a hardship to spend a day or two here.

Settled by the Germans in the 1890s, it's an easy town to explore on foot (though summers are blisteringly hot). Main sights, which are clustered around the downtown area, include the National Gallery (where you can often purchase works in the temporary exhibits), the remarkably good craft center, and some old German architecture. The city has a population of about 250,000 and growing, most of which resides in the largely black township of Katutura. If you have a few free hours, a visit to Katutura makes an interesting half-day expedition that gives visitors at least an idea of how the majority of urban Namibians live. Windhoek is also home to the country's brewing industry—a holdover from its days as a German colony—and a guided visit to the brewery is possible.

GETTING HERE AND AROUND

Namibia's main point of entry is Hosea Kutako International Airport. It's a small, bustling, modern airport that's a scenic 45-km (28-mile) drive from Windhoek. The smaller Eros Airport handles local flights and charters. Once in the country you can make use of scheduled flights or charter flights that service all domestic destinations.

Licensed shuttle companies (look for a sticker that shows they're registered with the NTB) offer service from Hosea Kutako International Airport to Windhoek's city center; the pickup and drop-off point is at the taxi stand on Independence Avenue, next to the Tourist Information Center. Expect to pay N$250–N$300 each way. Many larger hotels run a courtesy shuttle service to and from the airport. "Radio taxis" (taxis with radio contact to the dispatch) are available, but negotiate the price before you get in. Check on current fares at the airport information counter.

Intercape Mainliner runs buses between Windhoek and Swakopmund, as do other smaller and reliable shuttle services. Information on these is available at the Tourist Information Center in both cities.

If you're only in Windhoek for 24 hours or so, you won't need a car. It's an easy city to walk around in, and taxis are available everywhere. Always negotiate with the driver before getting into the taxi. Hotels also provide shuttle service.

That said, if you plan to drive to Swakopmund or any of the parks, you can rent a car here. Gas is on sale in all towns, but if you're planning a long journey between towns, fill up in Windhoek before you leave.

If you've got three days or so to spare and you're headed to or from the coastal resort of Swakopmund, then consider traveling on the Desert Express. The train departs from Windhoek on Friday around midday, and from Swakopmund on Saturday around 3 pm, arriving the next day around 10:30 am. Your first stop on the outward journey from Windhoek is Okapuka Ranch, where you'll watch lions being fed, after which you get back on the train and enjoy a splendid dinner yourself. The train parks in a siding for the night, then leaves early in the morning so you can catch a spectacular sunrise over the desert. Later, you get a chance to walk in the Namib when the train stops in the dunes between Swapkopmund and Walvis Bay. If you do the return journey, you'll be taken to see the San rock paintings at Spitzkoppe. The train has 24 air-conditioned, small but comfortable cabins with en suite facilities. Longer journeys to Etosha are available. One-way fares from Windhoek to Swakopmund start at N$3,500 per person sharing, and are all-inclusive of meals and activities.

African Extravaganza specializes in shuttle services, scheduled safaris, charter tours and fly-ins, self-drive options, day excursions, and transfers. But as Windhoek is a small town and easy to walk around in, your best bet is to stay in the city and see what's going on there. Ask your hotel concierge or guesthouse owner for up-to-date information, or check out the Tour and Safari Association website (⊕ *www.tasa.na*) for a comprehensive list of registered operators describing their specialties.

HEALTH AND SAFETY

If you need medical attention in Windhoek, consider the Medi-Clinic, an excellent private clinic, or the Roman Catholic Hospital. Ask at your accommodation for the nearest pharmacy.

Pickpockets work the city center, particularly the markets and the Post Street Mall. Lock your valuables away in the hotel safe, and carry only what you need. Never travel with expensive jewelry. Don't walk alone at night, and stick to well-lit areas.

VISITOR INFORMATION

The very helpful Tourist Information Bureau (run by the City of Windhoek) at the Post Street Mall provides information on Windhoek and environs; it's open weekdays 7:30–1 and 2–4:30. It also operates a kiosk on Independence Avenue next to the main taxi stand and opposite the Avani Windhoek Hotel and Casino. Also on Independence Avenue is the Tourist Information Center run by the Leading Lodges of Africa; here you can book accommodations and car rentals, and get advice about travel throughout the country. There's also a luggage storage facility and a small café with Wi-Fi.

The head office of the Namibia Wildlife Resorts (NWR) is also on Independence Avenue. Here you can get information on NWR lodging in all the parks and make bookings. The Namibia Tourism Board (NTB) has general information on Windhoek as well as the rest of Namibia, but isn't tailored to individual consultation. It's open weekdays 8–5.

Additionally, Windhoek City Tours now has a bus tour on the ubiquitous double-decker red buses that ply cities from London to Tokyo. Leaving twice daily at 9:30 and 2:30, the bus (N$185) is a pleasant zero-effort way to get your bearings and catch all the major sights in about two hours, with live commentary. Tickets and information are available at the Leading Lodge's Tourist Information Center on Independence Avenue.

ESSENTIALS

Airports Eros Airport. ☎ 61/295–5501 ⊕ www.airports.com.na. **Hosea Kutako International Airport.** ☎ 61/295–5600 ⊕ www.airports.com.na.

Bus Line Intercape Mainliner. ☎ 61/227–847 ⊕ www.intercape.co.za.

Car Rentals Avis. ☎ 61/233–166 ⊕ www.avis.co.za. **Budget.** ☎ 61/233–166 ⊕ www.budget.co.na. **Hertz.** ☎ 61/256–274 ⊕ www.hertz.co.za.

Tour Operator African Extravaganza. ☎ 61/372–100 ⊕ www.african-extravaganza.com.

Visitor Information City Tourist Office. ✉ 39 Post St. Mall, Windhoek ☎ 61/290–2092, 61/290–2401 ⊕ www.windhoekcc.org.na. **Namibia Tourism Board** (NTB). ✉ Haddy and Sam Nujoma Dr., Windhoek ☎ 61/290–6000 ⊕ www.namibiatourism.com.na. **Namibia Wildlife Resorts** (NWR). ✉ 189 Independence Ave., Windhoek ☎ 61/285–7200 ⊕ www.nwr.com.na. **Windhoek City Tours.** ✉ 41 Nickel St., Prosperita ☎ 61/275–300 ⊕ www.senseofafrica-namibia.com.

EXPLORING

TOP ATTRACTIONS

Namibia Crafts Centre. On Tal Street in the old breweries building behind the Avani Windhoek Hotel and Casino, the Namibia Crafts Centre offers some truly beautiful and unique pieces of work. Dozens of stalls showcase the work of more than 1,500 rural craftspeople, and include items such as particularly fine woven baskets, striking and original beadwork, distinct Caprivian pots, handmade contemporary jewelry, eye-catching prints, and much more. Be sure to check out the Omba Arts Trust stall, where changing exhibits of truly stunning work done by women from disadvantaged communities can be viewed and purchased. ⊠ *40 Tal St., Windhoek* ☎ *61/242–2222.*

National Gallery. This small but lovely museum features contemporary Namibian art. The somewhat ho-hum permanent exhibit downstairs features German-Namibian painters from the 20th century. Head upstairs, where cool contemporary lithographs by young Namibian artists line the walls, and regularly changing temporary exhibits feature very good work by Namibian and other African artists, most of which is for sale. A small café and shop adjoin. ⊠ *John Meinart St. at Robert Mugabe Ave., Windhoek* ☎ *61/231–160* ⊕ *www.nagn.org.na* ⊠ *Suggested donation N$20.*

Post Street Mall. At this open-air market known for its colorful sidewalk displays of curios, crafts, and carvings of all kinds, international tourists and businesspeople rub shoulders with Herero women in full traditional Victorian dress. Keep an eye out for the meteorites mounted on slender steel columns. These meteorites hit the earth during the Gibeon meteorite shower, which rained down some 600 million years ago, the heaviest such shower known on earth. ■TIP➡ There are some curios and beadwork on sale here but be sure to check out the sidewalk curio market farther down on Independence Avenue. ⊠ *Post St., Windhoek.*

WORTH NOTING

Bushman Art Gallery. This souvenir and curio shop on bustling Independence Avenue distinguishes itself from the rest with its fairly sizable collection of cult objects (religious, ceremonial, drums, etc.) and domestic utensils of local bushman and Himba tribes (not for sale). A large assortment of other carvings and antiques from around Africa adorn the walls and display cases. ⊠ *187 Independence Ave., Windhoek* ☎ *61/228–828, 61/229–131* ⊕ *www.bushmanart-gallery.com.*

Christuskirche. The Lutheran Christ Church is a good representation of German colonial architecture—a mixture of art nouveau and neo-Gothic dating from 1896. Although the church is sometimes locked, you can obtain a key from the nearby church office at 12 Fidel Castro Street (down the hill from the church). ■TIP➡ You must book in advance to be able to go inside. ⊠ *Robert Mugabe Ave., Windhoek* ☎ *61/236–002* ⊗ *Closed Sat. and Sun.*

Katutura. Created in the late 1950s for the forced evictions of blacks from the town center, Windhoek's vast African township now houses an estimated 60% of the city's population and makes for an interesting trip. Be sure to visit the Oshetu Market ("our market"), where northern Namibian fare like mopane worms and dried patties of a type of local spinach are sold, and whose bustling meat market includes a barbeque area where the adventurous can try succulent slices of all types of roasted meat, dipped by locals in a mixture of salt and chili. Most tours will include a visit to Penduka, an NGO (a nongovernmental organization set up by the UN) to empower women. Here you can meet the women who have learned to manufacture beads and fabrics for sale. ■TIP➡ Be sure to go with a guide, who can both navigate the dirt roads and provide commentary on what you're seeing; Katu Tours does this via bicycle and it's one of the best ways to experience it. ⊠ *SL10*

Soweto Market, Independence Ave., Kautura, Windhoek ☎ *61/210–097* 🌐 *www.katutours.com* 🎫 *Tours N$750 per person.*

Owela Display Centre. With displays on everything from archaeology to natural history to ethnology, this rather musty but endearing museum makes up in information (on densely formatted placards) for what it lacks in style; it's part of the larger National Museum of Namibia next door. The exhibit on the San, including refreshingly critical commentary on the bushman as a constructed concept, and a discussion on the exploitation of that concept, is worth noting. The Independence Museum located just down the road in the enormous flashy building, contains more exhibits on the history of Namibia and the struggle for independence; and it has a decent restaurant on the top floor with a great view of the city. ✉ *Robert Mugabe St., Windhoek* ☎ *61/302–230 Museums Association of Namibia* 🌐 *www.museums.com.na* 🕓 *Closed Sat. and Sun.*

Tintenpalast. The handsome circa-1912 (Palace of Ink) is fronted by beautiful formal gardens. Formerly the administration offices of the German colonial government, the two-story building now houses the National Assembly. One-hour tours are given weekdays at 9, 10, and 3. Nearby is the **Office of the Prime Minister,** decorated in mosaics, indigenous woods, and murals. Security guards will give informal tours on request. ✉ *Robert Mugabe Ave., Windhoek* ☎ *61/288–9111* 🎫 *Free* 🕓 *Closed daily noon–1 pm.*

WHERE TO EAT

$ CAFÉ 🍴 **Craft Café.** Located at the Craft Centre in downtown Windhoek this bustling café is as good for you as it is popular. They mostly serve generous portions of healthy fare—huge open-faced sandwiches on freshly baked bread, gorgeous salads, quiches, and all manner of smoothies and milkshakes—with a good dose of delightful cake and treats to balance it out. **Known for:** freshly squeezed fruit and vegetable juices; home-baked cheesecake that melts in your mouth. [$] *Average main: US$5* ✉ *40 Tal St., Windhoek* ☎ *61/249–974* 🌐 *www.craftcafe-namibia.com.*

$$ GERMAN FAMILY 🍴 **Joe's Beerhouse.** Tuck into generous portions of German and Namibian food at this popular Windhoek institution. The interior, filled with Joe's personal collection of memorabilia, is a great place to sit, but outside in the boma by a roaring fire is perfect for sipping a quaff glüwein (mulled wine) or Camelthorn Brewery's Sundowner beer, a local lager. **Known for:** great vibe and music; large menu with many choices—especially pork and venison; wide selection of craft beers. [$] *Average main: US$14* ✉ *160 Nelson Mandela Ave., Windhoek* ☎ *61/232–457* 🌐 *www.joesbeerhouse.com.*

$$ EUROPEAN 🍴 **Leo's at the Castle.** Arguably Windhoek's only true fine-dining establishment—with a price tag to match—Leo's is literally in a castle on a hill. The small chandelier-dazzled dining room has fabulous views of the city and the haute cuisine is both gorgeously prepared and presented. **Known for:** outstanding service; excellent wine selection; gorgeous view over Windhoek. [$] *Average main: US$16* ✉ *Hotel Heinitzburg, 22 Heinitzburg St., Windhoek* ☎ *61/249–597* 🌐 *www.heinitzburg.com.*

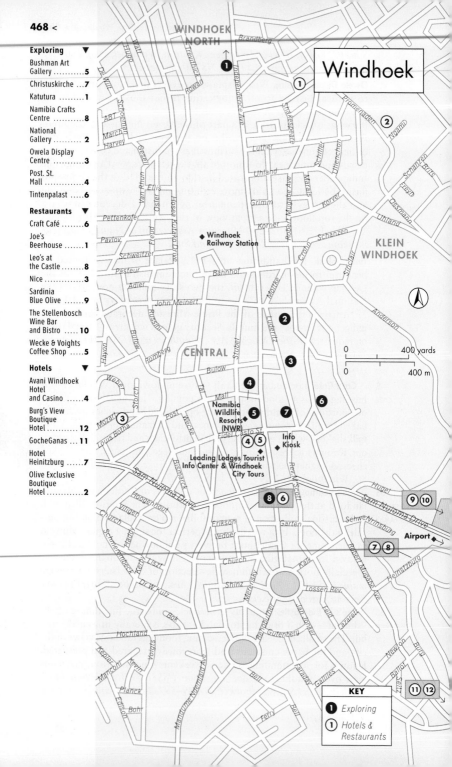

Windhoek

WINDHOEK NORTH

KLEIN WINDHOEK

CENTRAL

Windhoek
Railway Station

Namibia
Wildlife
Resorts
(NWR)

Info
Kiosk

Leading Lodges Tourist
Info Center & Windhoek
City Tours

Airport

KEY

① *Exploring*

① *Hotels &
Restaurants*

$$ ECLECTIC Fodor's Choice ★ 🍴 **Nice.** One of Windhoek's hippest places to wine and dine is the restaurant showcase for the Namibian Institute of Culinary Education. With an emphasis on local ingredients and a multitude of influences, trainees supervised by head chefs produce delicious fare. **Known for:** trendy dishes like tuna tartar and oryx with poached pear; sophisticated atmosphere; producing some of Namibia's top chefs for lodges around the country. [$] *Average main: US$15* ✉ *2 Mozart St. (corner of Hosea Kutako Dr.), Windhoek* ☎ *61/300–710* 🌐 *www.nice.com.na.*

$$ ITALIAN 🍴 **Sardinia Blue Olive.** Windhoek's offering of classic Italian cuisine has a touch of Namibian-inspired mains like oryx and lamb shank. Despite being 250 miles from the ocean their seafood is impressive—try the calamari starter with crispy squid-heads in a light lemon garlic sauce—and the deep-pan pizzas are as cheesy as it gets. **Known for:** deep-pan pizzas; classic Italian- and Mediterranean-style food; decent wine list. [$] *Average main: US$12* ✉ *Schoemans Bldg., Sam Nujoma Dr., Windhoek* ☎ *61/258–183* 🕓 *Closed Mon.*

$ STEAKHOUSE 🍴 **The Stellenbosch Wine Bar and Bistro.** A favorite restaurant among locals, this bistro-style steak house champions perfectly prepared Namibian meat and first-rate South African wine. The fairly large menu can be overwhelming, but only because it's all so delicious. **Known for:** selection of grass-fed beef classic steaks; matchless wine selection at good range of prices; prompt and professional service. [$] *Average main: US$10* ✉ *320 Sam Nujoma Dr., Bougain Villas, Windhoek* ☎ *61/309–141* 🌐 *www.thestellenboschwinebar.com* 🕓 *Closed Sun.*

$ BAKERY 🍴 **Wecke & Voigts Coffee Shop.** Among the craziness of downtown Windhoek this little lunch café is located on the main Independence Avenue; it's the perfect quick bite to see you through a busy day of sightseeing or shopping. Whether you sit in their amiable kitchen-style café, which is just inside the famous Wecke and Voigt's department store, or if you just grab a ready prepared *brötchen* from the counter, this place will keep you coming back for more. **Known for:** Rohhack Brötchen; irresistible cakes and desserts; fast, efficient service. [$] *Average main: US$5* ✉ *Gustav Voigts Centre, Independence Ave., Windhoek* ☎ *61/377–000.*

9

WHERE TO STAY

$ HOTEL 🏨 **Avani Windhoek Hotel and Casino.** Known locally as the Sands (as it has just recently changed its name from the Kalahari Sands Hotel and Casino), this hotel has pleasant rooms that give the property just enough character to make it comfortable and elegant. **Pros:** centrally located; most of downtown Windhoek is within walking distance; impressive breakfast buffet. **Cons:** navigating the entrance and parking area (if self-driving) can be confusing; the area is popular with vagrants. [$] *Rooms from: US$199* ✉ *Gustav Voigts Centre, 129 Independence Ave., Windhoek* ☎ *61/280–0000 hotel, 10/003–8977 central reservations* 🌐 *www.minorhotels.com/en/avani/windhoek* 🛏 *172 rooms* 🍽 *Breakfast.*

$ HOTEL 🏨 **Burg's View Boutique Hotel.** This boutique hotel is built on top of one of the hills in Klein Windhoek and combines a polished elegance with a touch of Namibian flavor. **Pros:** wonderful views over Windhoek; staff who are willing to go the extra mile; excellent Wi-Fi and business facilities. **Cons:** terribly steep driveway that can be rather hair-raising (they are on a hill, after all); not walking distance to town but close to big shopping mall. Ⓢ *Rooms from: US$200* ✉ *Burg St. at Chateau St., Klein Windhoek* ☎ *61/229–904* ⊕ *www.burgsview. com* ↝ *10 rooms* ⏇ *Breakfast.*

$ 　📷 **GocheGanas.** Just on the outskirts of Windhoek, this well-appointed
HOTEL lodge has all the safari charm and sophistication of a luxury lodge. **Pros:** close to Windhoek but far enough away to feel like a real safari lodge; wellness village, spa, and hot pool; excellent service. **Cons:** limited wine selection; restaurant feels a little sparse and hollow. Ⓢ *Rooms from: US$220* ✉ *Windhoek* ⊹ *20 km (12 miles) along D1463 to South of Windhoek* ☎ *61/224–909* ⊕ *www.gocheganas.com* ↝ *16 suites* ⏇ *Some meals.*

$ 　📷 **Hotel Heinitzburg.** This is your chance to stay in a turn-of-the-20th-
HOTEL century castle, a white fort with battlements set high on a hill and commissioned by a German count for his fiancée in 1914. **Pros:** lavishly decadent interior styling; great personalized service; five-minute drive from city center. **Cons:** rooms don't have tons of natural light (it's a castle, after all); the decor and bathrooms are a little dated. Ⓢ *Rooms from: US$237* ✉ *22 Heinitzburg St., Windhoek* ☎ *61/249–597* ⊕ *www. heinitzburg.com* ↝ *16 rooms* ⏇ *Breakfast.*

$$ 　📷 **Olive Exclusive Boutique Hotel.** Windhoek's premier boutique hotel, the
HOTEL Olive Exclusive, with its six large suites each decorated thematically
Fodor's Choice according to each of Namibia's regions, is an upmarket treat either
★ before or after your safari. **Pros:** beautifully appointed and spacious suites; in-house spa therapist; excellent restaurant; wonderful staff and management. **Cons:** the view onto the hills of Windhoek and a flourishing olive grove is decent but could seem spoiled by shabby housing on one side; you need a car to get around. Ⓢ *Rooms from: US$298* ✉ *22 Promenaden St., Klein Windhoek* ☎ *61/383–890* ⊕ *www.theolive-namibia.com* ↝ *7 suites* ⏇ *Breakfast.*

BEACH ESCAPES

You don't come to Namibia for beaches, but if you do fancy a dip in the freezing Atlantic waters, Swakopmund, the country's only real beach resort, is your best bet.

SWAKOPMUND

Although the desert continues to sweep its remorseless way toward the mighty Atlantic and its infamous Skeleton Coast, humans have somehow managed to hang on to this patch of coastline, where Swakopmund clings to the edge of the continent. The first 40 German settlers, complete with household goods and breeding cattle, arrived here with 120 German colonial troops on the *Marie Woermann* in the late 19th century. Today, instead of the primitive shelters that the early settlers built on the beach to protect themselves from sand and sea, stands Swakopmund, or "Swakops," as the resort town is affectionately known. There's something surreal about Swakops. On the one hand, it's like a tiny European transplant, with its seaside promenade, sidewalk cafés, fine German colonial buildings, trendy bistros, friendly and neat-as-a-pin pensions, and immaculate boarding houses and hotels. On the other hand, this little town is squashed between the relentless Atlantic and the harsh desert, in one of the wildest and most untamed parts of the African continent—something you might understandably forget while nibbling a chocolate torte or sipping a good German beer under a striped umbrella.

Swakops makes for a different, unique beach escape because of its history and surreal surroundings. It's one of the top adventure centers in Africa, second only to Victoria Falls in Zimbabwe. Adrenaline junkies can try their hand (or feet) at skydiving, sandboarding, kayaking, dune-buggying, paragliding, or wave-skipping in a light aircraft. The less adventurous (but romantic) can take day, moonlight, sunrise, or sunset horseback or camel rides through the riverbeds and up into the moon-like landscape. The curious can partake in one of the fabulous "little five" living-desert tours through the dunes that represent the northern extent of the Namib-Naukluft *(see Essentials below)*. There are also lots of curio shops and commercial art galleries, making Swakops great for shopping, and the dining options are improving all the time.

WHEN TO GO

Keep in mind that the town is packed with vacationing Namibians and South Africans at Christmas, New Year's, and Easter, so avoid these times if you can. The sea keeps temperatures relatively comfortable year-round, and positively chilly outside of summer.

GETTING HERE AND AROUND

The closest airport, handling domestic and international flights, is about a 45-minute drive from Swakopmund at Walvis Bay. *For more information on flights and carriers, see Air Travel in the Planning section, above.*

Intercape Mainliner runs buses between Windhoek and Swakopmund. The Town Hoppers shuttle service also runs a daily shuttle between Windhoek and Swakopmund for N$270 one-way. For an additional fee, they'll provide door-to-door pickup and/or drop-off. There are no reliable bus services within Swakopmund for visitors.

If you have the time, it's worth renting a car to drive from Windhoek to Swakopmund. It's a very scenic and easy four-hour drive, about 368 km (228 miles) on the B1, a good paved road. Once in Swakopmund, it's easy to find your way around. With a car, you'll also be able to visit the Cape Cross seal colony and drive farther north toward the Skeleton Coast, or drive 30 km (19 miles) south to Walvis Bay, where numerous outdoor activities originate. *(For more information on Walvis Bay, see Walvis Bay section below.)* A two-wheel-drive vehicle is fine, but if you intend on visiting Sandwich Harbour or Sossusvlei in Namib-Naukluft Park, then four-wheel drive will give you more access and better viewing (and is essential for Sandwich Harbour).

If you arrange to rent a car in advance at any of the reliable agencies, you'll be met at Walvis Bay Airport. The car-rental agencies also have offices in Swakopmund.

For more information on train travel between Windhoek and Swakopmund, see Windhoek's Getting Here and Around section, above.

SAFETY AND PRECAUTIONS

Swakops is a very safe little town, but you should always be aware of potential pickpockets. Lock your valuables away in the hotel safe, and carry only what you need. Never travel with expensive jewelry. Don't walk alone at night, and stick to well-lit areas.

Cottage Private Hospital is a private clinic. Ask at your accommodation about the nearest pharmacy.

TIMING

Swakopmund is both a pleasant place in itself and offers a surprising array of activities and good shopping, as well as some culinary variety if you've been on safari for a while. Visitors generally stay two nights, but three to four nights is better if you really want to partake in a few of the outdoor activities for which this area is famous (several of which happen in Walvis Bay, a 40-minute drive south), as well as relax and stroll around the town itself.

VISITOR INFORMATION

Namib-I, the tourist information center, provides excellent national and local information, maps, and more.

CONTACTS

Airport Walvis Bay Airport. ☎ *64/271–102* ⊕ *www.airports.com.na.*

Bus Line Intercape Mainliner. ☎ *61/227–847* ⊕ *www.intercape.co.za.*

Car Rentals Avis. ✉ *Swakopmund Hotel and Entertainments Centre, 2 Theo-Ben Guribab Ave., Swakopmund* ☎ *64/402–527.* **Crossroads 4x4 Hire.** ✉ *3 Henties Bay Rd., Swakopmund* ☎ *64/403–777* ⊕ *www.crossroads4x4hire. com.* **Hertz.** ✉ *Walvis Bay Airport, Walvis Bay* ☎ *64/200–853* ⊕ *www.hertz. co.za.* **Town Hoppers Shuttle.** ✉ *Otavi St., , Ane Court Shop 2, Swakopmund* ☎ *64/407–223* ⊕ *www.namibiashuttle.com.*

Emergency Contacts Ambulance/Hospital. ☎ *64/405–731.* **Police.** ☎ *64/10111.*

Hospital Cottage Medi-Clinic. ✉ *Franziska van Neel St., Swakopmund* ☎ *64/412–200* ⊕ *www.mediclinic.co.za.*

Visitor Information Namib I Tourist Information. ✉ *28 Sam Nujoma Ave., at Hendrik Witbooi St., Swakopmund* ☎ *64/404–827.*

EXPLORING
TOP ATTRACTIONS

Kristall Galerie. This sizable gallery houses the largest known quartz-crystal cluster in the world—an awesome natural wonder more than 520 million years old and weighing 14,000 kilograms. Numerous smaller but no less beautiful chunks of Namibian minerals and gems, including a wide variety of quartz crystals, rainbow tourmalines, and other semi-precious stones, are also on display. Some great souvenirs can be had in the adjoining large gift shop and high-end jewelry boutique to allow you to take home a unique piece of Namibia. ✉ *Tobias Hainyeko at Theo-Ben Gurirab Ave., Swakopmund* ☎ *64/406–080* ⊕ *www.namib-iangemstones.com* 🎫 *N$20* ⊗ *Closed Sun.*

FAMILY **The Living Desert Snake Park.** With more than 25 species of Namibian snakes, lizards, chameleons, and scorpions, this small museum will excite herpetologists large and small. Several of Southern Africa's most dangerous snakes can be seen in the flesh here, including the black mamba and puff adder. Snake feedings take place on Saturdays at 10. ✉ *59 Sam Nujoma Ave., at Otavi Bahnhof, Swakopmund* ☎ *64/405– 100, 081/128–5100* 🎫 *N$30* ⊗ *Closed Sun.*

Swakopmund Dunes. Though you may have already visited higher or more visually stunning dunes, the Swakop dunes have the unique distinction of being the subject of a truly fascinating tour that introduces visitors to the numerous—and normally invisible—creatures thriving in this surreal ecosystem. Both Chris Nel, the operator of Living Desert Namibia tours and Tommy Collard, of Tommy's Tours, are passionate and well-informed characters who tend to leap out of 4x4s to catch the desert's perfectly camouflaged lizards, geckos, and snakes. A visit here is a unique, educational, and often humorous experience. ✉ *Swakopmund* ☎ *64/461–038* ⊕ *www.tommys.iway.na.*

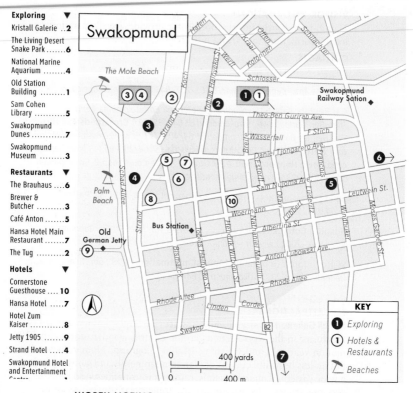

Swakopmund

KEY

❶ *Exploring*

① *Hotels &
Restaurants*

⛱ *Beaches*

WORTH NOTING

FAMILY **National Marine Aquarium.** The small, attractive aquarium showcases great displays of marine life in its tanks, including a huge main tank that can be viewed from different angles. A great feature is the walk-through tunnel. It's a worthwhile attraction if you are traveling with kids and is a great way to spend half an hour or so. ■**TIP**→ **The bigger fish, especially the sharks, are fed around 3 pm so try to time your visit for then.** ⊠ *South Strand St. (at the southern end), Swakopmund* ☎ *64/410–1214* 💰 *N$10* ⊘ *Closed Mon.*

Old Station Building. Probably Swakops's most notable landmark, the gorgeous, historic Old Station Building was built in 1901. Declared a national monument in 1972, this magnificent example of German colonial architecture came to life again in the early 1990s, when it was restored and renovated in a style evoking the charm and nostalgia of the old railway days. Don't miss the huge bustling lobby—a remnant of the building's former life as a railway station. Today, the building houses the Swakopmund Hotel and Entertainment Centre, which includes a movie theater, casino, spa, and two restaurants. ⊠ *2 Theo-Ben Gurirab Ave., Swakopmund* ⊕ *www.legacyhotels.co.za.*

Sam Cohen Library. As in Windhoek, there are lots of historic German buildings dating to the turn of the 20th century, most of them in perfect condition. The railway station, the prison, the Woermann House, the Kaserne (barracks), the Lutheran church, and the district court look more like illustrations from some Brothers Grimm fairy tale than the working buildings they once were. You can usually purchase a book with detailed information about these buildings from the Sam Cohen Library, which is worth a visit for its impressive collection of Africana books, archives of old newspapers (many in German), and vast photo collection (though note the N$50 users' fee to browse the archives). This library began its life with five books and now has more than 10,000 volumes. ⊠ *Sam Nujoma St., at Windhuker St., Swakopmund* ☎ *64/402–695* 🖃 *Free (N$50 browsing fee)* ⊗ *Closed weekends (except every 2nd Sat. of the month).*

Swakopmund Museum. The largest private museum in Namibia, this old and somewhat musty building down by the lighthouse and founded in 1951 houses a surprisingly large and varied collection of items. Displays on everything from natural history, archaeology, and ethnology to the German colonial period may be a bit dated in presentation, but are nonetheless informative and worth a look. ⊠ *Strand St., just below the lighthouse, Swakopmund* ☎ *64/402–046* 🖃 *N$25* ☞ *No credit card facilities.*

BEACHES

Though Namibia is hardly a beach destination, if you really want some sand and sun time, head to the Mole and adjacent Palm Beach, Swakops's most popular beaches (in front of the lighthouse). Keep in mind that this isn't Mauritius or the Caribbean: the sea can be treacherous, and the temperature usually runs in the lower 50s. Both of these beaches are a short walk from the center of town, and there are numerous cafés and restaurants along here to stop for a quick drink or bite to eat. The beach is sheltered by a breakwater, so its calm waters attract crowds, especially on the weekends; if you do swim out, beware of the strong currents just off the breakwater. There's a paved walkway that heads north along the beach if you need to stretch your legs. You can also head to the jetty at the southern end of the beach for a stroll. The southern side of the jetty is for walkers, while the northern side is reserved for fishing.

The Mole Beach. The designated swimming beach at Swakopmund, The Mole, is actually a failed engineering project. In 1899 the South Africans controlled the closest harbor at Walvis Bay, so attempts were made to build a harbor at Swakopmund. The engineer, FW Ortloff, failed to take into account the force of the Benguela current flowing down the length of Namibia and dumping desert sands on the shore. The result is the promontory you see today with The Mole now forming a secluded swimming beach. A short walk from the center of town, the beach is serviced by a number of restaurants and small cafés; the closest hotel is the Hotel Zum Kaiser. The Atlantic Ocean is generally cold and rough and unfortunately the town closed its heated Olympic-size swimming pool, so if you're set on swimming, you'll have to brave it. Lifeguards are on duty during the summer. **Amenities:** lifeguards (in summer), parking (free), toilets. **Best for:** sunsets, swimming. ⊠ *A. Schad Promenade, Swakopmund.*

Palm Beach. At a manageable 500 meters (1,640 feet), Palm Beach, which stretches along the western side of Swakopmund and effectively forms the western border, is the recommended beach for gentle walking. Swimming isn't encouraged due to rough waters and strong currents (and the icy Atlantic waters). Instead stroll from the north, starting at The Mole beach, and watch the sun go down in the west. Enjoy a sundowner on Swakopmund's famous jetty and if you're hungry try the festive scene at the famous Tug restaurant. The palms the beach is named after are set back against the access road offering limited shade. Busy in summer, but quiet in winter, Palm Beach is also often in fog due to the cold air of the Atlantic hitting the heat of the desert. Set just back off Beach Road, Hotel Zum Kaiser is the closest accommodation to the beach. **Amenities:** food and drink, parking, toilets. **Best for:** sunsets, walking. ⊠ *A. Schad Promenade, Swakopmund.*

WHERE TO EAT

$ ✕ **The Brauhaus.** A Swakopmund institution, the Brauhaus is a typical
GERMAN   German restaurant where the beer flows and the big wooden tables invite long sit-downs over hearty lunches and dinners. The German fare—schnitzel, bratwurst, and rosti (similar to a potato pancake)—is excellent, but if goulash and sauerkraut don't do it for you, there is a large selection of steaks and game meat, as well as seafood and even a few pasta and vegetarian options. **Known for:** hearty German fare; good selection of beers; great vibe especially Saturdays. $ *Average main: US$8* ⊠ *The Arcade 22, Sam Nujoma Ave., Swakopmund* ☎ *64/402–214* ⊕ *www.swakopmundbrauhaus.com* ⊘ *Closed Sun.*

$$ ✕ **Brewer & Butcher.** One of the in-house restaurants at the new Strand
STEAKHOUSE   Hotel, this genuine steak house has an inviting and lively atmosphere that will set you at ease at once. The steaks are A+ and the craft beers from the in-house microbrewery pair well with a succulent piece of Eland steak (game) or an Eisbein (a large roasted ham hock), but consider sharing the latter as the portion is big. **Known for:** juicy beef steaks; venison skewers served large and succulent; in-house craft beer and microbrewery on-site. $ *Average main: US$15* ⊠ *An der Mole, Swakopmund* ☎ *64/411–4410* ⊕ *www.strandhotelswakopmund.com.*

$ ✕ **Café Anton.** The palm-shaded terrace at this classic little café is a
CAFÉ   good place to take a break after perusing the curio market around the lighthouse. Watch the world go by while you savor scrumptious home-baked cakes and pastries, or enjoy a late afternoon tea with hazelnut triangles, custard-filled danishes, or croissants. **Known for:** chocolate Florentiner cookies; Black Forest cake; apple strudel. $ *Average main: US$4* ⊠ *Schweizerhaus Hotel, 1 Bismarck St., overlooking the Mole, Swakopmund* ☎ *64/400–331* ⊕ *www.schweizerhaus.net.*

$$ ✕ **Hansa Hotel Main Restaurant.** Full of old-world charm, the restaurant
EUROPEAN   in this perfectly restored 1905 German colonial building (the hotel itself has earned plenty of accolades) is the perfect place for that special-occasion dinner. The service is impeccable, the wine list excellent, and the menu is a broad selection of good, rich food such as venison steak and Namibian seafood delicacies. **Known for:** rich venison steaks; hearty oxtail stew; first-class service. $ *Average main: US$16* ⊠ *3 Hendrik Witbooi St., Swakopmund* ☎ *64/414–200* ⊕ *www.hansahotel.com.na.*

$$ **✕ Jetty 1905.** This restaurant, situated right at the end of Swakopmund's
SEAFOOD famous Jetty 1905, is a cocoon of warmth where guests can sip wine
and eat world-famous oysters while watching the Atlantic Ocean heave
around them. Seafood is the recommended food choice—try the grilled
sardines starter or the finger-licking-good grilled prawns—but there are
no-seafood items as well. **Known for:** great location; fresh and well-
prepared sushi; fresh Swakopmund oysters. $ *Average main: US$16*
✉ *The Jetty 1905, Molen Rd., on the Pier, Swakopmund* ☎ *64/405–664*
⊕ *www.jetty1905.com* ☽ *Closed Mon. No lunch Tues.–Thurs.*

$$ **✕ The Tug.** It's all about location at the Tug, which, as its name suggests,
SEAFOOD is actually an old tugboat that has been raised up and moored next to
the jetty. The restaurant is known for its fresh seafood—especially the
local oysters—which are some of the best in the world, but there are
creative seafood alternatives like venison or ostrich stir-fry. **Known
for:** famous Namibian oysters; incredible location. $ *Average main:
US$16* ✉ *The Strand, Swakopmund* ☎ *64/402–356* ⊕ *www.the-tug.
com* ☽ *No lunch Mon.–Fri.*

WHERE TO STAY

Several of the lodging establishments listed don't have air-conditioning,
but because of the cool climate this is actually standard practice in the
smaller guesthouses. They all have fans for use in summer, and it's rarely
so hot that the average person would consider air-conditioning necessary. For much of the year, having a heater indoors is more of an issue.

$ **▦ Cornerstone Guesthouse.** Walking into Cornerstone one is struck by the
B&B/INN lovely manicured garden and the pleasantly homey ambience. **Pros:** great
breakfast; personalized friendly service; lovely garden. **Cons:** one room
looks onto parking area instead of garden; often fully booked. $ *Rooms
from: US$136* ✉ *40 Hendrik Witbooi St., Swakopmund* ☎ *64/462–468*
⊕ *www.cornerstoneguesthouse.com* ⇱ *6 rooms* ❍ *Breakfast.*

$ **▦ Hansa Hotel.** This old-world grand dame gives guests a Belle Epoque–
HOTEL era feeling with its hushed solicitude, gleaming brass, thick carpets, and
Fodor's Choice manicured garden. **Pros:** lovely extras like a house library with a great
★ selection of books; gorgeous old bar with a fireplace; amazing restau-
rant. **Cons:** could be a bit stuffy for the younger crowd; there are no sea
views. $ *Rooms from: US$183* ✉ *3 Hendrik Witbooi St., Swakopmund*
☎ *64/414–200* ⊕ *www.hansahotel.com.na* ⇱ *58 rooms* ❍ *Breakfast.*

$ **▦ Hotel Zum Kaiser.** This three-story boutique hotel by the beach—with
HOTEL its tones of silver, champagne, and taupe, and modern art and orchid
displays—is all contemporary elegance and comfort. **Pros:** many of
the rooms have a partial sea view; amazing roof bar with great sunset
views; little bistro next door for easy dinners. **Cons:** Wi-Fi is spotty;
some rooms feel a little cramped. $ *Rooms from: US$95* ✉ *4 Sam
Nujoma Ave., Swakopmund* ☎ *64/417–100* ⊕ *www.hotelzumkaiser.
com* ⇱ *21 rooms* ❍ *Breakfast.*

$ **▦ Strand Hotel.** This large beachfront property, Swakopmund's newest
HOTEL hotel, is built right on Mole Beach overlooking the Atlantic Ocean.
Pros: all the amenities you could want or need; elegant rooms with gorgeous bathrooms; excellent in-house restaurants; a personal approach in
spite of its size. **Cons:** restaurants are often fully booked; the standard
rooms don't have step-out balconies. $ *Rooms from: US$151* ✉ *An*

9

der Mole, A. Schad Promenade, Swakopmund ☎ *61/207–5360 reservations, 64/411–4308* 🌐 *www.strandhotelswakopmund.com* 🛏 *125 rooms* 🍴 *Breakfast.*

$$ HOTEL FAMILY 🏨 **Swakopmund Hotel and Entertainment Centre.** At this hotel within the 1901 Old Station Building, the huge bustling lobby is a reminder of the building's previous incarnation as a railway station. **Pros:** conveniences of a large hotel with numerous facilities; lovely lobby architecture and pleasant (though unheated) pool. **Cons:** lack of real character or intimacy; often used as a business or conference center; no-smoking rooms exist, but those sensitive to smoke may smell occasional smoke. [$] *Rooms from: US$329* ✉ *2 Theo-Ben Gurirab Ave., Swakopmund* ☎ *64/410–5200* 🌐 *www.legacyhotels.co.za* 🛏 *90 rooms* 🍴 *Breakfast.*

SPORTS AND THE OUTDOORS

Africa's second adventure-activity capital after Livingstone, Swakopmund is the departure point for all manner of tours that make use of its surreal location between the dunes and the sea. Daytime, moonlight, sunrise, and sunset horseback rides are possible with Okakambe Trails. Desert Explorers, Outback Orange, and the Swakopmund Skydiving Club can organize skydiving over the dunes, sandboarding, and quad-bike (ATV) trips. The Living Desert Tour is highly recommended, as is a 4x4 day trip to Sandwich Harbour, with its rich bird life and spectacular views. Numerous sea-based tours are also available but most depart from Walvis Bay. Finally, Namib Tracks & Trails can organize all manner of trips, including day trips a bit farther afield to sights like the amazing rock formations and bush paintings at Spitzkoppe or the seal colony at Cape Cross.

TOUR OPERATORS

Desert Explorers. ✉ *Nathaniel Maxuilili St., Swakopmund* ☎ *64/406–096 mobile, 81/124–1386 mobile* 🌐 *www.namibiadesertexplorers.com.*

Living Desert Tour. ✉ *Swakopmund* ☎ *64/405–070, 81/127–5070* 🌐 *www.livingdesertnamibia.com.*

Namib Tracks & Trails. ✉ *14A Sam Nujoma Ave., Swakopmund* ☎ *64/416–820* 🌐 *www.namibia-tracks-and-trails.com.*

Okakambe Trails. ✉ *Erf 378 Swakopmund river plots, Swakopmund* ✣ *11 km (7 miles) east of Swakopmund on the B2 to Windhoek, next to the camel farm* ☎ *64/402–799* 🌐 *www.okakambe.iway.na.*

Outback Orange. ✉ *44 Nathaniel Maxuilili St., Swakopmund* ☎ *64/406–096, 81/129–2380 mobile* 🌐 *www.outback-orange.com.*

Swakopmund Skydiving Club. ✉ *Hanger 13B, Swakopmund* ✣ *5 km (3 miles) east of Swakopmund on B2, near airport turn-off* ☎ *64/405–671* 🌐 *www.skydiveswakopmund.com.*

Tommy's Tours and Safaris. ✉ *Swakopmund* ☎ *81/128–1038* 🌐 *www.tommys.iway.na.*

SHOPPING

African Art Jewellers. A cut above the rest, the original and African-inspired designs and materials used by this fine jeweler are worth checking out. ✉ *1 Hendrik Witbooi St., Swakopmund* ☎ *64/405–566* 🕐 *Closed Sun.*

Art Africa. A lovely emporium of high-quality crafts and curios from all over Namibia, as well as other parts of Africa. Items include rural art, contemporary jewelry, ceramics, leather products, masks, baskets, and funky whimsical crafts. ⊠ *Shop 6, The Arcade, Sam Nujome St., Swakopmund* 🕾 *64/463–454.*

Die Muschel. This beautiful book and coffee shop in the center of Swakopmund, specializes in gorgeous coffee-table books of African landscapes, people, and animals, as well as a great selection of field guides, maps, and other books about Namibia and Southern Africa. It's a perfect spot to buy postcards and find a new book to read for the rest of your trip. ⊠ *Brauhaus Arcade at Tobias Hainyeko St., Swakopmund* 🕾 *64/402–874* ⊕ *www.muschel.iway.na.*

Peter's Antiques. This store has been described as an antique store, a curio shop, and a museum. Whether you're looking for something to buy or not, it's worth a visit to meet and chat with the proprietor, who is very amiable and full of information about Namibia. ⊠ *24 Tobias Hainyeko St., Swakopmund* 🕾 *64/405–624* ⊕ *www.peters-antiques. com* ⊗ *Closed daily 1–3 pm.*

WALVIS BAY

One of southern Africa's most important harbor towns, the once-industrial Walvis Bay has recently developed into a seaside holiday destination with a number of pleasant lagoon-front guesthouses and several good restaurants—including one of Namibia's best, Lyon des Sables. The majority of water activities advertised in Swakopmund actually depart from Walvis's small waterfront area, and there's an amazing flamingo colony residing in the Bay's 3,000-year-old lagoon.

WHEN TO GO

Like Swakopmund, Walvis Bay enjoys a mild climate. Although most of the local Christmas and Easter holidaymakers head to Swakops, the overflow can spill out here, so it can get crowded during these times.

GETTING HERE AND AROUND

About 15 km (9 miles) east of town, the Walvis Airport serves the region (including Swakopmund) and has direct flights to South Africa. The major car-rental companies are located at the airport. Thirty kilometers (18 miles) from Swakopmund, the drive takes about 40 minutes on the B2. The town itself lacks attractions, and most visitors will head straight to the Walvis Bay lagoon. Here you'll find the majority of accommodations; the waterfront, from where almost all activities (both sea- and land-based) depart; and a handful of restaurants. Most everything in the lagoon area is within walking distance.

SAFETY AND PRECAUTIONS

Be sure to turn your lights on when driving between Walvis and Swakops, even in the daytime. Locals say that the way light reflects between the dunes and the sea impairs depth perception.

TIMING

Most of Walvis's activities, including bird-watching, boat tours, and 4x4 day trips to Sandwich Harbour, depart relatively early. As such, spending the night before such an activity is certainly worthwhile. Given the new accommodations and restaurants in town, if time allows and you plan on participating in more than one activity, two nights wouldn't be wasted.

WHERE TO EAT

$ SEAFOOD 🍴 **Anchors @ The Jetty.** This is the quintessential seaside restaurant to satisfy your appetite for seafood and a view. Sitting right on the water's edge, Anchors is the perfect spot to sip a glass of wine and taste the freshest west coast oysters or basic fish-and-chips while mesmerized by the sparkling ocean. **Known for:** the best west coast oysters; grilled calamari; postcard-type sunsets over the Atlantic Ocean. [$] *Average main: US$9* ✉ *Waterfront, Walvis Bay* ☎ *64/205–762* 🕒 *Closed Mon.*

$$ MEDITERRANEAN 🍴 **Flamingo Villa Restaurant.** The in-house restaurant at the Flamingo Villa Boutique Hotel, with a stunning view of the Lagoon, is probably the best fine-dining establishment in Walvis Bay. With exceptional attention to detail and service, the menu combines flavors of Europe and the Mediterranean with Namibian ingredients. **Known for:** seafood paella; cocktails at sunset; venison steaks. [$] *Average main: US$12* ✉ *30 Kavambo Nujoma Dr., Meersig, Walvis Bay* ☎ *64/205–631* 🌐 *www.flamingovillana.com.*

$$ SEAFOOD 🍴 **The Raft.** The Raft enjoys a spectacular view from its perch out over beautiful Walvis Bay Lagoon. Divided into two parts—bar to the right, restaurant to the left—this warm and friendly establishment seems to be a favorite with locals. **Known for:** melt-in-your mouth fresh linefish; fresh west coast oysters; great location. [$] *Average main: US$12* ✉ *Esplanade, on the lagoon, Walvis Bay* ☎ *64/204–877* 🌐 *www.theraftrestaurant.com.*

WHERE TO STAY

$ B&B/INN 🏨 **Egumbo Lodge.** This gorgeous guesthouse is located in a large thatch-roof, nine-room home. **Pros:** gorgeous decor; great location on the lagoon; amazing wine and whiskey collection. **Cons:** only a few rooms have lagoon views. [$] *Rooms from: US$197* ✉ *42 Kovambo Nujoma Dr., on the lagoon, Walvis Bay* ☎ *64/207–700* 🌐 *www.egumbolodge.com* 🛏 *9 rooms* 🍽 *Breakfast.*

$ HOTEL 🏨 **Flamingo Bay Boutique Hotel.** This hotel has one of the most spectacular views of the Walvis Bay Lagoon with its peaceful flamingos and idyllic sunsets. **Pros:** views over the lagoon; personal and attentive service; first-class restaurant. **Cons:** some of the soft furnishings are a little garish in places. [$] *Rooms from: US$135* ✉ *30 Kovambo Nujoma Dr., Walvis Bay* ☎ *64/205–631* 🌐 *www.flamingovillana.com* 🛏 *17 rooms* 🍽 *Breakfast.*

$$ HOTEL 🏨 **Pelican Point Lodge.** Built from the old Lighthouse and Port Authority building, this completely unique lodge is as beautiful as it is stark. **Pros:** unique and emotive lodge; incredible 360-degree view of the ocean; personal service. **Cons:** no electricity after 10 pm; long and very bumpy ride to get out there (it is remote, after all). [$] *Rooms from: US$360* ✉ *Pelican Point, Walvis Bay* ☎ *64/221–282, 81/800–9301 mobile* 🌐 *www.pelicanpointlodge.com* 🛏 *10 suites* 🍽 *Some meals.*

SPORTS AND THE OUTDOORS

The most popular activities here are the seal and dolphin tours, fishing, kayaking, and day trips to Sandwich Harbour.

Catamaran Charters. Catamaran Charters also runs a seal and dolphin cruise on a 45- or 60-foot catamaran. The four-hour cruise, which sets sail at 8:30 am, visits Pelican Point and the lighthouse, with almost guaranteed dolphin and seal sightings along the way. ⊠ *Atlantic St., Unit A, Walvis Bay* ☎ *64/200–798* ⊕ *www.namibiancharters. com* ☜ *N$720.*

Eco-Marine Kayak Tours. If you want to peacefully paddle the calm waters of Walvis Bay and enjoy the scenery and up-close encounters with marine and bird life, try Eco-Marine Kayak Tours. Their five-hour trips start at 7:45 and can be combined with a Sandwich Harbour tour. ⊠ *Walvis Bay Waterfront, Walvis Bay* ☎ *64/203–144, 81/293–144 mobile* ⊕ *www.emkayak.iway.na.*

Sandwich Harbour 4x4. Sandwich Harbour 4x4 runs an excellent day trip to the dunes that includes a hearty lunch (with oysters and sparkling wine). Expect to drive over the dunes as if it was a series of roller coasters. They also run bird-watching trips and combination trips (a boat trip and the dunes, or kayaking and the dunes). ⊠ *Waterfront, Atlantic St., Unit B, Walvis Bay* ☎ *81/147–3933* ⊕ *www.sandwich-harbour.com.*

Sun Sail Catamarans. Sun Sail Catamarans has daily departures at 8:15 to Pelican Point. During the four- to five-hour cruise you'll likely see seals, dolphins, numerous sea birds, and whales (in season). Fresh oysters, sparkling wine, and snacks are served on board. ⊠ *Walvis Bay Waterfront, Walvis Bay* ☎ *81/788–6800* ⊕ *www.sunsailnamibia.com.*

9

VICTORIA FALLS

WELCOME TO VICTORIA FALLS

TOP REASONS TO GO

★ **World-Class Phenomenon.** Not only can you experience Victoria Falls and the Batoka Gorge from every angle—the sheer size of this wonder fosters the delightful illusion of exclusivity.

★ **The Adrenaline Rush.** Looking for an adventure to get your heart pounding? From bungee jumping to white-water rafting and skydiving, Victoria Falls truly has it all.

★ **Perfectly Indulgent Relaxation.** Massages are offered on the banks of the Zambezi River, sumptuous food is served wherever you turn, and there are few sights on earth that rival watching the spray of the Falls fade from rainbow to starlight while enjoying cocktails at the end of the day.

★ **Intact Africa.** The warm, rich heart of Africa is proudly showcased in a region governed by people who have lived here for centuries, adeptly utilizing the very latest in ecotourism and benefiting from environmentally conscious development.

Victoria Falls is in Southern Africa and physically provides a natural border between Zambia and Zimbabwe. Each country has a national park that surrounds the Falls (Mosi-oa-Tunya National Park in Zambia and Victoria Falls National Park in Zimbabwe), as well as a town (Livingstone in Zambia and Victoria Falls in Zimbabwe) that serves as the respective tourist center for each country. The fissure currently framing the Falls stretches over a mile, roughly from northwest to southeast. Livingstone lies to the north and the town of Victoria Falls immediately to the south of the Falls. The official border between the countries is within walking distance of the compact town of Victoria Falls but around 10 km (6 miles) from Livingstone. The stretch between the Falls border and town center on the Livingstone side should not be attempted on foot because of the dangers of wandering elephants, the African sun, and the occasional opportunistic thief.

1 **Livingstone, Zambia.** Named after the famous Dr. David Livingstone, the town, just 10 km (6 miles) north of the Falls, was established in 1900 and was once Zambia's capital city. Its main street, Mosi-oa-Tunya Road, still boasts examples of classic colonial, and the occasional ramshackle building. In past years, the much-publicized political unrest in Zimbabwe has often caused tourists to choose Livingstone rather than the quieter town of Victoria Falls on the Zimbabwean side as a base for exploration of the area.

2 **Victoria Falls, Zimbabwe.** The town of Victoria Falls hugs the Zimbabwean side of the Falls on the Zambezi's southwestern bank. The view of the Falls and the gorge is spectacular from Zimbabwe. At one time, the town was the principal tourist destination for the area. It continues to be perfectly safe, more relaxed than Livingstone, and cheaper, and the general atmosphere has greatly improved as tentative stability has gradually returned to the area in recent years.

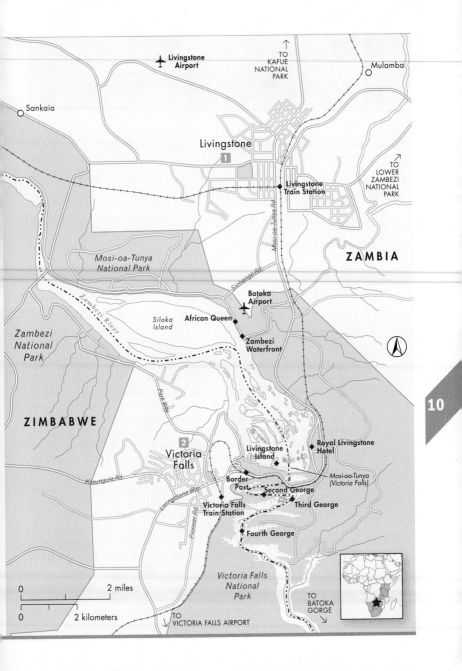

Livingstone Airport

TO KAFUE NATIONAL PARK

Mulamba

Sankaia

Livingstone

1

Livingstone Train Station

TO LOWER ZAMBEZI NATIONAL PARK

Mosi-oa-Tunya National Park

ZAMBIA

Mosi-oa-Tunya Rd

Sichanga Rd

Zambezi River

Batoka Airport

Siloka Island

African Queen

Zambezi Waterfront

Zambezi National Park

ZIMBABWE

Park Way

Victoria Falls

2

Livingstone Island

Royal Livingstone Hotel

Kazungula Rd

Border Post

Second George

Mosi-oa-Tunya (Victoria Falls)

Third George

Livingstone Way

Victoria Falls Train Station

Fourth George

Pioneer Rd

10

Victoria Falls National Park

TO BATOKA GORGE

0		2 miles
0		2 kilometers

TO VICTORIA FALLS AIRPORT

Updated by
Christopher
Clark

Roughly 1,207 km (750 miles) from its humble origins as an insignificant spring in northern Zambia, the Zambezi River has grown more than a mile wide. Without much warning the river bends south, the current speeds up, and the entire mass of water disappears into a single fissure. More than 1 million gallons of water rush over a vertical, 328-foot-high drop in the time it takes an average reader to reach the end of this paragraph. The resulting spray is astounding, the brute force forming a cloud of mist visible 64 km (40 miles) away on a clear day.

The settlements of Livingstone in Zambia and Victoria Falls in Zimbabwe both owe their existence to the Zambezi and the Falls. Though they're located in different countries and intriguingly diverse in character, they function almost like two sides of one town. Crossing the border is a formality that generally happens with minimum fuss. Zambia spoils guests with an overabundance of top-class safari lodges along the Zambezi, and this strong competition has resulted in an emphasis on personalized service, which enables you to tailor your visit. Livingstone is determined to remain the favored destination.

The political strife that's dogged Zimbabwe in years gone by has dissipated to some degree, at least in this part of the country. Severe shortages of basic necessities are now rare. The town of Victoria Falls has generally escaped the worst of the sporadic bouts of political turmoil, but not the reputation. However, the relative absence of large numbers of travelers is a luxury in itself, and this area currently provides good value for money, and is perfectly safe for tourists.

The region as a whole deserves its reputation as an adventure center and offers adrenaline-inducing activities by the bucketful. The backdrop for any of these is stunning, and the safety record nothing less than spectacular.

WHEN TO GO

If you're at all sensitive to heat and humidity, visit May through August, when it's dry and cool, with pleasant days and cool to cold nights. The winter bush is dry, with most of the grass having died down, and the leaves fallen from the trees. The advantage is improved game-viewing, and most other adventure activities are more comfortable in the cooler weather. This is also the time when the mosquitoes are less active, although it remains a malaria area year-round, and precautions should always be taken.

The rainy season starts sometime around late October or early November and generally stretches well into April. As the heavens open up, the bug population explodes with mosquitoes, and the harmless but aptly named stink bug seemingly runs the show for brief periods of the day. Of course, the abundance of insect life also leads to great bird-watching. Although the rain showers tend to be of the short and spectacular kind, they can interfere with some activities, especially if your visit to the area is brief. Try to arrange excursions for the early hours of the day, as the rain generally falls in the late afternoon.

Peak flow for Victoria Falls occurs in late April and May, when rafting and visiting Livingstone Island might not be possible. If your visit coincides with school vacations in South Africa, the area can become quite crowded.

10

LIVINGSTONE, ZAMBIA

This marvelous old town, once the government capital of Northern Rhodesia (now Zambia), boasts a wealth of natural beauty and a surplus of activities. After a few decades of neglect it's recently recast itself as Zambia's tourism and adventure capital.

There's a tangible whiff of the past here: historic buildings outnumber new ones, and many local inhabitants live a life not that dissimilar to the one they would have experienced 50 years ago. Livingstone handles the surge of tourists with equal parts grace, confidence, banter, and annoyance.

Many visitors to this side of the Falls opt to stay in one of the secluded safari-style lodges on the Zambezi River. The Zambian experience sprawls out along the many bends of the large river and time ticks in a very deliberate African manner.

PLANNING

GETTING HERE AND AROUND

South African Airways and Comair/British Airways regularly fly from Johannesburg into Livingstone International Airport, 5 km (3 miles) out of town. The flight is a comfortable hop, less than two hours in duration, and the airport is small and friendly, with helpful staff to speed you on your way. ■TIP→ **If at all possible, don't check your luggage in Johannesburg and always lock suitcases securely, as luggage theft in South Africa is an everyday occurrence.**

There's a perfectly reasonable traffic code in Zambia. Unfortunately, not many people have ever heard of it. You would do well to leave the driving to your local guides or negotiate an all-inclusive rate with a taxi driver recommended by your hotel or lodge for the duration of your stay. Note that taxis are generally not allowed to cross the border, so if you want to visit Zimbabwe, you'll have to book a tour that includes transfers. Once at the border, it's feasible to walk into and around Victoria Falls town or rent a bicycle.

FAST FACTS ABOUT ZAMBIA

Size 752,618 square km (290,587 square miles)

Number of National Parks 20. Kafue National Park, South Luangwa National Park, Lower Zambezi National Park, Mosi-oa-Tunya National Park (Victoria Falls National Park). There is also a growing number of private game reserves.

Population 16.6 million

Big Five The gang's all here.

Language Zambia has between 70 and 80 recorded languages, of which 42 are main dialects. Luckily English is the official language, and it's widely spoken, read, and understood.

Time Zambia is on CAST (Central African Standard Time), which is two hours ahead of Greenwich mean time and seven hours ahead of North American Eastern Standard Time. It's the same as South Africa.

Capital Lusaka.

Drives on the Left

If you insist on renting a car, you should know that some of the roads have more potholes than tar. You don't necessarily need a 4x4, but it's not a bad idea, especially if you want to go off-road at all. Voyagers has two offices in Livingstone: Mosi-oa-Tunya Road (opposite Ngolide Lodge) and Livingstone Airport. Hemingway's rents out Toyota Hilux Double Cabs (similar to the Toyota Tacoma), fully equipped with tents and other camping equipment—you can even hire a driver! Costs start from about US$220 per day for a fully equipped vehicle.

■ TIP→ If you plan to add the popular Kafue and Lower Zambezi camps to your trip, you should book your transfers together with your accommodations through a travel agent or with your camp reservations, as air-transfer companies change hands and/or minds quite often in Zambia. A travel agent or camp will also assure that connection times work to your best advantage if they're responsible for the transfers.

ESSENTIALS

The Zambian government is curbing the use of U.S. dollars, and increasingly, places accept only Zambian *kwacha (ZMW)*. The kwacha comes in denominations of ZMW2, ZMW5, ZMW10, ZMW20, ZMW50, and ZMW100 bills. Coins start at 5 *ngwee* (the local equivalent of cents) and work up to ZMW1. At the time of this writing, the conversion rate was about ZMW9 to US$1.

Tipping is less common in Zambia because service charges are included, but it's appreciated. Small notes or 10% is appropriate. Gas-station attendants can be tipped, but tip a taxi driver only on the last day if you've used the same driver for a number of days.

Zambia has a 17.5% V.A.T. and a 10% service charge, which is included in the cost or itemized on your bill. International banks along Mosi-oa-Tunya Road in Livingstone have ATMs and exchange services. Banking hours are generally weekdays 8–2 (although some do open the last Saturday of the month). Many bank ATMs accept

10

only Visa. It's also worth noting that queues for ATMs can get very long during working hours.

■TIP→ **You may be invited to do a little informal foreign exchange by persuasive street financiers. Resist the temptation—it's not worth the risk of being ripped off or arrested.** There are many reputable exchange bureaus throughout town, though they're sometimes flooded with dollars and low on kwacha, generally toward the end of the month. MasterCard and Visa are preferred by business owners and banks to American Express or Diners Club. Business owners always prefer cash to credit cards, and some smaller hotels levy fees up to 10% to use a credit card.

You'll need a valid passport and visa to enter Zambia. Nationals of any country not on the Zambian Immigration Referred Visa list can simply purchase a visa on entering the country. At this writing a standard U.S. single-entry visa costs US$50, and a single-entry and transit visa cost the same. Day-trip visas cost US$20 (often included in the cost of prebooked activities, so check with your booking agent). If you plan to return to Zambia in the near future, you'll need a multiple-entry visa, or you'll have to buy another visa on your return. Multiple-entry visas and visas for nationals from countries on the referred visa list (⊕ *www. zambiaimmigration.gov.zm*) can be purchased only at Zambian Missions abroad and not on arrival.

For minor injuries, a test for malaria, or the treatment of non-life-threatening ailments, you can go to the Rainbow Trust Mwenda Medical Centre, Southern Medical Centre, or Dr. Shafik Hospital. For serious emergencies, contact SES (Specialty Emergency Services). There are a number of pharmacies in town including Health and Glow Pharmacy, Link Pharmacy, and HK Pharmacy. Pharmacies are generally open weekdays 8–8, Saturday 8–6, and Sunday 8–1.

Wild animals abound throughout this area (even in the center of town from time to time) and must be given a lot of physical space and respect. You must also remember that Zambia is relatively poor. There are tourism police, but opportunistic thieving still happens occasionally. Although crime in this area is generally nonviolent, losing your money, belongings, or passport will result in spending the remainder of your trip with various officials in stuffy, badly decorated offices instead of sitting back on the deck of your sunset cruise with drink in hand.

As for the water, it's always advisable to drink bottled water, although the tap water in Zambia is generally considered safe. Should you develop any stomach upset, be sure to contact a physician, especially if you're running a fever, in order to rule out malaria or a communicable disease. Do remember to mention your visit to a malaria area to your doctor in the event of illness within a year of leaving Africa.

Telephone rates in Zambia are much cheaper and more stable than those in Zimbabwe. Check numbers very carefully, as some are Zimbabwean mobile phones. Zambian towns and cities generally have good cell coverage, but some of the remote lodges may not. If you have any trouble dialing a number, check with a hotel or restaurant owner, who should be able to advise you of the best and cheapest alternative.

International roaming on your standard mobile phone is also an option, as coverage is quite extensive. Alternatively, you could purchase a local SIM card with pay-as-you-go fill-ups—this is probably your cheapest option. Pay phones aren't an option, and the costs of all telephone calls out of the country can be exorbitant.

The country code for Zambia is 260. When dialing from abroad, drop the initial 0 from local area codes and cell-phone numbers. Note that all telephone numbers are listed as they're dialed from the country that they're in. Although the number for operator assistance is 100, you'll be much better off asking your local lodge or restaurant manager for help.

ABOUT THE RESTAURANTS

Game meat is something of a delicacy in Zambia, but superior free-range beef and chicken are available everywhere. The local bream, filleted or whole, is excellent, and the staple starch, a thick porridge similar to polenta—*nshima*—is worth a try; use your fingers to eat it (you'll be given a bowl for washing afterward). Adventurous? Try *macimbi* or *vinkuvala* (sun-dried mopane worms) or *inswa* (flash-fried flying ants) during the flood season.

Meals are taken at regular hours, but during the week, restaurants close around 10. Dress is generally casual, but this part of Africa easily lends itself to a little bling, so you'll never be out of place in something more glamorous.

ABOUT THE LODGES

It's advisable to make both flight and lodge reservations ahead of time. Lodges tend to have all-inclusive packages; hotels generally include breakfast only. All hotels and lodges quote in U.S. dollars but accept payment in other major currencies at unfriendly exchange rates. It might be best to take an all-inclusive package tour because meals can be exorbitantly expensive. A 10% service charge is either included or added to the bill (as is the value-added tax) in both countries, which frees you to include an extra tip only for exceptional service. Although air-conditioning can be expected in the hotels, lodges tend to have fans.

■ TIP➜ Travel with a sarong (locally available as a chitenge), which you can wet and wrap around your body, guaranteeing a cooler siesta.

Restaurant and hotel reviews have been shortened. For full information, visit Fodors.com.

WHAT IT COSTS IN U.S. DOLLARS			
$	**$$**	**$$$**	**$$$$**
Restaurants	under $12	$12–$20	$21–$30	over $30
Hotels	under $250	$250–$450	$451–$600	over $600

Prices in the restaurant reviews are the average cost of a main course at dinner or, if dinner isn't served, at lunch; taxes and service charges are generally included. Prices in the lodging reviews are the lowest cost of a standard double room in high season.

VISITOR INFORMATION

Although the Zambia National Tourist Board (next to the museum; open weekdays 8–1 and 2–5, Saturday 8–noon) is very helpful and friendly, you might be better off visiting Jollyboys (behind the Livingstone Museum; open daily 7 am–10 pm) for comprehensive and unbiased advice.

Airlines Comair/British Airways. ☎ 213/32–2827 ✉ contactba.kenya@ba.com ⊕ www.britishairways.com. **South African Airways.** ☎ 213/323–031 ⊕ www.flysaa.com.

Car Rental Companies Hemingway's. ☎ 0213/32–3097, 0977/86–6492 ⊕ www.hemingwayszambia.com. **Voyagers.** ☎ 0213/32–2753, 0213/32–3259 ⊕ www.voyagerszambia.com.

Embassies U.S. Embassy. ✉ Ibex Hill. (eastern end of Kabulonga Rd.), Lusaka ☎ 0211/35–7000 ⊕ zm.usembassy.gov.

Emergency Services Fire. ☎ 993. **General emergencies.** ☎ 999, 112 from mobile phones. **Police.** ☎ 991. **SES Emergency Medical Assistance.** ☎ 737 in Zambia ⊕ www.ses-zambia.com.

Hospitals Rainbow Trust Mwenda Medical Centre. ✉ Lusaka Rd., about 1 mile from center of Livingstone, Livingstone ☎ 213/32–3519. **Dr. Shafik Hospital.** ✉ Katete Rd., Livingstone ☎ 213/32–1130. **Southern Medical Centre.** ✉ House 9, 1967 Mokambo Rd., Livingstone ☎ 213/32–3547.

Visitor Information Jollyboys. ✉ 34 Kanyanta Rd., Livingstone ☎ 0213/32–4229 ⊕ www.backpackzambia.com. **Zambia National Tourist Board.** ✉ Tourist Centre, Mosi-Oa-Tunya Rd., Livingstone ☎ 0213/321–487 ⊕ www.zambiatourism.com.

CHOBE: A GREAT DAY TRIP

If it's serious game-viewing you desire, join a one-day excursion to Chobe National Park in Botswana. A trip will cost you about US$200 and usually includes transfers from Livingstone, a morning boat cruise, lunch with a drink, and an afternoon game drive. Reservations must be in writing and prepaid for both. To make reservations, see Bushtracks, in Sports and the Outdoors, for more information.

EXPLORING

FAMILY **Batoka Gorge.** Just below the Falls, the gorge forms an abyss between the countries with edges that drop away from the cliffs of both Zambia and Zimbabwe. Each successive sandstone gorge is numbered in sequence starting from the youngest (First Gorge to the Fifth Gorge), followed by Songwe Gorge and finally the official Batoka Gorge; it is common for all these gorges to be referred to collectively as The Gorge or Batoka Gorge. Batoka Gorge is more than 120 km (75 miles) long with vertical walls that are an average of 400 feet high (the Zambezi river water levels fluctuates up to 65 feet between the wet and dry season). On the Zambian side, the gorge is surrounded by the Mosi-oa-Tunya National Park, which contains a tropical rain forest that thrives on the eternal rainfall from the Falls. Victoria Falls National Park in Zimbabwe surrounds the other side of the gorge. Operators from both countries offer excursions to what is reputed to be the world's best one-day white-water

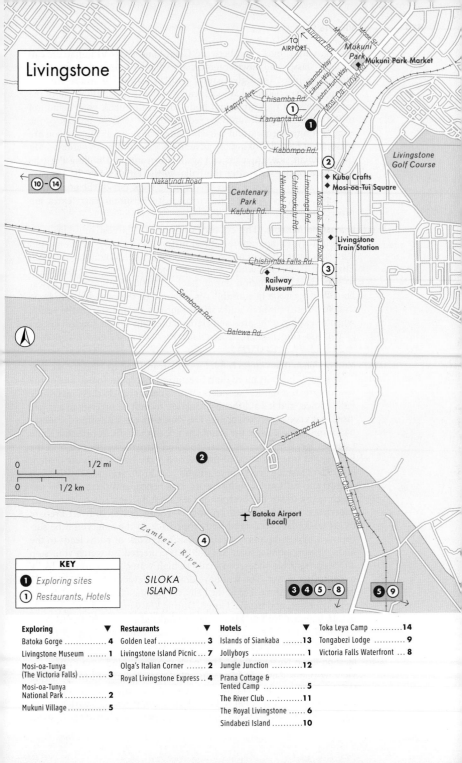

Livingstone

KEY

- ① *Exploring sites*
- ① *Restaurants, Hotels*

rafting, with rapids rated between Class I and Class VI (amateurs can do only Class V and down commercially) that have been given evocative nicknames like "The Ugly Sisters" and "Oblivion." If you're "lucky" enough to experience what locals call a "long swim" (falling out of the raft at the start of a rapid and body surfing through), your definition of the word *scary* will surely be redefined. The walk in and out of the gorge is quite strenuous on the Zimbabwe side, but as long as you are reasonably fit and looking for adventure, you need no experience. On the Zambian side, travelers can walk down into the Boiling Pot (the first bend of the river after the Falls) in the First Gorge. It's an easy walk down and slightly more challenging walk out of the gorge (lots of steps), but even young children enjoy it—be sure to carry extra sun protection and water. ⊠ *Livingstone.*

FAMILY   **Livingstone Museum.** The country's oldest and largest museum contains history, ethnography, natural history, archaeology sections, and materials ranging from newspaper clippings to photographs of Queen Elizabeth II dancing with Kenneth Kaunda (Zambia's first president) to historical information dating back to 1500. Among the priceless David Livingstone memorabilia is a model of the mangled arm bone used to identify his body and various journals and maps from the period when he explored the area and claimed the Falls for the English queen. ⊠ *Mosi-oa-Tunya Rd., between civic center and post office, Livingstone* ☎ *213/32–4429* ⊠ *USD$5.*

FAMILY   **Mosi-oa-Tunya (The Victoria Falls).** Literally translated as "the Smoke that Thunders," the Falls more than lives up to its reputation as one of the world's greatest natural wonders. Words can never do these incredible Falls justice, and it's a difficult attraction to fully appreciate in a single visit, as it's constantly changing. The Zimbabwean side offers famously panoramic views, while the Zambian side of the Falls features the Knife Edge bridge, which allows guests to stand virtually suspended over the Boiling Pot (the first bend of the river after the Falls), with the deafening water crashing everywhere around you. From around May through August the Falls are a multisensory experience, and there may be too much spray to see the bottom of the gorge. In high season the entire experience can be summed up in two words: power shower! Prepare to get soaked. If you stand with your back to the sun, you'll be surrounded by a symphony of rainbows. A network of paths leads to the main viewing points; some are not well protected, so watch your step and wear sensible shoes, especially at high water, when you are likely to get dripping wet. You will have dramatic views of the full 1½ km (1 mile) of the ironstone face of the Falls, the Boiling Pot directly below, the railway bridge, and Batoka Gorge. During low water levels, it's possible to take a guided walk to Livingstone Island and swim in the **Devils Pool,** a natural pond right on the lip of the abyss. ⊠ *Mosi-oa-Tunya Rd., just before border post, Livingstone* ⊠ *USD$10.*

FodorsChoice
★

FAMILY   **Mosi-oa-Tunya National Park.** This park is a quick and easy option for viewing plains game. In fact, you are almost guaranteed to spy white rhinos. You can also visit the Old Drift graveyard, as the park marks the location of the original settlement of Livingstone. The park's guides are very knowledgeable, and while you're free to explore on your own, the roads do get seriously muddy in the rainy season, and a guide who knows where to drive becomes a near-necessity. ■TIP→ It's best to find out about park entry details from your accommodations or a local tour operator, as park management can be less than helpful. ✉ *Sichanga Rd., off Mosi-oa-Tunya Rd., 3½ km (2 miles) from Livingstone, Livingstone* 🖂 *$10 per person per day and $16 per vehicle per day.*

FAMILY **Mukuni Village.** Fascinated by the history, customs, and traditions of the area? Local guides can escort you on an intimate visit inside a house and explain the customs of the village. This is not a stage set but a very real village, so your tour will be different depending on the time of day. It is customary to sign in the visitors' book and to pay a small fee to your guide. ✉ *Livingstone.*

A THREE-HOUR TOUR

Many park guides are well informed, but the ultimate Mosioa-Tunya National Park experience is this three-hour guided walking safari with **Livingstone Walking Safaris**. Not only can you see the endangered white rhino and other plains game, but your professional guide and park scout will impart detailed information on birding, flora, and the modern use of plants by local people. Walks are conducted early in the morning and late in the afternoon and cost US$80, including transfers within Livingstone, park fees and refreshments. ☎ *213/32–2267* ⊕ *www. livingstonerhinosafaris.com.*

WHERE TO EAT

$$
\begin{array}{ll}
\end{array}
$$

$$ **INDIAN** ✕**Golden Leaf.** The Moghuls themselves might declare a meal here a feast. Spicy but not hot, the curries are lovingly prepared from ingredients imported from India. **Known for:** authentic ambience and food; good variety of curries; great service. $ *Average main: $18* ✉ *110 Mosi-oa-Tunya Rd., opposite Ngolide Lodge, Livingstone* ☎ *213/32–1266* ⊗ *No dinner Mon.*

$$$$ **ECLECTIC** **FAMILY** **Fodor'sChoice** ★ ✕**Livingstone Island Picnic.** Available throughout the year whenever the water levels are low enough, this is a spectacular dining option. Livingstone Island is perched right on the edge of the void, where you'll dine at a table dressed with linen and gleaming silver on a delicious organic lunch (with salads) served by attentive waiters. $ *Average main: $120* ✉ *Livingstone Island, Livingstone* ☎ *213/32–7450* ⊗ *Closed a couple of months around Feb.–June, depending on water levels. No dinner.*

$ **ITALIAN** **FAMILY** ✕**Olga's Italian Corner.** This restaurant delivers a double whammy. Not only does it serve genuine homemade Italian food prepared from fresh local ingredients, it's also part of an NGO project that trains and benefits the local youth. **Known for:** its strong social conscience; probably the best pizza in Zambia; good value for money. $ *Average main: $10* ✉ *20 Mokambo Rd., Livingstone* ☎ *213/32–4160* ⊕ *www.olgasproject. com* ▭ *No credit cards.*

$$$$ **SOUTH AFRICAN** **Fodor'sChoice** ★ ✕**Royal Livingstone Express.** Walking the long stretch of red carpet alongside Locomotive 156 while it blows steam and rumbles in preparation for its journey is an ultimately exciting and romantic Vic Falls experience. Dinner guests are seated in either the Wembley or Chesterfield

10

dining carriage (both exquisitely restored) while the historic steam train pulls you through a bustling shanty town, over the Sinde River Bridge, and then back through Mosi-oa-Tunya National Park at sunset, or on Wednesday and Saturday the train stops to watch the sunset on the magnificent Victoria Falls Bridge. **Known for:** unashamedly decadent decor; stellar romantic sunsets; delectable menu. $ *Average main: $170 ⊠ Km 0 of the Mulobezi line on Mosi-oa-Tunya Rd., Livingstone ☎ 27/11–469–9300 ⊕ www.royal-livingstone-express.com ⊘ Closed Mon. and Tues.*

WHERE TO STAY

$$$$
RESORT
Fodor'sChoice
★

🏨 **Islands of Siankaba.** The lodge, located on two beautiful forested islands in the Zambezi River about 48 km (30 miles) upstream from Victoria Falls, was awarded the Environmental Certificate by the Environmental Council of Zambia in 2002. **Pros:** beautifully secluded location; innovative design; easy access to Chobe National Park just across the border into Botswana. **Cons:** 40-minute transfer from Livingstone; not for those on a tight budget; bugs galore in the rainier months. $ *Rooms from: $1176 ⊠ Livingstone ✛ 40 km (25 miles) from Livingstone along Nakatindi Rd. on the Zambezi ☎ 097–772–0530 ⊕ www.siankaba.net* ➽ *7 rooms* ⦿ *All-inclusive.*

$
B&B/INN

🏨 **Jollyboys.** The entire design of this small establishment is user-friendly, inviting, and certainly aimed at both private relaxation and easy interaction with other travelers. **Pros:** very central location; free daily transfers to the Falls; social atmosphere. **Cons:** the lodge and camp are for backpackers, so are pretty basic; not for those looking for tranquil accommodations surrounded by nature; can get a bit rowdy. $ *Rooms from: $55 ⊠ Kanyanta Rd., Livingstone ☎ 213/324–229, 213/324–756 ⊕ www.backpackzambia.com ⊟ No credit cards* ➽ *24 rooms* ⦿ *No meals.*

$
B&B/INN
FAMILY

🏨 **Jungle Junction.** The vibe of California and Marrakesh in the '60s and '70s is alive and well at this collection of thatch huts and campsites along the banks of the Zambezi, 52 km (32 miles) upstream of the Falls. **Pros:** good value for money; a great way to combine an educational canoe trip with a basic overnight camp; the perfect balance between comfort and a real commune with nature. **Cons:** this might be too basic for travelers who like their little luxuries; meals, fishing, and transfers are charged separately; guests have to bring their own towels. $ *Rooms from: $50 ⊠ Livingstone ✛ 52 km (32 miles) upstream from Victoria Falls, on Zambezi River ☎ 097/872–5282 ⊕ www.junglejunction.info ⊟ No credit cards* ➽ *8 huts* ⦿ *No meals.*

$
B&B/INN
FAMILY

🏨 **Prana Cottage & Tented Camp.** Taking its name from the Sanskrit for breathing, this exclusive camp offers the perfect opportunity for taking just that, a breather. **Pros:** this is the best value for an exclusive stay in the area; remote location, yet only 10 minutes from Livingstone and 10 minutes from the entry to Mosi-oa-Tunya Park at the Falls; friendly and personal service. **Cons:** if you don't have a car, you can feel a little isolated; Wi-Fi can be patchy; rooms in the self-catering house are a little bland. $ *Rooms from: $150 ⊠ Off Mosi-oa-Tunya Rd., Livingstone ☎ 0979–959–981 ⊕ www.pranazambia.com ⊟ No credit cards* ➽ *14 rooms* ⦿ *Breakfast.*

Continued on page 501

The first European to set eyes on the Falls was the explorer and missionary Dr. David Livingstone in the mid-1850s. Overcome by the experience he named them after the English queen, Victoria.

VICTORIA FALLS

Expect to be humbled by the sheer power and majesty. Expect to be deafened by the thunderous noise, drenched by spray, and overwhelmed at the sight. Expect the mighty swath of roaring, foaming Victoria Falls—spanning the entire 1-mile width of the Zambezi River—to leave you speechless.

On a clear day the spray generated by the Falls is visible from 31 miles (50 km) away—the swirling mist rising above the woodland savanna looks like smoke from a bush fire inspiring their local name, Mosi-Oa-Tunya, or the "Smoke that Thunders." The rim of the Falls is broken into separate smaller falls with names like the Devil's Cataract, Rainbow Falls, Horseshoe Falls, and Armchair Falls.

The Falls, which are more than 300 feet high, are one of the world's seven natural wonders and were named a UNESCO World Heritage Site in 1989. Upon seeing Victoria Falls for the first time Dr. David Livingstone proclaimed, "Scenes so lovely must have been gazed upon by angels in their flight." Truer words were never spoken.

WATCH OUT

Unlike other great waterfalls, the Zambezi has no rapids to warn of the approaching drop. One moment you'll be in calm placid waters; the next you'll be hurtling over the edge.

FALLS FACTS

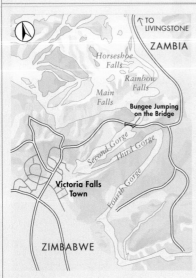

you might be able to catch a moonbow or lunar rainbow (a nighttime version of a rainbow) in the spray. The rest of the year offers its own charms with dry season–only activities like visiting Livingstone's Island, swimming in the Devil's Pool, and walking along the bottom of the Falls.

TO ZIM OR TO ZAM

Honestly? *Both* sides are great, but if you have to choose one, take the following into consideration: The Zambian side has more than four times the physical Falls frontage of Zimbabwe, but you're mostly looking across the gorge which means that Zimbabwe offers four times the visual display. Zimbabwe definitely has the most spray, the most rainbows, the best flat stone pathways for easy access, and the only views of the incredible Devil's Cataract. Rain forests with exotic flowers can be enjoyed on the Zimbabwe side year round and on the Zambian side during high water. Adventure seekers will love the Zam side's steep steps, the trail into the Boiling Pot, the slick Knife Edge bridge, and, during low water season visits to Livingstone Island, swimming in the Devil's Pool.

CROSSING THE FALLS

Built in 1905, Victoria Falls Bridge is one of the few useful remnants of the Colonial era. An important link in former South African Prime Minister Cecil John Rhodes's dream of creating the Cape-to-Cairo railway—it was never finished—the bridge continues to provide a convenient link between Zimbabwe and Zambia. It also offers a knockout view of the Falls and the Zambezi River raging through the Gorge, plus the added bonus of watching adrenaline junkies taking the 364-foot bungee plunge.

FORMATION OF THE FALLS

A basaltic plateau once stood where the Falls are today. The whole area was once completely submerged, but fast-forward to the Jurassic Age and the water eventually dried up. Only the Zambezi River remained flowing down into the gaping 1-mile-long continuous gorge that was formed by the uneven cracking of the drying plateau. The river charges through the ancient gorges creating some of the world's best commercial white water rapids.

WHEN TO GO

The Falls are spectacular at any time, but if you want to see them full, visit during the high water season (April–June) when more than 2 million gallons hurtle over the edge every second. The resulting spray is so dense that, at times, the view can be obscured. Don't worry though, the frequent gusts of wind will soon come to your aid and your view will be restored. If you're lucky to be there during a full moon,

Naming the Falls

Dr. David Livingstone, a Scottish medical doctor and missionary, visited Victoria Falls in 1855 and is widely credited with being the first European to document the existence of this natural wonder. He named it Victoria Falls in honor of his queen, although the Makololo name, Mosi-oa-Tunya (literally, "the Smoke that Thunders"), remains popular. Livingstone fell madly in love with the Falls, describing them in poignant prose. Other explorers had slightly different opinions. E. Holub could not contain his excitement and spoke effusively of "a thrilling throb of nature," A. A. de Serpa Pinto called them "sublimely horrible" in 1881, and L. Decle (1898) declared ominously that he expected "to see some repulsive monster rising in anger" at any moment. The modern traveler has the luxury of exploring every one (or all) of these perspectives. There's so much to do around the Falls that the only limitations will be your budget and sense of adventure or your lack thereof.

$$$$
HOTEL
The River Club. With split-level rooms that cling to the edge of the great Zambezi, The River Club puts a modern spin on a Victorian house party. **Pros:** beautiful location with stunning views of the Zambezi; a/c and enclosed rooms are pluses for those who don't want to give up too many modern conveniences; excellent service. **Cons:** colonial decor may not be Zambian enough for some travelers; 20-minute drive from town for any activities that are not run in-house; food not quite up to the standard of some other top lodges in the area. $ *Rooms from: $920* ✉ *Livingstone* ✛ *About 18 km (11 miles) upstream from Victoria Falls town, on Zambezi River, down same road as Tongabezi* ☎ *211/39–1051* ⊕ *www.theriverclubafrica.com* ✎ *11 rooms* ⦿ *Some meals.*

$$$$
HOTEL
The Royal Livingstone. This high-volume, high-end hotel has an incredibly gorgeous sundowner deck, arguably on the best spot on the river, just upstream from the Falls. **Pros:** location, location, location; the level of service here is definitely that of a five-star international hotel; there is direct access to the Falls via a resort gate that opens onto the eastern cataract. **Cons:** volume of people can lead to occasional problems, omissions, and errors; it can feel a little impersonal; stay clear if colonial nostalgia isn't your thing. $ *Rooms from: $660* ✉ *Livingstone Way, Livingstone* ☎ *27/11–780–7810* ⊕ *www.suninternational.com* ✎ *173 rooms* ⦿ *Breakfast.*

$$$$
RESORT
Fodor'sChoice
★
Sindabezi Island. This is the most environmentally friendly property on the Zambezi. **Pros:** lovely views of the national park on the Zimbabwean side from parts of the island; if you're lucky, elephants might swim across the Zambezi and graze a few meters from your bed; service is top-notch. **Cons:** it's very open, so if you are a bit nervous in the African bush, this might not suit you; there's no pool; it's difficult to get to. $ *Rooms from: $1190* ✉ *Livingstone* ✛ *About 19 km (12 miles) upstream from Victoria Falls, on Zambezi River* ☎ *213/32–7450, 213/32–7468* ⊕ *www.tongabezi.com* ✎ *5 rooms* ⦿ *All-inclusive.*

$$$$
RESORT
Toka Leya Camp. Spread out along the banks of the Zambezi River, the tents are set up on stilts, surrounded by a wooden deck that you

10

can sit on and watch the world and the Zambezi River go by. **Pros:** the camp is close to Livingstone and all of the activities offered in the area; there's a small spa on the banks of the river; almost all your activities are included in the rates. **Cons:** the decor makes it feel a bit like a hotel as opposed to a bush camp; prices will be prohibitive to many; not the most remote of the riverfront camps. $ *Rooms from: $1540 ⊠ Livingstone ✢ On the Zambezi River, 12 km (7½ miles) upstream from Victoria Falls* ☎ *11/807–1800* ⊕ *www.wilderness-safaris.com* ⇗ *12 rooms* ⦿ *All-inclusive.*

$$$$
RESORT
Fodor'sChoice
★

Tongabezi Lodge. If you're looking for a truly idyllic African experience, this is it. **Pros:** the original open-fronted lodge; owner offers personal service and thoughtful touches; management is environmentally focused and community aware. **Cons:** the use of local materials for building and decoration might not meet luxury standards for some; interaction with others is limited—though some might count this as a pro; a bit of a distance from town and most activities. $ *Rooms from: $1310 ⊠ Livingstone ✢ About 19 km (12 miles) upstream from Victoria Falls, on Zambezi River* ☎ *213/32–7468* ⊕ *www.tongabezi.com* ⇗ *11 suites* ⦿ *All-inclusive.*

$
RESORT

Victoria Falls Waterfront. There's a hive of happy activity here ranging from opportunistic monkeys relieving unsuspecting tourists of their lunch to serious late-night boozing. **Pros:** great location right on the river with beautiful sunsets; many of the adventure activities in the area are managed from the Waterfront; very social atmosphere at the bar. **Cons:** can be very noisy as it caters to campers and backpackers; food can still be inconsistent; Wi-Fi only available around the restaurant area. $ *Rooms from: $225 ⊠ Sichango Rd., just off Mosi-oa-Tunya Rd., Livingstone* ☎ *213/968–320606* ⊕ *www.thevictoriafallswaterfront.com* ⇗ *47 rooms* ⦿ *Breakfast.*

SPORTS AND THE OUTDOORS

Livingstone can compete with the best as far as indulging the wildest fantasies of adrenaline junkies and outdoor enthusiasts goes. You can reserve activities directly with the operators, let your hotel or lodge handle it, or book through a central booking agent.

BOATING

African Queen. Truly the monarch of the river, the *African Queen*—no relation to the movie—is an elegant colonial-style riverboat. Their sunset cruises offer the maximum style and splendor. ⊠ *Livingstone* ☎ *097/877–0175* ⊑ *2-hr sunset cruise with open bar and snacks from US$75.*

CANOEING

A gentle canoeing trip on the upper Zambezi is a great opportunity to see birds and a variety of game. Many of the lodges upriver have canoeing as an inclusive activity, but trips are also run by a number of companies, which are all reputable.

Bundu Adventures. Bundu Adventures offers custom-made canoe and white-water rafting trips that range from half-day outings to multiday excursions. ⊠ *1364 Kabompo Rd., Livingstone ✢ The office is at the*

The thundering roar of Victoria Falls and its many rainbows leave visitors speechless.

same location as The Gemstone Grill in Livingstone ☎ 213/32–4407 ⊕ www.bunduadventures.com ✉ From US$120 for a half-day cruise.

FLYING

Batoka Sky. Batoka Sky offers weight-shift Aerotrike twin-axis micro-lighting (flying jargon for what resembles a motorized hang glider) and helicopter flights over the Falls and through the gorges. There's a minimum of two passengers for helicopters. You are issued a flight suit (padded in winter) and a helmet with a headset, before you board the microlight, but you may not bring a camera for safety reasons. Batoka Sky has been operating since 1992, and has a 100% microlighting safety record. Flights are booked for early morning and late afternoon and are dependent on the weather. Transfer and a day visa, if you are coming from Victoria Falls, are included. The Helicopter Gorge picnic includes lunch and drinks for a minimum of six people. ✉ Livingstone's Adventure, Just off Sichango Rd., Livingstone ✛ Near the Chrismar Hotel Livingstone ☎ 213/32–3589 ⊕ www.livingstonesadventure.com ✉ US$180–US$350, depending on length of flight and aircraft; Helicopter Gorge, US$440.

JETBOATING

FAMILY **Jet Extreme.** If you want some thrills and speed but rafting seems a bit daunting, or you can't face the walk in and out, you'll probably enjoy jetboating with Jet Extreme. A new cable-car ride, included in the cost of the jetboat ride, means no more strenuous walking out of the gorge. Jetboating can be combined with a rafting excursion, as the jetboat starts at the end of the rafting run, or with a helicopter trip out of the gorge. ■ TIP→ **The rafting and helicopter must be booked separately,**

gorge. ■TIP→ The rafting and helicopter must be booked separately, although big operators like Safari Par Excellence and Livingstone's Adventure offer combinations. Children over seven can jetboat if they are accompanied by an adult. ✉ *Safpar at David Livingstone Safari Lodge, Livingstone* ☎ *213/320–606* ⊕ *www.livingstonesadventure.com* 💲 *US$125 for 30 minutes.*

RAPPELLING AND SWINGING

Zambezi Eco Adventures. For something completely different, Zambezi Eco Adventures (formerly Abseil Zambia) has taken some specially designed heavy-duty steel cables, combined them with various pulleys and rigs, one dry gorge, and a 100% safety record to entertain both the fainthearted and the daring. ⚠ Keep in mind that you will have to climb out after the gorge swing and the rappel. Work up an appetite for more daring drops by starting on the zip line (or flying fox). You run off a ramp while attached to the line, and the sensation is pure freedom and surprisingly unscary, as you are not moving up or down. Next rappel down into the 175-foot gorge, and, after you climb out, try it again facing forward. It's called a rap run. You're literally walking down the cliff face. End the day with the king of adrenaline activities, a whopping 175-foot, 3½-second vertical free-fall swing into the gorge. ✉ *Batoka Gorge, Livingstone* ☎ *213/32–1188* ⊕ *www.zambeziecoadventures.com* 💲 *From $80.*

TOURS

Bushtracks. This operator runs one-day excursions to Botswana's Chobe National Park. The trip includes transfers from Livingstone, a morning boat cruise, lunch with a drink, and an afternoon game drive. Bushtracks is also your best bet for a visit to the Mukuni Village. Reservations must be prepaid for both. ✉ *Livingstone* ☎ *213/32–3232, 11/469–9300 in Johannesburg* ⊕ *www.bushtracksafrica.com* 💲 *Chobe National Park, US$200; Mukuni Village, US$50.*

Livingstone Rhino Walking Safaris. Many park guides are well informed, but the ultimate Mosi-oa-Tunya National Park experience is this three-hour guided walking safari. Not only can you see the endangered white rhino and other plains game, but your professional guide and park scout will impart detailed information on birding, flora, and the modern use of plants by local people. Walks are conducted early in the morning and late in the afternoon and cost US$75, including transfers within Livingstone, park fees, and refreshments. ✉ *Livingstone* ☎ *213/32–2267* ⊕ *www.livingstonerhinosafaris.com* 💲 *$80.*

Safari Par Excellence. Half- and full-day rafting excursions to Batoka Gorge are available through Safari Par Excellence. A cable car transports rafters out of the gorge, so you only have to climb down—secure shoes, dry clothes, a baseball cap to wear under your helmet, and plenty of sunscreen are essential. River-boarding (hop off the raft onto a body board and surf suitable rapids) excursions, game drives, river cruises, canoeing, and rafting are also available, as are trip combinations such as a helicopter-and-rafting trip. Combo trips are a good option if your time is limited or you just want to go wild. ✉ *David Livingstone Safari*

Lodge, Livingstone ☎*213/32–0606* ⊕*www.safpar.net* ✐*Rafting US$150 half-day, US$175 full-day; river-boarding from US$185.*

SHOPPING

Kubu Crafts. This stylish home-decor shop features locally made furniture in hardwood and wrought iron. There's also a selection of West African masks and weavings and the work of numerous local artists. Local curios are attractively displayed and screened for quality. Kubu Crafts also provides both fair employment and training opportunities for the community. ✉*Mosi-O-Tunya Sq., 133 Mosi-Oa-Tunya Rd., Livingstone* ☎*213/32–0230* ⊕*www.kubucrafts.com.*

Mukuni Park Market. Although the park at the entrance to the Falls has stalls where you can find stone and wood carvings and simple bead and semiprecious-stone jewelry, the real gem of an African bazaar lies in the center of town, at Mukuni Park Market. ■TIP→ **This is the place to try your hand at bargaining.** You'll be quoted top dollar initially, but shop around. Look out for individual and unusual pieces, as it is occasionally possible to find valuable antiques. The market is open daily approximately 7–6. ✉*Mosi-oa-Tunya Rd. at Libala Dr., Livingstone.*

ZAMBIAN SAFARI CIRCUIT

If you are eager to see more of Zambia than just Livingstone and the Victoria Falls area, Lower Zambezi National Park and Kafue National Park (one of the biggest parks in Africa) are spectacular destinations teeming with big game and first-class luxury lodges. Both are within a few hundred kilometers (62 miles) of Livingstone. Most lodges and hotels in and around Livingstone can arrange transfers either by road or by air.

EXPLORING

Kafue National Park. Kafue is Zambia's oldest and largest national park, covering a massive 2,240,000 hectares (about the size of Wales in the United Kingdom), which also makes it one of the largest parks in Africa and, for that matter, the world. Thanks to its size, variety of ecosystems, and the sustenance provided by the beautiful Kafue River, this park is absolutely teeming with game, from the popular heavyweights like lions, elephants, and leopards to one of Africa's largest wild dog populations—right through to rare species such as lechwe and yellow-backed duiker and more than 400 types of bird. The park is an easy two-hour drive from Livingstone. Despite all its highlights, the park remains largely wild and unexplored, particularly the northern reaches. But this may be the park's number one draw. There are a handful of first-rate campsites and luxury lodges dotted in and around the edges of the park, almost all of which offer typically Zambian attention to detail in terms of service and providing the real bush experience. ✉*Livingstone* ⊕ *About 175 km (110 miles) from Livingstone via the T1* ☎*213/321–404* ⊕*www.zambiatourism.com.*

Lower Zambezi National Park. Lower Zambezi National Park may not be Zambia's biggest or best-known national park, but these are two of the main reasons it's so worth a visit. The whole park retains a unique

10

feeling of untouched African wilderness, and you certainly wouldn't think you were just a few hours from the urban hubs of Livingstone and Lusaka. When on game drives or guided bush walks through the park, you can go for hours without seeing another car, but the density of big game is astonishing. The vegetation and landscapes are spectacularly diverse, too, ranging from rugged, forested mountain escarpments to wide-open plains punctuated only by the occasional lonely baobab or palm tree. All six of the park's luxury and secluded camps are along the lush banks of the mighty Zambezi river, which serves as the natural southern border to the park as well as between Zambia and Zimbabwe's Mana Pools on the other side of the river. Lower Zambezi is a particularly special place for canoeing safaris and boat cruises, and is also a favorite with fishing aficionados. The quickest and easiest way to get to the park is to fly from Livingstone to Lusaka and then take a short chartered flight to Royal Airstrip within the park. ✉ *Lusaka* ☎ *213/321–404* 🌐 *www.zambiatourism.com.*

WHERE TO STAY

$$$$ RESORT FAMILY

🏨 **KaingU Safari Lodge.** KaingU Safari Lodge is a small camp comprised of a family house with two bedrooms and six classic en suite safari tents. **Pros:** Africa untouched in all its glory; the owners have a true commitment to environmental and community development; very friendly service. **Cons:** road transfers from Lusaka take 5–6 hours; the area has less big game than some other areas of the park; food is a little unspectacular for a top-end lodge. [$] *Rooms from: $840* ✉ *Livingstone* ✣ *South Kafue, 400 km (250 miles) north of Victoria Falls* ☎ *097/784–1653* 🌐 *www.kaingu-lodge.com* 💳 *No credit cards* 🛏 *9 suites* 🍴 *All-inclusive.*

$$$$ RESORT Fodor's Choice ★

🏨 **Old Mondoro Camp.** The legend of a great white-maned lion that used to call this area its home lives on in the name of this camp, which is Shona for the "king of cats." If you're looking for an African adventure of the original epic variety, then you need to stay at Old Mondoro. **Pros:** great game drives led by top-notch wildlife guides; one of the best places to see leopards; best walking area in the Lower Zambezi. **Cons:** the open rooms have only canvas flaps to ward off the wild at night, and this might be too daring for some; difficult to get to for those wanting to self-drive; not for those who need mod cons. [$] *Rooms from: $2400* ✉ *Lower Zambezi National Park* ✣ *142 km (88 miles) from Lusaka; Old Mondoro is a 1-hr motorboat ride or a 2-hr game drive from its sister camp, Chiawa. Jeki Airstrip is only a 30-minute game-drive away from Old Mondoro and can be reached via 2-hr flight from Livingstone or a 40-minute flight from Lusaka* ☎ *211/261–588* 🌐 *www.chiawa.com/old-mondoro* 🕓 *Closed Nov.–May 1* 🛏 *5 tents* 🍴 *All-inclusive.*

$$$$ RESORT

🏨 **Sausage Tree Camp.** There is no formal dress code, but this camp offers the perfect backdrop for throwing practicality to the wind and dressing up for dinner. **Pros:** elephants are regular visitors; stunning riverside location; gorgeous food. **Cons:** its remote location makes it very expensive and time-consuming to reach; no fences to keep wildlife at bay, so not for the faint of heart; not open all year-round. [$] *Rooms from: $1544* ✉ *Lower Zambezi National Park, 140 km (85 miles) from Lusaka, Livingstone* ☎ *097/657–9155* 🌐 *www.sausagetreecamp.com* 🕓 *Closed Nov. 20–Apr.* 🛏 *8 rooms* 🍴 *All-inclusive.*

VICTORIA FALLS, ZIMBABWE

Victoria Falls started with a little curio shop and slowly expanded until the 1970s, when it became the mecca around which the tourist phenomenon of Victoria Falls pivoted. The political problems following independence have been well documented in the press worldwide and have certainly taken their toll, as has poaching in Zambezi National Park to the northwest. (If you really want to have the African game experience, take a day trip to Chobe National Park, only 70 km/44 miles away in Botswana.)

However, the country has regained some semblance of political stability and the town of Victoria Falls enjoys the happy coincidence of being a curio shopper's paradise inside a national park. This means you can literally buy an elephant carving while watching the real McCoy march past the shop window. The town has an easygoing feel and is extremely compact. Almost all the hotels are within walking distance, and the Falls are only 10 minutes away on foot. The main road that runs through town and goes to the Falls in one direction and to the airport in the other is called Livingstone Way. Park Way is perpendicular. Most of the shops, banks, and booking agents can be found on these two streets, and this part of town is also where most of the hawkers operate. ■TIP➔ **Give these vendors a clear berth, as their wares are cheap for a reason (the boat cruise is substandard, it's illegal to change money, etc.).**

PLANNING
GETTING HERE AND AROUND
Tourists have gradually returned to Victoria Falls. If you choose to fly in and out of Victoria Falls Airport, most hotels will provide free shuttle service; book in advance.

ZIMBABWE FAST FACTS

Size 390,757 square km (150,872 square miles)

Number of National Parks 10. Hwange National Park; Victoria Falls National Park; Mana Pools National Park and Gonarezhou National Park are the most visited. Zimbabwe also has a small handful of exclusive private concessions and private game reserves, mostly concentrated around Victoria Falls.

Population 16.5 million

Big Five The gang's all here.

Language Zimbabwe has three official languages: English, Shona, and Ndebele. Although the number of native English speakers is small, English is widely understood and used.

Time Zimbabwe is on CAST (Central African Standard Time), which is two hours ahead of Greenwich mean time and seven hours ahead of North American Eastern Standard Time. It's the same as South Africa.

Capital. Harare

Drives on the left

Hotels can summon reputable taxis quickly and advise you on the cost. Tipping isn't mandatory, but change is always appreciated.

Airlines Air Zimbabwe. ☎ 263/457–5021 ⊕ www.airzimbabwe.aero. **Comair/ British Airways.** ☎ 013/42274, 013/4–2388 ⊕ www.british-airways.com. **South African Airways.** ☎ 11/978–5313 ⊕ www.flysaa.com.

Airport Victoria Falls Airport. ✉ *Livingstone Way, Victoria Falls* ☎ *013/4–4428.*

ESSENTIALS

Zimbabwe's currency used to be the Zimbabwe dollar, but now foreign currency is the only acceptable method of payment. Carry U.S. dollars in small denominations and stick to U.S. dollars for all activity payments to Zimbabwe-based operators (all activities are quoted in U.S. dollars). Credit card facilities aren't always readily available. (You'll also find Western Union banks in Victoria Falls and Livingstone, should you need to do cash transfers.)

It's possible to buy point-of-entry visas for Zimbabwe for US$60 for a single entry. If you leave Zimbabwe for more than 24 hours, you'll need to buy another to reenter (unless you bought a double-entry visa for US$75). Visas can be purchased from a Zimbabwean embassy before departure (application for multiple-entry visas can only be lodged here), but it'll almost certainly be more trouble and generally cost more than buying them at the border.

The political situation in Zimbabwe is currently fairly stable, but the damage from the lengthy dictatorship and internal strife is still very apparent. Prices have stabilized and basic goods have reappeared on the shelves, but the tourist capital of Victoria Falls has not yet regained its status as a prime international destination. All the activities, shopping, and dining options on offer on the Zimbabwean side can also be enjoyed across the border in Zambia—without any of the uncertainty and potential for sudden political and economic upheavals that could result in cancellations or threats to visitors' safety. ■ TIP→ **The Victoria Falls town and tourism industry has managed to build itself up in a remarkably short time. The political situation is still not 100% resolved, but for now, Zimbabwean lodges offer good value and service.**

MARS (Medical Air Rescue Services) is on standby for all emergencies. Dr. Nyoni is a trauma specialist and operates a hospital opposite the Shoestring Lodge. Go to Victoria Falls Pharmacy for prescriptions.

Male homosexuality is illegal in Zimbabwe—female homosexuality isn't mentioned in law—and same-sex relationships receive no recognition. Attitudes are slowly improving, but it's advisable to be extremely circumspect.

It's always a good idea to leave ample space in your luggage for common sense when traveling to Victoria Falls. Wild animals abound throughout this area (even in the center of town) and must be given a lot of physical space and respect.

As for the water, it's always advisable to drink bottled water. Should you develop an upset stomach, be sure to contact a physician, especially if you're running a fever, in order to rule out malaria or a communicable disease. Do remember to mention your visit to a malaria area to your doctor in the event of illness within a year of leaving Africa.

Embassies U.S. Embassy. ⊠ *172 Herbert Chitepo Ave., Box 4010, Harare* ☎ *04/25–0593* ⊕ *www.usembassy.gov/zimbabwe.*

Emergency Services Medical Air Rescue Services. ⊠ *Flat No. 1, Stanley House, 3rd St., opposite Shoestring, Victoria Falls* ☎ *013/4–4764* ⊕ *www.mars.co.zw.*

The country code for Zimbabwe is 263. When dialing from abroad, drop the initial 0 from local area codes. Ask a hotel or restaurant manager for exact telephone numbers and costs, should you wish to make any telephone calls from within Zimbabwe.

ABOUT THE RESTAURANTS

In Zimbabwe, excellent game meat such as warthog, crocodile, and various antelope species are a commonly found speciality in the lodges, hotels, and touristy restaurants; at the more local joints in town, hearty chicken and beef stews are more common. The local bream, filleted or whole, is always a good bet, and the staple starch, a stiff porridge similar to polenta—known as *sadza* this side of the border—is worth a try; use your fingers to eat it. Adventurous? Try *macimbi* or *vinkuvala* (sun-dried mopane worms), which are a favored Zimbabwean delicacy. Excellent high teas are a regular feature at hotels and camps, one of the more favorable legacies of British colonialism.

Meals are taken at regular hours, but during the week restaurants close around 10. Dress is generally pretty casual, like most things in Victoria Falls.

10

ABOUT THE LODGINGS

It's advisable to make both flight and lodge reservations ahead of time. Most of the luxury safari camps and lodges offer all-inclusive packages; hotels generally include breakfast only. All hotels and lodges quote in U.S. dollars; while some will accept payment in other major international currencies, this is not a suggested option due to the unfavorable exchange rates. Having said that, accommodation on this side of the border is generally much more affordable than in Zambia. A 10% service charge is either included or added to the bill (as is the V.A.T.) in both countries, which frees you to include an extra tip only for exceptional service.

Restaurant and hotel reviews have been shortened. For full information, visit Fodors.com.

WHAT IT COSTS IN U.S. DOLLARS			
$	$$	$$$	$$$$
Restaurants	under $12	$12–$20	$21–$30	over $30
Hotels	under $250	$250–$450	$451–$600	over $600

Prices in the restaurant reviews are the average cost of a main course at dinner or, if dinner isn't served, at lunch; taxes and service charges are generally included. Prices in the lodging reviews are the lowest cost of a standard double room in high season.

VISITOR INFORMATION

The Victoria Falls Publicity Association is fairly well stocked with brochures. It's open weekdays 8–1 and 2–4 and Saturday 8–1. You could also choose to seek advice from one of the many safari companies in town.

EXPLORING

FAMILY **Victoria Falls Bridge.** A veritable monument to Cecil Rhodes's dream of completing a Cape-to-Cairo rail line, this graceful structure spans the gorge formed by the Zambezi River. It would have been far easier and less expensive to build the bridge upstream from the Falls, but Rhodes was captivated by the romance of a railway bridge passing over this natural wonder. A net was stretched across the gorge under the construction site, which curiously prompted the construction workers to go on strike for a couple of days. They resumed work only when it was explained that they would not be expected to leap into it at the end of every workday. Although the workers did not share the current adrenaline-fueled obsession with jumping into the abyss, the net probably had a lot to do with the miraculous fact that only two people were killed during construction. The bridge was completed in only 14 months, and the last two cross-girders were defiantly joined on April 1, 1905.

To get onto the bridge, you first have to pass through Zimbabwean immigration and customs controls, so bring your passport. Unless you decide to cross into Zambia, no visa is necessary, though you will need a gate pass.

Depending on crowds, the simple procedure can take from five minutes to a half hour. The border posts are open daily from 6 am to 10 pm, after which the bridge is closed to all traffic. From the bridge you are treated to a fabulous view of the river raging through Batoka Gorge, as well as a section of the Falls on the Zambian side. An added bonus is watching the bungee jumpers disappear over the edge. ⊠ *Livingstone Way, Victoria Falls* ⊕ *www.victoriafallsbridge.com.*

FAMILY
Fodor's Choice
★

Victoria Falls National Park. Plan to spend at least two hours soaking in the splendors of this park. Avoid the crowds and the heat by getting there as early as possible. Bring snacks and water, and supervise children extremely well, as the barriers are by no means safe. Babies and toddlers can be pushed in a stroller. If you visit the Falls during the high-water peak, between April and June, you'd do well to carry a raincoat or umbrella (you can rent them at the entrance) and to bring along a waterproof, disposable camera because you *will* be drenched in the spray from the Falls, which creates a permanent downpour. Be prepared for limited photo opportunities due to the mist. ■TIP→ **Leave expensive cameras, cell phones, and wristwatches in your hotel or lodge safe.**

The constant drizzle has created a small rain forest that extends in a narrow band along the edge of the Falls. A trail running through this dripping green world is overgrown with African ebony, Cape fig, Natal mahogany, wild date palms, ferns, and deep-red flame lilies. A fence has been erected to keep non-fee-paying visitors at bay. Clearly signposted side trails lead to viewpoints overlooking the Falls. The most spectacular is **Danger Point,** a perilous rock outcropping that overlooks the narrow gorge through which the Zambezi River funnels out of the **Boiling Pot,** but be careful, as this viewpoint is hazardously wet and precarious. In low-water months (September–November) most of the water goes over the Falls through the **Devil's Cataract,** a narrow and mesmerizingly powerful section of the Falls visible from **Livingstone's statue.** Around the full moon the park stays open late so you can see the lunar rainbow formed by the spray—a hauntingly beautiful sight. Early morning and late afternoon are the best times to see the daylight rainbows most vividly. A booklet explaining the formation and layout of the Falls is available from the Victoria Falls Publicity Association for a small fee. ⊠ *Off Livingstone Way, Victoria Falls* ☎ *013/42–294* ⊒ *US$30.*

WHERE TO EAT

At the peak of Zimbabwe's political problems, shortages of even the most basic foods, like vegetables, were an everyday occurrence. Since the adoption of the USD as the official currency, however, hotels and restaurants have been able to restore some sanity, and in a short time, have been able to reestablish their unique flair for first-rate hospitality while maintaining a healthy dose of local flavor.

$
CAFÉ

✕ **The Africa Cafe.** Find refuge on a hot day at The Africa Cafe in The Elephant's Walk Shopping and Artist's Village. The chef creates simple, delicious food, using ingredients freshly picked from the Happy Hippo Organic Herb and Veggie Garden, found just behind the restaurant.

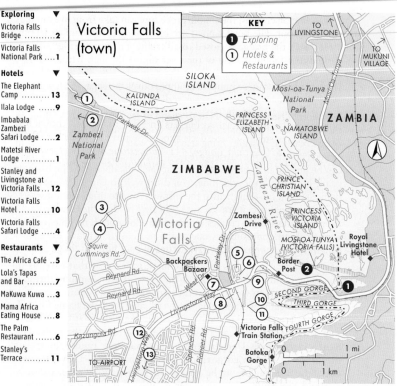

Victoria Falls (town)

Known for: friendly service; game meats; funky decor. $ *Average main: $10* ⊠ *Adam Stander Rd., Victoria Falls* ☎ *077/225–4552* ⊕ *www.elephantswalk.com.*

$$ ✕ **Lola's Tapas and Bar.** Lola's offers authentic Spanish flair combined

TAPAS with African touches in its cuisine and decor and is popular with the younger backpacker crowd. It's cool and open with tables and chairs spilling out onto a shaded courtyard. **Known for:** laid-back atmosphere; excellent central location; friendly staff. $ *Average main: $20* ⊠ *8 Landela Complex, Livingstone Way, in the tourist center, Victoria Falls* ☎ *013/4–2994.*

$$ ✕ **MaKuwa Kuwa.** Perched above a game-rich waterhole at the Victoria

AFRICAN Falls Safari Lodge, a spectacular view awaits diners at this memorable dining spot. On offer at breakfast is a combination of both cold and hot dishes; lunch ranges from great salads to huge gourmet burgers; dinnertime guests are treated to local a cappella performers. **Known for:** unique dining/game-viewing combo; expansive views; decent cocktails. $ *Average main: $20* ⊠ *Victoria Falls Safari Lodge, 471 Squire Cummings Rd., Victoria Falls* ☎ *013/432–1120* ⊕ *www.africaalbidatourism.com* 🍽 *Jacket required.*

$$ ✕ **Mama Africa Eating House.** This is a good local food experience as the

AFRICAN menu offers typical Zimbabwean dishes along with other African food and the atmosphere is colorful and celebratory. Tuesday and Friday nights are "Africa Nights" with a buffet dinner and live music from the local jazz band. **Known for:** local flavor; unpretentious atmosphere; traditional dishes including game meats and the famous mopane worms. $ *Average main: $15* ⊠ *Landela Complex, Matcalfe Rd., Victoria Falls* ☎ *013/4–1725* ⊕ *www.mamaafricaeatinghouse.com.*

$$
AFRICAN
✕ **The Palm Restaurant.** With tables flowing out onto the deep veranda of Ilala Lodge, the Palm has old-world grandeur with delicious modern cuisine. The lunch menu mixes light Mediterranean-style dishes with popular pub favorites such as burgers and fish-and-chips. **Known for:** great location; stellar service; decent cocktails at the poolside bar. $ *Average main: $20* ⊠ *Ilala Lodge, 411 Livingstone Way, Victoria Falls* ☎ *0213/284–44732, 0213/284–4739* ⊕ *www.ilalalodge.com.*

$$$$
MODERN BRITISH
Fodor's Choice
★
✕ **Stanley's Terrace.** A trip to Victoria Falls isn't complete without high tea (3 pm–6 pm) on the Victoria Falls Hotel's terrace. A multilayered cake stand filled with an array of delicious treats, including cakes, tarts, and sandwiches, is served with a pot of tea or coffee. The hotel is very grand, and although some of the furnishings are a little tired, the view out over the gorge and onto the bridge and falls is unforgettable. **Known for:** unforgettable vistas; colonial decadence; the occasional warthog running across the lawn. $ *Average main: $40* ⊠ *The Victoria Falls Hotel, 2 Mallet Dr., Victoria Falls* ☎ *013/4–4751* ⊕ *www.victoriafallshotel.com.*

WHERE TO STAY

With the introduction of the U.S. dollar as the official currency, there's no longer the rocketing inflation. However, an all-inclusive package tour is still a good bet in this area. Electricity and voltage are the same in Zimbabwe and South Africa.

$$$$
RESORT
Fodor's Choice
★
🏕 **The Elephant Camp.** From the deck of your luxurious tented suite, you gaze out across the bush and down to the Batoka Gorge and the "smoke" rising up from Victoria Falls, just 10 km (6 miles) away. **Pros:** every suite has a plunge pool that's most welcoming in the summer months; peaceful location; spectacular views. **Cons:** even though it's in the middle of a national game park, you'll be disappointed if you're there to see a variety of game; the kind of elephant encounters on offer here remain controversial; very expensive for this side of the Falls. $ *Rooms from: $1134* ⊠ *Victoria Falls* ✛ *10 km (6 miles) outside of Victoria Falls, on Livingstone Way (road to the airport)* ☎ *213/284–4571* ⊕ *www.theelephantcamp.com* ⤳ *12 suites* ❏ *All-inclusive.*

$$
HOTEL
FAMILY
🏨 **Ilala Lodge.** The lodge's elegant interior design is tempered with thatch roofs, giving it a graceful African look. **Pros:** great central location; family-friendly; only 10 minutes from the Falls by foot. **Cons:** the location in town can ruin expectations if you are keen on the peace of the African bush; the noise from passing helicopters can be disturbing; patchy Wi-Fi. $ *Rooms from: $426* ⊠ *411 Livingstone Way, Victoria Falls* ☎ *213/284–4737* ⊕ *www.ilalalodge.com* ⤳ *34 rooms* ❏ *Breakfast.*

$$$$
RESORT
🏨 **Imbabala Zambezi Safari Lodge.** Imbabala is a charming lodge an hour's drive from Victoria Falls Airport, set about a hundred meters from the

10

river's edge. **Pros:** authentic Zambezi River and bush experience; lots of activities for those traveling with kids; wonderful staff. **Cons:** the chalets all look out onto the main lawn, so other guests walk past the front of them; the lodge isn't far from Kazungula and the noise from the late-night revellers on the Zambian side can detract a little from the experience; not for those who want to be close to the amenities in town. $ *Rooms from: $694* ⊠ *Kazungula Rd., Victoria Falls* ⊕ *70 km (43 miles) from Victoria Falls* 🕾 *013/4–4571* ⊕ *www.imbabalazambez-isafarilodge.com* ⇝ *9 rooms* ⊙| *All-inclusive.*

$$$$
ALL-INCLUSIVE
FAMILY
Fodor'sChoice
★

🏠 **Matetsi River Lodge.** About 40 km (25 miles) upstream from Victoria Falls lies Matetsi Water Lodge, which is at the center of Matetsi Game Reserve, the largest private game reserve in Zimbabwe. **Pros:** superb personal butler service; 13 km (8 miles) of exclusive Zambezi waterfront that's bordered on both sides by unfenced national parks; interpretative wildlife experience with extensive information on fauna, flora, and history available for the telling by all the guides. **Cons:** 30 minutes from town; most of the adrenaline activities have to be sought elsewhere; the lodge is child-friendly, which might put off those looking to escape their own kids. $ *Rooms from: $1300* ⊠ *Victoria Falls* ⊕ *On southern banks of Zambezi River, 40 km (25 miles) upstream from Victoria Falls* 🕾 *11/809–4300 reservations to South African office* ⊕ *www.andbeyond.com* ▭ *No credit cards* ⇝ *18 suites* ⊙| *All-inclusive.*

$$$$
B&B/INN
Fodor'sChoice
★

🏠 **Stanley and Livingstone at Victoria Falls.** It's almost surreal to step from the surrounding bushveld into the meticulously composed rooms of this small hotel, which is set on a 6,000-acre private game reserve. **Pros:** rooms have a/c; 10 minutes outside town; unbelievably over-the-top and decadently indulgent decor. **Cons:** the design of this lodge owes very little to Africa; you might find yourself wanting to use words like "mahvelous" a lot!; service can be impersonal at times. $ *Rooms from: $672* ⊠ *Victoria Falls* ⊕ *Off Ursula Rd., 13 km (8 miles) south of Victoria Falls town* 🕾 *213/284–4571* ⊕ *www.stanleyandlivingstone. com* ⇝ *17 suites* ⊙| *Breakfast.*

$$
HOTEL

🏠 **Victoria Falls Hotel.** Hotels come and go, but this landmark built in 1904 has retained its former glory as a distant, stylish outpost in empire days, while pandering to today's modern tastes, needs, and wants. **Pros:** one of the very best views of the Falls—it does not come closer than this!; world-famous high teas; easy access to town and all its amenities. **Cons:** hotel is slightly run-down in parts; it's big and busy, so can feel impersonal; service is sometimes patchy. $ *Rooms from: $401* ⊠ *2 Mallet Dr., Victoria Falls* 🕾 *213/284–4751* ⊕ *www.victoriafallshotel. com* ⇝ *161 rooms* ⊙| *Breakfast.*

$$
HOTEL
FAMILY
Fodor'sChoice
★

🏠 **Victoria Falls Safari Lodge.** The lodge's location is atop a natural plateau that perfectly frames the African sunset against a private waterhole frequented by various game throughout the entire year. **Pros:** fabulous architecture; beautiful location; great African sunsets are guaranteed. **Cons:** can get quite busy; a little bit of a distance from the town's amenities. $ *Rooms from: $434* ⊠ *471 Squire Cummings Rd., Victoria Falls* 🕾 *213/284–3211* ⊕ *www.victoria-falls-safari-lodge.com* ⇝ *72 rooms* ⊙| *Breakfast.*

SPORTS AND THE OUTDOORS

The town of Victoria Falls was the epicenter of extreme adventures for many years. But at the peak of Zimbabwe's civil unrest, many of the adventure operators either closed down or moved to the Zambian side. Livingstone took over as the gateway to the Victoria Falls, the Zambezi River, and all the activities associated with them. Over the last few years, however, the Zimbabwean side has made a remarkable comeback, with companies such as Adventure Zone, Wild Horizons, and the original Shearwater offering all manner of thrills.

Adventure Zone. This is a one-stop booking agent for bungee jumping, upper Zambezi River canoeing, white-water rafting, Victoria Falls Bridge tour, transfers, and many other activities Victoria Falls has to offer. ⊠ *Shop No. 4, Phumula Centre, Victoria Falls* ☎ *213/4–4424* ⊕ *www.adventurezonevicfalls.com.*

Shearwater. One of the oldest operating companies in Victoria Falls (thrill-seeking since 1982) and unique in that it owns and operates the majority of activities available in Victoria Falls, Shearwater can put you in a helicopter or raft, or on an elephant or boat cruise. ⊠ *Park Way Ave. at Fox Rd., Victoria Falls* ☎ *213/4–4471* ⊕ *www.shearwatervictoriafalls.com.*

Wild Horizons. Need to get around? Wild Horizons runs transfers in and around Victoria Falls, Livingstone, and Chobe, including airport pickups and drop-offs as well as multiday tours and cross-border transfers between Zambia, Zimbabwe, and Botswana. They also operate a range of adrenaline activities in and around the Falls. ⊠ *310 Park Way Ave., Victoria Falls* ☎ *213/284–4571* ⊕ *www.wildhorizons.co.za.*

10

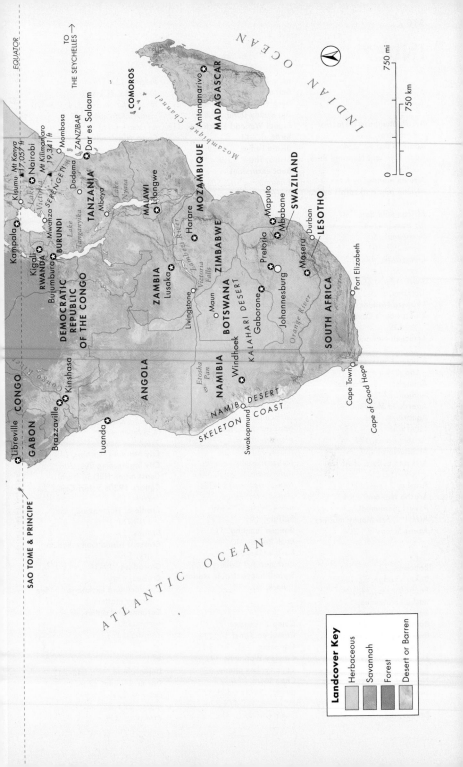

INDEX

PHOTO CREDITS

ABOUT OUR WRITERS

 Claire Baranowski spent an idyllic childhood in a small town in Zimbabwe before moving to South Africa. Today she works in London as a travel writer and editor. Her favorite travels include backpacking in Laos and beach escapes in the Caribbean and Sri Lanka, but the most magical have been on safari in Africa.

 Charlotte Beauvoisin ditched her 9 to 5 life in London to fulfill her teenage dream of living in Africa as a VSO (Voluntary Service Overseas... think Peace Corps) volunteer with the Uganda Conservation Foundation. As soon as the plane door opened, Uganda felt like home. Her award-winning travel blog Diary of a Muzungu documents her nine years in East Africa and her love of eating grasshoppers.

 Colleen Blaine is a travel writer based along South Africa's famous Garden Route. Her years living in and exploring all corners of Namibia, Botswana, Zimbabwe, Mauritius and South Africa have helped her share her knowledge and passion for Southern Africa through writing. A regular contributor to a variety of local and international publications and blogs, she loves to travel like a local and is inspired by stories about people, conservation, and nature. By her own admission she could not live without olives, wine, or wide open spaces.

 Christopher Clark is a British freelance journalist, writer, and wanderer based in Cape Town, South Africa. He's worked and traveled in 14 African countries, writing about everything from luxury safaris in the Serengeti to conflict in the Democratic Republic of Congo. His work has appeared in publications including Al Jazeera, CNN, Lonely Planet, NPR, Travel Africa and Vice.

 Leah Feiger is a freelance travel writer and researcher based in Rwanda. Raised in Hong Kong, London, and Chicago, her international upbringing was the perfect jumpstart to life on the road. Her travels include scuba diving with bull sharks in South Africa, summiting Mt. Kilimanjaro in Tanzania, gorilla trekking in Rwanda, and rafting the Zambezi in Zambia. Short bus rides and fresh mangoes are her favorites.

 Brought up in the UK, James Gifford was lucky enough to be introduced to the wilds of Africa at an early age. After travelling to all seven continents, he finally settled in Botswana in 2006 where he has forged a career as an award-winning photographer and writer. Although assignments often drag him kicking and screaming to upmarket lodges, he is happiest camping solo in the bush, sleeping on top of his vehicle with just a mosquito net separating him from the ubiquitous stars.

 Linda Markovina is a freelance photography and travel journalist with a home base in South Africa. She and her husband have lived and traveled extensively through East and West Africa for the past 13 years, including driving up both coastlines. She has written for various local and international publications garnering awards in the process as one of the directors of the expedition team of Moving Sushi, a nonprofit company that unlocks scientific data on ocean systems in Africa. Her focus is on conservation, travel, the natural world around us and how we as people interact with it...as long as it has nothing to do with snakes. Snakes give her the willies.

Originally from London, Lizzie Williams has been exploring Africa for two decades—first as a tour leader and now as a prolific guidebook author and travel writer. She's visited 20 African countries and more than 100 parks and reserves, and as well as being a safari specialist, is an expert at negotiating African border crossings. When not on the road, Lizzie lives in beautiful Cape Town.

Our South Africa chapter was updated by Mary Holland, Barbara Noe Kennedy, and Lee Middleton.